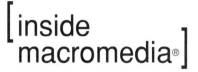

[inside
macromedia® **]**

AUTHORWARE®
6

Scott J. Wilson, Ph.D.

Jennie Thornton

ONWORD PRESS
——*——
THOMSON LEARNING™

Australia Canada Mexico Singapore Spain United Kingdom United States

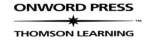

ONWORD PRESS
THOMSON LEARNING
™

Authorware 6.0 [Inside Macromedia]
Scott Wilson, Jennie Thornton

Business Unit Director:
Alar Elken

Executive Editor:
Sandy Clark

Acquisitions Editor:
James Gish

Editorial Assistant:
Jaimie Wetzel

Executive Marketing Manager:
Maura Theriault

Channel Manager:
Fair Huntoon

Marketing Coordinator:
Karen Smith

Executive Production Manager:
Mary Ellen Black

Production Manager:
Larry Main

Production Editor:
Tom Stover

Full Production Services:
Liz Kingslien
Lizart Digital Design, Tucson, AZ

NOTICE TO THE READER

We would like to thank the following parties for allowing us to include material from them within our book and exercises. *Images:* Corel digital imagery © 2001, Corel Corp. and PhotoDisc digital imagery © 2001, PhotoDisc, Inc. *Audio:* David Bennett Productions.

Website Pros., thank you for letting us share some of the screen designs we created together. Chris Volion, thank you for contributing your illustrations.

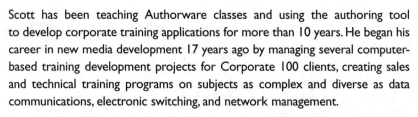

About the Authors

Scott J. Wilson, Ph.D.

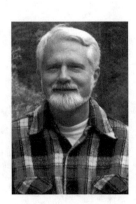

Scott has been teaching Authorware classes and using the authoring tool to develop corporate training applications for more than 10 years. He began his career in new media development 17 years ago by managing several computer-based training development projects for Corporate 100 clients, creating sales and technical training programs on subjects as complex and diverse as data communications, electronic switching, and network management.

He left a corporate position as training manager and started his own training company, where he managed the development of thousands of hours of multimedia and Web applications for Fortune 500 clients. His company served as an authorized Macromedia developer, training center, and software reseller over the course of 12 years.

Scott managed the development of projects ranging from end-user software simulations to policy training for corporate managers; from sales and product training for retail and direct sale environments to performance support tools for executives; and from complex hardware simulations for line engineers to counseling strategies for middle managers.

Currently Scott is Vice President of Instructional Architecture, a training/consulting firm helping corporations investigate, design, develop, and implement training/corporate needs over company intranets, the Internet, and more traditional delivery media.

Scott received his Ph.D. in Instructional Design and Research Methodology from Florida State University. He has actively served in the interactive and training communities, and has given presentations at both national and regional conferences on many topics related to interactive multimedia and training.

Scott is a coauthor among and instructional architect of numerous books published in the OnWord Press *Inside Macromedia* series.

Jennie Thornton

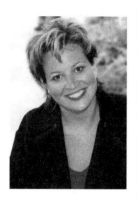

Jennie Thornton is one of the most recognized faces in the Authorware community today. She has been designing and developing multimedia-training projects for the last 13 years. Her extensive guru-knowledge-level of Authorware, her proven ability to produce award-winning interactive training projects, and her audience-pleasing teaching style have made her a sought-after Authorware expert.

Jennie began her career working for Fortune 100 companies to develop and design computer-based training using Authorware as a primary tool. After working in the corporate environment for four years, Jennie struck out on her own as a consultant to help other companies leverage the power that Authorware affords the development process. Based in San Francisco, California, Jennie has extensive experience consulting with all types of clients, which range from NASDAQ "Hot 100" firms to large corporations and governmental agencies.

Jennie's Authorware stand-up training curriculum is the most sought-after curriculum in the Authorware community today. Her unique insight into the needs of Authorware users allowed Jennie to contribute to the release of Authorware 6 by serving on the Authorware Advisory Council. As a member of the council, Macromedia asked for her input for the product's latest release.

Jennie has also maintained an active involvement with the Authorware (AWARE) community. Jennie has spoken at the Macromedia User Conference; presented numerous training sessions at the major Authorware conference, TAAC; and has delivered the keynote address at the European Authorware Conference. In recognition for her efforts, her past projects have been awarded the ASTD Blue Ribbon Award and Macromedia's People's Choice Award for Outstanding Corporate Training.

Acknowledgments

First and foremost we want to thank the thousands of students who have attended our classes during the past ten years. Your enthusiasm and probing questions have not only increased our enjoyment of teaching but have helped us become better at what we do.

We want to extend our deepest gratitude to Dan Clinger, Authorware guru and Director of Development at the Media Shoppe, for his eagle-eyed technical review of this book. His comments and encouragements indeed made this book the cutting-edge guide we envisioned it to be.

We would also like to thank the many people at Macromedia with whom we have worked over the years, including those in the Authorized Training Program, Authorized Developer Program, and Value-Added Reseller Program, as well as those on the Technical Support, Marketing/Trade Events, and Development/Engineering teams. Especially we want to thank the Authorware product team of Jamil Zainasheff, Christian Vescia, Stefan van As, Mike Baker, John Mayer, Tom Neuhold-Huber, Vickie Chapman, Ron De Medeiros, and Andrew Chemey. Without their tireless commitment, Authorware 6 would not have been such a successful release.

Finally, we want to thank the many people at OnWord Press/Thomson Learning for their help and encouragement: Jim Gish, for helping us bring this comprehensive book into existence and for helping us target the Inside Macromedia series; Thomas Stover for his technical expertise and work behind the scenes; Jaimie Wetzel for helping us keep organized and on track, and for countless other means of support; Liz Kingslien of Lizart Digital Design for her outstanding production work and very enjoyable working relationship; Daril Bentley for his invaluable, professional, and painstaking editing; and Vince Nicotina for his work on the CD-ROM.

We also want to extend our gratitude to the following reviewers for offering their expertise and constructive criticism: Robert Bremmer, Art Institute of Portland; Thom Gillepsie, Indiana State University; Tara Holod, Allentown Business School; and Justin West, Holyoke Community College.

From Scott

I would like to thank Jennie for the tremendous effort, enthusiasm, and dedication she has brought to this book, which like the Energizer bunny, just seemed to "keep on growing." In this world of change, whatever may next present itself to you . . . Bon Appetit.

A special thanks to Robert Milton, a friend and colleague who first introduced me to Authorware back when dinosaurs still roamed the earth. Robert, as one of the very early Authorware masters, you have kindly shared your expertise, wit, and humor with literally thousands, encouraging those who have learned from you to become skilled craftspersons in their own right.

I want to thank God and my fellow human beings for the many valuable lessons that have been provided to me along the way. May I have the strength and insight to gain from these lessons. Marie-Claire, my wise and beautiful wife, thank you from the bottom of my heart for your continued support, faith, and love.

From Jennie

First, I would like to thank the Authorware community. You are the people that make Authorware sing and dance and thrive every year. Without your efforts the world of adult learning would be a much less interactive place.

A very special thanks to Scott Wilson, my coauthor. You were there with me every step of the way and I will never be able to fully repay you for giving me the opportunity to see my vision realized.

A great accolade to Myles O'Connor. Without your hard work, this book would not be as comprehensive as it is. Thanks also to the following at the Media Shoppe: Dan Clinger, Jeff McGuire, Kevin Knapp, Wade Wells, and Robin Baker.

I would like to thank the gurus of Authorware who have inspired my career. Joe Ganci, I am proud to call you a dear friend. Stefan van As, your insistence has kept me active in the AWARE community. Mark Henry, you have galvanized the AWARE community with TAAC. Erik de Bruin, Bart van de Rotsheide, Peter Brouwers, and Jeroen Diderik; EuroTAAC is a wonderful success and you are true pioneers. Steve Howard, Mark Bainbridge, and Bernard Davis thanks for taking EuroTAAC to the next level. Ron Lubensky, Chris Swenson, Joe Francis, Michael Mizen, Andrew Poulos, David Linder, and Mark Steiner – you all consistently amaze me with your commitment and brilliance. Robert Milton, you were my first teacher, your contacts and advice launched my career, and I will always be in your debt. Dan Clinger, a deep thanks for teaching me how to "dive" into Authorware like a true guru – you are an inspiration.

Special acknowledgment to those at the training centers that have made me feel like part of the family over the years: to Lonnie Smith at In-House Productions, thanks for believing in me year in and year out; and to Leslie, Bill, Amy, Jennifer, and Phyllis at CIBER Training in San Francisco, you are the best.

To my family – Carl, Jerilyn, and Adam Thornton – my secret weapons, thanks for instilling in me the firm belief that nothing is impossible.

To my friends, who remind me that the universe has endless possibilities if you just remain open to them: Dan Carr for the atheistic inspiration, Julie Crew for the spiritual cleansing, Jill Heller-Hager for reminding me that I have made a difference, and Charlie Schoening for making my life so much easier in the early days.

Finally, to the friends and colleagues that were taken from my life on September 11, 2001, to all of you I promise to live my life fully and joyfully.

Thank you, all of you, for contributing to my life and my knowledge and my joy over the years. I have been truly blessed to know all of you.

CHAPTER 10

Creating Interactions – Part One 269

CHAPTER 11

Creating Interactions – Part Two 307

CHAPTER 15

The Framework Icon Structure 463

CHAPTER 16

Organizational and Navigational Structures 519

CHAPTER 17

Application: Basic-level Menu/Topic Structures 549

CHAPTER 21

CHAPTER 22

CHAPTER 23

Preface

If you want to learn Macromedia's Authorware 6, the multimedia/Web authoring tool that has revolutionized the way interactive applications are developed, you have picked up the right book.

We know Authorware inside and out. We have been teaching Authorware in authorized Macromedia training centers for 10 years, since its debut into the Windows environment with Authorware 1.0.

Our book allows you to tap into the real-world experience of instructors who are also successful developers in the multimedia and Web development industry. Through the use of our many Tips, Shortcuts, and occasional Cautions, we provide you with the benefit of this "true and tested" experience.

We designed our book from the ground up to be the essential hands-on resource for Authorware users, from beginners to those who are more advanced. We focus on what you need most: concentrating on the most frequently used features and functions, and presenting the information within the context of "hands-on" learning.

Those who have taken our Authorware courses are among the best trained in the industry. Why? Because our teaching method is based on a classroom-tested model of instruction. It works, whether you are learning in a classroom or on your own.

Our learning strategies are centered on the concept of "learn by doing." With numerous exercises and screen capture illustrations, you will build your experience base as you work through our book.

We focus on the "need to know" functions of Authorware, and help you get down to the business of building leading-edge interactive applications – fast. We provide a "real-world" focus that reflects the development needs, project objectives, and Authorware functionality typical of professional Authorware applications.

We deliver the professional experience of successful Authorware developers. You will learn the valuable tips and shortcuts that only the experts know. We hope you find our book valuable and have some fun along the way!

Scott Wilson and Jennie Thornton

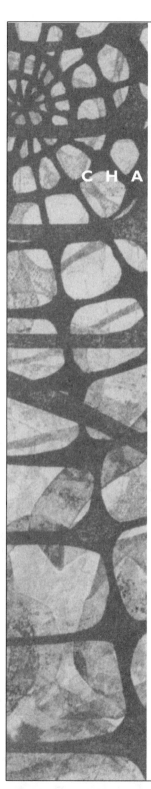

C H A P T E R

I

Getting Started

Introduction

This chapter provides a brief introduction to Authorware, as well as information on using the book and the companion CD-ROM. The chapter concludes with a brief review of the new features in Authorware 6. We hope you will find our book helpful in your quest for knowledge and that you will find Authorware a powerful and productive tool to use. By the end of the chapter you will be able to:

- *List the learning strategies used in this book*
- *Describe the Quick Access icons used in this book*
- *Create a directory on your computer for saving the exercises you will work with in this book*
- *Locate necessary exercise files on the companion CD-ROM*
- *Open the Authorware 6 program*
- *List the new features of Authorware 6*

An Overview of Authorware

Computer-based training (CBT) started out on mainframe computers prior to the existence of personal computers (PCs). Shortly after the appearance of the PC in the early 1980s, companies began creating authoring programs that could be used to create and deliver instructional material on these new desktop computers. In the early days, these software programs could be classified into one of two categories: programming languages or authoring systems. Programming languages were very powerful but typically difficult to use. Authoring systems were much easier to use but limited in what they could do. Since then, literally hundreds of authoring/programming tools have appeared and disappeared from the CBT/multimedia marketplace.

From its first days on the Macintosh and early emergence into the Windows environment, Authorware quickly established itself as one of the leading authoring tools in the multimedia industry. Authorware's rapid growth in popularity and steady capture of market share arose from its unique combination of ease of use and ever-increasing functionality.

The heart of Authorware's ease of use lies in the fact that it is truly a "What-You-See-Is-What-You-Get" (WYSIWYG) authoring environment. You create a presentation sequence by simply dragging icons from an icon palette to a flowline and arranging them in the order you choose. To place content (text and graphics) into the program you open (double click on) a Display icon and use a text tool to type whatever text you want, directly where you want it.

You can also import text and graphics created in other programs. Once on screen, the text and/or graphics can be moved anywhere you want, again using Authorware's WYSIWYG interface. All common text attributes can be modified directly on screen.

In addition to the very visual and easy-to-use icon/flowline method, Authorware includes hundreds of built-in functions and variables (Authorware's "programming" capability) that provide increased functionality. Authorware allows you to create your own custom variables (you will get a lot of practice doing this later in the book) to achieve a wide range of objectives.

Although Authorware can be described as an authoring tool for creating multimedia and Web applications in general, its strength lies in its ability to create, deliver, and keep record of highly interactive learning/training applications that can be delivered on CD-ROM, LANs/WANs, company intranets, or over the Internet. With Authorware, you can easily create interactions that require that the learner become engaged in the learning process, without the use of programming.

Creating Applications: Art and Technical Skills

Learning how to use Authorware (or any other authoring software program) is only one aspect of what is required to create a functional and professional-looking multimedia or Web program. Generally there are many different skill sets involved. These skills may exist within a single individual or may be represented in the composite skills that exist among a team of people. At a minimum, this set of skills (see figures 1-1 and 1-2) should include proficiency in:

- *Design and layout principles*
- *Artistic creativity and execution*
- *Writing (text and narration)*
- *Program, message, and instructional design*
- *Audio and video techniques*
- *Use of the authoring software*
- *Project management*

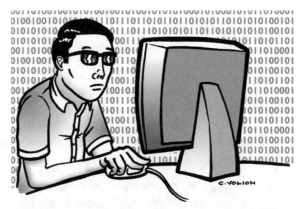

Fig. 1-1. Authorware applications require technical skill.

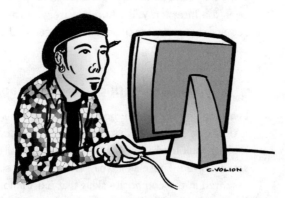

Fig. 1-2. Authorware applications require artistic talent.

Although the focus of this book is to help you learn how to use the Authorware software program, the acquisition of these technical skills should be considered within the context of other skills that may be required. The extent to which you may need these other skills will depend to a large extent on the type of application you are creating, its intended use, and how "professional" you want the result to be.

We realize that many readers may not have an art background. Therefore, the exercises included in this book do not require an art background, although they can be enhanced on your own if you do have artistic talent. In the beginning exercises, you will be asked to draw simple objects, as a means of introduction to the drawing tools. If you do have artistic talent, we encourage you to take creative license to modify and embellish the subject matter. In later exercises, artwork is supplied with the exercises so that you can create more realistic and professional-looking projects.

Instructional Approach

Because of the many features and functions, Authorware may at first seem intimidating. We do not want to overwhelm you with a lot of details all at once, and therefore begin by introducing the aspects of Authorware that are the most practical and most commonly used to build programs in the real world.

With this book you have an opportunity to learn Authorware in an intuitive way while practicing some of the techniques and shortcuts typically used by developers in creating Authorware products for real-world applications. Each chapter builds upon the last, adding new features of Authorware to your builder's toolbox.

The chapters within our book break up the material into "learning chunks" that are about right for most people during a single session, whether you are learning on your own or using this book within a classroom setting. The learning strategies used within these chapters are centered on the concept of "learning by doing." These learning strategies are a synthesis of the authors' many-year experience in teaching Authorware as Authorized Macromedia Training Providers. Understanding the intent behind these learning strategies may help you to most effectively use them in learning the Authorware software program.

Learning Strategies

The following describe components of this book intended to maximize the learning experience and to make the process as organized and easy to follow as possible.

- **Introduction:** *Each chapter begins with a brief introduction to topics covered, including a list of learning objectives.*

- **Conceptual overviews:** *Provide an overview of the subject matter before delving into the narrowly focused details of building something.*

- **Guided tours:** *Some chapters may include a structured "walkthrough" of how to perform tasks such as making menu/window selections or looking at the various properties or options listed. A guided tour is not really an exercise, but follows the notion of learning by actively "looking and doing."*

- **Practice exercises:** *Most chapters will include hands-on experience (see figure 1-3), introducing the basic skills of using tools and techniques to build structures typical of real-world applications. The scope of an exercise is fairly narrow, focusing on the concepts and skills introduced in the chapter. The content is generally simple so that the emphasis remains on building structures and using techniques and is not dependent on preexisting artistic or programming talent. Again, please feel free to modify and embellish exercise content.*

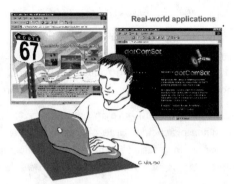

Fig. I-3. Hands-on learning.

Each practice exercise includes the following project elements, which reflect aspects of the real-world development process.

- **Description:** *Provides a general description of the purpose of the exercise and of the components used within it. Generally, real-world projects include a project description, although they are typically much more detailed than those found in these exercises.*

- **Take a Look:** *Asks you to make use of the companion CD-ROM by loading and playing a file that is the completed version of the exercise you are about to create. This section includes notes on aspects of the exercise you should pay attention to as you examine it.*

- **Storyboard, On Screen:** *Provides screen captures of what will be seen on screen when the exercise is completed, to serve as a printed reference. A storyboard that includes on-screen descriptions or illustrations is a vital real-world project deliverable.*

- **Storyboard, Behind the Scenes:** *Provides screen captures illustrating the authoring structures used in the completed version of the exercise, to serve as signposts for development. A storyboard that includes programming descriptions or illustrations is a vital real-world project deliverable.*

- **Go Solo:** *You will see this icon immediately following the storyboard sections. At this point in an exercise, you should have the information necessary to complete the exercise on your own, and you are encouraged to give it a try. If you need help, however, you can use the step-by-step instructions that follow.*

- **Step-by-step instructions:** *For those who would like structured help with the details of the tasks involved in the exercise. The numbered steps state what needs to be done, whereas the lettered sub-steps describe how to perform a given step.*

- **Summary:** *Each chapter concludes with a bulleted list of the major concepts and topics presented.*

Application Chapters and Project

Each application chapter focuses on an exercise that serves as a component of a real-world application. Combined, these components constitute a complete Authorware application project. Each application exercise provides hands-on experience in building structures that synthesize concepts and skills learned across several preceding chapters.

The companion CD-ROM contains the completed version of each application exercise. Therefore, you may skip over some content areas and still be able to work on other parts of the application project. Each application exercise contains the same subsections as the practice exercise, with one difference: the step-by-step instructions are not included (so that you can master the material on your own).

Icons for Quick Information

The Inside Macromedia series uses the following icons that highlight particular types of information.

CD-ROM icon: Indicates that material from the companion CD-ROM is necessary at this point in an exercise or tour.

Note icon: Provides information to which you will want to pay particular attention.

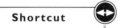

Tip icon: Provides information intended to make aspects of an exercise or tour easier to learn or more effective or efficient when put into practice.

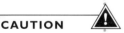

Shortcut icon: Provides a more efficient method as an alternative to the steps described in the text.

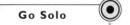

Caution icon: Provides helpful suggestions for avoiding actions that might result in lost time and effort.

Go Solo icon: Indicates that at this point you have enough information to take control of the exercise and attempt to complete the exercise on your own.

Using the Book on Your Own

Each book in the Inside Macromedia series is designed to be used either on your own or within a classroom setting. Those of you who use this book to learn Authorware on your own will find that you are guided through the process and given the freedom to modify what you want. The learning strategies employed in this book are the product of many years of teaching and learning on the part of the authors.

Keep in mind that there are generally several approaches to building something. You may end up performing exercises using steps (or sequences of steps) different from those outlined in this book, which is fine if your structure does what it needs to do. Note also that the step-by-step instructions provide two levels of detail.

- **Numbered steps:** *State what needs to be done.*
- **Lettered sub-steps:** *Describe how to perform particular steps.*

Using the Book Within a Classroom

As instructors for Authorware, Director, Flash, Dreamweaver, UltraDev, Fireworks (and others), we also think these same learning strategies (presented somewhat differently) are equally effective in the classroom. In the classroom, we use the book as a point of reference and organizational guide for the presentation of material. As a point of reference, we do not read from the book, nor ask students to do so. Rather, we use the book to organize the classroom presentation. We encourage students to take notes, right in the book. In regard to the elements used in this book, in the classroom we employ the following strategies for each chapter covered.

- **Conceptual overviews:** *We present an overview of the chapter, with each instructor adding his or her additional details or points of emphasis.*
- **Guided tours:** *Using a projection device attached to the instructor's computer, as a class we walk through the essence of a particular tour.*
- **Practice exercises:** *Using a projection device, as a class we walk through the beginning of an exercise, including use of the following elements found in this book.*

  Take a Look: *We look at the completed version of an exercise, pointing out noteworthy characteristics.*

  Storyboard: *We use the completed version to look at what is on screen and what is programmed (making reference to the illustrations in the book).*

  Go Solo: *For the beginning exercises and those involving more difficult concepts, the instructor (using the projection device) leads the class through the initial process of putting together the Authorware structure. Thereafter, we ask students to complete the exercise on their own. We occasionally stop the class and point out common difficulties. As students continue on their own, we suggest that they first look at the numbered steps that state what needs to be done, and then try to figure out how to perform those steps on their own, falling back on the lettered sub-steps if they need help.*

Instructor help: We walk around the classroom, providing help and additional information as needed.

Tips: Each instructor contributes his or her own additional information based on professional experience.

Application exercises: We have found that the application exercises are an excellent means of helping students integrate, practice, and solidify their newly learned skills, in an environment in which they can receive help and guidance if they so choose. Depending on the content of an exercise and the characteristics of a particular class, our instructors will either put the class in "workshop" mode (in which students work on the exercises by themselves) or begin an exercise as a collective effort, subsequently having students finish the exercise on their own.

Getting Your Computer Ready

The sections that follow discuss the knowledge base and skills you should bring to the use of this book in regard to your system's interface, hard drive, and other components.

Prerequisite Knowledge

It is assumed that you already have the skills necessary to work in the basic Windows environment prior to undertaking learning Authorware. Specifically, you should be able to:

* *Use the mouse and keyboard for basic input and selection*
* *Select and drag objects using the mouse*
* *Resize windows*
* *Locate directories (folders)*
* *Locate files within directories*
* *Create and name directories*
* *Copy files*

Preparing Your Computer's Hard Drive

Throughout the course of this book, you will be creating many Authorware files you will want to save on your computer. To make it easier to locate these files and follow the book's discussion of them, it is strongly recommended that you create a new directory (folder) on your computer's hard drive for storing these files.

(NOTE)

On the root directory
of your computer's
hard drive, create a
directory (folder)
named *SaveWork*, as
indicated in figure 1-4.

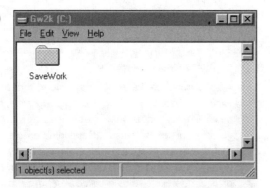

Fig. 1-4. Create a new directory named SaveWork.

About the Companion CD-ROM

This book includes numerous learning activities that make use of preexisting
Authorware files and a variety of media elements. All of these files and elements are contained on the companion CD-ROM. It is recommended that
you perform the steps that follow so as to become familiar with how the
material on the companion CD-ROM is integrated with the book and how
you can make the most efficient use of this material.

1. Place the companion CD-ROM into your computer's CD-ROM player.

2. There is an auto-run program that will open a menu, offering details
   about the CD-ROM content. Examine all of the options in the program.
   When finished, quit this program.

3. Use your computer to view the content of the companion CD-ROM.

4. Figure 1-5 shows the main directory structure of the companion CD-
   ROM. Familiarize yourself with this structure.

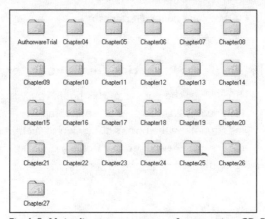

Fig. 1-5. Main directory structure of companion CD-ROM content.

Note the following regarding folder organization of the companion CD-ROM content.

- **Chapters:** *There is a folder for each chapter in the book. Each chapter folder contains all Authorware and media files needed for the guided tours, practice exercises, and application exercises for that chapter.*

- **Adobe Reader:** *Within this folder is a program file that will install Adobe's Acrobat Reader. This reader is required for displaying and printing several files that provide additional reference material and learning aids for Authorware.*

File Extensions and Descriptions

The following are descriptions of the file extension names that appear in this book.

- **.a6p:** *Authorware file; un-packaged, editable program file.*

- **.a6r:** *Authorware file; packaged without the runtime file.*

- **.exe:** *Executable file; Authorware files that have been packaged with the runtime file have this extension (along with any other Windows-executable files). Packaged Authorware files may not be edited.*

- **.aam:** *Authorware files that have been published for the Authorware Web Player.*

- **.htm:** *Authorware files with this file extension have been published for a Web page (this format also used by many HTML editors).*

- **.fla:** *Flash movie file; editable movie files.*

- **.swf:** *Shockwave files; exported Flash files that cannot be edited but can be played using the standalone Flash Player and that can be embedded in HTML files.*

- **.mov:** *Movie file format; Authorware can play Movies in QuickTime video format.*

- **.wav:** *Sound file format; one of many that can be imported and played within Authorware.*

- **.gif:** *Graphic file format; one of many that can be imported into Authorware.*

- **.png:** *Graphic file format; one of many that can be imported into Authorware.*

- **.bmp:** *Graphic file format; one of many that can be imported into Authorware.*

- **.jpg:** *Graphic file format; one of many that can be imported into Authorware.*

Opening a New File in Authorware

After you have successfully installed Authorware on your computer, you can open it like any other Windows software by performing the following steps.

1. From the Windows Start button, select the Programs category.

2. Select the *Macromedia Authorware 6* folder.

3. Double click on the Authorware 6 icon (see figure 1-6).

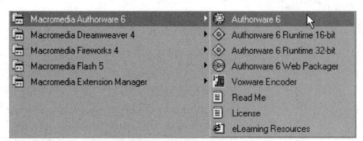

Fig. 1-6. Selecting Authorware in Windows.

4. As Authorware opens, it presents an opening title screen. The exact appearance of this screen (see figure 1-7) will differ, depending on whether you have a commercial version that can be used to develop and distribute Authorware programs or an educational version that can only be used in the educational institution and not for commercial distribution.

·T/P·

You can speed up the erasure of this opening title screen by clicking on it.

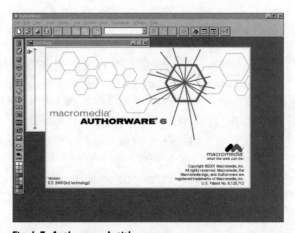

Fig. 1-7. Authorware's title screen.

5. Once the title screen has erased, you will note the appearance of a New File dialog window (see figure 1-8) for creating Knowledge Object program files. These knowledge objects are designed to help inexperienced authors create simple template structures, into which content can be quickly added. You do not need at this point to make either selection, but as a point of explanation the following are descriptions of these options.

- *Knowledge Object Application: Selecting this option brings up a wizard that systematically asks you a number of questions, and based on your responses automatically creates a simple presentation type of Authorware structure that includes learner/user navigational controls. You place text and graphics into the application as it is run for the first time.*

- **Knowledge Object Quiz:** *Selecting this option brings up a wizard that systematically asks you a number of questions pertaining to the type of questions you want to include in a quiz. After you have finished with the wizard, the quiz structure is automatically created, providing for the input of questions, responses, and feedback as the quiz is run for the first time.*

6. Close this window by clicking on the X in the upper right-hand corner of the New File window title bar (see figure 1-8).

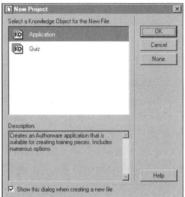

Fig. 1-8. Knowledge Object New File window.

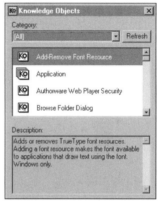

Fig. 1-9. Knowledge Object library window.

7. As soon as you close the previous window, another dialog window opens for the Knowledge Object library window (see figure 1-9). You are not going to use knowledge objects for quite a while, so at this point close this window by clicking on the X in the upper right-hand corner of the Knowledge Object library title bar.

8. You should now see Authorware's main interface, including menus, toolbar, Icon palette, and flowline. These elements of Authorware's interface are discussed in detail in Chapter 3.

What's New in Authorware 6

Authorware 6's new features can roughly be categorized into three somewhat overlapping areas: extended media capabilities, interface additions and improvements, and increased performance and power. The sections that follow discuss the new features in these three categories.

Extended Media Capabilities

Media Synchronization now provides the capability to directly synchronize icons or Map icons to Sound and Movie icons, based on either elapsed time or position. As you will see in Chapter 5, you can easily create presentational sequences in which text bullets are synced to the delivery of specific key points in a narration audio track. In addition, Authorware 6 now supports the MP3 sound format.

With the new RTF Objects editor, you can input the basic design and content of your Authorware project or any other RTF file. As you will see in Chapter 20, the editor allows you to add text, graphics, Authorware variables and expressions, and hot text. With RTF Knowledge objects, you can display external RTF documents within the Authorware Presentation window. This means you can dynamically link to external rich text documents created in the RTF Objects editor, with text assets remaining easy to update without re-authoring.

One-button publishing integrates and automates all steps in what used to be referred to as the packaging and distribution process. As you will see in Chapter 22, one-button publishing now makes it possible to prepare applications for the Web, CD-ROM, or corporate network with the click of a button. There are options that allow you to package and publish your application in several formats at the same time. With just one step, you can publish Authorware applications without runtime (*A6R* format), for the Web Player (*AAM* format), and for a Web page (*HTM* format). This new feature allows you to define customizable and reusable settings and will automatically identify and collect many of the support files needed (Xtras, DLLs, and UCDs). The Authorware Web Player, which downloads Authorware 6 content over the Web, is 40% smaller than previously.

Interface Additions and Improvements

In Authorware 6, you can create and add your own custom commands (any type of executable file, *.EXE*) to the new Commands menu. The behaviors of the items in the Commands menu are similar to those of the Authorware Knowledge objects.

Several improvements have been made to the Calculation window. You can now change the calculation preferences; insert a symbol, divider line, or message box; and view the ASCII value of the selected character in a function or variable. A number of general interface improvements have also been, including the following.

- *Sixteen colors can now be used to assign colors to icons on the flowline or in a library, to help categorize or quickly identify common functionality or subject content.*

- *Empty icons on the flowline or in a library can now be easily identified by their gray color. Icons with content are black.*

- *You can now adjust the size of the Functions and Variables dialog boxes.*
- *A color column has been added to library windows, allowing you to sort icons in the library by color.*
- *The default file type for libraries is .A6L instead of all files.*
- *The number of recent files displayed when you open a file has been increased to 10.*
- *New keyboard shortcuts have been added.*
- *Two commands have been moved to the Windows menu: Close Window and Close All Windows.*

Increased Performance and Power

You can extend your application with nearly any ActiveX control using communications that support extended properties and methods of ActiveX controls. The XMLParser Xtra allows Authorware applications to read, parse, and make use of the content of *XML* documents. This means you can create dynamic data-driven applications by importing external data stored in Web-standard *XML* files.

The Hot Spot, Hot Object, True/False, Single Choice, and Multiple Choice assessment question knowledge objects have been updated to allow for the import and export of question content stored in *XML* files that conform to the IMS Question Test Interoperability (QTI) version 1.1 standard. This means you can export a question to an *XML* file and import an *XML* file.

Many new properties, functions, and variables are provided with Authorware 6. Over 100 new properties are now available to the *GetIconProperty* and *SetIconProperty* functions. Several changes have been made to the *PWInt.x32* Xtra. The *PWInt.x32* Xtra now supports the *IsCourseChanged*, *IsLibraryChanged*, *CMISetAICCVersion*, and *CMIGetAICCVersion* functions. You can track student activity with enhance data-tracking capabilities with the SCO Metadata editor, which conforms to ADL-SCORM specifications.

Summary

- *Authorware quickly established itself as one of the leading authoring tools in the multimedia industry. The heart of Authorware's ease of use lies in the fact that it is truly a "What-You-See-Is-What-You-Get" (WYSIWYG) authoring environment. The following learning activities used within the book are designed to accommodate different learning styles and situations.*

  Guided tours: *Structured walkthroughs of how to perform tasks, such as making menu/window selections.*

Practice exercises: Introductory hands-on experience of the basic skills involved in using tools and performing processes.

Application exercises: Provide hands-on experience in building structures that combine the concepts and skills learned across several chapters.

- *The Inside Macromedia series uses a number of icons that highlight particular types of information.*

- *All files you work on in the exercises in this book will be saved in a directory you must create on the root directory of your computer's hard drive. This directory (folder) should be named SaveWork.*

- *This book incorporates numerous learning activities that make use of preexisting Authorware files and a variety of media elements. All of these files and elements can be found on the companion CD-ROM.*

- *Authorware 6 can be opened in the Windows environment, much like any other software program. As you open Authorware, note that you will not make use of knowledge objects during most exercises in the book. Therefore, you can close the first two dialog windows that appear, as they pertain to knowledge objects.*

- *Authorware 6 incorporates a number of new features, described in this chapter.*

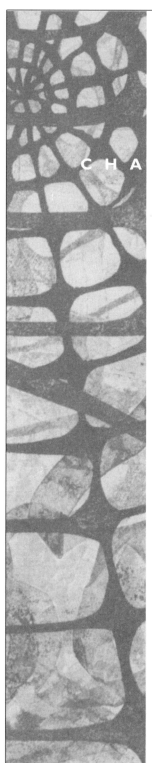

C H A P T E R 2

Multimedia
and Web
Development

Introduction

In the old days (all of 15 years ago), a multimedia presentation referred to a scenario in which several slide projectors were synchronized with music to create a multiple-screen presentation. Viewers of these presentations were typically not as impressed with the result as those who struggled mightily to put everything together.

Today, multimedia refers to a computer-created and delivered presentation that might involve the use of on-screen text, audio narration, graphics, photographs, music, animation, and video. The delivery medium might involve a computer and CD-ROM, traditional LAN/WAN, company intranet, or the Internet. Multimedia applications are developed to achieve a wide range of goals, for a wide range of audiences.

Regardless of the type of application you are creating or the authoring tool selected to build it, there are a number of common issues related to the development of any multimedia project. Although the major focus of this book is to help you learn how to use Authorware, it is important preliminarily to have an understanding of these common multimedia issues. To cover these critical issues adequately would require an entire book; thus, discussion here serves as a brief introduction only. By the end of this chapter you will be able to:

- *Describe various project/courseware characteristics*
- *Describe a number of issues of particular concern regarding Web delivery*
- *List a number of delivery considerations that will impact the way you create your application*
- *Describe a variety of presentational and instructional strategies*
- *Describe a structured project development process that will help you maintain sanity and stay on target*
- *Describe a number of issues and processes that should be part of your project standards*
- *List all of the individual roles or skill sets required for the complete multimedia team*

Project/Courseware Characteristics

Let's begin by looking at some typical characteristics of multimedia and Web projects. Obviously, the type of application will dramatically influence the characteristics, but this overview will consider some of the most salient features, providing a general description of the "look and feel" of a typical multimedia/Web project or course. You will explore the interface, media elements, and additional features.

Interface

The interface generally includes the components of overall screen design, navigational controls and guides, and content area layout.

Screen Design

There can be at least nine main types of application screens, each with a common and unifying "look and feel." Each type of screen is designed to serve a different purpose. The nine main types of screens are:

- *Title and program information screens*
- *Log-in screen*
- *Menu screens*
- *Introduction or objectives screen*
- *Content screens (with a variety of screen layouts)*
- *Exercise/simulation screens (with a variety of screen layouts)*
- *Quiz/test screens (with a variety of screen layouts)*
- *Message, feedback, and overlay screens*
- *E-commerce screens*

Figures 2-1 through 2-8 were taken from a single application, to illustrate the common "look and feel" across eight types of screens. Illustrations of a variety of layout designs for content screens and a sample e-commerce screen are included in material to follow.

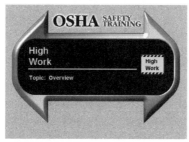

Fig. 2-1. Title screen.

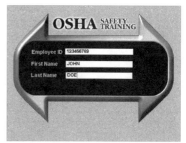

Fig. 2-2. Log-in screen.

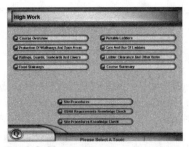

Fig. 2-3. Menu screen.

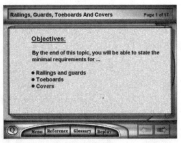

Fig. 2-4. Objectives screen.

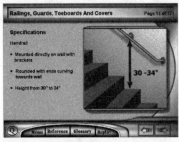

Fig. 2-5. Content screen.

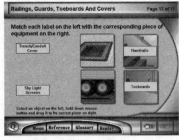

Fig. 2-6. Exercise screen.

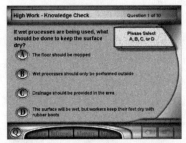

Fig. 2-7. Quiz screen.

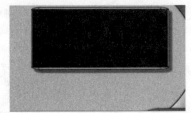

Fig. 2-8. Overlay screen.

Navigational Controls and Guides

The navigation scheme for most applications is hierarchical, consisting of a main menu, module menus, and structured topics. From the main menu, any of the module menus may be selected. Within each of the module menus, any of the topics may be selected. Once a topic has been selected, the user proceeds through the topic information and interactive screens. The Main and Module menus are shown in figures 2-9 and 2-10, respectively.

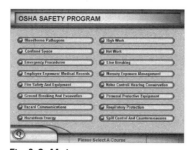

Fig. 2-9. Main menu.

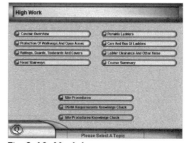

Fig. 2-10. Module menu.

Figure 2-11 shows a typical topic-level screen, with three design areas: the navigational guides at the top of the screen, the content area occupying most of the screen, and the navigational controls at the bottom. Navigational controls generally provide the user with the ability to proceed forward and backward, access main and module menus, and quit from each screen. Within applications delivered via CD-ROM, many developers will place the navigational controls at the bottom of the screen. With Web-based delivery, navigational controls tend to be located either at the top of screen or on the left.

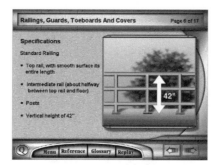

Fig. 2-11. Topic content screen.

Figure 2-12 shows a close-up of the navigational control buttons located at the bottom of the topic content screen, and figure 2-13 shows a close-up of the navigational guides located at the top of the screen.

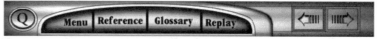

Fig. 2-12. Navigational (learner) controls at bottom of screen.

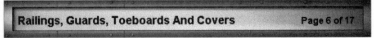

Railings, Guards, Toeboards And Covers   Page 6 of 17

Fig. 2-13. Navigational guides at top of screen.

Navigational guides consist of any relevant information that can be provided to the learner to indicate where he or she is currently located within the application. These guides include information such as course title, module title, topic title, and page x of y (within a topic).

Content Area Layout

Given the design and placement of navigational controls and guides, the rest of the area on the screen will generally show a variable combination of text (headlines, body text, and text bullets), graphics, and animation. This content area can be designed and the elements laid out in any number of ways, depending on the nature of the project. Figures 2-14 through 2-22 are from a Web application, but the different layouts of the content area can be equally effective within a project for CD-ROM delivery.

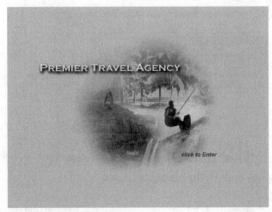

Fig. 2-14. Title screen.

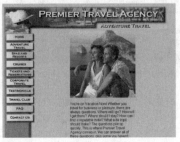

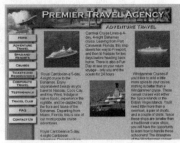

Fig. 2-15. Content area: layout design 1.   *Fig. 2-16. Content area: layout design 2.*

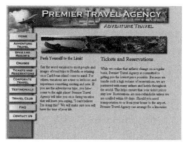

Fig. 2-17. Content area: layout design 3.

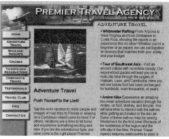

Fig. 2-18. Content area: layout design 4.

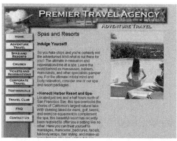

Fig. 2-19. Content area: layout design 5.

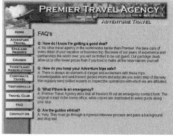

Fig. 2-20. Content area: layout design 6.

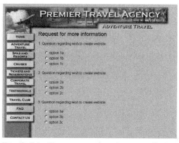

Fig. 2-21. Content area: layout design 7.

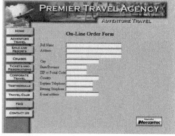

Fig. 2-22. E-commerce screen.

Media Elements

Multimedia (CD-ROM or Web) applications can use any combination of media, including on-screen text, audio narration, music/sound effects, graphics, animation, and digital movies.

On-screen Text

On-screen text can consist of headlines, body text, or text bullets using any number of standard text fonts, sizes, and colors. Text standards should be created prior to, and approved of, as part of the prototype phase of development. This topic is explored in greater detail later in this chapter.

Audio Narration

Depending on the type of application, equipment, and audience, the presence and extent of audio narration used will vary from project to project. One strategy (especially with CD-ROM delivery) is to use audio narration to convey the bulk of details, supporting the main points with text and graphics on screen. With Internet delivery, you may want to shift this emphasis and incorporate more of the details as text, leaving the audio narration light, in that many users may be limited by narrow-bandwidth modem access.

Music/Sound Effects

Again, depending on the type of application, you may or may not want to use music or sound effects to increase user interest in your application. Even within more traditional instructional projects, very brief musical introductions/transitions and strategic sound effects can help enliven the subject presented.

Graphics

Graphics can be created or purchased to represent a wide range of styles and quality, including line drawings, clip art, custom-created high-resolution graphics, photographic images, or any combination of these.

Animation

Animation can consist of rather simple and inexpensive 2D path animation that can be created within Authorware, more sophisticated Flash animation, or very expensive 3D effects typical of the commercial television and movie industries. Budget and anticipated delivery equipment requirements will generally dictate your choice here.

Digital Movies

Digital movies can be recorded, edited, and included within almost any budget, with the caveat that you generally get what you pay for (better equipment and talent for better results).

Additional Features

The following are other features that may be involved in a multimedia project. These include user tracking, bookmarks, and installation programs. These are discussed in the sections that follow.

User Tracking

User log-in is a frequently requested feature to be included in multimedia applications. Generally when a user enters the program for the first time, she will be prompted to enter a first and last name among other relevant information. This information can be stored along with topic completion and test score information, using a variety of methods explored in detail later in this book. You will get hands-on experience building a log-in structure and storing student information.

Bookmark

Analogous to its print-based cousin, CBT (computer-based training) applications have long included a feature that allows a learner to "sign off" from the program, bookmark the "page," and return to this exact location the next time he "signs in" to the program. As an alternative to this "page"-level bookmarking, you can build smaller topics that are more easily completed, and then automatically bookmark the menu by indicating which topics have been completed. One reason for doing this bookmarking at the menu level instead of at the page level is that few learners remember the context of the bookmarked page they return to. Starting and finishing a properly sized topic seems to make better instructional sense.

Installation Program

You will also probably want to include an installation program that will allow the user to easily run your application from a CD-ROM, and to copy and run it from a standalone computer or over a network. There are several off-the-shelf products available that can help you do this relatively easily. Setup Factory, for example, is probably a little easier to use for non-programmers, whereas a program such as Installation Shield offers greater capabilities.

Considerations for Web Delivery

In addition to the many characteristics that are a part of all multimedia projects, delivering an Authorware application within a browser environment requires that additional factors be taken into consideration. These factors are not related to Authorware or its capabilities as much as to the technical limitations or requirements of the browser environment. The material that follows explores the more salient issues you may encounter with Web delivery. If you are planning to deliver your application within a Web environment, you will need to consider these factors as part of the project design process, as they could significantly impact the design.

Lowest Common Denominator

From the very early days of CBT, developers have always had to design and develop applications to meet the "lowest common denominator" in terms of the user's computer equipment. In other words, the application must be capable of running on a computer typical of the target audience. Previously, finding the lowest common denominator meant considering the typical user's computer in terms of CPU speed, hard drive size, monitor resolution and maximum number of colors, the presence/absence of a sound card, and the presence/absence/speed of a CD-ROM player.

Related to the lowest common denominator issue is the question of where one draws the line. Requiring higher computer specifications has generally meant that applications could include greater capabilities, whereas lower computer requirements has generally meant that more people would have access to it. Our industry has always had to face this trade-off between greater capability and greater potential audience. *Where to draw the line* has been the challenge. The story continues.

In the early days, CBT was either developed for the PC or Mac. After awhile, cross-platform delivery became possible, which meant that the lowest common denominator then had to accommodate the PC/Mac differences in monitor display, color palettes, text fonts, and sound compatibility. With today's computer technology, many of the early issues concerning finding the lowest common denominator have gone away, although some of the PC/Mac issues still remain. In today's Web environment, probably the most important factor regarding finding the lowest common dominator is related to bandwidth and connection speed.

Bandwidth

In regard to bandwidth, the first consideration is the size of the "pipe" that will be used to distribute the content to be developed. In other words, how fast can the content be downloaded or transmitted from the server to the user's computer? The technology related to this issue is changing by the month. At this point, bandwidth can be classified into roughly three categories: very high-speed connections, high-speed connections, and low-speed connections.

Very High-speed Connections

Browser environments connected via LAN, T1, and T3 phone connections represent large "pipes" that can deliver content just about as effectively as that associated with CD-ROM delivery. This type of connection is typical of many company intranets. Many IT departments, however, are still wary about permitting movies to run over their networks, as this not uncommonly leads to traffic gridlock. Again, the associated streaming technologies in this area may dramatically change this situation in the near future. Typically this environment fully supports the use of audio and even large bitmapped graphics without impacting download performance or impeding network traffic.

High-speed Connections

ISDN, DSL, ADSL, and cable modem connections all promise (at least in their advertisements) to deliver high-speed connections to the Internet. In addition to the caution mentioned previously, you should also be careful about the size of bitmapped graphics. Large, uncompressed graphics will tend to take a lot of time to download. You can try compression formats such as JPEG, or you may want to limit the size of graphics to no larger than about a quarter of the screen. This type of connection generally supports the use of audio, but you will occasionally encounter audio anomalies using it.

Low-speed Connections

This type of connection consists of a 28.8- or 56-K modem connection, on which actual throughput is slow compared to other types of connections. In this environment, you will definitely need to be careful about the size of bitmapped graphics, and generally should use audio somewhat sparingly, as frequent audio glitches are typical. Even though this situation is changing, most home connections are low speed and will likely continue to be so for at least a while longer. If the home user is an important and significant aspect of your target audience, your lowest common denominator will need to include low-speed connections, which in turn will have a significant impact on your design.

Use of Graphics

There are two general types of graphic formats: vector graphics and raster (bitmapped) graphics. These formats are explored in detail in Chapter 4. Vector graphics have a much smaller file size than their bitmapped graphic cousins. On the other hand, most of us are probably more familiar with, and more likely to use, bitmapped graphics. Authorware supports and will import several bitmapped formats.

In addition to appearance, graphics differ in the way they are formatted and displayed. Various graphic formats differ in the way they compress and store the information about a graphic. In regard to Internet use, this is very important, because the greater the compression the smaller the file size, and the shorter the download time.

If you reduce the number of colors used in your image, you will reduce file size. However, you must weigh potential file reduction against image quality reduction. Generally, as you decrease the number of colors you also decrease the quality of the graphic.

Graphic Formats on the Internet

The following are summaries of graphic formats commonly used on the Web, including the main characteristics of each format. You might try saving an image in more than one format and then check its file size and quality to determine the format you want to use for a particular image.

- **JPEG/JPG (Joint Photographic Experts Group)**

    Best for photorealistic images (as opposed to line drawings). Use for images that require more than 256 colors and for scanned photographs.

    Supports millions of colors.

    You can adjust the compression ratio for the graphic. The more you compress an image, the smaller the resulting file size. Usually a graphic compressed to 80% or so of its original size will look just about the same as 100% but will be smaller in file size, thereby downloading much faster. Compressing even further will reduce file size more but may produce a noticeable loss of fidelity.

- **GIF (Graphics Interchange Format, CompuServe)**

    Images with repetitive areas of solid color compress best when exported as gif. This is probably the best choice for non-photographic images, black-and-white and grayscale photographs and graphics, cartoon-like graphics, logos, graphics with transparent areas, and animations.

    Very small file size and therefore download very quickly.

    Supports only 256 colors (8-bit or lower).

- **PNG (Portable Network Graphic)**

    The png format was created as a cross-platform file format. It is a lossless compression, meaning that no quality loss occurs when the image is saved. It internally contains the characteristics for the authoring system so that viewing software (such as browsers) can display the image correctly.

    Supports 8-, 16-, and 32-bit color.

Guidelines for Using Graphics on the Web

The following are some additional guidelines for creating and using graphics on the Web toward minimizing download time.

- *Split a large image into multiple files. You can accomplish this "splicing" within your graphics software program.*

- *Pre-load images whenever possible.*
- *Compress images and use fewer colors to decrease the size of images.*

Use of Sound

When recording audio for Web delivery it is important to keep file size small. Macromedia solutions include the sound formats *vox* and *swa*. The *swa* stands for Shockwave Audio, a specially compressed sound file. When you create an *swa* file you can trade quality for compression ratio: the higher the compression ratio, the smaller the file size. You might want to use a higher compression (with lower quality and smaller file size) when delivering over the Internet, and lower compression (higher quality and larger file size) for delivery over intranets. Files in the *swa* format are created in Authorware by selecting the menu option Xtras | Other | Convert *wav* to *swa*.

The vox format is Voxware's voice compression format. Authorware ships with the Voxware Encoder for converting *wav* files to the *vox* format. The sound compression ratios on *vox* files are nearly 30 to 1 over a normal *wav* file.

Use of Movies

Movies are very large media elements that are typically not very good candidates for including within Web-based applications, especially with modem access to the Internet. However, with the ever-expanding use of high-bandwidth access and rapidly advancing streaming technology, the more frequent use of this media element may soon become a reality.

Use of Flash

Flash animations provide small-size files and can be easily played within an Authorware application. Flash files can be published in a QuickTime (*.mov*) format and played via the Movie icon. The native Flash format can be played via Authorware's Flash sprite.

Presentational/Instructional Strategies

A wide range of strategies can be used to present or display the content of your multimedia application. The particular strategies selected for your project will be influenced by the type of application, the capabilities and imagination of the development team, the specifications of the delivery environment, and the requirements set by the customer. Although not exhaustive, the material that follows provides an overview of the possibilities that exist, including basic approaches, software application training, and learning reinforcers.

Basic Approaches

Basic approaches include strategies that provide a variety of presentational and interactive structures used to present information or actively solicit the user's involvement in the program. These approaches are explored in the sections that follow.

Conceptual Overviews

This type of strategy provides general overviews, using variable combinations of text, graphics, movies, and animation to illustrate concepts, functions, procedures, relationships, paper forms, computer screens, and general guidelines. The structure is linear, generally with forward- and backward-moving paging available. This structure is referred to as a "page turner," implying that it is both linear and noninteractive.

Layered Information

"Layering" is an effective method that accommodates users of varying levels of experience, requirements, or interest. Information is layered or categorized by its usefulness to the audience. The first layer targets an audience that requires general information about a topic. It presents the content using text and graphics, video, or animation. The second layer targets an audience that requires or would like additional information. The user can access the second layer from the first layer by selecting an on-screen button or by clicking on a "hot spot" that indicates more information is available. The second layer is optional and is only seen if the learner selects the button/hot spot to access the additional information.

Interactive Learning Techniques

With interactive techniques, the user becomes actively engaged in the learning process. The user might be asked to drag and place objects in their correct order, drag components and assemble an entire object, type in information, press a key, or correctly select hot spots or objects. Conditions can be structured, progress can be monitored, and evaluation can be recorded. Authorware makes building these interactive structures very easy, frequently with no "programming" involved. Once a particular Authorware interactive structure has been built, it can be reused very easily.

Vignettes and Scenarios

This approach involves a "storyline" involving events and characters, which provides a real-world context for decisions the learner is typically asked to make. Vignettes are structures with generally just a few screens, providing quick character/situation background information before requiring the learner to make some sort of decision based on the information provided. Scenarios are longer, involving greater detail, multiple decision points, and the possibility of multiple resulting paths.

Gaming Techniques

A variety of gaming techniques can be used to create and deliver material in a more interesting and engaging context. Gaming strategies can resemble the formats seen on television, and the creative mind can create a game concept from scratch. Gaming strategies offer fun to both user and creator of the game. Games can also be used as informal or graded user tests, and to capture and record student names and results.

Software Application Training

The entire multimedia industry (beginning with CBT) really began with the use of computers to teach learners how to use computer application software. A multitude of CBT applications have been created to teach a wide range of software programs. A variety of instructional strategies can be incorporated in the development of the components of computer-based training applications. The sections that follow explore such strategies.

Presentation Method

The first option is an instructional presentation method using screen captures to illustrate and describe tasks and functions within the application. Simulation of the software is *not* included. However, this strategy employs either static screen shots with attendant audio and text-based explanations or a video-cam presentation. This method is noninteractive but is generally easier, faster, and far less expensive to create than an interactive application. On the other hand, its instructional effectiveness does not match the simulation techniques described in the following sections.

Guided Practice

Via simulated practice using realistic customer data, this strategy incorporates detailed, step-by-step instructions on how to perform specific software functions. This strategy simulates the actual functioning of at least portions of the software, using customer data similar to that the learner will encounter on the job. Opportunities for the user to receive feedback are often built into this instructional design. This strategy is on the very high end of interactivity and is much more expensive and time-consuming to construct than a less interactive application.

Self-directed Practice

This type of practice strategy is similar to guided practice but differs in that it provides general information about a task rather than specific instructions on how to perform the task. It encourages user independence by requiring the user to apply newly acquired skills via simulated practice of the software application. This approach also incorporates realistic customer data but assumes greater preexisting knowledge on the part of the user. Where mastery and job performance are critical, it is a good strategy to combine guided practice with self-directed practice to reinforce learning and performance.

Case Study

This strategy involves the ultimate simulation exercise, in which students deal with simulated customer calls or data geared toward practice in making decisions, processing requests, and so on. Under this scenario, users have the luxury of making mistakes in a simulated, multimedia situation without fear of the potential negative consequences of real-life situations. Typically no instruction is given; rather, the case study is used to evaluate mastery of performance skills taught previously through guided and self-directed practice. Generally, all of the learner's decisions are recorded and evaluated.

Live Practice with Workbook

This strategy uses printed workbook exercises coordinated with a customer's on-line software application, in a mock situation (i.e., not connected to real customer data and records). This type of exercise allows the user to practice with the actual software and simulated customer data. However, this situation does not provide immediate feedback to the learner nor does it evaluate mastery. The advantage of this approach is that is less expensive and more quickly created than the simulation strategies previously described.

Learning Reinforcers

A number of other strategies can be used to support and expand on information and skills addressed through any of the previously discussed strategies. The strategies in this category are generally used in combination with or as an adjunct to a "main" strategy. The following are useful reinforcement techniques.

Electronic Post-it Notes

This technique involves adding a small overlay screen on top of a primary content or exercise screen, to highlight or emphasize a common problem, suggest a solution, or provide other important information.

Animation

Simple animation can often add considerable instructional value in helping users see and understand relationships, processes, and procedures. Animation also tends to increase user attention and interest in the learning process.

Reference

This strategy and design feature provides instant access to various types of important information, including terms, concepts, computer screens, and field definitions.

Job Aids

This strategy provides a variety of methods for helping users master specific material required to increase job performance. There are many possibilities for what such job aids might look like. As one example, you can create structures for "electronic flash cards" for learners whose jobs can be performed much more effectively if they can easily remember a number of job-related codes or terms.

User Progress and Competency Testing

This strategy evaluates a user's mastery of the material with test items matched to learning objectives. Periodic non-graded progress quizzes and graded competency tests can be constructed and delivered (as well as results recorded and maintained) very easily within Authorware. These structures can randomly select test items, per objective, resulting in each user receiving a unique test.

Project Development Process

The development of any project will generally involve at least four broad phases: *analysis* (examining what needs to be done and for whom), *design* (what will be included and what will it look like), *development* (putting the thing together), and *evaluation* (determining if what was created is what was intended). Each one of these steps can be broken down into far greater detail, depending on the type of project involved. The sections that follow examine each of these steps in greater detail.

Analysis

Before beginning the task of creating something it is a good idea to find out why you are doing it, what purpose it is supposed to serve, and who is going to use it. Such an analysis might be as simple as posing and answering a few questions, such as the following.

- *Who is the intended primary audience?*
- *Is there a secondary audience?*
- *What is the purpose of the application (e.g., to entertain, to teach skills, to provide information, and so on)?*
- *What outcome is expected from the audience after experiencing the application? Are they expected to be able to do something, use something, or have general knowledge about something, or to simply relax and laugh or smile?*
- *Do you need to formally evaluate whether the user "got it" or not?*
- *Will most members of the audience have the same prior knowledge or experiences or will the background and skills vary widely among users?*
- *What types of computer configurations will the application be placed on (you need to find out the lowest common dominator)? What is the processor speed? Will they have audio capability? What is the monitor resolution? Do they have CD-ROM players? Are they on a LAN and/or Web-based network?*

You may want to add questions to this list, depending on the type of project you intend to develop. It is often a good idea to include representatives of the intended target audience as members of the development review team. They can provide ongoing feedback as to whether the project is meeting their needs.

Even if you are creating a multimedia project for your own enjoyment, you may want to ask yourself questions such as this before you start. The answers will give you a target to aim for. Periodically, come back and review your answers to these questions as you are developing your project.

Design

The design phase includes specifying *what* and *how* in great detail. Again, depending on the application, there may be more or fewer elements involved in this phase. The sections that follow explore components to be taken into consideration.

Design Document

A design document is a written statement that should include at a minimum the following information.

- *Audience description*
- *General project objectives*
- *General project description*
- *Detailed content outline*
- *Description of presentational/instructional strategies (correlated to content)*
- *Description of project standards*

- *Development schedule*
- *Assumptions*

Project Standards

The foundation of quality control is the project standards that are proposed, reviewed, and revised/accepted as part of the design process. Quality rests on subsequently adhering to such standards. Standards should exist for text (e.g., text fonts, size, and color), writing (e.g., style, grammar, and punctuation), screen design (e.g., layout design and colors), navigational controls (e.g., usability, location, and functionality), organizational structures (e.g., project, menu, and topic), and functionality. All visual standards should be illustrated with the use of a design prototype developed and reviewed/accepted as part of the early design process. Writing standards and guidelines are typically presented for review as a printed document.

Design Prototype

A design prototype is an on-screen illustration and demonstration of the menu structure, navigational controls, functionality, and all project standards relevant to screen design (e.g., format and color), text (e.g., font, size, and color), graphic quality (e.g., image size, format, and performance), animation (e.g., image size, format, and performance), and audio/video media (e.g., quality and performance). Typically, this prototype does not contain project content but just enough text and images to convey standards.

Development

The best advice that can be given about the development phase is to be careful and do a good job in the analysis and design phases. The more you plan up front, the fewer mistakes you will make during development. Multimedia/Web projects are created in environments in which a lot of mistakes can be made very quickly. If you are creating something for fun, making mistakes is generally not a big deal. In fact, we probably learn most from making mistakes. On the other hand, if you have budget and time constraints, making a lot of mistakes can sink the ship before it sets sail.

In organizing the development phase and minimizing the potential for mistakes, some type of structured development process is critical. To effectively manage the development of complex multimedia/Web projects, you will need to create and strictly adhere to a process similar to that suggested by the following chart. Mutually agreed-upon delivery dates for these phases should also be established prior to beginning the project.

Development Phase	Responsible Party
Project Definition	
Award contract	Customer
Initial project meeting	Customer and developer
Gather information and consult subject matter experts	Customer and developer
Technical specifications set	Customer and developer
Content "frozen"	Customer
Project Design	
Develop design document	Developer
Deliver design document to customer	Developer
Review design document	Customer
Revise design document	Developer
Sign-off of design document	Customer
Design Prototype	
Develop design prototype (interface/standards)	Developer
Deliver design prototype to customer	Developer
Review design prototype	Customer
Revise design prototype	Developer
Sign-off of design prototype	Customer
Content Development	
Write scripts (screen text, audio narration)	Developer
Develop graphic concepts	Developer
Create storyboard (text, narration, graphic concepts)	Developer
Deliver storyboard to customer	Developer
Review storyboard	Customer
Revise storyboard	Developer
Sign-off of storyboard	Customer
Media Production	
Create graphics and animation	Developer
Record and digitize audio/video	Developer
Running First Draft	
Program running draft	Developer
Quality check running draft	Developer
Deliver running draft to customer	Developer
Review running draft	Customer
Revise running draft	Developer
Sign-off of running first draft	Customer
Final Version	
Program final version	Developer
Quality check final version	Developer
Deliver final version to customer	Developer
Sign-off of final version	Customer

Evaluation

Often people think of the evaluation phase in terms of giving a quiz to the learners to see if they "got it" or not. This is certainly one type of evaluation, but perhaps a more fundamental question is does the project do what it was intended to do? Does it meet the requirements of the original objectives? There are different means to address this more fundamental question, depending on the specific goals and type of application.

One method to help ensure that the project achieves its goals is through the use of a quality control and review process. The highly structured development process with customer review and sign-off at each phase is the backbone of developing high-quality multimedia/Web projects that meet the specifications set forth by the customer at the outset of the project.

Structured phase review not only ensures that the project remains on target but provides a means of progressively reviewing project components to ensure adherence to quality standards. With this methodology, design and suggested treatments are approved before executing the actual production of those elements. As elements are created, they are reviewed for quality and adherence to objectives prior to further development.

Phase/Component Internal Review

Before beginning each phase, project standards pertinent to the current phase should be reviewed by the project team and monitored by the project manager throughout the development of each phase. At the conclusion of each phase, group members and the project manager should review each deliverable prior to the customer's review. The review and acceptance process for each phase should be recorded and reviewed by management.

Project Testing

In addition to thorough quality control testing on the phase/component level, the assembled project should undergo separate quality control procedures. Separate and distinct quality control reviews should be conducted for the following.

- *Content accuracy of each screen (reviewing text, graphics, audio, and video segments)*
- *Functionality of each screen (forward, backup, hot spots, and interactivity)*
- *Functionality of common features (buttons for main menu, module menu, quit, glossary, and so on)*

- *Functionality of menus (main to module menu, module menu to topic level, and so on)*
- *Installation program tested on applicable computer platforms*
- *Functionality of installed program*

Project Change Request

Once a development phase has been reviewed and signed off, subsequent requests by the customer for additions or changes should be considered project change requests. A project change request generally results in an increase in cost of development and an increase in the time needed for development. Consider the following.

- *Any customer-requested modifications, changes, or additions outside the scope of the original design or that impact a previously approved phase should be considered project changes.*
- *A project change request generally impacts the delivery date and results in additional cost.*
- *The development team should provide a cost and time impact estimate for each project change request.*
- *A Project Change Request form should be filled out and signed by the designated customer representative.*
- *Project development should not proceed with the project change request until it has been approved and signed by the designated customer representative and returned to the developer's project manager.*

Project Team Members and Skill Sets

Although a single person can create a multimedia project individually, it is more often the case that multimedia/Web projects are worked on by a number of people, each with different skill sets. Multimedia/Web projects generally involve many hours of work, with the high potential for mistakes, and a clear need for skilled efforts, close cooperation, and structured organization.

In some ways, multimedia/Web development is much like the working environment and collaborative efforts required of the many people who typically produce a movie. Who knows, maybe by the end of the book you will feel like a "mini-Spielberg" or "mini-Lucas"?

With a small project, you may end up playing all the roles yourself. With larger projects, team members may have specific individual roles or may have multiple roles. At a minimum, you can have a lot of fun either being a "one-man band" or part of a multimedia team. The sections that follow discuss team members and skill sets typical of most multimedia/Web projects.

Audience

Before you begin any multimedia project, it is important to know who the intended target audience is for the project and what they are expected to get out of it. It might seem strange, but the first team member is sometimes overlooked once the excitement of the development process begins. The more you know about the intended audience, the more likely you will be successful in creating and delivering an application that will meet their needs.

Customer

The customer is the person or entity who has requested the project in the first place. The customer may be within your own school, department, company, or organization, or might be someone or some entity on the outside. The ultimate customer may be different from those who have asked you to create the project.

In the business world, the ultimate customer is the person or organization who will be paying for the project. Does this person or organization have any needs (in addition to those of the audience) this multimedia project must satisfy? These additional needs might include items such as reducing the number of complaints they receive, looking "good" in the eyes of other people, departmental politics, and other agenda items. These additional needs may not always be obvious and may not be open for inquiry, but may influence the successful outcome of your project.

Customer's Project Coordinator

There may be many people as part of the customer team, each with her own perspective about how things should be done. It is critical to establish and clearly identify a central person on the customer's team that all information about the project will flow through.

If there are several people involved in the review process, the customer's project coordinator must consolidate all of these review comments. This person will also be responsible for either personally approving or getting approval for each development sign-off phase. Without a competent person playing this important role, you may find yourself in need of a straitjacket.

Development Project Manager

The project manager for the development team is the team captain responsible for coordinating all aspects of the development process and supervising the efforts of all team members. It is important for the project manager to have an understanding of the skills required of each team member and the organizational skills to manage not only people but a process that tends to get out of kilter very quickly. Again, without a competent person playing this role you may need to have your resultant high blood pressure treated.

Content (or Instructional) Designer

This is the person who not only creates the overall master plan on how the project's content will be organized and sequenced but envisions and describes the details of what strategies should be used to present the content. Within applications that are instructional, educational, or training related, this position is generally held by an instructional designer experienced with how computer-based multimedia can provide interactive events that engage the user in the learning process. The computer's ability to provide this interactive engagement is a significant factor that differentiates multimedia from other instructional media (books, video, audiotape, and so on).

Subject Matter Expert

If you are lucky, the customer will provide as part of their team a person who is very knowledgeable about whatever content is being presented in the application you are building. If the customer does not provide the subject matter expert (SME), you may need to find or educate one quickly (obviously this involves a far greater risk of inaccuracies).

If an SME is provided, this person may not be familiar with multimedia or the project, or may not have very much time to provide you with the help you will probably need. If you carefully describe exactly what type of information you need from the SME, and perhaps show him examples of "how" you would like that information given to you, you will have a far better chance of getting what you need the first time around.

Writer

The writer not only must be able to clearly express the content at the level required of the audience but must have adapted these skills to the multimedia environment. Multimedia presentations can be generally broken down to the "screen" level, with the requirement that each screen must clearly express the central message of that screen through the use of on-screen text, narration, and/or graphics. The space available for text on screen is very limited and therefore must be concise and must support but not duplicate whatever narration is being carried in the audio track. These multimedia characteristics impose additional requirements that print-based writers may not be familiar with.

Editor

The editor not only must have the skills of the multimedia writer but must be familiar with the content and have a broad vision to maintain consistency of style and treatment across all portions of the project.

Art Director

In the same light that the content designer is responsible for the approach and treatment of content, it is the art director who is responsible for the overall visual "look and feel" of everything the user/learner sees, including screen designs, learner control panels, graphics, text styles, and so on. Multimedia projects tend to be very visual, involving many graphic elements, and it is therefore likely that the art director will supervise and coordinate the efforts of several graphic artists, as well as maintaining a consistent visual "look and feel" across all art created.

Graphic Artists

Graphic artists are responsible for creating graphics, animations, icons, screen backgrounds, menu screens, and title screens. Most frequently these graphic elements are created in software programs other than your authoring software. These software programs may include Fireworks, Flash, FreeHand, Photoshop, and other graphic programs. For small projects with limited budgets that are going to be distributed internally, you may end up using clip art as an alternative to a graphic artist. However, remember that most of the time you get what you pay for, so be careful about cutting back too much in this department.

Audio/Video Talent

If you have a small, low-budget project, you or someone else on your team may end up recording the narration or becoming the actors for the video. For larger projects with larger budgets, you will probably end up using professional talent. Just in case there is any doubt in your mind: yes, using professional talent will result in a far superior audio or video product.

Sound/Video Technicians

For smaller projects, relatively inexpensive equipment can be used to record audio and video segments. You will need both sound and video software to digitize and edit whatever you record. Someone on your team will have to do this. For larger projects, you may want to use the services of a professional recording studio and/or video crew.

Author/Programmer/Developer

Regardless of the title, this team member is responsible for creating the authoring structure and placing the content into that structure. Different levels of authoring experience among team members can easily be addressed by dividing tasks according to levels of difficulty. Creating pre-built topic and interactive structures in Authorware will help accommodate the use of developers with varied skill levels.

Authoring/Programming/Developer Manager

The manager of the authoring team is generally responsible for either creating or selecting the basic structures and templates to be used within the project. The manager will need to assign work tasks, supervise the work being performed, and maintain a standard approach to the development of the project.

Summary

- *Multimedia refers to a computer-created and delivered presentation that might involve the use of text on screen, audio narration, graphics, photographs, music, animation, and video. The delivery medium might involve a computer and CD-ROM, traditional LAN/WAN, company intranet, or the Internet. Multimedia applications are developed to achieve a wide range of goals, for a wide range of audiences.*

- *Multimedia applications generally include a number of common features, including an interface, media elements, and additional features. Details of each category were provided earlier in the chapter.*

- *In addition to the many characteristics that are a part of all multimedia projects, delivering an Authorware application within a Web environment requires that additional factors be taken into consideration. These factors are not really related to Authorware or its capabilities as much as to the technical limitations or requirements of a browser environment. These factors include finding the lowest common denominator, bandwidth, use of graphics, use of sound, use of movies, and use of Flash.*

- *Presentational and instructional strategies include basic strategies, software application training, and learning reinforcers. Details of each category were provided earlier in the chapter.*

- *The project development process involves a very structured schedule with designated responsibilities for both the customer and development team. A detailed process and schedule has been provided earlier in this chapter.*

- *Project standards need to be established and maintained for a large variety of development issues, including text standards, writing standards, screen design, navigational controls, project structures, and functionality. All visual standards should be illustrated with the use of a running design prototype, with writing standards and guidelines presented in printed format.*

- *The complete multimedia team involves the following roles or skill sets: intended audience, customer, customer's project coordinator, development project manager, content designer, subject matter expert, writer, editor, art director, graphic artists, audio/video talent, sound/video technician, authors/programmers, and the authoring/programming manager.*

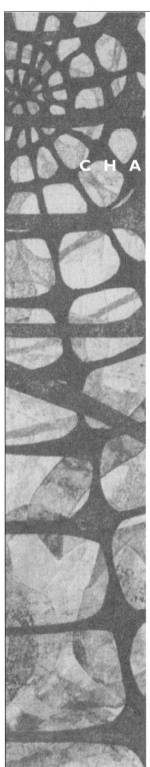

C H A P T E R

3

The Authorware Interface

Introduction

Authorware was originally created and has been continually improved to make your task as a multimedia developer easier to understand and easier to accomplish. A great deal of this ease of use can be attributed to the highly visual approach Authorware takes to the input and sequencing of information. Authorware is truly a "what you see is what you get" (WYSIWYG) authoring environment. Authorware's interface is the foundation of its WYSIWYG capability. There are five components of the interface you work with as "author": menus, toolbar, Icon palette, Design window, and control panel. A sixth component of the interface, the Presentation window, you use as "viewer." By the end of this chapter you will be able to:

- *Describe the general functionality of each Authorware pull-down menu*
- *Explain the use of the toolbar*
- *Describe each icon in the Icon palette*
- *Describe the use of the Design window*
- *Describe the use of the Presentation window*
- *Describe the use of the control panel*
- *Locate Authorware's File Properties function*
- *Explain important screen size and resolution issues*

The main interface components you work with as author are illustrated in figure 3-1. Other interface components are discussed later in the chapter.

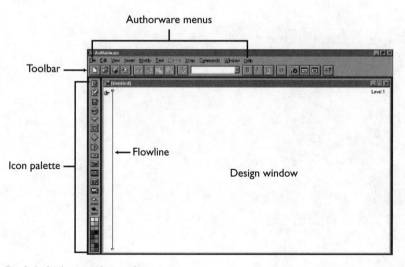

Fig. 3-1. Authorware's interface.

Authorware Menus

Authorware's menus (see figure 3-2) and many of the options within the menus are fairly typical in organization and function of those found in many Windows-based software programs. The sections that follow provide general descriptions of the functionality of each menu, along with an illustration and a few notes about the more common options. You will receive more details about the options in each menu as they are encountered in the process of performing exercises.

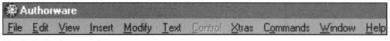

Authorware

File   Edit   View   Insert   Modify   Text   Control   Xtras   Commands   Window   Help

Fig. 3-2. Authorware's menus.

Menu Option Keyboard Shortcuts

As you look at the illustration for each Authorware menu, note that to the right of many of the options is a combination of letters, symbols, and special keys that constitute Authorware's keyboard shortcuts for these designated menu options. As you begin working with Authorware using this book, directions will point you to menu selections, including options within menus. However, as you continue with the practice exercises, keyboard shortcuts will be included either in exercise steps or in a Tip associated with a step.

File Menu

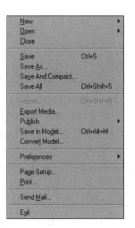

New	▶
Open	▶
Close	
Save	Ctrl+S
Save As...	
Save And Compact...	
Save All	Ctrl+Shift+S
Import...	Ctrl+Shift+R
Export Media...	
Publish	▶
Save in Model...	Ctrl+Alt+M
Convert Model...	
Preferences	▶
Page Setup...	
Print...	
Send Mail...	
Exit	

Options in the File menu (figure 3-3) pertain to operations you can perform on Authorware files, library files, models, and media. The common options include creating a new file (New), opening an existing file (Open), and saving a file (Save). The Print option offers a wide variety of choices in printing part of, or an entire, Authorware file. Save and Compact is a useful addition. As you create and delete icons in Authorware, the file size frequently is not reduced by the same amount as the material you have removed. Save and Compact not only saves the file but gets rid of any unused file space.

Fig. 3-3. File menu.

In the course of this book you will use the Import Media option to bring in graphics that have been created in other software packages. Authorware supports the following graphic formats: *wmf, pict, gif, jpeg, xResLRG, png, Photoshop 3.0, targa, tiff, emf,* and *bmp.* You will also use the Save In Model and Convert Model options to create and apply reusable icon structures called *models.* The Publish option is covered in detail later in the book.

(NOTE)

To import or play back *pict* image files on a Windows computer, you must have QuickTime 4.0 installed.

Edit Menu

The options of the Edit menu (figure 3-4) are common to most Windows software packages. These include Cut, Copy, Paste, Select All, and of course the indispensable Undo. You can use these options with icons on the flowline or objects within a display area. Find and Find Again are Authorware's version of a "Replace" option. The two related Change Properties options allow you to change one or more properties associated with selected icons.

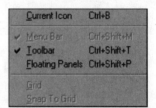

Fig. 3-5. View menu.

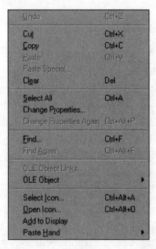

Fig. 3-4. Edit menu.

View Menu

The options listed in the View menu (figure 3-5) provide the capability to turn on or off various tool and formatting options. You will make use of these during the exercises. The Grid option displays a pattern of lines (visible within the Display icon), whereas the Snap To Grid option automatically aligns text or graphic objects to this pattern of lines. (Unfortunately, you cannot vary the size of the grid pattern.) If you are viewing the Presentation window and select the Current Icon option, Authorware will jump to "authoring mode" and show you the current icon on the flowline.

Insert Menu

The options listed in the Insert menu (figure 3-6) provide the capability to import into Authorware media that have been created elsewhere. The Insert | Image option can be used within an open Display icon to import a graphic using the same formats as those found under the File | Import option. The Insert | Icon option can be used to insert (from the menu) any icon found on the Icon palette, as well as the Knowledge Object icon. You might find of particular interest the Media option, which will insert Flash, QuickTime, and Animated GIF files using a special Sprite icon associated with each media type.

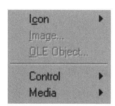
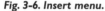

Fig. 3-6. Insert menu.

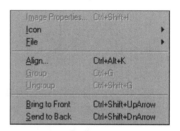

Fig. 3-7. Modify menu.

Modify Menu

The options of the Modify menu (figure 3-7) provide the capability to change the characteristics of icons, files, and objects. You will note that the Icon and File options have sub-menus, listing a number of additional options for each. Modify | Icon | Properties and Modify | File | Properties are options you will make use of extensively during the exercises, and therefore details on these options are provided later in the book.

The Align option helps you select objects and line them up relative to one another. The Group option is used two ways. It can group multiple selected objects located within an open display area. The group object is then treated as if it were a single object. In this case, the Ungroup option "breaks up" a selected group, returning the individual objects of which it was formed. The Group option can also be used to wrap a Map icon around selected icons on the flowline, thereby grouping these icons. In this case, the Ungroup option will "dissolve" a selected Map icon and place whatever icons it contains back on the flowline. Bring to Front and Send to Back allow for arrangement of objects on top of or behind each other, within a Display icon. Exercises will provide you with ample opportunity to practice using many of the options discussed here.

Text Menu

The Text menu (figure 3-8) options are common to word processors and desktop publishing programs. They determine or modify the attributes associated with text objects. Font, Size, Style, Alignment, Apply Styles, and Define Styles are all options you are probably familiar with, but you will get a lot of practice modifying these attributes in the Authorware environment. The Scrolling option creates a scrolling text window with a scroll bar the user can drag to see additional information within the window.

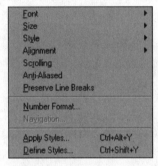

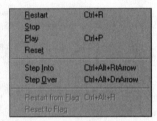

Fig. 3-8. Text menu.   **Fig. 3-9. Control menu.**

Control Menu

All options under the Control menu (figure 3-9) are pertinent to running/viewing either the entire file or a portion of it. You will make use of some of these options later. Authorware makes it very easy to jump back and forth between authoring mode and presentation mode (seeing the application as a viewer).

Xtras Menu

The Xtras menu (figure 3-10) offers several options. Library Links opens a window that displays the names of icons in the flowline that are either linked or have broken links to a library. The Spelling option provides a handy spell checker, and the Icon Size Report option generates a list of icon names and sizes.

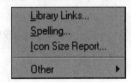

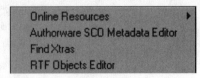

Fig. 3-10. Xtras menu.   **Fig. 3-11. Commands menu.**

Commands Menu

The new Commands menu (figure 3-11) adds the ability to access a number of commands from this menu structure. The Online Resource option offers sub-menu choices providing access to the resources listed. Selecting the Authorware SCO Metadata Editor opens an editor that can be used to record the metadata with your package that conforms to ADL-SCORM specifications (for additional information on this, see Authorware's Help function). The Find Xtras option is used to assist in locating the Xtras that are needed for your Authorware application. The RTF Object Editor is used to create or edit RTF objects without leaving Authorware. The editor includes the ability to add images, paste in Authorware expressions and graphics.

Window Menu

The options of the Window menu (figure 3-12) control the display (or absence) of a variety of information windows. Of greatest interest will be the Inspectors option, and the sub-options Line, Mode, Fill, and Color. These inspectors allow you to change the attributes associated with text and graphic objects. The Functions and Variables options open the same windows as those accessed from the toolbar.

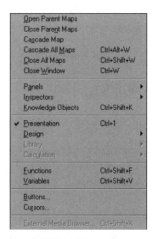

Fig. 3-12. Window menu.

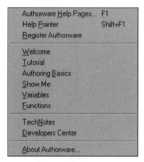

Fig. 3-13. Help menu.

Help Menu

The options of the Authorware Help menu (figure 3-13) offer a variety of approaches to obtaining additional information. The TechNotes and Developers Center options offer on-line connections to the Macromedia Web site, which offers historical and technical information.

Toolbar

As is the case with most Windows-based software programs, Authorware's toolbar contains icon-based shortcuts to the program's most frequently used menu options. Figure 3-14 shows the toolbar, with each of its icon buttons labeled.

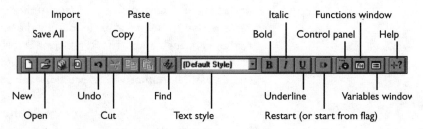

Fig. 3-14. Authorware toolbar.

Icon Palette

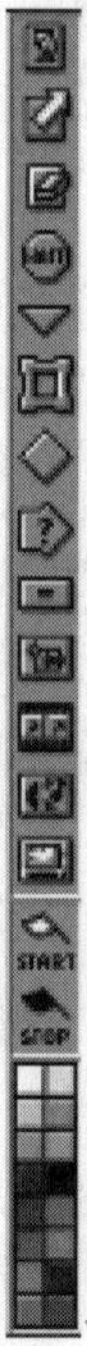

The Icon palette (figure 3-15) contains the building blocks (icons) that form the foundation of any Authorware application you create. Icons from this palette are dragged to the flowline and arranged to create Authorware structures.

In the sections that follow, you will find a brief description of each icon contained in the Icon palette. The name of each icon in the palette pretty much tells you what that icon does. More detailed descriptions of the characteristics and properties of each icon are presented in later chapters, as you begin to work with a specific type of icon.

A new feature in Authorware 6 is a visual indication as to whether an icon contains content. When you first drag an icon from the Icon palette to the flowline or to a library, the icon will appear gray. After you have placed content in it, the icon will appear black. This visual indicator works with icons placed directly on the flowline, within a structure attached to the flowline or within a library.

Fig. 3-15. Icon palette.

Display Icon

Fig. 3-16. Display icon.

As its name implies, the Display icon (figure 3-16) is used to present text or graphics on screen. Once the Display icon has been placed on the flowline, you can double click on it to open the display area within the Presentation window (see figure 3-17). After you have opened a Display icon, you will also notice the appearance of a toolbox containing tools that can be used to create and place objects in the display area. Authorware's File and Insert menus also provide the capability to import both text and graphics into this display area.

·T/P·

The presence of the toolbox within the Presentation window is a visual indicator that you are in the authoring mode within the opened display area of either a Display icon or Inter-action icon. Look carefully at the toolbox in figure 3-17. Note that the left-hand side of the toolbox shows a small illus-tration of a Display icon, indicating that this is the display area of a Display icon. Compare the toolbox in figure 3-17 with the toolbox in figure 3-25, where you will see a toolbox that contains a small illustration of an Interaction icon.

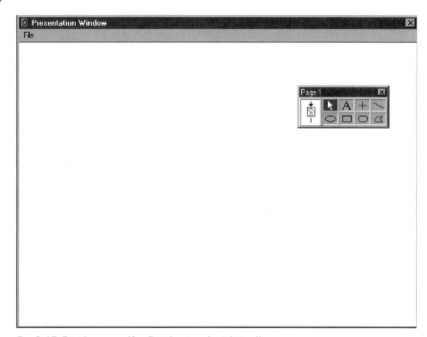

Fig. 3-17. Display area (for Display icon) with toolbox.

The display area is truly a WYSIWYG environment, as you can add, modify, and manipulate text and graphic objects directly on screen. As you will see in Chapter 4, the Display icon also includes a transition property, which allows you to use special effects to display the content of the icon as it is first being shown on screen.

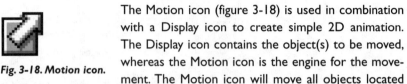
·TiP·

Authorware does not distinguish multiple objects located within a single Display icon. Therefore, if you want to move one object and not others, you will want to place the object to be moved within a Display icon by itself, and then link the Motion icon to this Display icon. Place all other displayed objects within a separate Display icon that is not linked to the Motion icon.

Motion Icon

Fig. 3-18. Motion icon.

The Motion icon (figure 3-18) is used in combination with a Display icon to create simple 2D animation. The Display icon contains the object(s) to be moved, whereas the Motion icon is the engine for the movement. The Motion icon will move all objects located within the Display icon to which it is linked. As you will see later, the Motion icon offers a variety of motion paths. Although the results produced with the Motion icon cannot compete with the animation obtainable with Flash or another animation program, the Motion icon can be used to quickly and inexpensively create simple animation to increase user interest and understanding.

Erase Icon

There are two methods by which you can erase objects from the screen. The first involves the use of an Erase icon (figure 3-19). When an Erase icon is encountered on the flowline, it will erase any icons linked to it. You can very easily link icons to be erased by simply opening the Erase icon and using the mouse to click on whatever objects you want to erase.

Fig. 3-19. Erase icon.

As mentioned previously, Authorware does not distinguish multiple objects located within a single icon, and will therefore erase all objects within an icon designated to be erased. You can also remove an icon from the linked list, so that it will no longer be erased. The same set of transitions available for the Display icon is available with the Erase icon, to apply special effects as objects are erased from the screen. The second method of erasing icons involves the use of the Authorware functions *EraseIcon* and *EraseAll*.

·TiP·

Normally you might use a single Display icon to display multiple objects on screen. If, however, you wish to leave some objects on screen as you erase others, you will need to place the objects that remain on screen in one Display icon, and place those to be erased in a second Display icon. Splitting up the objects in this way allows you to use the Erase icon to erase one Display icon (and its objects) while the other objects remain on screen.

Wait Icon

Fig. 3-20. Wait icon.

When Authorware encounters a Wait icon (figure 3-20) on the flowline, it will pause the program. The Wait icon can be set to pause for a length of time or wait for the user to press any key, click the mouse on the screen, or select an on-screen button. The Wait icon has additional options to show/hide a button and show/hide a clock counting down the time remaining.

Navigate Icon

Fig. 3-21. Navigate icon.

The Navigate icon (figure 3-21) is used to branch from one location in the flowline to a designated second location. The Navigate icon offers a variety of settings, which will be covered in more detail as you work with the Framework icon. The Navigate icon can be used in conjunction with the Framework icon only.

Framework Icon

Fig. 3-22. Framework icon.

The Framework icon (figure 3-22) serves as an excellent foundation for creating a variety of Authorware structures, including paging structures and menu structures. The Framework icon has a built-in navigation control panel, including forward, backup, and exit buttons (as well as others). The Framework icon can also be used to easily create hyperlinked structures for glossaries, help files, and other information sources.

Decision Icon

Fig. 3-23. Decision icon.

The Decision icon (figure 3-23) is a branching structure that allows the author/programmer to determine which path the user will proceed along. The Decision icon is strictly a branching/routing structure with no display area associated with it. The author may set the Decision icon's logic to follow either sequential or random order, along with several other properties.

Interaction Icon

Fig. 3-24. Interaction icon.

The Interaction icon (figure 3-24) represents the foundation of Authorware's ability to easily produce highly interactive learning applications with little or no programming on your part. The Interaction icon offers a wide variety of methods (response types) the learner can use to interact with the program. You will get extensive practice in using most of these response types in the chapters that follow.

·T/P·

Look carefully at the toolbox shown in figure 3-25. The left-hand side shows a small illustration of an Interaction icon, indicating that you are looking at the display area of an Interaction icon. Note the difference in the toolboxes in figures 3-17 and 3-25.

The Interaction icon is distinguished by two important capabilities. First, it has a display area similar to the Display icon that can be used to display text and graphics on screen. Double clicking on the Interaction icon opens this display area. Figure 3-25 shows the Interaction icon's display area and its associated toolbox. The Interaction icon's second capability provides a branching structure that requires a response from the learner. There is a wide range of response types that can be handled by the Interaction icon.

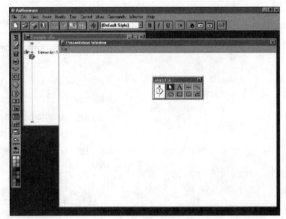

Fig. 3-25. Interaction icon's display area and toolbox.

The Interaction icon differs from the Decision icon in two important respects. First, the Decision icon does not have a display associated with it, whereas the Interaction icon does. Second, although both of these icons are branching structures, they differ as to who controls the branching decision. With the Decision icon, the author determines which path will be taken. With the Interaction icon, the user selects the path to be taken. As you will see later, during the exercises, you can create very useful Authorware structures using a combination of both Interaction icons and Decision icons.

The Calculation icon can be used to create and store developer comments that can be placed next to the Authorware structure to which they relate. These comments can serve as an invaluable development technique and cannot be misplaced as paper-based notes can.

If you are going to place comments within a Calculation icon, make sure you start each new line with a double hyphen (--). The double hyphen tells Authorware to ignore anything else that follows. Otherwise, Authorware will try to interpret whatever you have written as a function or variable, and will most often return an error message. You will practice using the Calculation icon for on-line notes during exercises found later in the book.

Calculation Icon

Fig. 3-26. Calculation icon.

The Calculation icon (figure 3-26) has neither display nor branching capability by itself. The Calculation icon is like an empty box. Programming statements can be written within a Calculation icon located on the flowline, within an icon structure, or directly attached to another icon. In Authorware, these programming statements are referred to as variables or functions. As a Calculation icon is encountered, whatever variables or functions are located within the icon are executed at that time. The Calculation icon can also be used to create developer's comments that never appear on screen (see following Tip).

Map Icon

Fig. 3-27. Map icon.

The Map icon (figure 3-27) has no display or branching capability. The Map icon is also like an empty box. However, in this case it holds other icons. The Map icon can be used to group icons that perform a similar task, or to group icons simply for the purpose of creating more space on the flowline. When a Map icon is opened, a second flowline appears within this Map icon. This second flowline exists on level 2, whereas the root flowline exists on level 1.

In this way, Map icons can be used to nest one flowline within another, within another, and so on. In other words, you can place a Map icon within a Map icon, within a Map icon, and so on, creating a multi-level structure. In figure 3-28 you will note that there is a Map icon (Topic One) on the level 1 flowline. Within this Map there are two Display icons (Topic 1-A and Topic 1-B) and another Map icon (Sound files). These icons exist on level 2 flowlines. Inside the Sound files Map icon there are three Sound icons that exist on the level 3 flowline.

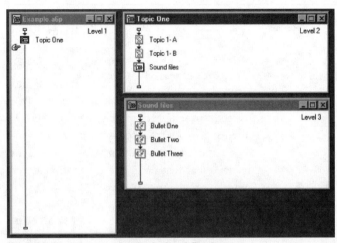

Fig. 3-28. Maps containing multi-level flowlines.

The inquiring mind might ask how many levels can be created. The practical answer to this question is more than you really want to use. Especially in the beginning, creating Authorware structures that contain more than five or six levels will probably lead to confusion and difficulty in locating authoring segments.

Digital Movie Icon

Fig. 3-29. Digital Movie icon.

The Digital Movie icon (or more simply, Movie icon), shown in figure 3-29, provides the capability to seamlessly play a digital movie within an Authorware application. The Movie icon is very easy to use and allows the author to set the Start frame and End frame, so that you can play either a portion of a movie file or the entire thing. The movie file itself remains an independent file that must be included when you distribute your Authorware program. The Movie icon is linked to the movie file and plays that movie through the Authorware interface.

The Movie icon can import a variety of formats, including Video for Windows, QuickTime, MPEG, Director, FLC/FLI, and bitmapped sequences. Some of these formats require software drivers in order to play the movie within a Windows application. You can also use Authorware's Insert menu (Insert | Media) to include Flash movies, QuickTime movies, and animated *gifs*. The Insert | Media option does not use a Movie icon but instead inserts a special Sprite icon associated with the media type you have selected. As you advance in the use of Authorware's functions, you will probably discover that there are also media functions that can be used to play movie files.

Sound Icon

Fig. 3-30. Sound icon.

With the use of the Sound icon (figure 3-30), you can very easily include narration, music, and sound effects within an Authorware application. There are a variety of options within the Sound icon that provide additional control. The Sound icon supports several digital audio formats, including *aiff*, *pcm*, *swa*, *vox*, *wav*, and *mp3*. Unlike movies, which will always remain as independent files on disk, with the Sound icon you have the choice of either creating a link and leaving the sound file on disk or importing the sound file into the Sound icon (so that it becomes part of the Authorware file).

Audio files tend to be fairly large. The sound file characteristics selected during the digital recording process will dramatically affect the size of the resulting file. Make note of the fact that as you import sound files using Sound icons your Authorware file will quickly become large.

There are advantages and disadvantages associated with linking to or importing sound files. Especially in the beginning, you will probably find it easier to simply import sound files into the Sound icon. As you advance in the use of Authorware's functions, you will discover that there are also media functions that can be used to play sound files.

Video Icon

Fig. 3-31. Video icon.

You will probably never use the Video icon (figure 3-31), as it is associated with the old technology of video disc players. This icon is not used in the exercises in this book. You may find additional information about this icon in your Authorware reference manual and on Macromedia's Web site.

Start Flag

Fig. 3-32. Start flag.

The Start flag (the white flag), shown in figure 3-32, and the Stop flag (the black flag) are very useful tools for viewing, testing, and troubleshooting sections of your Authorware structure. The Start flag can be dragged to the flowline to indicate where you want to begin the viewing, testing, and troubleshooting process.

Stop Flag

Fig. 3-33. Stop flag.

The Stop flag (black flag), shown in figure 3-33, may be dragged to the flowline to indicate where you want to stop the viewing, testing, and troubleshooting process.

Icon Color Palette

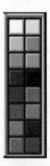

Fig. 3-34. Icon Color palette.

The Icon Color palette (figure 3-34) contains 16 colors that may be assigned to icons on the flowline. You may want to use these colors to categorize icons by common function, subject, or some other meaningful classification scheme. You can assign a color to an icon by first selecting the icon and then selecting one of these 16 colors.

Design Window

The Design window (figure 3-35) contains the main flowline, the vertical line that serves as the foundation upon which all Authorware sequences and structures are built. The process of building an Authorware structure is accomplished by dragging icons from the Icon palette to the flowline. The particular icons you select and the placement of those icons on the flowline determine how your content is presented.

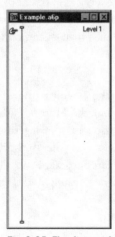

Fig. 3-35. Flowline within the Design window.

You can also add scrollbars to the Design window by clicking the right mouse button (within the Design window) and selecting the scrollbars option. This option adds horizontal and/or vertical scrollbars when the current dimensions can not display all of the flowline. We suggest, however, that the use of scroll-bars (especially in the beginning) may not be a good idea, as you may forget that icons are off-screen. Instead of using the scrollbars, you can use Map icons to group icon structures and increase the amount of room available on the flowline.

In the first couple of exercises you will build structures that will be placed directly on the main flowline. As you will soon discover, building structures in this way not only takes up a lot of room on the flowline but more importantly does not offer other important features needed for interactive applications. After the first few exercises, you will soon begin to build structures that expand horizontally (from left to right on the X axis).

·T*i*P·

Authorware "reads" the flowline in a particular order, much like we do in the English language. Authorware reads the flowline from top to bottom, left to right.

Control Panel

The Control panel is a floating window that contains controls that provide easy access to the playback, restart, or pausing of an Authorware program file. The Control panel can be opened within the authoring environment by select-ing Window | Control. The controls are similar to VCR play/stop buttons, as you can see in figure 3-36. The Show/Hide button on the right-hand side opens up a Trace window that can be used to debug the flowline structure.

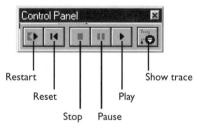

Restart
Reset
Stop   Pause
Play
Show trace

Fig. 3-36. Control panel.

Presentation Window

All elements of the Authorware interface you have examined so far have been viewed from the perspective of the Authorware author/programmer. The next interface element, the Presentation window, is examined from the perspective of the learner or user. The Presentation window is what the user or learner sees after the Authorware program file has been packaged and distributed for use. The size of the Presentation window within the computer monitor is dependent on the resolution setting of the Authorware file relative to the resolution of the monitor settings in Windows. See figures 3-43 and 3-44 for illustrations of two different examples of the Presentation window as seen from within the authoring environment.

Authorware provides you (as author/programmer) with the ability to quickly switch back and forth between the flowline (where the programming structure is built) and the Presentation window, where the results of that structure can be viewed. In fact, because Authorware is truly a WYSIWYG environment, almost anything you see within the Presentation window can be modified by you (author) on the fly. You will have a lot of practice doing this throughout exercises in the book.

The size and location of the Presentation window on your computer screen is dependent on two factors: your computer monitor's resolution setting within Microsoft Windows and the resolution setting within Authorware's file properties (Modify | File | Properties). You can examine the difference these settings can make within the authoring environment (on your computer) and when the Authorware application is packaged and run on a user's computer. However, to see these differences you first need some experience setting Authorware's file properties.

Guided Tour 3A: Authorware File Properties

Before you start creating anything in Authorware, it is generally a good idea to define at least a few properties that will apply to the entire Authorware file. In the following guided tour, you are going to change a few of the default settings.

1. Start by opening a new file, as follows.
    a) Select File | New.
    b) Close the two dialog windows that have opened by clicking on the X in the upper right-hand corner of each window. These windows pertain to the use of Knowledge objects, which you will not be using for quite a while. See figures 3-37 and 3-38.

·T/P·

An even quicker method of jumping back and forth is making use of a shortcut keyboard combination: simultaneously press the Control (Ctrl) and J keys. If you are currently on the flowline, you will jump to the Presentation window for the current location. If you are currently viewing the Presentation window, Ctrl + J will jump back to the flowline.

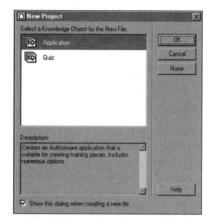

Fig. 3-37. Close the New File
knowledge object dialog window.

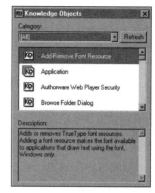

Fig. 3-38. Close the Knowledge
Objects dialog window.

    c)   You should now be looking at an empty flowline.

2.   Place an icon on the flowline, name it, and then add a little content, as follows.

    a)   Move your mouse to the Icon palette and click on the Display icon. While holding the left mouse button down, drag the Display icon to the flowline. Let go of the mouse button. You now have one icon on the flowline.

    b)   Select the Display icon on the flowline by clicking on it. Note that the "untitled" icon name is now highlighted. Type *Page 1*. You have now given this icon the name of *Page 1*. Note that the color of the Display icon is gray, indicating that it contains no content. This is a new feature of Authorware 6.

    c)   Double click on the Display icon to open it. Notice the toolbox, indicating that you are in authoring mode. In addition to the tools, the toolbox also displays the name of the current Display icon, *Page 1*, as well as a small picture of a Display icon.

    d)   Click on the Text tool to select it. See figure 3-39.

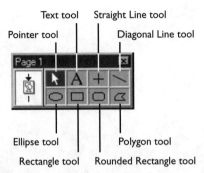

Text tool   Straight Line tool
Pointer tool   Diagonal Line tool

Ellipse tool   Polygon tool
Rectangle tool   Rounded Rectangle tool

Fig. 3-39. Tools in the toolbox.

e) As you move the cursor arrow away from the toolbox, it changes to an I-bar cursor. Click the I-bar cursor anywhere on screen and a new text object opens. Type in the word *Dog* and click on the Pointer tool in the toolbox to close the text object.

f) To close the Display icon, click on the X in the Toolbox (or you could click on the X in the upper right-hand corner of the Presentation window).

g) Notice that the color of the Display icon is now black, indicting that the icon now has content in it.

3. Now it is time to take a look at this Display icon through the Presentation window, as follows. Make note of what you see here, because you are going to change some of these properties in steps to follow.

a) Click on the Restart button in the toolbar. See figure 3-14 if you need help locating the button.

b) You should now be looking at the word *Dog* on a white background.

c) Look at the two bars at the very top of the screen. The topmost bar is the Title bar. Using the File Properties window (figure 3-40), you could enter the title of the program and have it appear in this Title bar on every screen in the packaged program.

d) Look at the second bar containing the word *File*. Click on the word *File* and notice that it opens a pull-down menu containing a Quit option. As you develop your own Authorware applications, pull-down menus you create for your user will all appear on this bar, located side by side to the right of this File menu.

e) Close the Presentation window by clicking on the X in the upper right-hand corner of the window.

4. Many Authorware developers create a custom user interface that does not make use of these two bars. The exercises in this book will *not* use these bars either, so let's remove these bars to recapture the use of this

screen space, as follows. You will look at some other file properties as you modify these options.

a) The file properties are in the Modify menu. Select Modify | File | Properties.

b) You should now be looking at a dialog window of file properties. See figure 3-40.

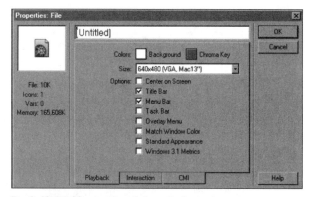

Fig. 3-40. File Properties dialog window.

5. Notice that there are three tabs on the bottom of this dialog window: Playback, Interaction, and CMI. If your computer screen does not look like that shown in figure 3-40, make sure the Playback tab has been selected.

6. Look at the top of the dialog window for a field named *Colors/Background*. The default background color for every display area in this file is currently white, as you may remember seeing in step 3b. Change the default background color, as follows.

a) Click on the white square, to the left of the word *Background*. This opens Authorware's Color palette, shown in figure 3-41.

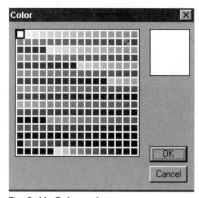

Fig. 3-41. Color palette.

b) Select the color you want for the background by clicking the mouse on that color. To close the Color palette, click on the OK button or on the X in the upper right-hand corner of the Color palette.

7. Note under Options at the center of the File Properties dialog window that there are check marks beside Title Bar and Menu Bar. It is the presence of these check marks that caused the appearance of the two bars in the Presentation window you saw in step 3c.

8. Examine the interface depicted in figure 3-42. This interface is typical of the screen design used by many developers of computer-based training. The header bar at the top of each screen is used to display program information such as module name, topic name, and page count. The navigational control panel at the bottom of screen contains all buttons for accessing movement capability within the program (forward, back, module menu, and so on).

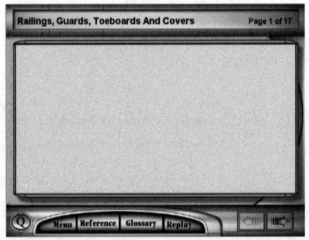

Fig. 3-42. Interface showing header bar at the top and navigational control panel at the bottom.

9. Throughout the exercises in this book, you are going to create (and/or use) a custom header bar. Thus, you will *not* be using pull-down menus, and therefore need to turn off the display of the title bar and menu bar, as follows.

a) Click your mouse on the check marks beside the Title Bar and Menu Bar options to remove them. In a step to follow you will confirm that both the title and menu bars no longer appear on screen.

10. Immediately above the Title Bar option is an option that will center the display of the Presentation window on screen. Click in the box next to the Center on Screen option to place a check mark there.

11. The next File Properties setting to look at is Size (computer screen resolution). Perform the following.
    a) Click on the down arrow next to the Size field to open a pull-down menu.
    b) The three most often used settings for PC users are 640 x 480, 800 x 600, and 1024 x 768. A more in-depth discussion of the impact of this setting is presented in the following section.
    c) Leave the size at 640 x 480. Close the pull-down menu, with 640 x 480 selected.

12. Before you close the File Properties window, take a look at the Title field at the very top of the window. Currently it displays *(Untitled)*. This is where you could type in a title for your course or application. The title you enter here will show up in the title bar (*if* you select this option by placing a check mark next to it) in the Presentation window of a packaged Authorware file.

13. Close the File Properties window by clicking on the OK button in the upper right-hand corner.

14. Now it is time to take another look at the Presentation window. Perform the following.
    a) Click on the Restart button in the toolbar.
    b) You should now be looking at the word *Dog,* but this time on the background color you just selected.
    c) You will also note that neither the title bar nor menu bar appear on screen.
    d) If your monitor is set to 640 x 480 (in Windows), the Presentation window will fill the entire screen. If your monitor (in Windows) is set to a higher resolution, the Presentation window should be displayed in the center of you computer monitor.

15. You are now finished with the guided tour, which has introduced you to the next topic: screen resolution issues.

Screen Resolution

The Size setting under the File Properties dialog window (figure 3-40) deserves further explanation. Notice that the default is set to 640 x 480. This setting determines the size of the Authorware Presentation window during playback, both in authoring mode as a program file and as a packaged (or final) file.

·T/P·

Center on Screen positions the Presentation window in the center of the computer's monitor but is only noticeable when running a low-resolution Authorware program (e.g., 640 x 480) on a high-resolution (800 x 600) monitor. Otherwise, the Presentation window takes up the entire screen.

·T/P·

Whatever name you enter in the Title field will only appear if the Title Bar option has been selected *and* the Authorware file has been packaged. Do not expect the title to change while you are in authoring mode.

Chapter 2 discussed in detail a number of issues concerning identifying the lowest common denominator of computers typical of your viewing audience. In regard to resolution, this means that if most of the people who will be viewing your program have computers with Windows set to 640 x 480 screen resolution, this is the Authorware setting you should choose. You may find that most computers in corporate America these days can support at least 800 x 600. However, this may not be true of home users.

An Authorware program created with the File Property set to a lower resolution (e.g., 640 x 480) will play on a higher-resolution (800 x 600) computer. The reverse, however, is not true. An Authorware program set to 800 x 600 will not play properly on a computer set to 640 x 480.

Another relevant factor related to the Windows/Authorware resolution issue is the size and appearance of the Presentation window within the authoring environment. If your Windows and Authorware settings are the same, the Presentation window will fill the entire screen. If on the other hand your Windows resolution is set higher than your Authorware resolution, you will be able to see both the Presentation window and the Authorware menus/toolbar.

Figures 3-43 and 3-44 show the difference in the Presentation window running at the two different resolution sizes. Notice that when Windows and Authorware are set the same, the Presentation window fills the entire screen (figure 3-43). In this situation, to gain access to Authorware's menus while the Presentation window is running you have to use either keyboard commands or jump to the flowline to select the menu. With Windows set at a higher resolution, the Presentation window appears on screen and there is enough room for Authorware's menus and the Icon palette to be displayed (figure 3-44).

·T/P·

This Authorware/ Windows resolution issue is an important one that you should not overlook. If you attempt to play a high-resolution Authorware program on a low-resolution computer monitor, you will notice that a significant portion of the content is off screen. Unfortunately, there is no quick fix. You will end up recreating the program practically from scratch, at the lower resolution.

NOTE

Unless noted otherwise, screen captures and instructions in this book are based on the assumption that Windows is set to 800 x 600 and Authorware is set to 640 x 480 resolution.

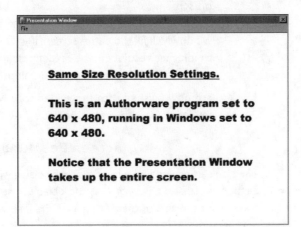

Fig. 3-43. Windows and Authorware set to same resolution.

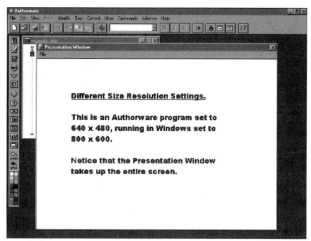

Fig. 3-44. Windows set to higher resolution than Authorware.

Summary

- *The Authorware menus and many of the options found within the menus are fairly typical in organization and function of menus found in many Windows-based software programs.*

- *The five interface components actively used by the Authorware author are the menus, toolbar, Icon palette, Design window, and control panel. The sixth interface component is the Presentation window, which displays whatever the user will see.*

- *Before you start creating anything in Authorware, it is generally a good idea to define at least a few properties that will apply to the entire Authorware file. The file properties are located in the Modify menu (Modify | File | Properties).*

- *There are several important issues relevant to screen size and resolution. It is generally suggested that you select the lowest common denominator of computers typical of your viewing audience. A program created in low resolution will play on a high-resolution computer. The reverse, however, is not true. A high-resolution program cannot be properly played on a low-resolution computer screen.*

- *The Windows operating system resolution of the computer you are working on will affect how your Authorware environment will appear.*

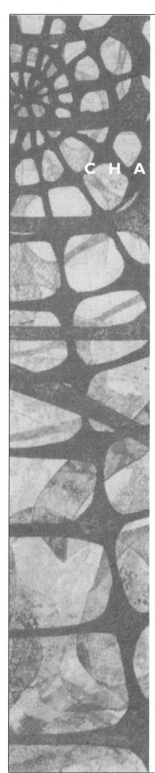

CHAPTER 4

Creating Display

Elements

Introduction

In this chapter you are going to start creating simple structures in Authorware. You will begin with the tools in the toolbox, learn some tricks about text objects and "depth," and then create a simple presentation sequence using Display icons, Wait icons, Erase icons, and a Map icon. By the end of the chapter you will be able to:

- *Create simple objects using the tools in the toolbox*
- *Use the inspectors to modify objects*
- *Describe the characteristics of the Display, Wait, Erase, and Map icons*
- *Create simple text displays and transitions*
- *Create timed and interactive pauses*
- *Create display/erase sequences with transitions*

Guided Tour 4A: Toolbox Basics

As its name implies, the Display icon is used to display objects (text or graphic) on the screen. Text and graphic objects can either be imported into the Display icon from external files or can be created "from scratch" using the tools within the toolbox. As you will see in a later chapter, the display area within the Interaction icon incorporates the same capabilities and characteristics as the Display icon. In the following you will take a look at these tools and get some experience in using them.

1. Start by opening a new file.
   a) Select File | New | File.
   b) Close the two dialog windows that have opened by clicking on the X in the upper right-hand corner of each window. (These windows pertain to the use of Knowledge objects, covered in a later chapter.)
   c) You should now be looking at an empty flowline.

2. Next you will need to place a Display icon on the flowline.
   a) Use the mouse and click on the Display icon in the Icon palette.
   b) While holding down the mouse button, drag the Display icon to the flowline and let go. See figure 4-1.

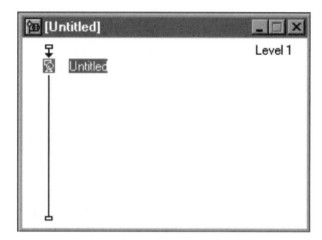

Fig. 4-1. Display icon on flowline.

Give each icon you place on the flowline a name descriptive of what is contained within the icon, or use some other logical naming convention. Try to use a name that is unique for each icon. Using unique names is generally a good idea, but becomes a necessity when naming icons used with animations and drag-and-drop interactions.

3. A really good production habit to get into is to name every icon you place on the flowline. Go ahead and do this now.

   a) The untitled Display icon on the flowline should still be highlighted (if not, simply touch it with the mouse cursor). The gray color indicates that it does not contain content.

   b) Give the highlighted icon a name by simply typing it while the title is highlighted. Type the name *Graphics*.

4. To take a look inside the Display icon, perform the following.

   a) Open the Display icon by double clicking on it.

   b) You are now looking at an empty Display icon with the toolbox ready to use.

   c) Take a look at the toolbox in figure 4-2, showing the descriptive labels of each tool.

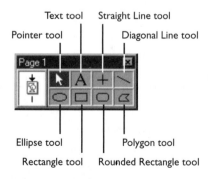

Fig. 4-2. Tools within the toolbox.

5. The first tool is the Pointer. It is used to select and reposition objects on screen. When using any of the other tools in the toolbox, the mouse cursor becomes active, takes on different shapes, and will create objects when the mouse is clicked anywhere on screen. After using these other tools, select the Pointer tool to return the mouse cursor to its normal state.

6. To use the Text tool to create text, perform the following.
   a) Click on the Text tool.
   b) As you move the cursor away from the toolbox, note that the cursor turns into an I-bar. Move the I-bar cursor over to the far left of the screen. Click on the screen.
   c) An open text object has appeared. Type in anything you want, but make sure to type at least *two* lines of text.
   d) Note that as you continue to type and reach the far right side of the text object, the text automatically word wraps just like a word processor.
   e) Close the text object by clicking on the Pointer tool.

7. Now try moving the text object around the screen.
   a) Using the Pointer tool, click on the text object.
   b) While holding down the mouse button, drag the text object to some other location on screen.

8. To change the margins of the text object, perform the following.
   a) Make sure you have the text object selected (if not, click on it). A selected object will have handlebars.
   b) Now use the Pointer tool and click on the right-hand handlebar of the text object. While holding the mouse button down, move the handlebar to the left, making the margin narrower.
   c) You have instantly created a new right-hand margin. See figures 4-3 and 4-4.

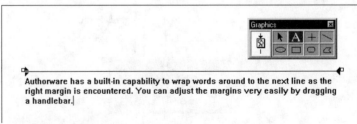

Authorware has a built-in capability to wrap words around to the next line as the right margin is encountered. You can adjust the margins very easily by dragging a handlebar.

Fig. 4-3. Text object with original margin.

In the authoring mode, you can move any object in an open display area by selecting the Pointer tool, clicking on the object, holding down the left mouse button, and dragging the object to the new location.

·T/P·

It is generally a good idea to select the Pointer tool every time you are finished creating some object and before you try selecting any object on screen. A very common problem occurs when you try to select an object while another tool is still active. As an example, you may end up creating a lot of tiny lines if you try to select an object while the Line tool is still active, or a lot of tiny rectangles if the Rectangle tool is still active. This is true with each of the tools, except the Text tool. Accidentally creating and closing an empty text object results in no text object being formed. In order to select and move an object within the display area, you will need the Pointer tool; it is just good practice to immediately select it as soon as you are done with any of the other tools.

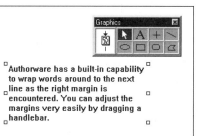

Authorware has a built-in capability to wrap words around to the next line as the right margin is encountered. You can adjust the margins very easily by dragging a handlebar.

Fig. 4-4. Text object with narrower margin.

After selecting any of the graphic tools in the toolbox, the cursor changes to a cross-hair cursor as you move the cursor away from the toolbox. Note the difference between the cross-hair cursor and the I-bar cursor used for text objects.

With the Pointer tool you can also drag the handlebars on any graphic object to increase or decrease the object's size.

If you hold down the Shift key before (and as) you create the circle or rectangle, you will be able to create a "perfect" ellipse (circle) or rectangle (square) of any size.

9. The next tool you will use is the Straight Line tool.
   a) Click on the Straight Line tool. As you move the cursor away from the toolbox, it turns into a cross-hair cursor.
   b) Click the cross-hair cursor somewhere on screen.
   c) As you hold the mouse button down, drag the cursor to the right and then let go.
   d) Try creating several lines. Note that the Straight Line tool allows you to draw lines that are either horizontal, vertical, or at 45-degree angles.

10. Next is the Diagonal Line tool, which allows you to draw a line at any angle.
    a) Click on the Diagonal Line tool and try drawing a few lines.
    b) Unlike the other line tool, the Diagonal Line tool allows you to create lines drawn at any angle.

11. Moving now to the bottom left corner of the toolbox, you will find the Ellipse tool.
    a) Click on the Ellipse tool.
    b) Click the cursor on a vacant part of the screen. While holding down the mouse button, drag the cursor to the right and downward. You can create any size and shape circle with this tool.

12. Now use the Rectangle tool.
    a) Click on the Rectangle tool.
    b) Click the cursor on a vacant part of the screen. While holding down the mouse button, drag the cursor to the right and downward. Try creating a few rectangles using this tool.

13. Next is the Rounded Rectangle tool, which creates rectangles with rounded corners. The Shift key trick (see Tip at left) works with this tool as well (a square with rounded corners).
    a) Click on the Rounded Rectangle tool.

b) Click the cursor on a vacant part of the screen. While holding down the mouse button, drag the cursor to the right and downward. Try creating a few rounded rectangles using this tool.

14. The last tool to be used in this section is the Polygon tool. This one is a little bit different.

a) Click on the Polygon tool.

b) Click on a vacant area of the screen. Let up on the mouse button and move the cursor. Note that the cursor seems "stuck" to the line as you move it around.

c) Click on the screen at a second location. You have just anchored a second point of the polygon and the line is still stuck to the cursor.

d) Move the cursor and click on another location. A third anchor point was just created.

e) Create several more anchor points. When you are finished drawing, double click to close the polygon.

15. As a final task, perform the following.

a) Click on the Pointer tool.

b) Click on one of the handlebars of the polygon. Drag the handlebar in one direction or another.

c) Note that you can increase or decrease the size but cannot change the number of sides of this graphic figure.

d) Click on one of the rectangles. Drag a handlebar in one direction or another. Again, you can change the size and shape but cannot change the fact that it is a four-sided figure.

That is all there is to the basic tools, but there is more to learn about the attributes associated with the objects you have just created. You will be introduced to these attributes in the next section, a tour of Authorware's inspectors.

Guided Tour 4B: Authorware's Inspectors

There are several attribute panels, known as inspectors, that can be used only with graphic or text objects located in a Display icon or the display area associated with an Interaction icon. These are simple but important tools that allow you to modify the attributes or characteristics of whatever objects you create within Authorware. The sections that follow explore these tools.

Using the Mode Inspector

To try your hand at using the Mode inspector, perform the following steps.

1. You should already have a file open from the last guided tour (if not, open a new file by selecting File | New | File).

If you close the polygon with the last point right next to the first (origin) point, the polygon will have a line around the entire object. If, on the other hand, you close the polygon with the last and first points at different locations, there will not be a line between these points, although you may still have a fill color (fills are discussed in the following section).

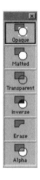

Fig. 4-5.
Modes
inspector.

Shortcut

The Modes inspector
can also be opened /
closed by double
clicking on the Pointer
tool in the toolbox, or
by using the keyboard
shortcut Ctrl + M.

NOTE

You may find the
Inverse Mode handy
for positioning graphics
that share common
elements or graphic
elements that are
contained in different
icons. You can set the
Mode to Inverse for
positioning, then change
the Mode back to
Matted or Transparent
when the elements are
aligned properly.

2. Before looking at the inspectors, select a color for the background of the Presentation window (as seen in a Display icon).
    a) Select Modify | File | Properties.
    b) In the dialog window that has opened, click on the Background color box. Select any color. Close the Color palette.
    c) Click on the OK button to close the dialog window.

3. Now let's take a quick look at the Modes inspector, located in the Window menu.
    a) Select Window | Inspectors | Modes.
    b) The Modes inspector should now be open on your screen. See figure 4-5.

4. Note the following characteristics of each of the options listed.

    * ***Opaque:*** *Object covers whatever is beneath it. Colors are displayed normally, with white displaying as white. Bitmapped objects generally display faster when in this mode, as compared with other modes. Opaque is the default mode for bitmapped objects.*

    * ***Matted:*** *Color is displayed normally with any white color interior to the image displaying as white, but white outside the image removed to allow the background (color or objects) to show through.*

    * ***Transparent:*** *Colors are displayed normally, but any white areas within the image become transparent, allowing whatever is beneath the object to show through these transparent areas.*

    White must be "pure white" (R-0, G-0, B-0 or #FFFFFF) for the Matted or Transparent Modes to take effect. If you want some white parts matted or transparent and other "white parts" to not include this effect, then use another color very close to white (but not "pure white") for those areas that you want to remain solid "white." These "close-to-white" areas will still be perceived by the user as being white but will not be affected by the Modes.

    * ***Inverse:*** *An object is displayed normally if it is on a white background. With colored backgrounds (or colored objects underneath), the colors of the object in front are inverted and white parts are transparent. You may want to experiment before using this option.*

    * ***Erase:*** *Makes an object invisible if it is displayed on the background color chosen in the Modify | File | Properties window.*

5. Now apply some of these Mode attributes to a text object. You should have one from the last guided tour.
    a) The Display icon should still be open (if not, double click on it).

b) Note that the text object contains black text with a white background for the entire text object.

c) What if you want get rid of the white background so that the text appears on the colored background you selected in the last guided tour.

d) Selecting the Transparent mode in the Mode inspector is how you can make the text object's background transparent so that the colored background shows through.

e) Try it. With the text object selected, select the Transparent mode in the Mode inspector.

f) Experiment with the other modes and other objects, if you wish.

Using the Fills Inspector

The following takes a quick look at the Fills inspector, located in the Window menu.

1. Select Window | Inspectors | Fills. The Fills inspector should now be open on your screen. See figure 4-6.

2. Note the following about the Fills inspector.

   - *With an appropriately selected graphic object, you can easily create a fill pattern using any of the patterns shown in figure 4-6.*

   - *You can use this tool with any graphic created with the Rectangle, Rounded Rectangle, Ellipse, and Polygon tools. You cannot use it with text, bitmaps, and lines.*

   - *The White Box option uses the background color (selected in the Color inspector).*

   - *The Black Box option uses the foreground color (selected in the Color inspector).*

3. Click on one of the rectangle objects. Click on any fill pattern. Try a couple of patterns if you wish.

Using the Color Inspector

The following takes a quick look at the Colors inspector, located in the Window menu.

1. Select Window | Inspectors | Color. The Color inspector should now be open on your screen. See figure 4-7.

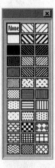

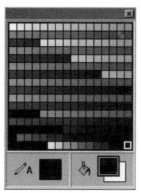

Fig. 4-7. Color inspector.

2. Note the following about the Color inspector.

If you want to change the color of an object, first select the object, and then select the color attribute you want to change (pencil/line, foreground or background). Then select from the Color palette the color you want. The following are components of the Color inspector with which you should be familiar.

- *Color palette: The largest portion of the Color inspector consists of the Color palette, displaying the wide variety of colors available for lines (and outlines), interior foregrounds, and interior backgrounds. To select a color, simply click the mouse cursor on it.*

- *"Pencil" (line) Color: In the lower left-hand corner you will see a pencil icon. Clicking on this icon will allow you to change the color of text objects, lines, and the outlines of rectangles, rounded rectangles, ellipses, and polygons. Whatever color you choose will remain the default color for the line color until the end of the current session or until you change the Pencil color again.*

- *Foreground Color: The foreground color selector is located on the lower right-hand side, top box. It will not affect text display. This option is used to change the foreground color of graphic objects created with tools in the toolbox, as well as to change fill patterns.*

- *Background Color: The background color selector is located on the lower right-hand side, bottom box. It is used to change the background color for text (for Opaque and Matted modes) and to define the background color of rectangles, rounded rectangles, ellipses, and polygons. This option can also be used with fill patterns.*

3. Try using the Color inspector on one of the rectangles you created previously. Click on a rectangle. Now click on the Pencil icon and click on a color in the palette. The outline of the rectangle should now have the color you selected.

4. Click on the Foreground Color box and click on a color.

5. Click on the Background Color box and click on a color. Look at the results. Try a few others if you wish.

Using the Line Inspector

The following takes a quick look at the Line inspector, located in the Window menu.

1. Select Window | Inspectors | Line. The Line inspector should now be open on your screen. See figure 4-8.

2. Note the following about the Line inspector.

- *Can be used with an object created with any of the graphic tools in the toolbox*

- *Modifies the line width of lines, rectangles, ellipses, and polygons*

- *Arrowheads may be added in lines*

3. Click on any the objects you created previously. Click on any of the line widths in the Line inspector. Note that you can also add arrowheads to any of the line objects.

You will have plenty of opportunity to work with the inspectors throughout the rest of the book. Keep the flowline open for the next guided tour.

Guided Tour 4C: Display Icon Properties

In Chapter 3 you looked at a few properties associated with the entire file. It is also important to look at the properties and attributes associated with all types of icons. As each icon is introduced within the book, the details of its associated properties are introduced. Because you have already started to work with the Display icon, let's start by looking at the properties associated with this icon. These options are located in the Modify menu.

1. The file should still be open from the last guided tour. Jump to the flowline and select the Display icon. Select Modify | Icon | Properties. The Properties window for the Display icon should now be open. See figure 4-9.

Shortcut

The Line inspector can be opened / closed by double clicking on the Straight Line tool or the Diagonal Line tool. Or you can use the keyboard shortcut Ctrl + L.

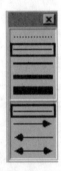

Fig. 4-8.
Line inspector.

T/P

Authorware treats all objects in a single Display icon the same, assigning all objects within it whatever properties you select for the icon. If you want to distinguish one object from another or give objects different properties, you can place each object in a separate Display icon.

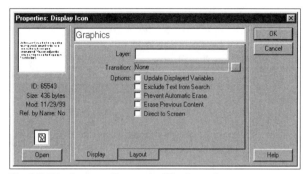

Fig. 4-9. Display icon Properties/Display tab.

2. Notice that there are two tabs in this window: Display and Layout. The Display tab should already be selected and on top; but if it is not, select it.

3. There are no properties you need to change at the moment. However, note the following about the Display tab options.

   • **Layer:** *Determines the position (front to back) of all objects in the current icon, relative to objects on screen but located in other Display icons. The same layer number is assigned to all objects in the current icon. Lower layer numbers are on the bottom (toward the back), whereas higher layer numbers are on top (toward the front). The default layer is 0 (zero). Movies and ActiveX controls always play in front (on top) of everything else.*

   • **Transition:** *Clicking on the box located to the right of this label will open a Transition dialog window where a number of different display effects can be viewed. Whatever Transition effect is selected here will be used as the contents of the Display icon first presented on screen. You will also see a similar dialog window and effects when the Erase icon is examined.*

   • **Update Displayed Variables:** *When checked, variables that are displayed or embedded on screen are automatically updated whenever the values change.*

   • **Exclude from Text Search:** *When checked, Authorware will exclude the selected icon from a text search initiated by the user. This affects all text objects in the current icon.*

   • **Prevent Automatic Erase:** *When checked, whatever objects exist within the current Display icon can only be erased with an Erase icon and are prevented from being erased with the automatic erase functions associated with other icon structures.*

   • **Erase Previous Content:** *When checked, Authorware will erase all previously displayed objects at the same layer or below before displaying the content of the current Display icon.*

·T/P·

You can arrange (front to back) different objects located within a single Display icon using the Modify | Bring to Front or Modify | Send to Back options. However, relative to objects in other Display icons, all objects in a single icon have the same layer value.

- **Direct to Screen:** *When checked, Direct to Screen will display objects in the current icon in front of any other objects located in other icons.*

4. Now let's look at the Layout tab. Select the Layout tab. See figure 4-10.

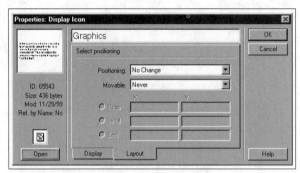

Fig. 4-10. Display icon Properties/Layout tab.

5. There are no properties you need to change at the moment. Note the following about the Layout tab options.

- **Positioning:** *Defines the on-screen position of all objects within the current icon, relative to the entire screen, an area, or path.*

- **Movable:** *As author, you can determine whether the user can move objects in this icon according to the following options.*

  On Screen: *The user can move the object anywhere on screen as long as it remains entirely on screen.*

  Anywhere: *The user can move an object anywhere, even off the screen.*

  On Path: *The user can move an object along a defined path (Positioning Path is selected in conjunction with X-Y Positions).*

  In Area: *The user can move an object within a defined area (Positioning In Area is selected).*

- **X-Y Positions:** *Use the Base and End coordinates to define an area in which the object can appear or a path the object can appear on (in conjunction with Movable).*

Practice Exercise 4-1: Creating Visual Depth

Description

In this exercise you are going to apply some basic principles of visual design. To increase visual interest and appeal as you develop Authorware projects, you may want to create the illusion of depth with the objects on screen. In

By default, the user will not be able to move any object on screen after the Authorware file has been packaged. Therefore, if you want the user to be able to move an object (for instance, in relationship to a drag-and-drop exercise), indicate that it can be moved by selecting one of the options under Movable.

the arts (painting, photography, and now multimedia), the use of highlights and shadows can help create the illusion of objects being 3D.

Look at the simple objects (figures 4-11 and 4-12) you are about to create. Top and left of the objects you can see highlights (where light reflects from the surface). To the right of and below the object, you can see shadows (created by the object blocking the light). The highlights and shadows are based on the assumption that there is a bright light source located in the upper left-hand section of the screen. The highlights appear on raised objects, on the sides facing the light source (the left and top edges). The shadows appear on the sides opposite the light source (the right and bottom edges).

You can easily create this type of illusion with highlights and shadows, even with the simple tools included in Authorware's toolbox. In this exercise you will create text and graphic objects with highlights and shadows. The following are elements covered in this exercise.

- *Placing content within a Display icon*
- *Using the text and graphic tools in the toolbox*
- *Using Authorware's inspectors*
- *Using the Modify menu options to modify stacking order (front to back positioning) of objects within a single Display icon*
- *Using the Modify menu to create a single grouped object from multiple single objects*
- *Creating simple highlights and shadows*

Take a Look

Before beginning this exercise, let's take a look at the exercise in its completed state so that you can clearly see what you are about to build.

1. You probably have a file open already from the previous guided tours. There is no need to save this file, unless you want to. Close the file by clicking on the X in the upper right-hand corner of the Design window.

CD-ROM

2. The completed exercise is located on the companion CD-ROM. To work with the CD-ROM file, perform the following.
   a) Place the companion CD-ROM in your CD-ROM drive.
   b) In Authorware, select File | Open | File and use the browse function to locate the CD-ROM.
   c) Within the CD-ROM, locate the folder named *Chapter04*. Double click on the *Chapter04* folder and you will see a number of files within it.
   d) Locate and double click on the file named *Exer4-1* to open the file.

e) You will see a message window appear, warning you that the file you are opening is locked and that you will not be able to save changes (you cannot save changes to the CD-ROM). Click on OK.

3. At the top of the flowline you will see two Display icons. One icon is named Text Tricks. The other icon is named Graphics Tricks.

4. Double click on the Text Tricks icon. You are now looking at examples of text with drop shadow and text with highlights. Note that with the example of drop shadow text, the shadow (the black copy of the text) is located slightly to the right and below the red copy of the text. With the highlighted text example, the white copy of the text is located slightly to the left and above the red copy of the text. Close this Display icon by clicking on the X in the upper right-hand corner of the toolbox (or on the X in the Presentation window).

5. Double click on the Graphic Tricks icon. You are now looking at an example of a graphic with shadows and highlights. Note the following about the completed exercise.

   • *Inside the Display icon named Text Tricks, there are two text objects. Each text object has been "grouped" so that if you use the menu option Modify | Ungroup you can see that there are actually two copies of the same text, each copy being a different color and offset slightly from the first copy.*

   • *Inside the Display icon named Graphic Tricks, there are multiple graphic objects. If you use the Menu option Modify | Ungroup you can see these many objects.*

   • *The illusion of depth is based on the assumption that there is a bright light source in the upper left-hand corner of the screen. With a raised, 3D object, shadows are cast on the right side and below the object. Highlights are seen on the left and top edges.*

Storyboard: On Screen

Figure 4-11 shows what the Display icon Text Tricks will look like when completed. Figure 4-12 shows what the Display icon Graphic Tricks will look like.

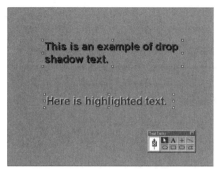

Fig. 4-11. Display icon Text Tricks.

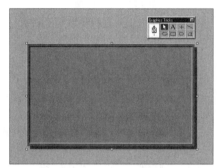

Fig. 4-12. Display icon Graphic Tricks.

Storyboard: Behind the Scenes

Figure 4-13 shows what the flowline will look like when completed.

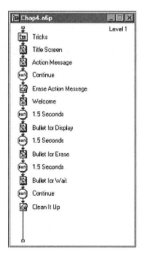

Fig. 4-13. Completed flowline.

Step-by-Step Instructions

1. Start by opening a new file and changing the file properties.
   a) Select File | Open | File.
   b) Close the two Knowledge Object dialog windows that have opened by clicking on the X that appears in the upper right-hand corner of each Knowledge Object window.
   c) You should now be looking at an empty flowline.
   d) Select Modify | File | Properties.
   e) Locate the Colors option toward the top of the dialog window that opens. Click on the Background color box to open the Color palette. Click on a medium shade of gray.
   f) Click on the OK button in the lower right to close the Color palette.
   g) Click on the check marks beside the Title Bar and Menu Bar options to remove the check marks.
   h) Click on the OK button to close the File Properties window.

2. Now let's place some Display icons on the flowline.
   a) Take your mouse over to the Icon palette and click on the Display icon. While holding down the mouse button, drag a copy of the Display icon to the flowline and let go.
   b) Drag a second copy of a Display icon to the flowline and drop it beneath the first one.

3. It is generally a good idea to give every icon on the flowline a unique name.
   a) Click on the first Display icon, which highlights as "untitled." Type in *Text Tricks*.
   b) Click on the second Display icon and type in *Graphic Tricks*.
   c) Your flowline should now look like that shown in figure 4-13.

4. Create a drop shadow for a text object.
   a) Double click on the Text Tricks icon. The Display icon, Text Tricks, should now be open. (Note the presence of the toolbox.)

NOTE

The text and inspector attributes you have just selected (Arial font, 24 point, bold, transparent) will remain the default settings until you either change them again or close Authorware. In fact, any of the attributes selected from the Text menu or with the use of one of the inspectors remains the default attribute until changed or the program is closed.

Shortcut

Keyboard Shortcuts:
Edit | Copy – Ctrl + C
Edit | Paste – Ctrl + P
Open Mode inspector –
Ctrl + M
Open Color inspector –
Ctrl + K

b) Click on the Text tool.

c) Move the cursor to the left portion of the screen. Click the I-bar cursor on the screen. You should now see an open text object. Type in *This is an example of drop shadow text.* Click on the Pointer tool in the toolbox to close the text object.

d) Change the text font. Make sure you still have handlebars around the text object (if not, click on the text object with the Pointer tool). You should now see handlebars. Select Text | Font and then select Arial. (You may have to use the scroll window to locate Arial.)

e) Establish the font size. Select Text | Size and click on 24 point.

f) Establish one last text attribute. Select Text | Style | Bold.

g) You are not done, however. Note that the black text object has a white background color. Change the background attribute to transparent so that the gray screen color will show through. With the text object still selected, select Window | Inspectors | Mode.

h) In the Mode inspector that opens, click on the Transparent mode. Click on the X to close this inspector.

i) You need a second copy of this text object. Click on the text object. Select Edit | Copy. Click the mouse somewhere on screen. Select Edit | Paste. You now have a second copy of the text object.

j) Now change the color of this second copy. There should still be handlebars around this second copy (if not, simply touch the text object with the cursor). Select Window | Inspector | Color. The Color inspector should now be open. Click on the Pencil icon in the lower left corner. Click on any one of the red color boxes you see in the Color palette. The second copy of the text object should now be red.

·T/P·

As you create multiple objects in a Display icon, each new object will appear in front of (layered on top of) the last object. In other words, the first object created will be the furthest in the background, whereas the last object created will be most toward the front.

If your black copy of the text object is in the foreground, with the red copy in the background, you probably changed the color of the first copy of the text object. This has an easy fix. Click on the black copy of the text object. Select Edit | Send to Back. The black copy should now be behind the red text object. Note that there also is a Bring to Front option listed in the Edit menu.

Shortcut

Keyboard Shortcuts:
Edit | Select All –
Ctrl + A
Modify | Group –
Ctrl + G
Modify | Ungroup –
Ctrl + Shift + G

k) Leave the Color inspector open but move it out of the way. Click on the gray bar at the top of the Color inspector and while holding down the left mouse button drag the Color inspector out of the way (but not off screen).

l) Drag the red text object to directly overlay the black copy, so that the red copy completely covers the black copy. You can use the cursor arrow keys for fine alignment. If the black copy appears on top of the red copy, see the Tip at left for help.

m) With the red copy selected, press the Up cursor arrow twice and the left cursor arrow twice. You have now created an example of a drop shadow. The black copy is 2 pixels to the right and 2 pixels underneath the red copy. See figure 4-11.

n) Select Edit | Select All to select both text objects. Select Modify | Group to create a single grouped object from the two individual text objects. Grouping the objects will allow you to move the drop shadow text around without accidentally getting the two text objects out of alignment.

5. Now you will create highlights.

a) Click on the Text tool. Click the I-bar cursor where there is room on the screen. You should now see an open text object. Type in *Here is highlighted text.* Click on the Pointer tool to close the text object.

b) You should now have a red text object.

c) You need a second copy of this text object. Click on the text object. Select Edit | Copy. Click the mouse somewhere on screen. Select Edit | Paste. A second copy of the text appears.

d) Change the color of this second copy. The Color inspector should still be open (if not, open it by selecting Window | Inspectors | Colors). There should still be handlebars around the second copy of the text. Click on one of the white color boxes you see in the Color palette. The second copy of the text object should now be white.

e) Drag the white text object to the red copy. You will note that the white copy is on top of the red copy. However, you want it behind the red. With the white text object selected, select Edit | Send to Back. Select the red copy and position it so that it completely covers the white text. You can use the cursor arrow keys for fine alignment.

f) Press the Down cursor arrow twice and the right cursor arrow twice. You have now created an example of highlighted text with the white copy 2 pixels on top of and 2 pixels to the left of the red copy. See figure 4-11.

g) Click the mouse to the upper left of both of these text objects and hold the mouse button down as you drag the expanding "elastic marquee" around the handlebars for both objects (thereby selecting both objects). Select Modify | Group to create a single grouped object from these two individual text objects.

6. You are now going to use the previous methods along with a new spin for the graphics. You will create a rectangle that will look like it is floating on the screen, with a shadow beneath it. The rectangle will also have a border that looks like it is raised above the surface (like a picture frame). There will be highlights on this border on the outside top and left edges and on the inside lower and right edges. The border will also have shadows on the inside left and upper edge. You may want to refresh your memory by looking at figure 4-12.

a) Double click on the Display icon Graphic Tricks to open it.

b) First select the colors you want to use. You will want to create a rectangle with an interior color that is lighter than the frame color. The Color inspector should still be open. Click on the Pencil icon in the lower left of the Color palette. Click on a medium blue. This will be the color of the rectangle's frame. In the lower right of the Color palette, click on the Foreground Color box. Click on a blue that is a couple shades lighter than the blue you chose for the frame.

c) You will want the rectangle to use a thick line for the frame. Select Window | Inspectors | Line. With the Line inspector open, select the thickest line shown in the inspector. Leave the Line inspector open, but move it to the side.

d) Select the Rectangle tool from the toolbox.

e) Click the cross-hair cursor (from the Rectangle tool) in the upper left-hand corner of the screen and drag the cursor to the lower right, so that you have a rectangle that is about 7 inches wide by 6 inches high. You now have a blue rectangle with a slightly darker frame. Click on the Pointer tool.

f) You need a second copy of this graphic object. Click on the rectangle. Select Edit | Copy. Click the mouse somewhere on screen. Select Edit | Paste. A second copy of the rectangle appears.

g) Now change the color of the second rectangle. There should still be handlebars around the second rectangle. The Color palette should still be open (if not, open it by selecting Window | Inspectors | Color). Click on the Pencil icon and then the color medium/dark gray. Click on the Foreground Color box and click on the same gray.

h) With the gray rectangle still selected (handlebars around it), select Edit | Send to Back.

i) Drag and position the blue rectangle in the center of the screen.

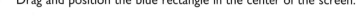

Shortcut

Keyboard Shortcut:
Open Line inspector –
Ctrl + L

j) Drag and position the gray rectangle so that it lies underneath the blue rectangle, slightly below and slightly to the right. You now have a shadow underneath the blue rectangle.

k) Additional details will help. The Line inspector should still be open (if not, select Window | Inspectors | Lines). Select a narrow line width. In the open Color palette, select the Pencil icon and then select white.

l) Select the Straight Line tool from the toolbox. Draw a line the same length as the top of the rectangle, about 1/2 inch above and parallel to the top edge of the blue rectangle. Draw a second line the length of the left edge of the rectangle, about 1/2 inch to the left and parallel to the left edge of the rectangle. Select the Pointer tool. Position these "highlights" (white lines) so that they just touch the *outside* upper edge and *outside* left edge of the rectangle and join each other on the outside corner, as indicated in figure 4-14.

·T/P·

It is often easier to draw objects on the side and then drag them where they belong rather than create multiple objects on top of one another.

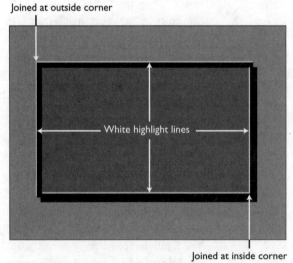

Joined at outside corner

White highlight lines

Joined at inside corner

Fig. 4-14. White lines as positioned in steps l and o.

NOTE

Holding down the Shift key prior to selecting an object allows you to continue to add objects to a selected group, as you select each additional object. Without the Shift key down, as you select one object the previous object becomes unselected.

m) Click on the long highlight line. Hold down the Shift key as you click on the shorter highlight line. Both lines should now be selected (have handlebars around them). Select Edit | Copy to make a copy of these lines in the clipboard.

n) Click the cursor above the rectangle. Select Edit | Paste to paste a second copy of both lines in an empty area of the screen.

o) Drag these highlights one at a time inside the rectangle so that the longer line is just touching the interior bottom edge of the frame and the shorter line is just touching the interior right-hand frame. These inside lines should also touch *each other* in the *lower right-hand corner*. See figure 4-14.

p) Add shadows on the inside of the rectangle. You should still have lines in the clipboard. Click the cursor in an empty part of the screen. Select Edit | Paste to place another copy of both lines on the screen.

q) With both of these lines still selected, go to the Color inspector and select the Pencil icon, and then select a black color. In the Line inspector, select a slightly thicker line. Drag the longer black line to the inside of the rectangle and place it so that it just touches the inside top frame of the rectangle border. Position the smaller line on the left inside edge of the rectangle. You may need to adjust the length of each of these two lines to make them fit. These two black lines should meet in the upper left corner, inside the rectangle border. See figure 4-15.

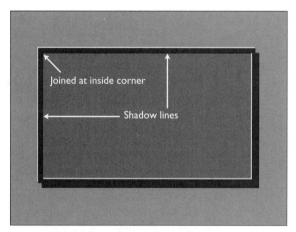

Fig. 4-15. Black lines positioned as shadows.

r) There are many graphic elements in this creation. If you try to move this figure you will quickly get some of these elements out of alignment by mistake. Therefore, let's group them. Select Edit | Select All and then Modify | Group.

s) With these simple concepts of highlights and shadows, you can help create the illusion of depth, providing greater visual interest.

7. Save the file you have been working on, as follows.

a) If you have not yet created a folder (or directory) on your computer's hard drive, do that now. Name the folder *SaveWork*.

b) Select File | Save. In the dialog window that appears, use the browse function to locate the folder (on your hard drive) named *SaveWork*, and type in *Exer4-1*.

Guided Tour 4D: Wait Icon Properties

As its name implies, the Wait icon causes an Authorware program to pause when this icon is encountered on the flowline. A couple of different events can trigger Authorware to continue past a Wait icon. These events, in addition to other options, constitute the properties associated with the Wait icon.

1. The Authorware file *Chap4* should still be open from the previous exercise. If it is not, open it.

2. Drag a Wait icon from the Icon palette to the bottom of the flowline.

3. Double click on the Wait icon. You are now looking at a dialog window for the Wait icon properties. See figure 4-16.

·T/P·

You can open the same dialog window by selecting a Wait icon on the flowline and then selecting Modify | Icon | Properties.

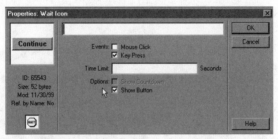

Fig, 4-16. Wait icon properties.

4. At the top of the dialog window you will see the Icon Title field, in which the icon name appears. At this point the icon is untitled.

5. Next to the Events field, you will see two options: Mouse Click and Keypress. If you click on the box next to Mouse Click, a check mark will appear and the Wait icon will wait for this action from the user before proceeding. In a similar manner, placing a check mark next to Keypress will require Authorware to wait for this event from the user before proceeding.

6. In the Time Limit field, you can type in a number requiring that Authorware wait that number of seconds before proceeding down the flowline.

7. If more than one of these options has been indicated, Authorware will move forward on the flowline with the first triggering event, whichever event happens first.

8. Selecting Show Counter from the Options field will result in the appearance of a Clock icon in the Presentation window, which will show the remaining time. This option is only available when a time limit has been entered. When this option is selected, you will note a small icon of a clock in the upper left-hand corner of the current dialog window.

9. The next option, Show Button, will display a Continue button in the Presentation window, requiring the user to click on the button to proceed. When this option is selected, you will also note a small icon of the Continue button in the upper left portion of the current dialog window.

10. The top area on the left side of this dialog window shows you what will appear on screen with the options you have selected: a small picture of the Continue button or the Counter icon. Below this area are some statistics about this icon.

11. That is all the properties for the Wait icon. Click on the Cancel button to close the window. You do not need to save this icon, so select and delete it.

Guided Tour 4E: Erase Icon Properties

The Erase icon can be used to erase any object (text, graphic, photograph, animation, or digital movie) from the Presentation window. It is worth noting that although you will use the Erase icon extensively during the first several chapters of this book, after that you will see how to use the automatic erase functions associated with other icons.

1. The Authorware file *Chap4* should still be open from the previous guided tour. If it is not, open it.

2. Drag an Erase icon from the Icon palette to the bottom of the flowline.

3. Double click on the Erase icon. You are now looking at a dialog window for the Erase icon properties. See figure 4-17.

You can open the same dialog window by selecting an Erase icon on the flowline and then selecting Modify | Icon | Properties.

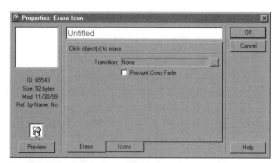

Fig. 4-17. Erase icon properties.

4. Note that there are two tabs for this dialog window: Erase and Icons. Let's take a look at the Erase tab options first (if you need to, select this tab).

5. At the top of the dialog window you will see the Icon Title field, where the icon name appears. At this point the icon is untitled.

·T/P·

This is a really great feature in Authorware. Simply place an Erase icon on the flowline and run the program. Authorware will automatically stop on the "empty" Erase icon. You can now click on the objects on screen that you want to erase (again, WYSIWYG). As you start to develop on your own, you will find this capability very convenient.

·T/P·

This capability to list and see icons being erased is a very useful feature in troubleshooting erase problems.

6. On the next line you have the instructions "Click object(s) to erase." You will use this capability soon.

7. The next field is Transition. Click on the small button to the right of this label. A dialog window now opens, offering a wide variety of erase effects. You will try out several of these in the next exercise. Click on the OK button to close the Transition dialog window.

8. The last field on this tab, Prevent Cross Fade, refers to an assumption that Authorware makes. If there are more than one Erase or Display icon on the flowline and they are using the same erase/display transition, Authorware will by default link these transitions. If you do not want the transitions linked, select the Prevent Cross Fade option, which will result in each icon transition being treated separately.

9. Click on the Icons tab. The top two lines (name of icon and instructions) are the same as you just saw with the Erase tab.

10. Next, you have a display area where you can either choose to list the icons currently selected (to be erased by the current Erase icon) or list the icons that will not be erased (will be preserved).

11. The top area on the left side of this dialog window shows you some statistics about this icon.

12. That is all the properties for the Erase icon. Click on the Cancel button to close this window. You do not need to save this icon, so select and delete it.

Guided Tour 4F: Map Icon Properties

Unlike the other icons in the Icon palette, the Map icon does not do anything active. It does not have any display, erase, branching, or media capabilities. The Map icon is like an empty container. The inside of a Map icon can hold other icons, structures built with icons, or other maps.

1. The Authorware file *Chap4* should be open from the previous guided tour. If it is not, open it.

2. Drag a Map icon from the Icon palette to the bottom of the flowline.

3. Select the Map icon on the flowline and select Modify | Icon | Properties. You are now looking at a dialog window for the Map icon properties. See figure 4-18.

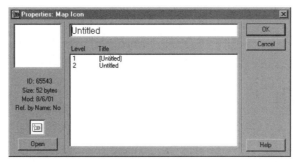

Fig. 4-18. Map icon properties.

4. As you can see, there are no options to select, because the Map icon does not really do anything. What this window does show is the current level of the selected map, and the levels above it.

5. The top area on the left side of this dialog window shows you some statistics about this icon.

6. That is all for the Map icon. Click on the Cancel button to close this window. You do not want to save this icon, so select and delete it.

Let's continue by working on an exercise.

Practice Exercise 4-2: Simple Text Display Sequence

Description

In this exercise, you will create a simple linear sequence that displays one object at a time, using a combination of timed pauses and a mouse click required to proceed from one screen to the next. The following elements are covered in this exercise.

- *Placing Display icons on the flowline*
- *Modifying Display icon properties for transitions*
- *Using the toolbox to create objects*
- *Using the Text menu to set text attributes*
- *Placing Wait icons (with timed waits and continue buttons)*
- *Using the inspectors to change modes and color*
- *Using the Group and Ungroup options*
- *Placing Erase icons on the flowline (with transition effects)*
- *Placing Map icons on the flowline*

Take a Look

Before beginning the exercise, let's take a look at the exercise in its completed state so that you can clearly see what you are about to build.

CD-ROM

·T/P·

Authorware will only open one file at a time, closing the current file as you open or create another file. The trick to having two Authorware files open simultaneously is to open two copies of the Authorware program at the same time, each program with a different file. You can then use the Alt + Tab keys to toggle back and forth between the two copies of Authorware. You may find this technique useful when you want to copy and paste structures from one program into another, using the Windows clipboard to help accomplish this task.

1. Select File | Open | File and on the companion CD-ROM locate the folder named *Chapter04* and the file named *Exer4-2* within this folder. Double click on *Exer4-2* to open the file.

2. You may see a message window on screen as you attempt to open *Exer4-2*. The prompt asks you whether you want to save changes to the file currently open (from the guided tours). In this case, you do not want to save the changes, so just select No. A message window will appear, warning you that the file you are opening is locked and that you will not be able save changes. Click on OK.

3. The file *Exer4-2* should now appear in Authorware. Click on the Restart button in the toolbar to play the file from the top of the flowline. Note the following about the completed exercise.

    • *On the first screen you see, after you click on the Continue button, one of the text objects erases, but the other stays on screen. As the text is erased, an erase transition is used.*

    • *After the first text object is erased, another text object replaces it, followed by a timed display of three bullet points. As each new text object is displayed, it is displayed using a transition effect.*

    • *After the sequence has been displayed, and you click on the last Continue button, everything on screen is erased, using an erase transition.*

Storyboard: On Screen

Figure 4-19 shows the first screen (note the presence of the Continue button). Figure 4-20 shows the second screen before any text bullets have appeared. Figure 4-21 shows the first text bullet, whereas figure 4-22 shows the completed screen.

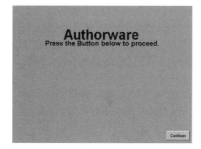

Fig. 4-19. First screen in sequence.

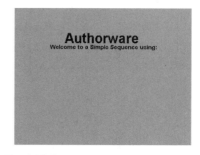

Fig. 4-20. Second screen, before text bullets appear.

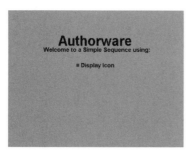

Fig. 4-21. Adding the first text bullet.

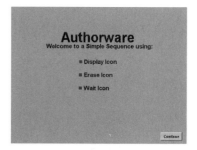

Fig. 4-22. Final appearance after sequence is complete.

Storyboard: Behind the Scenes

The flowline in figure 4-23 shows all icons, their placement, and their names as everything should appear after you have finished this exercise.

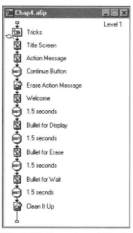

Fig. 4-23. Completed flowline.

Go Solo

If you think you can create the exercise on your own, do so. If you want help, continue with the step-by-step instructions.

Step-by-Step Instructions

1. Let's open the file you started earlier in this chapter (or if you wish, you can use the copy included in the *Chapter04* directory on the companion CD-ROM).

    a) Select File | Open | File. In the dialog window that appears, use the browse function to locate on your computer's hard drive the folder *SaveWork* and the file within it named *Exer4-1*. Double click on *Exer-1* to open the file.

    b) *Exer4-1* should now be open.

2. You need to clean up the flowline before proceeding.

    a) Click the mouse in the very upper left-hand corner of the flowline. While holding down the left mouse button, drag the mouse down to the right so that you select both of the Display icons with the elastic marquee. Let go of the mouse button. Both of the icons should now be selected.

    b) Select Modify | Group. You should now see an untitled Map icon instead of the Display icons. Do not worry, you have not lost them. In a manner of speaking, you have "wrapped" a map around the Display icons.

    c) The Map icon is currently untitled. Give it a name. The icon title should be highlighted, so just type in *Tricks*.

    d) Double click on Tricks (the Map icon). You should now see a second flowline inside the Map icon, with the Display icons present. Note that in the upper right-hand corner of this second window there is a label indicating that you are now inside this map and looking at the level 2 flowline. See figure 4-24.

·T/P·

You can place maps within maps ad nauseam, but probably do not want to go any deeper than five or six levels, or you will find yourself losing track of where things are located.

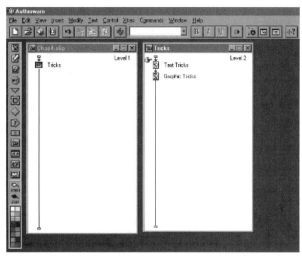

Fig. 4-24. Level 1 flowline on the left; level 2 flowline (inside the Map Icon) on the right.

    e)   Close the map by clicking on the X in the upper right-hand corner of the open Map title bar (level 2).

3.   To make sure you view only the exercise you are about to create when the file is run, drag the white Start flag from the Icon palette to the flow-line and place it immediately below Map icon *Tricks*. You will build the exercise below this flag.

4.   Let's create the structure first, and then name all elements, before putting in any content. See figure 4-23 as a point of reference.

    a)   Drag a Display icon to the flowline and drop it immediately below the white flag. Name this icon *Title Screen*.

    b)   Drag a second Display icon and place it below Title Screen. Name this icon *Action Message*.

    c)   Drag a Wait icon and place it below the last icon. Name it *Continue*.

    d)   Drag an Erase icon and place it below the Wait icon. Name it *Erase Action Message*.

    e)   Drag another Display icon and place it below the Erase icon. Name it *Welcome*.

    f)   Drag another Wait icon and place it below Welcome. Name it *1.5 Seconds*.

    g)   Drag another Display icon and place it below the Wait icon. Name it *Bullet for Display*.

h) Drag another Wait icon and place it below Bullet for Display. Name it *1.5 Seconds*.

i) Drag another Display icon and place it below the Wait icon. Name it *Bullet for Erase*.

j) Drag another Wait icon and place it below Bullet for Erase. Name it *1.5 Seconds*.

k) Drag another Display icon and place it below the Wait icon. Name it *Bullet for Wait*.

l) Drag another Wait icon and place it below Bullet for Wait. Name it *Continue*.

m) Drag an Erase icon and place it at the very bottom. Name it *Clean It Up*.

The structure is now complete. Your flowline should now look like that shown in figure 4-23. Now on to the content.

5. On the toolbar, click on the white Start Flag button to run the file from the white flag.

6. Authorware has now stopped and has opened up the first Display icon (*Title Screen*) on the flowline. Note the presence of the toolbox showing the icon's title. You will now put the content into this Display icon, but will first set the text attributes before you start typing.

a) Set the Font option first. Select Text | Font and then select Arial. If you do not see Arial, see the Tip at left for help.

b) Now establish the text size. Select Text | Size and 36. If you do not see 36, see the second Tip at left for help.

c) Now enter the content. Click on the Text tool in the toolbox. Move the I-bar cursor toward the left and top of the screen and click the left mouse button. In the text object that has now opened, type in *Authorware*. Click on the Pointer tool in the toolbox.

d) Select Modify | Icon | Transition. In the dialog window that opens, in the left column select Internal (if it is not already selected) and in the list appearing on the right select Build Down. Click on the OK button to close the Transition dialog window.

e) Click on the X in the toolbox to close this first Display icon.

7. Authorware is still in Run mode and with the closing of the first icon moves to and stops on the second empty Display icon, *Action Message*.

Should you accidentally drop out of Run mode at this point or at any time in the following steps, from the flowline you can simply double click on the icon indicated within a particular step to open it and pick up with the content entry instructions. Alternatively, you can click on the white Start Flag button

·T/P·

You may find the development approach used here to be an efficient method of constructing and testing Authorware structures. If you build and name the structure first, you can then run/play the file to put in the content. Authorware will stop on empty icons, providing you the opportunity to add content on the fly. Or if you wish, you can simply work off the flowline, double clicking on each icon as you want to work on it.

·T/P·

If Arial is not listed at first, select Other. A Font dialog window will open. Use the scroll window to find and select Arial. Remember that this list is showing you what is on your computer. The font you select here may not be available on the end user's computer unless you use a stan-dard Windows font. Note that as you select a font the display area below will show you a sample of what the font looks like. Click on the OK button to close the Font dialog window.

on the toolbar to rerun the program from the white flag. Run the program until you stop on the first empty icon.

a) Click on the Text tool in the toolbox. Move the I-bar cursor toward the left and below the first text object. Click the cursor on the screen, and in the text object that has now opened type in *Press the button below to proceed.*

b) Note that the text size is still 36, which is too large for this and the other text you will be entering. You need to resize it. Click on the Pointer tool to close the text object (there should now be handlebars around this text object). Select Text | Size and select 18.

When changing any text attribute, make sure the text is selected first, before changing the attribute. You can highlight text in an open text object, much like you do in a word processor. Whatever attributes you choose are applied to the selected portions of the text only. Alternatively, with a selected and closed text object, any attributes you choose are applied to all text within the text object.

c) Select Modify | Icon | Transition. In the dialog window that opens, in the left-hand column select Internal (if not already selected) and in the list column appearing on the right select Build Down. Click on the OK button to close the Transition window.

d) Making sure you have the Pointer tool selected first, you can click on and drag either of the two text objects and place them wherever you think they look best (remember that you will soon be adding text bullets). See figure 4-22 as a point of reference.

e) Why did you use two Display icons, one for each text object? Think about this as you continue. The Note at left provides the answer.

f) Click on the X in the toolbox to close this icon.

8. Notice that you now see a Continue button on screen. It is probably located in the upper left-hand corner. Simultaneously press the Ctrl and P keys to pause the program. Click on the Continue button and while holding the mouse button down drag the button down toward the bottom right of the screen. Let go of the mouse button when you have the Continue button where you want it.

9. Simultaneously press the Ctrl and P keys to put the program back in Run mode. Click on the Continue button to proceed. You have now stopped on an empty Erase icon, which you will now use to erase the message "Press the button."

Notice that because you have named all the icons to be descriptive of what they contain, as you now look at the dialog window the Icon Title field tells you what to erase (Erase Action Message). It cannot be emphasized enough how much it will help you more efficiently build and troubleshoot your Authorware programs if you will first take the time to descriptively name the icons you place on the flowline.

a) Immediately beneath the field for the icon title, Authorware is giving you instructions (*Click object(s) to erase*). Click on the text object *Press the Continue Button* to proceed. This message should now be erased from the screen.

b) The text object has been erased, but let's add an erase transition. With the dialog window still open, note that the next field is Transition. Click on the box next to Transition and it will open the Erase Transition window. Select Internal (if it is not already selected) in the left-hand window, and then select Remove Down in the right-hand window. Click on OK to close the Transition window.

c) Click on the Icons tab and note the small picture of the Display icon *Action Message* as being erased by this Erase icon.

d) Click on the OK button to close the Erase icon and the program proceeds and stops on the next empty Display icon named *Welcome*. Click on the Text tool in the toolbox and move the I-bar cursor to the left, beneath the first text object. Click the cursor on the screen to open the text object and type in *Welcome to a Simple Sequence using:*.

e) Click on the Pointer tool to close the text object, and select Modify | Icon | Transition. In the Transition dialog window that opens, select Internal and Build Down. Click on OK to close the Transition window.

f) Click on the X in the toolbox to close this icon and proceed to the next Wait icon. You will come back later and change this to a timed response. For now, click on the Continue button to proceed.

g) You are now looking at the next empty Display icon, *Bullet for Display* (note its name in the toolbox title bar). Click on the Text tool in the toolbox and move the I-bar cursor to the left, beneath the welcome message. Click the cursor on the screen to open the text object and type in *Display Icon*.

h) Click on the Pointer tool to close the text object and then select Modify | Icon | Transition. In the Transition dialog window that opens, select Internal and Build to Right. Click on OK to close the Transition window.

i) Add a graphic. Select File | Import. Use the browse function in the Look In field to locate on the companion CD-ROM the folder named *Chapter04*. Inside this folder, locate and double click on the graphic file named *Bullet.bmp*. The bullet should now be on screen. Use the mouse to drag and position the bullet to the left of the text object.

You may want to copy the bullet graphic from the current Display icon and paste it into the next Display icon, instead of importing it. To do this, first select the graphic and then select Edit | Copy. When you open the next Display icon, click the Paste hand where you want the graphic to appear and then select Edit | Paste. You may find the copy/ paste operation to be more efficient than importing the same graphic several times. Later in the book, you will learn an even more efficient way of reusing elements (using libraries).

Shortcut

Ctrl + J is a keyboard shortcut from earlier versions of Authorware, which still works in the current version. If you are currently in Run mode, Ctrl + J will jump to the flowline. If you are currently on the flowline, Ctrl + J will jump to the Presentation window for the currently selected icon.

j)   Click on the X in the toolbox to close this icon and proceed to the next Wait icon. For now, click on the Continue button to proceed.

k)   You are now looking at the next empty Display icon, *Bullet for Erase.* Click on the Text tool and move the I-bar cursor beneath the first bullet. Click the cursor on the screen to open the text object and type in *Erase Icon.*

l)   Click on the Pointer tool to close the text object and then select Modify | Icon | Transition. In the Transition dialog window that opens, select Internal and Build to Right. Click on OK to close the Transition window.

m) Add a graphic. Select File | Import. Use the browse function in the Look In field to locate and double click on the graphic file named *Bullet.bmp.* Use the mouse to drag the bullet to the left of the text object. See the Tip at left.

n)   Click on the X in the toolbox to close this icon and proceed to the next Wait icon. For now, click on the Continue button to proceed.

o)   You are now looking at the next empty Display icon, *Bullet for Wait.* Click on the Text tool and move the I-bar cursor beneath the second bullet. Click the cursor on the screen to open the text object and type in *Wait Icon.*

p)   Click on the Pointer tool and select Modify | Icon | Transition. In the Transition dialog window that opens, select Internal and Build to Right. Click on OK.

q)   Add another bullet via the method you have been using or by using the copy/paste method of the previous Tip. Use the mouse to drag the bullet to the left of the text object.

r)   Click on the X in the toolbox title bar to close this icon, and proceed to the next Wait icon. Click on the Continue button to proceed.

s)   The last Erase icon is now waiting for you to erase everything. Simply click the mouse on every object you see on screen. With the dialog window still open, click on the box next to Transition, and it will open the Erase Transition window. Select Internal in the left-hand window, and Remove Down in the right-hand window. Click on OK.

10. Now let's go back to the flowline and change three of the Wait icons to be timed responses. Simultaneously press the Ctrl and J keys to jump to the flowline.

a)   Double click on the first Wait icon labeled *1.5 Seconds.* In the Wait Icon Properties dialog window, in the Time Limit field, type in *1.5.* In the Options field, click on the box next to Show Button to remove the check mark (deselect it). Click on the OK button.

b) Repeat step *a* for the second and third 1.5-second Wait icons, to change them to timed responses, with no button showing.

11. That should be it. Click on the white Start Flag button in the toolbar to run from that flag. Go through the sequence. If you see something on screen you want to change, simultaneously press the Ctrl and P keys to pause the program. To move an object, just drag it to where you want it. To edit a text object, double click on it (note how you are now in the Display icon containing that text object; see the toolbox?) and select the Text tool. Double click on the text object. Edit as you wish.

12. To save your work, select File | Save As and type in *Chap4*.

Summary

- *In the first guided tour (4A), you were presented with the basics of the toolbox and what each tool is used for.*

- *The toolbox is available for use within an open Display icon or the display area associated with an Interaction icon. The toolbox contains the basic tools used to create both text and simple graphic forms: Pointer, Text tool, Straight Line tool, Diagonal Line tool, Ellipse tool, Rectangle tool, Rounded Rectangle tool, and Polygon tool.*

- *In the second guided tour (4B), you took a closer look at Authorware's inspectors, available from the Window menu. These include the Mode inspector, the Fills inspector, the Color inspector, and the Line inspector.*

- *Each icon within Authorware's Icon palette includes a variety of properties and attributes. In guided tour 4C, you looked at the properties of the Display icon, which are located on one of two tabs: Display and Layout.*

- *In the first practice exercise (4-1) you learned some simple techniques (drop shadow and highlighting) for creating the illusion of depth for text objects and graphics.*

- *In guided tour 4D, you looked at the properties of the Wait icon, including the Icon Tile field, the events Mouse Click and Keypress, Time Limit, Show Counter, and Show Button.*

- *In guided tour 4E, you looked at the properties for the Erase icon, which are organized under the Erase tab and the Icons tab.*

- *In guided tour 4F, you saw how the properties of the Map icon simply display the flowline level contained within the map.*

- *In the second practice exercise (4-2), you created a simple presentation sequence using Display icons, Wait icons, Erase icons, and a variety of transitions.*

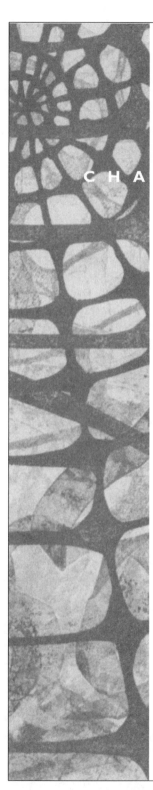

C H A P T E R

5

Importing

External Media

Introduction

To this point, the only objects you have included in Display icons have been text and graphic objects created using the toolbox. However, projects typically incorporate a variety of media, including high-resolution graphics, narration, sound effects, music, movie clips, and animation. These media elements are often created in external programs and imported into Authorware. Authorware can also import text that has been created in external word processors.

In this chapter you will get the opportunity to practice importing these various media elements into Authorware. You will also try out a new feature of Authorware 6, called Media Synchronization.

As you will see shortly, the Sound icon and the Movie icon make it very easy to include both sound and movies within any Authorware application. With a click of a button, you can load/link these media elements. The Sound and Movie icons provide control over these media, and in combination with the new Media Synchronization feature (and other icons such as the Display icon) allow you to easily orchestrate these media elements. The guided tours and practice exercises in this chapter focus on these capabilities.

In addition to learning how to use these media elements within Authorware, this chapter also provides some background information about sound and movie properties and the impact they have when played in a variety of delivery environments. By the end of this chapter, you will be able to:

- *Import graphics using the File menu and the Insert menu*
- *Import text*
- *Use library elements on the flowline*
- *Create and use a library*
- *Describe the general process of recording and preparing sound files for use within Authorware*
- *Import sound and use the Sound icon on the flowline*
- *Describe the general process of recording and preparing movie files for use within Authorware*
- *Import movies and use the Movie icon on the flowline*
- *Use the Media Synchronization feature with the Sound icon and the Movie icon*
- *Describe the general strengths and limitations of extended media use in the LAN/WAN, intranet, and Internet environments*

Guided Tour 5A: Importing Graphics

Within the display area of both the Display icon and Interaction icon, Authorware provides a basic toolbox that allows you to create text objects and very simple graphics. Most Authorware developers obtain and import graphics created in external programs. Graphics created from scratch can be created in graphics programs such as Freehand, Fireworks, and Photoshop. There are also a large number of vendors selling a wide variety of "clip" media, including photographs, graphics, background patterns, buttons, and other visual elements. This book incorporates visual elements from PhotoDisc and Corel.

You import a graphic created in another program into the display area of a Display icon or an Interaction icon. You use the menu option Insert | Image or File | Import to accomplish this task. You will work with both during this tour.

1. Start by opening a new file and modifying its properties.
    a) Select File | New | File.
    b) Close the two Knowledge Object dialog windows that have opened by clicking on the X that appears in the upper right-hand corner of each window.
    c) You should now be looking at an empty flowline.

2. Create a Display icon in which to place the graphic.
    a) Drag a Display icon to the flowline.
    b) Name the icon *Rushmore*.
    c) Open *Rushmore* by double clicking on it.

3. Use the Insert menu to import a single image at a time, which provides you with the opportunity to preset a few attributes before you bring the image into Authorware. Go ahead and try it.
    a) Select Insert | Image.
    b) The Properties/Image dialog window should now be open. See figure 5-1.

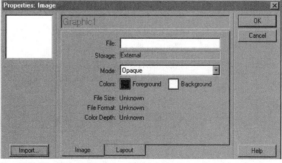

Fig. 5-1. Properties/Image dialog window.

4. Let's take a closer look at the Properties/Image dialog window.

    a) You can use the settings in this dialog window to modify a number of attributes that will affect the visual characteristics of the image. You will try out a few of these settings in material to follow.

    b) Click on the Import button, located in the lower left-hand corner of the dialog window.

    c) The *Import which file?* dialog window now opens. See figure 5-2.

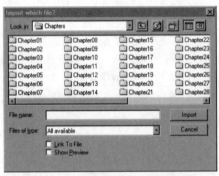

Fig. 5-2. Import which file? *dialog window.*

    d) Look to the right of the Look In field and locate the Down arrow. Click on this arrow. This opens a browse function that allows you to select whatever computer device (hard drive, CD-ROM drive, and so on) and folder you want to look in.

    e) Make sure the companion CD-ROM is in your computer's CD-ROM player.

    f) Select the CD-ROM drive for your computer (D, E, or another drive).

    g) On the companion CD-ROM, locate the folder named *Chapter05*. Double click on the *Chapter05* folder to open it. Locate and select (single click) on the file named *Rushmore.jpg*.

    h) At the bottom of the current dialog window *(Import which file?)* there are four fields worth looking at in detail.

      • *The* File name *field shows you the name of the currently selected file.*

      • *The* Files of type *field has a Down arrow on the right that opens a pull-down selection list that allows you to specify which type of file you want to view in the browse window. The options listed here are the graphic file formats Authorware supports and is capable of importing. Authorware supports the following graphic formats: WMF, PICT, GIF, Jpeg, XRes LRG, Photoshop 3, Targa, TIFF, EMF, and BMP. Leave this option set to All Available.*

- *Placing a check mark in the* Link to File *field will result in the image remaining as an external file linked to the current icon within Authorware. When Authorware encounters the current icon with the link, it "makes a call" to the external file, and then takes the content of the file and displays the result in the current icon using whatever image properties have been selected. If you modify the content of this external file, the revisions are automatically updated wherever the file was linked within the Authorware flowline.*

- *By placing a check mark in the last field,* Show Preview, *a small window opens on the right-hand side of the* Import which file? *dialog window, which shows a small thumbnail view of the currently selected graphic.*

i)   Select Show Preview by placing a check mark by it. You should now be able to see a small thumbnail of the Mount Rushmore graphic you are about to import. This option allows you to preview the graphic without actually importing it into Authorware.

j)   Click on the Import button, located on the right-hand side of the dialog window.

k)   You have now imported a graphic into Authorware. You may not be able to see the graphic very well because the Properties/Image dialog window is in the way. Click the mouse on the top title bar for the dialog window, and while holding down the mouse button drag the dialog window temporarily out of the way in order to view the graphic.

l)   Let's return our attention to the Properties/Image dialog window. Note that there are two tabs in this dialog window: Image and Layout. The Image tab is probably already selected; but if not, select the Image tab.

m)   Let's take a closer look at the options on the Image tab.

- *The File field shows the complete path and file name of the graphic file you just imported.*

- *The Storage field currently indicates Internal because when you imported the graphic you did not place a check mark beside the Link option. The graphic has actually been brought into and will be stored within the current Authorware file. If you had placed a check mark beside the Link option, the Storage field would read External, indicating that the image is a linked object stored in an external file.*

- *Note that the third field, Mode, has a Down arrow with a pull-down menu. Click on the Down arrow to view the list. Most of these options are the same as those of the Mode inspector. Most of the time you will probably want to keep the graphic set to the opaque mode. The last option here, however, is new. An alpha channel is a transparency setting for all or part of an image. The transparency can vary from clear to opaque. The alpha channel effect makes the image appear to blend in with whatever image is behind it.*

- *The Colors fields Foreground and Background can be used with an imported black-and-white image, to replace the black/white with colors you select for foreground and background from a color palette.*

- *The File Size, File Format, and Color Depth fields show characteristics of the imported graphic. These settings cannot be changed within Authorware, but instead just show you the information.*

n) You are not going to change any of these settings, but make sure the mode is still set to Opaque.

o) Let's take a look at the Layout tab. Click on the Layout tab. The following are descriptions of the options on this tab.

- *The first field is Display. Click on the Down arrow to see the list of options here. The option you select in this field will alter the remaining options listed on the tab.*

  As Is: Displays the image with no modifications.

  Cropped: Shows a rectangular section of the image. Use the last field on the tab (the Placement field) to select which rectangular section of the image you want displayed. The other options are used to define further characteristics of the rectangle to be displayed.

  Scaled: Allows you to either reduce or enlarge the graphic as a percentage of the original size.

- *The Position option includes fields in which you can enter X and Y coordinates to specify where you want the upper left-hand corner of the image to be positioned.*

- *The Size option includes fields in which you can enter X and Y coordinates to specify the width and height of the image. (Not available when As Is has been selected.)*

- *The Uncropped/Unscaled field shows the original size of the image. (Only available when Cropped has been selected.)*

- *The Placement field allows you to select which rectangular section of the image you want to display. (Not available when Scaled has been selected.)*

- *The Scale % field allows you to enter a percentage (X and Y) when you want to either reduce or enlarge the image (only available if the Scaled option has been selected).*

p) You are not going to change any of these settings. Click on the OK button in the upper right-hand corner to close the Properties/Image dialog window.

·TIP·

Resizing bitmapped graphics after they have been imported into Authorware is generally not a good idea because the quality of the image frequently falls apart during the resizing. This is especially true regarding attempts to enlarge the size of the graphic. As a rule of thumb, it is far better to create a graphic in an external graphic program, at the size you want, than to resize a graphic after it is in Authorware.

q) Click on the graphic and while holding down the mouse button move the graphic around on the screen. Place it anywhere on screen you want. As you have just seen, importing graphics into Authorware is very easy.

r) Click on the X in the Presentation window (or toolbox) to close the Display icon.

5. Now let's try the second method of using menu options to import graphics into Authorware. You will use the File menu, as follows.

a) Drag a Display icon to the flowline, placing it below the *Rushmore* Display icon.

b) Name the icon *Tools*.

c) Open *Tools* by double clicking on it.

d) Select File | Import. Note that the *Import which file?* dialog window now opens. This is a little different from the Insert | Image method, which opened the Properties/Image dialog window first.

e) Probably the most important difference between using the previous method and the File | Import option is that this method allows you import multiple objects at the same time. Let's give it a try.

f) There is one very important difference between this version of the *Import which file?* dialog window and the version you saw earlier. This version has a Plus (+) button in the lower right-hand corner. See figure 5-3.

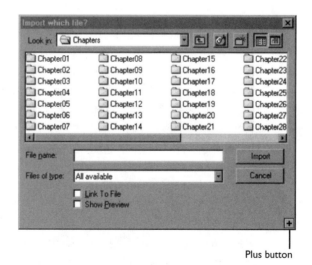

Plus button

Fig. 5-3.** **Import which file?** **dialog window containing the Plus (+) button.

g) Click on the Plus (+) button. A new File to Import section has now been added to the right, which will allow you to make multiple selections.

h) Use the browse function in the *Look in* field to locate on the companion CD-ROM the folder named *Chapter05* (it may already be positioned there). Locate and single click on the file *Drill.jpg*.

i) Click on the Add button located on the right. You should now see *Drill.jpg* listed on the right.

j) Click on the file *saw.jpg*. Click on the Add button on the right. You should now see *saw.jpg* listed on the right.

k) Click on the file *screwdriver.jpg*. Click on the Add button on the far right. You should now see *screwdriver.jpg* listed on the right.

l) Click on the Import button in the center of the dialog window.

m) You should now be looking at three graphics of tools. All three graphics are now selected. Click the mouse cursor on the vacant background to deselect the objects. Use the mouse to move the objects one at a time to any location you want.

n) Simultaneously importing multiple graphics into Authorware is very easy. Select File | Save. Use the browse function to locate the folder *SaveWork* on your computer's hard drive. Type in the file name *Ch5Tours*.

Let's move on. Leave this file open, as you will continue to use it.

Guided Tour 5B: Importing Text

Frequently development team members who do not know Authorware write the scripts (text-on-screen and audio narration) for multimedia projects. The writers will generally use a word processor to create and edit these scripts. There are a couple of good reasons to consider creating scripts using a word processor.

First, scripts are typically edited numerous times in the internal review process and as the client reviews the script. Word processors are better suited to this extensive editing process. Second, in allowing writers to use a tool they already know how to use (the word processor), it saves a great deal of time and expense in not having to train them how to use Authorware.

You might ask, however, whether this means the script has to be retyped to get it into Authorware. Hopefully, you have already guessed that the answer to this question is no. There are actually a couple of ways to get preexisting text into Authorware.

In the "old days," before importing text was an option, the process was still pretty easy. In fact, you can still use this method for small amounts of text. Start by opening a word processor along with the appropriate document. Minimize the word processor. Then open Authorware, and drag a Display icon to the flowline and open it. Next, press the Alt and Tab keys simultaneously to "roll over" to the word processor. Next, select whatever text is to appear in a single Display icon and copy it to the clipboard. Next, press Alt + Tab to "roll over" to Authorware, where you paste the text into the open Display icon. Close this Display icon, drag a new Display icon, and copy/paste, copy/paste, and so on.

Macromedia introduced the ability to import text files into Authorware. Importing text files is a much more efficient method. However, before getting into this process, a quick review of Save options in a word processor may help.

As you may know, saving a file in a word processor's native format (e.g., in Microsoft Word, the *.doc* format) not only saves the text you have typed but whatever formatting you have selected. It also saves many normally unseen control characteristics that are unique to that particular word processor. Importing a file with all of these control characteristics does not work because Authorware is not able to recognize these control characteristics.

Another option in a word processor is to save a file using a text-only (*.txt*) format. This option, however, will save only the text, losing whatever formatting you may have used. Authorware does recognize and can import the text-only (*.txt*) format, which is fine if you do not use formatting or if the text has formatting (in the native document) you do not want to use in Authorware.

The last and most efficient way (prior to Authorware 6) of importing text involves first having writers use the text formatting standards established as part of your project design. Then save the word document using the *.rtf* (Rich Text Format) option. Finally, import the *.rtf* file into Authorware, quickly and easily making use of preexisting and preformatted text script. You will practice this method in the steps that follow.

Authorware 6 has introduced yet another couple of methods of importing text: using the RTF Editor and using the RTF Knowledge object. These methods are covered in a later chapter. Let's start with the easiest method: importing an *.rtf* file directly into a Display icon.

1. The file *Ch5Tours* should already be open from the last guided tour. (If it is not, select File | Open and use the browse function to locate the *SaveWork* folder on your computer's hard drive. Then locate, select, and open the file *Ch5Tours*.)

2. Drag a new Display icon from the Icon palette to the flowline, placing it below the other icons already on the flowline. Name this new Display icon *Text*.

3. Double click on the Display icon *Text* to open it.

4. Click on the Text tool in the toolbox and then click the I-bar cursor somewhere on screen to open a text object.

5. Select Window | Inspector | Modes. Then click on the Transparent option.

6. Select File | Import. The *Import which file?* dialog window now opens. Use the browse function to locate the *Chapter05* folder on the companion CD-ROM. Locate and single click on the file named *SampleText.rtf*.

7. Click on the Import button on the right-hand side of the dialog window. You should now be looking at another dialog window, RTF Import. See figure 5-4.

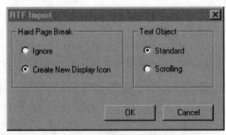

Fig. 5-4. RTF Import dialog window.

8. As the script is being written for the text to be used for on-screen display, make it part of the procedure to have the writer insert a hard page break (in the word document) after every "screen" of text. In this way, the text for each "screen" will be on its own page in the word processor. This may seem like a waste of paper, but it will save you time.

   If you use hard page breaks in your word processor, when you encounter the dialog window shown in figure 5-4, your work in Authorware will be made very easy. If you leave the default settings shown here as they are (Create New Display Icon and Standard), as you import the text, each "screen" of text will be placed into its own Display icon, using a standard text object.

   If you select the Ignore option, all text will be placed in a single text object. The Scrolling Text Object option will place the imported text into a scrolling text object instead of a standard text object.

The issues of "why open a text object" and "why select Transparent" are revisited after a few more steps. You will see that opening a text object and selecting the text attributes you want before importing will save you a lot of time.

9. Leave the default settings (Create New Display Icon and Standard) as they are. Click on the OK button. You should briefly see a pop-up window with a blue progress bar to confirm the import process.

10. In the open Display icon you should be looking at the first screen of text, including the text formatting used in the word processor. Close this Display icon by clicking on the X in the Presentation window (or toolbox).

11. You should now see two new Display icons on the flowline. Open each Display icon to view its content. Each new icon has a "screen" amount of text in it.

12. Do you see how the text in each new Display icon has a transparent attribute? If you had not opened a text object and selected the Transparent mode before importing the text, you would now have to go back to each icon and change this attribute (assuming you wanted the Transparent mode for your text objects).

13. Save the file and then close it (select File | Save and then File | Exit).

Guided Tour 5C: An Introduction to Libraries

The use of libraries in the development of Authorware projects will both save you time and significantly reduce the file size of the Authorware files you are working with. A library is a special type of file that can be used to store "reusable parts," which are basically icons you use frequently. You can place Display icons, Interaction icons (without other icons attached to them), Sound icons, and Movie icons in a library file. Libraries are frequently used to store media elements (e.g., graphics, sound files, and screen templates) you may want to use in multiple locations. Let's jump in and see how libraries work.

1. Start by opening a new file.
   a) Select File | New | File.
   b) Close the two dialog windows that have opened by clicking on the X that appears in the upper right-hand corner of each window.
   c) You should now be looking at an empty flowline.

2. Open a new library file.
   a) Select File | New | Library.
   b) You should now see a new library file on screen, along with the empty flowline. See figure 5-5.

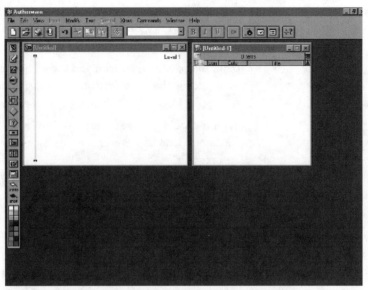

Fig. 5-5. New untitled library file and untitled Authorware file.

3. Place some graphics into the Authorware file.
   a) Drag three (3) Display icons to the flowline.
   b) Name these new icons *One*, *Two*, and *Three*.
   c) Double click on *One* to open the Display icon.
   d) Select File | Import. Use the browse function to locate the companion CD-ROM and the *Chapter05* folder on it. Locate and click on the file *Trees.bmp*. Click on the Import button.
   e) Select Modify | File | Properties. The Properties/File dialog window has opened. Look in the upper left-hand corner of this dialog window, which shows file statistics. These statistics are for the Authorware file. Note that there are currently three icons and zero variables in the Authorware file. The file size is about 775 K. Close the dialog window. Close the Display icon.
   f) Double click on *Two* to open the Display icon. You will import the same graphic.
   g) Select File | Import. Use the browse function to locate and click on the file *Trees.bmp*. Click on the Import button. Close the Display icon.
   h) Double click on *Three* to open the Display icon. You will import the same graphic.
   i) Select File | Import. Use the browse function to locate and click on the file *Trees.bmp*. Click on the Import button. Close the Display icon.

j) Select Modify | File | Properties. Note that there are now three icons with a file size of approximately 1,539 K. Write down this file size so that you can use it for comparison later. Close the dialog window.

4. Now let's see how the library might help.

a) Drag the Display icon *One* to and drop it inside the library.

b) Delete the Display icons *Two* and *Three*.

c) Select Modify | File | Properties. Note that there is currently one icon and that the file size is unchanged from the number you wrote down. Close the dialog window.

d) Now let's try a different variation. Drag six (6) copies of *One* from the library to the flowline.

e) Have you noticed anything about these Library icons on the flowline? Note that their labels are in italic. The italic icon label is a visual indication that the icon is from the library.

f) Now for some magic. Select Modify | File | Properties. Look at the file statistics, at the file size in particular. The file size should still be about the same as the file size you wrote down. Why didn't the file get any bigger, in spite of the fact that you placed six copies of the graphic on the flowline?

The answer is that in this case you were using icons from the library and the graphics do not really exist on the flowline. The graphic only exists in the library. What you see on the flowline are icons linked to the Display icon in the library. Look at the small symbol to the left of *One* in the library. This symbol indicates that *One* contains a link on the flowline. See figure 5-6. Close the dialog window.

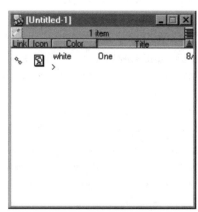

Fig. 5-6. Link symbol to left of One in the library.

5. Let's look at another great feature of the library.

·T/P·

Authorware does not immediately release "memory" after icons are deleted. If you were to save this file and check the file size afterward, you would see a large reduction. However, a word to the wise: before publishing your Authorware file, make sure to use the Save and Compact option to perform a better job of releasing memory associated with deleted icons.

a) Double click on any one of the Display icons on the flowline. Look carefully at the toolbox. Notice that all tools are grayed out. Click the mouse on the graphic. Drag the graphic to another location. Close this icon.

b) What conclusion can be drawn? The content of Library icons on the flowline can be repositioned but *cannot* be edited on the flowline.

c) However, here is a neat trick. Double click on *One* in the library. Note that all tools in the toolbox are active. Click on the Text tool. Click the I-bar cursor somewhere on the screen. Type in *Can you see the forest for the trees?* Close this icon.

d) Double click on any icon on the flowline. Note that the text you just typed in the Library icon now appears in an icon on the flowline. Close this icon. Open another icon on the flowline.

e) What conclusion can be drawn? Any modification to the content of an icon in the library will be automatically updated in all correspondingly linked icons on the flowline.

6. Select File | Exit to close the file without saving it.

Using Sound in Your Applications

When incorporating sound into your projects, think about your purpose for adding it. Some sounds may be used as a background to set a certain tone. Music and environmental sounds can evoke a particular mood or feeling. Sound can be very effective in this way.

Other uses of sound can include playing a sound effect in response to a user's action, such as a click as the user selects a button. This sound lets the user know that the program is responding to an action. Sound can serve a number of important functions for your project.

- *Music and sound tracks* can add dynamic support to on-screen graphics or animation, as well as increase the general level of user/viewer interest in your project.

- *Narration* (audio track) can provide information that either supports or adds to what is presented via text, graphics, and/or animation.

- *Sound effects* can accompany user actions, provide additional feedback concerning a user response or required action, and be used as a technique to arrest and focus the user's attention on a particular point of interest.

If you have your sound files prepared for you in the appropriate digital format, you may not need to read the following section. However, it is more likely that you will at some point be faced with the question "Where do I get the sound files I need for my Authorware application?"

Any change to the content of a Library icon is automatically updated to all linked copies of that icon located on the flowline. This feature can be a very important labor-saving technique, especially in situations in which you may have software screen captures or graphics you will want to use multiple times, but also when you expect that these screen captures or graphics may change in the future.

When it is time to update the screen capture, simply open the appropriate icon in the library, change the graphic, and close the Library icon. The graphic is updated where that linked icon appears on the flowline. What could be easier?

Prerecorded Music and Sound Effects

One answer to the question of "where" is to purchase sound effects or music tracks from vendors that make such products available for multimedia use. There are thousands of sound effects that have been recorded, and almost as many music segments representing a wide range of music styles. Typically these sound files are supplied on CD-ROM or can be downloaded, with at least a couple of file format types available for each selection.

There are also a few software programs you can purchase that allow you to select a preexisting recording and edit it in a variety of ways, including changing the length (time) of the music segment to fit your specific time requirement.

Assuming you can find the selections you need, the next and equally important factor in the use of prerecorded sound files is being very careful about examining the license agreement in terms of what limitations and obligations you may have. Your best bet is to look for music and sound effects products that very clearly state "Royalty Free Use" of their sound files. In other cases, you may need to pay a small licensing fee.

Be advised that per copyright law you cannot use the commercially recorded popular music you listen to on your stereo without prior written permission (and probably a fee with restrictions of use) from the producer, publisher, and/or performer of that music. However, this may be an option under copyright law "fair use" statute, but this requires complying with, for example, stipulations that the distribution of your application is not for sale and is intended for a small, targeted audience. It is best to check first before spending a lot of time and effort working with something you may not be able to use.

Using Professional Talent and Studios

There are times when you will not be able to purchase "clip" sound files but must record your own. For example, you may find yourself in need of high-quality professional narration to accompany the text, graphics, or animation that appears on screen. Without question, the most professional results will be achieved by using professional talent and a recording studio.

Most talent agencies will provide you with recorded samples of work from a variety of their clients, so that you can select the voice or two that best meets your project's specific needs. You can then sit in the studio during the recording to ensure proper pronunciation or vocal emphasis by the performer.

You will need to provide performers and the studio technician copies of the script to be recorded. You might want to break the script down, so that each audio file you need (per screen or per sequence) is identified and provided to you as a separate file. This means that you should also provide the file name for each file. Organize and plan ahead. Get everything ready before you go to the studio. Studio time is expensive, and wasted time is wasted money.

The technician at the recording studio will probably ask you a number of questions pertaining to the format and properties of the sound files to be delivered to you (these properties are briefly discussed in the next section). The recording studio will be able to provide a CD-ROM with the digital sound files, ready to be imported into Authorware.

Recording Your Own Sound

The sections that follow discuss factors to consider in recording sound yourself.

Necessary Equipment

If you have little or no budget, what then? Actually this should not be a problem; recording sound is pretty easy to do. At a minimum, you will need three things, with a fourth component recommended.

- *Sound card in your computer*
- *Microphone*
- *Sound-editing software*
- *Tape recorder (recommended, not required)*

Sound Card

You probably have a sound card in your computer already. Even if you do not plan to record sound, any computer intended to run your application with sound must have a properly installed sound card (most computers now include a built-in sound port).

Almost all sound cards will include at least two input ports, one for use with a microphone and a second as a line input for use with another playback device (such as tape recorder or CD player). Most of these input ports require a standard "Sony" plug. The sound card combined with the use of the sound editing software will capture and convert sound into a digital format recognized by the computer and by Authorware.

Microphone

The quality of a microphone can vary quite a bit, but you should not have to spend more than about $50 to get a fairly decent one. Alternatively, you can rent one. Either way, a "unidirectional" or limited-range microphone to help eliminate background sounds you do not want recorded. Inexpensive microphones will probably have a "Sony" plug that can be plugged directly into the computer's microphone input. If you are not going to use a tape recorder, an inexpensive microphone will do fine.

Sound-editing Software

You may have a "lite" version of software already, as some type of sound-editing software is generally included with sound cards. There is also a Windows utility that provides the basics needed for recording and limited editing. If you are going to do more than a little recording, you may want to purchase a more full-featured sound-editing software program that will help you do this work more quickly and efficiently.

Tape Recorder

Even though you can connect the microphone directly to the computer and record using the sound-editing software, there are a few good reasons for using a tape recorder. First, sound files can quickly take up a lot of space on your computer's hard drive. How many selections are you going to record? How many times are you going to have to repeat the selection to get a good "take"? Just think of the many times you have observed a television or movie scene in which the prompter says "Take 5," "Take 10," and so on. Even professional talent needs to repeat lines to achieve the desired result.

Every "take" will gobble up a lot of hard drive space. If you will be doing more than a little recording, you may want to get a decent recorder with a decent microphone and record first into the tape recorder. You can then identify the "good" takes and transfer these to the computer via the "line output" from the tape recorder into the "line input" of the sound card. Use the sound-editing software just as you would with direct microphone use.

The Recording Environment

You will want to find a nice quiet place to record your narration. This generally means away from windows, high-traffic (vehicle and people) areas, elevators, stairways, doors that open/close frequently, and loud voices next door. You will be surprised at how many stray (unintentional) sounds you may pick up as you record. You may not even hear them until you listen to the recording later.

If the description of this "nice quiet place" has just eliminated all possibilities at your normal place of work during the day, you may want to consider this same place at night or during the weekend, or find a quieter alternative.

Position your performer so that when the microphone is aimed directly at his/her mouth, it will be pointing to the quietest area of the room. Unless you have a microphone stand and other equipment, it will probably be easier to have your performer sit comfortably at a table, with the microphone mounted in a stable position directly in front of the speaker's mouth.

You will need to experiment, but will probably want to place the microphone no further than 8 to 12 inches from the speaker's mouth. Try to avoid anyone holding the microphone in-hand, as this is will undoubtedly produce unwanted noise. Make sure there is room for the speaker to place the script (maybe on a typist's copy stand) so that it can be easily read. Holding and turning pages will also, more than likely, produce unwanted noise.

The computer and/or tape recorder should be placed well out of range of the pickup pattern from the microphone. Figure 5-7 shows one possible arrangement of your recording space.

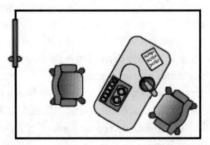

Fig. 5-7. Example of a recording arrangement.

Properties of Sound Files

Life has been described as a continuous stream of changing events. If we listen to a rock band playing, we hear a constantly changing series of different notes, varying loudness, changing beat, changing instruments, and so on. In the digital world of computers, if we want to record and play back this sound, we need to capture and represent this continuous stream of events as a long series of individual "moments frozen in time."

Each digital "frozen moment" is a sample of that music at a specific point in time. Our ability to digitally represent the live music is significantly influenced by three properties related to how we "sample" or capture these individual moments. These properties include sampling rate, size of sample, and mono/stereo capability.

Summary of Properties

As a point of reference for these properties, examine figure 5-8, which shows the dialog window used to set up properties for recording sound files in Sound Forge (Sonic Foundry).

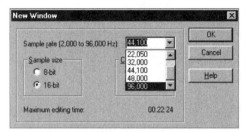

Fig. 5-8. New Data dialog window in Sound Forge.

Sampling Rate

Sampling rate refers to how many times per second a "sample" is taken. The sampling rate is generally measured in hertz (Hz). The pull-down menu for Sampling Rate allows you to select a rate ranging from 2,000 to 96,000 Hz.

The higher the sampling rate (the higher the number), the better the quality of your digital representation of the music. However, as you increase the sampling rate, you also increase the size of the resulting sound file. For most computer applications you will probably find that a sampling rate somewhere between 12,000 and 22,000 Hz will do the trick. However, the end result is also influenced by the other two sound properties.

Sample Size

Sample size refers to how big the "container" is that you use to store the "sample." If you use a large container, you will have a lot more room to store a lot more information about the sample. Typically most computer systems provide 8- or 16-bit containers(see figure 5-8, left-hand side). Sound cards are described as either 8-bit or 16-bit. As you might imagine, 16-bit sound files offer considerably better quality over 8-bit, but again they are considerably larger than 8-bit files. Experiment, but you may find that you can use 8-bit for most sound effects, whereas music and narration will sound best using 16-bit.

Channels

Files can offer multiple channels (stereo), each channel handling different information, or a single channel (mono), playing the same information on both sound speakers (see figure 5-8, right-hand side). For games and other applications for which you are trying your best to create a more realistic environment, you may want to try stereo. For most training applications, however, you probably will not add much to the quality by using stereo, and with the additional down side that stereo adds significantly to file size, you will probably want to employ mono.

Format

Format refers to the characteristics of the file type used for the sound file. Authorware 6 supports several sound file formats, described in the following. The format you choose will generally be determined by the capabilities of the computers and environment your application will be delivered into.

Sound File Types Supported by Authorware

You can import the following file types into Authorware: AIFF, PCM, SWA, VOX, WAV and MP3. In the Windows environment, WAV has been by far the most widely used format. Authorware 6 introduced support for MP3, as it is a compressed audio file format that features high quality with small file size.

Guided Tour 5D: Sound Icon Properties

Authorware is capable of playing sound files using either of two completely different approaches: use of the Sound icon or use of Authorware functions. Most of the time you will probably use the Sound icon, as it offers very easy and convenient control of sound files within your application. Let's take a quick look at the Sound icon and its properties.

1. Use the file *Ch5Tours* you created earlier. Select File | Open and use the browse function to locate the *SaveWork* folder on your computer's hard drive. Next, locate, select, and open the file *Ch5Tours*.

2. Drag a Sound icon to the flowline and drop it below everything else that is already there.

3. Examine the properties associated with the Sound icon, as follows.
    a) Make sure the Sound icon is selected (highlighted).
    b) Select Modify | Icon | Properties (or double click on the icon).
    c) The Properties/Sound Icon dialog window should now be open (see figure 5-9). There are three parts of this window you will take a closer look at: the left-hand side, the Sound tab, and the Timing tab.

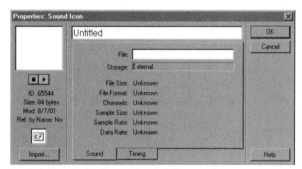

Fig. 5-9. Properties/Sound Icon dialog window.

4. As you have seen with other icons, the left-hand upper portion provides information specific to this particular icon that most of the time you will not care too much about. However, note that at the top of this section there appears to be a mini-control panel with a Stop/Pause button and a Play button. These controls can be used to play and pause the sound file after it has been imported. The Import button is on the bottom of this section.

a) Click on the Import button. You should now see the *Import which file?* dialog window, similar to the dialog you used to import graphics. See figure 5-10.

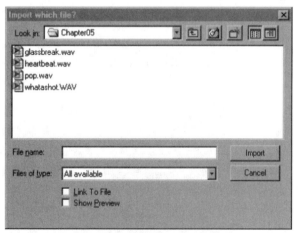

Fig. 5-10. Import which file? *dialog window.*

CAUTION

One word of caution here. Make sure the directory/folder structure (for any externally linked files) used during author-ing is the same as that used for the distributed application. If the location of the externally linked files for the distributed version is different from what was authored, Authorware will not be able to find the files, and an error message will result.

CD-ROM

- **Look in:** *This pull-down menu is exactly the same as those you have seen before, allowing you to browse through the file/folder structure to locate and select files.*

- **File Name:** *This field shows you the name of the currently selected file.*

- **Files of Type:** *This pull-down menu allows you to select a particular sound file type to be listed, or list all available sound types.*

- **Link to File:** *This field, on the bottom of window, is the other important choice to be made from this dialog window. The default setting is without a check mark. Set this way, as you import a sound file, it will become an internal part of the Authorware file. In contrast, placing a check mark in this field will provide a link to a sound file that remains external and does not become part of the Authorware file.*

- **Show Preview:** *This field is not relevant to importing sound files.*

b) Use the Look in Field option to locate on the companion CD-ROM the *Chapter05* folder. Now locate and single click on the file *glassbreak.wav*. Click on the Import button. You should see the Progress window appear on screen, showing a blue progress bar during the importing process. With a small file, the Progress window will appear and disappear quickly. If you link to an external file, the Progress window will not appear.

5. Click on the Sound tab (it may already be selected). Note that this tab provides a lot of information about a file, after it has been imported (see figure 5-11). The sound properties previously described are listed here. At the top of this tab, you can also see the file's name and whether it has been imported internally or whether it remains as an external file, linked to this icon.

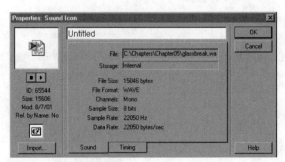

Fig. 5-11. Sound tab.

6. Click on the Timing tab (see figure 5-12). Examine this tab, starting from the top and working your way downward.

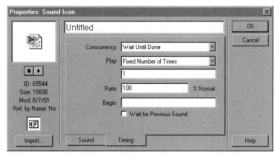

Fig. 5-12. Timing tab.

- **Concurrency:** *This is the first time you have seen this type of field. Click on the pull-down menu and you will see the following options.*

    Wait Until Done: *The default setting that will hold any forward movement on the flowline until after this current sound icon is finished playing.*

    Concurrent: *Means that the current sound icon will start playing, and as it does, Authorware will continue down the flowline. The sound will continue to play as Authorware does whatever else is called for as it continues on the flowline.*

    Perpetual: *Means that the sound is always available. Perpetual is generally used in conjunction with a function or variable that turns the sound on and off.*

- **Play:** *This field has two lines, the first being a pull-down menu containing the following choices. The second line supports use of the first line.*

    Fixed Number of Times: *Makes use of the second line for the manual entry of a number to indicate how many times the sound file should be played.*

    Until True: *Makes use of the second line for the manual entry of a logical variable used to turn the sound on and off. Until True is generally used with the Perpetual setting in the Concurrency field.*

- **Rate (% of Normal):** *This field can be used to play back the sound file at a slower or faster speed than originally recorded. The number you enter is considered a percentage of the original (100%) speed. For example, 50 would be played at half the speed of the original. You may want to experiment with this field first, as it does not always result in what you might think.*

- **Begin:** *This field is used in conjunction with a function or variable to create a condition that triggers the playing of the sound file.*

- **Wait for Previous Sound:** *With a check mark in this field, Authorware will completely finish playing the previous Sound icon before beginning to play the current Sound icon. Without the check mark, Authorware will stop* *playing (cut off) the previous Sound icon as soon as it encounters the current Sound icon that contains this setting.*

7. Click on the Cancel button to close this Sound icon.

8. Leave the file open, as you will continue to use it.

Using Movies in Applications

Many of the same possibilities mentioned earlier about sound files are also true of movie files, although the depth of these possibilities is generally much more limited. The sections that follow focus on the differences between the two media, rather than on a reiteration of material that applies to both sound and movie files.

Prerecorded Movie Files

There are vendors that offer products with prerecorded movie clips. The number of subject areas and the selections within these categories are typically limited when compared to the vast possibilities available for sound and music. Movie files are generally supplied on CD-ROM in QuickTime (*.mov*), Video for Windows (*.avi*), and MPEG formats.

The earlier caution regarding the license agreement for sound files is equally valid for movie files. Examine the license agreement carefully, with "Royalty Free Use" being your best bet. Likewise, do *not* use commercially recorded video/movie segments without prior written permission (and probably a fee with restrictions of use) from the producer and/or publisher (i.e., the copyright holder).

Using Professional Talent and Studios

If you want high-quality, professional movie segments, your best choice will be the services of professional on-screen and behind-the-camera talent. Again, talent agencies will furnish samples of work to help you choose the on-screen talent. Although you can engage the services of a professional studio for recording, another choice is hiring a free-lance professional video crew for location shooting. The studio or video crew will then edit what has been shot and should be able to supply you with whatever digital movie format you want, delivered on a CD-ROM.

Recording Your Own Movies

The sections that follow discuss aspects you need to be aware of in regard to recording movies.

Necessary Equipment

For low or nonexistent budgets you can record and edit your own movie segments, which is fairly easy to do. At a minimum, you will need three things, with a fourth component recommended.

- *Video capture card in your computer*
- *Video camera*
- *Video editing software*
- *Video tape recorder (recommended, not required)*

Video Capture Card

There is a wide range in quality and price of video capture cards, from a few hundred dollars to thousands of dollars. Most video capture cards will include an input port that will allow you to directly connect a video camera to the card, although it is highly recommended that you record the original on a video tape machine or camcorder and later transfer the selected "takes" to the computer.

Video files are a great deal larger than sound files, taking up hard disk space very quickly. The video capture card combined with the use of the video editing software will capture and convert video segments into a digital format recognized by the computer and by Authorware. You (and your audience) do *not* need a video capture card to play back the video segments, but you may need to distribute a software driver to play the movie segments.

Video Camera

If you have a "home" video camera (VHS format), this will work fine. However, if you need to buy a camera, it is suggested that you spend a little extra and get an SVHS format camera, as this will give you somewhat higher resolution (quality). You can also look at digital video cameras, but make sure any selection you might make can provide the video formats and hardware connection you need.

Video-editing Software

With the purchase of the video capture card, you probably also received a "lite" version of a video-editing software. If you are going to do more than a little recording, you may want to purchase a more full-featured video-editing software program that will help you do this work more quickly and efficiently.

Video Tape Recorder (Camcorder)

Even though you can connect the camera directly to the computer and record using the video-editing software, for the same reasons as suggested for sound you will probably want to use a video tape recorder or camcorder instead. You can then identify the "good" takes and transfer these to the computer via the "line output" from the recorder into the "line input" of the video capture card. Use the video-editing software just as you would with direct microphone use.

The Recording Environment

If you are shooting video with sound, all of the comments regarding recording sound are also true of video. There are, however, some additional considerations for video recording.

First, you will need to be careful about lighting. Assuming you do not have access to professional video lights, you may want to shoot the segments where plenty of light will fall on the subject. Second, make sure you can "see" what is most important as you shoot. Do you want to use a "long" shot so that the audience can see action as people walk around, or do you want a close-up showing facial expressions or something being held in the actor's hand? Third, get rid of the "clutter" that should not be seen, which distracts the audience's attention from what is important.

Properties of Movie Files

Let's return to the notion of life as a continuous stream of changing events. As for sound, movies should capture and represent this stream of events as a continuous series of individual "moments frozen in time." Each digital movie "frozen moment" is a sample of what we see at a specific point in time, like the frames of a movie. The ability to digitally capture video is significantly influenced by properties similar to those of sound. These properties include frame rate, image size, and data compression.

Frame Rate

When video or film is digitized for use in a computer, the process creates digital still shots or frames, similar to what can be seen by holding a piece of movie film up to a light. The speed at which these still shots are captured and played back influences the quality of the digital representation of "real" life. The more frames per second (fps), the higher the quality.

A movie film projected in a classroom plays back at about 30 fps. The appropriate computer frame rate setting is heavily influenced by the capabilities of the computer itself. Computers with very fast CPUs, high-speed disk drives, and a lot of RAM are capable of playing digital movies at 30 fps or higher. The appropriate frame rate for digital movies displayed at about 1/4 the size of a computer monitor's screen is about 15 fps. All three of the properties listed here interact and influence one another and the resulting performance.

Image Size

There are a series of standard image sizes for digital video, from 160 x 120 pixels, to 240 x 180 pixels, to 320 x 240 pixels, to full screen. Some software programs provide the capability for nonstandard sizes. 160 x 120 is pretty small for most video clips, with 320 x 240 being the most commonly used size, as it tends to be the best trade-off of quality versus performance.

Data Compression

To accurately represent a visual "moment in time," a great deal more information must be captured (and played back) than is required for sound alone. Because large amounts of data need to be dealt with very quickly, hardware and software devices have been created that mathematically reduce (compress) the data needed. High-speed disk drives can be used to capture "raw" digital information, but almost always you will end up using a compression utility to reduce the data stream and file size.

There are a wide variety of standard (and nonstandard) compression routines out there. Whatever compression you use for creating the movie clip, just remember that the user must also possess this compression routine or software driver to play the digital movie.

Guided Tour 5E: Movie Icon Properties

Like the Sound icon, Authorware is capable of playing movie files via icon or Authorware functions. Most of the time you will probably use the Movie icon, as it offers very easy and convenient control of movie files within your application.

Authorware can also use a sprite to load and control a QuickTime movie. Using a sprite with a QuickTime movie is explored in the 5F guided tour. For now, let's take a quick look at the Movie icon and its properties.

1. You should still have the file *Ch5Tours* open from the last guided tour. If not, select File | Open and use the browse function to locate the *SaveWork* folder on your computer's hard drive. Next, locate, select, and open the file *Ch5Tours*.

·T*i*P·

If you use a movie, make sure to include the necessary software drivers and Xtras to properly play these movies. Xtras are extensions that add capabilities to the standard Authorware application. Many Xtras have been developed by independent third parties.

2. Drag a Movie icon to the bottom of the flowline and let go.

3. Name this Movie icon *Golf*.

4. Examine the properties associated with the Movie icon.
   a) Make sure the Movie icon is selected (highlighted).
   b) Select Modify | Icon | Properties (or double click on the Movie icon).
   c) The Properties/Move Icon window should now be open (see figure 5-14). There are four parts of this window to be examined more closely: left-hand side and Movie, Timing, and Layout tabs.

5. The left-hand side of the Properties/Movie Icon window and the Import button (bottom of the panel) are pretty much the same as for the Sound icon. Note that the control buttons at the top of this section also include Step Forward and Step Back. After selecting certain movie file types, the Options button will become active, providing additional choices.

6. Import a movie.
   a) In the lower left-hand corner of the dialog window, click on the Import button.
   b) You should now be looking at the *Import which file?* dialog window. Use the browse function and locate the companion CD-ROM and the *Chapter05* folder. Now locate and single click on the file *Golf.avi*. Click on the Import button.
   c) Click on the title bar of the dialog window, and while holding down the mouse button drag the dialog window out of the way.
   d) You should now be looking at a movie of a golfer ready to take a swing (see figure 5-13).

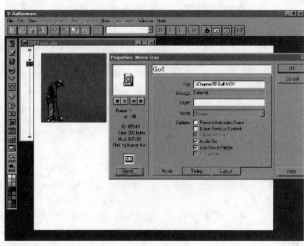

Fig. 5-13. First frame of the golf movie.

If you are going to use QuickTime movies, you are better off selecting the Insert | Media | QT option. This option will circumvent certain driver and other issues.

e) In the Controller panel in the upper left-hand corner of the dialog window, click on the Play button. You should be able to hear the club hit the ball, see the ball move (missing the hole), and hear the crowd's empathetic reaction. Play it again, Sam (if you would like to).

f) Move the dialog window back to the center of the screen. In the following you will explore the tabs and change a few settings.

7. Select the Movie tab (it already may be selected). See figure 5-14. Let's look at the fields, starting at the top and working downward.

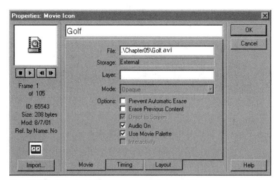

Fig. 5-14. Movie tab.

- **File:** *You should be looking at the file and path name of the movie file you just imported.*

- **Storage:** *Indicates whether the movie is internal or external to the Authorware application.*

- **Layer:** *Use the Layer text box to set up the selected digital movie's layer position. The layer position determines the movie's position from back to front relative to other objects on the screen. External movies always play in front of other objects.*

- **Mode:** *For all external movies, the mode will be assigned the Opaque value.*

- **Prevent Automatic Erase:** *Place a check mark here to prevent the movie from being erased by the automatic erase options set in other icons. The only way to remove an image of a movie protected by this option is to use an Erase icon.*

- **Erase Previous Content:** *Place a check mark here to erase all objects placed on screen from previously displayed icons. When you select this option, Authorware erases all objects (on the same or lower layer) before displaying the content of the current digital Movie icon.*

- **Direct to Screen:** *Place a check mark here to always play the movie in front of any other objects on the screen. Turn off Direct to Screen if you want to assign a movie to a layer other than the one in front. Externally* *stored movies are always played direct to screen, in front of other objects. Direct to Screen is available only in Opaque mode.*

- **Audio On:** *Place a check mark here to play the sounds included in a movie file. If the type of movie you loaded does not support sound, this option is grayed out.*

- **Use Movie Palette:** *Place a check mark here to use the digital movie's color palette instead of the Authorware color palette. This option is not available for all movie formats.*

- **Interactivity:** *Place a check mark here to allow users to interact with a Director movie, by clicking the mouse or pressing keys to continue, for example.*

a) Several of the options listed previously are grayed out and not available with our current movie. The options you are most likely to use are Audio On and Use Movie Palette.

b) Click on Audio On to remove the check mark. Click on the Play button in the dialog window. Audio is removed. Click on Audio On again to replace the check mark.

c) The most common situation in which you will want to remove the check mark from Use Movie Palette when you already have a bitmapped graphic on screen. As the movie begins to display, you may see a color flash or shift in colors. This flash or shift indicates that there is a palette conflict between the palette being used for the graphic and the palette being used for the movie. Sometimes the easiest solution is to remove the check mark from Use Movie Palette and let the movie use the same palette being used for the graphic. If this action does not solve the situation (or makes it worse), you will have to find another solution.

8. Select the Timing tab (see figure 5-15). Let's look at the fields, starting from the top and working downward.

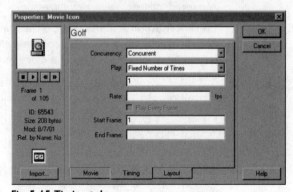

Fig. 5-15. Timing tab.

- **Concurrency:** *This field contains the same options as the Sound icon.*

    Wait Until Done: *The default setting that will hold any forward movement on the flowline until the current Movie icon is finished playing.*

    Concurrent: *Means that the current Movie icon will start playing, and as it does Authorware will continue down the flowline. The movie will continue to play as Authorware does whatever else is called for as it continues on the flowline.*

    Perpetual: *Means that the movie is always available. Perpetual is generally used in conjunction with a function or variable that turns the sound on and off.*

- **Play:** *This field offers the following options available from a pull-down menu.*

    Repeatedly: *Will play the movie over and over, until either it is erased or paused using a function.*

    Fixed Number of Times: *Enter the number of times you want the movie to play. If you enter 0, Authorware will display the first frame. A variable can be entered into this field.*

    Until True: *Will play the movie repeatedly until the condition entered in the field below becomes true. As an example, if you enter the system variable MouseDown, the movie plays repeatedly until the user presses the mouse button.*

    Only While In Motion: *Available for PICS movies. The movie's first frame is displayed on the screen but the movie is only played while a motion icon is moving it or it is dragged by the user. This option is useful for special effects such as simulating walking or jumping. This option is not available for externally stored movies.*

    Times/Cycle: *Generally used in conjunction with animation. The value entered limits the number of times the movie plays during each repetition of the animation. When you use the Times/Cycle option, Authorware adjusts the movie playback speed to complete the indicated number of plays during each repetition of the animation.*

    Controller Paused: *The movie is paused when first displayed, waiting for the user to click on the Controller Play button.*

    Controller Play: *For QuickTime movies, this option displays the movie controller on the user's screen so that the user can freeze frames, back up, play slowly, and otherwise control the movie. The movie starts playing immediately when displayed, unless the Controller Paused option has been selected.*

- **Rate:** *Use this field to set the speed of an externally stored movie if its format supports adjustable speeds. Enter a number or variable name to speed up or slow down the movie. If the speed is too fast to display all frames at the selected rate, Authorware skips frames to approximate the chosen speed, unless you have enabled the Play Every Frame option.*

- **Play Every Frame:** *Enable Play Every Frame to play a movie as fast as possible without skipping frames, but no faster than specified in the Rate field. Using this option may result in the movie playing at different speeds on different systems, but it generally yields the best results. This option is available for internally stored movies only.*

- **Start Frame and End Frame:** *Use the Start Frame and End Frame entry boxes to set the range of frames you want to play. When you first load a movie, the numbers of the first and last frames in the movie file appear in the Start Frame and End Frame boxes. If you want to play only specific movie frames, enter frame numbers, or enter variables or expressions that result in frame numbers in these boxes.*

a) Oh yeah, this tab we can play with! But first, close the Movie icon by clicking on the OK button.

b) Drag a Display icon to the flowline, placing it below the Movie icon. Name this icon *Movie Text*.

c) Double click on *Movie Text*. Use the Text tool and type in *And the putt stops just short of the pin*. Close this Display icon.

d) Drag the white Start flag from the Icon palette and place it immediately above the Movie icon.

e) Double click on the Movie icon *Golf*. Click on the Timing tab.

f) Just so you can clearly see the difference, click on the Concurrency pull-down menu and select the Wait Until Done option. Click on the OK button to close the Movie icon.

g) Click on the white Start Flag button in the Authorware toolbar to run the file from the white flag.

h) As you watch, the movie plays completely first, and then you see the text appear.

i) Double click on the Movie icon. Click on the Concurrency pull-down menu and select the Concurrent option. Click on the OK button to close the Movie icon.

j) Click on the white Start Flag button in the Authorware toolbar to run the file from the white flag. This time, as the movie begins to play the text displays immediately.

k) Double click on the Movie icon. Click on the Play pull-down menu and select the Fixed Number of Times option. In the field below, type in *2*. Click on the OK button to close the Movie icon.

l) Click on the white Start Flag button in the Authorware toolbar to run the file from the white flag. Like before, as the movie begins to play the text immediately appears and now the movie plays through twice. If you having been observing carefully, you have probably noted that the text does not reflect what is happening in the movie. The putt curves and goes past the pin. It does not stop short of the pin, as the text indicates. You need to fix this.

m) Double click on the Movie icon. Toward the bottom of the dialog window, in the End Frame field, type in *45*. Go to the field below Fixed Number of Times and change the *2* to a *1*. Click on the OK button to close the Movie icon.

n) Click on the white Start Flag button in the toolbar and take a look. The text now reflects what is happening in the movie.

o) Press Ctrl + J to jump to the flowline.

p) Double click on the Movie icon so that you can look at the next tab.

9. Select the Layout tab (see figure 5-16). Let's look at the fields, starting at the top and working downward.

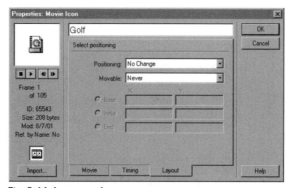

Fig. 5-16. Layout tab.

- **Positioning:** *Defines the position of the movie within the current icon, relative to the entire screen, area, or path.*

- **Movable:** *As author, you can determine whether the user can drag the movie according to the following options.*

  On Screen: *The user can move the movie anywhere on screen as long as it remains entirely on screen.*

  Anywhere: *The user can move the movie anywhere, even off the screen.*

  On Path: *The user can move the movie along a defined path (used in conjunction with X-Y Positions).*

  In Area: *The user can move the movie within a defined area (used in conjunction with X-Y Positions).*

- **X-Y Positions:** *Use the Base and End coordinates to define an area in which the object can appear or path the object can appear on (used in conjunction with the On Path or In Area option in the Movable field).*

10. There really is not anything to change here. Go ahead and save the file. Select File | Save.

Practice Exercise 5-1: Sound Synchronization

Media Synchronization is a new feature in Authorware 6. It provides the capability to use the Sound icon or Movie icon as a foundation upon which to attach other icons and determine how they will perform together. To this point you have been working with single icons on the flowline, so this will be the first icon structure you will build, simple as it may be.

As you first begin to work with the Media Synchronization feature, you will probably want to attach Display icons to either a Sound icon or a Movie icon. One common design requirement is to have text bullets appear on screen in conjunction with either narration or a movie being played. The Media Synchronization feature can make it easy to meet this design requirement.

Description

In this exercise you are going to create a very simple icon structure that will use the new Media Synchronization feature of Authorware 6. The foundation of the structure is the Sound icon. You will use a background graphic of a golf club house, an announcer's voice (narration sound file), and a couple of Display icons that contain text bullets that will need to be synchronized to the narration track. The following elements are covered in this exercise.

- *Creating text objects*
- *Importing external graphics*
- *Importing a sound file and selecting various sound options*
- *Using the Media Synchronization feature to link text display to narration*

Take a Look

Before beginning the exercise, let's take a look at the exercise in its completed state so that you can clearly see what it is you are about to build.

CD-ROM

1. Select File | Open and locate on the companion CD-ROM the folder *Chapter05*. Locate the file *Exer5-1* and double click on it.

2. The file *Exer5-1* should now appear in your copy of Authorware. Click on the Restart button on the toolbar to play the file from the top of the flowline.

3. Note the following properties of this completed exercise.

NOTE

Each time you open an Authorware file from the CD-ROM, you will encounter a prompt window that states the file is locked and you will not be able to save any changes. Just click on the OK button and move on.

- *The graphic of the clubhouse appears immediately, followed by the beginning of the narration.*
- *Just as the announcer says "From the time you tee off," the text bullet displays.*
- *Just as the announcer says "Five minutes," the text bullet displays.*
- *Just as the announcer says "Eight swings," the text bullet displays.*
- *Just as the announcer says "Foursome behind will play through," the text bullet displays.*
- *After the narration finishes, a Continue button appears.*
- *After you click on the Continue button, everything on screen erases.*

Storyboard: On screen

Figure 5-17 shows what the completed exercise will look like on screen after you have finished.

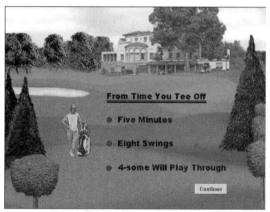

Fig. 5-17. Completed exercise on screen.

Storyboard: Behind the Scenes

Figure 5-18 shows what the completed exercise will look like in the design window after you have finished.

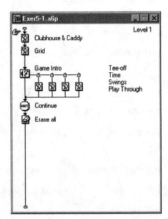

Fig. 5-18. Completed design window.

Step-by-Step Instructions

Go Solo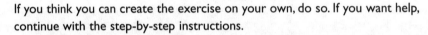

If you think you can create the exercise on your own, do so. If you want help, continue with the step-by-step instructions.

1. You need to open a new file for this exercise. Select File | New | File. Close the two Knowledge Object dialog windows that open by clicking the X in the upper right-hand corner of each window.

2. You should now be looking at a new flowline.

3. Save the file on your hard drive by selecting File | Save. Use the browse function to locate the *SaveWork* directory on your hard drive. Type in the name *Chap5-1* and click on the OK button.

4. Set the File properties.
    a) Select Modify | File | Properties.
    b) Click on the Colors/Background color box. In the Color palette that opens, click on a dark green.
    c) Make sure the Size field is set to 640 x 480.

NOTE

d) Click on the Title Bar box to remove the check mark.
    e) Click on the Menu Bar box to remove the check mark.

Do *not* place the Grid Display icon on the flowline yet. You will place the Grid Display icon in material to follow.

    f) Click on the OK button to close the Properties/File dialog window.

5. Drag most of the required icons to the flowline and arrange them to create the icon structure you want. See figure 5-18 for reference.
    a) Drag a Display icon to the flowline. Name it *Clubhouse & Caddy*.
    b) Drag a Sound icon to the flowline and drop it below the Display icon. Name the Sound icon *Game Intro*.

c) Drag a Display icon and drop it to the *right* of the Sound icon. Name it *Tee-off*.

d) Drag a second Display icon and drop it to the *right* of the Display icon *Tee-off*. Name it *Time*.

e) Drag a third Display icon and drop it to the *right* of the Display icon *Time*. Name it *Swings*.

f) Drag a fourth Display icon and drop it to the *right* of the Display icon *Swings*. Name it *Play Through*.

6. Now that you have the icon structure, let's add the content for *Clubhouse & Caddy*.

a) Double click on the first Display icon to open *Clubhouse & Caddy*. Select File | Import.

b) In the *Import which file?* dialog window that opens, use the browse function to locate your CD-ROM drive and the *Chapter05* folder on it.

c) Locate and single click on the file *Clubhouse.bmp*. Click on the Show Preview field at the bottom of the window to place a check mark there. Click on the Import button.

d) The graphic of the clubhouse should now be within the Display icon and positioned correctly on the screen. If you need to adjust the position/location of the graphic, click your mouse on it and move it as you see fit.

e) Select File | Import. In the *Import which file?* dialog window that opens (it should already be pointing into the *Chapter05* folder on the CD-ROM), locate and single click on the file *Caddie.bmp*.

f) Click on the Import button on the right.

g) The graphic of the caddie should now be in the Display icon. You will note that it has a white background. Let's change this to transparent. There should still be handlebars around the graphic, indicating that it is selected (if not, select it). Select Window | Inspectors | Modes. Select the Transparent option. Drag the caddy to the left. You will make final adjustments to the caddy's location in material to follow.

h) Click on the X to close the icon.

7. Establish the Sound icon.

a) Double click on the Sound icon *Game Intro*.

b) In the lower left-hand corner, click on the Import button.

c) In the *Import which file?* dialog window that opens, use the browse function to locate the CD-ROM drive and the *Chapter05* folder on it. Locate and single click on the sound file *GameIntro.wav*. Click on the Import button on the right. You should see a blue progress bar as the sound file is imported into Authorware.

Shortcut

After you have located a graphic file name with the browse function, you can simply double click on it to import it.

Shortcut

The following are keyboard shortcuts for the inspectors.
– Lines (Ctrl + L)
– Fills (Ctrl + D)
– Modes (Ctrl + M)
– Colors (Ctrl + K)

d) Click on the Timing tab. The settings you need should already be set, as they are the defaults, but check to make sure. Set Concurrency to Wait Until Done. Set Play to Fixed Number of Times, with *1* in the field below.

e) In the upper left-hand corner of the dialog window, click on the Play button to hear the narration.

f) When the narration is finished, click on the OK button to close the Properties/Sound Icon dialog window.

8. Add the content to the Display icon *Tee-off*.

a) Double click on the Display icon *Tee-off*.

b) You need to add some text to this Display icon. Select the text attributes first. Select Text | Font. Click on the Other option. In the Font dialog window that opens, use the pull-down menu and locate the font Arial Black or some other font you want to use. Click on the OK button. Select Text | Size. Click on the 14 point size.

c) Move the I-bar cursor to about the middle of the screen. Click the mouse on the screen to open the text object. Type in *From Time You Tee Off*. Click on the Pointer tool to close the text object.

d) Now for a little visual highlight with a line, but first the attributes. Press the Ctrl and L keys simultaneously (keyboard shortcut) to bring up the Line inspector. Click on a thick line format (perhaps not the thickest). Now for color. Press the Ctrl and K keys simultaneously (keyboard shortcut) to bring up the Color inspector. Click on the Pencil icon in the lower left. Click on a black color. Leave all inspectors on screen, as you will use them later. Move them to the side if you want.

e) Now you can draw the line. Click on the Straight Line tool. Click the mouse and draw a line about the same length as the text you just typed in.

f) With the line still selected, select Edit | Copy to copy the line to the clipboard. Click on the Pointer tool and then click the mouse on the screen below the black line. Select Edit | Paste.

g) Handlebars should still be around the second copy of the line (indicating it is selected). The Color inspector should still be on screen (if not, press Ctrl + K). Click on the Pencil icon in the lower left of the inspector. Click on a dark red color. The second line should now be red.

h) Move the red line so that it is slightly below the text. Do not be concerned about exact alignment, as you will be moving both objects in material to follow.

i) Click on the Pointer tool. Click on the black copy of the line. Select Modify | Send to Back so that the black line will be layered below (in

NOTE

If you copy an object to the clipboard and immediately paste it into the display area without clicking anywhere on screen, the object will be pasted in the exact location from which it was copied. You will want to do this sometimes, but in this case it is easier to work with the two objects separated. By clicking the mouse on the screen and then pasting, the object will be pasted at the approximate location of where you clicked the mouse on the screen.

back of) the red line. Click on the black line and drag it so that it lies underneath the red line, but slightly below and to the right of the red line (so that it looks like a shadow, as in the exercises in Chapter 4).

j) Select the red and black copies of the lines (click on one, hold the Shift key down, click on the second) and select Modify | Group so that the lines are grouped.

k) Close the Display icon by clicking on the X.

9. Establish the Display icon *Time*.

a) Hold the Shift key down and double click on the Display icon *Time*.

b) Click on the Text tool. The text attributes were already set in the previous step.

c) Move the I-bar cursor so that it is slightly below the middle of the screen and below the previous text object. Do not be too concerned about lining up the text objects, as you will do this using a grid pattern in material to follow. Click on the screen to open a text object, and type in *Five Minutes*.

d) Click on the Circle tool. Hold the Shift key down as you click the cross-hair cursor on the screen, and then draw a very small circle. Let's call this small circle a bullet for the text points.

e) Click on the Pointer tool. The Color inspector should still be on screen (if not, press Ctrl + K). There should still be handlebars around the circle. Click on the Pencil icon in the Color inspector. Click on a black color. Click on the Foreground color box in the lower right corner of the Color inspector. Click on a dark red. Your circle (bullet) should now have a black line with a dark red fill.

f) Move the red bullet so that it is slightly to the left of the text. Do not be concerned about exact placement, as you will align everything in material to follow.

g) With the bullet selected, select Edit | Copy to place a copy of the red bullet into the clipboard.

h) Click on the X to close the icon.

10. Establish the Display icon *Swings*.

a) Hold the Shift key down and double click on the Display icon *Swings*.

b) Click on the Text tool.

c) Move the I-bar cursor so that it is slightly below the middle of the screen and a little below the previous text and bulleted objects. Click on the screen to open a text object and type in *Eight Swings*.

d) Select Edit | Paste to paste a copy of the red bullet into this Display icon.

e) Move the red bullet so that it is slightly to the left of the text you just typed.

    f) Click on the X to close the icon.

11. Establish the Display icon *Play Through*.

    a) Hold the Shift key down and double click on the Display icon *Play Through*.

    b) Click on the Text tool.

    c) Move the I-bar cursor so that it is slightly below the middle of the screen and a little below the previous text and bulleted objects. Click on the screen to open a text object, and type in *Foursome Will Play Through*.

    d) Select Edit | Paste to paste a copy of the red bullet into this Display icon.

    e) Move the red bullet so that it is slightly to the left of the text you just typed.

    f) Click on the X to close the icon.

12. Establish the media synchronization for *Tee-off*.

    a) Note the small symbol directly above the Display icon *Tee-off*. This symbol looks like a very small clock, which is the symbol for media synchronization properties.

    b) Double click on the Synchronization Properties icon immediately above *Tee-off*. You are now looking at the Properties/Media Synchronization dialog window (see figure 5-19).

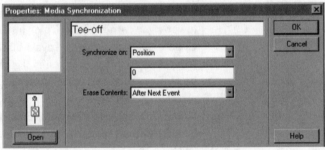

Fig. 5-19. Properties/Media Synchronization dialog window.

    c) In the first field, *Synchronization on*, click on the pull-down menu and select the Seconds option.

    d) In the second (blank) field, type in *1*.

    e) In the last field, Erase Contents, click on the pull-down menu and select the Don't Erase option.

    f) In the upper right corner, click on the OK button.

13. Establish the media synchronization for *Time*.

    a) Double click on the Synchronization Properties symbol above *Time*.

b) In the first field, *Synchronization on*, click on the pull-down menu and select the Seconds option.

c) In the second (blank) field, type in *2.1*.

d) In the last field, Erase Contents, click on the pull-down menu and select the Don't Erase option.

e) In the upper right-hand corner, click on the OK button.

14. Establish the media synchronization for *Swings*.

a) Double click on the Synchronization Properties symbol above *Swings*.

b) In the first field, *Synchronization on*, click on the pull-down menu and select the Seconds option.

c) In the second (blank) field, type in *3.7*.

d) In the last field, Erase Contents, click on the pull-down menu and select the Don't Erase option.

e) In the upper right-hand corner, click on the OK button.

15. Establish the media synchronization for *Play Through*.

a) Double click on the Synchronization Properties symbol above *Play Through*.

b) In the first field, *Synchronization on*, click on the pull-down menu and select the Seconds option.

c) In the second (blank) field, type in *6.9*.

d) In the last field, Erase Contents, click on the pull-down menu and select the Don't Erase option.

e) In the upper right-hand corner, click on the OK button.

16. Now let's make a trial run. There are some fixes yet to perform.

a) Click on the Restart button in the toolbar (below the menus).

b) Let the narration and all text bullets display on screen. What a mess!

c) Double click on the text *From Time You Tee Off*. You are now in the Display icon named *Tee-off*. You should see the icon name *Tee-off* in the toolbox.

d) Note that all objects in this Display icon are selected. Click the mouse on the graphic of the clubhouse to deselect all objects. Now click on the text and move it to about the center of the screen. Refer to figure 5-20 as a point of reference for steps *d* through *n*.

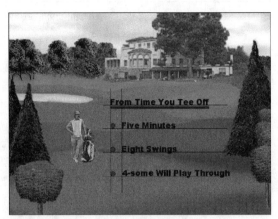

Fig. 5-20. On-screen alignment of objects.

e) Click on the grouped red and black lines and move them just below the *From Time You Tee Off* text.

f) Click on the caddy graphic and move it to the left.

g) Double click on the background clubhouse graphic. You are now in the Display icon named *Clubhouse & Caddy*.

h) Click on the Straight Line tool and draw several lines that will serve as a grid pattern to line up each of the text points and their corresponding bullets. See the grid shown in figure 5-20.

i) Click on one of the grid lines. Hold the Shift key down as you continue to click each grid line so that they are all selected (make sure you do not select the background graphic).

j) Place these grid lines in another Display icon. Select Edit | Group. Select Edit | Cut. Click on the X to close the icon.

k) Drag a Display icon to the flowline and drop it immediately below the *Clubhouse & Caddy* icon. Name this new icon *Grid*.

l) Double click on *Grid* to open this Display icon. Select Edit | Paste to place the grid lines in this new icon. Click on the X to close this icon.

m) Click on the Restart button to run the program again. Let the narration and all text bullets display on screen. If the grid lines are not where you want them, double click on a line and move the group of lines where you want them.

n) Double click on each text object, single click on the background (to deselect the multiple objects), and arrange all objects so that they line up with the grid line pattern. See figure 5-20 for reference.

17. Click on the Restart button and take another look.

It is generally a good idea to create different sets of grid line patterns (each grid for a particular purpose) as part of your project design standards and then keep these grid patterns in a library for use during development. However, when you do end up needing to create grid lines on-the-fly, by placing them in a separate Display icon, you can then place the pattern in the library and reuse it if necessary.

a) If you want to adjust any of the sync timing for any of the text bullets, double click on the appropriate Synchronization Properties symbol and change the time as you wish.

b) Run the program a few more times to get the timing the way you want it.

18. Drag a Wait icon to the bottom of the flowline. Name this icon *Continue*.

19. Drag an Erase icon to the bottom of the flowline. Name this icon *Erase All*.

20. Click on the Restart button.

21. When you encounter the Continue button, click on it.

22. When you encounter the Erase icon, click on every object you see on screen to erase everything. Click on the Transition pull-down menu (on the Erase tab) and select whichever transition you want to use.

23. Select File | Save.

Practice Exercise 5-2: Movie Synchronization

You began your first experience with Media Synchronization in practice exercise 5-1, working with the Sound icon. In that exercise you saw how easy it is to synchronize the appearance of text bullets to correspond with audio narration. In this exercise you will work with the Movie icon and will turn off the movie's audio track so that you can synchronize another series of sound effects to correspond with action in the movie. Again, you will see how easy this is to accomplish using Authorware's new Media Synchronization feature.

Description

In this exercise you are going to continue your golf game and gain further experience with the new Media Synchronization feature in Authorware 6. The foundation of the structure you will build is the Movie icon. You will use a background graphic of a golf green and will add a graphic of a caddy. You will turn off the audio track in the movie so that you can add your own series of sound effects, with a more playful end result. The sound effects will be synchronized with the action in the movie. The following elements are covered in this exercise.

- *Importing external graphics*
- *Playing a movie file*
- *Importing sound files*
- *Using the Media Synchronization feature to sync sound effects to action in the movie*

Take a Look

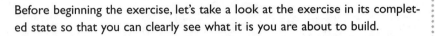

CD-ROM

Before beginning the exercise, let's take a look at the exercise in its completed state so that you can clearly see what it is you are about to build.

1. Select File | Open and locate on the companion CD-ROM the folder named *Chapter05*. Locate the file named *Exer5-2* and double click on it.

2. The file *Exer5-2* should now appear in your copy of Authorware. Click on the Restart button in the toolbar to play the file from the top of the flowline. Note the following properties of this completed exercise.

   • *The graphics of the golf green and caddie appear immediately, followed by a series of sound effects.*

   • *Just as the club hits the ball, you hear a pop.*

   • *As the ball moves toward the cup, you hear a heartbeat, adding suspense.*

   • *As the ball drops into the cup, you hear glass break.*

   • *As the sequence finishes, you hear the announcer say "What a shot!"*

   • *After you click on the Continue button, everything on screen erases.*

Storyboard: On screen

Figure 5-21 shows what the completed exercise will look like on screen after you have finished.

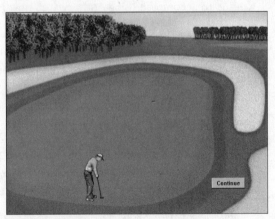

Fig. 5-21. Completed exercise on screen.

Storyboard: Behind the Scenes

Figure 5-22 shows what the completed exercise will look like in the design window after you have finished.

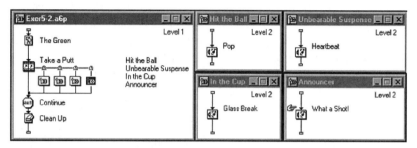

Fig. 5-22. Completed design window.

Step-by-Step Instructions

Go Solo

If you think you can create the exercise on your own, do so. If you want help, continue with the step-by-step instructions.

1. Open a new file for this exercise. Select File | New | File. Close the two Knowledge Object dialog windows that open by clicking on the X in the upper right corner of each window.

2. You should now be looking at a new flowline.

3. Save the file on your hard drive by selecting File | Save, and use the browse function to locate the *SaveWork* directory. Type in the name *Chap5-2* and click on the OK button.

4. Set the File properties.
    a) Select Modify | File | Properties.
    b) Click on the Colors/Background color box. In the Color palette that opens, click on a dark green.
    c) Make sure the Size field is set to 640 x 480.
    d) Click on the Title Bar box to remove the check mark.
    e) Click on the Menu Bar box to remove the check mark.

·T/P·

You want to synchronize sound to action in the movie. However, you cannot attach a Sound icon directly to the right of the Movie icon. As a work-around, drag a Map icon to the right of the Movie icon. The Map icon will attach to the Movie icon. You can then go inside the Map icon and place a Sound icon inside the Map icon. In this way you can very easily synchronize sound to action in the movie.

    f)   Click on the OK button to close the Properties/File dialog window.

5.   Drag all required icons to the flowline and arrange them to create the icon structure you want. See figure 5-22 for reference.

    a)   Drag a Display icon to the flowline. Name this icon *The Green*.

    b)   Drag a Movie icon to the flowline. Name this icon *Take a Putt*.

    c)   Drag a Map icon to the right of the Movie icon and drop it there to attach it to the Movie icon. Double click on the Map icon, so that you open a level 2 flowline within the Map icon. Drag a Sound icon to the level 2 flowline within the Map icon.

    d)   Click on the X of the Map icon so that it closes.

    e)   Click on the Map icon to select it. Select Edit | Copy to copy the Map icon (with a Sound icon within it) to the clipboard.

    f)   Click the mouse to the right of the first Map icon, to place the Paste Hand at this position.

    g)   Select Edit | Paste three times, so that you will have a total of four Map icons attached to the right of the Movie icon.

    h)   Single click on the first Map icon to select it. Name the Map icon *Hit the Ball*. Double click on the Map icon to open it. Single click on the Sound icon to select it. Name the Sound icon *Pop*. Click on the X on the Map to close it.

    i)   Single click on the second Map icon to select it. Name the Map icon *Unbearable Suspense*. Double click on the Map icon to open it. Single click on the Sound icon to select it. Name the Sound icon *Heartbeat*. Click on the X on the Map icon to close it.

    j)   Single click on the third Map icon to select it. Name the Map icon *In the Cup*. Double click on the Map icon to open it. Single click on the Sound icon to select it. Name the Sound icon *Glass Break*. Click on the X on the Map icon to close it.

    k)   Single click on the fourth Map icon to select it. Name the Map icon *Announcer*. Double click on the Map icon to open it. Single click on the Sound icon to select it. Name the Sound icon *What a Shot!* Click on the X on the Map icon to close it.

    l)   Drag a Wait icon to the flowline and drop it below the Movie icon. Name it *Continue*.

    m)   Drag an Erase icon to the flowline and drop it below the Wait icon. Name it *Clean Up*.

6.   Now to start adding the content. Let's begin with the first Display icon.

    a)   Double click on the Display icon *The Green* to open it.

    b)   In the *Import which file?* dialog window that opens (it should already be pointing into the *Chapter05* folder on the companion CD-ROM), locate and single click on the file *TheGreen.bmp*.

c) Click on the Import button on the right.

d) The graphic of the golf green should now be in the Display icon.

e) Click on the X to close the icon.

7. Add content to the Movie icon.

a) Double click on the Movie icon *Take a Putt*.

b) In the lower left corner, click on the Import button. In the *Import which file?* dialog window that opens (it should already be pointing to the *Chapter05* folder on the companion CD-ROM), locate and single click on the file *LongPutt.avi*. Click on the Import button on the right.

c) On the Movie tab, click on the box next to the Audio On field to *remove* the check mark.

d) Click on the OK button to close the Movie icon.

8. Add content to the first Map icon, *Hit the Ball*.

a) Double click on the Map icon *Hit the Ball*.

b) Double click on the Sound icon *Pop* located on the level 2 flowline.

c) In the lower left-hand corner, click on the Import button. In the *Import which file?* dialog window that opens (it should already be pointing to the *Chapter05* folder on the companion CD-ROM), locate and single click on the file *Pop.wav*. Click on the Import button on the right.

d) In the upper left of the Properties/Sound Icon dialog window that is still open, click on the Play button to preview the sound.

e) In the upper right-hand side of this dialog window, click on the OK button to close the window.

f) Click on the X to close the Map icon.

g) Double click on the Synchronization Properties symbol above this Map icon.

h) Change the Synchronize On field to be set for Seconds.

i) In the blank field below, type in *1*.

j) Click on the OK button to close the window.

9. Add content to the second Map icon, *Unbearable Suspense*.

a) Double click on the Map icon *Unbearable Suspense*.

b) Double click on the Sound icon *Heartbeat* located on the level 2 flowline.

c) In the lower left-hand corner, click on the Import button. In the *Import which file?* dialog window that opens, locate and single click on the file *heartbeat.wav*. Click on the Import button on the right.

d) Click on the Timing tab. The default setting for the Play field is Fixed Number of Times, which is okay. However, in the field below, type in *4*. This should play the heartbeat sound long enough. But in order to be able to sync the next sound with the movie image of the ball going into

---

NOTE

In the following steps, we suggest values to be entered in the blank Seconds field. Feel free to experiment and use whatever values you would like to.

---

the cup, we need to change another setting in this Sound icon so that the heartbeat can be cut off when needed. In the Concurrency field, use the pull-down menu and select Concurrent.

e)   In the upper left of the Properties/Sound Icon dialog window that is still open, click on the Play button to preview the sound.

f)   In the upper right-hand side of this dialog window, click on the OK button to close the window.

g)   Click on the X to close the Map icon.

h)   Double click on the Synchronization Properties symbol above this Map icon.

i)   Change the Synchronize On field to be set for Seconds.

j)   In the blank field below, type in *1.5*.

k)   Click on the OK button to close the window.

10. Add content to the third Map icon, *In the Cup*.

a)   Double click on the Map icon *In the Cup*.

b)   Double click on the Sound icon *Glass Break* located on the level 2 flowline.

c)   In the lower left-hand corner, click on the Import button. In the *Import which file?* dialog window that opens, locate and single click on the file *glassbreak.wav*. Click on the Import button on the right.

d)   In the upper left of the Properties/Sound Icon dialog window that is still open, click on the Play button to preview the sound.

e)   In the upper right-hand side of this dialog window, click on the OK button to close the window.

f)   Click on the X to close the Map icon.

g)   Double click on the Synchronization Properties symbol above this Map icon.

h)   Change the Synchronize On field to be set for Seconds.

i)   In the blank field below, type in *7.8*.

j)   Click on the OK button to close the window.

11. Add content to the last Map icon, *Announcer*.

a)   Double click on the Map icon *Announcer*.

b)   Double click on the Sound icon *What a Shot!* located on the level 2 flowline.

c)   In the lower left-hand corner, click on the Import button. In the *Import which file?* dialog window that opens, locate and single click on the file *whatashot.wav*. Click on the Import button on the right.

If you are careful to use the same color palette and shades of color in a background graphic as you do when creating a movie, you can seamlessly place a movie on top of the graphic so that it will look like they are both one creation. In this case the green of the movie exactly matches the green of the background graphic, so that it appears as though the entire screen is the movie. However, keeping the actual movie small will significantly improve the performance when the program is run.

    d) In the upper left of the Properties/Sound Icon dialog window that is still open, click on the Play button to preview the sound.

    e) In the upper right-hand side of this dialog window, click on the OK button to close the window.

    f) Click on the X to close the Map icon.

    g) Double click on the Synchronization Properties symbol above this Map icon.

    h) Change the Synchronize On field to be set for Seconds.

    i) In the blank field below, type in *9.2*.

    j) Click on the OK button to close the window.

12. Reposition the movie on screen.

    a) Click on the Restart button in the toolbar to run the program from the top.

    b) As soon as the movie begins to play, press Ctrl + P to pause the program.

    c) Click on the movie and drag it so that the cup in the movie is directly over the cup in the background graphic.

    d) Simultaneously press the Ctrl and P keys to resume play of the program.

    e) Repeat steps *a* through *d* until you are satisfied with the alignment.

13. Readjust the media synchronization for any of the Map icons if necessary.

    a) Click on the Restart button in the toolbar to run the program from the top.

    b) Simultaneously press the Ctrl and P keys to pause the play of the program.

    c) Simultaneously press the Ctrl and J keys to jump to the flowline.

    d) Double click on the Synchronization Properties symbol above the appropriate Map icon and adjust the time as necessary.

    e) Repeat steps *a* through *d* for whichever Map icons you want to.

14. Clean up.

    a) Click on the Restart button in the toolbar to run the program from the top.

    b) Let the program run until you encounter the Continue button.

    c) Simultaneously press the Ctrl and P keys to pause the play of the program.

    d) Drag the Continue button to whatever location you want.

    e) Simultaneously press the Ctrl and P keys to resume play of the program.

    f) Click on the Continue button.

    g) You should have now encountered the Erase icon. Click on every object on screen. Select an erase transition if you wish. Click on the OK button to close the Erase window.

15. Review.
   a) Click on the Restart button in the toolbar to run the program from the top. Let it go all the way to the end, erasing everything from the screen.
   b) With everything the way you want it, select File | Save.

Guided Tour 5F: Using a Sprite with QuickTime

Throughout this chapter you have seen how easy it is to use sound and movie clips within Authorware, with the use of the Sound and Movie icons. You have also had the experience of using the Media Synchronization feature with both of these icons to coordinate the display/presentation of various media elements.

Authorware makes it possible to call, control, and play QuickTime movies and Flash files using another element called a Sprite icon. QuickTime provides the ability to rotate, scale, and offset a QuickTime movie's image within its sprite's bounding rectangle. These capabilities go beyond what you will work with here, but for more information, consult Authorware's help pages.

1. Select File | New | File. Close the two Knowledge Object dialog windows that open.

2. Select Insert | Media | QuickTime. The QuickTime Xtra Properties window has opened. See figure 5-23. Let's take a quick look.

If you use these Sprite icons, you will have to make sure you also include the appropriate Xtras to support them. You will note that there is no Sprite icon in the Icon palette. However, you can easily insert a sprite using the Insert menu.

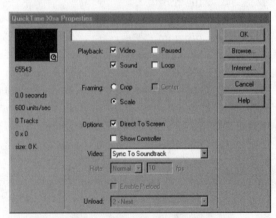

Fig. 5-23. QuickTime Xtra Properties window.

• **Buttons on the right:**

   Browse: *Use this button to locate and link a QuickTime movie file on your computer to the current QuickTime sprite.*

   Internet: *Use this button to locate and link a QuickTime movie file located at a URL address.*

- **Playback:**

  Video: *Placing a check mark here will cause the video portion of the movie file to be displayed.*

  Sound: *Placing a check mark here will cause the audio portion of the movie file to be heard.*

  Paused: *Placing a check mark here will display the first frame of the movie but will remain paused. If you want to give the user control to start the movie, make sure to place a check mark next to the Show Controller option.*

  Loop: *Placing a check mark here will cause the movie to continuously replay, until instructed to stop.*

- **Framing:**

  Crop: *Placing a check mark here will cause the movie to be displayed at its default size, with any part of the image outside the bounding box cropped.*

  Center: *Placing a check mark here will result in the QuickTime movie being centered within the sprite. With the check mark removed, the movie's upper left corner will be aligned with the sprite's upper left corner.*

  Scale: *Placing a check mark here will result in the movie being scaled to fit within the bounding box.*

- **Options:**

  Direct To Screen: *Place a check mark here to always play the movie in front of any other objects on the screen.*

  Show Controller: *Place a check mark here to display a controller panel with volume adjustment, and with play/pause controls for user control of the QuickTime movie.*

- **Video:**

  Sync To Soundtrack: *Selecting this option dictates that playing the soundtrack is most important, and video frames may be skipped to allow the sound to play without interruption.*

  Play Every Frame: *Selecting this option disables the soundtrack so that every frame may be played.*

3. To see what these settings do, you first need a QuickTime movie file.
   a) Click on the Browse button on the right.
   b) Locate the CD-ROM drive, and the *Chapter05* folder on it.
   c) Locate and select the file *golf.mov*.
   d) Click on the Open button.

4. Now let's change a few of these settings.

·T*i*P·

Using a sprite with a QuickTime movie, you can turn off the visual element by removing the check mark next to Video, and just play the sound track of the movie (with a check mark being left next to Sound).

    a)   Click on the box beside Show Controller to place a check mark there.

    b)   Click on the box beside Paused to place a check mark there.

    c)   Click on the OK button to close the window.

5.   Now let's take a look.

    a)   Click on the Restart button in the toolbar.

    b)   Click on the Play button in the controller that is on screen below the movie. Let the movie play through.

    c)   Simultaneously press the Ctrl and J keys to jump to the flowline.

6.   Double click on the QuickTime sprite. The Properties/Sprite Icon dialog window is now open. See figure 5-24. This is not the same dialog window you saw before. (You will see how to access the previous dialog window in material to follow.)

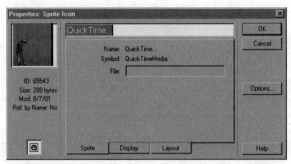

Fig. 5-24. Properties/Sprite Icon dialog window showing the Sprite tab.

7.   As you can see, there are three tabs in this dialog window: Sprite, Display, and Layout.

8.   First let's take a quick look at the Sprite tab. See figure 5-24. This tab provides you with information about the QuickTime sprite.

9.   Click on the Display tab. See figure 5-25. The options here are very similar to those found in the Display tab for the Display icon.

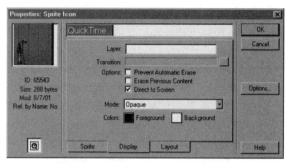

Fig. 5-25. Properties/Sprite Icon dialog window showing the Display tab.

10. Click on the Layout tab. See figure 5-26. The options here are very similar to those found in the Layout tab for the Movie icon.

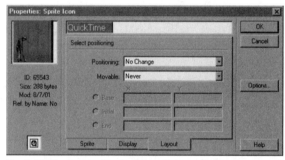

Fig. 5-26. Properties/Sprite Icon dialog window showing the Layout tab.

11. Click on the Options button to the right of the current dialog window. Here is the QuickTime Xtra Properties window you saw previously as you first inserted the QuickTime media from the Insert menu. Click on OK to close the QuickTime Xtra window. Click on OK to close the Properties window for the Sprite icon.

12. Keep the file open, as you will use it in the next tour.

Guided Tour 5G: Using a Sprite with Flash

There are several ways Flash files can be played in Authorware. First, Flash files can be exported from Flash as a QuickTime movie and played with the use of a Movie icon, just like any other movie. Second, as a QuickTime movie, a Flash file can be played within the QuickTime sprite you just worked with. Flash files can also be called, played, and controlled using Authorware's functions. Finally, you can also play the Shockwave (*.swa*) format of a Flash file using a Flash sprite. Let's take a quick look.

1. Use the same file that should be open from the last tour. If not, open a new file.

2. Select Insert | Media | Flash. The Flash Asset Properties window has opened. See figure 5-27. You can see that this property window is virtually the same as the QuickTime version, with just a minor difference toward the bottom, relating to the fact that Flash movies can be resized easily.

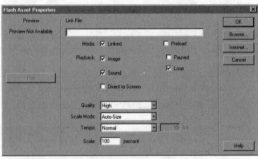

Fig. 5-27. Flash Asset Properties window.

3. Click on the Browse button on the right. Locate the CD-ROM and the *Chapter05* folder on it. Locate and select the file *SouthWest.swf*. Click on the Open button. Click on the OK button.

4. Click on the Restart button to start the program.

5. Click on the GO sign to move to an interactive menu screen.

6. Click on whichever cities you want, to learn interesting facts about the Southwest.

7. Click on the File pull-down menu in the Presentation window (upper left corner) and select Quit.

8. Double click on the Flash sprite and change whatever settings you want.

9. Select File | Quit. You do not need to save this file.

Enhanced Media in the Delivery Environments

The sections that follow discuss various avenues of delivery associated with the Authorware environment. These include local delivery, intranet delivery, and Internet delivery.

Delivery via Local Hard Drive, CD-ROM, and LAN/WAN

Projects intended for distribution via CD-ROM or LAN/WAN may include diverse instructional strategies and can be media rich, with full screen graphics, animation, narration, and music. Extensive use of video is best suited for

If you want to have some fun learning Flash and create this Southwest tour, see another of the books in the OnWord Press Inside Macromedia series at *www.onwordpress.com/ InsideMacromedia/ Flash5*.

hard drive or CD-ROM delivery (with a minimum speed of a 4X player). Limited video can be implemented over a LAN/WAN, but is highly dependent on specific hardware and traffic use issues.

The use of narration, music, and sound effects requires sound capability on each delivery machine, but generally does not present network performance problems. Performance may be significantly increased in the LAN/WAN environment with the distribution of copies of Authorware's "run" file to local computers.

Delivery via Intranet

The most important and defining characteristic (from the application development standpoint) is that these Web-based company intranets are typically "hard-wired" using high-bandwidth cable, connecting remote servers with dedicated high-bandwidth telephone lines. Company intranets typically exclude dial-up modem access. Using this description, intranet delivery poses no media or instructional design limitations. Authorware requires the appropriate Shockwave plug-in to be installed in each user computer's browser.

Delivery via Internet

Although Internet delivery provides the greatest capability in terms of access (available from any phone line, at any time, from anywhere), it does present several significant limitations, ultimately connected with the issue of the limited bandwidth of dial-up modems. Applications developed for this environment must be designed and created using care with the graphic palette, format, and size to achieve reasonable performance and artistic quality on varied delivery platforms. Narration must be sequenced and recorded carefully to minimize quality degradation during transmission. Quite effective animation can be utilized, whereas the use of video (though changing rapidly) is currently not recommended.

Summary

- *Authorware applications can use a wide variety of media, including high-resolution graphics, narration, sound effects, music, movie clips, and animation. Authorware can also import text created in an external program.*

- *The Sound icon and the Movie icon make it very easy to include both digital sound and movies within any Authorware application, offering very convenient control over these media elements.*

- *Sound files of prerecorded music and sound effects can be purchased. Typically these sound files are supplied on CD-ROM, with at least a couple of different* file formats available for each selection. Your best bet is to look for music and sound effects products that very clearly state "Royalty Free Use" of their sound files.

- Most Authorware developers obtain and import graphics that have been created in external programs. Graphics created from scratch can be created in graphics programs such as Freehand, Fireworks, and Photoshop.

- In Guided Tour 5A, you went through the process of importing graphics created in an external program and took a look at the various options associated with doing so.

- In Guided Tour 5B, you went through the process of importing text created in an external word processor and took a look at the various options associated with doing so.

- In Guided Tour 5C, you saw the advantages of using libraries within Authorware and learned how to create and use them for storing reusable parts.

- Sound can serve a number of important functions for your project, including music and sound tracks, narration, and sound effects.

- A professional recording studio will be able to create music and sound effects, and record any narration you may require. The cost of these services varies tremendously, depending on what you are asking for.

- You can also record your own narration, as it is pretty easy to do. At a minimum, you will need three things, with a fourth component recommended: a sound card in your computer, a microphone, sound-editing software, and a tape recorder (recommended, not required).

- There are four properties of sound files that collectively determine their quality and file size: sampling rate, sample size, channels, and format.

- In Guided Tour 5D, you explored the Sound icon properties and imported sound files into Authorware.

- Many of the possibilities associated with the use of sound files are also true of movie files, although the depth of these possibilities will generally be much more limited.

- To record your own digital movies, you will need three things, with a fourth component recommended: a video-capture card in your computer, a video camera, video editing software, and videotape recorder/camcorder (recommended, not required).

- There are three properties of movie files that collectively determine their quality and file size: frame rate, image size, and data compression.

- In Guided Tour 5E, you looked at the Movie icon properties and got experience importing a movie into Authorware.

- In Practice Exercise 5-1, you took a first look at Authorware's new Media Synchronization feature. In this exercise, you learned how to use a Sound icon as *the foundation and then synchronize the display of text bullets to the progress of a narration track, so that the bullets displayed just as the narrator was mentioning them.*

- *In Practice Exercise 5-2, you continued working with the new Media Synchronization feature. In this exercise, you learned how to use a Movie icon as the foundation and then synchronize the sound clips to the action happening on screen in the movie.*

- *In Guided Tour 5F, you took a quick look at how to use the QuickTime sprite to display and control QuickTime movies.*

- *In Guided Tour 5G, you took a quick look at how to use the Flash sprite to display and control shocked Flash files.*

- *Distribution of enhanced media over networks requires careful consideration. Extensive use of video is best suited for hard drive or CD-ROM delivery. Over a LAN/WAN, limited video can be implemented but is highly dependent on specific hardware and traffic use issues. The use of narration, music, and sound effects requires sound capability on each delivery machine, but generally does not present network performance problems.*

- *Company intranets typically exclude dial-up modem access. Using this description, intranet delivery poses no media or instructional design limitations. Authorware requires the appropriate Shockwave plug-in to be installed in each user computer's browser.*

- *Although Internet delivery provides greatest capability in terms of access, it does present several significant limitations, ultimately connected with the issue of the limited bandwidth of dial-up modems.*

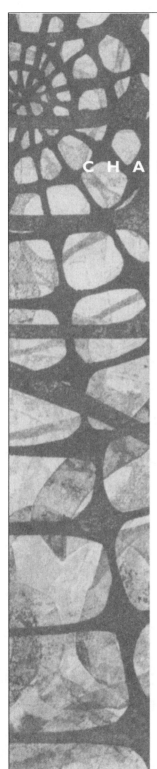

6

Creating

Sequences Using

the Decision Icon

Introduction

In Chapter 4 you created a simple structure that displayed text and graphics on screen, made use of various pausing techniques, and included display and erase transition effects. This type of structure (i.e., placing icons directly on the main flowline) is simple, but has significant shortcomings. First, this type of structure rapidly takes up the entire flowline. You can group icons into maps, but this is only a partial solution. The second shortcoming of this method is that it does not provide any other branching possibilities, including the ability to "back up" to previous screens.

In Chapter 5 you were introduced to the new Authorware 6 feature Media Synchronization. In the two practice exercises in that chapter you saw how icons could be attached to the right of the Sound and Movie icons, creating "mini-structures" for the purpose of synchronizing media elements.

In this chapter you will begin working with the Decision icon, which not only provides a better solution to sequencing information but presents true "branching" options. By the end of this chapter you will be able to:

- *Describe the chief characteristics of the Decision icon*
- *Create a Sequential Decision icon branching structure*
- *Create a Random Decision icon branching structure*
- *Create a Looping Decision icon branching structure*

Guided Tour 6A: Decision Icon Properties

The Decision icon is a simple device that can be used to determine which path the user will proceed along. You might say that the Decision icon is simply a branching structure without content. The Decision icon (see figure 6-1) looks like the diamond-shaped icon often used in flow charts to indicate one type of event; namely, a point at which one of multiple pathways can be chosen.

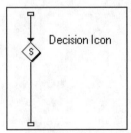

Fig. 6-1. Decision icon on the flowline.

The following are characteristics of the Decision icon it is important that you keep in mind.

- *It is strictly a branching structure.*
- *It has no display area or display capability.*
- *Its branching is defined by the author/programmer.*

1. Start by opening a new file.
    a) Select File | New | File.
    b) Close the two dialog windows that have opened by clicking on the X that appears in the upper right-hand corner of each window.
    c) Verify that you are now looking at an empty flowline.

2. Drag a Decision icon to the flowline and let go. Name the icon *Show Pages*.

3. A Decision icon is never used by itself (all it can do is control branching to other icons), so let's drag a few Display icons that will help illustrate how the branching in the Decision icon works.
    a) Drag a Display icon to the right of the Decision icon and let go.
    b) Drag three (3) more Display icons to the right of the first Display icon. See figure 6-2.
    c) Highlight each Display icon and name them, respectively, *Page 1*, *Page 2*, *Page 3*, and *Page 4*.
    d) Double click on the *Page 1* Display icon. Click on the Text tool. Click on the screen to open a text object and type in *Page 1*. Close this icon.
    e) Open each of the other Display icons and place text in each corresponding to its title. That is, inside Display icon *Page 2*, type in the text *Page 2*, and so on.
    f) Drag another Display icon to the flowline and drop it below the Decision icon.
    g) Name this new Display icon *Prove it to me*.
    h) Double click on this Display icon. Click on the Text tool. Click on the screen and type in *Here I am*. Close this icon.
    i) Select File | Save. Type in the name *Guided Tour*.

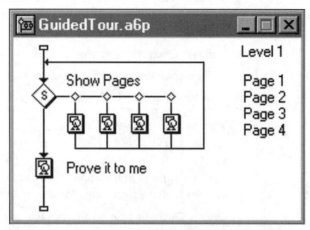

Fig. 6-2. Decision icon with four Display icons attached.

4. Now let's look at the properties associated with the Decision icon.
    a) Verify that the Decision icon is selected (highlighted).
    b) Select Modify | Icon | Properties (or simply double click on the Decision icon).
    c) The Properties/Decision Icon dialog window should now be open. See figure 6-3.

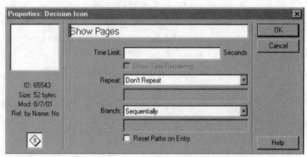

Fig. 6-3. Properties/Decision Icon dialog window.

5. There are no properties you need to change at the moment, but note the following descriptions of the options listed. As you look at the following properties, keep in mind the structure in figure 6-2; namely, a Decision icon with four Display icons attached. The properties of the Decision icon will determine which path (Display icon) will be selected and how often the repeat process will occur. The following are the options, starting from the top and working downward.

- **Icon Title Field:** *As in every icon property dialog window, the name of the current icon is displayed here.*

- **Time Limit:** *Provides the capability to limit the amount of time the user can spend within a decision structure. When the time elapses, Authorware exits the Decision icon regardless of the status of other options. You can enter a number for seconds or a variable expression.*

- **Show Time Remaining:** *If this box is selected, a small alarm clock appears on screen and graphically counts down the time remaining. This option is available only if the Time Limit option has been selected.*

- **Repeat:** *Provides a pull-down list of options to indicate how many times the structure should be repeated before exiting.*

  Fixed Number of Times: *Provides for the input of either a number or variable to indicate the number of times the decision paths are to be repeated. If the entry is less than 1 or greater than the number of attached icons, no branching occurs and Authorware drops straight through the Decision icon without entering any icons that might be attached to it.*

  Until All Paths Used: *Indicates that every icon attached to the Decision icon must be entered at least once before exiting.*

  Until Click/Keypress: *Indicates that the Decision paths should be repeated until the user presses a key or clicks the mouse button.*

  Until True: *Indicates that the Decision paths should be repeated until the value of the variable or expression in the Entry field below becomes true.*

  Don't Repeat: *Indicates that the Decision paths should be entered only once and then exited.*

- **Entry Field:** *This field (currently grayed out) becomes active only if the Until True repeat option is selected first. You can then enter a variable expression in this field as the condition the Until True option is looking for.*

- **Branch:** *Provides a pull-down list of options to indicate what type of branching logic should be used to determine which path to follow. Note that whatever choice is made here is reflected by the presence of a corresponding letter in the Decision icon, as seen on the main flowline: S (Sequential), A (Randomly to Any Path), U (Randomly to Unused Path), and C (To Calculated Path). See figure 6-4. These options are described in the following.*

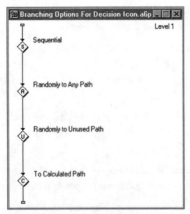

Fig. 6-4. Branching options for Decision icon.

> ***Sequential:*** *Sequentially selects each attached icon, one after another.*
>
> ***Randomly to Any Path:*** *Randomly selects any path each time the decision is made. A path might be selected again before other paths have been selected.*
>
> ***Randomly to Unused Path:*** *Randomly selects a path and will not select it again until all other paths have been selected.*
>
> ***To Calculated Path:*** *The path selected is based on the integer value of the number or variable typed into the Entry field below (e.g., 1st path = 1, 2nd path = 2, and so on).*

- ***Entry Field:*** *This field (currently grayed out) becomes active only if the Calculated Path option is selected first. You can then enter an integer or variable expression as the value the Calculated Path option is looking for.*

- ***Reset Paths on Entry:*** *Placing a check mark here resets the Decision icon as if it had not been previously run.*

To better understand these options, let's play a bit with the structure you have built.

6. Before you close the Decision icon dialog window, note that the default option for Repeat should still be set to Don't Repeat and that the option for Branch should still be set to Sequentially. Click on OK to close the dialog window.

7. Click on the Restart button. You should now be looking at the text *Here I am* on screen.

But why didn't the structure branch to the first path, so that you could see *Page 1* on screen before getting to *Here I am?* This suggests that there must be other factors to consider. Let's take a look at the properties of the "decision paths" attached to the Decision icon.

NOTE

The paths (icons) attached to a Decision icon are internally numbered from left to right, starting with 1 (one) in the leftmost position (closest to the Decision icon) and increasing in integer value as you move to the right.

Guided Tour 6B: Properties of the Decision Path

You have just looked at the properties of the Decision icon. However, this icon has some icons attached to it, and these attachments (paths) have properties you have not seen before.

1. Let's take a look.
    a) Select (highlight) the first Display icon attached to the Decision icon.
    b) Select Modify | Icon | Decision Path (or simply double click on the diamond symbol above the Display icon).
    c) The Properties/Decision Path dialog window should now be open. See figure 6-5.

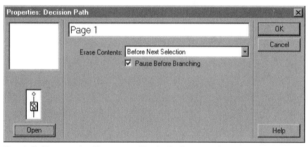

Fig. 6-5. Properties/Decision Path dialog window.

(NOTE)

The Before Next Selection choice will generally require the selection of the Pause Before Branching option or the use of a Wait icon within a Map icon. Otherwise, whatever is displayed in the path will probably be erased before you get a chance to see it. This is part of the reason you did not see *Page 1* when you ran the program previously.

2. There are no properties you need to change at the moment, but note the following descriptions of the options listed. As you look at the following properties, keep in mind the structure in figure 6-2; namely, a Decision icon with four Display icons attached. You are now looking at the properties associated with any of the paths (icons) attached to the Decision icon, as follows, starting from the top and working downward.

- ***Icon Title Field:*** *The name of the current icon is displayed here.*

- ***Erase Contents:*** *Unlike the Erase icon, this erase function is an automatic capability associated with the branching of the Decision icon. Erasing does not require an additional Erase icon but simply a choice of the following made in this pull-down window.*

    Before Next Selection: *With this selection, the content of whatever is displayed in this path (in the current example, a Display icon) will be erased before the next path (associated with this Decision icon) is entered.*

    Upon Exit: *This selection will display the content in the path and keep it on screen until the Decision icon is exited, at which time the content will be automatically erased.*

Don't Erase: Disables the automatic erase function associated with the current decision path (icon). Content displayed in the current path will stay on screen until erased with an Erase icon or other erase function.

- *Pause Before Branching:* Placing a check mark in this box will cause the program to pause, displaying a Continue button the user must click on to proceed.

3. Click on OK to close the decision path Properties window. Let's experiment; first with the Decision icon properties.
   a) Double click on the Decision icon.
   b) The default Branch option is fine; leave it as Sequentially.
   c) Click on the pull-down menu for the Repeat option. Set it to Until All Paths Used.
   d) Click on the OK button to close the dialog window.

4. Let's try running the program again, but be prepared to hit the wall.
   a) Click on the Restart button and on screen you should see *Here I am.*

You set the Decision icon to Until All Paths Used. Why didn't you see *Page 1, Page 2,* and so on?

5. If you were to run this program on a very old computer, with a slow processor, you would see *Page 1, Page 2,* and so on flash very quickly on screen. This suggests that there must be some other settings that have to be changed. Let's take a look around. Let's look at the Decision Path symbol, immediately above the *Page 1* Display icon.
   a) Double click on the Decision Path symbol.
   b) Click on the box next to the Pause Before Branching option.
   c) Click on the OK button to close the dialog window.

6. Examine the result of changing the Decision Path option.
   a) Click on the Restart button.
   b) You should now be looking at the text *Page 1* on screen, and you should see a Continue button. Selecting the Pause Before Branching option seems to have been the answer.
   c) Click on the Continue button and you should again see *Here I am.*

Note that you changed just one of the Decision Path properties. Therefore, you now need to change all of them.

7. Repeat step 5 for the Decision Path symbol above each of the other Display icons, setting them all to Pause Before Branching.

8. Examine the result.
   a) Click on the Restart button.

b) You should now be looking at the text *Page 1* on screen, and you should see a Continue button.

c) Click on the Continue button and you should see *Page 2*.

d) Keep clicking on the Continue button until you reach the text *Here I am*.

9. You have just built a Decision icon structure that uses sequential branching, until all paths are selected. Let's keep this structure separate, as you will be creating other structures. The easy way to do this is to place this structure within a Map icon, as follows.

a) Click the mouse in the upper left-hand corner of the flowline and, holding the mouse button down, drag the elastic marquee to the lower right to select all icons in this structure. Let go of the mouse. All icons have now been selected.

b) Select Modify | Group.

c) Name the new Map icon *Until All Paths Used*.

10. Instead of creating another structure from scratch, it is quicker to simply copy the structure you already have, as follows.

a) With the Map icon still selected, select Edit | Copy.

b) Click the mouse on the flowline below the first Map icon so that the Paste Hand cursor appears there.

c) Select Edit | Paste.

d) Name this second Map icon *Random, Unused Paths*.

11. Modify this second Map icon.

a) Double click on the Map icon *Random, Unused Paths*.

b) Double click on the Decision icon to open the dialog window.

c) In the Branch field, select the Randomly to Unused Path option.

d) Click on the OK button to close the dialog window.

e) Drag the white Start flag and place it above the Map icon *Random, Unused Paths*.

f) Click on the white Start Flag button in the toolbar.

g) Run through this segment. Click on the Continue button each time it is encountered. You should see the text for all pages appear, in random order. Once all pages have been displayed, you will then see *Here I Am*.

h) Select File | Save, and use the browse function to save this file into the *SaveWork* directory on your hard drive. Name the file *Chap6Tour*.

12. Before moving on to another structure, let's change another option of the current Decision icon structure.

a) Verify that the Map icon *Random, Unused Paths* is still open (i.e., you are looking at the level 2 flowline). If it is not, double click on the Map icon to open it.

b) Double click on the Decision icon to open the dialog window.

c) Click on the pull-down menu for the Repeat field. Select the Fixed Number of Times option.

d) In the blank field below the Repeat field (which has now become active), type in 2.

e) Click on the OK button to close the window.

f) Click on the white Start flag and take a look (make sure the white Start flag is still above the current Map icon). Click on the Continue button each time it is encountered. You should see two pages randomly selected and then the text *Here I Am*.

g) Close the Map icon by clicking on the X on the title bar of the level 2 design window.

13. Create one more structure.

a) Select the Map icon *Random, Unused Paths*.

b) Select Edit | Copy.

c) Click the Paste Hand on the flowline below this Map icon.

d) Select Edit | Paste.

e) Rename the copied Map icon *Random, Any Path*. Double click on this Map icon to open it.

f) Double click on the Decision icon to open the dialog window.

g) In the Repeat field, select Until All Paths Used.

h) In the Branch field, select Randomly to Any Path.

i) Drag the white Start flag so that it is above the current Map icon *Random, Any Path*.

j) Click on the white Start Flag button. Click on the Continue button each time it is encountered. You should see all pages displayed, with some pages being selected again, until all pages have been displayed. Eventually you arrive at the text *Here I Am*.

14. Click on the X on the title bar of the level 2 design window to close the Map icon.

15. Select File | Save.

That concludes the tour. Hopefully you have seen how the options for the Decision icon and the Decision Path properties are fairly logical. You now have three models to reference and work with. If you would like to experiment and change any of the settings in any of the Decision icon structures you have just built, go ahead and do so.

Practice Exercise 6-1: Creating a Text Bullet Sequence

Description

In this exercise, you will create a presentation sequence using a Decision icon. This type of sequence is useful for presenting the details of each of a multi-step process. In this exercise, the initial screen presents an overview of the four steps involved in developing a multimedia project. This list of steps remains on screen as each step in highlighted and additional details about that step are presented. As the presentation moves to the next screen, the highlight and details related to the first step are erased and replaced with a highlight and details about the second step; and so on. The Decision icon is set to Sequential Branching, with the Erase option set to Before Next Selection and with the Pause Before Branching option selected. The following elements are covered in this exercise.

- *Using text objects to highlight bulleted lists*
- *Creating a Decision icon sequence*
- *Setting Decision icon properties*
- *Setting Decision Path properties*

Take a Look

Before beginning the exercise, let's take a look at the exercise in its completed state so that you can clearly see what you are about to build.

1. Select File | Open and locate on the companion CD-ROM the *Chapter06* directory. Locate the file named *Exer6-1* and double click on it.

2. The file *Exer6-1* should now appear in your copy of Authorware. Click on the Restart button to play the file from the top of the flowline. Note the following properties of this completed exercise.

    a) The first screen displayed actually consists of four different Display icons that when combined display what is shown in figure 6-6.

    b) The Display icon *Grid for Sequence* has been left in the flowline to illustrate how it can be used to line up the various elements on screen. The grid lines would normally be removed prior to external viewing.

    c) It is important to note that the Display icon *Spaces* is not blank but contains a text object consisting of a couple of spaces (pressing the space bar to create it). If this icon were left blank, Authorware would stop on the empty icon and require an object to be placed within the icon.

CD-ROM

NOTE

We have noted before that each time you attempt to open an Authorware program or library file from a CD-ROM, you will see a message window warning the current file is locked and changes cannot be saved. In this case, there is an associated library file, and you will see this message twice. Just click on the OK button. This is our last reminder about this warning message. From here on, you'll remember ... right?

d) As each highlight appears, there are only three objects in each over-laying Display icon: the bullet, the red version of the word, and the details that explain that particular phase.

Storyboard: On screen

Figures 6-6 through 6-8 show various elements of the on-screen display. Figure 6-6 illustrates what the complete on-screen presentation will look like as the sequence first begins. Figure 6-7 shows the screen template. Figure 6-8 shows the content of the Display icon *Analysis*. In this icon there is a red copy of the word *Analysis*, which you will align so that when the program is run, it overlays the black copy of the same word (located in the Display icon *Screen Template* – see figure 6-7). The red word is being used to highlight the current phase being discussed. In this same icon, located over on the right, are details about the current phase (in this case, details about Analysis). The content of the other three Display icons is similar to that shown in figure 6-8, with text and placement appropriate to the particular phase.

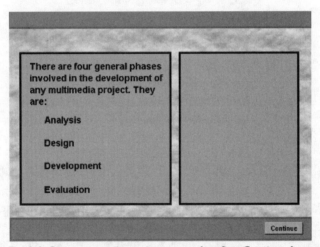

Fig. 6-6. On-screen presentation stopped at first Continue button.

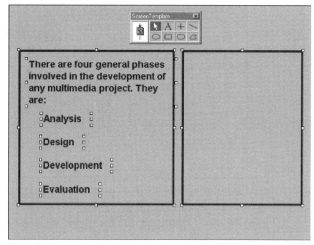

Fig. 6-7. Content of the Display icon Screen Template.

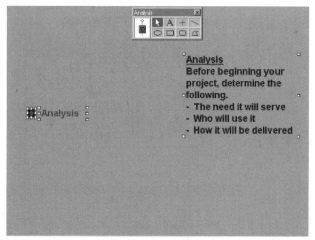

Fig. 6-8. Content of the Display icon Analysis.

Storyboard: Behind the Scenes

The design window shown in figure 6-9 illustrates all icons, their placement, and their names as they should appear after you have finished this exercise. The library you will be using appears in figure 6-9.

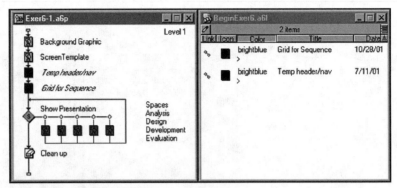

Fig. 6-9. Main flowline with icons.

The dialog windows shown in figures 6-10 and 6-11 illustrate the settings selected for the following exercise.

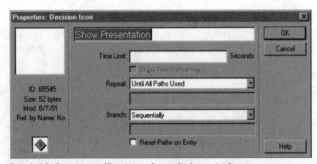

Fig. 6-10. Properties/Decision Icon dialog window.

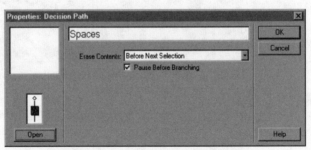

Fig. 6-11. Properties/Decision Path dialog window.

Step-by-Step Instructions

1. Begin by opening a new file for this exercise.

   a) Select File | New | File.

    b)   Close the two Knowledge Object dialog windows.

2.   Verify that you are now looking at a new flowline.

3.   Set up the file properties.
   a)   Select Modify | File | Properties.
   b)   Select whatever background color you want.
   c)   Make sure that Size is set to 640 x 480.
   d)   Remove the check marks beside the Tile Bar and Menu Bar options.
   e)   Click on the OK button to close the window.
   f)   Select File | Save and locate the *SaveWork* directory. Type in *Chap6-1* and click on the OK button.

4.   Start with icons from the Icon palette. You will come back and get some icons from the library in material to follow.
   a)   Drag two Display icons to the flowline. Name them *Background Graphic* and *Screen Template*.
   b)   Drag a Decision icon to the flowline and place it directly below the two Display icons on the flowline. Name this icon *Show Presentation*.
   c)   Drag five (5) Display icons to the *right* of the Decision icon. Name these icons *Spaces*, *Analysis*, *Design*, *Development*, and *Evaluation*.
   d)   Drag an Erase icon to the bottom of the flowline, below the Decision icon. Name this icon *Clean Up*.

5.   Establish the library items.
   a)   Select File | Open | Library. The Open Library dialog window opens.
   b)   Use the browse function to locate the CD-ROM drive and the *Chapter06* directory on it. Locate and select the file *BeginExer6.a6l*. Click on the Open button. The library should have opened.
   c)   Make sure the library is selected (click the mouse on it, if it is not). Select File | Save As. Use the browse function to locate the *SaveWork* directory on your computer's hard drive. Save it using the default name *BeginExer6.a6l*. You now have a copy of the library on your computer, in the *SaveWork* directory.
   d)   Drag the *Temp header/navigation* icon from the library to the flowline, and place it below the Display icon *Screen Template* (above the Decision icon *Show Presentation*).
   e)   Drag the *Grid for Sequence* icon from the library to the flowline, and place it below the *Temp header/navigation* icon.

6.   There is a lot of content to put in. Let's start at the top and work down.
   a)   Double click on Background Graphic to open this Display icon.
   b)   Select File | Import. The *Import which file?* dialog window opens. Use the browse function to locate the CD-ROM and the *Chapter06* direc-

tory on it. Locate and select the file *backgrnd.bmp*. Click on the Import button. Reposition the graphic on screen, if you need to.

   c) Close the Display icon.

7. You will have to create the content for the *Screen Template* icon from scratch.

   a) Double click on *Screen Template* to open this Display icon.

   b) First you will need to draw the two "text windows." Click on the Rectangle tool and draw two rectangles, as illustrated in figure 6-12. Use the Line inspector (Window | Inspector | Line) to make the line a little thicker than the default value. Use the Color inspector (Window | Inspector | Color) to give the rectangles an internal fill color (click on the Foreground color box in the inspector). Size and position the "text windows" as shown in figure 6-12.

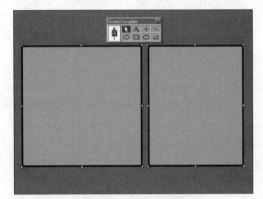

Fig. 6-12. Display icon **Screen Template.**

   c) Select the Text tool. Before your start typing, first select the text attributes. Select Text | Font and locate and select Arial. Select Text | Size and select 14. Select Text | Style | Bold. Finally, select Window | Inspector | Modes and select Transparent.

   d) Click the I-bar cursor on screen toward the top of the screen. Type in the following text.

There are four general phases involved in the development of any multimedia project. They are:

   e) Click the I-bar cursor on the screen below this first text object and type in the following items, each as a separate text object (in other words, there are four text objects below). Do not worry about placement of these objects; in material to follow you will use the grid lines to align them.

Analysis

Design
Development
Evaluation

    f)   Close the Display icon.

8.   Establish the content in the Display icons attached to the Decision icon.

    a)   Double click on the Display icon *Spaces*.

    b)   Click on the Text tool. Click the I-bar cursor on the screen and press the space bar twice, so that there are now two text "spaces" in the text object. It is important to put some object in this Display icon; otherwise, Authorware will stop and open the Display icon here, because it is designed to stop on empty icons.

    c)   Close the Display icon.

    d)   Double click on the Display icon *Analysis*.

    e)   Click on the Text tool. Click the I-bar cursor on the right-hand side of the screen. Type in the following as a single text object.

Analysis: Before beginning your project, determine the following:

- The need it will serve
- Who will use it
- How it will be delivered

    f)   With the text object still open, highlight the word *Analysis* and then click on the Underline button in the toolbar. Click on the Pointer tool to close the text object. Make sure to click the cursor on the background to "unselect" the text object. Click on the Underline button in the toolbar to remove the underline style as the default style. Close the Display icon.

    g)   Double click on the Display icon *Design*.

    h)   Click on the Text tool. Click the I-bar cursor on the right-hand side of the screen. Type in the following as a single text object.

Design: The design phase includes creation of the following:

- Design document
- Project standards
- Design prototype

    i)   With the text object still open, highlight the word *Design* and then click on the Underline button in the toolbar. Click on the Pointer tool to close the text object. Make sure to click the cursor on the background to "unselect" the text object. Click on the Underline button in the toolbar to remove the underline style as the default style. Close the Display icon.

j)   Double click on the Display icon *Development*.

k)   Click on the Text tool. Click the I-bar cursor on the right-hand side of the screen. Type in the following as a single text object.

Development: The development phase includes creation of the following:

    - Script for text and narration
    - Graphics concepts
    - Media elements
    - Authorware program file

l)   Close the Display icon (click on the X).

m)   Double click on the Display icon *Evaluation*.

n)   Click on the Text tool. Click the I-bar cursor on the right-hand side of the screen. Type in the following as a single text object.

Evaluation: The evaluation phase involves assessment of the following:

    - Does the project meet the targeted need?
    - How effectively can the target audience use the project?

o)   With the text object still open, highlight the word *Evaluation* and then click on the Underline button in the toolbar. Click on the Pointer tool to close the text object. Make sure to click the cursor on the background to "unselect" the text object. Click on the Underline button in the toolbar to remove the underline style as the default style. Close the Display icon.

p)   Select File | Save to make sure you do not lose all the work you have done to this point.

9.   Establish the properties of the Decision icon.

    a)   Double click on the Decision icon *Show Presentation*. You should now be looking at the Properties/Decision Icon dialog window.

    b)   In the Repeat field, select Until All Paths Used.

    c)   In the Branch field, leave the default setting of Sequentially.

    d)   Click on the OK button to close the dialog window.

10.   Establish the Decision Path properties for each of the Display icons attached to the Decision icon.

    a)   Double click on the small diamond symbol directly above the Display icon *Spaces*.

    b)   In the Properties/Decision Path dialog window that has opened, note that the Erase Contents field should display the default option Before Next Selection.

    c)   For the next option, place a check mark in the Pause Before Branching field.

    d) Click on the OK button to close this dialog window.

    e) Repeat steps *a* through *d* for the Decision Path properties for each of the remaining Display icons *Analysis*, *Design*, *Development*, and *Evaluation*.

11. Now is a good time to fix the alignment of the basic elements, before you add the "highlights."

    a) Click on the Restart button.

    b) Simultaneously press the Ctrl and P keys to pause.

    c) Double click on the text *There are four general phases involved in the development of any multimedia project. They are:* and place this text object where you want it to appear (see figure 6-13). Resize the margins if you want to.

    d) Double click on the grid lines. You will have to be careful to click right on the line and not the background graphic. Note that the grid lines have been "grouped."

    e) Move the grid lines so that the leftmost vertical line aligns with the left edge of the first letter T in the text and so that the uppermost horizontal line aligns with the bottom of the letter T. See figure 6-13.

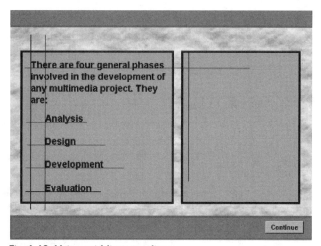

Fig. 6-13. Using grid lines to align.

    f) Click on each of the words *Analysis*, *Design*, *Development*, and *Evaluation* and line them up according to the grid lines. Use figure 6-13 as reference.

12. Now let's make use of a shortcut that will save you time in adding the "highlights" and bullets.

    a) Try to perform the following step carefully, so that you do not accidentally knock any of the words out of alignment. Click on *Analysis*.

While holding the Shift key down, click on *Design*, *Development*, and *Evaluation*. All four words should now be selected.

b) Select Edit | Copy to copy these words to the clipboard.

c) Close the current icon. Simultaneously press the Ctrl and J keys to jump to the flowline.

d) Double click on the Display icon *Analysis*. Being careful to not click the mouse cursor anywhere except to make the menu selection, select Edit | Paste. The four words should now appear in this icon.

e) Note that the four words you just pasted have handlebars around them, in addition to the text object on the right. Hold the Shift key down as you click on the text object on the right. This deselects this object. At this point, the four words you pasted should be the only objects selected.

f) Press Ctrl + K to bring up the Color inspector. Click on the Pencil icon in the lower left. Click on a red color. All four words should now be red. Single click on the background to deselect all objects.

g) Click on the Circle tool. Draw a very small circle that you will use for a text bullet. With this bullet still selected, click on the color black. The line of the circle is now black. Click on the Foreground Color box in the lower right of the Color palette. Then click on the same red color you chose before. You should now have a red bullet, outlined in black. If the line is too thick, use the Line inspector to reduce the line thickness.

h) Click on the Pointer tool and position the bullet to the left of the word *Analysis*. Do not worry about the alignment at this point.

i) Carefully select the bullet and all four words. Press Ctrl + C to copy these five objects to the clipboard.

j) Deselect all objects by clicking on the background. Click on the text objects *Design*, *Development*, and *Evaluation*. Press the Del key to delete them. What is left is the highlight for *Analysis*, the bullet, and the details. Close the Display icon.

k) Double click on the Display icon *Design*. Press Ctrl + V to paste the content into this icon. Press the space bar to deselect all objects. Click on *Analysis*. While holding down the Shift key, click on *Development* and *Evaluation*. Press the Del key to delete these objects. What is left is the highlight for *Design*, the bullet, and the details. Close the icon.

l) Double click on the Display icon *Development*. Press Ctrl + V to paste the content into this icon. Press the space bar to deselect all objects. Click on *Analysis*. While holding down the Shift key, click on *Design* and *Evaluation*. Press the Del key to delete these objects. What is left is the highlight for *Development*, the bullet, and the details. Close the icon.

·T/P·

In the previous step, you copied four words into the Clipboard. In a new Display icon, if you carefully select Edit | Paste without clicking anywhere else on the screen, Authorware will paste whatever is in the Clipboard into the exact same location that it was in, when it was copied.

Shortcut

Press the Spacebar to deselect all objects.

m) Double click on the Display icon *Evaluation*. Press Ctrl + V to paste the content into this icon. Press the space bar to deselect all objects. Click on *Analysis*. While holding down the Shift key, click on *Design* and *Development*. Press the Del key to delete these objects. What is left is the highlight for *Evaluation*, the bullet, and the details. Close the icon.

13. Run the program to see what needs to be aligned.
    a) Click on the Restart button.
    b) The program should have stopped for a Continue button. Press Ctrl + P to pause. Click on the Continue button and move it down to the lower right corner. The text *The general phases* should already be aligned, as well as the four text objects. Press Ctrl + P to return to Play mode.
    c) Click on the Continue button. You should now see a red copy of *Analysis* and additional text about analysis. Press Ctrl + P to pause. Double click on the red word *Analysis*. Click on the background to deselect all objects, and then click on and position the red *Analysis* so that it overlays the black copy of *Analysis* exactly (or you can offset it a little, so that the black acts as a shadow). Drag the bullet to the left of *Analysis* and use the grid to align it. Drag the detailed text object to the right and use the grid there to align it. You may need to resize the margins so that the text fits within the boundaries of the right-hand frame. See figure 6-14. Press Ctrl + P to return to Play mode.

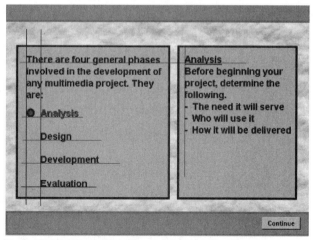

Fig. 6-14. Alignment for bullet, red Analysis, and details.

d) Click on the Continue button. You should now see a red copy of *Design* and additional text about design. Press Ctrl + P to pause.

Double click on the red word *Design*. Click on the background to deselect all objects, and then click on and position the red word *Design* so that it overlays (or offsets) the black copy of *Design*. Drag the bullet to the left of *Design* and use the grid to align it. Drag the detailed text object to the right and use the grid there to align it. You may need to resize the margins so that the text fits within the boundaries of the right-hand frame. Press Ctrl + P to return to Play mode.

e) Click on the Continue button. You should now see a red copy of the word *Development* and additional text about development. Press Ctrl + P to pause. Double click on the red word *Development*. Click on the background to deselect all objects, and then click on and position the red *Development* so that it overlays (or offsets) the black copy of *Development*. Drag the bullet to the left of *Development* and use the grid to align it. Drag the detailed text object to the right and use the grid there to align it. Resize the margins. Press Ctrl + P to return to Play mode.

f) Click on the Continue button. You should now see a red copy of the word *Evaluation* and additional text about evaluation. Press Ctrl + P to pause. Double click on the red word *Evaluation*. Click on the background to deselect all objects, and then click on and position the red *Evaluation* so that it overlays (or offsets) the black copy of *Evaluation*. Drag the bullet to the left of *Evaluation* and use the grid to align it. Drag the detailed text object to the right and use the grid there to align it. Resize the margins. Press Ctrl + P to return to Play mode.

g) Click on the Continue button.

14. Clean up.

a) You should have now exited the Decision icon and arrived at the empty Erase icon.

b) Simply touch whatever you see on screen to erase it (remember that the icons attached to the Decision icon had the automatic erase capability set to Before Next Selection, but the Display icons on the main flowline need to be erased with an Erase icon).

15. Save the file on your hard drive by selecting File | Save.

Practice Exercise 6-2: Decision Icon "Attraction" Loop

Description

In this exercise you will use a Decision icon set to loop continuously until a user clicks the mouse. In the multimedia industry, this type of structure is frequently called an "attraction" loop and is generally created for a self-standing multimedia kiosk. Animation and sound plays continually, with the intent that it will attract someone's attention and draw the potential audience member to interact with the kiosk. You are going to create a very simple loop, with very simple content, focusing on the Authorware structure. Later you can use this same structure and add much nicer animation and content. The following elements are covered in this exercise.

- *Creating text and graphic objects*
- *Creating a Decision icon sequence*
- *Setting Decision icon properties*
- *Setting Decision Path properties*

Take a Look

Before beginning the exercise, let's take a look at the exercise in its completed state so that you can clearly see what it is you are about to build.

CD-ROM

1. Select File | Open and locate on the companion CD-ROM the directory *Chapter06*. Locate and select the file *Exer6-2* and double click on it.

2. The file *Exer6-2* should now appear in your copy of Authorware. Click on the Restart button to play the file from the top of the flowline. Note the following properties of this completed exercise.

   - *Different colored circles are randomly flashing on screen.*

   - *The animation continues until you click the mouse on the screen.*

   - *The Decision icon branch option is set to Randomly to Unused Path, with the Repeat field set to Until Click/Keypress. The Decision Path properties are set to the Erase option of Before Next Selection, with No Pause.*

Storyboard: On screen

Figures 6-15 and 6-16 show you what the finished presentation will look like. Figure 6-15 shows the Display icon *Panel*. Figure 6-16 shows the Display icon *Blue Circle* within the first Map icon.

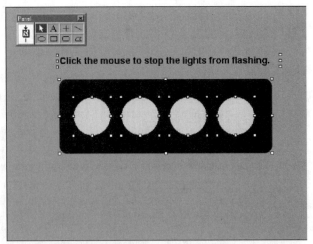

Fig. 6-15. Display icon **Panel.**

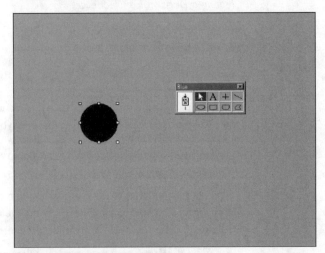

Fig. 6-16. Display icon **Blue Circle.**

Storyboard: Behind the Scenes

The flowline shown in figures 6-17 and 6-18 illustrates all icons, their placement, and their names as they should look when you are finished with this exercise.

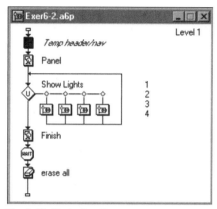

Fig. 6-17. Main flowline.

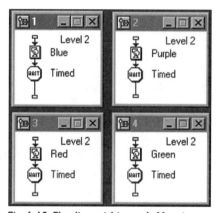

Fig. 6-18. Flowline within each Map icon.

Step-by-Step Instructions

1. Begin by opening a new file for this exercise.
   a) Select File | New | File.
   b) Close the two Knowledge Object dialog windows.

2. Verify that you are now looking at a new flowline.

3. Set up the file properties.
   a) Select Modify | File | Properties.
   b) Select whatever background color you want.
   c) Make sure Size is set to 640 x 480.

Go Solo

T/P

If you had not used a Map icon, but instead had dragged a Display icon directly to the right of the Decision icon, you would have been faced with one of two possible problems. First, the Decision Path properties only allow the presence or absence of a continue button; there is no Time Limit option here. Using continue buttons will destroy the ability of the structure to function as an attraction loop. Without the continue buttons (try it if you want), the loop flashes the lights much too quickly.

Using Map icons to the right of the Decision icon, you can place a Display icon (for the colored circle) and a Wait icon within the Map icon. Because the Wait icon has a Time Limit option, you can experiment with the length of the pause needed to have the lights flash (or whatever animation you substitute in the future) at whatever timing interval you want.

    d) Remove the check mark beside the options Tile Bar and Menu Bar.

    e) Click on the OK button to close the window.

    f) Select File | Save and locate the *SaveWork* directory. Type in *Chap6-2* and click on the OK button.

4. Create the icon structure.

    a) Drag a Display icon to the flowline. Name this icon *Panel*.

    b) Drag a Decision icon and place it directly below the Display icon on the flowline. Name this icon *Show Lights*.

    c) Drag a Map icon from the Icon palette and place it to the right of the Decision icon. Name it *1*.

    d) Double click on the Map icon to open it. Drag a Display icon and place it on the flowline within this Map icon. Leave this icon untitled for the moment.

    e) Drag a Wait icon and place it on the flowline within the Map icon, below the Display icon. Name the Wait icon *Timed*.

    f) Double click on the Wait icon, and in the Time Limit field type in *1*. In the Events field, click on the Keypress box to remove the check mark. In the Options field, click on the Show button box to remove the check mark. Close the Wait icon.

    g) Close the Map icon.

    h) Select the Map icon. Select Edit | Copy.

    i) Click the mouse to the right of the Map icon to place the Paste Hand there. Select Edit | Paste. Repeat this two more times to paste three (3) copies of the Map icon (so that you will end up with four Map icons to the right of the Decision icon).

    j) Name the Map icons you just pasted *2*, *3*, and *4*.

    k) Drag a Display icon and place it on the flowline below the Decision icon. Name it *Finish*. Double click on this icon. Click on the Text tool. Type in *Finished*. Close this icon.

    l) Drag a Wait icon and place it on the flowline below the Display icon *Finish*. Name it *Continue*.

    m) Drag an Erase icon and place it on the flowline below the Wait icon. Name it *Clean Up*.

5. Return to the first Display icon, *Panel*, and add some content. See figure 6-15 as a point of reference for the following steps.

    a) Double click on the Display icon *Panel* to open it.

    b) For the background rectangle, select the Rounded Rectangle tool in the toolbox. Draw a large, rounded rectangle.

    c) Select Window | Inspectors | Color. In the lower right, click on the Foreground Color box and then click on whatever color you want for the interior of the rectangle. Leave the Color inspector open.

d) Create some yellow circles. You may find it easier to create the first circle outside the rectangle and then move it inside the rectangle. Select the Circle tool and while holding down the Shift key (to get a perfect circle) click and drag the cursor to create one circle (but remember that you must have room for four circles within the rectangle). Select the Pointer tool. The Foreground Color box in the Color inspector should still be selected. The circle you just drew should also still be selected. Select the color yellow. Your circle should now be yellow.

e) Drag this first circle into the far left portion of the rectangle and align it. If you think you need to make the circle either smaller or larger, hold the Shift key down and drag any of the corner handle bars to proportionally resize the circle. Resize it so that four circles of the same size will fit within the rectangle.

f) With the circle selected (handlebars around it), select Edit | Copy. Click the mouse somewhere on screen and select Edit | Paste. Paste two more copies of the circle, so that you end up with a total of four (4) yellow circles.

g) Drag the three new circles into place and align them all to appear as shown in figure 6-15.

h) Select the Text tool. Select Text | Font and then Arial. Select Text | Size and then 14. Click the I-bar cursor on screen and type in *Click the mouse to stop the lights flashing*. Click on the Pointer tool and position the text object above the panel.

i) Single click on the first yellow circle. While holding down the Shift key, click on the other three yellow circles so that all four circles are selected (but do *not* include the rectangle). Select Edit | Copy to copy all yellow circles to the clipboard. Close the icon.

6. Now let's go inside the first Map icon.

a) Double click on Map icon *1*.

b) Select the "untitled" Display icon and name it *Blue*.

c) Double click on this Display icon to open it. Being careful to not click the mouse cursor anywhere except to make the menu selection, select Edit | Paste to paste the four yellow circles within the display area. Press the space bar to deselect all objects.

d) Click on first circle to the left. The Color inspector should still be open (if not, open it by pressing Ctrl + K). Click on the Foreground Color box in the lower right. Click on a blue color. Leave the Color inspector open.

e) Select the other three yellow circles you pasted here and delete them.

·T/P·

Although you've seen a similar Tip previously, this copy/paste method is important so the concept is being repeated here for the current exercise.

In the previous step, you copied four yellow circles into the Clipboard. In a new Display icon, if you carefully select Edit | Paste without clicking anywhere else on the screen, Authorware will paste whatever is in the Clipboard into the exact same location that it was in, when it was copied. Using this copy/paste method, you can easily change the color of one of the pasted circles, delete the others and have a new colored circle that will be exactly aligned to overlay a corresponding yellow circle. Follow along with the steps in the exercise, as you continue to work with this copy/paste method.

f)	Close this Display icon. Click on the title bar for Map icon *1* and drag it to the side. Click on a corner of the Map icon and drag it to make the icon smaller. Leave the Map icon open.

7.	Now let's go inside the second Map icon.
   a)	Double click on Map icon *2*.
   b)	Select the "untitled" Display icon and name it *Purple*.
   c)	Double click on this Display icon to open it. Being careful to not click the mouse cursor anywhere except to make the menu selection, select Edit | Paste to paste the four yellow circles within the display area. Press the space bar to deselect all objects.
   d)	Click on second circle to the left. The Color inspector should still be open (if not, open it by pressing Ctrl + K). Click on the Foreground Color box in the lower right. Click on a purple color. Leave the Color inspector open.
   e)	Select the other three yellow circles you pasted here and delete them.
   f)	Close this Display icon. Click on the title bar for Map icon *2* and drag it to the side. Leave the Map icon open.

8.	Now let's go inside the third Map icon.
   a)	Double click on Map icon *3*.
   b)	Select the "untitled" Display icon and name it *Red*.
   c)	Double click on this Display icon to open it. Being careful to not click the mouse cursor anywhere except to make the menu selection, select Edit | Paste to paste the four yellow circles within the display area. Press the space bar to deselect all objects.
   d)	Click on third circle to the left. Click on a red color in the Color palette. Leave the Color inspector open.
   e)	Select the other three yellow circles you pasted here and delete them. Click on the title bar for Map icon *3* and drag it to the side. Leave the Map icon open.
   f)	Close this Display icon. Click on the title bar for Map icon *3* and drag it to the side. Leave the Map icon open.

9.	Now let's go inside the fourth Map icon.
   a)	Double click on Map icon *4*.
   b)	Select the "untitled" Display icon and name it *Green*.
   c)	Double click on this Display icon to open it. Being careful to not click the mouse cursor anywhere except to make the menu selection, select Edit | Paste to paste the four yellow circles within the display area. Press the space bar to deselect all objects.
   d)	Click on the last circle to the right. Click on a green color. Leave the Color inspector open.

e)   Select the other three yellow circles you pasted here and delete them.

f)   Close this Display icon. Click on the title bar for Map icon *4* and drag it to the side. Make the Map icon smaller. Leave the Map icon open.

10. Select File | Save.

11. Set a temporary condition for the Decision icon properties.

a)   Double click on the Decision icon *Show Lights*. In the dialog window that opens, find the Repeat field and select Until All Paths Used.

b)   Temporarily leave the Branch field with the default setting of Sequential. (You will change this setting in material to follow. Here you are going to use the Sequential branch to help align the structure.)

12. Establish the final alignment.

a)   Click on the Restart button. As soon as you see the blue circle, immediately press Ctrl + P to pause. If you need to, align the blue circle so that it perfectly overlays the first yellow circle in the rectangle. Press Ctrl + P again to resume play.

b)   As soon as you see the purple circle, immediately press Ctrl + P to pause. If you need to, align the purple circle so that it perfectly overlays the second yellow circle in the rectangle. Press Ctrl + P again to resume play.

c)   As soon as you see the red circle, immediately press Ctrl + P to pause. If you need to, align the red circle so that it perfectly overlays the third yellow circle in the rectangle. Press Ctrl + P again to resume play.

d)   As soon as you see the green circle, immediately press Ctrl + P to pause. If you need to, align the green circle so that it perfectly overlays the last yellow circle in the rectangle. Press Ctrl + P again to resume play.

13. Clean up.

a)   You should have now exited the Decision icon and encountered the Continue button. Click on the Continue button.

b)   You should have now encountered the empty Erase icon. Simply click on whatever you see on screen to erase it. (The only thing to be erased should reside within the Display icon *Panel*, in that the icons attached to the Decision icon had their automatic erase capability set to Before Next Selection.) Close the Erase icon.

14. Reset the Decision icon properties.

a)   Double click on the Decision icon *Show Lights*. In the dialog window that opens, find the Repeat field and select Until Click/Keypress.

b)   In the Branch field, change the setting to Randomly to Unused Path.

15. Save the file by selecting File | Save.

16. Click on the Restart button and take a look.

Summary

- In Chapter 4 you created a simple structure using Display, Wait, and Erase icons placed directly on the main flowline. This type of linear structure on the main flowline has significant shortcomings. In this chapter, the Decision icon was introduced to solve some of these problems and to introduce additional features.

- In the first guided tour, you looked at the Decision icon properties.

- The Decision icon is a branching structure in which the author predetermines the path the user will follow. The Decision icon does not have a display area associated with it, although Display icons (and other types of icons) can be attached to the Decision icon.

- The Decision icon's Repeat setting includes the options Fixed Number of Times, Until All Paths Used, Until Click/Keypress, Until True, and Don't Repeat.

- The Decision icon can branch sequentially, randomly to any path, randomly to unused paths, or to a calculated path.

- In the second guided tour, you looked at the properties of the Decision path, where you saw that this structure includes an automatic erase function and the ability to pause with the use of a Continue button.

- The first practice exercise focused on creating a structure with sequential branching.

- The second practice exercise centered on creating an "attraction" loop in which paths are selected randomly. The loop continues until there is some input from a user.

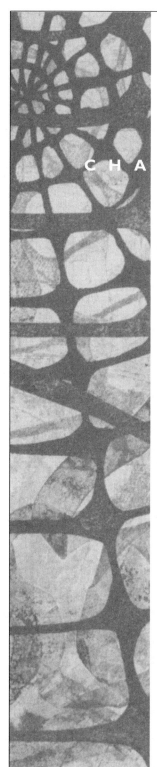

CHAPTER 7

Creating Simple

Animation

Introduction

As you saw in Chapter 5, Authorware can very easily play animation that has been created in an external program such as Flash. In this chapter you will see how Authorware provides the capability to easily create simple 2D motion in your application. The animation you produce will certainly not compete with a Hollywood production or even a Flash animation, but it can significantly help learners better understand concepts, processes, or procedures you may be trying to convey via your application.

Animation can be combined with interactive structures to create learning strategies that are both fun and challenging. Even in the most linear presentation sequences, motion can enhance user interest and help focus attention on points being presented.

The great thing about creating animation with Authorware's built-in motion capabilities is that most animation can be created quickly, with limited resources; will generally have a "light footprint"; and will perform relatively well over both LANs and Web-based networks. At the end of the chapter you will be able to:

- *Create a direct-to-point animation*
- *Modify the origin and destination points of a direct-to-point animation*
- *Create a motion path animation*
- *Modify the origin, destination, and interim points of a motion path animation*
- *Add, delete, and change properties of interim points of a motion path animation*
- *Use the layer and timing properties of the Motion icon to enhance animation*

Guided Tour 7A: Motion Icon Properties

Typically you will place the object you want to move in a Display icon and use the Motion icon as the "engine" to accomplish the movement. Although there are several types of motion paths built into the Motion icon, this chapter focuses on the two most common types, including exercises in which you will build both types. Let's take a quick look at the Motion icon and its properties.

1. Start by opening a new file.
   a) Select File | New | File.
   b) Close the two dialog windows that have opened.
   c) Verify that you are now looking at an empty flowline.

2. Drag a Motion icon to the flowline. Examine the properties associated with the Motion icon.
   a) Verify that the Motion icon is selected (highlighted).
   b) Select Modify | Icon | Properties (or you can simply double click on the Motion icon).
   c) The Properties/Motion Icon dialog window should now be open. See figure 7-1. This window consists of three parts: the left-hand side, the Motion tab, and the Layout tab.

Shortcut

You can also right mouse click on the Motion icon and then select Properties from the menu that opens.

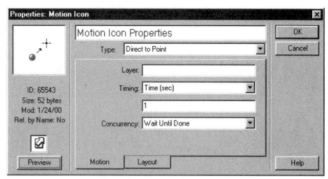

Fig. 7-1. Properties/Motion Icon dialog window.

3. As you have seen with other icons, the left-hand side, upper portion provides information specific to the Properties/Motion icon (which most of the time you will not care too much about). This area displays a small picture of the type of motion selected, and will indicate the object to be moved (after the object has been selected). The Preview button on the bottom of this section can be used to take a quick look at the animation after you have created it.

4. The Motion tab should already be selected (if not, select it). The following are the fields under this tab, starting from the top and working down.

   • **Type:** *Provides a menu of available motion types.*

     Direct to Point: *The default animation type. This motion type will move an object in a straight line from its current position to the destination you specify.*

     Direct to Line: *Moves an object from its current position to a calculated position on a line.*

     Direct to Grid: *Moves an object from its current position to a calculated position on a grid.*

     Path to End: *Moves an object along a path that you define, from the base point to the end point. There can be multiple points between.*

Path to Point: *Moves an object along a path (of multiple points) and stops at any point along the path, depending on a calculated value. The path can consist of straight and curved segments.*

NOTE

We suggest that you do not use negative numbers (integers less than 1) in the Layer field of the Motion icon. Instead you can use the strategy employed in Exercise 7-2.

- **Layer:** *Animated objects always appear on top of non-animated objects unless the layer of either object is changed in the Motion icon or in the Display icon properties. If more than one object is animating at once, the animation started last will appear on top.*

- **Timing:** *This field controls the speed of the animation. It can be established via Time or Rate options.*

    Time: *Number of seconds in which to complete the animation. Animation will take the number of seconds specified regardless of distance to be covered. This value can be a variable. The lower the number of seconds, the quicker the animation.*

    Rate: *Objects move approximately 1 inch (72 pixels) per the number of seconds specified.*

- **Entry field:** *This field is used to enter a number or variable to represent the time or rate.*

NOTE

When first dragging the object to be animated, the number of seconds you take to move it will be inserted into the Rate box.

- **Concurrency:** *This field is used to indicate how Authorware should process the icon, per the following options.*

    Wait Until Done: *Authorware completes the current animation before proceeding on the flowline.*

    Concurrent: *Authorware begins the animation and then proceeds down the flowline. Whatever icons are encountered are acted on as Authorware continues with the animation.*

    Perpetual: *Makes the motion available whenever an associated condition becomes true.*

- **Last field:** *The name and function of the last field changes, depending on what Type and Currency have been selected, as follows.*

    Direct to Point: *Used with this option, the last field does not exist.*

    Direct to Line, Direct to Grid, and Path to Point: *Used with any of these options, the last field is defined as Beyond Range, an option for specifying, as follows, what should happen when the value or variable is outside the base and end values.*

    Stop at Ends: *Moves the object to whichever end point of the line is closest to the value.*

    Loop: *Moves the object to the appropriate scaled position.*

    Go Past Ends: *This option is available only for Direct to Line or Direct to Grid. Moves the object to the appropriate position even if that point is beyond the defined base or end point.*

·T*i*P·

System variables can be used with animation. These system variables include *Animating, Moving, Display X, Display Y, PathPosition, Position X,* and *Position Y.*

Path to End: *Used with this option, the last field is defined as Move When, which is used to set a condition to specify whether an object should move. Authorware moves the object only when the condition is True. When it is False, Authorware ignores the Motion icon. If you leave this field empty, Authorware moves the object only when it first encounters the icon.*

5. Select the Layout tab. This tab includes the following fields, starting from the top and working down.

    *   **Type:** *Exactly the same as described for the Motion tab.*
    *   **Instructions:** *Authorware will tell you what needs to be done. The instructions provided here will change, depending on what needs to be done at any particular point.*
    *   **Object:** *Displays the name of the icon linked to the current Motion icon. This field remains blank until an object is linked.*
    *   **Coordinates:** *The selection you make under Type will dramatically influence the rest of the fields for the Layout tab. You may enter numbers or variables into any active field entry position.*

Practice exercise 7-1, which follows, will give you a sense of how the Motion icon works.

Practice Exercise 7-1: Direct-to-Point Motion

Description

In this exercise you are going to create a simple animation involving archery. You may not quite have the accuracy of William Tell shooting an apple sitting on someone's head, so you will need to be content with clicking on a button to shoot an arrow at a target...a safe distance away.

The initial steps in the exercise will intentionally create a common animation mistake so that you can see the problem and the solution. You will also see how easy it is to change the origin and destination points of the Direct to Point motion type. The following elements are covered in this exercise.

*   *Designating a target*
*   *Designating an object of movement*
*   *Setting the Motion icon properties for Direct to Point*
*   *Correcting a common animation problem*
*   *Changing the origin and destination points*

Take a Look

CD-ROM

Before beginning the exercise, let's take a look at the exercise in its completed state so that you can clearly see what it is you are about to build.

1. Select File | Open and locate on the companion CD-ROM the directory *Chapter07*. Locate the file *Exer7-1* and double click on it.

2. The file *Exer7-1* should now appear in your copy of Authorware.

3. Click on the Restart button to play the file from the top of the flowline.

4. Click on the Continue button on screen to shoot the arrow.

Note the following properties of this completed exercise.

*   *After clicking on the Continue button, the arrow is the only object that should move.*

*   *The arrow's animation path is a straight line, from the origin to the destination.*

Storyboard: On screen

Figures 7-2 through 7-4 show you what the finished presentation will look like. Figure 7-2 shows the complete presentation on screen. Figure 7-3 shows what is inside the Display icon *Target*. Figure 7-4 shows what is inside the Display icon *Arrow*.

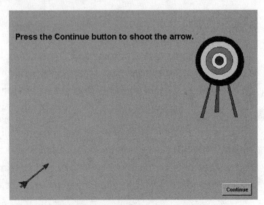

Fig. 7-2. Finished presentation on screen.

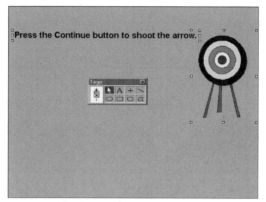

Fig. 7-3. Display icon **Target**.

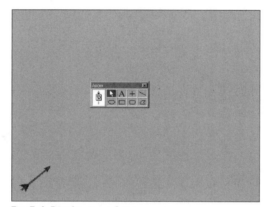

Fig. 7-4. Display icon **Arrow**.

Storyboard: Behind the Scenes

Figure 7-5 shows the main flowline (with all icons, their placement, and their names) as it should look when you are finished with this exercise. Figure 7-6 shows the settings inside the Motion icon *Move the Arrow*.

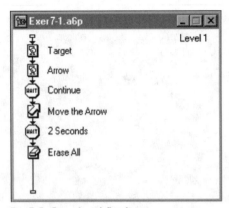

Fig. 7-5. Completed flowline.

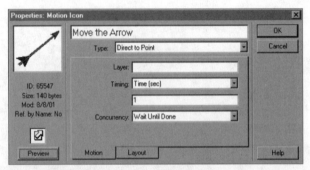

Fig. 7-6. Properties/Motion Icon dialog window for the **Move the Arrow** icon.

Step-by-Step Instructions

1. Select File | New | File. Close the two Knowledge Object dialog windows.

2. Verify that you are now looking at a new flowline.

3. Set up the file properties.
   a) Select Modify | File | Properties.
   b) Select whatever background color you want.
   c) Make sure Size is set to 640 x 480.
   d) Remove the check marks beside the Tile Bar and Menu Bar options.
   e) Click on the OK button to close the window.
   f) Select File | Save and locate the *SaveWork* directory. Type in *Chap7-1* and click on the OK button.

4. Create the beginning of the icon structure.
   a) Drag a Display icon to the flowline. Name this icon *Target*.
   b) Drag a second Display icon to the flowline. Name this icon *Arrow*.

Go Solo

    c)   Drag a Wait icon to the flowline. Name this icon *Continue*.

    d)   Drag a Motion icon to the flowline. Name this icon *Move the Arrow*.

    e)   Drag another Wait icon to the flowline. Name this icon *2 Seconds*.

    f)   Drag an Erase icon to the flowline. Name this icon *Erase All*.

5.   Add the content for the Display icon *Target*.

    a)   Double click on the Display icon *Target*.

    b)   Select Insert | Image.

    c)   In the dialog window that has opened, in the lower left, select Import.

CD-ROM

    d)   Use the *Look in* field's browse function to locate on the companion CD-ROM, in the *Chapter07* directory, a graphic file named *BullsEye.bmp*. Select this graphic and click on the Import button. In the Mode field of the open dialog window, select Transparent. Click on the OK button.

    e)   Position the bull's-eye graphic in the upper right-hand corner of the screen. Close this icon.

6.   Add the content for the Display icon *Arrow*. The following intentionally incorporates a mistake (which you will correct in material to follow).

    a)   Double click on the Display icon *Arrow*.

    b)   Select Insert | Image.

    c)   In the dialog window that has opened, in the lower left, select Import.

CD-ROM

    d)   Use the *Look in* field's browse function to locate on the companion CD-ROM, in the *Chapter07* directory, a graphic file named *Arrow.bmp*. Select the graphic and click on the Import button. In the Mode field of the open dialog window, select Transparent. Click on the OK button.

    e)   Position the Arrow graphic in the lower left-hand corner of the screen.

    f)   Select the Text tool. Click the I-bar cursor on screen and type in the following.

        Press the Continue button to shoot the arrow.

    g)   Position the message on the top of the screen. Close this icon.

7.   The easiest way to connect the Motion icon to the object to be moved is to run the program.

    a)   Click on the Restart button.

    b)   You should now see on your screen the bull's-eye, the message, the arrow, and a Continue button.

    c)   Click on the Continue button.

    d)   The Properties/Motion Icon dialog window has opened. The Motion tab is probably being displayed (if not, click on it). Note that Motion Type is probably already set to Direct to Point (the default). If this is not the case, use the pull-down window and select Direct to Point.

NOTE

Note that as soon as you touched the object to be moved, three things happened. First, a small picture of the object to be moved appeared in the upper left-hand corner of the Properties/Motion Icon dialog window. Second, the name of the icon containing the object you touched was displayed in the Object field beneath the message line. Third, the first instructional message was replaced with a second instructional message.

e) Select the Layout tab.

f) Note immediately under the Motion Type field the instruction *Click object to be moved*.

g) Click on the arrow displayed on screen.

h) A new instructional message has appeared: *Drag object to destination*. Click and drag the arrow to the bull's-eye.

8. Do you see anything wrong with this picture? Rerun the program and take another look.

a) Click on the Restart button.

b) You should now see on your screen the bull's-eye, the message, the arrow, and a Continue button.

c) Click on the Continue button.

d) What is moving? Both the arrow and the message. Why?

In Chapter 4, in regard to Display icon properties, it was pointed out that Authorware does not really distinguish multiple objects within a single Display icon. In this exercise, you can clearly see that this is the case, as currently Authorware is treating both objects within the Display icon (the arrow and text message) as one object and is moving them both. Remember that any object you want to move must be placed in a Display icon by itself.

9. Let's correct the problem of both arrow and message moving.

a) Simultaneously press the Ctrl and P keys to pause. Double click on the message *Press the Continue button*.

b) You should now be in the Display icon *Arrow*, with handlebars around both objects. Click on the background to deselect both objects. Click on the text object. Cut the message from this icon by simultaneously pressing the Ctrl and X keys. Now the only object in this icon is the arrow graphic.

c) Jump to the flowline by pressing Ctrl + J.

d) Double click on the Display icon *Target* to open it.

e) Paste the message by pressing Ctrl + V. Position the message at the top of the screen.

f) Jump to the flowline by pressing Ctrl + J.

TIP

As you dropped the arrow at the bull's-eye, the X and Y coordinates of the destination appeared in the Destination field of the Layout tab. For a more exact location, you can also type in the X and Y coordinates for the destination point.

10. Establish the Wait icon settings.

a) Double click on the Wait icon *2 Seconds*.

b) Remove any check marks in the Event fields Mouse Click and Keypress. In the Time Limit field, type in 2. Place a check mark beside the Show Countdown option.

c) Click on the OK button to close the dialog window.

11. Clean up.

a) Click on the Restart button.

b) Click on the Continue button to shoot the arrow. The arrow should move to the target.

c) After seeing the countdown for a 2-second wait, the Property/Erase Icon dialog window should now be open.

d) Note that the instructional message tells you exactly what needs to be done. Click on every object you see on screen to erase it.

12. Changing the origin point for the arrow is very easy. Proceed as follows.

a) Jump to the flowline (Ctrl + J).

b) Open (double click on) the Display icon *Arrow*.

c) Move the arrow to a different location on screen. Close the icon.

d) Click on the Restart button. The arrow should start from a different location.

e) Click on the Continue button and the arrow still goes to the original destination point.

13. Change the destination point.

a) Click on the Restart button, so that the target is now on screen.

b) Jump to the flowline (Ctrl + J).

c) Double click on the Motion icon *Move the Arrow*.

d) Drag the arrow to a new destination point. Close the dialog window.

e) Click on the Restart button.

f) Click on the Continue button to shoot the arrow. You can see that changing the destination point is also very easy.

14. Let's do a little house cleaning.

a) Jump to the flowline (Ctrl + J).

b) Select Edit | Select All to highlight all icons on the flowline.

c) Select Modify | Group to "wrap a map" around these icons.

d) You should now see an untitled Map icon on the flowline. Name this Map icon *Direct to Point*.

15. Save the exercise by selecting File | Save.

Practice Exercise 7-2: Single-Path-to-End Motion

Description

In this exercise you will create another type of simple animation in which you will define a path for the movement of a ball. The icon structure here is very similar to that of the previous exercise. You will also change the origin and destination points, as well as add and delete points to the path of animation and change the path properties from linear to circular. As a grand finale you will change the layer properties so that the ball will pass behind one box and in front of another. The following elements are covered in this exercise.

- *Designating an object of movement*
- *Selecting Motion icon properties*
- *Creating and modifying a path for animation*
- *Adding and deleting path points*
- *Changing origin and destination points*
- *Changing path properties from linear to circular*
- *Creating layering effects for animation*

Take a Look

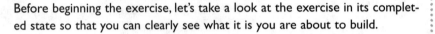

CD-ROM

Before beginning the exercise, let's take a look at the exercise in its completed state so that you can clearly see what it is you are about to build.

1. Select File | Open and locate on the companion CD-ROM the directory *Chapter07*. Locate the file *Exer7-2* and double click on it.

2. Verify that the file *Exer7-2* has appeared in your copy of Authorware.

3. Click on the Restart button to play the file from the top of the flowline.

4. Click on the Continue button.

Note the following properties of this completed exercise.

- *The motion path for the ball is not a linear path but changes in direction.*
- *The ball moves "on top of" the red box but "behind" the blue box.*

Storyboard: On screen

Figures 7-7 through 7-10 show you what the finished presentation will look like. Figure 7-7 shows the complete presentation. Figure 7-8 shows what is inside the Display icon *Message and Red Box*. Figure 7-9 shows what is inside the Display icon *Blue Box*. Figure 7-10 shows what is inside the Display icon *Ball*.

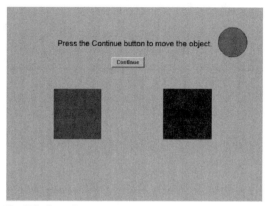

Fig. 7-7. Complete presentation screen.

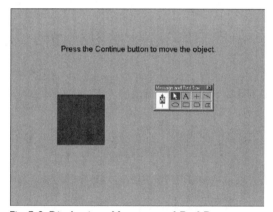

Fig. 7-8. Display icon **Message and Red Box.**

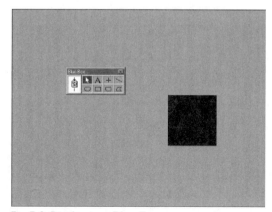

Fig. 7-9. Display icon **Blue Box.**

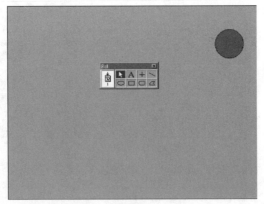

*Fig. 7-10. Display icon **Ball**.*

Storyboard: Behind the Scenes

Figure 7-11 shows the main flowline (containing all icons, their placement, and their names) as it should look when you are finished with this exercise. Figure 7-12 shows the Properties/Motion Icon dialog window for the Motion icon *Move the Ball*. Figure 7-13 shows the Properties/Display Icon dialog window for the Display icon *Blue Box*.

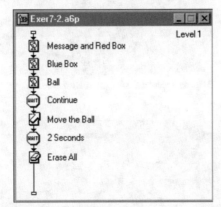

Fig. 7-11. Completed flowline.

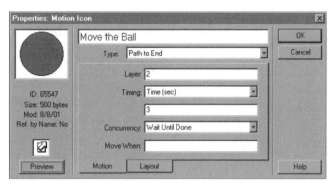

Fig. 7-12. Properties/Motion Icon dialog window for **Move the Ball.**

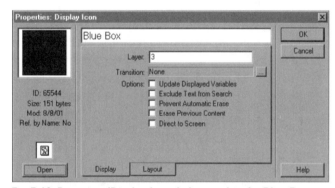

Fig. 7-13. Properties/Display Icon dialog window for **Blue Box.**

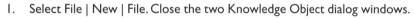

Step-by-Step Instructions

Go Solo

1. Select File | New | File. Close the two Knowledge Object dialog windows.

2. Verify that you are looking at a new flowline. Select File | Save and type in *Chap7-2.*

3. Create the beginning of the icon structure, as follows.

    a) Drag a Display icon to the flowline. Name this icon *Message and Red Box.*

    b) Drag a second Display icon to the flowline. Name this icon *Blue Box.*

    c) Drag a third Display icon to the flowline. Name this icon *Ball.*

    d) Drag a Wait icon to the flowline. Name this icon *Continue.*

    e) Drag a Motion icon to the flowline. Name this icon *Move the Ball.*

    f) Drag another Wait icon to the flowline. Name this icon *2 Seconds.*

    g) Drag an Erase icon to the flowline. Name this icon *Erase All.*

4. Add content to the icons created in step 3.

a) Double click on the Display icon *Message and Red Box.* Select the Text tool and type in the following.
Press the Continue button to move the object.
Position the text at the upper center of the screen.

b) Select the Rectangle tool and draw a square about 2 inches high. Position this square on the left-hand side of the screen.

c) Press Ctrl + K to open the Color inspector. With handlebars still around the square, select the Foreground Color tile and select a red color. The square should now be red.

d) Close this first Display icon.

e) Double click on the Display icon *Blue Box.* Select the Rectangle tool and draw a square about 2 inches high. Position this square on the right-hand side of the screen.

f) The Color inspector should still be open. With handlebars still around the square, select the Foreground Color tile and select a blue color. This second square should now be blue.

g) Close this icon.

h) Double click on the Display icon *Ball.* Select the Ellipse tool and draw a circle about an inch in diameter. Place the circle in the upper right-hand portion of the screen.

i) The Color inspector should still be open. With handlebars still around the circle, select the Foreground Color tile and then select a green color. The circle should now have a green color in it.

j) Close this icon.

5. Connect the object to the Motion icon.

a) Click on the Restart button.

b) You should now see a red box, a blue box, the ball, the message, and a Continue button.

c) Press Ctrl + P to pause the program.

d) Single click on and drag the Continue button so that it is slightly below the text message.

e) Return to Play mode by pressing Ctrl + P.

f) Click on the Continue button.

g) The Properties/Motion Icon dialog window should be open, and the Motion tab should be displayed. Note that Motion Type is set (by default) to Direct to Point. From the pull-down window, select Path to End.

h) Select the Layout tab. Note the instructional message *Click object to be moved.* Click on the ball.

By holding down the Shift key prior to starting to draw, you can constrain the shape to a circle.

Here you are placing the object to be moved in a separate icon. If you were to place it in the same icon as the message, the message would move along with the ball.

i) The instructional message now reads *Drag object to create path*. Drag the ball (not the triangle) so that its path crosses over the red box. Let go of the mouse.

j) The message has changed again to *Drag object to extend path*. Move the ball (not the triangle) to a second location on the screen. Let go of the mouse.

k) Move the ball to a third location on screen.

l) Continue to extend the path for several more points. Make sure the path crosses over both boxes.

m) When you are finished with the paths, look in the lower left-hand corner of the dialog window. Select the Preview button.

n) The ball is probably going too fast. Let's slow it down some. Select the Motion tab. About in the center of the window you will see a Timing field. Below this field is another field with a number 1 in it. Click the cursor in this second field and replace the 1 by typing in *3*. Click on the OK button to close the window.

o) Double click on the Wait icon *2 Seconds*. Remove all check marks and in the Time Limit field type in *2*.

p) Click on the white Start Flag button and view the results of your animation. Click on the Continue button.

q) You should now have encountered the empty Erase icon *Erase All*. Click on everything on screen to erase everything.

r) Select File | Save to save your work to this point.

6. Modify the motion path a couple of different ways.

a) Jump to the flowline by pressing Ctrl + J.

b) Double click on the Motion icon *Move the Ball*.

c) Move an existing point. Single click on one of the triangles on the motion path. Note that it changes to a solid black triangle (indicating that it is the point selected). Hold the mouse button down and drag this point to some other location. Single click on and drag another triangle to another location. Obviously, moving the points is easy to do.

d) Add a new point. Single click on the line with no triangle on it. Note that you have now added a new point you can either leave in its current position or move to a new location. You can add as many points as you wish. If a triangle on the motion path happens to transform into a circle, examine step 6h to find out why it did so.

e) Delete a point. Single click on an existing point. Select the Layout tab (if it is not currently selected). Note that toward the lower, mid-right portion of the tab there are the Edit Points options Undo and Delete. Pressing the Delete button will delete whatever point is currently selected (is currently black). Undo will undo the last action.

You may want to experiment with circular path points. As you add more circular points, the paths can become somewhat bizarre. By changing the position of some points and the circular/linear nature of other points, you may better achieve the effect you are looking for.

The default layer value is zero (0), with lower numbers being toward the back and higher numbers toward the front. You are assigning a 1 to the red box, a 2 to the animation path, and a 3 to the blue box so that the animation (2) should be in front of the red box (1) but behind the blue box (3).

·T/P·

It is not necessary to open a Display icon to access its properties. Simply select the icon you wish to modify, and then select Modify | Icon | Properties.

f) Change the origin point. Single click on the first point you created and drag it to a new location.

g) Change the destination point. Single click on the last point you created and drag it to a new location.

h) Change the point property (circular and linear). Double click on any existing triangle in the path. Note that the triangle changes to a solid circle and that the path on either side of this point changes to a circular nature. Double clicking on this same point changes it back to a triangle, and the paths on either side to linear paths.

7. Now for the grand finale. You have probably noticed that to this point the ball passes in front of each box. Change this so that the ball will pass in front of the red box and behind the blue box.

a) Jump to the flowline (Ctrl + J).

b) Double click on the Display icon *Message and Red Box*. Note that there are two objects inside this icon: the message and the red box.

c) Select Modify | Icon | Properties. Select the Display tab in the dialog window that opens. Note the Layer field just below the Icon Title field. Type *1* in the Layer field. Click on the OK button to close this window. Close this icon.

d) Single click on the Display icon *Blue Box* (that is, select it without opening it).

e) Select Modify | Icon | Properties. Select the Display tab in the dialog window that opens. Locate the Layer field just below the Icon Title field. Type *3* in the Layer field. Click on the OK button to close this window.

f) Single click on (select) the Motion icon *Move the Ball*.

g) Select Modify | Icon | Properties. Select the Motion tab in the dialog window that opens. Locate the Layer field just below the Icon Title field. Type *2* in the Layer field. Click on the OK button to close this window.

h) Click on the Restart button and view the results of your animation. The ball should pass in front of the red box and behind the blue box.

i) Jump to the flowline (Ctrl + J).

j) Click the cursor just above and to the left of the first Display icon and while holding down the mouse button use the expanding marquee to select all icons that are part of the current exercise. Select Modify | Group and name the resulting Map icon *Path to End*.

k) Select File | Save to save your work.

Practice Exercise 7-3: Multiple Simultaneous Motion

Description

In this exercise you will create multiple-path animations of cars that will all run simultaneously along a predefined "Grande Prix" racecourse (path). A sound will play as the last car crosses the finish line. You will have to employ a temporary means of having the sound wait for the last car. The better means of providing this function lies in the use of a variable covered in material in a later chapter. The following elements are covered in this exercise.

- *Designating multiple objects for simultaneous movement*
- *Selecting Motion icon properties for multiple objects*
- *Creating a temporary timing solution*

Take a Look

CD-ROM

Before beginning the exercise, let's take a look at the exercise in its completed state so that you can clearly see what it is you are about to build.

1. Select File | Open and locate on the companion CD-ROM the directory *Chapter07*. Locate the file *Exer7-3* and double click on it.

2. The file *Exer7-3* should now appear in your copy of Authorware.

3. Click on the Restart button to play the file from the top of the flowline.

4. Click on the Continue button.

Note the following properties of this completed exercise.

- *All cars move at the same time.*
- *The red car is the last over the finish line.*
- *The sound does not play until the red car crosses the finish line.*

Storyboard: On screen

Figures 7-14 through 7-16 show you what the finished presentation will look like. Figure 7-14 shows the complete presentation. Figure 7-15 shows what is inside the Display icon *Track*. Figure 7-16 shows what is inside the Display icon *Green Car*. (The Display icons for the blue and red cars are identical except for color.)

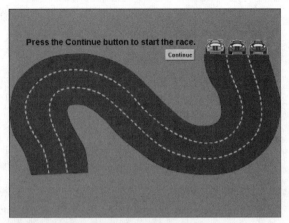

Fig. 7-14. The complete presentation screen.

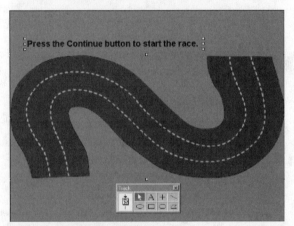

Fig. 7-15. Display icon **Track**.

Fig. 7-16. Display icon **Green Car**.

Storyboard: Behind the Scenes

Figure 7-17 shows the main flowline (containing all icons, their placement, and their names) as it should look when you are finished with this exercise. Figure 7-18 shows the Properties/ Motion Icon dialog window for *Move the Green Car* (similar to that for *Move the Blue Car*). Figure 7-19 shows the Properties/Motion Icon dialog window for *Move the Red Car*. Note that the red car is the last car to cross the finish line.

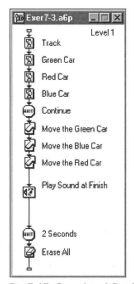

Fig. 7-17. Completed flowline.

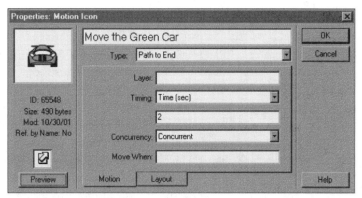

Fig. 7-18. Properties/Motion Icon dialog window for Move the Green Car.

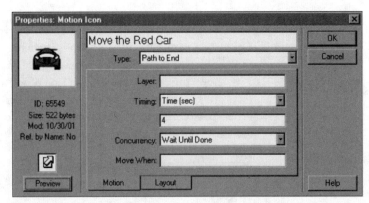

Fig. 7-19. Properties/Motion Icon dialog window for Move the Red Car.

Step-by-Step Instructions

1. Select File | New | File. Close the two Knowledge Object dialog windows.

2. Verify that you are looking at a new flowline. Select File | Save and type in *Chap7-3*.

3. Create the beginning of the icon structure below the two Map icons.

    a) Drag a Display icon to the flowline below the previous Map icons. Name this icon *Track*.

    b) Drag a second Display icon to the flowline. Name this icon *Green Car*.

    c) Drag a third Display icon to the flowline. Name this icon *Red Car*.

    d) Drag a fourth Display icon to the flowline. Name this icon *Blue Car*.

    e) Drag a Wait icon to the flowline. Name this icon *Continue*.

    f) Drag a Motion icon to the flowline. Name this icon *Move the Green Car*.

    g) Drag a second Motion icon to the flowline. Name this icon *Move the Red Car*.

    h) Drag a third Motion icon to the flowline. Name this icon *Move the Blue Car*.

    i) Drag a Sound icon to the flowline. Name this icon *Play Sound at Finish*.

    j) Drag a Wait icon to the flowline. Name this icon *2 Seconds*.

    k) Drag an Erase icon to the flowline. Name this icon *Erase All*.

4. Supply content to the Display icons.

    a) Double click on the Display icon *Track*. Select Insert | Image. In the dialog window that opens, click on the Import button (lower left). Use the pull-down menu to locate the *Chapter07* directory. Locate and select the graphic file *Track.png*. Click on the Import button. Position the track mid-screen.

Go Solo

NOTE

The order of the icons that you are being asked to create in step 3 is different from what is seen in figure 7-14. Please follow the order suggested in step 3, in that we want to show you a "problem" and its solution a little later in the exercise.

b) While still inside the *Track* icon, select the Text tool and type in the following instruction to the user.
Press the Continue button to start the race.
Position the text above the track. When finished, jump to the flowline (Ctrl + J).

c) Double click on the Display icon *Green Car*. Select Insert | Image. Click on the Import button. In the *Chapter07* directory, locate and select the graphic file *GreenCar.png*. Click on the Import button. In the open dialog window, in the Mode field, select Matted. Close the dialog window. You will position the car later. When finished, jump to the flowline (Ctrl + J).

d) Double click on Display icon *Red Car*. Select Insert | Image. Click on the Import button. In the *Chapter07* directory, locate and select the graphic file *RedCar.png*. Click on the Import button. In the open dialog window, in the Mode field, select Matted. Close the dialog window. You will position the car later. When finished, jump to the flowline (Ctrl + J).

e) Double click on the Display icon *Blue Car*. Select Insert | Image. Click on the Import button. In the *Chapter07* directory, locate and select the graphic file *BlueCar.png*. Click on the Import button. In the open dialog window, in the Mode field, select Matted. Close the dialog window. You will position the car later. When finished, jump to the flowline (Ctrl + J).

f) Double click on the Wait icon *2 Seconds*. Remove the check marks beside the Mouse Click and Key Press options. In the Time Limit field, type in 2. Place a check mark beside Show Countdown. Click on the OK button to close the icon.

5. Carefully align all cars at the starting line. To accomplish this, you will use a trick you may recall from previous material.

a) You first need a point of reference for all cars. You have a natural one, the track. Double click on the Display icon *Track* to open it.

b) The track is now in Authorware's video memory. Jump to the flowline (Ctrl + J).

c) Hold down the Shift key as you double click on the Display icon *Green Car*. Position the green car at the starting line in the first racing lane on the left. When finished, jump to the flowline (Ctrl + J).

d) Hold down the Shift key as you double click on the Display icon *Red Car*. Note that the last thing on screen (both the track and the green car) are brought back onto the screen. Position the red car at the starting position of the middle racing lane. When finished, jump to the flowline (Ctrl + J).

> **NOTE**
>
> Remember that holding the Shift key down as you open a Display icon will redisplay whatever is in Authorware's video memory before it displays the new content of the icon it is in the process of opening. The previous content does not really exist in the current icon but is being displayed as a point of reference for you.

e) Hold down the Shift key as you double click on the Display icon *Blue Car*. Position the blue car at the racing lane on the right. When finished, jump to the flowline (Ctrl + J).

6. Link the cars to the Motion icons.

   a) Click on the Restart button.

   b) You should see on screen the track with all three cars lined up at the starting line. The Continue button should also be visible.

   c) Press Ctrl + P to pause. Drag the Continue button so that it is directly to the right of the message. Press Ctrl + P to return to Play mode.

   d) Click on the Continue button. The Properties/Motion Icon dialog window for the first unassigned Motion icon (*Green Car*) should now appear on screen.

   e) In the dialog window, select the Layout tab. In the Type field at the top, use the pull-down menu to locate and select Path to End. Note the instruction *Click object to be moved*. Click on the green car you see on screen. Drag and release the green car several times to create and extend the path within the racing lane for this car, similar to that shown in figure 7-20. Remember that you can click on the line to add points, and you can move an existing point by selecting it and dragging it to another location. When finished, click on the OK button to close the dialog window.

(NOTE)

Examine the Icon Title field in the dialog window for this first Motion icon. It should read *Move the Green Car*. This points out the importance of not only labeling each icon but using labels that are descriptive of what they do or contain. Without this label, you would have to flounder around trying to guess which car the current Motion icon should be linked to.

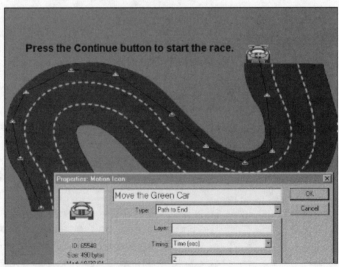

Fig. 7-20. Path along which to move the green car.

·**T/P**·

If you accidentally drop out of the sequence previously described, you can individually link each car to its corresponding Motion icon using the following process. From the flowline, get the cars and track on screen by running the program. Jump to the flowline (Ctrl + J). Hold the Shift key down as you double click on the Motion icon that needs to be linked (e.g., *Move the Red Car*). Select the Layout tab and then select Path to End. Click on the (for example) red car. Drag and release the red car several times to create and extend the path. You can repeat this process for whatever Motion icon needs to be linked. The key is to have the cars and track in video memory before trying to create the motion path.

f) The Properties/Motion Icon dialog window for the second unassigned Motion icon (*Red Car*) should now appear on screen. Select the Layout tab. In the Type field at the top, select Path to End. Click on the red car. Drag and release the red car several times to create and extend the path within the racing lane for the red car. When finished, click on the OK button to close the dialog window.

g) The Properties/Motion Icon dialog window for the third unassigned Motion icon (*Blue Car*) should now appear on screen. Select the Layout tab. In the Type field at the top, select Path to End. Click on the blue car. Drag and release the blue car several times to create and extend the path within the racing lane for the blue car. When finished, click on the OK button to close the dialog window.

h) Jump to the flowline (Ctrl + J).

7. Perform a couple of final tasks.

a) Double click on the Sound icon *Play Sound at Finish*. Click on the Import button (lower left). Locate and select the sound file *PlayFinish.wav* in the *Chapter07* directory on the companion CD-ROM. Click on the Import button. You should see a blue progress bar quickly display on screen as the sound is imported into Authorware. Click on the OK button to close the dialog window.

b) Double click on the Wait icon *2 Seconds*. Remove all check marks. In the Time Limit field, type in *2*. Place a check mark beside Show Countdown. Click on the OK button to close this icon.

8. Let's take a look at what you have at this point.

a) Click on the Restart button.

b) Click on the Continue button that appears.

c) You should see that each car moves, but one at a time. The sound plays and then there is a 2-second pause. Note that the cars do not "turn" as they go through curves. Verify that you have encountered the empty Erase icon.

Unfortunately, Authorware's animation cannot turn the object. If this effect is important to you, you might try developing the animation in Flash, where the cars can "lean" into the curves and change directions. You can then play the exported Flash animation as a movie within Authorware.

d) To erase everything on screen, click on everything you see.

e) Obviously you have some more work to do. Jump to the flowline (Ctrl + J).

9. Let's begin the fine-tuning by first dealing with the "one-at-time" movement.

   a) Double click on the Motion icon *Move the Green Car*. Select the Motion tab. Examine the Concurrency field at the bottom. It is currently set to Wait Until Done. Change this by selecting Concurrent. Click on the OK button to close this icon.

   b) Double click on the Motion icon *Move the Red Car*. Select the Motion tab. In the Concurrency field, select Concurrent. Click on the OK button.

   c) Double click on the Motion icon *Move the Blue Car*. Select the Motion tab. In the Concurrency field, select Concurrent. Click on the OK button.

10. Let's take another look.

    a) Click on the white Start Flag button.

    b) Click on the Continue button that appears.

    c) You should see that the cars all move at the same time, but much too quickly, and the red car may not be the last one to finish, as intended. The sound plays, but immediately after the cars have started to move.

11. Obviously there is more work to do. First tackle the timing problem.

    a) Double click on the Motion icon *Move the Green Car*. The Motion tab should already be selected (if not, select it). The Timing field is set to Time (sec). Just below this field, you will find the default setting of 1 (for 1 second). Change this value to a number that seems appropriate. Click on the OK button.

    b) Adjust the Timing field value (number of seconds) for all three Motion icons until the cars finish at different times, with the red car coming in last.

12. The sound still plays too soon. The real solution lies with the use of a variable. You have not been introduced to variables yet, but let's take a look at how to temporarily fix this problem.

    a) From the flowline, drag the Motion icon *Move the Red Car* from its current position and place it so that it is the last Motion icon in the sequence of cars on the flowline. See figure 7-14 for reference. You may have to adjust the timing so that the red car is the last over the finish line.

    b) Double click on the Motion icon *Move the Red Car*. Select the Motion tab. Change the Concurrency field back to Wait Until Done. This will hold forward progression on the flowline until after this icon has finished.

NOTE

The default settings should make sense out of what you observed. *Move the Green Car* was encountered on the flowline. Authorware waited as this Motion icon continued to move the green car. When this icon was finished, the program moved on to the next Motion icon, where the same play/wait sequence continued.

   c) After the *Move the Red Car* icon has finished, the program will drop down to the next icon (the Sound icon *Play Sound at Finish*) and play the sound.

13. Select File | Save to save your work.

Summary

- *Authorware's Motion icon provides the capability to easily add simple 2D motion to your application.*

- *These animations will generally have a "light footprint" and perform relatively well over both LANs and Web-based networks.*

- *In the first guided tour, you took a look at the Motion icon properties.*

- *At a minimum, animation involves the use of a Display icon, containing the object to be moved, and a Motion icon, which acts as the engine for the movement.*

- *In the first practice exercise, you created a simple direct-to-point animation. Direct-to-point animation moves the object from the origin to the destination along the most direct route. You can change the origin point by going inside the Display icon containing the object being moved and simply moving it to another location. The destination can be changed by opening the Motion icon and simply dragging the object to a new location.*

- *In the second practice exercise, you created a simple animation using a motion path. Path-to-end animation adds the ability to create and modify a specific path along which the object will move. There are several properties of the motion path that can be modified.*

- *In the third practice exercise, you created multiple animations that occurred simultaneously. Simultaneous animation can easily be created by placing each object to be moved in its own Display icon and linking each of these icons to a corresponding Motion icon. Properties within the Motion icon can be modified to achieve a variety of effects.*

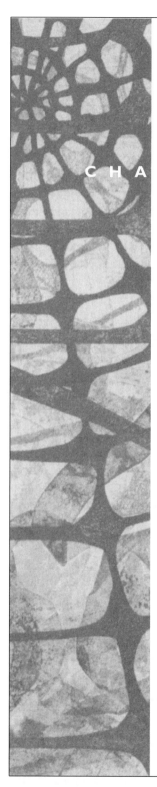

C H A P T E R

8

Application:

Creating the Basics

What Are the Application Project Exercises?

Throughout this book you will find a number of application chapters. These chapters differ from the others in that they will challenge you to combine the knowledge and techniques acquired from several previous chapters and apply these newly acquired skills to create part of a "real-world" Authorware project on your own.

Each application chapter focuses on performing a sequence of application exercises that combined with the other application chapters constitutes a fully functional application project titled *Inside Authorware 6*. Each application chapter constitutes a separate and distinct element of the overall application project. Each exercise in its completed form can be found on the companion CD-ROM. In this way, you can choose to create all of the application exercises on your own or complete whatever application exercises you would like to and integrate your work with the completed exercises supplied on the companion CD-ROM.

The overall application project, *Inside Authorware 6*, and all of the component exercises found in each of the application chapters are designed to reflect real-world content, structures, and project objectives. The exercises are designed to not only review what has been covered in the book but to "push a little past" what has been presented. In this way, you are provided with a means of applying what you know and are challenged to go further.

These exercises are structured so that you can refer to the completed version as you are creating the exercise on your own. This task is most easily accomplished by opening two copies of Authorware on your desktop, using one copy to view the completed version and the second to house the exercise you are currently working on. You can easily switch back and forth between the two Authorware copies by pressing Alt + Tab.

Also please look carefully at the Authorware flowline in each application exercise, as many blue Calculation icons labeled READ ME are included. Double click on these READ ME icons to reveal a wealth of additional information about the particular structure the icon is located close to.

Application Project Description

The application project involves creating an Authorware project (*Inside Authorware 6*) that includes creating Authorware structures and variables that meet most of the typical requirements found in most computer-based training applications in the corporate and educational environments. You will practice creating simple animation, content pages, content pages synced to sound events, interactive learning strategies, various question models, course and topic structures, menus with visual bookmarks, a sign-on structure that records data to disk, and many other capabilities.

The content deals with the new features of Authorware 6.0, the community of Authorware developers around the world, and some challenging tests of your Authorware knowledge. All of the media elements (text, graphics, sound, and movies), as well as some of the Authorware structures (in the form of Authorware models), are supplied on the companion CD-ROM. It is hoped the application project will help you solidify what you are learning about Authorware, having some fun along the way. The sections that follow describe the application exercises by chapter.

Chapter 8: Creating the Basics

In this chapter you will use what you have learned in chapters 1 through 7 to create different aspects of the basic elements found in many Authorware applications. In the first three exercises, you will create "animated" presentations using a variety of simple and quick techniques. Some of the techniques make use of the Motion icon, whereas others do not actually use the Motion icon but simulate animation. In the last exercise, you will have the opportunity to reinforce your skills using the Media Synchronization feature. Each of the exercises in this chapter will be incorporated into topic-level structures you will create in Chapter 17.

Exercise 8A: Simulating Drawing

This exercise simulates someone drawing lines on the screen, in "real time." In looking at what appears on screen, you may think that Authorware's Motion icon created this effect. However, this is not the case. A variety of other techniques can simulate animation effects.

Exercise 8B: Simple Motion

Simple 2D animation is quick and easy to create within Authorware. This exercise reinforces your animation skills by showing you how to create a continuously looping motion path.

Exercise 8C: Simulating 3D Motion

One limitation of Authorware's Motion icon is that it can only move an object around in what appears to be 2D space. In this exercise you will see how easy it is to create the illusion of 3D movement.

Exercise 8D: Media Synchronization

In this exercise you will create 12 groups of content, with each group synchronized to a Sound icon. The completed sequence will present an explanation of each of the icons on the Icon palette.

Chapter 14: Creating Interactive Structures

In this chapter you will create interactive structures that can be used as instructional learning strategies and quiz formats. The key to efficient Authorware development is creating interactive structures that require very little rework for reuse. Each of the exercises in this chapter emphasizes the benefits of carefully designing the learning activity interface before starting, and then making use of grid patterns developed during this design phase. The last two exercises are intermediate-level question structures, offering a generic capability without the complexity (or power) of the dynamic model you will explore in Chapter 26. Each of the exercises in this chapter will be incorporated into topic-level structures you will create in Chapter 17.

Exercise 14A: Interactive Learning Strategy 1

This learning activity illustrates an interactive strategy based on hot spots, which can be effectively used when there are multiple terms or concepts that must be learned or associated with additional information. Once the learning activity interface has been created, it can be reused with the same target words within seconds, or reworked with a different subject within moments.

Exercise 14B: Interactive Learning Strategy 2

This learning activity illustrates using the Drag and Drop response to require learners to correctly match descriptive labels with corresponding graphics. The key to rapid reuse is in effectively designing the interface, the objects, and a placement grid.

Exercise 14C: Interactive Learning Strategy 3

This learning activity uses the Drag and Drop response again, but this time to drag words to complete multiple sentences with missing phrases. The design and grid also play an important part in efficient reuse.

Exercise 14D: Interactive Learning Strategy 4

In this learning activity an "interactive" graphic is used to provide two layers of information to the learner. As the learner moves the cursor over a graphic of an icon, narration is triggered, stating what that icon is. If the user clicks on that same icon, a second layer of additional information is provided, including text and narration.

Exercise 14E: Creating a Basic Generic Question

In this exercise you will create a generic question structure that is both effective and efficient, requiring minimal effort to change content and scoring considerations. You will explore the details of the variables and structure used to facilitate this structure.

Exercise 14F: Creating a Generic Question for Multiple Correct Answers

In this exercise you will create a generic question structure in which there may be multiple correct answers. The learner may select and deselect answers until she is ready to have the answers evaluated.

Chapter 17: Basic-level Menu/Topic Structures

The sections that follow describe the application exercises within Chapter 17. In these exercises you will work with "smart" navigation and topic structures. In this chapter you will incorporate the content you created in Chapters 8 and 14.

Exercise 17A: Main Menu Framework with "Smart" Navigation

In this exercise you will create a graphical user interface (GUI), Main menu framework, and global navigational controls with "smarts." The Main menu will include visual status markers to indicate which topics have been selected. You will also add a Flash movie at the beginning of the file. This represents a basic-level interface and navigational controls. In Chapter 27 you will replace some of this structure with a more sophisticated, "dynamic" structure that offers easier maintenance and updating.

Exercise 17B: Topic Structures

In this exercise you will create three topic-level structures that incorporate the content created in Chapters 8 and 14. Each topic structure will include topic-level navigational controls with "smarts." You will also add a Replay button so that the content (text, narration, and animation) of each "page" can be replayed.

Chapter 21: Creating a Sign-on and Extra Features

The sections that follow describe the application exercises within Chapter 21. These include creating a sign-on application, using the RTF editor, linking to external graphics, and using ActiveX controls and event responses.

Exercise 21A: Creating a Sign-on Application and Connecting to a Database

In this exercise you will create a log-in structure to track the user's entry into the Authorware file, and then save that information to a custom variable. Every time the user returns to the file, he will be prompted for name and password to confirm user status. This exercise demonstrates the implementation of the log-in file examined in Chapter 18. Once the user has confirmed his identity, the information is stored in a database, using the structure outlined in Chapter 19.

Exercise 21B: Using the RTF Editor and Creating RTF Knowledge Objects

In Chapter 20, you learned how to use the new RTF Editor command to create Rich Text files that can be brought into Authorware or linked externally to make updating content easier than ever. In this exercise you will use the Create RTF Knowledge Object command to import a multi-page RTF document that will introduce you to some of the more recognizable names in the Authorware community. This RTF file will be displayed via a Framework paging structure. Using the system variable *CurrentPageID*, you will be able to display one page of the RTF document at a time.

Exercise 21C: Linking to External Graphics

In Chapter 20, you learned how to use the external media features in Authorware to speed your development and update files remotely. In this exercise you will use the Expression feature to dynamically pull in graphics based on the icon title of a display.

Exercise 21D: Using ActiveX Controls and Event Responses

In Chapter 20, you learned how to use ActiveX controls to display Web pages within Authorware. In this exercise you will create an interaction in which users can view various Web pages about Authorware and the properties about each page.

Chapter 27: Creating Dynamic Navigation Structures

The sections that follow describe the application exercises within Chapter 27. These include creating a subroutine quiz, creating a dynamic menu and navigation, and working with the Add Font Recourse Knowledge object.

Exercise 27A: Creating a Subroutine Quiz

In Chapter 23, you learned how to separate content from code, with the result of a flowline that is easier to update and to troubleshoot. In chapters 24 and 25 you learned how to populate lists with the *repeat loop* function. In this exercise, you will bring it all together to create a subroutine quiz with all of its data being called from an external file. The data will be stored in a list and will populate the quiz as needed. This exercise demonstrates the power and ease of use accomplished through the separation of content and structure.

Exercise 27B: Creating a Dynamic Menu and Navigation

In Chapter 17, you created a basic menu/topic structure that worked well. However, as you learned in Chapter 26, you can create a more sophisticated structure that is much easier to maintain and update. In this exercise you will enhance the menu and topic structures using variables and parent/child relationships. This produces a result in which content can be added or subtracted without affecting the dynamic structure.

Exercise 27C: Working with the Add Font Resource Knowledge Object

In this exercise you will use the Add Font Resource Knowledge Object to install a unique font onto the user's system. This will ensure that all of your content will display as you intended on any machine that your Authorware piece is delivered on.

Before You Start

Throughout the application exercises you will be asked to open two copies of Authorware at the same time. One copy of Authorware will read files from the companion CD-ROM, and the other copy will read files from the *SaveWork* directory on your computer's hard drive. For this learning strategy to work, you will need to place a second copy of the library files in the *SaveWork* directory. As is the case with files in the Windows environment, a single library file cannot be opened simultaneously by two applications (the two copies of Authorware).

1. Place the companion CD-ROM into the CD-ROM player in your computer.

2. Using either Windows Explorer or the My Computer icon, locate the *Chapter08* directory on the companion CD-ROM.

3. Open the *Chapter08* directory and locate the files Graphics.*a6l* and *Sounds.a6l*.

4. Copy these two files into the *SaveWork* directory located on your computer's hard drive.

5. Verify that these two files are now located in the *SaveWork* directory.

Application Exercise 8A: Simulating Drawing

Description

This exercise simulates someone drawing lines on screen, in "real time." In looking at what appears on screen, you may think that Authorware's Motion icon created the effect. However, this is not the case. A variety of other techniques can simulate animation effects. These techniques can be quickly created and implemented within your future applications. You will leave this exercise grouped within a Map icon to be placed within a topic structure (in Chapter 17).

Storyboard: On screen

Figure 8-1 shows what the finished exercise will look like on screen.

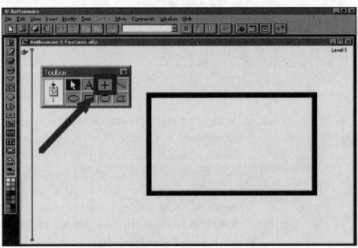

Fig. 8-1. Completed presentation on screen.

Storyboard: Behind the Scenes

Figure 8-2 shows the main flowline (with all icons, their placement, and their names) as it should look when you are finished with this exercise.

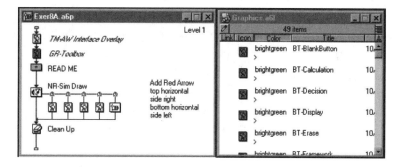

Fig. 8-2. Main flowline.

Step-by-Step Instructions

With guidance from the following generalized steps, perform this exercise on your own. Consult the completed exercise (*Exer8A.a6p*) on the companion CD-ROM for further guidance.

1. Open the file *Exer8A.a6p* located on the companion CD-ROM in the directory named *Chapter08*. Open the library file *Graphics.a6l*, located in the same directory. Run the program and see how it works. Jump to the flowline and examine the various icons and structures.

2. Open the Calculation icon labeled READ ME and read its content.

3. Leave this file open in this copy of Authorware.

4. Open another copy of Authorware, starting a new file. Open the library file *Graphics.a6l* located in the *SaveWork* directory of your hard drive.

5. When finished, make sure to save your exercise as *App8A* in the *SaveWork* directory on your computer's hard drive.

Application Exercise 8B: Simple Motion

Description

Simple 2D animation is quick and easy to create within Authorware. This exercise reinforces your animation skills by showing you how to create a continuously looping motion path. You will leave the exercise grouped within a Map icon, to be placed within a topic structure (in Chapter 17).

Storyboard: On screen

Figure 8-3 shows what the finished exercise will look like on screen.

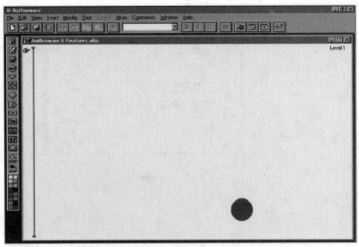

Fig. 8-3. Completed presentation on screen.

Storyboard: Behind the Scenes

Figure 8-4 shows the main and second-level flowlines (with all icons, their placement, and their names) as they should look when you are finished with this exercise.

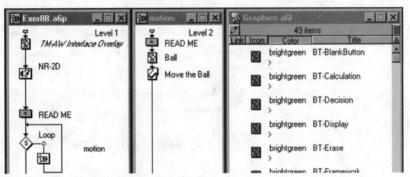

Fig. 8-4. Main and second-level flowlines.

Step-by-Step Instructions

With guidance from the following generalized steps, perform this exercise on your own. Consult the completed exercise (*Exer8B.a6p*) on the companion CD-ROM for further guidance.

1. Open the file *Exer8B.a6p* located on the companion CD-ROM in the directory named *Chapter08*. Open the library file *Graphics.a6l* located in the same directory. Run the program and see how it works. Jump to the flowline and examine the various icons and structures.

2. Open the Calculation icon labeled READ ME and read its content.

3. Leave this file open in this copy of Authorware.

4. Open another copy of Authorware, starting a new file. Open the library file *Graphics.a6l* located in the *SaveWork* directory of your hard drive.

5. When finished, make sure to save your exercise as *App8B* in the *SaveWork* directory on your computer's hard drive.

Application Exercise 8C: Simulating 3D Motion

Description

One limitation of Authorware's Motion Icon is that is can only move an object around in what appears to be 2D space. In this exercise you will see how easy it is to create the illusion of 3D movement. Actually, the easiest and best way to create the animation in this exercise is by using Macromedia's Flash to create the animation and then play that Flash movie from Authorware. However, this means that you will need a copy of Flash to accomplish the task. As an alternative to using Flash, the following exercise shows you how to create a simulated animation in Authorware. You will leave the exercise grouped within a Map icon, to be placed within a topic structure (in Chapter 17).

Storyboard: On screen

Figure 8-5 shows all balls being displayed simultaneously on screen so that you can see the relative position of each ball graphic.

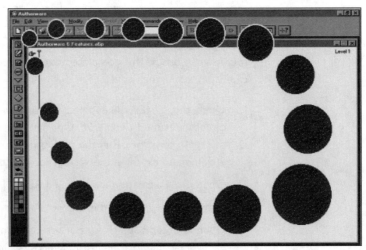

Fig. 8-5. All ball graphics on screen.

Storyboard: Behind the Scenes

Figure 8-6 shows the main and second-level flowlines (with all icons, their placement, and their names) as they should look when you are finished with this exercise.

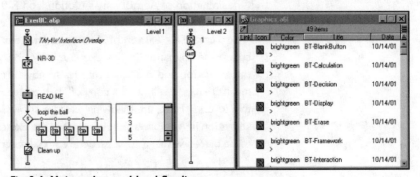

Fig. 8-6. Main and second-level flowlines.

Step-by-Step Instructions

With guidance from the following generalized steps, perform this exercise on your own. Consult the completed exercise (*Exer8C.a6p*) on the companion CD-ROM for further guidance.

1. Open the file *Exer8C.a6p* located on the companion CD-ROM in the directory named *Chapter08*. Open the library file *Graphics.a6l* located in

the same directory. Run the program and see how it works. Jump to the flowline and examine the various icons and structures.

2. Open the Calculation icon labeled READ ME and read its content.

3. Leave this file open in this copy of Authorware.

4. Open another copy of Authorware, starting a new file. Open the library file *Graphics.a6l* located in the *SaveWork* directory of your hard drive.

5. When finished, make sure to save your exercise as *App8C* in the *SaveWork* directory on your computer's hard drive.

Application Exercise 8D: Media Synchronization

Description

The main focus of this exercise is to reinforce your skills in using Authorware's Media Synchronization feature. You will be synchronizing the display of 12 content groups (information about 12 Authorware icons) with audio narration.

The exercise might have been designed so that all 12 groups were synchronized to a single Sound icon. However, the content is divided into 12 "pages" (corresponding to the 12 icons), using 12 Sound icons, with each Sound icon having several media elements synchronized with it. This approach will allow each "page" to be replayed once it is incorporated in a topic structure (in Chapter 17).

Storyboard: On screen

Figure 8-7 shows a representative sample of what one finished content page will look like on screen.

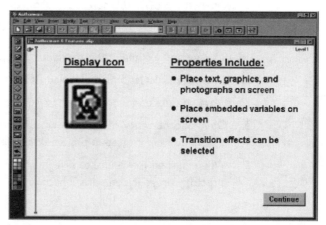

Fig. 8-7. Representative content page on screen.

Storyboard: Behind the Scenes

Figure 8-8 shows the main and second-level flowlines (with all icons, their placement, and their names) as they should look when you are finished with this exercise.

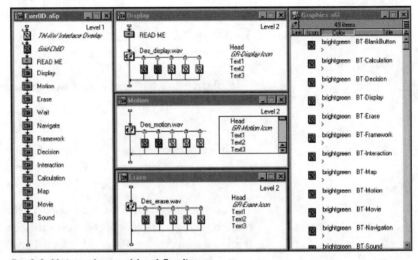

Fig. 8-8. Main and second-level flowlines.

Step-by-Step Instructions

With guidance from the following generalized steps, perform this exercise on your own. Consult the completed exercise (*Exer8D.a6p*) on the companion CD-ROM for further guidance.

1. Open the file *Exer8D.a6p* located on the companion CD-ROM in the directory named *Chapter08*. Open the library file *Graphics.a6l* located in the same directory. Run the program and see how it works. Jump to the flowline and examine the various icons and structures.

2. Open the Calculation icon labeled READ ME and read its content.

3. Leave this file open in this copy of Authorware.

4. Open another copy of Authorware, starting a new file. Open the library file *Graphics.a6l* located in the *SaveWork* directory of your hard drive.

5. When finished, make sure to save your exercise as *App8D* in the *SaveWork* directory on your computer's hard drive.

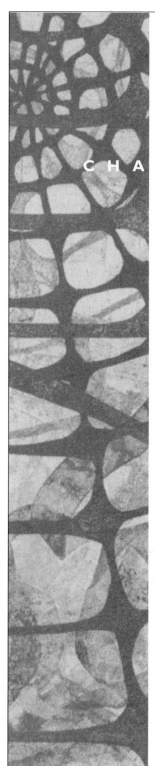

CHAPTER 9

Introducing

Interactivity

Introduction

In the beginning days of computer-based training (CBT) and for a few years thereafter, CBT courseware could accurately be described as reading facilitators. These CBTs were little more than the result of taking the words from books and putting them on a computer, sometimes including very simple and crude graphics. The user generally pressed the Enter key to move forward in the program. Early CBT programs did not even include backup and quit functions.

After a few years, course developers started inserting review questions after every few presentation screens. The insertion of these questions was seen by most people as a good thing, as it forced users to interact with the learning program. Thus the term *interactivity* made its way into the CBT environment. In fact, in those days, how "interactive" a course was came to be defined by how often questions where interspersed between presentation screens.

Development tools have changed dramatically since. With the birth and continual development of Authorware (and other authoring tools), the user has been able to interact with a learning application in a wide variety of ways previously unavailable. This chapter begins an exploration of the numerous ways Authorware can help you design and create interactive learning sequences. By the end of this chapter, you will be able to:

- *Describe the key characteristics of the Interaction icon*
- *List the interaction types offered in Authorware*
- *Work with the button response properties*
- *Describe the characteristics of the "pickup truck" interaction structure*
- *Create two versions of the "pickup truck" interaction structure*

Guided Tour 9A: Interaction Icon Properties

The Interaction icon is the heart of Authorware. The Interaction icon provides the capability for the user to interact with the learning program using a wide variety of instructional techniques. All of these instructional techniques are built into Authorware and are available "out of the box" to you as author/programmer, without having to perform any programming.

The Interaction icon combines the characteristics of the Display and Decision icons, and adds enhanced functionality. There are two important characteristics of the Interaction icon that distinguish it from the Decision icon. The Interaction icon includes the following.

- *Display screen and toolbox (similar to the Display icon)*
- *Branching determined by user selection*

In contrast, the Decision icon:

- *Does* not *include a display screen*
- *Does include branching determined by author/programmer*

Through the use of the Interaction icon, Authorware provides powerful capabilities to the author/programmer, all available with the simple click of the mouse. Let's take a quick look at the properties of the Interaction icon to see what is available.

1. Start by opening a new file.
    a) Select File | New | File.
    b) Close the two dialog windows that have opened.
    c) Verify that you are now looking at an empty flowline.

2. Let's take a look at the properties associated with the Interaction icon.
    a) Drag an Interaction icon to the flowline.
    b) Make sure the Interaction icon is selected (highlighted).
    c) Select Modify | Icon | Properties. (Or right mouse click on the icon and select Properties from the menu that opens.)
    d) The Properties/Interaction Icon dialog window should now be open. See figure 9-1. This window consists of five areas: left-hand side, Interaction tab, Display tab, Layout tab, and CMI tab.

NOTE

If you double click on the Interaction icon, you do not see the properties, but instead see the display screen that is part of the Interaction icon. This display area looks the same as a Display icon, including the presence and use of a toolbox.

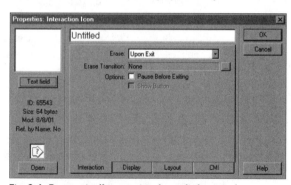

Fig. 9-1. Properties/Interaction Icon dialog window.

3. Examine the left-hand side of the window. This side of the window includes a small picture of the content contained in the display area of the icon, a Text Field button (which you will examine when you work with the Text Response type in Chapter 11), data about the icon, and the Open button on the bottom (which upon selection opens the display area associated with the icon).

4. Examine the Interaction tab. The following outlines the options of this tab, starting at the top and working downward.

    • **Icon Title:** *As you have seen previously, each icon property starts off with a field that displays the name of the current icon, or allows you to type in a name into this field.*

    • **Erase:** *Used to set automatic erase characteristics for the display area in this Interaction icon. This setting does not affect the erase characteristics of any icon that may be attached to this icon. The following are the options in this field.*

        Upon Exit: *The content in the Interaction icon display area will erase as the program exits the current interaction.*

        After Next Entry: *The content in the Interaction icon display area will erase after the user selects another option from the current Interaction icon.*

        Don't Erase: *Disables the current automatic erase feature. The content in the Interaction icon display area stays on screen until erased with an Erase icon or a higher-level erase function.*

    • **Erase Transition:** *As you have seen before, this field opens a dialog window that provides the capability to select from a wide variety of erase effects, using a variety of options and speeds.*

    • **Options:** *There is an additional option available that consists of the following:*

        Pause Before Exiting: *Placing a check mark here will cause the program flow to pause, waiting for either a mouse click or key press from the user.*

        Show Button: *Only active if the previously described pause option has been selected. Placing a check mark here will display a Continue button on screen during the pause.*

5. Examine the Display tab. Click on the Display tab. The following are the options of this tab, starting at the top and working downward.

    • **Layer:** *You can type in a number in this field to assign a position (back to front) to all content in the display area of the current Interaction icon. Higher numbers will position the current content toward the front, relative to the displayed objects from other icons with a lower number.*

    • **Transition:** *Selecting this field will open a dialog window very similar to the erase transitions seen before. In this case, these transitions affect the content of the current icon as it is being brought up for display on screen.*

    • **Options:** *You can place a check mark beside any of the following options.*

Update Displayed Variables: Automatically updates the current value of any Authorware variable embedded in the display area of the current icon.

Exclude Text from Search: Eliminates any text in the display area of the current icon from any user-initiated word searches.

Prevent Automatic Erase: Disables the current automatic erase function for the content of the display area. Current content will remain on screen until erased with either an Erase icon or higher-level automatic erase function.

Erase Previous Content: Erases anything on screen prior to displaying the content of the current icon.

Direct to Screen: Displays the content of the current icon in front of any other objects on screen.

6. Examine the Layout tab. Click on the Layout tab. The following are the options of this tab, starting at the top and working downward.

- *Positioning: This field uses the following options to determine where an object appears when it is displayed.*

  No Change: Objects will appear in the same locations as currently placed. Disables all options except Movable.

  On Screen: Objects must remain entirely on screen. Enter coordinates or variables in the Initial fields of the X and Y positions. The coordinates are always screen coordinates.

  On Path: Objects will appear at a point somewhere between the base and end points of a path, which must be specified in the X and Y coordinate positions.

  In Area: Objects will appear at a point within an area defined by the base and end points specified in the X and Y coordinate positions.

- *Movable: This field uses the following options to determine where (or if) the user can move (drag) the current objects displayed on screen.*

  Never: Objects displayed in the current icon cannot be moved by the user.

  On Screen: Objects displayed in the current icon can be moved anywhere on screen by the user, as long as the entire object remains on screen.

  Anywhere: The user can move objects anywhere, including completely off the screen.

- *X and Y Positions: Fields in this area become available only when the appropriate corresponding choices have been made in the Positioning and/or Movable fields. As X and Y positions become active, you can type in*

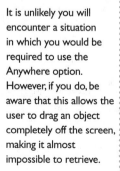

CAUTION

It is unlikely you will encounter a situation in which you would be required to use the Anywhere option. However, if you do, be aware that this allows the user to drag an object completely off the screen, making it almost impossible to retrieve.

239

whatever X/Y coordinates are appropriate for your application. You will use these positions in exercises to follow involving the Interaction icon.

7. Examine the CMI tab. Click on the CMI tab. The following are the options of this tab, starting at the top and working downward.

   - **Knowledge Track:** *Placing a check mark here turns on CMI tracking for the current interaction. When you turn tracking on, the Interaction All option in the File Properties dialog window in the CMI tab also needs to be on for tracking to take place.*

   - **Interaction ID:** *To specify the interaction's unique identifier. Authorware passes the ID you enter to the CMIAddInteraction function as the Interaction ID parameter.*

   - **Objective ID:** *To specify the objective ID the current interaction is associated with. Authorware passes the ID you enter to the CMIAddInteraction function as the Objective ID parameter. If you leave this field empty, Authorware uses the content of the variable IconTitle as the Objective ID parameter.*

   - **Weight:** *To indicate the relative importance of the interaction. Authorware passes the value you enter to the CMIAddInteraction function as the Weight parameter.*

   - **Type:** *To indicate the interaction type. Authorware passes the choice you make or the string you enter to the CMIAddInteraction function as the Type parameter. The Type parameters are as follows: Multiple Choice (C), Fill in the Blank (F), and From Field.*

As you can see, there are a lot of properties for the Interaction icon. In the following guided tour, you will explore interaction response types.

Guided Tour 9B: Interaction Response Types

Authorware provides you with a large number of interactive strategies you can select with the mere click of the mouse. For any given Interaction icon, you can include as many different response types as you wish. Of course, if you are going "mix and match" response types, hopefully you will do so guided by instructional design and/or common sense. Without performing any programming, let's take a quick look at the response type options Authorware provides.

1. Let's continue with the flowline you should still have open from the previous guided tour, which should be simply a single Interaction icon sitting on the flowline.

2. Drag a Map icon to the right of the Interaction icon and drop it just to the right of the Interaction icon. See figure 9-2.

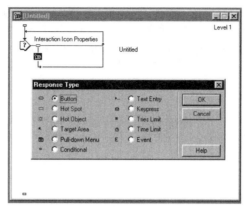

Fig. 9-2. Dropping an icon to the right of the Interaction icon.

3. You should now be looking at the Response Type dialog window. See figure 9-3. You will see this window only when you drag and drop an icon in the first position immediately to the right of an Interaction icon. At this point you can select any response type by simply clicking in the round selection box next to the response type you want to use.

    As you continue to drop other icons to the right of this first attached icon, all additional icons will be automatically assigned the response type you chose initially. A little later in this tour, you will see how you can change response types.

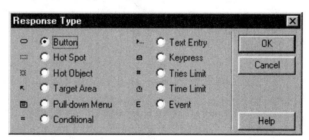

Fig. 9-3. Response Type dialog window.

4. Examine the Response Type dialog window. The following outline the options of this window.

    *   **Button:** *A 3D-looking button (appears to depress upon selection) that can use either the system button or custom buttons that you can create.*

    *   **Hot Spot:** *To set up any rectangular area as a selectable area the user can click or double click on, or position the cursor over, to trigger a response.*

- **Hot Object:** *To create an object the user can click or double click on, or position the cursor over, to trigger a response.*

- **Target Area:** *To allow the user to drag an object into a specified target area in the interaction display.*

- **Pull-down Menu:** *To create a pull-down menu, similar to that found in most software applications.*

- **Conditional:** *To create an interaction that will evaluate the condition or value of a given constant, variable, or function.*

- **Text Entry:** *Allows the user to type text into an entry field. User entries can be evaluated for specific or multiple values, or use wildcards.*

- **Tries Limit:** *Used to set a maximum number of attempts Authorware will allow the user.*

- **Time Limit:** *Used to set a maximum amount of time Authorware will allow the user.*

- **Event:** *Used to interact with Xtras that send events, such as ActiveX controls.*

5. Click on the OK button to close the dialog window. Now take a quick look at figure 9-4, which specifies the generic terminology we use to describe various parts of the interaction structure.

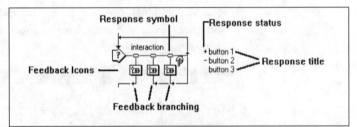

Fig. 9-4. Terminology associated with interaction parts.

- **Interaction icon:** *Serves as the platform from which the user makes selections. If the interaction is presenting a question for the user to answer, the Interaction icon contains the question stem.*

- **Feedback icons:** *Present whatever response has been designed, as the result of the user making a selection from the Interaction icon. If the interaction is presenting a question, the icons attached to the Interaction icon would present feedback concerning whatever choice the user selected.*

- **Feedback branching:** *The line directly below each attached icon illustrates the type of branching that has been designated. The branching options are Try Again, Continue, and Exit. With the Perpetual option chosen, there will be an additional return branch.*

- *Response Type symbol: Immediately above each attached icon there is a small graphic symbol representing the response type of that icon. Each type of symbol corresponds to the response type selection as illustrated in the Response Type dialog window. See figure 9-3.*

- *Response status: Each attached icon can be identified as a correct choice (+), an incorrect choice (−), or not judged (no symbol) relative to a selection made from the current Interaction icon.*

- *Response title: Name given to each attached icon.*

That completes this tour. In guided tour 9C, you will explore the Button Interaction response type.

Guided Tour 9C: Button Interaction Response

The Button Interaction response is the first type listed in the Response Type dialog window, and is perhaps the most widely used. Authorware makes it very easy to create interactive buttons of any size or style. Authorware will create the familiar Windows-style gray buttons that can be resized and positioned anywhere on the visible screen.

However, of even greater significance is the fact that Authorware includes a Button editor and library that provide the capability to very easily create custom buttons that have three functional states: button up, button down, and "rollover" (cursor passes over the button without the mouse being clicked). You can also link a sound file with a button, so that when the user selects a button it looks as though the button is being depressed (with an attendant "click" sound).

The Button Interaction Response option incorporates a variety of properties that provide power and convenience. Let's take a quick look.

1. Let's continue with what you have left over from the previous guided tour, which should be a single Interaction icon sitting on the main flow-line, with a Map icon attached to the right.

2. In the previous guided tour, you selected Button Response Type, so you should be set to proceed here.

3. Double click on the Response Type symbol for the Map icon to access the Properties/Response dialog window. The Response Type symbol is the tiny eclipse icon directly above the Map icon. See figure 9-4 for reference.

4. Verify that you are looking at the Properties/Response dialog window shown in figure 9-5. You will examine the following three parts of this window: left-hand side, Button tab, and Response tab.

You can alternatively highlight the Map icon and then select Modify | Icon | Response to bring up this same dialog window. Or use the keyboard shortcut Ctrl + E.

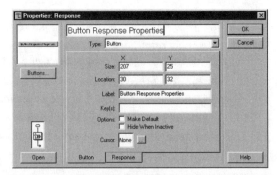

Fig. 9-5. Properties/Response dialog window for the button interaction.

5. Examine the left-hand side. This side of the window includes a small picture of whatever button is shown on screen, with a Buttons button directly beneath this picture that will access the Button editor and library. You will work with the Button editor and library in Chapter 15. On the bottom is an Open button, which upon selection will open the icon associated with the response.

6. At the top of every Response Type dialog window there will be two fields that will remain the same: Icon Title and Type. The Icon Title field displays the current title or allows you to type in whatever name you wish. The Type field is a menu listing of all Interaction Response types. This list is the same as that you saw when you first dragged an icon to the right of an Interaction icon. In this field, you can instantly change the interaction type by simply making another selection.

7. The Button tab should already be selected (if not, select it). The following are the options of this tab, starting at the top and working downward.

   • **Size:** *The X and Y entry fields for the Size option allow you to type in exact height and width specifications for the button associated with this interaction response. These fields are a great aid if you want to standardize the size of buttons (producing more professional-looking results).*

   • **Location:** *The X and Y entry fields for the Location option allow you to type in exact coordinates for the location of the button associated with this interaction response. These fields are a great aid if you want exact alignment of buttons (producing more professional-looking results).*

   • **Label:** *This field also displays the name of the current icon. There are options in the Button editor where you can indicate whether you want this label to appear on the button or not.*

   • **Key(s):** *Use this field to enter keyboard shortcuts users can press instead of clicking on the button. Enter alphanumeric keys by typing them; separate multiple keys with an "or" bar (|). Enter keys such as Tab, Enter, and*

Backspace by typing their names. See Authorware's Help for a complete listing of key names that can be used in this field.

- **Options:** *The following options are specific to the Button Interaction Response option.*

    Make Default: *If you are using a standard Authorware or system button from the Button library, selecting the Make Default option displays a heavy line around the button to let the user know that this button is the default choice. When a button is the default choice, pressing the Enter key is the same as clicking on this button. If you have created a custom button, this option is not available.*

    Hide When Inactive: *The default display of an inactive button is to be grayed out. Selecting this option completely removes the display of the button when it is not active or not available for selection.*

- **Cursor:** *Selecting this field brings up a Cursor library in which you can select a custom cursor from those in the library or add custom cursors to this library. With a custom cursor chosen, and Authorware in Run mode, the normal arrow cursor will change to whatever custom cursor you have chosen when the mouse is moved over the button.*

8. Examine the Response tab. Click on the Response tab. This tab will contain the same information and options for each Interaction Response type. The following are the features of this tab.

    - *Icon title and type:* *Previously described.*

    - *Scope Perpetual:* *Selecting this field keeps the interaction response available throughout an entire Authorware file or within a section of that file. This option is available for the following response types: Hot Spot, Hot Object, Target Area, Pull-down Menu, Button, and Conditional. Variables can be used to turn on and off the availability of these perpetual interaction responses.*

    - *Active If:* *This field is used to specify that the interaction response is available only when the condition entered in the Active If field is true. This field can be used in conjunction with response types Hot Spot, Hot Object, Target Area, Pull-down Menu, Keypress, Button, and Time Limit.*

    - *Erase:* *This field provides automatic erase capabilities for the current icon or in the case of a Map icon everything within the Map icon. This erase capability overrides all erase settings that may be contained within this Map icon. The following are the erase options.*

        After Next Entry: *Erases items in this current icon after the user is asked to enter another response or if the interaction is exited.*

        Before Next Entry: *Erases items in this current icon after displaying its content and before the user is asked to enter another response.*

T/P

Many developers like to use the Hide When Inactive option in combination with custom variables to control the presence or absence of buttons being displayed on screen. You will learn how to do this in Chapters 15 and 16.

T/P

Using this custom cursor feature is a very easy way to help give visual cues to the user that this object (the button) can be selected or is interactive. The key to using such visual cues, however, is that you be consistent, using the custom cursor on all buttons.

On Exit: *Leaves the current content on screen until the interaction is exited.*

Don't Erase: *Disables the automatic erase function, leaving current content on screen until an Erase icon or higher-level erase function is used to erase it.*

- **Branch field:** *This field tells Authorware where it should go next after displaying/executing the content of the current icon. The following are the branching options. See figure 9-6.*

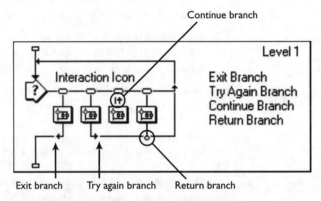

Fig. 9-6. Symbols for branching options associated with interaction responses.

Try Again: *Takes the branching arrow to the right, looping back to the Interaction icon to allow the user to make another selection.*

Continue: *Takes the branching arrow back up through the Response Type symbol to continue to the right, to allow Authorware to immediately check if any other interaction responses to the right might also match the current response.*

Exit Interaction: *Takes the branching arrow to the left and out of the current Interaction icon.*

Return: *Available only if Scope Perpetual has been selected. Takes the branching arrow straight downward, ending with a small circle. Upon hitting the circle, Authorware will return to whatever location the perpetual was called from and continue progress on the flowline at that location.*

- **Status:** *This field is used if you want Authorware to track performance. The options of this field are as follows. See figure 9-7.*

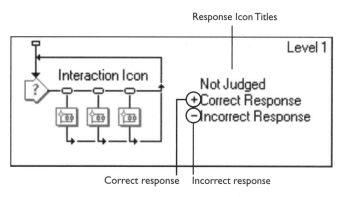

Fig. 9-7. Symbols for the Status field for interaction responses.

Not Judged: *The default setting indicates that Authorware will not track responses to this icon.*

Correct Response: *Indicates that the current icon is a correct response. On the flowline, a correct response is indicated with a plus sign (+) to the left of the icon's title.*

Wrong Response: *Indicates that the current icon is a wrong response. On the flowline, a wrong response is indicated with a minus sign (−) to the left of the icon's title.*

- **Score:** *In this field, you can enter the score you want to associate with this response. The score can be a positive value if the response is correct, or a negative value if the response is incorrect. You can also use an expression in this field.*

This completes this tour. Let's build a few interactive structures.

Practice Exercise 9-1:
Building a Generic Interaction Structure

As Authorware developers and trainers for over ten years, we have seen numerous approaches to developing Authorware structures. Many students have brought examples into class of Authorware structures developed by outside vendors. Some of these structures have been elegant and extremely efficient at what they do.

Other structures that have been brought into class resembled a huge plate of spaghetti with endless strands of entangled variables. Even in the best of cases, frequently these structures have been difficult for the novice and mid-level user to maintain or modify. (Let's leave the spaghetti code for those who are adept at such things, or for those who do not mind "Excedrin headaches.")

Authorware structures can be examined with three main criteria in mind: performance, efficiency, and ease of modification. When examining performance, it is most useful to consider performance from the user's perspective; that is, what the user sees and hears. Frequently performance can be measured in terms of time; for example, how long it takes for a graphic or media element to register or be written to the screen. Typically as developers, we would rather optimize than sacrifice performance.

Efficiency, on the other hand, is most often considered from the developer's perspective. For example, an efficient Authorware program might be characterized as one that offers increased functionality or capability while reducing the number of icons or scripting language being used to accomplish that functionality. Authorware's variables, functions, and global icon controls are frequently used to achieve an efficient Authorware structure. Another way to describe greater efficiency is through the use of global controls that can be set or modified in one or a few places versus the use of controls that are local and must be set or modified at numerous places. Global controls are much more efficient. However, they are frequently difficult for the novice user to modify or "repair" if accidentally "broken."

In considering the last criterion, ease of modification, the perspective taken depends on who will be making the modifications: an experienced developer or new Authorware user. Frequently it is the relatively new Authorware user who will be making modifications.

With this assumption in the mind, we have been willing to sacrifice efficiency in structure for the sake of making it easier for the new Authorware user to understand and modify an "inherited" Authorware project. The "Pickup Truck" interaction structure you will build in exercises that follow grew out of the same assumption: the willingness to sacrifice coding efficiency for the sake of ease of modification by a non-expert Authorware programmer.

Description

Over the years of teaching Authorware classes, we have referred to this structure as the "Pickup Truck" interaction structure because like a pickup truck it is durable and will do most of the things you want it to do. Equally important, this structure helps novice users more quickly troubleshoot display and erase problems associated with the Interaction icon and icons attached to it.

The foundation of the Pickup Truck structure lies in the use of an Interaction icon with attached Map icons. Generally, each of the Maps will contain a Display icon and a Wait icon. Throughout the rest of this chapter you will build the basic Pickup Truck Interaction structure and a couple of variations. The following elements are covered in this exercise.

- *Creating a Button Response Type interaction*
- *Creating a question stem that remains present as feedback is overlaid*
- *Creating a generic question/feedback template*

Take a Look

 CD-ROM

Before beginning the exercise, let's take a look at the exercise in its completed state so that you can clearly see what it is you are about to build.

1. Select File | Open and locate on the companion CD-ROM the directory *Chapter09*. Locate and double click on the file *Exer9-1*.

2. The file *Exer9-1* should now appear in your copy of Authorware. Click on the Restart button to play the file from the top of the flowline. Note the following properties of this completed exercise.

   - *The key to working with this Pickup Truck interaction structure involves drawing an imaginary vertical line between the Interaction icon on the left and the Map icons on the right, as illustrated in figure 9-8.*

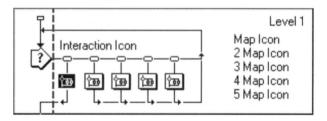

Fig. 9-8. Imagine a vertical line.

   - *There are two guidelines in regard to troubleshooting this Pickup Truck interaction structure: First, if there is a problem with the content in the "question stem" not erasing, pausing, or displaying as it should, try to solve the problem by looking to the left of the imaginary vertical line. Second, if there is a problem with the content for the "feedback" not erasing, pausing, or displaying as it should, try to solve the problem by looking to the right of the imaginary vertical line.*

   - *To modify or troubleshoot any erase, display, or pause issues concerning the question stem, the answer can be found by looking to the left of the imaginary line. Highlight the Interaction icon. Select Modify | Icon | Properties. See figure 9-9. The Properties/Interaction Icon dialog window allows you to change erase characteristics and/or add a pause before exiting. You will practice this in the exercises that follow.*

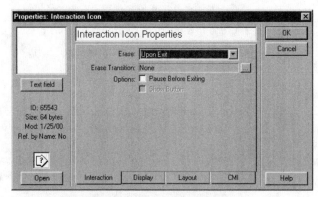

Fig. 9-9. Interaction Icon Properties dialog window.

- To change the content of the question stem, double click on the Interaction icon and make the changes inside the display area.

- To modify or troubleshoot any erase, display, or pause issues concerning the feedback, the solution can be found by looking to the right of the imaginary line.

    To change the erase characteristics, double click on the Response Type symbol above the feedback you want to change, select the Response tab, and change the option in the Erase field (see figure 9-10).

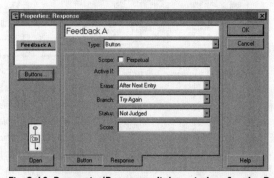

Fig. 9-10. Properties/Response dialog window for the Response tab.

    To change the pause, double click on the Map icon associated with the feedback and place or remove (depending on your desired outcome) a Wait icon at the bottom of the flowline inside this Map icon.

    To change the display, double click on the Map icon associated with the feedback and double click on the Display icon and add/modify text and or graphic objects.

Storyboard: On screen

Figures 9-11 and 9-12 show what the finished presentation will look like.

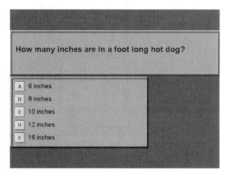

Fig. 9-11. Question stem and responses.

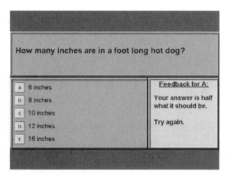

Fig. 9-12. After selecting the first answer, labeled A.

Storyboard: Behind the Scenes

Figure 9-13 shows the main and secondary flowlines (with all icons, their placement, and their names) as they should look when you are finished with this exercise.

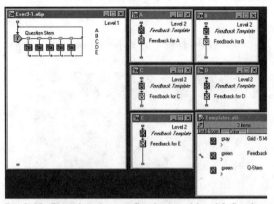

Fig. 9-13. Completed main flowline and level 2 flowlines inside Map icons.

Step-by-Step Instructions

1. Select File | New | File. Close the two Knowledge Object dialog windows.
2. Verify that you are now looking at a new flowline.
3. Set up the file properties.
   a) Select Modify | File | Properties.
   b) Select whatever background color you want.
   c) Verify that Size is set to 640 x 480.
   d) Remove the check marks beside the Tile Bar and Menu Bar options.
   e) Click on the OK button to close the window.
   f) Select File | Save and locate the *SaveWork* directory. Type in *Chap9-1* and click on the OK button.
4. Create the icon structure.
   a) Drag an Interaction icon to the flowline.
   b) Drag a Map icon to the right of the Interaction icon.
   c) The Response Type dialog window has opened. Button Response Type is the default setting. Click on the OK button to accept this default.
   d) Drag a second Map icon to the right of the first Map icon.
   e) Drag three more Map icons to the right of the Interaction icon.
5. Name these icons.
   a) Select the Interaction icon by touching the icon with the mouse, which also highlights the icon title. Type in the new icon name *Question Stem*.
   b) Select the first Map icon and type in (capital) *A*.
   c) Select the second Map icon and type in (capital) *B*.

d) Select the third Map icon and type in (capital) *C*.

e) Select the fourth Map icon and type in (capital) *D*.

f) Select the fifth Map icon and type in (capital) *E*.

6. As you create this interaction structure, you will want to make use of a screen design appropriate to multiple-choice questions.

a) Select File | Open | Library. In the dialog window that has opened, locate the *Chapter09* directory on the companion CD-ROM.

b) Select the library file *Templates.a6l*.

7. Create the background for the Interaction icon *Question Stem*.

a) Let's make use of a screen design template in the library. Locate the Q-Stem icon in the library. Double click on Q-Stem. Note that all objects in this icon have handlebars around them. Copy these objects to the clipboard by selecting Edit | Copy. Close the Library icon.

b) Double click on the Interaction icon *Question Stem*. You are now looking at the display area for this Interaction icon. Note that the buttons A, B, C, D, and E appear on screen. You will move these buttons in material to follow.

c) Select Edit | Paste to place a copy of the screen template into the display area.

8. Create the content for the question stem.

a) Select the Text tool in the toolbox.

b) Click the I-bar cursor on the text object that says *Put Question Stem Here* so that the text object opens. Highlight the current text and type in the following sentence (replacing what is there already):

How many inches are in a foot long hot dog?

Do not worry about the placement or alignment of the text right now. You will take care of that in material to follow.

9. Create the content for the question responses (also within the Interaction icon).

a) Click the I-bar cursor on the text object that says *Put Response A here*. Type in the following response: *6 inches*.

b) Click the I-bar cursor on the text object that says *Put Response B here*. Type in the following response: *8 inches*.

c) Click the I-bar cursor on the text object that says *Put Response C here*. Type in the following response: *10 inches*.

d) Click the I-bar cursor on the text object that says *Put Response D here*. Type in the following response: *12 inches*.

e) Click the I-bar cursor on the text object that says *Put Response E here*. Type in the following response: *16 inches*.

CD-ROM

·T*i*P·

You can drag library icons to the flowline to reuse them intact. In this case, you cannot copy an actual icon into a display area. However, you can take the content of that icon and paste it into the display area. Or you could have dragged the Q-Stem icon from the library and placed it on the flowline, immediately above the Interaction icon.

·T*i*P·

Note that the text object from the Library template already had previously defined text attributes. Therefore, when you clicked the I-bar cursor on it, the text you typed used these previously defined attributes. Templates that include "text samples" such as this (which use the attributes defined in your project's standards) will greatly increase your efficiency in creating display screens.

f) Leave this icon open.

10. Resize and align the buttons. There are two methods you can use to do this.

   a) Let's take a look at the quick and dirty method first. Single click on the A button that is on screen. Drag the A button to the left of the first response. Click on any one of the four corner handlebars and while holding down the left mouse button move the mouse to resize the button. You could continue to resize and reposition the button until you are satisfied with this location and size. However, there is better method to achieve standard-size buttons that are perfectly aligned with the responses.

   b) Double click on the A button. Examine the center of the dialog window. There are X and Y fields for the size of the button, and X and Y fields for the location of the button.

   c) To change the size of the button, click the cursor in the Size/X field and type in 30. Click the cursor in the Size/Y field and type in 30.

   d) To change the location of the button, click the cursor in the Location/X field and type in *15*. Click the cursor in the Location/Y field and type in *222*. See figure 9-14. Close the window.

When you are creating your own grid patterns, remember to account for the size and location of buttons.

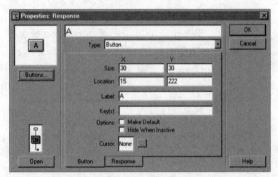

Fig. 9-14. Standardizing the size and location of buttons.

   e) Double click on the B button. Click the cursor in the Size/X field and type in *30*. Click the cursor in the Size/Y field and type in *30*. Click the cursor in the Location/X field and type in *15*. Click the cursor in the Location/Y field and type in *260*. Close the window.

   f) Double click on the C button. Click the cursor in the Size/X field and type in *30*. Click the cursor in the Size/Y field and type in *30*. Click the cursor in the Location/X field and type in *15*. Click the cursor in the Location/Y field and type in *298*. Close the window.

   g) Double click on the D button. Click the cursor in the Size/X field and type in *30*. Click the cursor in the Size/Y field and type in *30*. Click the cursor in the Location/X field and type in *15*. Click the cursor in the Location/Y field and type in *337*. Close the window.

h) Double click on the E button. Click the cursor in the Size/X field and type in *30*. Click the cursor in the Size/Y field and type in *30*. Click the cursor in the Location/X field and type in *15*. Click the cursor in the Location/Y field and type in *375*. Close the window.

i) Jump to the flowline (Ctrl + J keys).

11. Add feedback for each response.

a) Double click on the A Map icon (associated with the A button), opening it. From the library, drag the Display icon *Feedback Template* to the flowline inside this Map icon. Drag a Display icon from the Icon palette and place it on the level 2 flowline, below the *Feedback Template* Display icon. Label this new Display icon *Feedback for A*. Double click on this Display icon to open it. Click on the Text tool, click the I-bar cursor somewhere on the screen, and type in *Feedback for A*. To create a second text object, click the I-bar cursor somewhere else on screen and type in the feedback *Your answer is half what it should be. Try again*. Do not worry about the placement of these text objects. You will establish that in material to follow.

b) Double click on the B Map icon, opening it. From the library, drag the Display icon *Feedback Template* to the flowline inside this Map icon. Drag a Display icon from the Icon palette and place it on the level 2 flowline, below the *Feedback Template* Display icon. Label this new Display icon *Feedback for B*. Double click on this Display icon to open it. Click on the Text tool, click the I-bar cursor on the screen, and type in *Feedback for B*. Click the I-bar cursor somewhere else on screen and type in the feedback *Your answer is still short. Try again*.

c) Double click on the C Map icon, opening it. From the library, drag the Display icon *Feedback Template* to the flowline inside this Map icon. Drag a Display icon from the Icon palette and place it on the level 2 flowline, below the *Feedback Template* Display icon. Label this new Display icon *Feedback for C*. Double click on this Display icon to open it. Click on the Text tool, click the I-bar cursor on the screen, and type in *Feedback for C*. Click the I-bar cursor somewhere else on screen and type in the feedback *Your answer may be right after cooking the dog. Try again*.

d) Double click on the D Map icon, opening it. From the library, drag the Display icon *Feedback Template* to the flowline inside this Map icon. Drag a Display icon from the Icon palette and place it on the level 2 flowline, below the *Feedback Template* Display icon. Label this new Display icon *Feedback for D*. Double click on this Display icon to open it. Click on the Text tool, click the I-bar cursor on the screen, and type in *Feedback for D*. Click the I-bar cursor somewhere else on screen and type in the feedback *Your answer is correct.*

e) Double click on the E Map icon, opening it. From the library, drag the Display icon *Feedback Template* to the flowline inside this Map icon. Drag a Display icon from the Icon palette and place it on the level 2 flowline, below the *Feedback Template* Display icon. Label this new Display icon *Feedback for E*. Double click on this Display icon to open it. Click on the Text tool, click the I-bar cursor on the screen, and type in *Feedback for E*. Click the I-bar cursor somewhere else on screen and type in the feedback *Your answer would only be considered correct in the state of Texas. Try again.*

12. Let's take a look at what you have at this point.

a) Click on the white Start Flag button in the toolbar.

b) Click on the A button. Press Ctrl + P to pause the program. Double click on the feedback window. Single click on the background to get rid of the selection handlebars. Single click on the text object *Feedback for A*. Position this object at the top of the feedback overlay window. Position the feedback text appropriately within the feedback window. Resize the margins of either of the text objects if necessary. Press Ctrl + P to play the program.

c) Click on the B button. Press Ctrl + P to pause the program. Double click on the feedback window. Single click on the background to get rid of the selection handlebars. Single click on the text object *Feedback for B*. Position this object at the top of the feedback overlay window (see figure 9-12). Position the feedback text appropriately within the feedback window. Resize the margins of either of the text objects if necessary. Press Ctrl + P to play the program.

d) Continue this process for C, D, and E, aligning both the feedback header (Feedback for X) and the feedback text.

13. Let's take a look at what is controlling the current display and erase characteristics.

a) Jump to the flowline (Ctrl + J).

b) Double click on the Response Type symbol for the A response.

c) Click on the Response tab at the bottom of the dialog window.

d) Examine the Erase Field. It is currently set to After Next Entry. Recall that upon selecting the A button, the feedback for A was displayed on screen and remained on screen until after you made a second selection. The erase description in this case accurately describes the resulting erase characteristic.

NOTE

The feedback for the first response is being displayed and will remain on screen until after you make another selection.

NOTE

The feedback for the second response is now displayed, and the feedback for the first response has been erased.

14. Let's take another look, observing what happens after you make each selection.

    a) Click on the Restart button and select each of the wrong answers (A, B, C and E). Note that the feedback for each wrong answer tells us to . . . Try Again. This is typical of self-mastery type of questions, where the answer is not being evaluated. The question becomes a learning event as the learner eventually "discovers" the correct answer.

    b) Click on the correct answer (D). Note that even after selecting the correct answer, we end up back at the question stem again. In fact, look at figure 9-13. This illustration clearly shows that each branch circles back to the question stem. We will take care of this situation in the next exercise. This is a work in progress.

15. Save your work to this point by selecting File | Save.

Practice Exercise 9-2: Completing the Generic Interaction Structure

Description

Let's change the structure you created in the previous exercise so that the feedback (with a Continue button) will be displayed after selecting an answer but erase *before* you return to the question stem to try again. The following elements are covered in this exercise.

- *Modifying a Button Response Type interaction*
- *Investigating structural elements that influence pause and erase characteristics*
- *Creating feedback that overlays the question stem*
- *Creating a generic interaction structure*

Take a Look

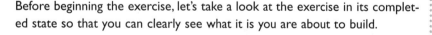

CD-ROM

Before beginning the exercise, let's take a look at the exercise in its completed state so that you can clearly see what it is you are about to build.

1. Select File | Open and locate on the companion CD-ROM the directory *Chapter09*. Locate and double click on the file *Exer9-2*.

2. The file *Exer9-2* should now appear in your copy of Authorware. Click on the Restart button to play the file from the top of the flowline. Take a look at the completed model and then see if you can figure out what changes you will need to make to achieve these results. Note the following properties of this completed exercise.

NOTE

The feedback is erased *before* you make another selection.

- *Select the A button. Note that the feedback for A is displayed on screen, with a Continue button below the text. Also note that all buttons have now disappeared. Click on the Continue button. Note that the feedback for A has erased, and all the buttons have reappeared.*

- *Select the B button. The feedback for B is displayed, with a Continue button. Click on the Continue button.*

- *Select the correct answer, D. Note that Authorware now exits the interaction and everything on screen erases, without an Erase icon.*

Storyboard: On screen

When you are finished with this exercise, your screen should look like that shown in figure 9-15 before you make a selection. This looks the same as in the last exercise. Figure 9-16 shows the screen after you select A. The difference is that the current exercise includes a Continue button, whereas the last exercise did not.

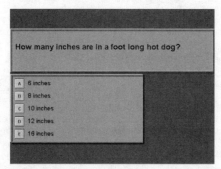

Fig. 9-15. Question stem before selection.

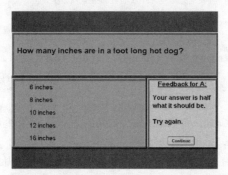

Fig. 9-16. Question stem after selecting the first answer, labeled A.

Storyboard: Behind the Scenes

When you are finished with this exercise, the main flowline and the flowline inside each Map icon should look like those shown in figure 9-17.

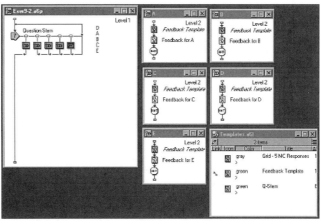

Fig. 9-17. Main flowline, and level 2 flowlines inside Map icons.

The settings for the Button tab and Response tab for the correct answer (D) should look like those shown in figures 9-18 and 9-19.

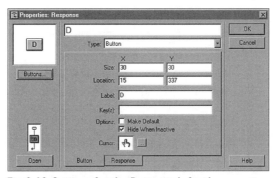

Fig. 9-18. Settings for the Button tab for the correct answer (D).

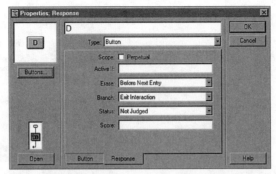

Fig. 9-19. Settings for the Response tab for the correct answer (D).

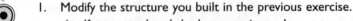

Step-by-Step Instructions

1. Modify the structure you built in the previous exercise.

   a) If you completed the last exercise and want to use the file you created, select File | Open | File and locate on your computer's hard drive the *SaveWork* directory and select file *Chap9-1*.
   Or

   b) If you did not complete the last exercise, select File | Open | File and locate on the companion CD-ROM the *Chapter09* directory and select file *Exer9-1*.

2. Select File | Save As and locate the *SaveWork* directory. Type in the name *Chap9-2* and click on the OK button.

3. You are going to modify the structure you have already created to achieve a different instructional result. First, let's change the erase characteristic for all feedback so that these responses will display after an answer is chosen but will erase *before* another selection is made (assuming the wrong answer is selected).

   a) Double click on the Response Type symbol above the *A* Map icon.

   b) Click on the Response tab.

   c) In the Erase field, select *Before Next Entry*.

   d) Click on the Button tab.

   e) Toward the bottom, find Options. Click in the box to the left of Hide When Inactive. This will make the answer buttons disappear when inappropriate for selection.

   f) We are also going to add another feature here, including the use of a custom cursor. At the very bottom of the window, there is the Cursor option, with an empty field next to it. To the right of the empty field is a button. Click on this button. The Cursor Library is now open. Use the scroll bar on the right to scroll down to the bottom. Click on the "Hand Cursor." Click on the OK button to close the Cursor library. Now while in the Run mode, as the user moves the cursor over the button, the standard cursor will change to the Hand cursor, visually indicating that the button is "selectable."

g) Click on the OK button to close the dialog window.

4. Add the Continue button.
   a) Double click on the *A* Map icon.
   b) Drag a Wait icon to the flowline inside the *A* Map icon, below the Display icon.
   c) Click on the white Start Flag button.
   d) Click on the A button. Pause the program (Ctrl + P). Drag the Continue button so that it is centered at the bottom of the overlay window for the feedback for A (see figure 9-16). Resume play (Ctrl + P). Click on the Continue button.

5. Examine the results of the previous changes.
   a) Click on the A button again.
   b) Click on the Continue button. Looks good.
   c) These changes should now replicate the completed model you looked at earlier in the "Take-a-Look" section. The feedback is displayed with a Continue button. After clicking on the Continue button, the feedback is erased as Authorware returns to the question stem so that another selection can be made.

6. Make the same changes for Map icons B, C, D, and E.
   a) Double click on the Response Type symbol above the *B* Map icon. Click on the Response tab. Select Before Next Entry in the Erase field. Click on the Button tab. Select Hide When Inactive. Select the option The Hand for the cursor style. Click on the OK button. Double click on the *B* Map icon. Drag a Wait icon to the flowline inside the *B* Map icon, below the Display icon.
   b) Double click on the Response Type symbol above the *C* Map icon. Click on the Response tab. Select Before Next Entry in the Erase field. Click on the Button tab. Select Hide When Inactive. Select the option The Hand for the cursor style. Click on the OK button. Double click on the *C* Map icon. Drag a Wait icon to the flowline inside the *C* Map icon, below the Display icon.
   c) Double click on the Response Type symbol above the *D* Map icon. Click on the Response tab. Select Before Next Entry in the Erase field. Click on the Button tab. Select Hide When Inactive. Select the option The Hand as the cursor type. Click on the OK button. Double

click on the *D* Map icon. Drag a Wait icon to the flowline inside of the *D* Map icon, below the Display icon.

d) Double click on the Response Type symbol above the *E* Map icon. Click on the Response tab. Select Before Next Entry in the Erase field. Click on the Button tab. Select Hide When Inactive. Select the option The Hand as the cursor type. Click on the OK button. Double click on the *E* Map icon. Drag a Wait icon to the flowline inside the *E* Map icon, below the Display icon.

7. Click on the white Start Flag button. Select each response. If you need to adjust or modify anything you see on screen, simply pause and make your adjustments. Resume play when ready.

8. You have probably noticed that you are still not done. For example, if you select the correct answer, *D*, the current branch characteristic is Try Again. For the correct response, the appropriate branch is to exit the interaction.
   a) Click on the Response Type symbol for *D*.
   b) Click on the pull-down menu in the Branch field.
   c) Select Exit Interaction.
   d) Click on the OK button.

9. Click on the white Start Flag button. Select *D*. Click on the Continue button. You should now have a blank screen, as you have exited the interaction.

10. Let's make it easier to locate the correct answer with the Exit branch, and distinguish it from the other responses.
    a) Select the Map icon *D*.
    b) Hold the mouse button down and drag the Map icon *D*, carefully placing it in the very first position to the right of the Interaction icon.
    c) Click on the Restart button and select a few answers. Changing the location of the Map icon should not have produced any change in how the interaction looks on screen or in how it functions.

11. Save your work by selecting File | Save.

The interaction that you have just built is a pretty solid question/feedback structure that is easy to modify and reuse. The instructional design here is to present the learner with a question; after an incorrect selection, overlay feedback and as the learner returns to the question to try again, the feedback is erased. With the selection of the correct answer, feedback is provided and the question is exited. This is one instructional design; in the next exercise you create a structure to reflect another instructional design.

CAUTION

If you happen to mistakingly drop the Map on the main flowline instead of in the very first postion to the right of the Interaction icon ... STOP ... and immediately select Edit | Undo. Otherwise, you will end up redoing all the settings for this Map as you drag it back into place.

Practice Exercise 9-3:
Modifying the Generic Structure to Erase a Stem

Description

In this exercise, the instructional design calls for a change to the previous structure. In this new variation, the goal is to erase the question stem after each selection, as you examine the feedback for that selection. There will still be a Continue button on the feedback screen. After you click on that Continue button, you will see the question stem again. This exercise will hopefully reinforce the idea that the Pickup Truck interaction structure is easy to understand and to modify. This is a useful structure when the feedback involves a large graphic. The following elements are covered in this exercise.

- *Modifying a Button Response Type interaction*
- *Investigating structural elements that influence pause and erase characteristics*
- *Creating feedback that replaces the question stem*
- *Creating a generic interaction structure*

Take a Look

| CD-ROM |

Before beginning the exercise, let's take a look at the exercise in its completed state so that you can clearly see what it is you are about to build.

1. Select File | Open and locate on the companion CD-ROM the directory *Chapter09*. Locate and double click on the file *Exer9-3*.

2. The file *Exer9-3* should now appear in your copy of Authorware. Click on the Restart button to play the file from the top of the flowline. Examine the completed model and then see if you can figure out what changes you need to make to achieve this result. Note the following properties of this completed exercise.

    - *Select the A button. Note that the question stem has been erased as the feedback for A is displayed on screen, with a Continue button below the text. Also note that all the buttons have now disappeared. Click on the Continue button. Note that the feedback for A has been erased, and all buttons have reappeared, along with the question.*

    - *Select the D button. The feedback for D is displayed with a Continue button. Click on the Continue button.*

Storyboard: On screen

When you are finished with this exercise, your screen should look like that shown in figure 9-20 before you make a selection, and like that shown in figure 9-21 after you make a selection.

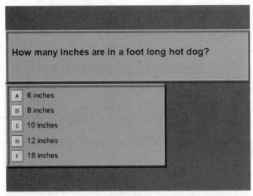

Fig. 9-20. Question stem before selection.

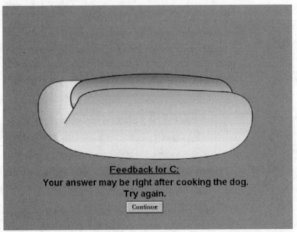

Fig. 9-21. After selecting C.

Storyboard: Behind the Scenes

When you are finished with this exercise, the main flowline and the level 2 flowline inside each Map icon should look like those shown in figure 9-22.

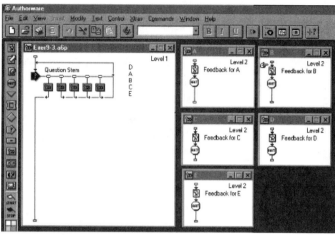

Fig. 9-22. Main flowline with level 2 flowlines.

The settings for the Properties/Interaction Icon dialog window should set as shown in figure 9-23.

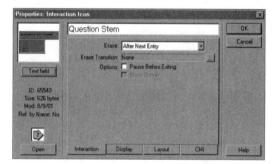

Fig. 9-23. Properties/Interaction Icon dialog window.

Step-by-Step Instructions

Go Solo

1. Modify the structure you built in the previous exercise.
   a) If you completed the last exercise, select File | Open | File and locate on your computer's hard drive the *SaveWork* directory and select the file *Chap9-2.*
   Or
   b) If you did not complete the last exercise, select File | Open | File and locate on the companion CD-ROM the *Chapter09* directory and select the file *Exer9-2.*

(NOTE)

In this case you want to change the erase characteristics of the question stem, and therefore you need to look to the left of the imaginary line.

Our new instructional design calls for erasing the question stem after a response has been chosen. The last two options listed in the Erase field, Upon Exit and Don't Erase, are clearly not what you want. The first option is what you want to choose, but unfortunately the label does not accurately describe the action actually taken. A more accurate label would read Before Next Entry.

2. Select File | Save As and locate the *SaveWork* directory. Type in the name *Chap9-3* and click on the OK button.

3. Instead of building this variation from scratch, let's use our previous model and make changes to it. You will change the erase characteristic for the Interaction icon *Erase Question*.
   a) Select the Interaction icon Question Stem.
   b) Select Modify | Icon | Properties.
   c) In the dialog window that opens, in the Erase field, select After Next Entry. Click on the OK button.

4. Change the feedback screens, so that each feedback screen displays a graphic along with the text.
   a) Double click on the *A* Map icon.
   b) Double click on the Display icon *Feedback for A*. Press the space bar to deselect all objects. Click on the overlay window and press the Delete key. The two text objects should remain.
   c) Select File | Import and in the dialog window that appears use the browse function to locate the *Chapter09* directory on the companion CD-ROM, and select the file *6inchDog.jpg*. Click on the Import button. While the graphic is still selected, select Modify | Send to Back. You should now be able to see the text.
   d) Arrange the objects on screen where you want them to be by selecting and moving them one at a time.

5. Test this change.
   a) Click on the Restart button to run to program.
   b) Click on the A button. The question stem should have been erased, being replaced by a full screen graphic of the 6-inch hot dog and text. Click on the Continue button. The question stem should reappear.

6. Make the same changes for Map icons *B, C, D,* and *E*.
   a) Double click on the *B* Map icon.
   b) Double click on the Display icon *Feedback for B*. Press the space bar to deselect all objects. Click on the overlay window and press the Delete key. The two text objects should remain.
   c) Select File | Import and in the dialog window that appears locate and select the graphic *8inchDog.jpg*. Click on the Import button. While the graphic is still selected, select Modify | Send to Back. You should now be able to see the text.
   d) Arrange the objects on screen where you want them to be by selecting and moving them one at a time.
   e) Double click on the *C* Map icon.

f)   Double click on the Display icon *Feedback for C.* Press the space bar to deselect all objects. Click on the overlay window and press the Delete key. The two text objects should remain.

g)   Select File | Import and in the dialog window that appears locate and select the graphic *10inchDog.jpg.* Click on the Import button. While the graphic is still selected, select Modify | Send to Back. You should now be able to see the text.

h)   Arrange the objects on screen where you want them to be by selecting and moving them one at a time.

i)   Double click on the *D* Map icon.

j)   Double click on the Display icon *Feedback for D.* Press the space bar to deselect all objects. Click on the overlay window and press the Delete key. The two text objects should remain.

k)   Select File | Import and in the dialog window that appears locate and select the graphic *12inchDog.jpg.* Click on the Import button. While the graphic is still selected, select Modify | Send to Back. You should now be able to see the text.

l)   Arrange the objects on screen where you want them to be by selecting and moving them one at a time.

m) Double click on the *E* Map icon.

n)   Double click on the Display icon *Feedback for E.* Press the space bar to deselect all objects. Click on the overlay window and press the Delete key. The two text objects should remain.

o)   Select File | Import and in the dialog window that appears locate and select the graphic *16inchDog.jpg.* Click on the Import button. While the graphic is still selected, select Modify | Send to Back. You should now be able to see the text.

p)   Arrange the objects on screen where you want them to be by selecting and moving them one at a time.

7.   Save your work by selecting File | Save.

Summary

- *The Interaction icon is the heart of Authorware. The Interaction icon provides the capability to the user to interact with the learning program using a wide variety of instructional techniques.*

- *All of these instructional techniques are built into Authorware and are available "out of the box" to you as author/programmer without doing any programming.*

- *In the first guided tour your looked at the Interaction icon properties.*

- *Characteristics of the Interaction icon include the following.*

    Display screen and toolbox (similar to the Display icon)

Branching determined by user selection

- *In contrast, the Decision icon:*

    Does not include a display screen

    Does include branching determined by author/programmer

- *The Interaction icon provides a number of properties, including automatic erase functions, erase transitions, branching options, and others.*

- *In the second guided tour, the interaction response types were looked at in detail.*

- *Authorware provides you with a large number of interactive strategies you can select with a click of the mouse, including the following.*

    Button: *A 3D-looking button (appears to depress upon selection) that can use the system button or custom buttons that you can create.*

    Hot Spot: *To set up any rectangular area as a selectable area the user can click or double-click on, or position the cursor over, to trigger a response.*

    Hot Object: *To create an object the user can click or double-click on, or position the cursor over, to trigger a response.*

    Target Area: *Use target area response when you want the user to drag an object into a specified area in the interaction display.*

    Pull-down Menu: *To create a pull-down menu like that found in most software applications.*

    Conditional: *To create an interaction that will evaluate the condition or value of a given constant, variable, or function.*

    Text Entry: *Allows the user to type text into an entry field. User entries can be evaluated for specific values, multiple values, or wildcards.*

    Tries Limit: *Used to set a maximum number of attempts Authorware will allow the user.*

    Time Limit: *Used to set a maximum amount of time Authorware will allow the user.*

    Event: *Used to interact with Xtras that send events, such as ActiveX controls.*

- *The third guided tour examined Button interaction response properties.*

- *The focus of the first practice exercise was to build a generic interaction structure. This structure can help novice users more quickly troubleshoot display and erase problems associated with Interaction icons. The key to working with this interaction model involves drawing an imaginary vertical line between the Interaction icon on the left and the Map icons on the right.*

- *The focus of the second practice exercise was to complete the generic interaction so that the feedback was displayed, with a Continue button. The feedback was erased after the Continue button was pressed.*

- *The focus of the third practice exercise was to change the generic interaction so that the feedback is displayed full screen as the question stem is erased. The feedback was erased after the Continue button was pressed.*

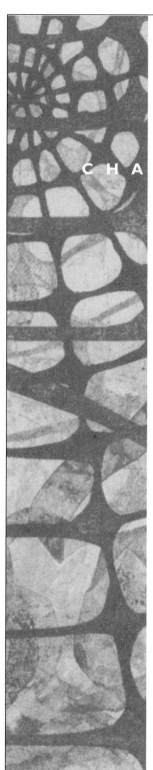

C H A P T E R

10

Creating

Interactions –

Part One

Introduction

From the previous chapter, you know that the button response is only one of many types of interactions Authorware is capable of providing, "out of the box" and without any programming. These other interaction response types greatly expand the possibilities for instructional strategies that actively engage the learner. These other strategies could not be accomplished if programming were restricted to the use of "button choices" only. In this chapter you will create interactive structures that not only illustrate the use of these other engaging strategies but can be reused later with your own content. By the end of the chapter you will be able to:

• *Describe the general capabilities and properties of the Hot Spot response type*

• *Create Hot Spot response interaction structures*

• *Describe the general capabilities and properties of the Hot Object response type*

• *Create Hot Object response interaction structures*

Guided Tour 10A: Hot Spot Interaction Response and Properties

The Hot Spot response type is most frequently used with photographs or graphic elements that do not lend themselves to buttons. In contrast to the button that is clearly visible on screen, the Hot Spot response does *not* have any visible indicator on screen. The Hot Spot uses an invisible rectangular "wireframe" that can be resized and positioned to correspond to the desired "hot spot" on a photograph or graphic. In other words, the graphic displayed on screen contains the only visual clue as to what the user needs to select. Let's take a quick look at the properties of the Hot Spot interaction response.

1. Start by opening a new file.
    a) Select File | New | File.
    b) Close the two dialog windows that have opened.
    c) Verify that you are now looking at an empty flowline.

2. Drag an Interaction icon to the flowline. Drag a Map icon and drop it to the right of the Interaction icon.

3. The Response Type window should now be open. Click on the Hot Spot option and then click on the OK button.

4. Double click on the Response Type symbol above the Map icon to access the dialog window for this Hot Spot interaction response.

5. You should be looking at the Properties/Response dialog window, shown in figure 10-1. There are three parts of this window, but we will only

·T*i*P·

You can also highlight the Map icon and then select Modify | Icon | Response to bring up this same dialog. Or you can highlight the icon and use the keyboard shortcut Ctrl + E.

briefly look at one of them, the Hot Spot tab. The left-hand side and the Response tab are identical to those you saw in Chapter 9 in regard to the Button interaction response, so we will not repeat them here.

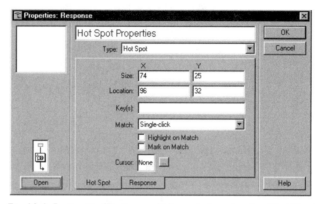

Fig. 10-1. Properties/Response dialog window showing Hot Spot tab.

6. Select the Hot Spot tab, if it is not already on top. See figure 10-1. Review the following explanations of the options on this tab.

    • **Size and Location fields:** *These fields are identical to those you saw in Chapter 9 in regard to the Button tab. The only difference is that instead of resizing and positioning a button, you are using the X and Y coordinates in these fields to establish what area (pixel locations) will register a match when the user clicks within this area. These coordinates define the hot spot "wireframe" for the current response.*

    • **Key(s) and Cursor fields:** *These fields are identical to those you saw in Chapter 9 for the Button tab.*

    • **Match:** *Use this field to define how the user can match the response. The options in this field are as follows.*

        Single-click: *The user clicks on the hot spot once to match this response. This is the default setting.*

        Double-click: *The user double clicks on the hot spot to match this response.*

        Cursor in Area: *Authorware matches this response when the user moves the cursor through the hot spot area without clicking.*

    • **Highlight on Match:** *Place a check mark in this field to display an inverse image of the hot spot when the user clicks on it. The inverse color is displayed until the user releases the mouse button. For example, if the hot spot area is white, it changes to black; if the hot spot is a color, it changes to its inverse color.*

- **Mark on Match:** *Place a check mark in this field to place a small square symbol in the inside left edge of the hot spot. The square is empty until the user matches the response. At that time, Authorware fills in the square.*

- **Cursor:** *You saw this field in regard to the Button response type in Chapter 9. This option allows you to select a custom cursor.*

In Practice Exercise 10-1 you will begin building a hot spot interaction.

Practice Exercise 10-1: Hot Spot Interaction

Description

In this exercise you will create an interactive strategy in which you ask the user to click the mouse on elements included in a graphic. Specifically, there will be a number of objects hanging on a pegboard from which you want to user to select the object most appropriate to general safety in regard to hiking on trails in the mountains.

The Button response type is great for text- or number-based selections. However, in this case you have graphic representations of the tools, so you will use the Hot Spot response type. In most cases you will want to provide feedback concerning incorrect selections, which you will do here. In addition, you will also include one hot spot that will trigger feedback when the cursor simply moves through the Hot Spot target area (the mouse click is *not* required). This "cursor in the area" action response is included not because the example requires it but because it demonstrates how to create one. The following elements are covered in this exercise.

- *Importing an external graphic and creating text objects*
- *Creating user feedback based on selection made*
- *Creating several Hot Spot responses triggered by a mouse click in the target area*
- *Creating a Hot Spot response triggered by passing the cursor through the target area*
- *Creating a "Catch-all-else" response area*
- *Selecting a custom cursor*
- *Enabling automatic erase functions*
- *Modifying branching functions of the Interaction icon*

Take a Look

Before beginning the exercise, let's take a look at the exercise in its completed state so that you can clearly see what it is you are about to build.

CD-ROM

1. Select File | Open and locate on the CD-ROM the directory named *Chapter10* and the file named *Exer10-1*. Double click on *Exer10-1*.

2. The file *Exer10-1* should now appear in your copy of Authorware. Click on the Restart button to play the file from the top of the flowline. Note the following properties of this completed exercise.

   • *When the cursor passes through a target area for each Hot Spot response, the normal arrow cursor will change to a hand cursor while it remains within the target area. As soon as the cursor leaves the target area, it changes back to the normal cursor symbol.*

   • *When you click on most of the hot spots, an overlay text window appears, providing feedback specific to that choice. This window also contains a Continue button. When the Continue button is selected, the feedback window is erased.*

   • *When the cursor passes through the DoubleClip hot spot, an overlay text window appears and remains on screen as long as the cursor is in the target area, providing feedback (with no Continue button). As soon as the cursor is moved out of the target area, the feedback window is erased.*

   • *If the user clicks on the screen anywhere outside a predefined hot spot for an object, an overlay text window appears providing generic feedback. This window also contains a Continue button. When the Continue button is selected, the feedback window is erased.*

   • *If the user selects a wrong answer, feedback is provided, and the user is returned to the interaction to try again.*

   • *If the user selects the correct answer, feedback is provided, and the user will then exit the interaction.*

   • *There are no erase icons used in this icon structure. All erasing is accomplished using the automatic erase function of the Interaction icon and the automatic erase function of responses.*

Storyboard: On screen

Figures 10-2 through 10-4 show you what the finished presentation will look like. Figure 10-2 shows what is inside the Interaction icon *Tools*. Figure 10-3 shows what is presented on screen for one of the feedback Display icons (*Rope*). Figure 10-4 shows what the Interaction icon looks like on screen when the icon is paused so that all Hot Spot wireframes can be seen.

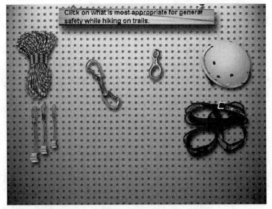

Fig. 10-2. Interaction icon **Tools.**

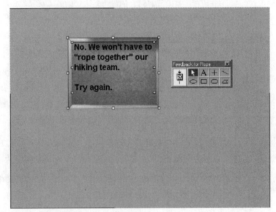

Fig. 10-3. Display icon **Rope.**

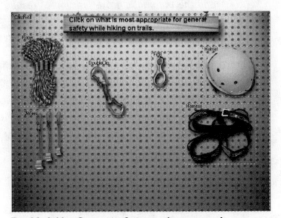

Fig. 10-4. Hot Spot wireframes when paused.

Storyboard: Behind the Scenes

Figure 10-5 shows the main and secondary flowlines (with all icons, their placement, and their names) as they should look when you are finished with this exercise. The settings for the *Rope* response are representative of most of the other responses. Figure 10-6 shows the Properties/Response dialog window for the Map icon *Rope* (for the Hot Spot tab), and figure 10-7 shows the Response tab. The *DoubleClip* response will be triggered by the cursor moving within the area, and therefore an additional graphic has been included to illustrate this setting. Figure 10-8 shows the Properties/Response dialog window for the Map icon *DoubleClip* (for the Hot Spot tab).

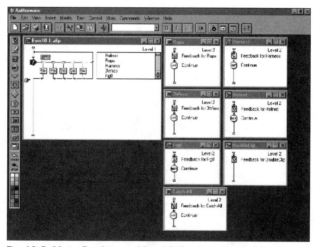

Fig. 10-5. Main flowline and level 2 flowlines inside Map icons.

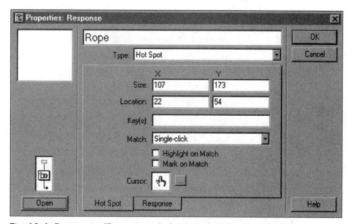

Fig. 10-6. Properties/Response dialog window for the Map icon Rope (Hot Spot tab).

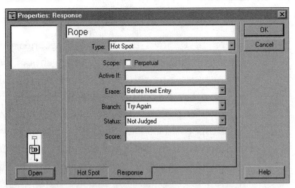

Fig. 10-7. Properties/Response dialog window for the Map icon **Rope** *(Response tab).*

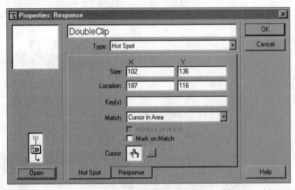

Fig. 10-8. Properties/Response dialog window for the Map icon **DoubleClip** *(Hot Spot tab).*

Step-by-Step Instructions

1. Select File | New | File. Close the two Knowledge Object dialog windows.

2. You should now be looking at a new flowline.

3. Set up the file properties.
    a) Select Modify | File | Properties.
    b) Select whatever background color you want.
    c) Verify that Size is set to 640 x 480.
    d) Remove the check marks beside the Tile Bar and Menu Bar options.
    e) Click on the OK button to close the window.
    f) Select File | Save and locate the *SaveWork* directory. Type in *Chap10-1* and click on the OK button.

4. Create the basic icon structure.

Go Solo

a) Drag an Interaction icon to the flowline. Name this icon *Tools*.

b) Drag a Map icon and place it to the right of the Interaction icon. The Response Type dialog window has opened. See figure 10-9. Select the Hot Spot option and then click on the OK button. Name this Map icon *Rope*.

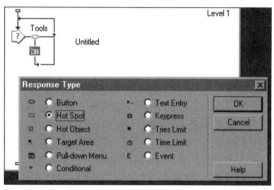

Fig. 10-9. Response Type dialog window showing Hot Spot option selected.

c) Drag another Map icon and place it to the right the Map icon *Rope*. Name this icon *Harness*.

d) Drag another Map icon and place it to the right of the Map icon *Harness*. Name this icon *3Wires*.

e) Drag another Map icon and place it to the right of the Map icon *3Wires*. Name this icon *Helmet*.

f) Drag another Map icon and place it to the right of the Map icon *Helmet*. Name this icon *Fig8*.

g) Drag another Map icon and place it to the right of the Map icon *Fig8*. Name this icon *DoubleClip*.

h) Drag another Map icon and place it to the right of the Map icon *DoubleClip*. Name this icon *Catch-All*.

5. Place icons inside the Map icons to provide feedback and pause functionality before the feedback is erased.

a) Double click on the Map icon *Rope*. Drag a Display icon to the level 2 flowline inside this Map icon. Name this Display icon *Feedback for Rope*. Drag a Wait icon to the level 2 flowline and place it below the Display icon. Label it *Continue*. Click on the X in the upper right-hand corner of the Map's title bar to close the Map icon.

b) Double click on the Map icon *Harness*. Drag a Display icon to the level 2 flowline inside this Map icon. Name this Display icon *Feedback for Harness*. Drag a Wait icon to the level 2 flowline and place it below the Display icon. Label it *Continue*. Close the Map icon.

·T*i*P·

Note that the Response Type dialog window did not open this time. Authorware assumed that because you previously selected Hot Spot for the last response type you would want this type again. Most of the time this assumption will be correct. However, you can always change the response type by double clicking on the Response Type symbol. This opens the dialog window for response types (see figure 10-8), in which you can use the Type field to make another selection.

c) Double click on the Map icon *3Wires*. Drag a Display icon to the level 2 flowline inside this Map icon. Name this Display icon *Feedback for 3Wires*. Drag a Wait icon to the level 2 flowline and place it below the Display icon. Label it *Continue*. Close the Map icon.

d) Double click on the Map icon *Helmet*. Drag a Display icon to the level 2 flowline inside this Map icon. Name this Display icon *Feedback for Helmet*. Drag a Wait icon to the level 2 flowline and place it below the Display icon. Label it *Continue*. Close the Map icon.

e) Double click on the Map icon *Fig8*. Drag a Display icon to the level 2 flowline inside this Map icon. Name this Display icon *Feedback for Fig8*. Drag a Wait icon to the level 2 flowline and place it below the Display icon. Label it *Continue*. Close the Map icon.

f) Double click on the Map icon *DoubleClip*. Drag a Display icon to the level 2 flowline inside this Map icon. Name this Display icon *Feedback for DoubleClip*. Close the Map icon. Do *not* place a Wait icon in this Map.

g) Double click on the Map icon *Catch-All*. Drag a Display icon to the level 2 flowline inside this Map icon. Name this Display icon *Feedback for Catch-All*. Drag a Wait icon to the level 2 flowline and place it below the Display icon. Label it *Continue*. Close the Map icon.

6. Set up the content: the graphic of the pegboard that includes all tools for the interaction.

a) Double click on the Interaction icon *Tools* to open the display area.

b) Select File | Import. The *Import which file?* dialog window opens.

c) On the bottom of this window, select Show Preview (place a check mark there).

d) Use the *Look in* Field to browse to the CD-ROM, and look in the *Chapter10* directory. Locate and select the graphic *Pegboard.jpg*. Click on the Import button.

e) Position the graphic in the display area.

f) Select the Text tool. Select Text | Font, and then select Arial. Select Text | Size, and then select 12. Select Text | Style, and then select Bold. Select Window | Inspectors | Modes, and then select Transparent.

g) Click the I-bar cursor on the wooden sign at the top of the pegboard and type in *Click on what is most appropriate for general safety while hiking on trails*.

h) Select the Pointer tool and resize the text margins and position of the text object so that it fits within the wooden sign (as illustrated in figure 10-2).

7. Create links to the various areas of the pegboard graphic.

a) Verify that the Interaction icon *Tools* is still open.

CD-ROM

·T*i*P·

If Arial is not on the list shown, select Other to bring up the Font dialog window. From the options listed, select Arial or a similar font.

NOTE

This step illustrates again why it is so important to label the icons with descriptive names. Because you did this labeling in step 4, you can now easily locate and position the appropriate wireframe hot spots over the appropriate area of the graphic.

NOTE

Remember that when Authorware is in Run mode, it will automatically stop on empty icons. In this case, the Display icon *Feedback for Rope* is empty and waiting for your input. The presence of a toolbox indicates that you are looking at an open display area (either a Display icon or the display area for an Interaction icon).

b) Carefully look for wireframes (the dotted-line rectangles that indicate hot spots) on screen and find the one labeled *Rope*. Click the cursor directly on one of the four sides of this wireframe rectangle. Hold the mouse button down and drag the wireframe rectangle so that it is on top of the picture of the rope. Release the mouse button. Click on one of the handlebars (gray squares) in the corner of the rectangle, and while holding down the mouse button drag the dotted line to change the shape of the target area. Drag and stretch the target area so that it is slightly larger than the area of the rope. See figure 10-10 for reference.

c) Locate, reposition, and enlarge each target hot spot over its corresponding graphic image. See figure 10-10 for reference.

d) When you have reached the Catch-All wireframe, stretch this rectangle so that it covers the entire screen.

e) When finished, your hot spots should look like those shown in figure 10-10.

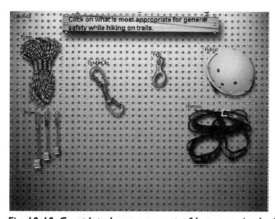

*Fig. 10-10. Completed arrangement of hot spots in the Interaction icon **Tools**.*

8. Add the content for each of the feedback Display icons. The easiest way to do this is to simply run the program.
   a) Click on the Restart button in the toolbar. You should now be looking at the pegboard containing all tools.
   b) Click on the image of the rope. Look carefully and you will see the toolbox for the Display icon *Feedback for Rope*, indicating that this icon is currently open on screen.
   c) Select File | Import. The *Import which file?* dialog window opens.
   d) Use the *Look in* field to browse to the CD-ROM, and look in the *Chapter10* directory. Locate and select the graphic *Overlay.jpg*. Click on the Import button.

e) Position the graphic so that it is adjacent to the rope.

f) Select the Text tool. Select Text | Size, and then select 14. Click the I-bar cursor on screen and type in *No. We won't have to rope together our hiking team. Try again.*

g) When finished typing, click on the Pointer tool, and then click on the X on the toolbox to close the display area. At this point, Authorware is still in Run mode, stopping only because it encountered the empty Display icon *Rope*. You should now see a Continue button. Press Ctrl + P to pause. Drag the Continue button and place it at the bottom of the overlay window. Press Ctrl + P to resume Play mode. Click on the Continue button.

h) Note that the feedback remains on screen. You will correct this in material to follow.

9. You should now be back at the pegboard (Interaction icon).

a) Click on the harness. You should see the toolbox for the Display icon *Feedback for Harness.*

b) Select File | Import. The *Import which file?* dialog window opens.

c) Use the *Look in* field to browse to the CD-ROM, and look in the *Chapter10* directory. Locate and select the graphic *Overlay.jpg*. Click on the Import button.

d) Position the graphic so that it is adjacent to the harness.

e) Select the Text tool. Click the I-bar cursor on screen and type in *No. We will not be rock climbing on our hike. Try again.* Click on the pointer tool to close the text object.

f) Select Edit | Select All. Then select Edit | Copy to copy the overlay graphic and text to the clipboard.

g) Click on the X on the toolbox to close the display area. You should now see a Continue button. Press Ctrl + P to pause. Drag the Continue button and place it at the bottom of the overlay window. Press Ctrl + P to resume Play mode. Click on the Continue button.

10. You should now be back at the pegboard (Interaction icon).

a) Click on the three-wire image. You should see the toolbox for the Display icon *Feedback for 3 Wires.*

b) Select Edit | Paste to paste a copy of the overlay graphic and text into the current Display icon.

c) Position the graphic and text so that they are adjacent to the three-wire image. The text is still appropriate, so there is nothing to change.

d) Click on the X on the toolbox to close the display area. You should now see a Continue button. Press Ctrl + P to pause. Drag the Continue button and place it at the bottom of the overlay window. Press Ctrl + P to resume Play mode. Click on the Continue button.

11. You should now be back at the pegboard (Interaction icon).
    a)   Click on the helmet. You should see the toolbox for the Display icon *Feedback for Helmet.*
    b)   Select Edit | Paste to paste a copy of the overlay graphic and text into the current Display icon.
    c)   Position the graphic and text so that they are adjacent to the helmet.
    d)   Select the Text tool. Click the I-bar cursor directly on the existing text object to open it. Select all text and delete it. Type in *Correct. The helmet offers the best overall protection for hiking.*
    e)   Click on the X on the toolbox to close the display area. You should now see a Continue button. Press Ctrl + P to pause. Drag the Continue button and place it at the bottom of the overlay window. Press Ctrl + P to resume Play mode. Click on the Continue button.

12. You should now be back at the pegboard (Interaction icon).
    a)   Click on the figure-eight clamp. You should see the toolbox for the Display icon *Feedback for Fig8.*
    b)   Select Edit | Paste to paste a copy of the overlay graphic and text into the current Display icon. The text is still appropriate, so there is nothing to change.
    c)   Position the graphic and text so that they are adjacent to the figure-eight clamp.
    d)   Click on the X on the toolbox to close the display area. You should now see a Continue button. Press Ctrl + P to pause. Drag the Continue button and place it at the bottom of the overlay window. Press Ctrl + P to play. Click on the Continue button.

13. You should now be back at the pegboard (Interaction icon).
    a)   Click on the double clip. You should see the toolbox for the Display icon *Feedback for DoubleClip.*
    b)   Select Edit | Paste to paste a copy of the overlay graphic and text into the current Display icon. The text is still appropriate, so there is nothing to change.
    c)   Position the graphic and text so that they are adjacent to the double clip.
    d)   Click on the X on the toolbox to close the display area. You will *not* see a Continue button, and you will be immediately returned to the interaction.

14. You should now be back at the pegboard (Interaction icon).
    a)   Click on the pegboard, but not on any object. You should see the toolbox for the Display icon *Feedback for Catch-All.*
    b)   Select Edit | Paste to paste a copy of the overlay graphic and text into the current Display icon.

c) Position the graphic and text so that they are in the middle of the screen.

d) Select the Text tool. Click the I-bar cursor directly on the existing text object to open it. Select all text and delete it. Type in *Please click directly on an object. Try again.*

e) Click on the X on the toolbox to close the display area. You should now see a Continue button. Press Ctrl + P to pause. Drag the Continue button and place it at the bottom of the overlay window. Press Ctrl + P to resume Play mode. Click on the Continue button.

15. Take a quick look at the current status of the structure.

a) Click on the Restart button.

b) Click on the rope. Click on the Continue button.

c) Click on the figure eight. Click on the Continue button.

d) Clearly you can see that the feedback erases "after the next selection," which is not how the completed model should be constructed. The completed model should show the feedback after the selection, bringing up a Continue button as the feedback is read. After you click on the Continue button, the feedback should erase before Authorware returns to the interaction.

16. You need to go back and change the erase characteristics concerning the feedback. While you are doing this, you will also select a custom cursor for each hot spot. According to guidelines you learned in regard to the Pickup Truck interaction structure, you should find the solution to these needed changes to the right of the imaginary line between the Interaction icon and the Map icons to the right.

a) Jump to the flowline (Ctrl + J).

b) Double click on the Response Type symbol for the first Map icon, *Rope.* You should now be looking at the Properties/Response dialog window, with the Hot Spot tab on top. Note that the Match field is set to *Single click* (which for most of the responses is fine). At the bottom of this tab, click on the button to the right of the Cursor field to open the Cursors library. Scroll to the bottom of the list and select the Hand cursor. Click on the OK button to close the library. Click on the Response tab. In the Erase field, select Before Next Entry. Click on the OK button to close this dialog window.

c) Double click on the Response Type symbol for the second Map icon, *Harness.* You should now be looking at the Properties/Response dialog window, with the Response tab on top. In the Erase field, select Before Next Entry. Click on the Hot Spot tab. At the bottom of this tab, open the Cursors library. Scroll to the bottom of the list and select the Hand cursor. Click on the OK button to close the library. Click on the OK button to close this dialog window.

·T*i*P·

You may notice that each time you open a Response Type symbol, whichever tab you were looking at previously (Hot Spot or Response) will by default be on top as you open the next dialog window. Authorware assumes that because you were looking at this tab last you will probably want to look at this same tab in the next Response Type symbol. Most of the time this assumption will be correct; but if not, simply click on the tab you want to look at. In these steps, you are actually changing values on both tabs, and whichever tab you work with last will appear on top as you open the next

d) Double click on the Response Type symbol for the third Map icon, *3Wires*. You should now be looking at the Properties/Response dialog window, with the Hot Spot tab on top. At the bottom of this tab, open the Cursors library. Scroll to the bottom of the list and select the Hand cursor. Click on the OK button to close the library. Click on the Response tab. In the Erase field, select Before Next Entry. Click on the OK button to close this dialog window.

e) Double click on the Response Type symbol for the fourth Map icon, *Helmet*. You should now be looking at the Properties/Response dialog window, with the Response tab on top. In the Erase field, select Before Next Entry. Click on the Hot Spot tab. At the bottom of this tab, open the Cursors library. Scroll to the bottom of the list and select the Hand cursor. Click on the OK button to close the library. Click on the OK button to close this dialog window.

f) Double click on the Response Type symbol for the fifth Map icon, *Fig8*. You should now be looking at the Properties/Response dialog window, with the Hot Spot tab on top. At the bottom of this tab, open the Cursors library. Scroll to the bottom of the list and select the Hand cursor. Click on the OK button to close the library. Click on the Response tab. In the Erase field, select Before Next Entry. Click on the OK button to close this dialog window.

g) Double click on the Response Type symbol for the sixth Map icon, *DoubleClip*. You should now be looking at the Properties/Response dialog window, with the Response tab on top. In the Erase field, select Before Next Entry. Click on the Hot Spot tab. At the bottom of this tab, open the Cursors library. Scroll to the bottom of the list and select the Hand cursor. Click on the OK button to close the library. For this particular response, you also want to change the Match field, which is currently set to *Single click*. Click on the pull-down menu for the Match field and select Cursor in Area. This will be a different type of response than the others, in that it will not require a mouse click to activate the response; simply bringing the cursor into the hot spot area will trigger the display of the feedback. Click on the OK button to close this dialog window.

h) Double click on the Response Type symbol for the seventh Map icon, *Catch-All*. You should now be looking at the Properties/Response dialog window, with the Hot Spot tab on top. Do *not* select a custom cursor. Click on the Response tab. In the Erase field, select Before Next Entry. Click on the OK button to close this dialog window.

17. Now for a little cleanup work.

a) Run the program and select each object, including the peg-board background.

b) For each selection, pause the program (Ctrl + P) and reposition the object or Continue button, if needed. Return to Play mode (Ctrl + P) to continue with the cleanup.

c) Note that as soon as you bring the cursor into the *DoubleClip* hot spot, the feedback displays and will continue to display as long as you keep the cursor in the area. As soon as you move the cursor out of this hot spot area, the feedback will erase.

18. What is missing? What happens when you select the correct answer? What should happen after selecting the correct answer?

a) After selecting the correct answer (*Helmet*), Authorware should branch to exit the interaction.

b) Jump to the flowline (Ctrl + J).

c) Double click on the Response Type symbol above the *Helmet* icon. The Response Type window should now be open.

d) Select the Response tab. Click on the Branch field and select Exit Interaction. Click on the OK button.

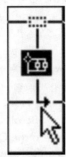

Fig. 10-11. Keyboard shortcut for changing the branch of a response.

e) You should now be back at the flowline. Select the Map icon *Helmet*. Hold the mouse button down and drag the Map icon *Helmet* all the way to the left and drop it so that it is now the very first Map icon to the right of the Interaction icon. Be careful as you perform this step. If you accidentally drop the Map icon on the main flowline, immediately select Edit | Undo.

f) Run the program. Click on the helmet. Click on the Continue button. You should have now exited the interaction.

19. Jump to the flowline (Ctrl + J).

20. Select File | Save, to make sure you do not lose what you have just created.

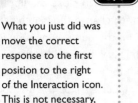

Shortcut

A keyboard shortcut to quickly change the branch of a response is to press and hold down the Ctrl key as you click on the branch symbol immediately below the response icon (see figure 10-11). As you keep clicking here, you will see that Authorware will rotate through the options available for branching. Simply stop when you reach the branch you wish to use.

·TiP·

What you just did was move the correct response to the first position to the right of the Interaction icon. This is not necessary, but it makes it easier to quickly see in the branching the correct answer (which exits the interaction) and the incorrect answers (which indicate "try again").

21. Now for a little reflective thinking (or head scratching). The wireframe for the Catch-All hot spot covers the entire screen, whereas each additional wireframe hot spot includes only a small section. However, these sections are also included within (overlap with) the Catch-All wireframe. See figure 10-12.

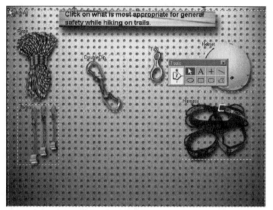

Fig. 10-12. Catch-All hot spot covers the entire screen.

If you click the mouse in the Rope hot spot, for example, why does Authorware assume the selection was meant for the Rope hot spot and not the Catch-All hot spot, even though this area is included within both wireframe hot spots?

The answer lies within the process of how Authorware "reads" the flowline. Authorware reads much like we do with the English language: from top to bottom, left to right. Examine the flowline in figure 10-13.

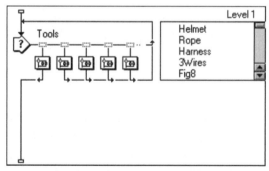

Fig. 10-13. Authorware "reads" each response from left to right.

Let's look at a concrete example. Assume that you run the program and when faced with the choice click on the 3Wires hot spot. Why does Authorware drop into the 3Wires response and not the Catch-All response?

After the mouse is clicked in the 3Wires hot spot, Authorware moves from the Interaction icon to the first response and evaluates "was the mouse clicked within this first hot spot area (Rope)?" The answer is no, and therefore Authorware continues to the right to the second response and evaluates "was the mouse clicked within this second hot spot area (Harness)?" The answer is again no, and therefore Authorware continues to the right to the third response and evaluates "was the mouse clicked within this third hot spot area (3Wires)?" The answer is now yes, and therefore Authorware drops into this Map icon and encounters the Display icon (containing text feedback) and the Wait icon.

22. To illustrate how important the order is, let's "break" the structure and change the order of the responses.
    a) Select and drag the *Catch-All* Map icon so that it resides in the first position immediately to the right of the Interaction icon. See figure 10-14.

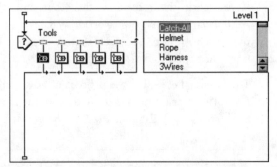

Fig. 10-14. Catch-All response now in first position, showing "broken" structure.

    b) Click on the Restart button.
    c) Click on the 3Wires image. You should now be reading the feedback for the Catch-All response: *Please click directly on an object. Try again.*
    d) Click on the Continue button and click on any other object. What you should see is that regardless of where you click Authorware will now always drop through the Catch-All response. Why is this?
    e) See figure 10-14 as reference. Let's walk through this example. Imagine that the user has clicked on the 3Wires image. After the mouse is clicked in the 3Wires hot spot, Authorware moves from the Interaction icon to the first response (which is now the Catch-

All response) and evaluates "was the mouse clicked within this hot spot area (anywhere on screen)?" The answer is yes, and will always be yes regardless of where you click on screen.

In some cases the placement order of the responses doesn't matter. On the other hand, sometimes the placement order does make a big difference. With that said, we'd like to offer the following rules of thumb regarding the order of interaction responses:

- *Place the correct response in the first position, immediately to the right of the Interaction icon.*

- *Place all incorrect responses next.*

- *Place the catch-all to the far right.*

    f)   To correct this "broken" structure, select and drag the Catch-All response back to the far right. Click on the Restart button, and test a couple of selections to make sure you have your interaction back in the normal working condition.

23. Save your work by selecting File | Save.

Guided Tour 10B: The Hot Object Interaction Response

As you saw in exercise 10-1, the "hot spots" are rectangular in shape. For Authorware, if you click inside the hot spot for "rope," it will trigger the Rope response, even if the mouse technically touches the pegboard within this area and not the rope. For situations such as the pegboard and the various items of equipment, it did not matter because most people would assume that if you clicked on the pegboard right next to the rope, you meant to click on the rope. However, what if you need to carefully distinguish objects that are of irregular shape, or that are very close together so that the rectangles from two objects overlap? Or what if the objects themselves overlap each other? In all of these cases, trying to use the Hot Spot interaction response would pose problems. Not to worry; Authorware has another solution.

The Hot Object interaction response is another interactive technique that provides the capability to meet special needs that rectangular hot spots do not address. With the Hot Object interaction response, there is no longer an area that is "hot." Instead, you identify *distinct objects* that are "hot." Every "hot object" must reside in its own Display icon (remember that Authorware does not distinguish objects within a single Display icon).

In the following, after taking a quick tour of the Hot Object response properties, you will build two Hot Object structures. The first exercise demonstrates how the Hot Object response allows you to distinguish overlapping objects; the second exercise illustrates how you can distinguish irregular, very closely placed objects. First, however, let's take a quick look at the properties of the Hot Object interaction response.

1. Start by opening a new file.
    a)   Select File | New | File.
    b)   Close the two dialog windows that have opened.
    c)   Verify that you are now looking at an empty flowline.

2. Drag an Interaction icon to the flowline. Drag a Map icon and drop it to the right of the Interaction icon.

3. The Response Type window should now be open. Click on the Hot Object option and then click on the OK button.

4. Double click on the Response Type symbol above the Map icon to access the dialog window for this Hot Spot interaction response.

5. You should be looking at the Properties/Response dialog window, shown in figure 10-15. There are three parts of this window, but we will briefly look at only one of them, the Hot Object tab.

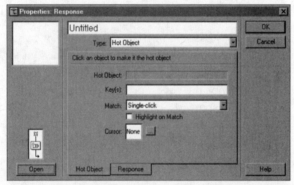

Fig. 10-15. Properties/Response dialog window showing Hot Object tab.

6. Select the Hot Object tab, if it is not already on top.

7. As you take a look at the fields on this tab, the only new addition is the message line that appears immediately under the Type field. After you click on the Hot Object the current response is to be linked to, the name of the icon that contains that Hot Object will be listed in the Hot Object field below the message line.

Practice Exercise 10-2:
Hot Object – Overlapping Objects

Description

In this exercise you are going to create an interactive strategy in which the user is asked to click the mouse on one of three overlapping objects. The content and graphics in this exercise are simple so that you can concentrate on the structure and move through it more quickly. The structure will also provide feedback concerning the current selection after the user has clicked on each object. The following elements are covered in this exercise.

- *Creating simple graphic and text objects*
- *Creating feedback to the user, based on selection made*
- *Creating several Hot Object responses triggered by a mouse click on the Hot Object*
- *Creating a Catch-all response area*
- *Selecting a custom cursor*
- *Enabling automatic erase functions*
- *Modifying branching functions of the Interaction icon*
- *Modifying the layering of objects displayed on screen*

Take a Look

CD-ROM

Before beginning the exercise, let's take a look at the exercise in its completed state so that you can clearly see what it is you are about to build.

1. Select File | Open and locate on the CD-ROM the directory named *Chapter10*. Locate and double click on the file named *Exer10-2*.

2. The file *Exer10-2* should now appear in your copy of Authorware. Click on the Restart button to play the file from the top of the flowline. Note the following properties of this completed exercise.

   - *When the cursor passes over a Hot Object, the normal arrow cursor will change to the custom Hand cursor while it remains over the Hot Object. As soon as the cursor moves off the object, it changes back to the normal cursor symbol.*

   - *When any Hot Object is clicked on, an overlay text window appears, providing feedback specific to that choice. This window also contains a Continue button. When the Continue button is selected, the feedback window is erased.*

- *If the user clicks on the screen anywhere other than on a Hot Object, an overlay text window appears providing generic feedback. This window also contains a Continue button. When the Continue button is selected, the feedback window is erased.*

- *If the user selects a wrong answer, feedback is provided and the user is returned to the interaction to try again.*

- *If the user selects the correct answer, feedback is provided and the user can then exit the interaction.*

- *There are erase icons in this icon structure used to erase Display icons that are not part of the structure that provides an automatic erase function.*

Storyboard: On screen

Figures 10-16 through 10-20 show you what the finished presentation will look like. Figure 10-16 shows the content of the Display icon *Catch-All*, as the large rectangle is being dragged to cover the entire screen. Figure 10-17 shows the content of the Display icon *Square*. Figure 10-18 shows the content of the Display icon *Circle*. Figure 10-19 shows the content of the Display icon *Triangle*. Figure 10-20 shows the completed presentation on screen before a selection is made.

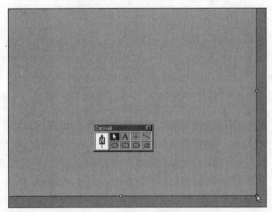

Fig. 10-16. Display icon **Catch-All** *as rectangle is positioned.*

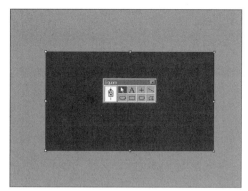

Fig. 10-17. Display icon **Square**.

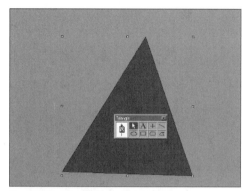

Fig. 10-18. Display icon **Triangle**.

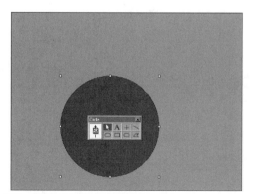

Fig. 10-19. Display icon **Circle**.

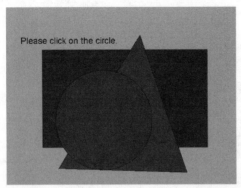

Fig. 10-20. Complete presentation on screen before selection.

Storyboard: Behind the Scenes

Figure 10-21 shows the main and secondary flowlines (with all icons, their placement, and their names) as they should look when you are finished with this exercise.

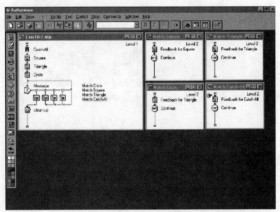

Fig. 10-21. Main flowline with secondary flowlines.

Step-by-Step Instructions

Go Solo

1. Select File | New | File. Close the two Knowledge Object dialog windows.

2. Verify that you are now looking at a new flowline.

3. Set up the file properties.
    a) Select Modify | File | Properties.
    b) Select whatever background color you want.
    c) Make sure Size is set to 640 x 480.

NOTE

The Hot Object response is different from the Hot Spot response, in that each "hot object" is located in its own Display icon, whereas all Hot Spot responses were visually seen as part of a single graphic in the single display area of the Interaction icon. For any object to be designated as a "hot object," it must reside in its own Display icon.

NOTE

By now you should be seeing a similarity in the structure built for each of the interaction exercises (it is the Pickup Truck inter- action structure); namely, an Interaction icon with attached Map icons containing a Display icon and a Wait icon. There will be small variations in each, depending on the specifics of the response type you are working with.

    d) Remove the check marks beside the Tile Bar and Menu Bar options.

    e) Click on the OK button to close the window.

    f) Select File | Save and locate the *SaveWork* directory. Type in *Chap10-2* and click on the OK button.

4. Establish what will become the "hot objects."

    a) Drag four Display icons to the flowline.

    b) Name these Display icons *Catch-All*, *Square*, *Triangle*, and *Circle*.

5. Create the interactive structure.

    a) Drag an Interaction icon to the flowline below *Triangle*. Name this icon *Message*.

    b) Drag a Map icon to the right of the Interaction icon. The Response Type dialog window has opened. Select the Hot Object option and then click on the OK button. Name this Map icon *Match Square*.

    c) Drag another Map icon to the far right. Name this icon *Match Triangle*.

    d) Drag another Map icon to the far right. Name this icon *Match Circle*.

    e) Drag another Map icon to the far right. Name this icon *Match Catch-All*.

6. Place icons inside the Map icons to provide feedback and a pause func- tion before the feedback is erased.

    a) Double click on the Map icon *Match Square*. Drag a Display icon to the level 2 flowline inside this Map icon. Label the Display icon *Feedback for Square*. Drag a Wait icon to the level 2 flowline and place it below the Display icon. Label it *Continue*. Click on the X in the upper right-hand corner of the Map icon's title bar to close the Map icon.

    b) Double click on the Map icon *Match Triangle*. Drag a Display icon to this level 2 flowline and place it below the Display icon. Label the Display icon *Feedback for Triangle*. Drag a Wait icon and place it below the Display icon. Label it *Continue*. Close the Map icon.

    c) Double click on the Map icon *Match Circle*. Drag a Display icon to this level 2 flowline and place it below the Display icon. Label the Display icon *Feedback for Circle*. Drag a Wait icon and place it below the Display icon. Label it *Continue*. Close the Map icon.

    d) Double click on the Map icon *Match Catch-All*. Drag a Display icon to this level 2 flowline and place it below the Display icon. Label the Display icon *Feedback for Catch-All*. Drag a Wait icon and place it below the Display icon. Label it *Continue*. Close the Map icon.

7. Add content to the hot object Display icons.

    a) Double click on the Display icon *Catch-All*. In this icon, you want to cover the entire screen with a background graphic that will help you with the Catch-All response. Select the Rectangle tool and draw a large square. Select the Pointer tool. Select Window | Inspectors |

Colors. The square you drew should still have handlebars around it (if not, click on the square). Click on the foreground color box in the lower right of the Color window and then select whatever color you wish. Your square should now be that color. Click on the rectangle and drag it toward the upper left corner of the screen, pushing the left top edge off the screen. Click on the rectangle's handlebar in the lower right-hand corner. Drag this handlebar so that the rectangle is stretched toward the very bottom of the lower right-hand corner of the screen. Click on the rectangle and reposition it so that it covers the entire screen area. (See figure 10-16 for reference.) Close the Map icon.

b) Double click on the Display icon *Square*. Select the Rectangle tool and draw a large square. Select the Pointer tool. Select Window | Inspectors | Colors. The square you drew should still have handlebars around it (if not, click on the square). Click on the foreground color box in the lower right of the Color window and then select whatever color you wish. Your square should now be that color. Position the square with reference to figure 10-17. Close the Map icon.

c) Double click on the Display icon *Triangle*. Select the Polygon tool and draw a large triangle. The Colors inspector should still be open. Select the Pointer tool, click on the foreground color box, and select a different color for the triangle. Position the triangle with reference to figure 10-18. Close the Map icon.

d) Double click on the Display icon *Circle*. Select the Ellipse tool and draw a medium-size circle. The Colors inspector should still be open. Select the Pointer tool, click on the foreground color box, and select a different color for circle. Position the circle with reference to figure 10-19. Close the Map icon.

8. Create the content for the Interaction icon.
   a) Double click on the Interaction icon *Message*.
   b) Select the Text tool. Select Text | Font, and then select Arial. Select Text | Size, and then select 18. Select Window | Inspectors | Mode, and then select Transparent. Click the I-bar cursor on screen and type in *Please click on the circle*.
   c) Select the Pointer tool and reposition the text object as shown in figure 10-20.

9. To finish creating the content, go inside each of the feedback Display icons in the attached Map icons.
   a) Inside the Map icon *Match Square*, double click on the Display icon *Feedback for Square*. Select File | Import and on the companion CD-ROM, in the *Chapter10* directory, locate and select the file *Overlay.jpg*.

CD-ROM

Click on the Import button. Position the graphic in the upper left corner of the screen. Select the Text tool. Click the I-bar cursor on screen and type in *Sorry, this is the square. Try again.* Position the text so that it fits within the overlay graphic. Press Ctrl + C to copy the graphic and text objects to the clipboard. Close the Display icon and the Map icon.

b) Inside the Map icon *Match Triangle*, double click on the Display icon *Feedback for Triangle*. Press Ctrl + V to paste the graphic overlay window and a text object into this Display icon. Select the Text tool and click the I-bar cursor directly on the existing text object. Delete the existing text and replace it with *Sorry, this is the triangle. Try again.* Close the Display icon and the Map icon.

c) Inside the Map icon *Match Circle*, double click on the Display icon Feedback for Circle. Press Ctrl + V to paste the graphic overlay window and a text object into this Display icon. Select the Text tool and click the I-bar cursor directly on the existing text object to open it. Delete the existing text and replace it with *Yes, you are correct. This is the circle.* Close the Display icon and the Map icon.

d) Inside the Map icon *Match Catch-All*, double click on the Display icon *Feedback for Catch-All.* Press Ctrl + V to paste the graphic overlay window and a text object into this Display icon. Select the Text tool and click the I-bar cursor directly on the existing text object. Delete the existing text and replace it with *No, please click on an object. Try again.* Close the Display icon and the Map icon.

10. Create the link between each object and its corresponding response Map icon. If you make a mistake or otherwise get lost during the linking process that follows, here are a few suggestions:

- *Run the program so that you see each of the hot objects on screen.*

- *If response dialog windows come up, cancel them.*

- *From the flowline, hold the Shift key down and double click on the Response Type symbol for the Map icon corresponding to whatever hot object you are trying to link to.*

- *Click on the graphic of the hot object you want to link to, and then click on the OK button to close the dialog window.*

- *Repeat this process for the other objects.*

a) Click on the Restart button to run the program.

Again, note that the naming convention for the icons is descriptive of what they actually do. As you will see, when linking the hot objects to their responses and feedback, descriptive labels are essential. This logic is used throughout most exercises and in most real-world applications.

b) You should now see the open Properties/Response dialog window for the Match Square response (examine the Icon Title field, which again is why you use descriptive labels). Click on the graphic of the square to link this response to the graphic. The Hot Object tab is on top. Select the Cursor field, and locate and select the Hand custom cursor. Click on the OK button to close the Cursor library. Click on the Response tab. In the Erase field, select Before Next Entry. Click on the OK button to close the dialog window.

c) You should now see the open Properties/Response dialog window for the Match Triangle response. Click on the graphic of the triangle to link this response to the graphic. The Response tab is on top. In the Erase field, select Before Next Entry. Click on the Hot Object tab. Select the Cursor field, and locate and select the Hand custom cursor. Click on the OK button to close the Cursor library. Click on the OK button to close the dialog window.

d) You should now see the open Properties/Response dialog window for the Match Circle response. Click on the graphic of the circle to link this response to the graphic. The Hot Object tab is on top. Select the Cursor field, and locate and select the Hand custom cursor. Click on the OK button to close the Cursor library. Click on the Response tab. In the Erase field, select Before Next Entry. Click on the OK button to close the dialog window.

e) You should now see the open Properties/Response dialog window for the Match Catch-All response. Click on the background rectangle that covers the entire screen to link this response to the graphic. Because this graphic covers the entire screen, the user will not perceive this as an object but rather as a background color. However, if the user clicks on this background color, and not on an object, you can use this response to provide a catch-all type of feedback.

The Response tab is on top. In the Erase field, select Before Next Entry. There is no need to go to the Hot Object tab, as there is *no* custom cursor for this response. Click on the OK button to close the response window.

11. Now a little cleanup work.

a) Run the program and select the square. Pause the program (Ctrl + P) and reposition the object or Continue button, if needed.

b) For both the triangle and circle, continue this cleanup process.

12. Finally, we need to change the branch for the correct answer so that it will exit the interaction.

a) Double click on the Response Type symbol above the Map icon *Match Circle*. The Response Type window should now be open.

d) Select the Response tab. Click on the Branch field and select Exit Interaction. Click on the OK button.

c) Run the program. Click on the circle. Click on the Continue button. You should have now exited the interaction.

13. But what is still on screen? Why are the graphics of the background color, circle, square, and triangle still there?

a) The answer is that these graphics are all located in Display icons located on the main flowline above the Interaction icon. Located where they are, these Display icons do not have an automatic erase function available for use. You will have to use an Erase icon to erase them.

b) Drag an Erase icon to the bottom of the flowline.

c) Run the program. Click on the circle. Click on the Continue button. You should have now exited the interaction and encountered the empty Erase icon. Look at the message line inside the response window for the Erase icon and do as it suggests: click on the square, the circle, the triangle, and the background color (rectangle). Click on the OK button to close the Erase icon. Your screen should now be empty.

14. Save your work by selecting File | Save.

15. Before moving on, let's do a quick review concerning layers. In this exercise, you used four Display icons at the top of the flowline: *Catch-All*, *Square*, *Triangle*, and *Circle*. This order was specified in the exercise so that the largest objects would be created first, with the smallest object (the circle) being created last. As you run the program, these objects are displayed with the last object on top. Using this particular order allows you to see all objects without doing anything else.

a) However, look at what happens when you change the order. Select and drag the Display icon *Catch-All* and place it below the Display icon *Circle*. Click on the Restart button. What you see now is that the background color (large rectangle that covers the entire screen) covers up everything else on screen.

b) Without changing the order of any of the other objects, let's change how these objects are displayed in terms of which object is on top of or behind another.

c) Select the Display icon *Catch-All*. Select Modify | Icon | Properties. The Properties/Display Icon dialog window has opened. In the Layer field, click the cursor in this field and type in a *1*. You will place this large rectangle (the background color) in the far background. The lower the number, the further toward the background; the higher the number, the more toward the front. Click on the OK button.

d) Select the Display icon *Square*. Select Modify | Icon | Properties. Click the cursor in the Layer field and type in a *3*. Click on the OK button.

e) Select the Display icon *Triangle*. Select Modify | Icon | Properties. Click the cursor in the Layer field and type in a *2*. Click on the OK button.

f) Select the Display icon *Circle*. Select Modify | Icon | Properties. Click the cursor in the Layer field and type in a *4*. Click on the OK button.

g) Click on the Restart button. You should notice that the objects are now displayed in a different layer order.

16. You do not need to save the revised layering, and because you previously saved the completed file, simply select File | Close.

Practice Exercise 10-3: Hot Object – Irregular Objects

Description

This exercise is very similar to the last Hot Object exercise, but this time the objects are irregular and placed closely together. This exercise involves the same structure you used previously, but you will be using graphics of three U.S. states. You will arrange them so that they appear as a single map of the Southeast. Try to complete this exercise without looking at the step-by-step instructions. The following elements are covered in this exercise.

• *Importing graphics and creating text objects*

• *Creating feedback to the user, based on selection made*

• *Creating several Hot Object responses triggered by a mouse click on the Hot Object*

• *Selecting a custom cursor*

• *Enabling automatic erase functions*

• *Modifying branching functions of the Interaction icon*

Take a Look

CD-ROM

Before beginning the exercise, let's take a look at the exercise in its completed state so that you can clearly see what it is you are about to build.

1. Select File | Open and locate on the companion CD-ROM the directory named *Chapter10*. Locate and double click on the file *Exer10-3*.

2. The file *Exer10-3* should now appear in your copy of Authorware. Click on the Restart button to play the file from the top of the flowline. Note the following properties of this completed exercise.

a) Note that the graphic objects are definitely not rectangular (when in Transparent mode).

b) When the cursor passes over a Hot Object, the normal arrow cursor will change to a hand cursor while it remains over the Hot Object. As soon as the cursor leaves, it changes back to the normal cursor symbol.

c) When any Hot Object is clicked on, an overlay text window appears, providing feedback specific to that choice. This window also contains a Continue button. When the Continue button is selected, the feedback window is erased.

d) In this exercise, you will not include a catch-all response.

e) If the user selects a wrong answer, feedback is provided and the user is returned to the interaction to try again.

f) If the user selects the correct answer, feedback is provided and the user can then exit the interaction.

g) There are erase icons in this icon structure used to erase the Display icons that are not part of the structure that provides an automatic erase function.

Storyboard: On screen

Figures 10-22 through 10-25 show you what the finished presentation will look like. Figure 10-22 shows what is inside the Display icon *Florida*. Figure 10-23 shows what is inside the Display icon *Alabama*. Figure 10-24 shows what is inside the Display icon *Georgia*. Figure 10-25 shows what the interaction looks like with all states and instructions positioned appropriately.

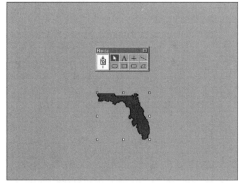

Fig. 10-22. Display icon **Florida.**

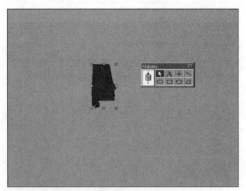

*Fig. 10-23. Display icon **Alabama**.*

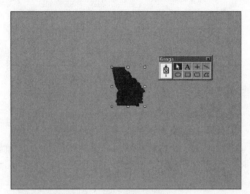

*Fig. 10-24. Display icon **Georgia**.*

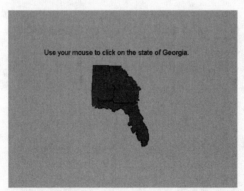

Fig. 10-25. Complete display for the interaction.

Storyboard: Behind the Scenes

Figure 10-26 shows the main and secondary flowlines (with all icons, their placement, and their names) as they should look when you are finished with this exercise.

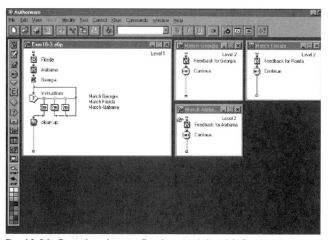

Fig. 10-26. Completed main flowline with level 2 flowlines.

Step-by-Step Instructions

Go Solo

The design and structure of this exercise is identical to the last Hot Object exercise. It is strongly suggested that you try to complete this exercise on your own, with just the aid of the information provided in the two previous "Storyboard" sections. After you have tried on your own and find that you need some help, then take a look at the step-by-step instructions.

1. Select File | New | File. Close the two Knowledge Object dialog windows.

2. Verify that you are now looking at a new flowline.

3. Set up the file properties.
   a) Select Modify | File | Properties.
   b) Select whatever background color you want.
   c) Make sure Size is set to 640 x 480.
   d) Remove the check marks beside the Tile Bar and Menu Bar options.
   e) Click on the OK button to close the window.
   f) Select File | Save and locate the *SaveWork* directory. Type in *Chap10-3* and click on the OK button.

4. Establish what will become the "hot objects."

a) Drag three Display icons to the flowline.

b) Name these Display icons *Florida, Alabama,* and *Georgia.*

5. Drag an Interaction icon to the flowline below the word *Georgia.* Name this icon *Instructions.*

a) Drag a Map icon and place it to the right of the Interaction icon. The Response Type dialog window has opened. Select the Hot Object option and click on the OK button. Name this Map icon *Match Florida.*

b) Drag another Map icon and place it to the right of the Map icon *Match Florida.* Name this icon *Match Alabama.*

c) Drag another Map icon and place it to the right of the Map icon *Match Alabama.* Name this icon *Match Georgia.*

6. Place icons inside the Map icons to provide feedback and a pause function before the feedback is erased.

a) Double click on the Map icon *Match Florida.* Drag a Display icon to the level 2 flowline inside this Map icon. Label the Display icon *Feedback for Florida.* Drag a Wait icon to the level 2 flowline and label it *Continue.* Close the Map icon.

b) Double click on the Map icon *Match Alabama.* Drag a Display icon to the level 2 flowline inside this Map icon. Label the Display icon *Feedback for Alabama.* Drag a Wait icon to the level 2 flowline and label it *Continue.* Close the Map icon.

c) Double click on the Map icon *Match Georgia.* Drag a Display icon to the level 2 flowline inside this Map icon. Label the Display icon *Feedback for Georgia.* Drag a Wait icon to the level 2 flowline and label it *Continue.* Close the Map icon.

7. Let's tackle the content for the "hot object" Display icons first.

a) Double click on the Display icon *Florida.* Select File | Import and on the companion CD-ROM, locate the *Chapter10* directory. Locate and select the file *Florida.bmp.* Click on the Import button. Select Window | Inspectors | Modes, and then select Transparent. Leave the Modes inspector open. Position the graphic temporarily at the bottom of the screen. Close the Display icon.

b) Double click on the Display icon *Alabama.* Select File | Import and on the companion CD-ROM, locate the *Chapter10* directory. Locate and select the file *Alabama.bmp.* Click on the Import button. Use the inspector to set the graphic's mode to Transparent. Position the graphic temporarily to the far left. Close the Display icon.

c) Double click on the Display icon *Georgia.* Select File | Import and on the companion CD-ROM, locate the *Chapter10* directory. Locate and

CD-ROM

select the file *Georgia.bmp*. Click on the Import button. Use the inspector to set the graphic's mode to Transparent. Position the graphic temporarily to the far right. Close the Display icon.

8. Create the content for the Interaction icon.
   a) Double click on the Interaction icon *Instructions*.
   b) Select the Text tool. Select Text | Font, and then select Arial. Select Text | Size, and then select 18. Select Window | Inspectors | Mode, and then select Transparent. Type in *Use your mouse to click on the state of Georgia.*
   c) Select the Pointer tool and reposition the text object as shown in figure 10-25.

CD-ROM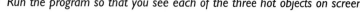

9. Next let's tackle the content for each of the feedback Display icons in the attached Map icons.
   a) Inside the Map icon *Match Florida*, double click on the Display icon *Feedback for Florida*. Select File | Import and on the companion CD-ROM, in the *Chapter10* directory, locate and select the file *Overlay.jpg*. Click on the Import button. Position the graphic in the lower right corner of the screen. Select the Text Tool. Type in *No, but this is a great place for vacations. Try again.* Select both the graphic overlay window and the text object. Press Ctrl + C to copy both objects to the clipboard. Close the Display icon.
   b) Inside the Map icon *Match Alabama*, double click on the Display icon *Feedback for Alabama*. Press Ctrl + V to paste the graphic overlay window and text object into this Display icon. Select the Text tool. Click the I-bar cursor directly on the text object. Delete the existing text and replace it with *No, but this is also the name of a great country band. Try again.* Position the overlay and text to the left. Close the Display icon.
   c) Inside the Map icon *Match Georgia*, double click on the Display icon *Feedback for Georgia*. Press Ctrl + V to paste the graphic overlay window and text object into this Display icon. Select the Text tool. Click the I-bar cursor directly on the text object. Delete the existing text and replace it with *Yes, this is the state of Georgia.* Position the overlay window and text at the upper right of the screen. Close the Display icon.

10. Create the link between each object and its corresponding response Map icon.

If you make a mistake or otherwise get lost during the linking process that follows, here are a few suggestions:

• *Run the program so that you see each of the three hot objects on screen.*

- *If response dialog windows come up, cancel each one until there are no more of them.*

- *From the flowline, hold the shift key down and double click on the Response Type Symbol for the Map icon corresponding to whatever hot object you are trying to link to.*

- *Click on the graphic of the hot object you want to link to, then click on the OK button to close this dialog window.*

- *Repeat this process for the other objects.*

   a) Click on the Restart button to run the program.

   b) You should now see the open Properties/Response dialog window for the response Match Florida. Click on the graphic of Florida to link the response to the graphic. The Hot Object tab should already be on top. Select the Cursor field, and locate and select the Hand custom cursor. Click on the OK button to close the Cursor library. Click on the Response tab. In the Erase field, select Before Next Entry. Click on the OK button to close the dialog window.

   c) You should now see the open Properties/Response dialog window for the response Match Alabama. Click on the graphic of Alabama to link the response to the graphic. The Response tab should be on top. In the Erase field, select Before Next Entry. Click on the Hot Object tab. Select the Cursor field, and locate and select the Hand custom cursor. Click on the OK button to close the Cursor library. Click on the OK button to close the dialog window.

   d) You should now see the open Properties/Response dialog window for the response Match Georgia. Click on the graphic of Georgia to link the response to the graphic. The Hot Object tab should be on top. Select the Cursor field, and locate and select the Hand custom cursor. Click on the OK button to close the Cursor library. Click on the Response tab. In the Erase field, select Before Next Entry. Click on the OK button to close the dialog window.

11. Let's position the states so that they look like they are all part of the same map.

   a) Run the program so that all states are on screen.

   b) Jump to the flowline (Ctrl + J).

   c) Hold the Shift key down as you double click on the Display icon *Florida*. Drag Florida so that it is positioned as shown in figure 10-25. Jump to the flowline (Ctrl + J).

   d) Hold the Shift key down as you double click on the Display icon *Alabama*. Drag Alabama so that it is positioned as shown in figure 10-25. Jump to the flowline (Ctrl + J).

e) Hold the Shift key down as you double click on the Display icon *Georgia*. Drag Georgia so that it is positioned as shown in figure 10-25. Jump to the flowline (Ctrl + J).

12. Change the branch for the correct answer so that it will exit the interaction.
    a) Double click on the Response Type symbol above the Map icon *Match Georgia*. The Properties/Response Type dialog window should now be open.
    b) Select the Response tab. Click on the Branch field and select Exit Interaction. Click on the OK button.
    c) Select the Map icon *Match Georgia* and move the Map icon so that it is the first Map icon immediately to the right of the Interaction icon.

13. Let's add the Erase icon to clean up the Display icons that are outside any automatic erase structure.
    a) Drag an Erase icon and place it below the Interaction icon *Instructions*.
    b) Run the program. Click on Georgia. Click on the Continue button. You should have now exited the interaction and encountered the empty Erase icon. Click on Florida, Alabama, and Georgia. Click on the OK button to close the Erase icon. Your screen should now be empty.

14. Save your work by selecting File | Save.

Summary

- *The Hot Spot response type is most frequently used with photographs or graphic elements that do not lend themselves to "button" functionality.*

- *In contrast to the Button response, in which a button is clearly visible on screen, the Hot Spot response does not have any visible indicator on screen. The Hot Spot uses an invisible rectangular wireframe that can be resized and positioned to correspond to the desired "hot spot" on a photograph or graphic. In other words, the graphic contains the visual clue as to what the user needs to select.*

- *In practice exercise 10-1, you created an interactive structure that asked the user to select (click on) the tool most appropriate for hiking. The selection interaction contained a pegboard full of equipment.*

- *The Hot Object interaction response can be used to distinguish objects that are of irregular shape, or that are very close together, or when the objects themselves overlap. With the Hot Object interaction response, there is no longer an area that is "hot." Instead, you identify distinct objects that are "hot."*

- *The key difference in the structure for hot objects (in contrast to the structure for hot spots) is that every "hot object" must be displayed in its own Display icon (remember that Authorware does not distinguish objects within a single Display icon).*

- In practice exercise 10-2, you created an exercise that asked the user to select (click on) one of three overlapping objects. Practice exercise 10-3 demonstrated how this response type can be used to distinguish irregular objects in close proximity, such as the example of states constituting part of the southeastern United States.

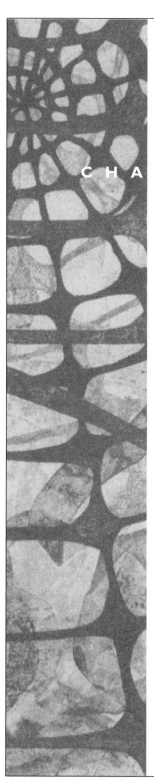

C H A P T E R

11

Creating

Interactions —

Part Two

Introduction

As you have seen in previous chapters, Authorware provides many different types of interactive responses "out of the box," without any programming. In this chapter, you will have the opportunity to work with the rest of the response types that do not require the use of variables. These response types include the Target response, the Tries Limit response, the Text Entry response, the Time Limit response, the Keypress response, and the Pull-down Menu response. By the end of the chapter you will be able to:

- *Describe the general capabilities and properties of the Target response type*
- *Create Single-target response interaction structures*
- *Create Multiple-target response interaction structures*
- *Describe the general capabilities and properties of the Tries Limit response type*
- *Create Tries Limit response interaction structures*
- *Describe the general capabilities and properties of the Text Entry response type*
- *Create Text Entry response interaction structures*
- *Describe the general capabilities and properties of the Time Limit response type*
- *Create Time Limit response interaction structures*
- *Describe the general capabilities and properties of the Keypress response type*
- *Create Keypress response interaction structures*
- *Describe the general capabilities and properties of the Pull-down Menu response type*
- *Create pull-down response interaction structures*

Guided Tour 11A: Target Interaction Response and Properties

The Target response type can serve as the foundation of many types of interactive strategies. In each interaction, the user is required to click on and drag-drop (frequently referred to as "drag-and-drop" interactions) an object from one location to another. Authorware's ease in creating drag-and-drop interactions distinguishes itself from many other development tools in the marketplace. The drag-and-drop technique can be implemented in a wide variety of ways. Figures 11-1 through 11-5 illustrate but a few of the many interactive strategies possible.

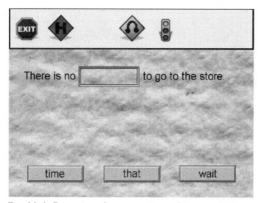

Fig. 11-1. Dragging the correct word to complete a sentence.

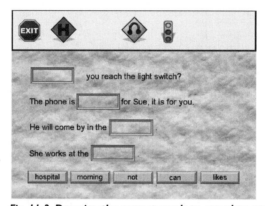

Fig. 11-2. Dragging the correct words to complete several sentences.

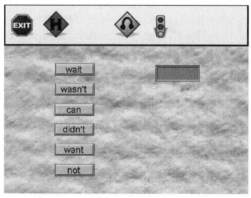

Fig. 11-3. Drag the word that has just been pronounced (via audio track).

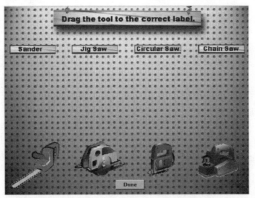

Fig. 11-4. Dragging objects to an appropriate category.

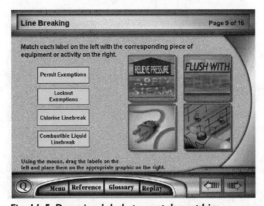

Fig. 11-5. Dragging labels to match graphics.

Each object to be dragged is placed in its own Display icon. The Target response uses an invisible rectangular wireframe (visible in the authoring mode only) that can be resized and positioned to correspond to the desired target at which the object should be dropped. The Target response requires that the target be made visible through the use of a graphic, in that the target wireframe is not visible to the user. Although the wireframe for the Target response looks very similar to the wireframe of the hot spot (while in authoring mode), they respond very differently to user interactions. The wireframe for a Target response is programmed to accept objects being dropped within this area, whereas the Hot Spot wireframe is programmed to accept mouse clicks. Let's take a closer look at this response type.

1. Start by opening a new file.
   a) Select File | New | File.
   b) Close the two dialog windows that have opened.

c) You should now be looking at an empty flowline.

2. Drag an Interaction icon to the flowline. Drag a Map icon and drop it to the right of the Interaction icon.

3. The Response Type dialog window should now be open. Click on the Target option and then click on the OK button.

4. Double click on the Response Type symbol above the Map icon to access the dialog window for this Target interaction response.

5. You should be looking at the Properties/Response dialog window for the Target interaction response. There are three parts of this window, but we will briefly look at only one of them, the Target tab. The left-hand side and the Response tab are identical to those you have seen previously, and therefore an explication of them is not repeated here.

6. Select the Target tab, if it is not already on top. See figure 11-6.

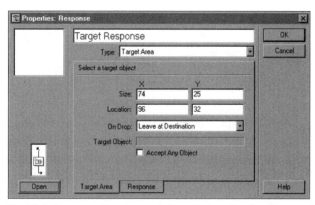

Fig. 11-6. Properties/Response dialog window showing Target tab.

7. Most of these options are very similar to those found on the Hot Spot tab. Examine the following regarding these options.

- **Size and Location:** *These fields are identical to those you have seen on the Button tab and Hot Spot tab. In this tab you can use the X and Y coordinates to precisely place the target wireframe.*

- **On Drop:** *Use this field to select what you want Authorware to do if the correct object has been dropped within the target area.*

  Leave at Destination: *The object is simply left wherever the user dropped it on screen. This is the default setting.*

  Put Back: *This option returns the object to whatever location it was in before the user started dragging it. This option is generally used for*

Shortcut

Select the Map icon and then press Ctrl + E to open the Properties/Reponse dialog window.

incorrect match responses. By "putting back" the object, it is visually (and hopefully intuitively) clear that this was an incorrect response.

Snap to Center: This option takes the object and moves it to the center of the target area, aligning the center of the object with the center of the target area. This option is frequently used for the correct response. By snapping the object to the center of the target area, there is a visual confirmation that the response is correct.

- **Target Object:** Remains grayed out until a single target object has been selected by clicking on it. After the object has been selected, the name of the icon that contains the object appears in this field.

- **Accept Any Object:** Placing a check mark in this field will allow Authorware to correctly match any object that is dragged and dropped within the specified target area. This option is frequently used in a catch-all response in which multiple objects can be dragged to multiple target areas.

Let's get to work building a single target interaction.

Practice Exercise 11-1: Single-target Drag and Drop Interaction

Description

In this exercise you are going to create an interactive strategy in which you ask the user to drag a graphic of a power tool to the correctly labeled area of a pegboard. In Chapter 9 you required that the user click on objects that were already located on a pegboard. In this exercise, the user is required to be a little more active by selecting and dragging the object to the correct location, dropping it within the target area.

Unlike many of the other interactions you have already created, this response type generally does not require that text-based feedback be provided to the user for incorrect or correct selections. As you just read about in the preceding guided tour, the Put Back and Snap to Center options (located on the Target tab) often provide adequate feedback to the user. If you are working with an audience or particular content that requires text-based feedback, you can always add a Display icon (for the feedback) and a Wait icon within the level 2 flowline within each Map icon. The following elements are covered in this exercise.

- *Importing an external graphic and creating text objects*
- *Creating user feedback for incorrect responses based on the Put Back option*
- *Creating user feedback for the correct response based on the Snap to Center option*

- *Creating a Single-target area response triggered by an object being dropped within the target area*

- *Creating a "Catch-all-else" target area triggered by an object being dropped within this area*

- *Enabling automatic erase functions*

- *Modifying branching functions*

Take a Look

CD-ROM ✳

Before beginning the exercise, let's take a look at the exercise in its completed state so that you can clearly see what it is you are about to build.

1. Select File | Open and locate on the companion CD-ROM the directory named *Chapter11*. Within this directory, locate and double click on the file named *Exer11-1*.

2. The file *Exer11-1* should now appear in your copy of Authorware. Click on the Restart button to play the file from the top of the flowline. Note the following properties of this completed exercise.

   - *When you drag and drop the object to an incorrect area, the object returns to where it was originally located.*

   - *For an incorrect response there is no text-based feedback and you can try again.*

   - *When you drag and drop the object to the correct area, the object snaps to the center of the target area.*

   - *For the correct response there is no text-based feedback and the program exits the interaction.*

   - *This is a subtle point, but notice that when you first run the program the pegboard appears before the tool.*

Storyboard: On Screen

Figures 11-7 through 11-9 show you what the finished presentation will look like. Figure 11-7 shows the complete presentation on screen. Figure 11-8 shows the display area for the Interaction icon *DragAndDrop*. Figure 11-9 shows the display area for the Display icon *JigSaw*.

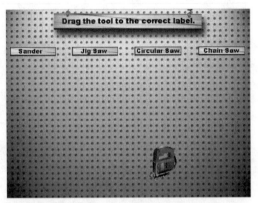

Fig. 11-7. Complete presentation on screen.

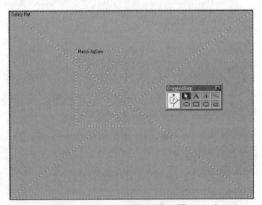

Fig. 11-8. Interaction icon **DragAndDrop** showing target areas.

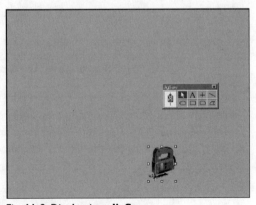

Fig. 11-9. Display icon **JigSaw**.

Storyboard: Behind the Scenes

Figure 11-10 shows the main and secondary flowlines (with all icons, their placement, and their names) as they should look when you are finished with this exercise. Figure 11-11 shows the Properties/Response dialog window (Target tab) for the Map icon *Match JigSaw*. Figure 11-12 shows this same tab for the Map icon *Safety Net*.

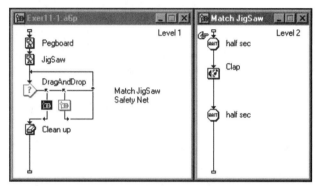

Fig. 11-10. Main flowline with level 2 flowline inside **Match JigSaw.**

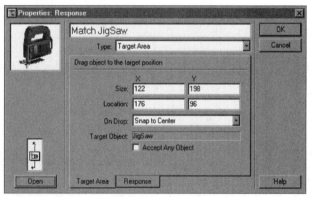

Fig. 11-11. Properties/Response dialog window showing Target tab for **Match JigSaw.**

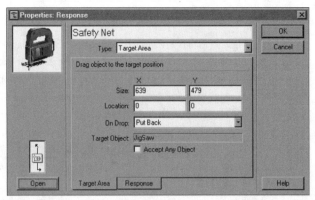

*Fig. 11-12. Properties/Response dialog window showing Target tab for **Safety Net**.*

Step-by-Step Instructions

1. Select File | New | File. Close the two Knowledge Object dialog windows.

2. Verify that you are now looking at a new flowline.

3. Set up the file properties.
   a) Select Modify | File | Properties.
   b) Select whatever background color you want.
   c) Make sure Size is set to 640 x 480.
   d) Remove the check marks beside the Tile Bar and Menu Bar options.
   e) Click on the OK button to close the window.
   f) Select File | Save and locate the *SaveWork* directory. Type in *Chap11-1* and click on the OK button.

4. Create the basic icon structure.
   a) Drag two display icons to the flowline. Name these icons *Pegboard* and *JigSaw*.
   b) Drag an Interaction icon to the flowline and place it below the Display icons. Name this icon *DragAndDrop*.
   c) Drag a Map icon and place it to the right of the Interaction icon. The Response Type dialog window has opened. Select the Target option and then click on the OK button. Name this Map icon *Match JigSaw*.
   d) Drag another Map icon and place it to the right of the first Map icon. Name this Map icon *Safety Net*.
   e) Drag an Erase icon to the bottom of the flowline and name it *Clean up*.

5. Add the content to the Display icon *Pegboard*.
   a) Double click on the Display icon *Pegboard*.
   b) Select File | Import. The *Import which file?* dialog window opens.

Go Solo

You could place the content of the Display icon *Pegboard* inside the display area of the Interaction icon *DragAndDrop*. A small disadvantage of doing this, however, is that when the user first encounters this interaction she will first see the jigsaw and then the pegboard. It is only a split-second difference, but it looks more professional if you first display the background (pegboard) and then the object (jigsaw). To accomplish this, place the background graphic on the flowline first, followed by another Display icon containing the draggable object. The Interaction icon follows, with the Target responses attached to it.

If you try to reposition either graphic at this point, both will move, because they are both selected. You may notice it may seem a little difficult to deselect the objects by clicking on them. You can press the space bar to deselect all objects, and then select the object you want.

Because you will be positioning text objects over graphic objects that are about the same size, you may find it helpful to use a center alignment for the text objects and then either stretch or reduce the size of the text object margins so that they are a different width than the sign graphic. This will make it easier to select either of the objects. If you do not follow this tip, you may find it difficult to distinguish (and select) one of these objects from the other. You can also use the Tab key to move the current selection from one object on screen to another.

c) On the bottom of this window, select Show Preview (place a check mark there).

d) In the lower right-hand corner of this window, click on the plus (+) button to expand the window.

e) Use the *Look in* field to browse to the companion CD-ROM, and look in the *Chapter11* directory.

f) Locate and single click on the graphic *EmptyPegboard.bmp*. Click on the Add button located on the far right.

g) Locate and single click on the graphic *sign-pegboard.bmp*. Click on the Add button located on the far right.

h) Click on the Import button located in the lower center area of the window to import both graphics at the same time. You should now see both graphics in the Display icon.

i) While both graphics are still selected (have handlebars around them), select Window | Inspectors | Modes. Click on the Transparent mode option to get rid of the white borders on the outside of each graphic.

j) Both objects are currently selected. Hold down the Shift key as you click on the small sign you just imported. This will deselect the sign graphic, leaving the background graphic selected. Position and resize the pegboard graphic in the display area, if you need to.

k) Click on the sign graphic. Press Ctrl + C to copy the sign to the clipboard. Press Ctrl + V three (3) times so that you end up with a total of four (4) sign graphics. Position the signs as shown in figure 11-8.

l) Select the Text tool. Select Text | Font | Arial. Select Text | Size | 12. Select Text | Style | Bold. Select Text | Alignment | Center. Select Window | Inspectors | Modes | Transparent (or Ctrl + M).

m) Click the I-bar cursor on the background of the pegboard and create four (4) separate text objects. Type in *Sander, Jigsaw, Circular Saw,* and *Chain Saw*. Either stretch or reduce each text object's margins so that they are different than the width of the sign. Position each text object over one of the signs, as shown in figure 11-7.

n) Select Text | Size | 18. Click the I-bar cursor on the background of the pegboard and create one more text object. Type in *Drag the tool to the correct label*. Position this text object over the large sign at the top, as shown in figure 11-7.

6. Add the content to the Display icon *JigSaw*. This will be much quicker.
a) Double click on the Display icon *JigSaw*.
b) Select File | Import. The *Import which file?* dialog window opens.
c) Use the *Look in* field to browse to the companion CD-ROM, and look in the *Chapter11* directory.

    d)   Locate and select the graphic *JigSaw.bmp*. Click on the Import button. You should now see the graphic in the Display icon.

    e)   While the graphic is still selected, select Window | Inspectors | Modes. Click on the Transparent mode option to get rid of the white borders on the outside of the graphic.

    f)   Position the graphic toward the bottom of the pegboard.

    g)   Select Modify | Icon | Properties. Click on the Layout tab. In the Movable field, select On Screen. This will allow the user to move the object that is displayed in this icon (the jigsaw), but it can only be moved on screen and cannot be dragged out of sight (off screen).

7.   And now for some fun. Let's connect the object with the correct target area.

    a)   Click on the Restart button on the toolbar.

    b)   Verify that you are now looking at the Properties/Response dialog window for *Match JigSaw*.

    c)   The Target Area tab should be on top (but if not, click on it).

    d)   Toward the top of the Target Area tab there is an instructional message *Select a target object.*

    e)   Click on the title bar of the dialog window and drag it out of the way so that you can see the graphic of the jigsaw. Click on the jigsaw. You should now see a picture of the jigsaw in the upper left-hand corner of the dialog window. This shows you the object to which the current response is linked.

    f)   Note that the instructional message has now changed. It now states *Drag object to the target position.*

    g)   Drag the graphic of the jigsaw and drop it so that it rests just below the sign labeled *Jigsaw*.

    h)   Click on and drag the handlebars and sides of the wireframe to resize and reposition the target area so that it encompasses both the sign and a reasonable area below and around the jigsaw. See figure 11-8 as reference.

    i)   In the center of the Target Area tab there is a field named On Drop. Click on the pull-down menu and select Snap to Center. Remember that this is the correct response; that is, dragging the graphic of the jigsaw to the appropriately labeled sign. It is a nice visual touch to snap the graphic to center, providing the user with visual feedback that the interaction is functioning and that the correct target has been found.

    j)   Click on the Response tab. In the Branch field, select Exit Interaction.

    k)   Click on the OK button to close the dialog window. You should now see the dialog window for the Safety Net response.

·T/P·

If you accidentally closed this second dialog window along with the first one, click on the Restart button. The dialog window for the unlinked Safety Net response should appear on screen. If this does not work (from the flowline), double click on the response symbol for the Safety Net to open this dialog window.

8. Connect this link to provide visual feedback that the user has dropped the graphic in the wrong location. You want to be able to detect this "drop" everywhere on screen, outside the correct target area.

   a) Verify that you are now looking at the Properties/Response dialog window for *Safety Net*.

   b) Click on the Target Area tab.

   c) As you saw before, toward the top of the Target Area tab there is an instructional message *Select a target object*.

   d) Click on the title bar of the dialog window and drag it out of the way so that you can see the graphic of the jigsaw. Click on the graphic of the jigsaw. You should now see a picture of the jigsaw in the upper left-hand corner of the dialog window.

   e) Note that the instructional message has now changed. It now states *Drag object to the target position*. In this case, the safety net target area is the entire screen. Therefore, you do not have to drag the object anywhere.

   f) Click on and drag the handlebars and sides of the wireframe to resize and reposition the target area so that it encompasses the entire screen. See figure 11-8 for reference.

   g) In the On Drop field, click on the pull-down menu and select Put Back. You are now working with the incorrect (catch-all) response; that is, dragging the graphic of the jigsaw to anywhere on screen, outside the correct target area. Authorware will "put back" the graphic object to its original location once the object has been dropped. Most people understand this visual feedback to mean that they got it wrong.

   h) Click on the Response tab. Verify that the Branch field is set to Try Again.

   i) Click on the OK button to close the dialog window.

9. Let's take a look at what you have now.

   a) Click on the Restart button. Authorware should now be at the interaction, waiting for you to drag an object.

   b) Drag the object and drop it beside the Chain Saw sign. It should have returned to its starting location. Try a couple more incorrect drag-and-drop operations.

   c) Drag the object to the correct target: *JigSaw*. You should now be looking at the Erase icon. Click on the graphic of the jig saw, the only object that has not already erased (because it is outside the automatic erase functions of the Interaction icon).

   d) Click on the Restart button. Drag the object to the correct target. You can see that you are not done because as soon as you dropped the object in the correct target area the entire exercise erased.

·T*i*P·

If you think you need to provide text-based feedback as well, you can open the Map icon *Safety Net* and place both a Display icon and Wait icon on the level 2 flowline inside this Map icon. Make sure to set the Response tab's Erase field to Before Next Selection.

NOTE

As you are working with Drag-and-Drop interactions, you will soon discover that it is not difficult to accidentally grab and drag the background graphic instead of the object you intended. After the program has been packaged, the user will not be able to drag the background (or any object whose properties have not been set to Movable). In authoring mode, you are able to move any object on screen. In this type of situation, however, it would be nice to be able to "lock" background graphics in place so that you do not accidentally move them. After variables have been introduced in Chapter 12, you will learn how you can lock objects in place, even in authoring mode.

10. Let's modify the structure so that it waits a little bit before the erase happens, as well as provide a little positive feedback while we are at it.

a) Double click on the Map icon *Match JigSaw* to open it.

b) Drag a Wait icon and place it on the level 2 flowline inside the Map icon. Name it *half sec*.

c) Drag a Sound icon and place it on the level 2 flowline, placing it below the first Wait icon. Name the Sound icon *Clap*.

d) Drag another Wait icon and place it on the level 2 flowline, below the Sound icon. Name it *half sec*.

e) Examine figure 11-10 for a reference of what the level 2 flowline should look like at this point.

f) Double click on the first (top) Wait icon to open the dialog window. Remove all check marks. Click the cursor in the Time Limit field and type in *.5* (that is, a period and a 5, for half a second). Click on the OK button to close the dialog window.

g) Double click on the bottom Wait icon to open the dialog window. Remove all check marks. Click the cursor in the Time Limit field and type in *.5*. Click on the OK button to close the dialog window.

h) Double click on the Sound icon to open the dialog window. In the lower left corner, click on the Import button. The *Import which file?* dialog window opens. Use the browse function to locate the *Chapter11* directory on the companion CD-ROM. Select the *Clap.wav* file. Click on the Import button. You should see the blue progress bar briefly on screen. In the upper left corner, click on the Play button to preview the sound. Click on the OK button to close the dialog window.

i) Close the Map icon.

11. Let's take another look.

a) Click on the Restart button.

b) Drag the object and drop it on a couple of incorrect locations.

c) Drag the object to the correct target: *JigSaw*. You should now experience a brief pause, hear an applause, followed by another brief pause. The exercise should then exit and erase.

12. Save your file. Good work!

Practice Exercise 11-2:
Multiple Target Drag-and-Drop Interaction

Description

Now that you have mastered the drag-and-drop technique with a single object and target area, it is time to tackle multiple objects with multiple target areas.

To save time and effort you will copy and paste the previous exercise and will make additions and modifications to this beginning structure. If you would rather build this exercise from scratch, go ahead and do so. You should be able to look at the "Storyboard" section and have enough information to create the interaction on your own, if you are so inclined.

As a reminder, to let Authorware distinguish unique objects, each object must be placed in its own Display icon. This means that instead of a single Display icon, such as in the previous exercise, you will now have four Display icons, each with a separate tool. For each target object there will need to be a unique target area for that object. In other words, you will also have four target responses and corresponding target areas.

What about the safety net? Will you need four target responses, one for each object? There is a better solution that avoids this, as you will see in material to follow. Let's jump in. The following elements are covered in this exercise.

- *Copying and reusing an existing interaction structure*
- *Creating user feedback for incorrect responses based on the Put Back option*
- *Creating user feedback for the correct response based on the Snap to Center option*
- *Creating multiple Target Area responses with multiple target objects*
- *Creating a "Catch-all-else" target area for multiple target objects*
- *Enabling automatic erase functions*
- *Modifying branching functions*

Take a Look

CD-ROM

Before beginning the exercise, let's take a look at the exercise in its completed state so that you can clearly see what it is you are about to build.

1. Select File | Open and locate on the companion CD-ROM the directory named *Chapter11*. In this directory, locate and double click on the file named *Exer11-2*.

2. The file *Exer11-2* should now appear in your copy of Authorware. Click on the Restart button to play the file from the top of the flowline. Note the following properties of this completed exercise.

    - *When you drag and drop any object to an incorrect area, the object returns to where it was originally located.*

    - *For an incorrect response there is no text-based feedback and you can try again.*

- When you drag and drop an object to the correct area, the object snaps to the center of the target area.

- For the correct response there is no text-based feedback and the program exits the interaction.

- Note that there is a Done button on screen. Clicking on this button allows the user to exit the interaction. This is a temporary solution. The real solution involves the use of a variable. After you have been introduced to variables in a later chapter, you will revisit this exercise to create a better "exit" solution.

Storyboard: On Screen

Figures 11-13 and 11-14 show you what the finished presentation will look like. Figure 11-13 shows the complete presentation on screen. Figure 11-14 shows the display area of the Interaction icon *DragAndDrop*.

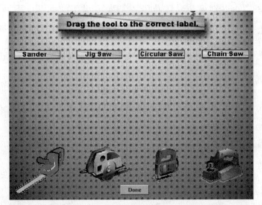

Fig. 11-13. Complete presentation on screen.

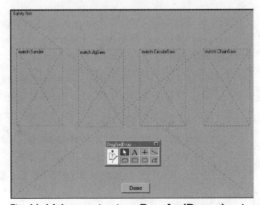

*Fig. 11-14. Interaction icon **DragAndDrop** showing all target areas.*

Storyboard: Behind the Scenes

Figure 11-15 shows the main and secondary flowlines (with all icons, their placement, and their names) as they should look when you are finished with this exercise. Figure 11-16 shows the Properties/Response dialog window and Target tab for the Map icon *Match JigSaw*. Figure 11-17 shows this same tab for the Map icon *Safety Net*.

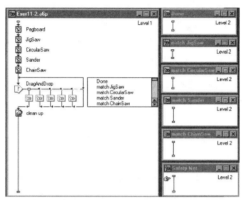

Fig. 11-15. Main flowline with all level 2 flowlines.

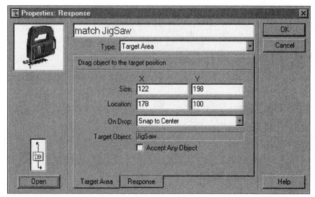

Fig. 11-16. Properties/Response dialog window showing Target tab for Match JigSaw.

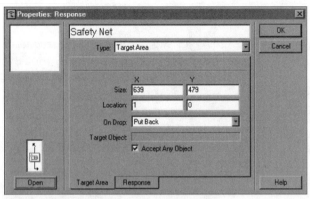

Fig. 11-17. Properties/Response dialog window showing Target tab for Safety Net.

Step-by-Step Instructions

Go Solo

1. Start with the completed version of the previous exercise. You can use either the file you created and saved on your hard drive or the completed version found on the companion CD-ROM.

    a) Open *Chap11-1.a6p* from the *SaveWork* directory on your computer's hard drive.

        Or

        Open *Exer11-1.a6p* from the companion CD-ROM's *Chapter11* directory.

    b) Select File | Save As and save this file as *Chap11-2.* into the *SaveWork* directory on your computer's hard drive.

CD-ROM

2. Add the other objects, which are more tools.

    a) Drag three (3) Display icons to the flowline and place them below the Display icon *JigSaw* (and above the Interaction icon *Tools*). Name these icons *CircularSaw*, *Sander*, and *ChainSaw*.

    b) Double click on the Display icon *CircularSaw*.

    c) Select File | Import. The *Import which file?* dialog window opens. Use the *Look in* field to browse to the companion CD-ROM, and look in the *Chapter11* directory.

    d) Locate and select the graphic *CircularSaw.bmp*. Click on the Import button. You should now see the graphic in the Display icon.

    e) While the graphic is still selected, select Window | Inspectors | Modes. Click on the Transparent mode option to get rid of the white borders on the outside of the graphic. Leave the inspector open.

    f) Position the graphic at the bottom of the pegboard.

g) Select Modify | Icon | Properties. Click on the Layout tab. In the Movable field, select On Screen. Close the icon.

h) Double click on the Display icon *Sander*.

i) Select File | Import. The *Import which file?* dialog window opens. Use the *Look in* field to browse to the companion CD-ROM, and look in the *Chapter11* directory.

j) Locate and select the graphic *Sander.bmp*. Click on the Import button. You should now see the graphic in the Display icon.

k) While the graphic is still selected, click on the Transparent mode option.

l) Position the graphic at the bottom of the pegboard.

m) Select Modify | Icon | Properties. Click on the Layout tab. In the Movable field, select On Screen. Close the icon.

n) Double click on the Display icon *ChainSaw*.

o) Select File | Import. The *Import which file?* dialog window opens. Use the *Look in* field to browse to the companion CD-ROM, and look in the *Chapter11* directory.

p) Locate and select the graphic *ChainSaw.bmp*. Click on the Import button. You should now see the graphic in the Display icon.

q) While the graphic is still selected, click on the Transparent mode option.

r) Position the graphic at the bottom of the pegboard.

s) Select Modify | Icon | Properties. Click on the Layout tab. In the Movable field, select On Screen. Close the icon.

3. Add more target responses.

a) Drag three (3) Map icons and place them *between* the two Map icons that are already there. That is, place these to the right of the Map icon *Match JigSaw* but to the left of the Map icon *Safety Net*. Name these Map icons *Match CircularSaw*, *Match Sander*, and *Match ChainSaw*.

b) Click on the Restart button in the toolbar.

c) Verify that you are now looking at the Properties/Response dialog window for *Match CircularSaw*.

d) Click on the Target Area tab, if it is not on top.

e) Toward the top of the Target Area tab there is an instructional message *Select a target object*.

f) Click on the title bar of the dialog window and pull it out of the way so that you can see the graphic of the circular saw. Click on the graphic of the circular saw. You should now see a picture of the circular saw in the upper left-hand corner of the dialog window.

g) The instructional message now states *Drag object to the target position.* Drag the saw and place it below the sign for the circular saw.

h) Click on and drag the handlebars and sides of the wireframe to resize and reposition the target area so that it encompasses both the sign and a reasonable area below and around the circular saw. See figure 11-14 as reference.

i) Because you placed Map icons to the right of an existing icon in which the response properties had been set previously, Authorware assumed that when you dragged the new Map icons that you would want the same settings as those found in the first response. Let's check out this assumption.

j) Look at the On Drop field. It should already be set to Snap to Center. This Map icon is the correct response for dragging the circular saw to the appropriately labeled sign. Authorware assumed correctly in this case, and therefore you are ready to go on. (Actually there is a problem in the Response tab, but this is dealt with in material to follow because it will involve looking at the "big picture.")

k) Click on the OK button to close the dialog window.

l) Verify that you are now looking at the Properties/Response dialog window for *Match Sander.*

m) Click on the Target Area tab, if it is not on top.

n) Follow the guidance of the instructional message *Select a target object.*

o) Drag the dialog window out of the way so that you can see the graphic of the sander. Click on the sander. You should now see a picture of the sander in the upper left-hand corner of the dialog window.

p) The instructional message now states *Drag object to the target position.* Drag the sander and place it below the sign for the sander.

q) Click on and drag the handlebars and sides of the wireframe to resize and reposition the target area so that it encompasses both the sign and a reasonable area below and around the sander. See figure 11-14 as reference.

r) Click on the OK button to close the dialog window.

s) Verify that you are now looking at the Properties/Response dialog window for *Match ChainSaw.*

t) Click on the Target Area tab, if it is not on top. Follow the guidance of the instructional message *Select a target object.*

u) Drag the dialog window out of the way so that you can see the graphic of the chain saw. Click on the chain saw. You should now see a picture of the chain saw in the upper left-hand corner of the dialog window.

v) The instructional message now states *Drag object to the target position.* Drag the chain saw and place it below the sign for the chain saw.

w) Click on and drag the handlebars and sides of the wireframe to resize and reposition the target area so that is encompasses both the sign and a reasonable area below and around the chain saw. See figure 11-14 as reference.

x) Click on the OK button to close the dialog window.

4. What about the safety net?

a) Double click on the Response Type symbol for the Map icon *Safety Net*.

b) If the Target tab is not on top, click on it.

c) Look in the upper left-hand corner. As you can see, because you copied this structure from the first exercise, the safety net is currently linked to the jigsaw. Try clicking on the circular saw on screen. The picture now changes to the circular saw. Does this mean that you will have to include four safety nets, one for each object?

The answer is no. Look at the bottom of the Target tab and find the Accept Any Object option. Click on the box next to this option, so that a check mark appears there. Note that now there is no object depicted in the upper left-hand corner, as the safety net will now match any object dragged into its target area (which encompasses the entire screen).

5. Let's take a look at what the interaction looks like at this point.

a) Click on the Restart button.

b) Press Ctrl + P to pause. If you want to reposition any of the tools, go ahead and do so now. Single click on the object you want to move. Move it to where you want it. Single click on the next object, and so on. When finished, press Ctrl + P to resume play.

c) Drag any object to the appropriately labeled target area. You exited the interaction, right? This is no good; you need to be able to continue dragging objects.

d) Press Ctrl + J to jump to the flowline. Note that currently all of the correctly matched responses have exit interactions. Obviously this will not do. After the first attempt, you need to be able to continue to move objects; that is, you need to be able to "try again."

e) Double click on the Response Type symbol for the Map icon *Match JigSaw*. Click on the Response tab. In the Branch field, select Try Again. Click on the OK button.

f) Double click on the Response Type symbol for the Map icon *Match CircularSaw*. Click on the Response tab. In the Branch field, select Try Again. Click on the OK button.

NOTE

Remember as you saw demonstrated in exercise 10-1 that the reason the safety net catch-all response works as intended is that you have placed it on the far right side of the interaction. Authorware reads the responses from left to right, providing the opportunity to match a correct response before reaching the Catch-all response. If you want to review how this works, see steps 21 and 22 of exercise 10-1.

Shortcut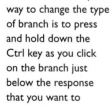

A reminder: The quick way to change the type of branch is to press and hold down the Ctrl key as you click on the branch just below the response that you want to change. Keep clicking until the appropriate branch is displayed.

327

g) Double click on the Response Type symbol for the Map icon *Match Sander*. Click on the Response tab. In the Branch field, select Try Again. Click on the OK button.

h) Double click on the Response Type symbol for the Map icon *Match ChainSaw*. Click on the Response tab. In the Branch field, select Try Again. Click on the OK button.

6. Let's try running the program again.

a) Click on the Restart button.

b) Drag any object to any incorrect location. It should return to its original location.

c) Drag any object to its correct target area. Drag the rest of the objects to their respective correct target areas.

d) Changing the branching to Try Again allows you to continue in the interaction until you have correctly dragged all objects. But what now? How do you get out of the interaction?

e) Press Ctrl + J to jump to the flowline. As you look at the flowline, you can see that it is "broken" (i.e., discontinuous). In other words, there is no flowline extending from the interaction structure down to the Erase icon, as shown in figure 11-18.

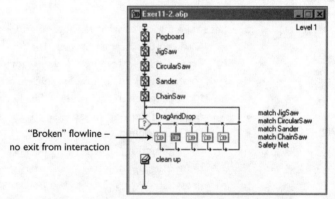

Fig. 11-18. Flowline is "broken," meaning no Exit interaction.

f) For a minute, think about what you need to do here, without worrying about how to do it.

In simple terms, you need to be able to keep dragging objects (as you can do now) until you have correctly matched all objects. This condition (i.e., all responses correctly matched) is actually an Authorware system variable, and it will be with the use of this variable that you can provide the actual solution to this situation. (This is covered in Chapter 12.)

g) However, because you have not learned variables yet, you will employ a temporary solution. Actually you have seen the temporary solution in an earlier exercise.

h) Drag a Map icon and carefully drop it in the very first position to the right of the Interaction icon (to the left of all existing Map icons). As you drop it, the Response Type dialog window opens.

i) Select the Button response. Name this icon *Done*.

j) Hold the Ctrl key down as you click on the branch for the Map icon *Done*. This should have changed the branch to an Exit branch.

7. Let's try running the program yet another time.

a) Click on the Restart button.

b) Press Ctrl + P to pause. Click on the Done button and position it where you want it. Press Ctrl + P to resume play. Drag all objects to their correct locations.

c) Click on the Done button to exit the interaction.

d) As you can see, although the pegboard and jigsaw were erased by the Erase icon (recall that you copied the starting structure from exercise 11-1), the new objects (circular saw, sander, and chain saw) are still on screen. There is an easy fix.

e) Press Ctrl + J to jump to the flowline.

f) Hold the Shift key down as you double click on the Erase icon. You should now be looking at the open dialog window for the Erase icon, as well as be able to see the unerased objects (circular saw, sander, and chain saw) on screen.

g) Click on the circular saw, sander, and chain saw to add each of these objects to the Erase icon's list of objects to be erased. Click on the OK button to close the dialog window.

8. One last time, run the program.

a) Click on the Restart button.

b) Drag each object to its correct target area.

c) Click on the Done button.

d) You should have exited the interaction, and all objects should have erased.

9. Save the file. This interactive response type is really fun to work with. You now have an excellent foundation to start working with it.

Holding the Shift key down as you open the Erase dialog window brings back to the screen whatever was on screen before you jumped to the flowline.

Guided Tour 11B:
Tries Limit Interaction Response and Properties

The next response type – Tries Limit – is generally used as an addition to an interaction that uses one of the previously discussed response types as the primary interactive strategy. As the name implies, Tries Limit allows the Authorware programmer to restrict the number of attempts the user is allowed with any given interactive structure. Let's take a look at the Tries Limit response.

1. Start by opening a new file.
    a) Select File | New | File.
    b) Close the two dialog windows that have opened.
    c) Verify that you are now looking at an empty flowline.

2. Drag an Interaction icon to the flowline. Drag a Map icon and drop it to the right of the Interaction icon.

3. The Response Type window should now be open. Click on the Tries Limit option and then click on the OK button.

4. Double click on the Response Type symbol above the Map icon to access the dialog window for this Tries Limit interaction response.

5. You should be looking at the Properties/Response dialog window for the Tries Limit interaction response. There are two tabs on this window, but we will briefly look only at the Tries Limit tab. The Response tab is identical to that you have seen before, so we will not repeat it here.

6. Select the Tries Limit tab, if it is not already on top. See figure 11-19.

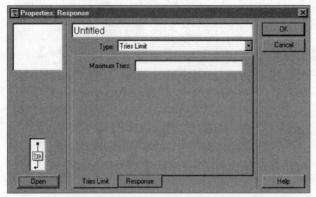

Fig. 11-19. Properties/Response dialog window showing Tries Limit tab.

7. As you can see, the tour will be very short because there is only one field on this tab, the Maximum Tries field. This blank field allows you to type in whatever number you want to use to limit the attempts on the interaction.

To see how this response type works, you will need an example to work with, which is supplied by practice exercise 11-3.

Practice Exercise 11-3:
Adding a Tries Limit Response

Description

In the last exercise using target areas, there were four objects to be dragged to four target areas. In this exercise you are going to copy that exercise and add a Tries Limit response so that the user will only be allowed seven (7) attempts to successfully complete the interaction. If the user successfully completes the interaction before the seventh attempt, he will exit the interaction.

However, on the seventh attempt, Authorware will automatically "match" the Tries Limit response and provide feedback to the user that the maximum number of attempts has been reached. As an additional instructional strategy and as part of this feedback, you will also create some animation to illustrate the correct placement of all objects. The following elements are covered in this exercise.

- *Copying and reusing an existing interaction structure*
- *Creating a Tries Limit response with an existing interaction*
- *Creating animation to illustrate the correct responses for a target area interaction*

Take a Look

CD-ROM

Before beginning the exercise, let's take a look at the exercise in its completed state so that you can clearly see what it is you are about to build.

1. Select File | Open and locate on the companion CD-ROM the directory named *Chapter11*. In this directory, locate and double click on the file named *Exer11-3*.

2. The file *Exer11-3* should now appear in your copy of Authorware. Click on the Restart button to play the file from the top of the flowline. Note the following properties of this completed exercise.

   - *Drag the objects to incorrect locations and note that on the seventh attempt you see feedback indicating that you have exceeded the number of attempts.*

   - *In addition to the text-based feedback within the Tries Limit response, after selecting the Continue button, you will see animation that moves all objects to their correct locations.*

Storyboard: On Screen

Figures 11-20 and 11-21 show you what the finished presentation will look like. Figure 11-20 shows the completed presentation on screen. Figure 11-21 shows the display area of the Interaction icon *DragAndDrop*.

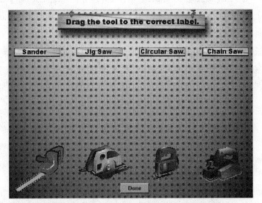

Fig. 11-20. Complete presentation on screen.

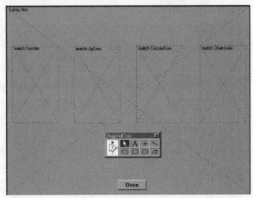

*Fig. 11-21. Interaction icon **DragAndDrop** showing all target areas.*

Storyboard: Behind the Scenes

Figure 11-22 shows the main and secondary flowlines (with all icons, their placement, and their names) as they should look when you are finished with this exercise. Figure 11-23 shows the Properties/Response dialog window and the Tries Limit tab for the Map icon *Exceed Limit*. Figure 11-24 shows the level 2 flowline inside the Map icon *Exceed Limit*.

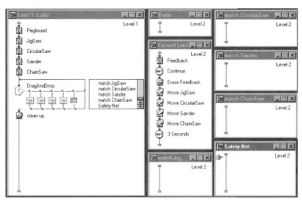

Fig. 11-22. Main flowline with all level 2 flowlines.

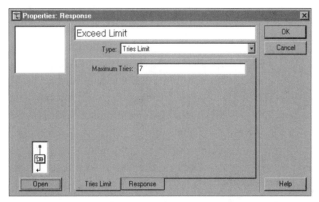

Fig. 11-23. Properties/Response dialog window showing Tries Limit tab for **Exceed Limit.**

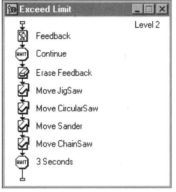

Fig. 11-24. Level 2 flowline inside Map icon **Exceed Limit.**

Step-by-Step Instructions

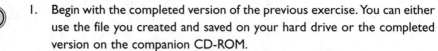

Go Solo

1. Begin with the completed version of the previous exercise. You can either use the file you created and saved on your hard drive or the completed version on the companion CD-ROM.

    a) Open *Chap11-2.a6p* from the *SaveWork* directory on your computer's hard drive.

        Or

        Open *Exer11-2.a6p* from the companion CD-ROM's *Chapter11* directory.

    b) Select File | Save As and save this file as *Chap11-3.a6p* into the *SaveWork* directory on your computer's hard drive.

2. Begin adding "new parts" to this structure.

    a) Drag a Map icon and carefully place it to the right of the Map icon *Done*. Note that Authorware assumed that you wanted a Button response, in that you dropped it to the right of an existing Button response. This assumption is incorrect, but very quick to correct.

    b) Name this new Map icon *Exceed Limit*.

    c) Double click on the Response Type symbol for the Map icon *Exceed Limit*.

    d) In the Type field, select Tries Limit. The interaction type changes to Tries Limit.

    e) In the Tries Limit field, type in 7.

    f) Click on the OK button to close the dialog window.

3. Add some text feedback for the Tries Limit response.

    a) Double click on the Map icon *Exceed Limit* to open the level 2 flowline within it.

    b) Drag a Display icon and place it on this level 2 flowline. Name the icon *Feedback*.

    c) Drag a Wait icon and place it on the level 2 flowline, below the Display icon. Name it *Continue*.

    d) Drag an Erase icon and place it on the level 2 flowline, below the Wait icon. Name it *Erase Feedback*.

    e) Double click on the Display icon. Select File | Import. Use the *Look in* field to locate the companion CD-ROM and the *Chapter11* directory on it. Select the file *Overlay.jpg* and click on the Import button. Position the overlay graphic in the center of the screen. Leave the Display icon open.

    f) Select Text | Font | Arial. Select Text | Size | 12. Select Text | Style | Bold.

g) Select the Text tool. Click the I-bar cursor on screen and type in these two sentences: *You have exceeded the maximum number of attempts. Watch as we show you the correct locations.*

h) Reposition the text on top of the overlay screen. Close the Display icon.

i) Drag four (4) Motion icons to the level 2 flowline and place them below the Erase icon. Name them *Move JigSaw, Move CircularSaw, Move Sander,* and *Move ChainSaw.*

j) Drag a Wait icon to the level 2 flowline and place it below the last Motion icon. Name this icon *3 seconds.*

k) Double click on the Wait icon. Remove both check marks in the option fields. Click the cursor in the Time Limit field and type in *3.* Click on the OK button to close the dialog window.

4. Connect the Erase icon and Motion icons to the objects.

a) Click on the Restart button.

b) Drag any object(s) to incorrect locations seven (7) times. You should now see the text feedback. Press Ctrl + P to pause. Reposition the text and Continue button so that they are where you want them. Press Ctrl + P to resume play.

c) Click on the Continue button.

d) You should have now encountered the Erase icon. Click on the overlay screen and feedback text only, leaving everything else on screen. Select an erase transition if you want one. Click on the OK button to close the Erase icon.

e) You should have now encountered the Properties/Motion Icon dialog window for *Move JigSaw.* Accept the Motion Type default setting Direct to Point. In the Concurrency field, select Concurrent. Click on the Layout tab, where you are instructed to *Click object to be moved.* Click on the jig saw. Drag the jig saw to the area immediately below the sign for JigSaw. Click on the OK button.

f) You should have now encountered the Properties/Motion Icon dialog window for *Move CircularSaw.* Click on the circular saw. In the Concurrency field, select Concurrent. Drag the circular saw to the area immediately below the sign for Circular Saw. Click on the OK button.

g) You should have now encountered the Properties/Motion Icon dialog window for *Move Sander.* In the Concurrency field, select Concurrent. Click on the sander. Drag the sander to the area immediately below the sign for Sander. Click on the OK button.

h) You should have now encountered the Properties/Motion Icon dialog window for *Move ChainSaw.* In the Concurrency field, select Concurrent. Click on the chain saw. Drag the chain saw to the area immediately below the sign for Chain Saw. Click on the OK button.

5. Let's test it out.
    a) Click on the Restart button.
    b) Drag the objects incorrectly so that you exceed the maximum number. You should see the feedback. Click on the Continue button. The animation should illustrate the correct location of each tool. After a 3-second pause, everything should erase.

6. There is a minor problem that you cannot fix yet. You will need a variable to offer a solution, but let's take a look.
    a) Click on the Restart button.
    b) Move three (3) of the objects to their correct locations. For the fourth, fifth, and sixth attempts, drag the object to incorrect locations. On the seventh attempt, drag the remaining object to its correct location. Note that you still received the feedback for exceeding the maximum attempts, even though you correctly matched all four objects.

    Take a look at the flowline. Authorware really has no other choice at this point. Even though you got the last object into the correct location, with the Try Again branch, Authorware circled back to the Interaction icon, where it read seven attempts and automatically triggered the Tries Limit response. (You will return to the solution to this exercise after you have learned a little about variables.)

7. Save the file.

Guided Tour 11C:
Text Entry Interaction Response and Properties

Authorware's next response type, the Text Entry interaction response, requires that the user use the keyboard and type in a response to whatever is being requested. This response type is used for traditional questions of the "fill-in-the-blank" nature as well as any time the user is asked for "free-form" data entries. These requests for user data may include information such as name, address, and so on. In fact, the Text Entry response is a foundation for most user log-in structures.

When you are using the Text Entry response for formal questions, especially when the results are being recorded, you will need to be careful about what answers you are willing to accept as correct and what options you use as part of this "answer judging" process. As you will see in material to follow, there are several options that can be selected or ignored in setting up Authorware's "answer judging."

Actually, you face this same situation if you are an instructor grading a "paper and pencil" test of fill-in-the-blank questions. What criteria are you going to use, and how strictly will you adhere to these? Hopefully before starting the grading process you have already considered what responses you will accept, as well as such considerations as whether you are going to count spelling or not. The difference here is that Authorware forces you to make all of these decisions up front, in selecting what to include in the answer judging and in what response patterns you use. Let's take a closer look.

1. Start by opening a new file.
   a) Select File | New | File.
   b) Close the two dialog windows that have opened.
   c) You should now be looking at an empty flowline.

2. Drag an Interaction icon to the flowline. Drag a Map icon and drop it to the right of the Interaction icon.

3. The Response Type window should now be open. Click on the Text Entry option and then click on the OK button.

4. Double click on the Response Type symbol above the Map icon to access the dialog window for this Text Entry interaction response.

5. You should be looking at the Properties/Response dialog window for the Text Entry interaction response. There are two tabs on this window, but we will briefly look only at the Text Entry tab. The Response tab is identical to that you have seen previously, and therefore we will not repeat it here.

6. Select the Text Entry tab, if it is not already on top. See figure 11-25.

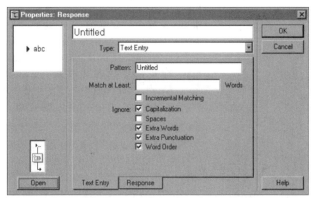

Fig. 11-25. Properties/Response dialog window showing Text Entry tab.

7. Examine the following fields and options on the Text Entry tab.

   • **Pattern:** *This field is where the anticipated answer is entered for this particular response. Whatever is entered here is what the user must type in* *to match this response. Note that whatever is entered in the Pattern field also becomes the title of the icon. Be careful with this response type, as the icon labels (titles) serve a dual purpose, unlike the icon title of most other response types. You can create a pattern that accepts multiple answers with the use of Authorware's "or" symbol, which is a pipe (|). For example, the entry of Bill | William in the Pattern field would accept either of these responses. You can also use the question mark (?) wild card for single characters or the asterisk (*) as a wild card for a word. See Authorware's Help feature or the Authorware manual's text entry rules for more information on these options.*

- **Match at Least:** *Enter a number in this field to indicate the minimum number of words (relative to the total number of words in the Pattern field) the user must enter to match this response.*

- **Incremental Matching:** *If the Pattern field contains more than one word, placing a check mark in this field will allow the user multiple opportunities to type in all required words. For example, if the pattern is George Washington, the user could type in Washington in the first attempt and George the second attempt and still be judged correct. To provide meaningful feedback to the user concerning partial answers, the use of the incremental matching can be a bit tricky.*

- **Ignore:** *This area includes a number of options that will be ignored by Authorware during "answer judging." The presence of a check mark next to the option means that it will be ignored.*

    Capitalization: *A check mark here means Authorware will not consider whether letters are lowercase or uppercase.*

    Spaces: *Be careful with this option. Authorware (and many programs) define a "word" as characters separated by a space on either side. Therefore, if for example the Pattern field included multiple words, Authorware would distinguish the words by identifying the spaces between letters. If you were to place a check mark in this field, Authorware would interpret the collection of letters and spaces as a single word (i.e., an unbroken string of characters).*

    Extra Words: *With this option selected, Authorware will ignore any additional words in the user's entry that may be present in the Pattern field, as long as the required words were entered. For example, if the Pattern field contained George Washington and the user typed in President George Washington without the check mark in the Extra Words option, Authorware would not match the response. If the check mark were included in the Extra Words option, Authorware would match the response.*

Extra Punctuation: With a check mark in this option, Authorware will ignore extra commas, periods, and other punctuation symbols. Perhaps the most common use of this option occurs in combination with the next option.

Word Order: With this option selected, Authorware will accept the words contained in the Pattern field in any order. A common example might be where there is the likelihood that the user may enter a person's name: first name, then last name (e.g., George Washington); or last name followed by a comma, then first name (e.g., Washington, George). Both Word Order and Extra Punctuation options would need to be selected for both of these possibilities to match.

Let's jump in and give it a try.

Practice Exercise 11-4: Fill-in-the-Blank Interaction

Description

In this exercise you are going to ask the user a geography question and require that he use the keyboard to type in the answer. Realizing the "stress" you might cause with this question, you will also anticipate some incorrect answers that might be entered and provide appropriate feedback. The following elements are covered in this exercise.

* *Creating a correct answer pattern for the Text Entry response*

* *Creating anticipated wrong answer patterns for the Text Entry response*

* *Creating a "Catch-all-else" pattern for the Text Entry response*

Take a Look

CD-ROM

Before beginning the exercise, let's take a look at the exercise in its completed state so that you can clearly see what it is you are about to build.

1. Select File | Open and locate on the companion CD-ROM the directory named *Chapter11*. In this directory, locate and double click on the file named *Exer11-4*.

2. The file *Exer11-4* should now appear in your copy of Authorware. Click on the Restart button to play the file from the top of the flowline. Note the following properties of this completed exercise.
    * *There is one correct answer that matches the correct answer pattern. Spelling counts.*
    * *There are a couple of other answers that are considered anticipated wrong answers.*

- *There is a response that will provide feedback for any response that was not anticipated.*

Storyboard: On Screen

Figures 11-26 and 11-27 show you what the finished presentation will look like on screen. Figure 11-26 shows the completed presentation. Figure 11-27 shows the Display icon *Feedback for McKinley.*

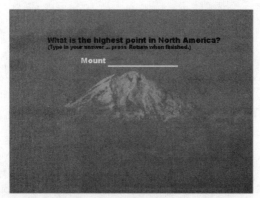

Fig. 11-26. Completed presentation on screen.

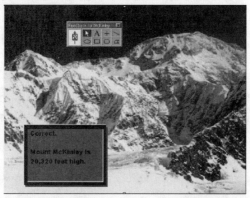

Fig. 11-27. Display icon **Feedback for McKinley.**

Storyboard: Behind the Scenes

Figure 11-28 shows the main and second-level flowlines (with all icons, their placement, and their names) as they should look when you are finished with this exercise. Figure 11-29 shows the Properties/Response dialog window (Text Entry tab) for the Map icon *McKinley.* Figure 11-30 shows this same tab for the catch-all Map icon (note that its label and pattern is *).

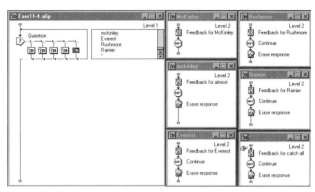

Fig. 11-28. Main flowline with all level 2 flowlines.

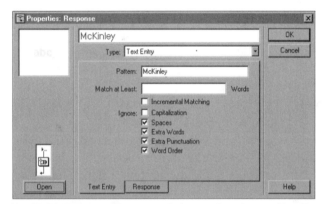

Fig. 11-29. Properties/Response dialog window showing Text Entry tab for McKinley.

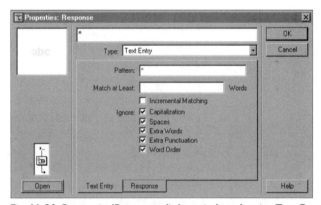

Fig. 11-30. Properties/Response dialog window showing Text Entry tab for *.

Step-by-Step Instructions

Go Solo

1. Select File | New | File. Close the two Knowledge Object dialog windows.

2. Verify that you are now looking at a new flowline.

3. Set up the file properties.
   a) Select Modify | File | Properties.
   b) Select whatever background color you want.
   c) Verify that Size is set to 640 x 480.
   d) Remove the check marks beside the Tile Bar and Menu Bar options.
   e) Click on the OK button to close the window.
   f) Select File | Save and locate the *SaveWork* directory. Type in *Chap11-4* and click on the OK button.

4. You are going to approach building this structure a little differently than previously. You will create this piece by piece so that you can more easily see what is going on with the answer judging. Begin with the question.
   a) Drag an Interaction icon to the flowline. Name it *Question*.
   b) Double click on the Interaction icon to open the display area.
   c) Select Text | Font | Arial. Select Text | Size | 14. Select Text | Style | Bold.
   d) Select the Text tool and click the I-bar on the screen. Type in *What is the highest point in North America?*
   e) Center this text at the top of the screen.
   f) Leave about an inch or so and create a second text object. Type in *Mount.*
   g) Set Text Size to *10*. Create a third text object. Type in *(Type in your answer. Press Return when finished.).*
   h) Drag this last text object directly beneath the question. See figure 11-26 for reference.
   i) Open the Color inspector (Ctrl + K). Select the word *Mount.* Change its color to white. Leave this inspector open, but move it aside.
   j) Select the Straight Line tool. Draw a white line to the right and slightly below the word *Mount,* to create a blank area for the user's answer.
   k) Select File | Import. Locate and select the graphic *mountain.bmp*. Click on the Import button. You should now see the graphic in the Display icon.
   l) Select Modify | Send to Back. You should now be able to see the graphic, as well as the text.
   m) Position the text or graphic if you need to.

5. Create the correct answer.
   a) Drag a Map icon to the right of the Interaction icon. In the dialog window that opens, select Text Entry. Click on the OK button.
   b) Double click on the Response Type symbol for the Map icon.
   c) The Text Entry tab should be on top (if not, select it).
   d) In the Pattern field, type in *McKinley*. (Note the use of capitalization in the answer. Also note that McKinley now becomes the name of the icon as well.)
   e) In the Ignore options, remove the check mark beside Capitalization (you will look for the correct lowercase/uppercase letters). Leave the rest of the check marks as they are, to be more liberal in our answer judging.
   f) Click on the Response tab. In the Erase field, select *Before Next Entry*. In the Branch field, select Exit Interaction. Click on the OK button to close the dialog window.
   g) Double click on the Map icon to open the level 2 flowline.
   h) Drag a Display icon and place it on the level 2 flowline. Name it *Feedback for McKinley*.
   i) Drag a Wait icon and place it on the level 2 flowline, below the Display icon. Name it *Continue*.
   j) Double click on the Display icon *Feedback for McKinley*. Select File | Import. Locate and select the graphic *McKinley.bmp*. Click on the Import button. You should now see the graphic in the Display icon. Locate and select the graphic *Blueover.bmp*. Click on the Import button. While the overlay graphic is still selected, select Transparent in the Mode inspector. Position the overlay window in the lower left corner.
   k) Select Text | Size | 14. Select Text | Style | Bold. Use the open Color inspector and select Black as the "pencil" color.
   l) Click the I-bar on screen and type in *Correct. Mount McKinley is 20,320 feet high.*
   m) Position the text over the overlay window, resizing the text margins as needed. Close this Display icon.

6. Let's take a look.
   a) Click on the Restart button.
   b) The Text Entry field is probably not located where you want it to be. The following fixes this condition. Type in anything, just so there is some text entered. Press Ctrl + P to pause. Double click on the text you just typed.
   c) You should now be looking at the Properties/Interaction Text Field dialog window. See figure 11-31. You have not seen this dialog win-

dow before. These properties are not for the Interaction icon and not for the feedback inside the Map icons. These properties are related to what the user is typing in. Let's take a closer look.

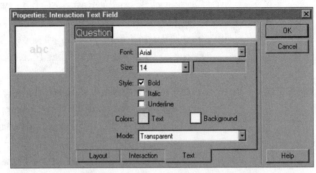

Fig. 11-31. Properties/Interaction Text Field dialog window showing Text tab.

d) Note that there are three tabs: Layout, Interaction, and Text.

e) Click on the Text tab, if it is not on top. See figure 11-31. All of these fields on the Text tab should be familiar and do not need much discussion. The first few are exactly what you think they are: Font, Size, and Style. The next are Colors, Text (for the color of the text), and Background (for the background behind the text, if Mode is set to Opaque). The last field is Mode.

f) Click on the Interaction tab. See figure 11-32. The following describe the options found on this tab.

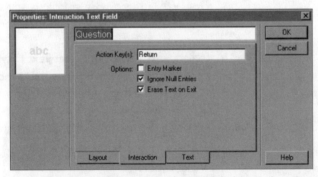

Fig. 11-32. Properties/Interaction Text Field dialog window showing Interaction tab.

- **Action Key(s):** *This field contains the key the user must press to complete the text entry so that Authorware can judge the entry. The Enter key (Enter) is the default Action Key. For software simulations, you may need to use the Tab key (Tab) to simulate data field entries. You can also use the "or" symbol (|) to accept either of the keys entered (Enter | Tab). See Authorware's Help function for other keys that can be entered here.*

- **Options:** *This field contains the following options:*

    Entry Marker: *The presence of a check mark in this field will result in a small, black triangular pointer appearing immediately to the left of the Text Entry field. The purpose of the pointer is to draw attention to the location of the Text Entry field. The blinking cursor will appear whether Entry Marker is selected or not. For most software simulations, you will want to turn off the display of the entry marker (remove the check mark).*

    Ignore Null Entries: *Placing a check mark here will cause Authorware to ignore the Action Key option if the user presses it without typing in anything else.*

    Erase Text on Exit: *Placing a check mark here will cause Authorware to erase, as the flow of the program leaves the interaction, whatever response the user types into the Text Entry field. If you remove the check mark, the user's response will remain on screen as the interaction is exited.*

g) Click on the Layout tab. See figure 11-33.

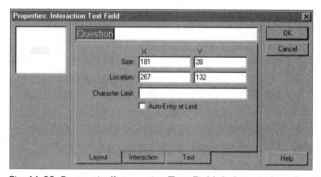

Fig. 11-33. Properties/Interaction Text Field dialog window showing Layout tab.

- **Size:** *This field includes the X and Y coordinates for the size of the Text Entry field that appears on screen. If the opaque or inverse modes are selected, the size of the field will be visible. If the transparent mode has been selected, the size will not be visible on screen, but the user's response will be constrained to this size.*

- **Location:** *This field includes the X and Y coordinates of where the text entry field is located on screen.*

- **Character Limit:** *This field provides you with the capability to establish a maximum number of characters the user may type in as a response to the interaction. Any additional characters typed will not be displayed and will be ignored by Authorware. If this field is left blank, the user can type in as many characters as will fit in the Text Entry field.*

- **Auto-Entry at Limit:** *If a number has been entered in the Character Limit field, placing a check mark in this option will cause Authorware to automatically judge the user's response, as if the Action key had been pressed.*

7. Now that you have had an overview on these tabs, you now need to change some of the settings.
   a) Click on the Text tab.
   b) In the Font field, use the pull-down menu and select Arial.
   c) In the Size field, use the pull-down menu and select 14.
   d) In the Style field, place a check mark beside the Bold option.
   e) Click on the Colors text box to bring up a color palette. Click on White. Click on the OK button to close the palette.
   f) In the Mode field, use the pull-down menu and select Transparent.
   g) Click on the Interaction tab.
   h) Remove the check mark beside the Entry Marker option.
   i) Click on the OK button to close the dialog window.

8. You should now be looking at the display area of the Interaction icon, with the format of the text you typed in changed in accordance with the settings you just established. Now you need to make some minor adjustments.
   a) Click on one of the handlebars on the right side of the wireframe (the Text Entry field). Stretch the field so that it is at least 3 inches wide.
   b) Click inside the wireframe, and while holding down the mouse button move the field to a location to the right of the word *Mount*.
   c) For fine alignment it is easier to use the arrow keys. Make sure the Text Entry field is still selected (has handlebars on it). Use your arrow keys to align the text in the Text Entry field with the word *Mount*. It may help to focus on the bottom of the text you entered, aligning it with the bottom of the letters in *Mount*. Do not try to line up the wireframe itself, as it will extend below the bottom of the word *Mount*.
   d) When you are finished, press Ctrl + J to jump to the flowline.

9. Let's test what you have at this point.
   a) Click on the Restart button.
   b) Type in *McKinley*. Press the Enter key.
   c) You should now see the feedback and a Continue button. Click on the Continue button.

10. You should have exited the interaction, with nothing left on screen. The response acts like it has been programmed to do. Let's try a variation.
    a) Click on the Restart button.

NOTE

Be careful in the use of the Auto-Entry option. Try to be consistent in how users need to respond to Text Entry interactions. Users may find it confusing if some Text Entry interactions require that they press a key (Enter) to complete their response and others do not.

    b)   Type in the answer using all lowercase letters: *mckinley*. Press the Enter key.

11. What has happened? You have returned to the interaction with the Text Entry field highlighted. Remember, you removed the check mark beside Ignore Capitalization, meaning that you want the user to use capital letters where appropriate. Therefore, Authorware has judged this last response as incorrect.

If you were to leave the interaction just like this, the user would have to have the insight to try again, this time using capital letters. Relying on insight is not a good instructional strategy. More importantly, it is the responsibility of the instructional designer to do a better job with the interaction. For one thing, if you are going to "count" capitalization, you should either inform the user of this up front or anticipate that some users will not use capitalization. From an instructional design standpoint, you really need to distinguish a number of types of responses, such as the following.

- *Correct response(s)*

- *Response that is correct except for capitalization*

- *Responses that are "good attempts" (reasonable but incorrect answers) or those wrong answers that are commonly mistaken for the correct answer*

- *Anything else that might be entered by the user*

12. At this point you have a response for the first category, the correct response. Let's create a response for the second category: the response that is correct except for capitalization. The easiest way to do this is to simply copy the correct response and make adjustments.

    a)   Select the Map icon *McKinley*. Press Ctrl + C to copy it to the clipboard.

    b)   Click the cursor to the right of the Map icon to place the Paste Hand cursor there. Press Ctrl + V to paste the copy to the right of the Map icon.

    c)   Double click on the Response Type symbol for this new response. Click on the Text Entry tab, if it is not already on top. You have a couple of possibilities here. To help distinguish this "almost correct" response from the correct response, change the entry in the Pattern field. Change all letters of this entry to lowercase: *mckinley*. Note that the icon's title is now also lowercase, allowing you (from the flowline) to distinguish this response from the correct response.

    d)   In the Ignore field, place check marks beside all options, making sure to include Capitalization. With the Pattern setting modified and with all of these options now being ignored, if the user were to type in *mckinley* using all lowercase, all uppercase, or any incorrect capitalization pattern (as long as the correct letters were used), this response would "catch" all of these "almost correct" responses.

e) Click on the Response tab. In the Branch field, select Try Again. Click on the OK button to close the dialog window.

f) You also need to change the feedback. Double click on the Map icon *mckinley*. Select the Display icon on the level 2 flowline and change the name of this Display icon to *Feedback for almost*.

g) Double click on this Display icon. Select the Text tool and click the I-bar cursor inside the text object that is there. Change the text so that it reads *Almost. You have the correct mountain, but the capitalization is incorrect. Please try again.*

h) Resize the margins and reposition the text if you need to. Close the icon.

13. Create a few responses for the third type of possible response: reasonable but incorrect answers.

a) Drag three (3) Map icons to the right of the Map icons already there. Name these icons *Everest*, *Rushmore*, and *Rainier*.

b) Double click on the Response Type symbol for *Everest*. Click on the Text Entry tab, if it is not already on top. Note that by default all options at the bottom have check marks beside them, and will therefore be ignored (the "most forgiving" scenario). Click on the Response tab. Note that Branch is already set to Try Again. Everything is just as you need it to be. Close the dialog window.

c) Drag a Display icon to the level 2 flowline, inside the Map icon *Everest*. Name the icon *Feedback for Everest*.

d) Double click on the Display icon. Select File | Import. Locate and select the file *Blueover.bmp*. Click on the Import button. Press Ctrl + M to open the Mode inspector, and then select Transparent. Position the overlay window in the lower left-hand corner of the screen.

e) Select Text | Arial | 14. Select the Text tool and type in *Sorry, Mount Everest is highest mountain in the world, but it is in Nepal. Try again.*

f) Position the text object so that it fits within the Overlay window. Close the Display icon.

g) Drag a Wait icon to the level 2 flowline and place it below the Display icon. Name the Wait icon *Continue*.

h) Select both the Display icon and the Wait icon. Copy this selection to the clipboard. Close the Map icon *Everest*.

i) Double click on the Map icon *Rushmore*. Click on the level 2 flowline to place the Paste Hand cursor here. Press Ctrl + V to paste the icons here. Rename the Display icon *Feedback for Rushmore*.

j) Double click on the Display icon and change the existing text so that it reads *Sorry, Mount Rushmore is famous, but for something else. Try again.*

k) Position the text object so that it fits within the Overlay window. Close the icon. Close the Map icon.

l) Double click on the Map icon *Rainier*. Click on the level 2 flowline to place the Paste Hand cursor here. Press Ctrl + V to paste the icons here. Rename the Display icon *Feedback for Rainier*.

m) Double click on the Display icon and change the existing text so that it reads *Sorry, Mount Rainier is high, but is not the correct answer. Try again.*

n) Position the text object so that it fits within the Overlay window. Close the icon. Close the Map icon.

14. Establish the last possible response type, the catch-all.

a) Drag one more Map icon to the far right.

b) Double click on the Response Type symbol. If the Text Entry tab is not on top, click on it.

c) What can you enter in the Pattern field that will "catch" anything that is typed in? Recall that there are two "wild card" symbols associated with this tab: the question mark (?) for single characters and the asterisk (*) for a word or words.

d) Click the cursor in the Pattern field and type in *.

e) Note that the title of the icon is now *. Everything else on the tab is fine as is. Close the dialog window.

f) Click the cursor on the level 2 flowline. Press Ctrl + V to paste the icons (which should still be in the clipboard) onto this flowline.

g) Rename the Display icon *Feedback for catch-all*.

h) Double click on the Display icon and change the existing text so that it reads *Sorry, that is not the correct answer. Please try again.*

i) Position the text object so that it fits within the Overlay window. Close the icon. Close the Map icon.

15. Save the file.

16. Let's test the file.

a) Click on the Restart button.

·T/P·

You can select multiple icons on the flowline either by clicking on one and holding the Shift key down as you click on the second or by clicking the cursor next to the upper left-hand corner of the Display icon and while holding the mouse button down dragging the expanding marquee to the lower right-hand corner, encompassing both icons, and then letting go.

b) Type in *McKinley* and press Enter. You should get feedback and a Continue button. Click on the Continue button. You should have exited the interaction.

c) Click on the Restart button.

d) Type in *Everest* and press Enter. You should get feedback and a Continue button. Click on the Continue button. You are now back to the interaction and can type again. However, your last response is still there, with the Text Entry field highlighted.

e) Press Ctrl + J to jump to the flowline. The following is a quick trick for "cleaning up" the Text Entry field. Double click on the Map icon *Everest*. Drag an Erase icon to the bottom of the level 2 flowline inside the Map icon *Everest*. Name this Erase icon *Erase User's Response*.

f) Click on the Restart button.

g) Type in *Everest* and press Enter. You should get feedback and a Continue button. Click on the Continue button. You should now see the dialog window for the Erase icon. Click on the word you just typed in: *Everest*. This word should have erased. Close the Erase icon.

h) Press Ctrl + J to jump to the flowline.

i) Select the Erase icon. Press Ctrl + C to copy it. Close the Map icon.

j) Open the Map icon *Rushmore*. Click the cursor at the bottom of the level 2 flowline inside the Map icon. Press Ctrl + V to paste the Erase icon here. Close the Map icon.

k) Open the Map icon *Rainier*. Click the cursor at the bottom of the level 2 flowline inside the Map icon. Press Ctrl + V to paste the Erase icon here. Close the Map icon.

l) Open the Map icon *. Click the cursor at the bottom of the level 2 flowline inside the Map icon. Press Ctrl + V to paste the Erase icon here. Close the Map icon.

m) Open the Map icon *mckinley*. Click the cursor at the bottom of the level 2 flowline inside the Map icon. Press Ctrl + V to paste the Erase icon here. Close the Map icon.

17. Let's test all answers again.

a) Click on the Restart button.

b) Type in each of the anticipated "almost correct" responses.

c) Type in anything else, to see if the catch-all picks up this response.

d) Make whatever position adjustments you need to.

18. Save the file.

Guided Tour 11D:
Time Limit Interaction Response and Properties

Much like the Tries Limit response type you worked with earlier in this chapter, the Time Limit response is generally used as an addition to an interaction that uses another response type as the primary interactive strategy. As the name implies, the Time Limit response allows the Authorware programmer to restrict the amount of time the learner is allowed to take on any given interactive structure. Let's take a look.

1. Start by opening a new file.
    a) Select File | New | File.
    b) Close the two dialog windows that have opened.
    c) Verify that you are looking at an empty flowline.

2. Drag an Interaction icon to the flowline. Drag a Map icon and drop it to the right of the Interaction icon.

3. The Response Type window should now be open. Click on the Time Limit option and then click on the OK button.

4. Double click on the Response Type symbol above the Map icon to access the dialog window for this Tries Limit interaction response.

5. You should be looking at the Properties/Response dialog window for the Time Limit interaction response. There are two tabs on this window, but we will briefly look only at the Tries Limit tab. The Response tab is identical to that you have seen previously, so we will not repeat it here.

6. Select the Time Limit tab, if it is not already on top. See figure 11-34.

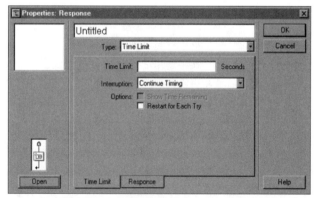

Fig. 11-34. Properties/Response dialog window showing the Time Limit tab.

7. The fields are:

- **Time Limit:** *This field is where you type in the maximum number of seconds you want to allow the user to remain in the interaction. After the time limit is exceeded, this response will be automatically activated.*

- **Interruption:** *The options included for this field can be used to turn off a timed interaction when the user goes to another activity during the interaction. As an example, if the user selects a perpetual interaction (such as selecting a pull-down menu) during a timed interaction, you can select what happens as Authorware leaves and then returns to the timed interaction with the following options:*

  Continue Timing: *This option is the default setting. It instructs Authorware to continue timing while the perpetual interaction is being conducted.*

  Pause, Resume on Return: *Select this option to stop the time while the perpetual interaction is being conducted. When Authorware returns to the timed interaction, it resumes counting down from the time that has already elapsed.*

  Pause, Restart on Return: *Select this option to stop the time while the perpetual interaction is being conducted. When Authorware returns to the timed interaction, it restarts the timing even if the time limit had already been exceeded before the perpetual activity began.*

  Pause, Restart if Running: *Select this option to stop the time while the perpetual interaction is being conducted. When Authorware returns to the timed interaction, it restarts the timing only if the time limit had not been exceeded before the perpetual activity began.*

- **Options:** *This consists of the following options:*

  Show Time Remaining: *Placing a check mark here causes a clock icon to be displayed on screen, showing the countdown of the time remaining. The clock can be moved by pausing while in run mode and dragging it to another location.*

  Restart for Each Try: *Placing a check mark here causes Authorware to restart the countdown each time the user matches a response.*

To see how this response type works, you will need an example to work with, which is supplied by practice exercise 11-5.

Practice Exercise 11-5: Adding a Time Limit Response

Description

In the last exercise the user was asked to type in an answer to a question. In that exercise you anticipated a number of "almost" responses and trapped all other responses with a wild card response with generic feedback indicating that the user needs to try again. As an instructional designer you also need to provide a "way out" if the user simply does not know the answer. With the addition of a Time Limit response, you can limit the maximum time the user is permitted on the question. When the maximum time has been exceeded, the response automatically triggers, providing the user with feedback and a means of continuing on the flowline. The following elements are covered in this exercise.

- *Copying and reusing an existing interaction structure*
- *Creating a Time Limit response with an existing interaction*

Take a Look

CD-ROM

Before beginning the exercise, let's take a look at the exercise in its completed state so that you can clearly see what it is you are about to build.

1. Select File | Open and locate on the companion CD-ROM the directory named *Chapter11*. In this directory, locate and double click on the file named *Exer11-5*.

2. The file *Exer11-5* should now appear in your copy of Authorware. Click on the Restart button to play the file from the top of the flowline. Note the following properties of this completed exercise.

   - *As you enter the interaction, there is a clock icon that begins to count down the time allowed for the interaction.*
   - *After the maximum time has been exceeded, feedback is presented that informs the user that the maximum time has been exceeded and provides the correct answer. The interaction is then exited.*

Storyboard: On Screen

Figure 11-35 shows what the complete presentation will look on screen when the exercise is finished.

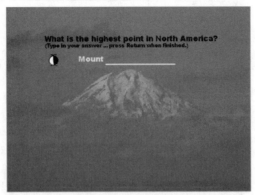

Fig. 11-35. Complete presentation on screen.

Storyboard: Behind the Scenes

Figure 11-36 shows the main and secondary flowlines (with all icons, their placement, and their names) as they should look when you are finished with this exercise. Figure 11-37 shows the Properties/Response dialog window (Time Limit tab) for the Map icon *Time Limit*.

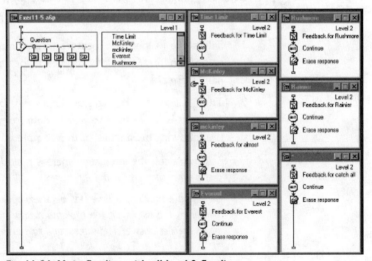

Fig. 11-36. Main flowline with all level 2 flowlines.

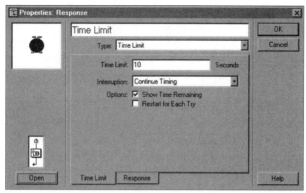

Fig. 11-37. Properties/Response dialog window showing Time Limit tab.

Step-by-Step Instructions

Go Solo

1. Start with the completed version of the previous exercise. You can either use the file you created and saved on your hard drive or the completed version on the companion CD-ROM.

    a) Open *Chap11-4.a6p* from the *SaveWork* directory on your computer's hard drive.

        Or

        Open *Exer11-4.a6p* from the companion CD-ROM's *Chapter11* directory.

    b) Select File | Save As and save this file as *Chap11-5.a6p* into the *SaveWork* directory on your computer's hard drive.

2. Begin adding "new parts" to this structure.

    a) Drag a Map icon and carefully place it immediately to the right of the Interaction icon.

    b) The Response Type dialog window is now open. Select Time Limit.

    c) Name this icon *Time Limit*.

    d) Double click on the Response Type symbol for this new Map icon.

    e) In the Time Limit field, type in *15*.

    f) Place a check mark beside the Show Time Remaining option.

    g) Click on the OK button to close the dialog window.

3. Add feedback for this new response.

    a) Double click on the Map icon *Time Limit*.

    b) Drag a Display icon to the level 2 flowline inside the Map icon *Time Limit*. Name this icon *Feedback for Time Limit*.

    c) Double click on this feedback icon. Select File | Import. Locate and select the graphic file *Blueover.bmp*. Click on the Import button. Open the Mode inspector and select Transparent. Position the Overlay window in the lower left-hand corner.

d) Select the Text tool. Select Text | Arial | 14. Type in *Sorry, you have exceeded the maximum time allowed. The correct answer is Mount McKinley.*

e) Position the text object so that it fits within the Overlay window. Close the Display icon.

f) Drag a Wait icon to the level 2 flowline and place it below the Display icon. Name this icon *Continue*.

4. Let's try it out.

a) Click on the Restart button.

b) As soon as the interaction begins, pause the program (Ctrl + P). Drag the clock and place it next to the question. Resume play (Ctrl + P). Type in several incorrect responses and let the time run out.

c) You should now see the appropriate feedback. Pause the program and drag the Continue button so that it is positioned at the bottom of the Overlay window. Resume play.

d) Click on the Continue button.

5. Save the file.

Guided Tour 11E:
Keypress Interaction Response and Properties

You will probably not use the next type of response very often, unless you are simulating software screens. The Keypress response looks for the user to press a single key or multiple keys simultaneously to trigger a response. Any key on the keyboard can be programmed as the matched response. Let's take a quick look.

1. Start by opening a new file.

a) Select File | New | File.

b) Close the two dialog windows that have opened.

c) Verify that you are now looking at an empty flowline.

2. Drag an Interaction icon to the flowline. Drag a Map icon and drop it to the right of the Interaction icon.

3. The Response Type window should now be open. Click on the Keypress option and then click on the OK button.

4. Double click on the Response Type symbol above the Map icon to access the dialog window for this Tries Limit interaction response.

5. You should be looking at the Properties/Response dialog window for the Keypress interaction response. There are two tabs on this window, but

we will briefly look only at the Keypress tab. The Response tab is identical to that you have seen previously, so we will not repeat it here.

6. Select the Keypress tab, if it is not already on top. See figure 11-38.

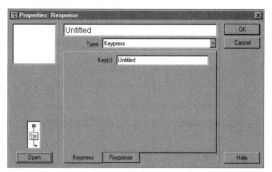

Fig. 11-38. Properties/Response dialog window showing Keypress tab.

7. You can see that this will be very short tour, as there is only one field.

- **Key(s):** *This field is where you type in the name of the key or keys you want the user to press. The following table lists the key names you can use in the Key field.*

Authorware Key Name	Windows Keyboard Key(s)
Alt	Alt
Backspace	Backspace
Break	Break
Clear	—
Cmd	Ctrl
Control	Ctrl
Ctrl	Ctrl
Delete	Del (Delete)
DownArrow	Down arrow
End	End
Enter	Enter
Escape	Esc
F1-F15	F1 through F15
Help	—
Home	Home
Ins or Insert	Insert (Ins)
LeftArrow	Left arrow
PageDown	Pg Dn
PageUp	Pg Up
Pause	Pause
Return	Enter
RightArrow	Right arrow
Shift	Shift
Tab	Tab
UpArrow	Up arrow

In practice exercise 11-6, you will create a quick interaction.

Practice Exercise 11-6:
Simple Keypress Interactions

Description

In this exercise you are going to ask the user to press a "normal" letter key on the keyboard. Feedback will be provided for both correct and incorrect responses. You will then create another interaction that looks for two keys to be pressed simultaneously. The following elements are covered in this exercise.

- *Creating a Keypress interaction in which a single key is the correct response*
- *Creating a Keypress interaction in which pressing two keys simultaneously is the correct response*
- *Creating feedback for both correct and incorrect responses*

Take a Look

CD-ROM

Before beginning the exercise, let's take a look at the exercise in its completed state so that you can clearly see what it is you are about to build.

1. Select File | Open and locate on the companion CD-ROM the directory named *Chapter11*. In this directory, locate and double click on the file named *Exer11-6*.

2. The file *Exer11-6* should now appear in your copy of Authorware. Click on the Restart button to play the file from the top of the flowline. Note the following properties of this completed exercise.

    - *In the first interaction, pressing either a lowercase or uppercase B key matches the correct answer.*
    - *In the second interaction, simultaneously pressing the Ctrl and A keys matches the correct answer.*
    - *Feedback is provided for both correct and incorrect answers.*

Storyboard: On Screen

Figure 11-39 shows what the finished presentation will look like on screen when the exercise is completed.

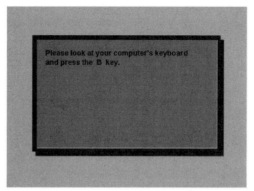

Fig. 11-39. Completed presentation on screen.

Storyboard: Behind the Scenes

Figure 11-40 shows the main and secondary flowlines (with all icons, their placement, and their names) as they should look when you are finished with this exercise. Figure 11-41 shows the Properties/Response dialog window (Keypress tab) for the first interaction. Figure 11-42 shows this same tab for the second interaction.

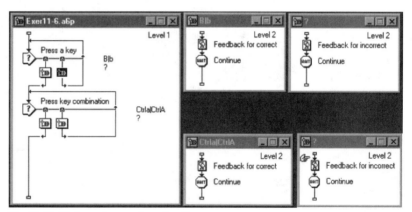

Fig. 11-40. Main and secondary flowlines.

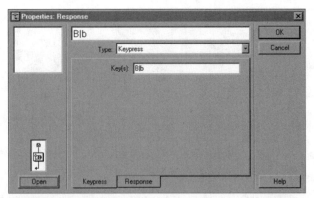

Fig. 11-41. Properties/Response dialog window showing Keypress tab for first interaction.

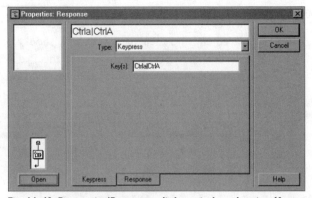

Fig. 11-42. Properties/Response dialog window showing Keypress tab for second interaction.

Step-by-Step Instructions

Go Solo

1. Select File | New | File. Close the two Knowledge Object dialog windows.

2. Verify that you are now looking at a new flowline.

3. Set up the file properties.

   a) Select Modify | File | Properties.

   b) Select whatever background color you want.

   c) Verify that Size is set to 640 x 480.

   d) Remove the check marks beside the Tile Bar and Menu Bar options.

   e) Click on the OK button to close the window.

   f) Select File | Save and locate the *SaveWork* directory. Type in *Chap11-6* and click on the OK button.

4. Begin creating the icon structure.

   a) Drag an Interaction icon to the flowline. Name the icon *Press a key*.

   b) Double click on the Interaction icon. Select File | Import. Locate and select the graphic file *ScrTemp4.bmp*. Click on the Import button. Open the Mode inspector and select Transparent. Leave the inspector open on the desktop.

   c) Select the Text tool. Select text attributes Arial 14 point and Bold. Type in *Please look at your computer's keyboard and press the B key*.

   d) Position the text object within the screen template. Close the Display icon.

   e) Drag a Map icon and drop it to the right of the Interaction icon. You should now see the Response Type dialog window. Select Keypress. (For the moment, you will not name this Map icon.)

   f) Double click on the Map icon. Drag a Display icon to the level 2 flowline. Name this icon *Feedback for correct*.

   g) Double click on the Display icon. Select File | Import. Locate and select the file *Blueover.bmp*. Click on the Import button. Using the Mode inspector, select Transparent.

   h) Select the Text tool. Select text attributes Arial and 14 point. Type in *Yes, you found the correct key*.

   i) Position the text object over the Overlay window. Close the icon.

   j) Drag a Wait icon to the level 2 flowline and place it below the Display icon. Name this icon *Continue*.

   k) Close the Map icon.

5. Establish the "answer judging."

   a) Double click on the Response Type symbol for the Map icon.

   b) Click the cursor in the Keypress field. Type in *B|b*. The pipe (|) character (the "or" symbol) is located on your keyboard above the Enter key. Hold down the Shift key and then press this key. What you have just entered will accept either B (uppercase) or b (lowercase).

   c) Note that the title of the Map icon has just become what you entered in the Keypress field: *B|b*. The Keypress and Text Entry responses both take on the "judged answer" for the name of the icon.

   d) Close the dialog window. This also works the other way around. Whatever you type in the Title field will also appear in the Keypress (Text Entry) field.

6. Let's try it out.

   a) Click on the Restart button.

   b) Type a lowercase *b*. You should now see feedback and a Continue button. Pause the program and reposition the Continue button so that it is located at the bottom of the screen template.

NOTE

The Keypress response is case sensitive. Therefore, if you do not care if a lowercase or uppercase letter is pressed, you will have to enter both possibilities in the Keypress field, as in B|b (read B or b).

c) Click on the Restart button.

d) Type an uppercase (using Shift) *B*. You should now see the same feedback you saw before. Click on the Continue button.

e) Click on the Restart button.

f) Type a lowercase *v* (or press any other key). Nothing happens.

·T/P·

You can also add a comment to the Title, without affecting the answer judging. First type in the appropriate answer (or title), then type in two hyphens and whatever comment you would like to add. Anything to the right of the hyphens will be ignored.

For example: *?–This is a wildcard.*

Authorware will only recognize the ?.

7. You need to check for and provide feedback for any other key that might be pressed. You are going to take advantage of what you already have by copying it.

a) Select the Map icon. Copy it to the clipboard. Paste a copy of the Map icon to the right of the first one.

b) Double click on the Response Type symbol for the second Map icon. Click the cursor in the Keypress field. Type in *?*. The question mark (?) acts as a wild card and will accept any key. Note that the name of this Map icon has now become *?*. Click on the OK button.

c) Double click on the Map icon *?*. Select the Display icon *Feedback for correct* and change this name to *Feedback for incorrect*.

d) Double click on the Display icon. Use the Text tool and change the existing text so that it reads *Sorry, that is the wrong key. Try again.*

e) Close the Display icon. Close the Map icon.

8. Let's see the result of what you just added.

a) Click on the Restart button.

b) Press any key. You should see the feedback for "incorrect," along with the Continue button. Click on the Continue button.

9. Save the file.

10. Now let's quickly create a similar structure, but one that accepts key combinations being pressed. You can do this more quickly by copying the previous structure and making modifications to it.

a) Click the cursor in the upper left-hand corner of the flowline. Hold the mouse button down as you drag the expanding marquee to the lower right-hand corner, so that you have selected all icons on the flowline. Copy the selection to the clipboard.

b) Click the cursor on the flowline below the current structure to place the Paste Hand cursor there. Paste the selection here.

c) Drag the White Flag and place it above the structure you just copied.

d) In the structure you just pasted in place, rename the Interaction icon *Press key combination*.

e) Double click on this Interaction icon. Use the Text tool and replace the existing text so that it reads *Please look at your computer's keyboard and press Ctrl + A.*

f) Close the Interaction icon.

g) Double click on the Response Type symbol for first Map icon to the right. In the Keypress field, replace what is there with *Ctrla|CtrlA*. This reads as the Control key plus a lowercase *a* or the Control key plus *A*. Close the dialog window.

h) The response and feedback for incorrect key presses is good as is.

11. Let's take a look at this second structure. Verify that the White Flag is located on the flowline immediately above the second structure.

a) Click on the White Flag button.

b) Press Ctrl + A. You should now see the feedback and a Continue button. Click on the Continue button.

c) Click on the White Flag button.

d) Press any key. You should see the feedback for "incorrect," along with the Continue button. Click on the Continue button.

12. Save the file.

Guided Tour 11F:
Pull-down Menu Interaction Response and Properties

Most developers these days provide the user with access to menus and other navigational controls through the use of static user control panels located at the top, bottom, or left edge of the screen. Typically these control panels include a variety of buttons that provide access to the main menu, module menu, and so on. If you are working with software simulations, you may want to use this next response type, Pull-down Menu, perhaps in combination with other response types.

1. Start by opening a new file.

a) Select File | New | File.

b) Close the two dialog windows that have opened.

c) Verify that you are now looking at an empty flowline.

2. Drag an Interaction icon to the flowline. Drag a Map icon and drop it to the right of the Interaction icon.

3. The Response Type window should now be open. Click on the Pull-down Menu option and then click on the OK button.

4. Double click on the Response Type symbol above the Map icon to access the dialog window for this Pull-down Menu interaction response.

5. You should be looking at the Properties/Response dialog window for the Pull-down Menu interaction response. There are two tabs on this window, but we will briefly look only at the Menu tab. The Response tab is identical to that you have seen previously, so we will not repeat it here.

6. Select the Menu tab, if it is not already on top. See figure 11-43.

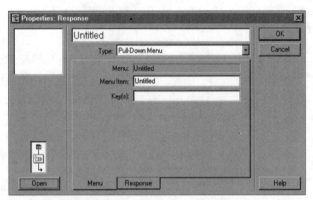

Fig. 11-43. Properties/Response dialog window showing Menu tab.

7. Examine the following fields of this tab.

- **Menu Item:** *This field is where you will type in the name of the item, choice, or command you want to appear on the menu you are creating. The actual menu name is taken from the name of the Interaction icon. The responses attached to the Interaction icon provide the items that will be found on that menu. The following options are used to format the menu items.*

  To dim a menu item, type a left parenthesis before the text you want to display, as in (text here.

  To display a blank line, documentation indicates using a left parenthesis, as in (. (Simply leaving the line blank also works.)

  To insert a separator line, documentation indicates a left parenthesis followed by a hyphen, as in (-. (Using just the hyphen also works.)

  To underline a letter and make it an accelerator key (so that when viewing the option in the menu the user can press this key instead of mouse clicking), type an ampersand (&) before the letter you want to underline.

  To place an ampersand (&) in the menu, type &&.

- **Key(s):** *Just as actual menu items have keyboard shortcuts for activating an item, keys you enter into this field will allow the user to employ them as shortcut keys for your menus. Authorware assumes that unless otherwise specified the Control (Ctrl) key is required. This means that whatever key you type into this field will be activated with the simultaneous pressing of the Ctrl key and the key you have entered. To specify that you want to use the Alt key instead of the Ctrl key, type in Alt_ and whatever other key you want to use.*

Let's create an example of a pull-down menu.

Practice Exercise 11-7: Pull-down Menu Interaction

Description

In this exercise you are going to build a single menu with options on that menu. You will then copy this structure a couple of times, modifying each new structure so that you will end up with three menus, each containing submenu items. The pull-down menu structure is most often used with the Perpetual status, so that the menus are available from any screen. You are not going to spend time making the screen "look pretty," but are going to use content you created previously, concentrating on building the structures. The following elements are covered in this exercise.

- *Creating a single menu that includes several items*
- *Creating formatting options with the menu items*
- *Copying and modifying the first menu to result in multiple menus*

Take a Look

CD-ROM

Before beginning the exercise, let's take a look at the exercise in its completed state so that you can clearly see what it is you are about to build.

1. Select File | Open and locate on the companion CD-ROM the directory named *Chapter11*. In this directory, locate and double click on the file named *Exer11-7*.

2. The file *Exer11-7* should now appear in your copy of Authorware. Click on the Restart button to play the file from the top of the flowline. Note the following properties of this completed exercise.

   - *There are four menus available at all times: File, Module 1 Menu, Module 2 Menu, and Module 3 Menu.*

   - *The File menu is "supplied" by Authorware by leaving the Menu Bar option checked under File Properties.*

   - *Each Module menu contains Topics, which can be selected by clicking on the item or pressing the key corresponding to the underlined letter in that item. Each Topic consists of a number of screens.*

Storyboard: On Screen

Figure 11-44 shows what the finished presentation will look like on screen when the exercise is completed.

Menus are located at the very top.

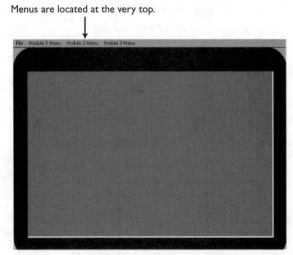

Fig. 11-44. Completed presentation on screen.

Storyboard: Behind the Scenes

Figure 11-45 shows the main flowline (with all icons, their placement, and their names) as it should look when you are finished with this exercise. Figure 11-46 shows the level 2 flowline inside the Map icon *Topic&A*. Figure 11-47 shows the Properties/Response dialog window (Menu tab) for this same Map icon.

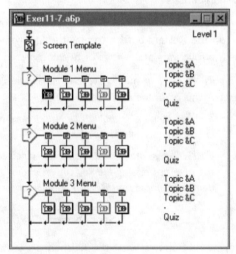

Fig. 11-45. Main flowline.

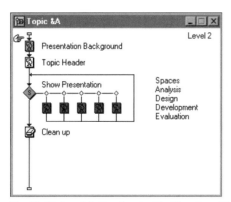

Fig. 11-46. Level 2 flowline inside Map icon **Topic&A.**

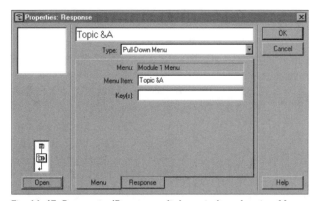

*Fig. 11-47. Properties/Response dialog window showing Menu
tab for Map icon* **Topic&A.**

Step-by-Step Instructions

Go Solo

1. Select File | New | File. Close the two Knowledge Object dialog windows.

2. Verify that you are now looking at a new flowline.

3. Set up the file properties.

   a) Select Modify | File | Properties.

   b) Select whatever background color you want.

   c) Verify that Size is set to 640 x 480.

   d) Remove the check mark beside the Tile Bar option.

   e) *Leave* the check mark beside the Menu Bar option.

   f) Click on the OK button to close the window.

   g) Select File | Save and locate the *SaveWork* directory. Type in *Chap11-7* and click on the OK button.

4. To save time you are going to use a preconstructed topic structure.
   a) Select File | Open | Files. Select the file *Structures.a6p* located in the *Chapter11* directory on the companion CD-ROM. (The current file will close as you open this new file).
   b) Select Edit | Select All to select both Map icons. Select Edit | Copy to copy the icons to the clipboard.
   c) Select File | Open | Files. Select the file *Exer11-7.a6p* in your *SaveWork* directory (from step 3).
   d) Click the cursor on the flowline to position the Paste Hand cursor there. Select Edit | Paste to paste the two Map icons from the other file into the current file.

5. Before you start to build the Pull-down interaction, let's take a quick look at what you just copied and pasted into this file.
   a) Drag the black Stop Flag and place it between the two Map icons.
   b) Click on the Restart button. You are now looking at a Decision icon structure you built in an earlier chapter. Click on the Continue button a few times. A text object has been added at the top of the screen that identifies that this is *Module 1 – Topic A*.
   c) Jump to the flowline (Ctrl + J).
   d) Drag the black Stop Flag back to the Icon palette and drag the white Start Flag and place it between the two Map icons.
   e) Click on the white Start Flag button on the toolbar. You are now looking at a question structure you built in an earlier chapter. Click on a few responses. The only thing added subsequently is a text object at the top of the screen that identifies that this is *Module 1 – Quiz*.
   f) Jump to the flowline (Ctrl + J).

6. Examine the structures inside these Map icons.
   a) Double click on the Map icon *Topic*. This should look very familiar.
   b) Right mouse click on the Display icon *Presentation Background*. Select Preview. This is the beginning screen display you have seen before. Click on the flowline to close the preview.
   c) Right mouse click on the Display icon *Topic Header*. Select Preview. Here is a single text object providing the module and topic names. This is the only text object you will have to change/update as you copy and paste this Map icon to create pull-down menus.
   d) Examine the other icons if you wish. Again, all of the icons should be familiar to you.
   e) Close the Map icon.
   f) Double click on the Map icon *Quiz*.

g) Right mouse click on the Display icon *Topic Header*. Select Preview. Here is a single text object providing the module and quiz names. This is the only text object you will have to change/update as you copy and paste this Map icon to create pull-down menus.

h) Examine the other icons if you wish. Again, all of these icons should be familiar to you.

i) Close the Map icon.

7. Begin building the pull-down menu structure.

a) Drag an Interaction icon and place it on the main flowline, below the two Map icons. Name the Interaction icon *Module 1*.

b) Drag the Map icon *Topic* and place it to the right of the Interaction icon. The Response Type dialog window opens. Select the option Pull-down Menu. Click on the OK button.

c) Double click on the Response Type symbol for the Map icon. Click on the Response tab. In the Erase field, select Before Next Entry. Click on the OK button.

8. Let's take a quick look at what you have so far.

a) Drag the white Start Flag and place it on the main flowline immediately above the Interaction icon *Module 1*.

b) Click on the Start Flag button on the toolbar.

c) You should see two menus at the top: File and Module 1. If you do not see any menus, you have probably mistakenly removed the check mark beside Menu Bar in the File Properties option. See step 1e.

d) Click on the File menu and select Quit. Obviously this is a "built-in" quit function that when the program has been packaged will drop the user out to the Windows desktop.

e) Click on the Start Flag again.

f) Click on the Module 1 menu and select Topic. Click on the Continue button a few times. This is the "foundation" for the operations you will perform in the following.

9. The screen looks a little naked without an interface, and so you need to add some more topics to this menu.

a) Drag a Display icon to the main flowline and place it immediately above the Interaction icon. Name the Display icon *Screen Interface*.

b) Double click on the Display icon. Select File | Import. Locate and select the graphic file *ScrTemp5.bmp*. Click on the Import button. Use the Mode inspector to set it to Transparent mode. Close the icon.

c) Select the Map icon *Topic*. Rename this icon *Topic A*.

d) Verify that the white Start Flag is above the Display icon *Screen Interface*.

e) Click on the white Start Flag button.

NOTE

The name of the menu you see at the top (Module 1) comes from the name of the Interaction icon that contains the Pull-down Menu response. This Interaction icon is named *Module 1*.

369

f) You should now see the screen interface. Select the Module 1 menu, and then select Topic A. Click on the Continue button a few times.

10. Let's add a little formatting to the menu item, as well as increase user convenience.

a) Jump to the main flowline (Ctrl + J).

b) Highlight the name of the Map icon. Modify the name again so that it reads *Topic &A*. (The & symbol is made by pressing Shift + 7.)

c) Click on the Start Flag button. Select Module 1 and press the A key.

(NOTE)

As you may remember from the guided tour regarding pull-down menus, placing an ampersand (&) before a word in the icon's title will place an underscore under the first letter and allow the user to press that letter key (an accelerator key) on the keyboard instead of clicking on the item.

11. Finish this first menu by adding some more topics to it, as well as a quiz.

a) Select the Map icon *Topic &A*. Copy it to the clipboard (Ctrl + C).

b) Click the cursor to the right of the Map icon so that the Paste Hand cursor appears there. Paste two (2) copies of the Map to the right of the Map icon, so that you end up with a total of three (3) Map icons.

c) Rename the second Map icon *Topic &B*. Rename the third Map icon *Topic &C*.

d) Double click on the Map icon *Topic &B*. On the level 2 flowline, double click on the Display icon *Topic Header*. Use the Text tool and modify the existing text so that it reads *Module 1 – Topic B*.

e) Close the Display icon. Close the Map icon.

f) Double click on the Map icon *Topic &C*. On the level 2 flowline, double click on the Display icon *Topic Header*. Use the Text tool and modify the existing text so that it reads *Module 1 – Topic C*.

g) Close the Display icon. Close the Map icon.

12. Add a quiz as the last item on the menu. It would be a good idea to visually separate the quiz from the three instructional topics. You will incorporate this "separation" by incorporating a divider line.

a) Drag a new Map icon to the far right of the Interaction icon, so that it will become the last Map icon to the right. Select this new Map icon and name the icon - (hyphen, *not* an underscore).

b) Click on the Start Flag. Select the menu. You should now see a divider line at the bottom of the menu. The divider line is the result of the hyphen acting as the name of the icon.

c) The Map icon *Quiz* is currently located at the top of the flowline. Drag it to the far right of the attached Map icons, so that it now becomes the last Map icon in the series.

d) Click on the Start Flag. Select any of the topics or the quiz. Everything should be working properly at this point.

e) Jump to the flowline.

13. To quickly create two more module menus, you can copy and paste the menu structure you have just finished building.

a)   Use your cursor and expanding marquee to select the Interaction icon *Module 1*, as well as all of the attached Map icons. Do not include the Display icon *Screen Interface*. Copy the selection to the clipboard.

b)   Click the cursor on the flowline below the current structure so that the Paste Hand cursor will appear here. Paste two (2) copies below the original.

c)   In the second copy, select the Interaction icon and rename it *Module 2*.

d)   In the third copy, select the Interaction icon and rename it *Module 3*.

e)   Click on the Start Flag. Why don't you see the Module 2 and Module 3 menus?

f)   Jump to the flowline.

14. Do you see anything wrong with this picture? See figure 11-48. The main flowline is "broken" or disconnected. The flowline does not continue from the first interaction to the second, or the second interaction to the third. This picture tells the entire story of why you currently cannot see the Module 2 or Module 3 menu.

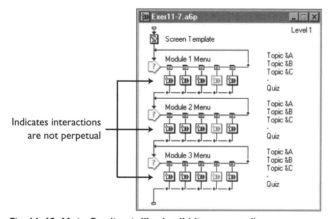

Fig. 11-48. Main flowline is "broken" (disconnected).

You need each of the module menus to be available all of the time, regardless of what screen you are on or which topic you are within. In Authorware, "being available all of the time" translates roughly as "perpetual."

a)   In the first structure, double click on the Response Type symbol for *Topic &A*. Click on the Response tab. Look at the top of this tab, and find the Scope option. Click on this box to place a check mark next to Perpetual. Close the dialog window. Place a check mark beside the Scope/Perpetual option in the Response tab for all Map icons attached to this first interaction.

b) Note what happens to the flowline as soon as you change the last response to Perpetual. It is now connected to the second interaction. Obviously this was the correct move. Let's keep going and change the rest.

c) In the second structure, double click on the Response Type symbol for *Topic &A*. Click on the Response tab. Click on the box to place a check mark next to Perpetual. Close the dialog window. Place a check mark beside the Scope/Perpetual option in the Response tab for all Map icons attached to this second interaction.

d) In the third structure, double click on the Response Type symbol for *Topic &A*. Click on the Response tab. Click on the box to place a check mark beside Perpetual. Close the dialog window. Place a check mark beside the Scope/Perpetual option in the Response tab for all Map icons attached to this third interaction.

15. Take a look at where you are now.

a) You can drag the white Start Flag back to the Icon palette or simply click in the "empty" box in the Icon palette, where the white Start flag normally resides.

b) Click on the Restart button.

c) You should be able to see all three module menus. Click on Module 2. Select a topic. Click on the Continue button a few times. Look at the header information. It still says Module 1. You still have a little fixing up to do.

d) Jump to the flowline.

e) In the second interaction structure, double click on *Map – Topic &A*. Double click on the Display icon *Topic Header*. Use the Text tool and modify the existing text so that it reads *Module 2 – Topic A*. Close the icon. Close the Map icon. Open *Map – Topic &B*. Open the Display icon. Modify the text so that it reads *Module 2 – Topic B*. Open *Map – Topic &C*. Open the Display icon. Modify the text so that it reads *Module 2 – Topic C*.

f) In the third interaction structure, open *Map – Topic &A*. Open the Display icon. Modify the text so that it reads *Module 3 – Topic A*. Close the icon. Close the Map icon. Open *Map – Topic &B*. Open the Display icon. Modify the text so that it reads *Module 3 – Topic B*. Open *Map – Topic &C*. Open the Display icon. Modify the text so that it reads *Module 3 – Topic C*.

16. That should do it. Let's take one more look.

a) Click on the Restart button.

b) Select menus, topics, and quizzes. All should be working properly.

·T/P·

After you learn the use of variables in Chapter 12, you will begin to use embedded variables in Topic Header Display icons so that you don't have to change all these topic headers manually.

17. Save the file.

Summary

- *By this time, hopefully you are convinced that Authorware provides the potential for a wide variety of interactive instructional strategies through the use of the Interaction icon. Authorware provides this capability "out of the box," with no programming necessary. As you will soon see, you can significantly increase the capabilities of the interaction with the use of variables and functions. However, these are neither required nor necessary for numerous interactive structures that can be created.*

- *In the first guided tour and practice exercises, you saw how Authorware provides the capability to create drag-and-drop interactions that require that the user actively engage in the instructional activity. This interactive structure can be used to require that the user drag single or multiple objects to their appropriate locations, to label objects, to sort and categorize objects, to assemble the parts of a whole, to complete a sentence, and many other types of input.*

- *The foundation of the Target response lies with objects being placed in separate Display icons on the top portion of the flowline, linked to responses placed to the right of the Interaction icon. The wireframe targets can be resized and positioned anywhere on screen. The wireframes are not visible to the user, and therefore each target must be represented by a graphic of some sort. As a reminder with this type of interaction, you will probably want to modify the properties of the icon where each draggable object resides so that it will be movable on screen only.*

- *The next interactive response type covered was the Tries Limit response. This response type allows the author to limit the maximum number of times the user can attempt the interaction. Generally the Tries Limit response is used as an adjunct to another type of interactive response, which serves as the primary interactive strategy.*

- *The Text Entry (i.e., fill-in-the-blank) response was the next response type covered. This response type requires that the user use the keyboard and type in a response, finishing the entry with an "Action key" that passes the entry on to Authorware for "answer judging." By default the Action key is the Enter key, but may be changed to many other possibilities. There are also many options, which the author can elect to include or ignore, that govern the latitude by which "answer judging" takes place. The Text Entry response type is also frequently used as the foundation of user log-in screens that require user input, which can then be captured and stored.*

- *The Time Limit response allows the author to specify the maximum amount of time the user may take while engaged in the interaction. Like the Tries Limit response, the Time Limit response is most often used in combination with another type of response, which serves as the primary interactive strategy.*

- *The Keypress response was then created and demonstrated within the context of situations in which the user was asked to press a particular key or a key combination on the keyboard. The Keypress interactive response is generally not used very frequently, but when used it is often within the context of a software simulation.*

- *Because most developers use navigational control panels, the Pull-down Menu response is not used very often these days. To use this response type, the file properties must include a check mark beside the Menu Bar option. To provide access to multiple menus, all items attached to all relevant menus must be set to Perpetual.*

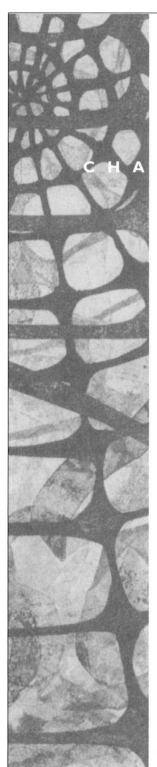

C H A P T E R

12

An Introduction

to Variables

and Functions

Introduction

Up to now you have created structures by simply using the available icons "out of the box"; that is, without any additional scripting or programming. If you do not want to get into scripting, you do not really need to. You can create menus, learner controls, and instructional presentations using a wide variety of interactive strategies, without any scripting necessary. However, if you are willing to "dip your toe" into the vast pool of Authorware's variables and functions, you can greatly increase the capabilities of your instructional presentations, as well as very easily capture, display, and record student information (including test/quiz data).

Before panic sets in, be reassured that you will never be writing code as it was done in the "old days," or even as it is still done today in other authoring tools. Most developers using Authorware access variables and functions through the use of pull-down menus, selecting the item in question by clicking on it. Sometimes the variable/function can be used "as is." Sometimes the variable/function may need to have a word or phrase added, or otherwise modified from the form pasted in automatically by Authorware.

There are a number of loyal Authorware programmers out there who really enjoy building anything, including the Eiffel Tower, with code. Most of you, however, will not need to push yourselves anywhere near this level of expertise. This and other chapters of this book supply you with the level of capability you need. By the end of the chapter you will be able to:

- *Provide a working definition of an Authorware variable*
- *Provide a working definition of an Authorware function*
- *Access variables within variable categories, from the Variable menu*
- *Embed and set properties to automatically update variables within a Display icon*
- *Use the Calculation icon with variables*
- *Use the enhanced Calculation editor*
- *Create custom variables*
- *Use the Conditional response type to modify existing interactions*
- *Systematically increase/decrease the value of a custom variable*

What Are Variables and Functions?

Authorware's variables and functions provide a scripting (i.e., programming) function that greatly expands Authorware's capabilities not only within its own program files but outward to interact with external programs and even directly with the computer's operating environment. You do not need to be a programmer to begin to use variables and functions. Much of time, you will be able to use a menu to select the item you want, and then click the mouse to have it pasted where you need to use it. Sometimes you can use the item "as is"; sometimes you may need to modify or add a word or phrase. Unless you are an Authorware guru, in no case will you ever have to write code from scratch.

Here you will begin using variables one step at a time. First, what are variables? What does the word *variable* mean in English? In general terms, it means "capable of change." Like a variable-rate loan means that the interest rate is not fixed but can change, a variable within Authorware has this same meaning: a value that can change. Such values are stored in Authorware's memory.

A variable is a "cubbyhole" in Authorware's memory that stores a value that can change. Authorware can distinguish three types of values that can be stored as a variable: numeric values (i.e., numbers that can be added, subtracted, and multiplied), logical values (i.e., true or false), and alphanumeric values (i.e., letters and/or words, referred to as strings). A variable can store a numeric value, where, for example, the value 10 can be changed by adding 3 to result in a new value of 13. The variable can store a logical value, where, for example, a True value can be changed to False. In the case of alphanumeric values, a variable can store, for example, a name, such as *Joe*, which can be changed to *Sally*.

A function within Authorware does something; that is, it performs a task. You can use a function, for example, to "write" information obtained from the learner and place this information in a text file on the computer's hard drive. You can use another function to instruct Authorware to "jump" from one Authorware file to another. You can use another function to quit the Authorware program.

There are variables and functions (known as system variables and system functions) supplied with Authorware, and those the developer creates (known as custom variables and custom functions). This division of variable types is outlined in the following.

System Variables

System variables are:

- *Predefined*
- *Updated by Authorware*
- *Categorized in the System Variable menu*
- *Automatically updated by the system*
- *Named using a convention that begins each word with an uppercase letter and that can use a combination of words with no spaces between words*

Custom Variables

Custom variables exhibit the following characteristics:

- *Must be defined by author.*
- *Must be updated by author.*
- *Are named using a convention that includes using a unique name of 40 characters or less. The name must start with a letter or underscore (_). Names are not case sensitive, but spaces are counted if used.*
- *Are listed in the Variable window, under the category of the current file name.*

System Functions

System functions are:

- *Predefined*
- *Categorized in the Function Variable menu*
- *Named using a convention that begins each word with an uppercase letter and that can use a combination of words with no spaces between words*

Custom Functions

Note the following regarding custom functions:

- *Many developers will not have the opportunity to create custom functions, as this often requires expert knowledge of the computer's operating environment*
- *Are generally created as a dynamic link library (DLL) or user code file (UCD)*

Using Variables

Variables can be inserted in the following:

- *Calculation icons or calculations attached to other icons*
- *Condition fields*
- *Options fields*
- *Text objects in display areas of Display icons or Interaction icons (referred to as an embedded variable)*

Embedded variables exhibit the following characteristics:

- *Are automatically placed within curly brackets ({}) when pasted into a text object from the Variable menu*
- *Must be placed within curly brackets when being typed directly into the text object*
- *The embedded variable name will be displayed in an open or active text object*
- *The current value of the embedded variable will be displayed in a closed text object*

• *To update embedded variables, the icon's property* Update Displayed Variables *must be selected*

Using Functions

Note the following regarding system function syntax.

• *Appears in the first line of the function's description, listed in the Function Window menu*

• *If there are arguments, they are enclosed in parentheses*

• *Includes quotes around any character string arguments*

• *Does not use quotes for variables included in arguments*

Guided Tour 12A: Introduction to System Variables

Before using system variables within an exercise, let's take a closer look at where they are located and how they are organized. You will also begin to work with the system variables *FullTime* and *ExecutingIconTitle* by embedding them within a Display icon.

1. Start by opening a new file.
    a) Select File | New | File.
    b) Close the two dialog windows that have opened.
    c) Verify that you are now looking at an empty flowline.

2. Let's take a look at the Variables window.
    a) Click on the Variables window located on the toolbar (on the far right, second from the last).
    b) You are now looking at the Variables dialog window. See figure 12-1.

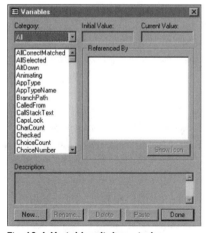

Fig. 12-1. Variables dialog window.

c) There are several sections to this window; we will briefly look at each section.

3. The first section is the Category pull-down menu and display window.

a) In the upper left-hand corner of the dialog window, you will see a pull-down menu under Category. Click on the menu. You can see that there are a number of categories listed.

b) Click on the Interaction category.

c) Beneath the Category pull-down menu, you will see a display window that lists all system variables related to the Interaction icon.

d) Use the scroll bar to the right of the display window to take a look at the system variables listed under Interaction.

e) Click on the Category pull-down menu and select the Time category.

4. Let's now look at the other sections in the Variables dialog window.

a) With the Time category already selected, click on *FullTime*. See figure 12-2.

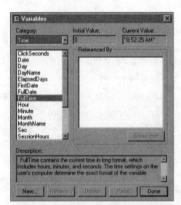

*Fig. 12-2. Variable window showing Time category with **FullTime** selected.*

b) Look at the Description section, toward the bottom. This section provides a description of the currently selected variable.

c) Look at the upper right-hand corner, at the Current Value option. This box shows you the current value of whatever variable is currently selected. In this case, it should be showing you the time of your system clock, at the moment you selected the variable.

d) To the left of Current Value is Initial Value. This box shows the initial value of the currently selected variable. This is most useful when working with custom variables.

e) Below the current and initial values is the Referenced By display window. This area will list all icons in the current file that include the currently selected variable. It is currently blank, because you have not placed it in the file yet.

f) The Show Icon button works in conjunction with the Referenced By window. If you select an icon in the Referenced By window and then click on the Show Icon button, Authorware will jump to the flowline, to the currently selected icon.

g) The buttons on the very bottom of the Variables dialog window perform the tasks as labeled.

5. Let's try working with a system variable. You will embed two variables, but must first have a place to put them.

a) Close the Variable window by clicking on the X in the upper right-hand corner.

b) Drag a Display icon to the flowline and name it *Show Title*.

c) Drag a Wait icon to the flowline and name it *2 seconds*.

d) Drag a Display icon to the flowline and name it *Show Time*.

e) Drag a Wait icon to the flowline and name it *2 seconds*.

f) Drag a Display icon to the flowline and name it *Last Icon*.

g) Drag a Wait icon to the flowline and name it *Continue*.

h) You should now have a structure that looks like that shown in figure 12-3.

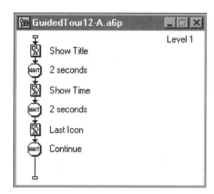

Fig. 12-3. Guided tour flowline.

6. Now that you have a structure to work with, let's dive in and create the first embedded system variable.

a) Double click on the Display icon *Show Title*.

b) Select the Text tool and click the I-bar cursor on screen to open a text object.

c) Click on the Variables Window button.

d) In the Category pull-down menu, select Icons.

e) In the list below Category, locate and single click on *ExecutingIconTitle*.

In other words, as the program moves down the flowline, the "executing icon" is the icon Authorware is currently "reading" and "performing" whatever task is involved with that icon. In our example, embedding the system variable *ExecutingIconTitle* (with Update Displayed Variables selected), will display the name of each icon's title as Authorware encounters it on the flowline.

f) Take a moment and read the description.

g) With the variable *ExecutingIconTitle* selected, click on the Paste button in the lower right.

h) You should now see the variable pasted in the open text object, displayed within curly brackets: {*ExecutingIconTitle*}.

i) Select the Pointer tool to close the text object. The closed text object should now read *Show Title*, which is the name of the current Display icon.

j) Select the Text tool and click the I-bar inside the existing text object, to open it. With the text object open, you should now be able to read the name of the variable again: {*ExecutingIconTitle*}. You may need to extend the text margins to read it more easily.

k) Select the Pointer tool again, to close the text object.

l) Select Modify | Icon | Properties. You should now be looking at the Properties/Display Icon dialog window. On the Display tab, in the Options area, place a check mark beside the Update Displayed Variables option. Click on the OK button to close the dialog window.

m) Close the Display icon.

n) Double click on the first Wait icon. Remove all check marks and enter 2 in the Time Limit field. Close the dialog window.

o) Double click on the second Wait icon. Remove all check marks and enter 2 in the Time Limit field. Close the dialog window.

7. Finish embedding the first system variable.

a) Double click on the Display icon *Show Time*.

b) Select the Text tool and click the I-bar cursor on screen to open a text object.

c) Click on the Variables Window button.

d) In the Category pull-down menu, select Time.

e) In the list below Category, locate and single click on *FullTime*.

f) Take a moment and read the description; it is pretty straightforward.

g) With the variable *FullTime* selected, click on the Paste button in the lower right.

h) You should now see the variable pasted in the open text object, within curly brackets: {*FullTime*}.

i) Select the Pointer tool to close the text object. The closed text object should now show you the current time of your system.

j) Select Modify | Icon | Properties. You should now be looking at the Properties/Display Icon dialog window. In the Options area, place a check mark beside the Update Displayed Variables option. Click on the OK button to close the dialog window.

k) Close the Display icon.

  l) Double click on the Display icon *Last Icon*. Select the Text tool and type in *Here I am*.

  m) Close the Display icon.

8. Let's take a look.

  a) Click on the Restart button.

  b) You should see the name of the current icon being displayed and watch as it is updated as Authorware moves on to the next icon. When you encounter the *Show Time* icon, your computer's current system time is displayed, and is updated as long as the program is in run mode. As Authorware continues, you can see the name of the current icon being displayed via the embedded variable.

You will have a great deal of practice using system variables as you continue. There is no need to save this file, unless you want to.

Guided Tour 12B:
Conditional Interaction and Properties

Now that you have been introduced to variables, you can go back and finish examining the Interaction response types by looking at one more interaction response, the Conditional response type. This response type is not dependent on the user doing anything. Rather, this type looks for some "condition," generally expressed as a variable. For example, you could use the system variable *AllCorrectMatched* to match the condition when the user has selected all correct responses attached to the Interaction icon. When that condition becomes true, you can set Authorware to automatically "jump" to this conditional response. The conditional response is frequently used in combination with another type of response that serves as the primary interactive strategy. Let's take a look.

1. Start by opening a new file.

  a) Select File | New | File.

  b) Close the two dialog windows that have opened.

  c) Verify that you are now looking at an empty flowline.

2. Drag an Interaction icon to the flowline.

3. Drag a Map icon and drop it to the right of the Interaction icon. The Response Type dialog window has now opened. Select the Conditional response (bottom of first column).

4. Double click on the Response Type symbol above the Map icon. You are now looking at the Properties/Response dialog window for the

Conditional response. (If it is not on top, click on this tab.) See figure 12-4. There are only two fields to consider.

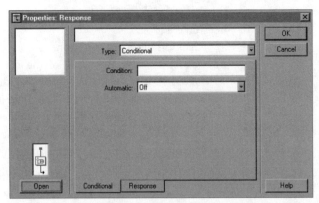

Fig. 12-4. Properties/Response dialog window for the Conditional response.

- **Condition:** *This field is where the expression is entered that Authorware should use to "match." You can either directly type in the expression or paste it in from the Variables window.*

- **Automatic:** *This field is used in combination with the Condition field. It tells Authorware what it should do when the condition has been met, given one of the following options.*

    Off: *Authorware matches the specified condition only when the user responds to the interaction and the condition is matched. Because the condition is not matched automatically, additional action is frequently required to "push" Authorware to move to the conditional response.*

    When True: *Authorware will automatically move to the response when the condition becomes true. This is probably the option you will use most often. It is also possible to inadvertently set up continuously looping interactions with this option, so you will need to pay attention when using it.*

    On False to True: *Authorware matches the conditional response only when the condition changes from true to false while Authorware is executing the Interaction icon. No user response is necessarily required for a match. You probably will not use this option very often.*

You can get a better idea of what the Conditional response is all about by working with it. Let's jump in.

Practice Exercise 12-1: Using a System Variable *(AllCorrectMatched)* to Evaluate Conditions

Description

In this exercise you are going to revisit an exercise you performed in Chapter 11. That exercise involved dragging multiple tools to multiple correct locations. In that exercise you were faced with a problem. On one hand, you needed to set the Branching option on each response to *Try Again* so that Authorware would circle back to the interaction and allow you to continue dragging the other objects.

On the other hand, this produced a "broken" (discontinuous) flowline, with no Exit branch to allow you out of the interaction and capable of continuing down the flowline. You created a temporary solution by providing a Done button that could be clicked on after you had correctly dragged all objects to their appropriate locations. The Done button supplied the interaction with an Exit branch and allowed you to leave the interaction and continue down the flowline.

In this exercise, you will be able to provide a better solution to this situation. You will use the Conditional response to evaluate the "condition" of having finished dragging all objects to their correct locations. In the language of Authorware, this condition might be expressed as "when the user has matched all correct responses attached to the Interaction icon." In fact, this condition is a system variable, *AllCorrectMatched*. The following elements are covered in this exercise:

- *Modifying an existing interaction structure by adding a Conditional response to it*
- *Using the Conditional response to evaluate the system variable* AllCorrectMatched
- *Setting each correct target response to a Correct status*

Take a Look

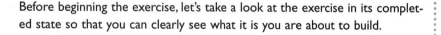

CD-ROM

Before beginning the exercise, let's take a look at the exercise in its completed state so that you can clearly see what it is you are about to build.

1. Select File | Open and locate on the companion CD-ROM the directory named *Chapter12*. Within this directory, locate and double click on the file named *Exer12-1*.

2. The file *Exer12-1* should now appear in your copy of Authorware. Click on the Restart button to play the file from the top of the flowline. Note the following properties of this completed exercise.

- *When you drag and drop the object to an incorrect area, the object returns to where it was originally located.*
- *For an incorrect response, there is no text-based feedback and you can try again.*
- *When you drag and drop the object to the correct area, the object "snaps" to the center of the target area.*
- *For the correct response, there is no text-based feedback and the program exits the interaction.*
- *When all objects have been moved to their correct target locations, Authorware will automatically "match" this condition and provide text-based feedback as well as applause.*

Storyboard: On Screen

Figure 12-5 shows what the finished presentation will look like on screen when the exercise is complete.

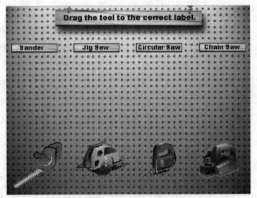

Fig. 12-5. Completed presentation on screen.

Storyboard: Behind the Scenes

Figure 12-6 shows the main and secondary flowlines (with all icons, their placement, and their names) as they should look when you are finished with this exercise. Figure 12-7 shows the Properties/Response dialog window and Conditional tab for the Map icon *AllCorrectMatched*.

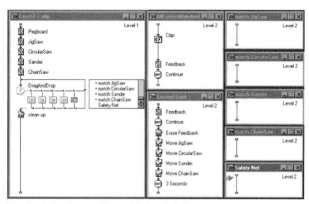

Fig. 12-6. Main flowline with level 2 flowlines.

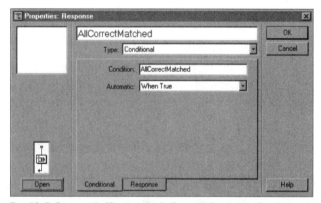

Fig. 12-7. Properties/Response dialog window with Conditional tab for AllCorrectMatched.

Step-by-Step Instructions

Go Solo

1. In a previous exercise you created an interaction you had to leave with a temporary solution because at the time you had no way to evaluate a condition. Now that you can evaluate a condition, let's revisit that multiple drag-and-drop exercise.

    a) Open *Chap11-3.a6p* from the *SaveWork* directory on your computer's hard drive.

    Or

    Open *Exer11-3.a6p* from the companion CD-ROM's *Chapter11* directory.

    b) Select File | Save As and save this file as *Chap12-1.a6p* into the *SaveWork* directory on your computer's hard drive.

2. Let's take a look at what you have. See figure 12-6 or look at your flow-line in Authorware.

   a) The first response to the right of the Interaction icon (i.e., the Done button) was the temporary solution.

   b) The Done button provided the Exit branch out of the interaction.

3. Let's simply reuse the Done button, converting it to a Conditional response.

   a) Double click on the Response Type symbol for the Done button.

   b) You are now looking at the Properties/Response dialog window. In the Type field, use the pull-down menu and select Conditional. The response type has now changed to Conditional.

   c) Click your cursor in the Condition field.

   d) Click on the Variables Window button. Click on the Category pull-down menu and select the Interaction category.

   e) Single click on the very first variable, *AllCorrectMatched*. Read the description of this variable at the bottom of the Variable window.

   f) In the variable description, pay particular attention to "with a Status of Correct."

   g) Click on the Paste button located in the lower right. (If the Paste button is grayed out, you probably forgot to place the cursor in the Condition field. Verify that this is done before trying to paste.)

   h) Click on the Done button to close the Variable window.

   i) The Properties window should still be open. In the Automatic field, select When True.

4. With settings you have just made, Authorware will automatically jump to this response when the condition *All responses with a "correct Status" have been matched* becomes true. What does "correct Status" mean? Let's take a closer look at a response that matches a particular object being dragged to the appropriate target area.

   a) Let's start with the Map icon *matchJigSaw*. Double click on the Response Type symbol for this Map icon.

   b) Click on the Response tab. Toward the bottom, look at the Status field. Select Correct. Click on the OK button to close this dialog window.

   c) Look to the right, at the name of this icon. Note that it now has a plus symbol (+) to the left of the icon name. See figure 12-8. Also note that this symbol is not part of the icon name, but resides in a separate location to the left of the name.

Status symbols appear here

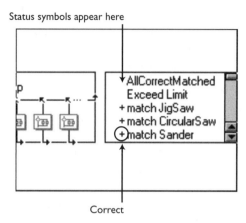

Correct

Fig. 12-8. Plus symbol (+) to left of icon name indicates a status of Correct.

On the Response tab, the Status field can be used to tell Authorware that the current response is a correct or incorrect response, or to simply leave it as Not Judged. By selecting either correct or incorrect, you are setting a "flag" in Authorware's memory to keep track of whether this response was chosen or not. In this case, if the user drags the graphic of the jigsaw to the target area for the jigsaw, this is a correct match. If the user drags the circular saw to the target area for the circular saw, this is also a correct match. In this exercise, there are four correct matches (responses), each of which must be set to a status of Correct Response.

If you are not judging an interaction or do not care about how the user responds to a particular interaction, it is far better to leave Status in its default setting of Not Judged. Selecting either a Correct or Wrong setting in this case unnecessarily takes up space in Authorware's memory. A few interactions set needlessly to correct/incorrect will not make any difference. However, if you end up with hundreds of interactions needlessly set to take up part of Authorware's memory, at some point you will see a negative impact on performance.

d) Double click on the Response Type symbol for the Map icon *match CircularSaw*. If the Response tab is not on top, click on it. In the Status field, select Correct. Click the OK button to close this dialog window.

e) Double click on the Response Type symbol for the Map icon *match Sander*. If the Response tab is not on top, click on it. In the Status field, select Correct. Click on the OK button to close this dialog window.

f) Double click on the Response Type symbol for the Map icon *match ChainSaw*. If the Response tab is not on top, click on it. In the Status field, select Correct. Click on the OK button to close this dialog window.

Shortcut

Similar to the shortcut you saw earlier (which allowed you to change branches from the flowline), there is also a shortcut for changing the status from the flowline. Try this if you wish. Hold the Ctrl key down as you click on the plus symbol (+) to the left of *matchJigSaw*. The status changes to a minus sign (-), a Wrong Response. Click on the minus sign and the status changes to a blank (Not Judged). Click one more time so that you end up with a plus symbol there.

5. Now you need to add the feedback for the Conditional response. Remember that the user will only get here after she has correctly matched all four objects.

   a) Double click on the Map icon *AllCorrectMatched*.

   b) Drag a Sound icon to the level 2 flowline inside this Map icon. Name the Sound icon *Clap*.

   c) Drag a Display icon to the level 2 flowline and drop it below the Sound icon. Name the Display icon *Feedback*.

   d) Drag a Wait icon to the level 2 flowline and drop it below the Display icon. Name the Wait icon *Continue*.

   e) Double click on the Sound icon. The Properties/Sound Icon dialog window opens. In the lower left-hand corner, click on the Import button. Use the browse function to locate the *Chapter12* directory on the companion CD-ROM. Locate and select the sound file *Clap.wav*. Click on the Import button. You should see a blue progress bar flash on your screen.

   f) In the Concurrency field, select Concurrent. Click on the OK button to close the dialog window.

   g) Double click on the Display icon. Select the Text tool. Select the text attributes Arial, 18, and Bold. Type in *Congratulations, you know your power tools*.

   h) Click on the Pointer tool to close the text object, leaving the text object still selected. Open the Mode inspector and set it to Opaque. Open the Color inspector and set the "pencil" color to black and the background (i.e., the box behind) color to a medium brown.

   i) Center the text object toward the bottom of the screen. Close the Display icon.

6. That should do it. Let's give it a try.

   a) Click on the Restart button.

   b) Drag each object to its correct target location.

   c) You should hear applause and see the feedback. Pause the program and reposition the Continue button.

7. Save the file.

Guided Tour 12C: Creating a Custom Variable Using the Calculation Icon

So far you have seen how you can place a system variable either within a display area (Display icon) or within the Condition field in a Conditional response type. However, most of the time when you use variables, you will probably not embed them, but will instead place them within Calculation icons either located directly on the flowline or attached to another icon.

The Calculation icon is like an empty box, a container in which you can place variables and functions. There is no display area associated with the Calculation icon, nor any branching capability. It is primarily a container used to hold variables and functions. You can also use Calculation icons to store developer's notes that can be viewed in authoring mode but will remain totally invisible to users in the packaged version of the file.

Earlier versions of Authorware expanded the Calculation icon with the addition of an editor that became part of the Calculation icon. Authorware 6 added several tools and capabilities that make working with the Calculation editor more convenient and efficient. Let's take a look at the Calculation icon and the Calculation editor via creating a custom variable.

(NOTE)

Normally, completed exercise files are not supplied with the guided tour, but are provided in this case because you are now working with your first custom variable. You can find these on the companion CD-ROM, in the *Chapter12* directory. The file's name in this case is *GuidedTour12-C.a6p*.

1. Start by opening a new file.
   a) Select File | New | File.
   b) Close the two dialog windows that have opened.
   c) Verify that you are now looking at an empty flowline.

2. Set up the file properties.
   a) Select Modify | File | Properties.
   b) Select whatever background color you want.
   c) Verify that Size is set to 640 x 480.
   d) Remove the check marks beside the Tile Bar and Menu Bar options.
   e) Click on the OK button to close the window.

3. Save the file as *GuidedTour12-C*.

4. Drag a Calculation icon to the flowline. Name it *Set First Value*.
   a) Select the Calculation icon.
   b) Select Modify | Icon | Properties. You are now looking at the Properties/Calculation Icon dialog window. There are no tabs or settings because this is just a box. See figure 12-9. The windows you see here will list the functions and/or variables contained within the Calculation icon. Click on the OK button to close this dialog window.

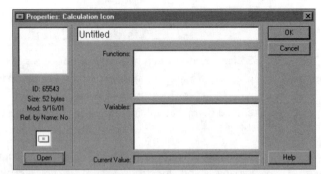

Fig. 12-9. Properties/Calculation Icon dialog window.

c) Double click on the Calculation icon. You are now looking at the Calculation editor. See figure 12-10. Most of the buttons are grayed out because the icon is empty. Let's put something in it first, and then come back and look at the buttons.

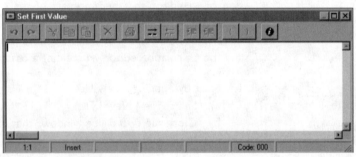

Fig. 12-10. Calculation editor.

5. As you create a new custom variable, Authorware will bring up a New Variable dialog window and ask that you fill in entries, to initially define the variable. The variable you are going to create is named *MyNumber*. Remember that a variable is a "cubbyhole" in Authorware's memory. When you first create and define this new variable, you will give it an initial value of 0 (zero). You will also type in a brief description of the new custom variable. When you first use the variable in the Calculation icon, you will assign the value 1 to the variable.

The initial value, 0, is associated with creating the variable. Thereafter, you will assign the variable a new value representing a particular occurrence (use). To see how this process works, continue with the following:

a) You are now going to use the assignment operator (:= . . . colon equals sign) to assign a value to a variable. Authorware's syntax when assigning a value to a variable is:

variable : = value

    b) The Cursor should be blinking in the blank Calculation icon.

    c) Type in *MyNumber := 1*.

In this step you are actually doing two things at once. First, you are creating a new custom variable called *MyNumber*. Second, as you are creating a new variable, you are also going to use it for the first time, assigning it a value of 1.

    c) Click on the X in the upper right-hand corner of the icon to close it.

    d) You should see an Authorware prompt window, asking if you want to save the changes to the Calculation icon. Click on the Yes button.

    e) If this custom variable had already been created or were a system variable, the icon would have simply closed after you clicked on the Yes button to save the changes.

    f) Because Authorware did not recognize the entry as either an existing custom variable or a system variable, it assumed you wanted to create a new custom variable and opened the New Variable dialog window. Note that the entry *MyNumber* is already in the Name field, as the name of the new variable.

    g) Click the cursor inside the Initial Value field. Type in *0* (a zero). This is the initial value that you are assigning to the variable as you create it. It is generally a good practice (but not required) to give an initial empty or null value to custom variables as you create them. For example, with numerical variables you could assign a 0 (zero); for logical variables, assign a FALSE; and for alphanumeric variables assign a "" (two sets of quotation marks). In a sense, the particular value you assign in this field is arbitrary. This is especially true if you follow "good programming practice" and initialize variables each time before you use them. You will see what we mean by "initialize variables" in the material that follows.

    h) Click the cursor inside the Description field. Type in *This custom variable will store the current value of my number*.

    i) Click on the OK button to close the New Variable dialog window.

6. Let's create a very simple structure to show the results of changing the value of the new custom variable.

    a) Drag a Display icon to the flowline and place it below the Calculation icon. Name this Display icon *Show Current Value*.

    b) Drag a Wait icon to the flowline and place it below the Display icon. Name it *Continue*.

    c) Drag a Calculation icon to the flowline and place it below the Wait icon. Name it *New Value 10*.

    d) Drag a Wait icon to the flowline and place it below the Calculation icon. Name it *Continue*.

·T/P·

This example is pretty simplistic. However, in real-world practice, it is an extremely useful habit (perhaps it should be a requirement) to document each new variable in the Description field. You may think you will remember what the variable is, but this is not difficult to forget when you have created many variables. By providing your variable documentation here, you cannot lose it (as you can lose or misplace paper). In addition, others who may work on this file later will have the benefit of being able to read first-hand what the variable is supposed to do.

e) Drag a Calculation icon to the flowline and place it below the Wait icon. Name it *New Value 20*.

f) Drag a Wait icon to the flowline and place it below the Calculation icon. Name it *Continue*.

g) Drag a Calculation icon to the flowline and place it at the very top of the flowline, above everything else that is there. Name it *Initialize Variable*.

7. Add content (text) to the Display icon.

a) Double click on the Display icon *Show Current Value*. This is where you are going to embed the new custom variable and set the icon's properties so that the variable will be automatically updated.

b) Select the Text tool. Set the text attributes to Arial, 14, Bold. Set the mode to Transparent.

c) Click the I-bar cursor on the screen to open a new text object. Type in the text *The current value of MyNumber is...*

d) Leave the text object open, with the cursor at the end of the text you just typed, and click on the Variables Window button.

e) In the Category pull-down menu, look at the very bottom, for the name of the current file, *GuidedTour 12-C*.

f) Single click on the category *GuidedTour 12-C*. You should now be looking at the list of custom variables in this file. There is only one because you created just one.

g) Click on the new custom variable *MyNumber*. You can now see the current entries within the Initial Value, Current Value, Referenced By window, and in the Description window. As a point of reference, at any point you wish, you can open this dialog window to modify the variable description.

h) Click on the Paste button. Click on the Done button. Keep the text object open for a moment.

As a note of caution, if the New Variable dialog window opens when you least expect it, do not dismiss it by clicking on the OK button (this will create a new variable). Instead, stop and look for a mistake, because unless you were intentionally trying to create a new variable you have made a mistake.

i) The text object on your screen should now look like that shown in figure 12-11, which shows a combination of regular text and the embedded variable *MyNumber*.

j) Select the Pointer tool to close the text object. Your text object should now look like that shown in figure 12-12, which shows regular text and the current value of the embedded variable.

·TiP·

Especially when you are first beginning to work with variables, it is a very good idea to open the Variables window, select the appropriate category (for custom variables, look at the very bottom of the category list for the name of the current file), and paste in the variable (as you have done here). This way, you minimize the risk of making errors. If you are working with custom variables and choose to not paste in the variables, but instead type them in, it is very easy to type the variable differently than you did initially, with the possible result of accidentally creating a second variable for this same thing.

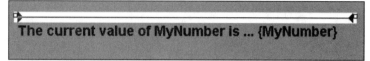

Fig. 12-11. Opened text object with regular text and embedded variable.

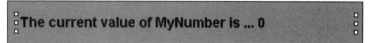

Fig. 12-12. Closed text object with regular text and current value of embedded variable.

    k)   Close the Display icon.

8.   Change the value of the new variable in two places.

    a)   Double click on the Calculation icon *New Value 10*. Make sure the cursor is inside the Calculation icon (it should already be there). Click on the Variable window. The category for your file name (*GuidedTour12-C*) should already be selected (if not, select it).

    b)   You should be able to see the name of the custom variable you created previously, *MyNumber*. Single click on it. Click on the Paste button to paste it inside the Calculation icon. Click on the Done button to close the dialog window.

    c)   The Calculation icon should now read *MyNumber*.

    d)   Continue the expression by typing in *:= 10*.

    e)   Use the cursor to highlight the entire expression *MyNumber := 10*.

    f)   Some of the buttons in the Calculation editor that were grayed out are now active. Let's take a quick tour of the buttons in the Calculation editor. Figure 12-13 shows each of these buttons labeled.

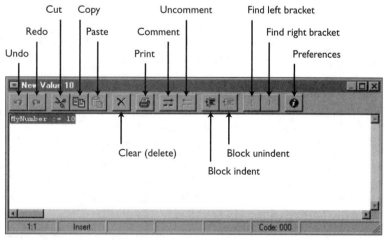

Fig. 12-13. Buttons within the Calculation editor.

The ability to include developer's notes within the Calculation icon is a tremendous production technique. By inserting a double hyphen on each line, your comments and notes are totally ignored by Authorware and are only visible within the authoring environment when the Calculation icon is opened.

As you have already seen in the application exercises in Chapter 8, we frequently use a Calculation icon for the sole purpose of recording developer's comments, naming these icons READ ME. Keeping your notes within the file and next to variable/ function locations ensures that the notes will not be lost and will be available to whomever works on the structure next.

As you continue working with variables and functions, you will also at times find it useful to "comment out" a particular expression temporarily, thereby having Authorware ignore it until you are ready to have it become active again as you remove the double hyphen.

- **Undo, Redo, Cut, Copy, Paste, Clear, and Print:** *These first seven buttons are for very common actions, duplicating most already found in the toolbar.*

- **Comment and Uncomment:** *These buttons provide the capability to include notes, comments, and in-file documentation within the Calculation icon. Clicking on the Comment button inserts two hyphens (--). Authorware will ignore anything to the right of a double hyphen. The Uncomment button removes the double hyphen.*

- **Block Indent, Block Unindent, Find Left Bracket, and Find Right Bracket:** *These buttons are used with more extensive and lengthy sections of expressions to help identify and distinguish sections of code.*

- **Preferences:** *This button accesses a dialog window containing five tabs that allow you to set numerous preferences related to the Calculation icon.*

g) The entire expression within the Calculation icon should still be highlighted. Click on the Copy button within the Calculation editor. Close the Calculation editor. Click on Yes (you do want to save). The Calculation icon should have closed.

h) Double click on the next Calculation icon, *New Value 20.* Click on the Paste button within the Calculation editor. Replace the 10 with 20. The modified entry should now read *MyNumber := 20.* Close the Calculation editor. Click on Yes (you do want to save). The Calculation icon should have closed.

i) Double click on the Calculation icon, *Initialize Variable,* at the very top of the flowline. Click on the Paste button within the Calculation editor. Replace the 10 with 0. The modified entry should now read *MyNumber := 0.* Close the Calculation editor. Click on Yes (you do want to save). The Calculation icon should have closed.

9. Now it is time to take a look.

a) Click on the Restart button.

b) You should now see the following on screen: *The current value of MyNumber is 1.*

c) Click on the Continue button.

d) You should now see the following on screen: *The current value of MyNumber is 10.*

e) Click on the Continue button.

f) You should now see the following on screen: *The current value of MyNumber is 20.*

g) You may have noticed that you never saw the results on screen of what is contained in the very first Calculation icon, *Initialize Variable.* The purpose of this Calculation icon is not for the user, it is a programming technique to make sure we know the current value of the variable before we start to use it. Although with this very simple example we don't really need to use it. It is generally a good programming practice to include a Calculation icon that "initializes all custom variables." The Calculation icon used in this way will specifically predefine the values of the variables you are about to use so that Authorware will start to use these variables within the current structure with known values. This is of particular importance if you reuse variables within the current file.

Congratulations! You have now seen how easy it is within Authorware to create a new custom variable and assign it new values.

10. Save the file.

Practice Exercise 12-2: Systematically Increasing/ Decreasing the Values of Custom Variables

Description

In the previous guided tour, you were introduced to creating a new custom variable and saw how to manually update or change its value. In this exercise, you will now move on to create a structure that will provide you the opportunity to learn a simple but very useful technique: how to systematically increase or decrease the value of a custom variable.

You are going to build a very simple "calculator" containing buttons that will add 1 or 10 or subtract 1 or 10. The current value is shown in the calculator's display panel. The following elements are covered in this exercise.

- *Creating a new custom variable*
- *Using a Calculation icon to initialize all variables before using them*
- *Creating a variable expression that will systematically increase or decrease the current value*

Take a Look

CD-ROM

Before beginning the exercise, let's take a look at the exercise in its completed state so that you can clearly see what it is you are about to build.

1. Select File | Open and locate on the companion CD-ROM the directory named *Chapter12*. Within this directory, locate and double click on the file named *Exer12-2*.

2. The file *Exer12-2* should now appear in your copy of Authorware. Click on the Restart button to play the file from the top of the flowline. Note the following properties of this completed exercise.

    - *The initial displayed value is 0.*
    - *Clicking on either Add button will add that value to the current value.*
    - *Clicking on either Subtract button will subtract that value from the current value.*
    - *Negative values are possible.*
    - *When you are finished with the interaction, you need to click on the Done button.*

Storyboard: On Screen

Figures 12-14 and 12-15 show what the finished presentation will look like on screen. Figure 12-14 shows the completed presentation on screen, in run mode. Figure 12-15 shows this same screen, but in the pause mode with the text object opened.

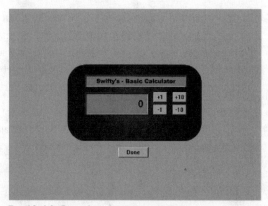

Fig. 12-14. Completed presentation on screen, in run mode.

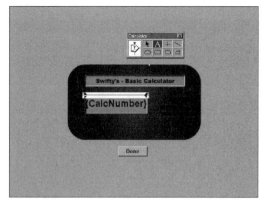

Fig. 12-15. Program paused, with text object opened.

Storyboard: Behind the Scenes

Figure 12-16 shows the main flowline (with all icons, their placement, and their names) as it should look when you are finished with this exercise. Figure 12-17 shows the interior of the Calculation icon *+1*.

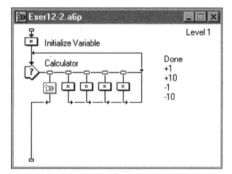

Fig. 12-16. Main flowline.

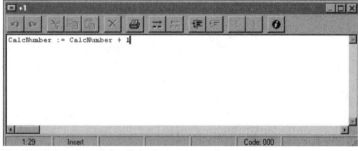

Fig. 12-17. Interior of the Calculation icon +1.

Step-by-Step Instructions

Go Solo

1. Select File | New | File. Close the two Knowledge Object dialog windows.

2. Verify that you are now looking at a new flowline.

3. Set up the file properties.
   a) Select Modify | File | Properties.
   b) Select whatever background color you want.
   c) Verify that Size is set to 640 x 480.
   d) Remove the check marks beside the Tile Bar and Menu Bar options.
   e) Click on the OK button to close the window.
   f) Select File | Save and locate the *SaveWork* directory. Type in *Chap12-2* and click on the OK button.

4. Create the basic icon structure.
   a) Drag an Interaction icon to the flowline. Name it *Calculator*.
   b) Drag a Calculation icon to the right of the Interaction icon. The Response Type dialog window opens. Select Button. Click on the OK button. Name this first Calculation icon *+1*.
   c) Drag three (3) more Calculation icons to the right of the first Calculation icon. Name these icons *+10*, *−1*, and *−10*.
   d) Drag a Map icon to the very first position to the right of the Interaction icon. The Response Type dialog window opens. Select Button. Click on the OK button. Name this Map icon *Done*.
   e) Drag one more Calculation icon and place it above the Interaction icon. Name it *Initialize Variable*.

5. Place the calculator graphic into the Interaction icon.
   a) Double click on the Interaction icon to open the display area.
   b) Select File | Import. On the companion CD-ROM, in the *Chapter12* directory, locate and select the graphic file *calculator.bmp*. Click on the Import button.
   c) Set the mode of the graphic to Transparent.
   d) Position the graphic in the center of the screen. Close the icon.

6. Position the buttons so that they look good on the calculator. You could do this by eye and just drag them to a position and resize each. To make this task a little easier, however, you are provided with some X-Y coordinates for positioning.
   a) Double click on the Response Type symbol for *+1*. In the Size fields, enter the following values: for X enter *35*; for Y enter *25*. In the Location fields, enter the following values: for X enter *368*; for Y

enter *214*. Click on the Cursor button and in the Cursor library select the Hand cursor type at the bottom of the list. Close the icon.

b) Double click on the Response Type symbol for *+10*. In the Size fields, enter the following values: for X enter *35*; for Y enter *25*. In the Location fields, enter the following values: for X enter *417*; for Y enter *214*. Click on the Cursor button and in the Cursor library select the Hand cursor type at the bottom of the list. Close the icon.

c) Double click on the Response Type symbol for *−1*. In the Size fields, enter the following values: for X enter *35*; for Y enter *25*. In the Location fields, enter the following values: for X enter *368*; for Y enter *245*. Click on the Cursor button and in the Cursor library select the Hand cursor type at the bottom of the list. Close the icon.

d) Double click on the Response Type symbol for *−10*. In the Size fields, enter the following values: for X enter *35*; for Y enter *25*. In the Location fields, enter the following values: for X enter *417*; for Y enter *245*. Click on the Cursor button and in the Cursor library select the Hand cursor type at the bottom of the list. Close the icon.

e) Double click on the Response Type symbol for *Done*. In the Size fields, enter the following values: for X enter *75*; for Y enter *25*. In the Location fields, enter the following values: for X enter *280*; for Y enter *350*. Click on the Cursor button and in the Cursor library select the Hand cursor type at the bottom of the list.

Click on the Response tab. In the Branch field, select Exit. Close the icon.

7. Create a new variable.

a) Double click on the Calculation icon *Initialize Variable*, located on top of the Interaction icon. Type in *CalcNumber := 0*. (Again, you are about to do two things: create and use a new variable, *CalcNumber*. Click on the X to close the icon. Click on the Yes button to save the Calculation changes.

b) The New Variable dialog window opens, with name of the new variable (*CalcNumber*) assigned. In the Initial field, type in *0* (a zero). In the Description field, type in *This custom variable will hold the current value of a number that is being modified with the use of the calculator*.

c) Click on the OK button to close the dialog window. The New Variable window should close, and the Calculation icon should close.

8. You have just created a new variable and have assigned a value to it. But how do you get this variable to appear in the calculator? The answer is by embedding the variable within the display area of the Interaction icon, as follows.

a) Double click on the Interaction icon.

·T/P·

Although it is not necessary in this case, it is generally good programming practice to set any custom variable you are about to use to a known value. Here, regardless of the initial value chosen when the variable was first created, you initialize (or set) the variable to whatever number you want to be displayed as the calculator first appears on screen. If you wanted a 10 to appear as the calculator first appears, you could do so very easily by placing the expression *CalcNumber := 10* in the *Initialize Variable* Calculation icon.

401

b) Select the Text tool. Set the text attributes Arial, 18, Bold, Right (alignment), Transparent.

c) Click the I-bar cursor on screen. Click on the Variables button. Select the category *Exer12-2.a6p* (the name of the current file). You should now see the new variable, *CalcNumber*. Single click on it. Click on the Paste button. Click on the Done button to close the Variable window.

d) With the text object open, you should see the embedded variable *{CalcNumber}*. Select the Pointer tool to close the text object. You should now see the current value, *0*. Again, if you want a particular number to appear when the Calculator is first displayed, you can place that number in the Calculation icon *Initialize Variable*. That number will then be displayed as you begin.

e) Position the text object so that it fits within the display window of the calculator.

f) Close the icon.

9. Create an expression that will take the current value of *CalcNumber* and add 1 to it, giving you a new value for *CalcNumber*. First take a look at the syntax (order) Authorware expects to see:

new value := current value + 1

That looks pretty easy. Try it.

a) Double click on the Calculation icon *+1*. Type in *CalcNumber := CalcNumber + 1*.

b) It is easier to understand the syntax if you start reading on the right side of the equals sign, as follows.

        := current value + 1
        := 0 (from the Calc icon - Initialize Variable) + 1
new value := 1

Look at the top of the flowline. As Authorware drops into the first Calculation icon, *Initialize Variable*, the variable *CalcNumber* is assigned the value 0. When the calculator first appears, it displays a 0, which is the result of the embedded variable *{CalcNumber}* set to automatically update the embedded variables. If the user now clicks on the *+1* button, the expression in the corresponding Calculation icon takes the current value (0) and adds 1 to that, resulting in a new value of 1.

c) Click on the X to close the icon. Click on the Yes button to save the calculation changes.

d) Double click on the Calculation icon *+10*. Type in *CalcNumber := CalcNumber + 10*.

e) Highlight the entire expression and click on the Copy button in the Calculation editor. Close the icon and save the changes.

     f)   Double click on the Calculation icon *–1*. Click on the Paste button in the Calculation editor. Change the expression so that it reads *CalcNumber := CalcNumber - 1.*

     g)   Close the icon and save the changes.

     h)   Double click on the Calculation icon *–10*. Click on the Paste button in the Calculation editor. Change the expression so that it reads *CalcNumber := CalcNumber - 10.*

     i)   Close the icon and save the changes.

10. Save the file.

11. Try it out.

     a)   Click on the Restart button. Click on whatever buttons you wish. The calculator should add +1 and +10 and subtract –1 and –10 from the current displayed value.

     b)   Click on the Done button to exit.

Summary

- *On one hand, Authorware provides the capability to create a wide range of interactive structures, without any scripting. On the other hand, if you are willing to "dip your toe" into the vast pool of Authorware's variables and functions, you can greatly increase the capabilities of your instructional presentations and very easily capture, display, and record student information (including test/quiz data).*

- *Most developers using Authorware will access a variable or function through the use of a pull-down menu, selecting the item in question by clicking on it. Sometimes the variable/function can be used "as is." Sometimes the variable/function may need to have a word or phrase added or be otherwise modified from the form pasted in automatically by Authorware.*

- *A variable is a "cubbyhole" in Authorware's memory that stores a value that can change. Authorware can distinguish three types of values that can be stored as a variable: numeric values (i.e., numbers that can be added, subtracted, multiplied, and so on), logical values (i.e., true or false), and alphanumeric values in the form of letters or words, referred to as strings.*

- *A function within Authorware does something; that is, it performs a task. You can use a function to write information obtained from the learner and place this information in a text file on the computer's hard drive. You can use another function to instruct Authorware to "jump" from one Authorware file to another. You can use another function to quit the Authorware program.*

- *System variables are:*

    Predefined

    Categorized in the System Variable menu

    Automatically updated by the system

> Named using a convention that begins each word with an uppercase letter and that can use a combination of words with no spaces between words

- *Custom variables:*

  Must be defined by the author.

  Must be updated by the author.

  Are named using a convention that includes using a unique name of 40 characters or less. The name must start with a letter or underscore (_). Names are not case sensitive but spaces are counted if used. (Names that are descriptive of what they do will make referencing or documentation more meaningful.)

  Are listed in the Variable window, under the category of the current file name.

- *System functions are:*

  Predefined

  Categorized in the Function Variable menu

  Named using a convention that begins each word with an uppercase letter and that can use a combination of words with no spaces between words

- *Note the following regarding custom functions.*

  Many developers will not create custom functions, as this requires knowledge of the computer's operating environment.

  Are generally created as a dynamic link library (DLL) or user code file (UCD).

- *In the first guided tour, you saw how to embed and automatically update two system variables. You used FullTime to display the current time, to the second. You used ExecutingIconTitle to show you the names of the icons as Authorware moved through the flowline.*

- *In the second guided tour, you took a quick look at the Conditional interaction response and its properties.*

- *In the first practice exercise, you returned to an exercise you created earlier, involving dragging four tools to their appropriately labeled places. In the earlier exercise, you had to use a temporary solution to exit the interaction, because at that time you had no way to evaluate whether all four objects had been placed in their correct locations. In this exercise, you used the system variable AllCorrectMatched to perform this evaluation, after you learned to change the status of each object's response to Correct.*

- *In the third guided tour, you created your first custom variable using a Calculation icon. You worked with the New Variable dialog window to define and create this new custom variable. You also took a quick tour of the Calculation editor.*

- *In the second practice exercise, you learned a simple but valuable variable expression that allows you to easily increase or decrease the current value of a particular custom variable.*

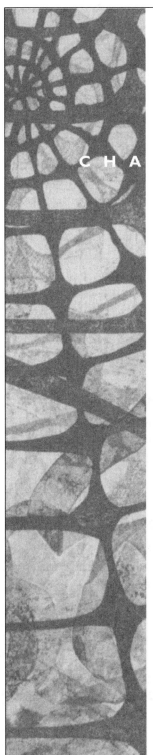

C H A P T E R

13

Nested Decision

and Interaction

Structures

with Variables

Introduction

Apparently you survived your introduction to variables and functions in Chapter 12. Hopefully you will continue to persevere, as you are about to undertake a "mission into deep space." In this chapter you will join the NASA (Nonexistent Authorware Spaced Associates) team to launch a backyard rocket, using Authorware's variables.

You will build a variety of icon structures; some nested one within another, in combination with both system and custom variables. Although most of you will probably not pursue launching rockets into space, the icon structures, concepts, and variables explored in this chapter should help you begin using variables within your own projects.

Unlike most chapters, the practice exercises in this chapter are related and sequenced to build upon one another. In this way, concepts and structures are introduced within reasonably sized sections. By the end of the chapter you will be able to:

- *Provide a working definition of nested structure*
- *Identify common sources of "erase errors" within nested structures*
- *Create a visual "button" with on/off control*
- *Modify the visual on/off button to include logical conditions and custom variables*
- *Create an icon structure to evaluate multiple True events*
- *Create a countdown sequence using a custom variable*
- *Create a perpetual "mission scrub" structure using a custom variable*
- *Create animation*

Guided Tour 13A: Capturing User Data Within a Nested Structure

When you first started working with Authorware, you placed Display icons directly on the main flowline, and placed text and graphics within these icons. To remove the text and graphics from view, you placed an Erase icon on the flowline and linked it to the Display icon. A little later you started creating icon structures with the Decision and Interaction icons, and saw how both of these structures include automatic erase capabilities.

In this extended guided tour you will be introduced to some of the consequences of nesting one structure within another. Nesting refers to placing an item within another, and generally also includes the connotation of a parent/child relationship. That is, the outside structure influences, directs, or controls the inside structure. You are also going to see how to capture user information using the *EntryText* system variable and place the result in custom variables. Let's get started.

NOTE

Again, since this guided tour is a little bit more involved, we have included a completed version of it on the CD-ROM. You can find it in the *Chapter 13* folder, named *GuidedTour13-A*.

1. Start by opening a new file.
   a) Select File | New | File.
   b) Close the two dialog windows that have opened.
   c) Verify that you are now looking at an empty flowline.
   d) Save the file as *GuidedTour13A*.

2. Create a very simple interactive structure.
   a) Drag an Interaction icon to the flowline. Name it *Get First Name*.
   b) Double click on the Interaction icon. Select the Text tool. Select whatever font and size you want. Type in *Please type in your First Name:*.
   c) Place the text object toward the top of the screen. Close the icon.
   d) Drag a Calculation icon to the right of the Interaction icon. The Response Type dialog window opens. Select Text Entry. Click on the OK button to close the window.
   e) Double click on the Response Type symbol. In the Pattern field, type in * (an asterisk).
   f) This asterisk (*) entry is a wildcard that will allow the user to type in any name.
   g) Click on the Response tab. In the Branch field, select Exit Interaction. Close the dialog window.

3. Create a variable expression that will allow you to capture whatever the user types in. To do this, you will use the *EntryText* system variable and then assign the content of this system variable to a new custom variable.

   Let's take a look at this system variable first. Click on the Variables Window button. Select the category Interaction. Look for and single click on *EntryText*. Read the description. *EntryText* is one system variable in Authorware's memory that will hold the content of whatever the user types in as a response to a Text Entry interaction. However, this variable only holds the content of the *very last entry*. When you reuse the variable, you lose its previous content.

   In this example you are going to ask for the first name using one interaction, and then use a second interaction to ask for the last name. After typing in the first name, the system variable *EntryText* will contain the user's first name. Moving to the second interaction, as the user types in the last name, the current content of *EntryText* is replaced by whatever is entered for the "last name" interaction.

NOTE

As a reminder, since you are assigning a value to a custom variable, you will need to use the assignment operator (:= ...colon equals sign). Authorware's syntax when assigning a value to a variable is: variable := value.

If you want to store each piece of information obtained from the user, you need other variables. Since Authorware doesn't have a second *EntryText* system variable, you will need to create some custom variables that will perform the tasks that we need.

Each time you capture user information using the system variable *EntryText*, you will immediately assign (place) the content of *EntryText* to a new custom variable, so that you can reuse *EntryText* and still preserve the information obtained.

Note that Authorware includes system variables for *FirstName* and *UserName*. In this guided tour you will not use these system variables but will create your own custom variables. In Chapter 18 (and following chapters), you will have experience working with the system variable *UserName*. Let's give it a try.

a) Double click on the Calculation icon. Type in *FName :=*. Leave the Calculation icon open.

b) Click on the Variables Window button. Select the category Interaction, and then select the variable *EntryText*. Read the description. Click on the Paste button. Click on the Done button.

c) The Calculation icon should now contain *FName := EntryText*. Again, the easiest way to read the expression is to start to the right of the equals sign.

EntryText – as the user types a response to the Interaction, whatever is typed is first stored in the *EntryText* variable. The value stored here is then := assigned to.

FName – the custom variable. It is like taking the contents in one box and copying it into another box.

d) Close the icon. Save the changes.

e) The New Variable dialog window should now be open, with *FName* already in the Name field.

f) Click the cursor in the Initial Value field. Type in two quotation marks ("") with no space between them. Previously, custom variables were used to store numbers, wherein you assigned initial values of zero (0). You are going to use *FName* to store words, and all words have to be enclosed by quotation marks. If you want to initialize a "word" variable, you can tell it to contain "nothing" with the use of double quotation marks with no space between them.

g) Click the cursor in the Description field and type in *This custom variable will hold the user's first name*.

h) Close the New Variable window.

4. Test what you have so far.

a) Click on the Restart button. You should now see the text *Please type in your First Name:*.

b) Type in your first name and press the Enter key.

c) Everything erases, because there are two automatic erase functions: one for the Interaction icon (where the text object is located), and a second erase function associated with the text field response.

5. Change these automatic erase functions so that they do not erase, so that you can leave the text prompt and user's response on screen as Authorware exits the interaction.

a) Select the Interaction icon. Select Modify | Icon | Properties. On the Interaction tab, at the top is the Erase field. Select Don't Erase.

b) Look at the upper left-hand corner of this same dialog window. Click on the Text Field button. (You can also see this dialog window by running the program, typing something in, pausing, and then double clicking on the response you typed in.)

c) Click on the Interaction tab. At the bottom there is the Erase Text on Exit option. Remove the check mark in this field (so that the user's response will stay on screen). Click on the OK button to close the Text field.

d) Click on the OK button to close the Response dialog window.

6. Now try it.

a) Click on the Restart button.

b) Type in your first name and press the Enter key.

c) Everything should still be on screen.

7. You have just modified the interaction so that the text and user response do not erase. But have you really captured and stored the first name? Let's build something that will test this.

a) Drag a Display icon to the bottom of the flowline. Name it *Prove It*.

b) Double click on the Display icon. Select the Text tool and type in *This is testing the First Name variable. The current value is...* (Do not close the text object.)

c) Click on the Variables Window button. In the Category field, select *GuidedTour13A.a6p* (the name of the current file). Select the custom variable *FName*. Click on the Paste button. Click on the Done button.

d) The text object should now read as follows:

This is testing the First Name variable. The current value is . . . {FName}.

e) Select the Pointer tool. Close the icon.

8. Conduct another test.

a) Click on the Restart button.

b) Type in your first name and press the Enter key.

c) The text prompt, the response you just typed, and *This is testing the First Name variable. The current value is...* (with the current value of *Fname*; whatever you just typed in) should all appear on screen.

9. Save the file.

10. You now have a structure that captures user information and leaves whatever it is on screen.

11. Let's "map" this first structure.

a) Use the cursor and elastic marquee to select both the Interaction icon and the Calculation icon to the right. (Do not select the Display icon at the bottom.)

b) Select Modify | Group. Name the Map icon *First Name*.

12. Now that you have a structure that works for the first name, copy it, modify it, and reuse it for the last name.

a) Select the Map icon *First Name*. Select Edit | Copy.

b) Click the cursor above the Display icon (and below the first Map icon) so that the Paste Hand cursor appears there. Select Edit | Paste. Rename this second Map icon *Last Name*.

c) Double click on the Map icon *Last Name*.

d) Rename the Interaction icon *Get Last Name*.

e) Double click on the Calculation icon (make sure you are in the level 2 flowline for *Last Name*).

f) Change the entry so that it now reads *LName := EntryText* (i.e., you have changed *FName* to *LName*).

g) Close the Calculation icon. Click on Yes to save changes.

h) The New Variable window is now open, with *LName* in the Name field. Click in the Initial Value field and type in "" (double quotation marks with no space between them).

i) Click the cursor in the Description field and type in *This custom variable will hold the user's last name.*

j) Click on the OK button to close the window. Your flowline should look like that shown in figure 13-1.

As mentioned in earlier chapters, when you copy, paste, and reuse a structure, it is very important that you have first finished changing everything that needs to be changed in the copied version. This will generally involve changing the outside label (to the Map icon), the inside labels (all icons inside the Map icon), the expression inside the Calculation icon (if appropriate), the text inside display areas of Interaction icons or Display icons, and the placement of the user text response field. If you do not change these you are likely to become confused as you begin testing the new structure.

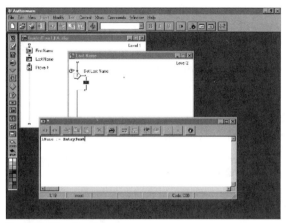

Fig. 13-1. Flowline in progress.

- k) Double click on the Interaction icon. Change the text so that it reads *Please type in your Last Name:.*
- l) Move the text object down about 2 inches.
- m) Move the text response field down about 2 inches, to the same level as the text object.
- n) Close the Display icon.

13. Add an embedded variable in the Display icon *Prove It.*
    - a) Double click on the Display icon. There should already be handlebars around the text object.
    - b) Select Edit | Copy.
    - c) Click the cursor about 2 inches below the first text object. Select Edit | Paste.
    - d) Select the Text tool and modify the second text object. You may want to paste in the variable name from the Variable window. The modified text object should now read *This is testing the Last Name variable. The current value is ... {LName}.*
    - e) Close the text object. If you now have a New Variable window open, you have made a mistake. Look carefully at how you have spelled what is inside the curly brackets: *{LName}.*
    - f) Close the icon.

14. Conduct another test.
    - a) Click on the Restart button.
    - b) Type in an entry for first name and press the Enter key.
    - c) Type in an entry for last name and press the Enter key.
    - d) You should see both prompts and entries and the two embedded variables showing the current values for *FName* and *LName.*

15. Save the file.

16. Create a nested structure.

    a) Drag a Decision icon to the flowline and place it below the Map icon *Last Name* and above the Display icon *Prove It*. Name the Decision icon *Get Names*.

    b) Drag the Map icon *First Name* to the right of the Decision icon.

    c) Drag the Map icon *Last Name* to the right of the Map icon. See figure 13-2.

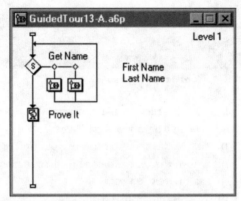

Fig. 13-2. Nested structure in progress.

    d) Double click on the Decision icon. In the Repeat field, select Until All Paths Used. Click on the OK button to close the icon.

17. Conduct another test.

    a) Click on the Restart button.

    b) Type in an entry for first name and press the Enter key.

    c) Type in an entry for last name and press the Enter key.

    d) Both text prompts and both user entries were erased. Why? You previously created a structure that worked fine. Why are these now being erased?

    e) Note that you are still capturing the content of what you typed in because you should be able to see it on screen from the embedded variables being displayed in the Display icon *Prove it*. But the prompts and initial text entries were erased.

18. The answer to the previous questions is that the structures you created previously have now been placed within another structure that also has an automatic erase function. The variable expressions remain unchanged by erase functions. Let's take a look.

a) Double click on the Decision Path symbol (small diamond above the Map icon) for *First Name*. Look at the Erase Contents field. It is currently set to Before Next Selection.

b) The erase setting for this Map icon governs (or controls) everything inside the Map icon. Therefore, even though you had the first structure working the way you wanted, once you place it inside a Map icon attached to either an Interaction icon or a Decision icon the structure is governed by the erase function in the response or decision path. The parent properties (Map icon) govern the child (structure inside the Map icon).

c) This is an easy fix. Simply change the Erase Contents field to Don't Erase. Close the dialog window.

d) Double click on the Decision Path symbol (small diamond above the Map icon) for *Last Name*. Change the Erase Contents field to Don't Erase. Close the dialog window.

19. Save the file.

20. Conduct another test.
    a) Click on the Restart button.
    b) Type in an entry for first name and press the Enter key.
    c) Type in an entry for last name and press the Enter key.
    d) Everything should still be on screen, and the embedded variables should now display the last entries you typed in.

21. It is important to remember that placing one structure inside another will place the inside content under control of the outside icon's properties.

Good job. You are ready for Deep Space Nine.

Practice Exercise 13-1: Nesting Decision Icons Within Interaction Responses

Description

The current exercise and the following three practice exercises in this chapter are all related to creating a mission control panel and launching a rocket. The development process has been broken into four phases, corresponding with concepts and structures that are relatively distinct. Each of these phases corresponds to a practice exercise. The following outlines what will be accomplished in each exercise.

- *Practice Exercise 13-1: Build a control panel with three lights. Each light can be turned on or off independently of any other light.*

- *Practice Exercise 13-2: Create variables and a variable expression that will be able to evaluate when all three lights are on.*

- *Practice Exercise 13-3: Create an icon structure and variable expression that will be able to count down and display seconds in real time, finally launching the rocket into space.*

- *Practice Exercise 13-4: Create an icon structure and variable expression that will be able to "scrub" (i.e., stop) the countdown process and then resume it.*

Obviously the content of the exercises is not the focus here. However, the content does make it easy to illustrate some important concepts, structures, and capabilities you will need as you begin to develop with Authorware on your own. The following elements are covered in this exercise.

- *Creating buttons that are visibly either on or off*

- *Creating an icon structure that provides a bipolar choice of on or off*

- *Troubleshooting common problems associated with nested structures*

Take a Look

CD-ROM

Before beginning the exercise, let's take a look at the exercise in its completed state so that you can clearly see what it is you are about to build.

1. Select File | Open and locate on the companion CD-ROM the directory named *Chapter13*. Within this directory locate and double click on the file named *Exer13-1*.

2. The file *Exer13-1* should now appear in your copy of Authorware. Click on the Restart button to play the file from the top of the flowline. Note the following properties of this completed exercise.

- *Each button can be turned on or off.*

- *Interaction with each button is totally independent of the other two buttons.*

Storyboard: On Screen

Figures 13-3 and 13-4 show what the finished presentation will look like on screen. Figure 13-3 shows the completed presentation on screen. Figure 13-4 shows one of the On buttons that resides in Display icon *Button 1 ON*.

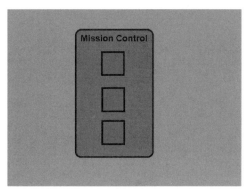

Fig. 13-3. Completed presentation on screen.

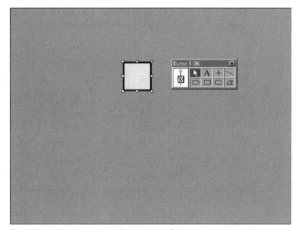

Fig. 13-4. Display icon **Button 1 ON.**

Storyboard: Behind the Scenes

Figure 13-5 shows the main flowline and level 2 flowlines (with all icons, their placement, and their names) as they should look when you are finished with this exercise. Figure 13-6 shows the Properties/Response dialog window for the Map icon *Button 1*. Figure 13-7 shows the Properties/Decision path dialog window for *Button 1 ON/OFF*.

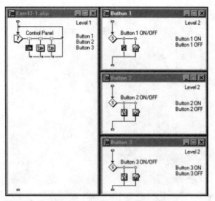

Fig. 13-5. Main and level 2 flowlines.

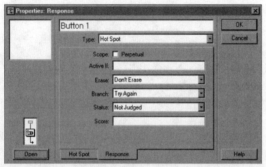

Fig. 13-6. Properties/Response dialog window for the Map icon **Button 1**.

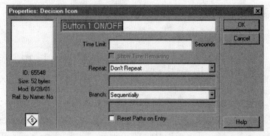

Fig. 13-7. Properties/Decision path dialog window for **Button 1 ON/OFF**.

Step-by-Step Instructions

Go Solo

1. Select File | New | File. Close the two Knowledge Object dialog windows.

2. You should now be looking at a new flowline.

3. Set up the file properties.

a) Select Modify | File | Properties.

b) Select whatever background color you want.

c) Verify that Size is set to 640 x 480.

d) Remove the check marks beside the Tile Bar and Menu Bar options.

e) Click on the OK button to close the window.

f) Select File | Save and locate the *SaveWork* directory. Type in *Chap13-1* and click on the OK button.

4. Create the basic control panel for our mission launch center.

a) Drag an Interaction icon to the flowline. Name it *Control Panel*.

b) Double click on the Interaction icon.

c) Use figure 13-3 as a reference.

d) Select the Rectangle tool. Select the following attributes: Line set to thick; Color set to black line and green fill.

e) Draw a large rectangle in the middle of the screen as the main control panel.

f) Select the Text tool. Select the following attributes: Font set to Arial; Size set to 18, Style set to Bold; Color set to Black. Type in *Mission Control*. Place the text object at the top of the control panel. Leave the icon open.

5. What about the buttons? Can you use the Button response to create the buttons you need? Unfortunately, the answer is no, not very easily. The Button response provides a means of creating a button that looks like it goes down when pressed and even has a rollover state. However, this is not what you need. In this case you need a button that looks like it is off and then looks like it is on.

To keep the focus on the structures and concepts, this exercise keeps the construction of the buttons pretty simple. You can represent an OFF button by using a dark gray rectangle (or circle if you would prefer). To represent an ON button, you can replace the dark rectangle with a light yellow one, positioning it in exactly the same place. Note that we will NOT be using the labels of On and Off, as you might do with the use of the Button response. Instead we will represent the ON condition with a bright yellow color (yellow rectangle) and the OFF condition with a dark gray color (gray rectangle).

You will begin by representing the button in the Off condition. When you click on the button, it converts to the On condition. You can use a Hot Spot response and place a wireframe around the OFF button, so that when the user clicks in the hot spot the program will overlay the ON button (a graphic the same size and location as the OFF button but colored to represent the On state). Start with this information and build one button first.

a) The OFF button needs to be present on the control panel, and therefore must be located inside the display area for the Interaction icon.

b) The display area for the Interaction icon should still be open (if not, open it). Select the Rectangle tool. Select the following attributes: Line set to medium thick; Color set to black line and medium gray fill.

c) Draw a small rectangle (or circle if you prefer) to represent one OFF button. Do not draw it too big, as this button should be sized so that eventually you will be able to fit three buttons this same size on the control panel.

d) Place the button at the top of the control panel.

e) Copy the OFF button to the clipboard (make sure to not include any other object).

f) Close the Interaction icon.

g) Drag a Map icon to the right of the Interaction icon. The Response Type dialog window opens. Select Hot Spot. Name the Map icon *Button 1*.

h) Double click on the Map icon. Drag a Display icon to the level 2 flowline. Name the Display icon *Button 1 ON*.

i) Double click on the Display icon. Select Edit | Paste. (Be careful to not click anywhere on screen before pasting.) You should now see a copy of the OFF button in the Display icon, in exactly the same position as it was on the control panel.

j) With the OFF button still selected, use the Color inspector to change the gray-colored fill to bright yellow. This is now an ON button. Close the Display icon.

k) Double click on the Response Type symbol for the Map icon *Button 1*. Drag the dialog window aside for the moment. You should see a wireframe and the control panel containing the OFF button. Drag and resize the wireframe so that it is slightly larger (and completely covers) the button.

l) Move the dialog window back so you can work with it. On the bottom of the Hot Spot tab, open the Cursor library and select the Hand custom cursor. Close the dialog window.

6. Let's try it.

a) Click on the Restart button. You should now be looking at the control panel containing an OFF button.

b) Click on the button. It should have turned on (become a yellow rectangle).

c) Click on the button again. It should remain on.

d) Jump to the flowline.

7. How do you turn the button off? There are at least two possibilities. You could overlay another OFF button, or use an Erase icon to erase the ON button. Assume the Erase icon strategy is used. But where are you going to put it?

Can you place the Erase icon below the Display icon *Button 1 ON*? No, not really. What you really need to do is create two paths: one for ON and one for OFF. This calls for a branching structure. You can create a branch with either an Interaction icon or a Decision icon. Frequently the choice as to whether to use an Interaction icon or a Decision icon can be based on who (the user or the programmer) is going to decide on which branch to select. Think about this for a minute.

On the outside level, you have an Interaction icon that contains the control panel. It has a Hot Spot response attached to it. When the program is run, the Interaction icon requires a response from the user. The user therefore clicks the mouse on the OFF button. Upon selection, Authorware moves into the flowline inside the Map icon for the selected hot spot. Who then decides whether the light inside the button will be OFF or ON?

The user chooses whether to select the button or not. However, once the button has been selected, the law of physics takes over. If the light is currently off, selecting the button turns the light on. If the light is on, selecting the button again turns the light off. This works just like the light switch on your wall. This is not a user choice but a programmer choice representing how bipolar physical events (such as the working of a light switch) actually work in the real world. Therefore, the structure inside the Map icon has to be a Decision icon. Take a look at figure 13-8. This is the Decision icon structure that you are about to build inside the Map icon for *Button 1*. See Tip to the left.

·T/P·

As you look at figure 13-8, you may want to go back and reread the last several paragraphs to give you a better understanding of the logic behind the structure you are about to build. The concepts here are important.

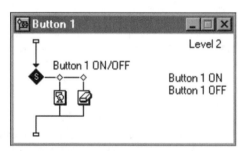

Fig. 13-8. Button 1, Hot Spot response, and level 2 flowline.

a) Drag a Decision icon to the level 2 flowline and place it below the Display icon. Name the Decision icon *Button 1 ON/OFF*.

b) Drag the Display icon *Button 1 ON* from its current position and place it to the right of the Decision icon.

c) Drag an Erase icon from the Icon palette to the right of where you just placed the Display icon. Name the Erase icon *Button 1 OFF.*

d) Double click on the Decision icon. The Properties/Decision Icon dialog window now opens. What settings do you need?

e) Click on the title bar of the dialog window and move it so that you can see both the dialog window and the level 2 flowline with the Decision icon.

f) Return to the dialog window. The default settings are: Repeat field set to Don't Repeat and the Branch field set to Sequentially. What do you need to change these fields to?

g) Think about the Branch field first. Do you want random selection or a calculation? No. The operation of a light switch produces a sequential event. That is, on to off serially. Authorware "knows" that there are only two paths attached to the Decision icon. When Authorware has sequentially gone through both, it simply starts over again with path 1. The branch therefore has to be sequential.

h) What about the Repeat field? If Authorware has just gone down path 1 to turn on the light, do you want to stay within the Decision icon structure and repeat the process until all paths have been used? No, the program should exit after the light is on and go back to the Interaction icon and let the user click on the button again. When the user clicks on the button a second time, Authorware drops into the Map icon and encounters the Decision icon. Authorware knows it has already been down path 1, and therefore now sequentially goes to the next path (path 2), where it encounters the Erase icon that will erase the ON light, leaving you with the OFF light on screen.

Let's try it.

8. As you build this structure you will encounter a couple of common "erase problems" that are typical of building nested structures. We'll go slowly, step-by-step so that you not only see the "problem" but will also understand how to fix it.

a) Click on the Restart button.

b) Click on the OFF button. Anything happen?

c) Try again. Click on the OFF button. You may be able to see a quick flash of yellow.

d) The yellow rectangle (the ON button) seems to be erasing right away. Why?

e)   Look at the level 2 flowline. You placed the Display icon within the Decision icon structure.

f)   Double click on the Decision Path symbol above the Display icon. Note that the Erase field is set to Before Next Selection. Change this to Don't Erase. Click on the OK button to close the dialog window.

g)   Click on the Restart button.

h)   Click on the OFF button. The button should change to the yellow ON button.

i)   Click on the ON button. The dialog window for the Erase icon appears. Move the dialog window aside. But where is the yellow ON button? You were supposed to be able to click on it to erase it with the icon. You just changed the erase function in the Decision path for the Display icon, but it looks like the yellow ON button got erased again by something else. Let's take another look. Click on the Cancel button to close the Erase icon dialog window.

j)   Look at the Decision icon structure. Even though you changed the automatic erase function inside the Decision Path symbol, the entire Decision icon structure is inside the Map icon *Button 1*, which also has an automatic erase function.

k)   Double click on the Response Type symbol for the Map icon. Click on the Response tab. In the Erase field, select Don't Erase. Click on the OK button to close the dialog window.

l)   Click on the Restart button.

m)   Click on the OFF button. The yellow ON button appears.

n)   Click on the ON button. The dialog window for the Erase icon appears. Move it aside. You should see the yellow rectangle (ON button). Click on the yellow square and the Erase icon will erase it.

o)   Click on the Restart button. Try turning the button on and off several times.

It looks like you have it!

9.   Actually, you have one button, but need three. Because this structure now works, creating the other two buttons is a matter of copying, pasting, and modifying the existing button structure. Remember, however, that it is vitally important when copying and pasting that you be very thorough about changing everything that needs to be changed. After you copy and paste the ON button, buttons 2 and 3 will be located in exactly the same place as button 1. The Hot Spot wireframes for buttons 2 and 3 will also correspond to button 1, and you will have to remember to move these as well.

a)   You first need to add OFF buttons for buttons 2 and 3. Double click on the Interaction icon.

b) Click the cursor on the background to deselect all objects. Select the OFF button. Copy it to the clipboard.

c) Paste two copies into the display area. Arrange all three OFF buttons so that they are similar to those shown in figure 13-3. Close the icon.

d) Close the Map icon, if it is still open.

e) Select the Map icon. Copy it to the clipboard. Paste two copies to the right of the first Map icon.

f) Change the outside labels. Change the names of Map icons 2 and 3 to *Button 2* and *Button 3*.

g) Open each Map icon and resize and reposition each level 2 flowline so that you can see both the main flowline and each of the three level 2 flowlines. (See figure 13-5.)

h) Inside the Map icon *Button 2*, rename the Decision icon as *Button 2 ON/OFF*. Rename the Display icon as *Button 2 ON*. Rename the Erase icon as *Button 2 OFF*.

i) Inside the Map icon *Button 3*, rename the Decision icon as *Button 3 ON/OFF*. Rename the Display icon as *Button 3 ON*. Rename the Erase icon as *Button 2 OFF*.

j) The level 2 flowlines should look like those shown in figure 13-9.

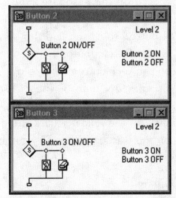

Fig. 13-9. All icon labels changed after the copy-and-paste procedure.

10. Perform the following to change the placement of the buttons 2 and 3 wireframes and corresponding ON yellow rectangles.

a) Click on the Restart button.

b) Pause (Ctrl + P). You should now see three wireframes, each labeled to correspond with a button (the benefit of labeling the icons). The wireframe for the Button 1 response should already be in place. Click on the wireframe for the Button 2 response and reposition it and resize it so that it is slightly larger and covers the OFF button 2. Do the same for the wireframe for the Button 3 response. When finished, your wireframes should look like those shown in figure 13-10.

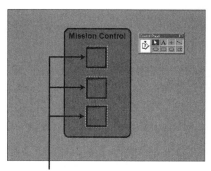

Hot Spot wireframes

Fig. 13-10. Hot Spot wireframes positioned over appropriate buttons.

   c)   Return to play mode (Ctrl + P).

   d)   Click on button 1 to turn it on, and again to turn it off. This should have worked without a problem.

   e)   Click on button 2 to turn it on. Note that the yellow rectangle for button 2 is in the location for button 1 (because you copied the entire Map icon). Therefore, pause, click on the yellow rectangle, and using the down arrow on your keyboard move the yellow rectangle down so that it is aligned perfectly over the OFF button 2. Return to play mode. Click on button 2. Click on button 2 again, and when you are convinced it is working leave it in the Off state.

   f)   Click on button 3 to turn it on. Note that the yellow rectangle for button 3 is in the location for button 1. Therefore, pause, click on the yellow rectangle, and using the down arrow on your keyboard move it down so that it is aligned perfectly over the OFF button 3. Return to play mode. Click on button 3. Click on button 3 again, and when you are convinced it is working leave it in the Off state.

   g)   Verify that all three buttons are working as intended.

11. Save the file.

Practice Exercise 13-2: Adding Custom Variables to Evaluate Logical Conditions

Description

In this exercise you are going to pick up where the last exercise left off. You will be creating some custom variables and a variable expression that will be able to evaluate when all three lights are on. Just like a real space mission, you cannot start the countdown until "all systems are go." The following elements are covered in this exercise.

- *Adding "logic" to visual buttons so that an ON button corresponds to a logical True*
- *Adding "logic" to visual buttons so that an OFF button corresponds to a logical False*
- *Adding a Conditional response and a variable expression capable of evaluating multiple True values*
- *Troubleshooting common problems associated with multiple custom variables and a variable expression*

Take a Look

Before beginning the exercise, let's take a look at the exercise in its completed state so that you can clearly see what it is you are about to build.

1. Select File | Open and locate on the companion CD-ROM the directory named *Chapter13*. Within this directory locate and double click on the file named *Exer13-2*.

2. The file *Exer13-2* should now appear in your copy of Authorware. Click on the Restart button to play the file from the top of the flowline. Note the following properties of this completed exercise.

- *Each button can be turned on and off.*
- *When all three buttons are in the On condition, Authorware exits the interaction.*

Storyboard: On Screen

Figure 13-11 shows what the finished presentation will look like on screen.

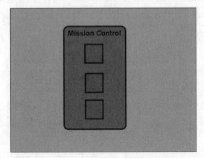

Fig. 13-11. Completed presentation on screen.

CD-ROM

Storyboard: Behind the Scenes

Figure 13-12 shows the main and levels 2 and 3 flowlines (with all icons, their placement, and their names) as they should look when you are finished with this exercise. Figure 13-13 shows the level 3 flowlines, inside Map icon *Button 1 ON*. Figure 13-14 shows the content of the Calculation icon *B1 True* on the level 3 flowline within Map icon *Button 1 ON*.

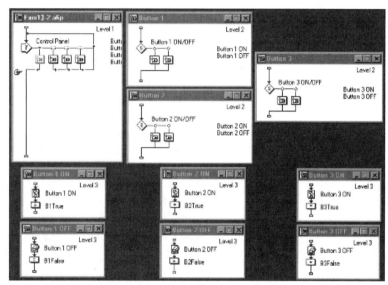

Fig. 13-12. Main and levels 2 and 3 flowlines.

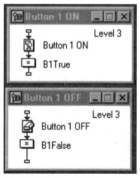

*Fig. 13-13. Level 3 flowlines within Map icon **Button 1 ON**.*

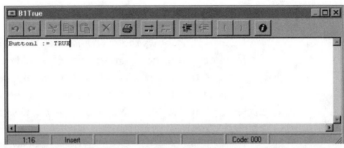

Fig. 13-14. Content of Calculation icon B1True within Map icon Button 1 ON.

Step-by-Step Instructions

Go Solo

1. In the first practice exercise of this chapter, you created a basic control panel containing functional lighted buttons. In the following you are going to pick up where that exercise left off.

    a) Open *Chap13-1.a6p* from the *SaveWork* directory on your computer's hard drive.

    Or

    Open *Exer13-1.a6p* from the companion CD-ROM's *Chapter13* directory.

    b) Select File | Save As and save this file as *Chap13-2.a6p* into the *SaveWork* directory on your computer's hard drive.

2. Let's take a look at what you have. Refer to figure 13-12 or look at your flowline in Authorware. As you can clearly see, there is no Exit branch from the interaction. In the previous exercise, you needed the Try Again branch for each button so that the user could continue to click on buttons. You now need to evaluate the condition in which all three button lights are on.

    In practice exercise 11-2 you were faced with a similar situation. You created a solution for this situation in practice exercise 12-1, in which you used the system variable *AllCorrectMatched* and set the status for each to Correct Response. However, that solution will not work in this situation because there is no "correct" response. That is, the light in the button is either on or off. This exercise uses a Decision icon to distinguish between the On and Off states, and the Decision icon does not have an option for Correct Status (a property of an Interaction response).

    However, what if you were to link a logical condition of True with the light being in the On state, and link the logical condition of False with the light being in the Off state? Let's examine how this might work.

3. Where are you going to make this link? One possibility is in the same place the light is turned on and off. In other words, inside the Map icon, as part of the Decision icon.

   How are you going to make this link? The answer is to create a custom variable (in this case named *Button1*) in which you can assign a value of True to the variable when the button 1 light is on, and assign a value of False when the button 1 light is off.

4. Create a variable corresponding to button 1. Where are you going to put a variable? The Calculation icon, of course. However, look at the Decision icon. It would be great if you could place a Calculation icon immediately below the Display icon *Button 1 ON*. However, as you discovered when working with the Decision icon, you cannot do this. You need to place the Display icon inside a Map icon, and then add a Calculation icon. There is an easy way to do this, as follows.

   a) Open each Map icon and arrange your workspace so that you can clearly see the main flowline and each of the three level 2 flowlines. Examine figure 13-15, so that you can see where you will arrive at the end of step e.

   b) Inside the Map icon *Button 1*, select the Display icon *Button 1 ON*. Select Modify | Group. You have just "wrapped" a Map icon around the Display icon. Notice that the Map icon automatically took the name *Button 1 ON* (same name as the Display icon it encompassed). This is fine, just leave it as is. Select the Erase icon *Button 1 OFF*. Select Modify | Group. You have just "wrapped" a Map icon around the Erase icon. Notice that the Map icon automatically took the name *Button 1 OFF* (same name as the Erase icon it encompassed). Again, this is what is expected.

   c) Inside the Map icon *Button 2*, select the Display icon *Button 2 ON*. Select Modify | Group. The Map icon is automatically named *Button 2 ON*. Select the Erase icon *Button 2 OFF*. Select Modify | Group. The Map icon is automatically named *Button 2 OFF*.

   d) Inside the Map icon *Button 3*, select the Display icon *Button 3 ON*. Select Modify | Group. The Map icon is automatically named *Button 3 ON*. Select the Erase icon *Button 3 OFF*. Select Modify | Group. The Map icon is automatically named *Button 3 OFF*.

   e) Open each Map icon you just created and make them small, arranging your workspace so that you can see all flowlines. Use figure 13-15 as a reference.

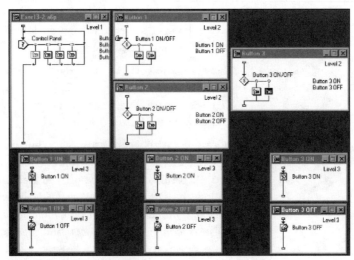

Fig. 13-15. All flowlines open.

5. Before we go any further, we would like to point out and emphasize real-world practices concerning naming conventions of icons and custom variables. As you begin your "Authorware career" you will need to pay particular attention to how you name custom variables: how you spell them and the presence or absence of spaces between words in the variable name. We suggest that you do NOT use spaces in variable names, but either capitalize the first letter in each word (StopLaunch) or use the underscore (Stop_Launch). The consequences of not paying attention to the "space" is dramatic. For example, typing in . . . "StopLaunch" in one place and "Stop Launch" in another place will create TWO variables. Again, you need to be very careful with variable names.

   You also need to be very careful to distinguish the names of icons from variable names. For example, you will notice that we have named Map icons Button 1, Button 2, etc. These names DO include a space, reflecting real-world practice. However, you will soon be creating the custom variables . . . Button1, Button2, Button3 . . . where there is NO space in the variable name.

   This may seem a little confusing at first, but it is a reflection of what you will find out there. Here are the points to remember: be very careful with variable names; do NOT place spaces in variable names; be careful to distinguish icon names from variable names. Good luck!

6. Now you are going to use Calculation icons and create custom variables so that you can create logical links to ON and OFF buttons.

·T/P·

It is your choice as to whether to include a space between a variable name and another part of the expression (such as the := symbol). You can use *Button1 := True* or *Button1:=True*. Just do not place a space within the variable name (as in *Button 1*).

a) Drag a Calculation icon and place it on the flowline inside the Map icon *Button 1 ON*. Place the Calculation icon under the Display icon. Name the Calculation icon *B1 True*.

b) Double click on the Calculation icon. Type in *Button1 := True*. (Note that there is no space between the *n* in button and the 1 that follows it.) Close the Calculation icon. Save the changes. The New Variable dialog window is now open, with *Button1* in the Name field. In the Initial Value field, type in *false* (with logical variables, this is generally the most conservative setting). In the Description field, type in *This variable will store a TRUE value when first button is ON and a FALSE value when first button is OFF*. Click on the OK button. The window and the icon should close.

c) Select the Calculation icon. Copy it to the clipboard. Paste it into the Map icon *Button 1 OFF*, below the Erase icon. Change the Calculation icon name to *B1 False*. Double click on the Calculation icon. Note that Authorware capitalized the word *TRUE*. Modify the expression to read *Button1 := False*. Close the icon. Save the changes. Because the variable *Button1* was created previously, the icon simply closed. Here you simply assigned another value to it.

d) Click the Paste cursor inside the Map icon *Button 2 ON*, below the Display icon. Paste the Calculation icon there. Change the Calculation icon name to *B2True*. Double click on the Calculation icon. Modify the expression to read *Button2 := True*. Close the icon. Save the changes. The New Variable dialog window is now open, with *Button2* in the Name field. In the Initial Value field, type in *false*. In the Description field, type in *This variable will store a TRUE value when second button is ON and a FALSE value when second button is OFF*. Click on the OK button. The window and icon should close.

e) Select the Calculation icon. Copy it to the clipboard. Paste it into the Map icon *Button 2 OFF*, below the Erase icon. Change the Calculation icon name to *B2False*. Double click on the Calculation icon. Modify the expression to read *Button2 := False*. Close the icon. Save the changes. Because the variable *Button2* was created previously, the icon simply closed.

f) Click the Paste cursor inside the Map icon *Button 3 ON*, below the Display icon. Paste the Calculation icon there. Change the Calculation icon name to *B3True*. Double click on the Calculation icon. Modify the expression to read *Button3 := True*. Close the icon. Save the changes. The New Variable dialog window is now open, with *Button3* in the Name field. In the Initial Value field, type in *false*. In the Description field, type in *This variable will store a TRUE value when third button is ON and a FALSE value when third button is OFF.* Click on the OK button. The window and icon should close.

g) Select the Calculation icon. Copy it to the clipboard. Paste it into the Map icon *Button 3 OFF*, below the Erase icon. Change the Calculation icon name to *B3False*. Double click on the Calculation icon. Modify the expression to read *Button3 := False*. Close the icon. Save the changes. Because the variable *Button3* was created previously, the icon simply closed.

h) Save the file.

6. Before building anything else, it would be a really good idea to thorough-ly test the custom variables you just created and make sure you have set the appropriate logical condition in each of the six Calculation icons. You can perform this quality control check using two separate and independ-ent methods.

- *Check logical conditions. There are two parts to this troubleshooting process: (1) check with all buttons on, and then (2) check with all buttons off.*

- *Visual inspection. Open each of the Calculation icons and look at the expression.*

7. Check the logical condition with all buttons turned on.
a) Click on the Restart button. Click on each button once, leaving each button on.
b) Click on the Variables Window button. In the Category field, locate and click on the category *Exer13-2.a6p* (name of the current file).
c) Click on the custom variable *Button1* created within this current file. The current value should be 1.
d) Click on the custom variable *Button2*. The current value should be 1.
e) Click on the custom variable *Button3*. The current value should be 1.
f) If any of your values were not 1, make sure to carefully complete step 9. You may want to skip to step 9 now and come back to redo step 7.

8. Check the logical Off condition.
a) Click on the Restart button. Click on each button twice, leaving each button off.
b) Click on the Variables Window button. In the Category field, locate and click on the category *Exer13-2.a6p* (name of the current file).
c) Click on the custom variable *Button1* created within this current file. The current value should be 0.
d) Click on the custom variable *Button2*. The current value should be 0.
e) Click on the custom variable *Button3*. The current value should be 0.

f) If any of your values were not 0, make sure to carefully complete step 9. You may want to do step 9 and come back to redo step 8.

9. Finally, especially if you found errors in either step 7 or 8, you should perform a visual inspection of the variable expression within each Calculation icon.

a) You should have only three custom variables listed with the current file: *Button1*, *Button2*, and *Button3*. (Again, variable names are sensitive to spaces within the variable name. Therefore, if you included a space in a Calculation icon or two, you may have created an extra variable by mistake.) If you have any additional variables, you have made a mistake.

b) Verify that you have *Button1*, *Button2*, and *Button3* listed in the category for the current file. Just ignore whatever other mistakes you may have made.

c) Open each Calculation icon and verify that you have the following expressions. Modify whatever you need to so that your Calculation icons contain the following expressions.

B1True *icon contains* Button1 := TRUE
B1False *icon contains* Button1 := FALSE
B2True *icon contains* Button2 := TRUE
B2False *icon contains* Button2 := FALSE
B3True *icon contains* Button3 := TRUE
B3False *icon contains* Button3 := FALSE

d) If you had to modify any of the variable expressions, it would be a good idea to retest the expressions by repeating steps 8 and 9.

10. Now that you have all the logical conditions working properly, it is time to evaluate when each button has been turned on (i.e., its logical condition is True). Hopefully you have guessed by now that you are going to attach a Conditional response type to the current Interaction icon.

a) Drag a Map icon and place it in the very first position to the right of the Interaction icon. You should now see the Response Type window, asking you to select which type of response you want. Select the Conditional response option.

b) Double click on the Response Type symbol for this new icon. The Conditional tab should be on top. (If it is not, click on it.)

c) The condition you want to evaluate is "when button 1 and button 2 and button 3 are all on." You can determine that a button is on by seeing if the corresponding custom variable is set to True. The condition you want to evaluate might be restated as "when *Button1* is true and *Button2* is true and *Button3* is true."

d) Click the cursor in the Conditional field. Click on the Variable Window button. Select the category *Exer13-2.a6p* (current file name). Click on *Button1*. Click on the Paste button. Click on *Button2*. Click on the Paste button. Click on *Button3*. Click on the Paste button. Click on the Done button. Use the cursor to click between the variables and type in spaces and ampersand (&) characters. When you are finished, you should have *Button1 & Button2 & Button3*. Or you could type in the following, if this method helps you understand better what is being evaluated: *Button1 = True & Button2 = True & Button3 = True.*

e) In the Automatic field, select When True. In other words, you want Authorware to automatically jump to this response when the condition is true (all three variables are true).

f) In trying to understand what is going on here, it might help to consider the two fields (Condition and Automatic) together. In plain English the result is "when *Button1* becomes True and *Button2* becomes True and *Button3* becomes True," then the program will automatically match the Conditional response and move into the flowline that is associated with the Conditional response.

g) After the Conditional response has been matched, you want the program to exit the interaction.

h) Click on the Response tab. In the Branch field, select Exit Interaction. Click on the OK button to close the dialog window.

11. Run a test and see if the structure is working at this point.

a) Drag a Display icon and place it on the very bottom of the flowline. Label this icon *Here I Am.*

b) Double click on the icon. Select the Text tool and type in *Here I Am.* Close the text object. Close the icon.

c) Click on the Restart button.

d) Click on buttons 1 through 3. You should now see the text *Here I Am.*

e) Click on the Variable window. The category *Exer13-2.a6p* should already be selected. (If it is not, select it.)

f) Click on the custom variable *Button1*. Look at the Current Value field. It should show a 1. Click on custom variables *Button2* and *Button3*. Each should show a Current Value setting of 1.

12. Save the file.

You are now ready for the countdown.

Practice Exercise 13-3: Creating a Countdown Structure Using a Custom Variable

Description

In this exercise you are going to pick up where the last exercise left off. Now that you have completed the control panel capable of having three lights turned on independently of one another and that can evaluate when all three lights are on, it is time to create a countdown structure and display the results on screen. As you might imagine, you will be creating more custom variables and building a looping structure that will probably come in handy some day as you are creating Authorware projects on your own. The following elements are covered in this exercise.

- *Creating an icon structure that can systematically subtract 1 from the current time value to show real-time seconds being counted down*

- *Modifying the countdown structure so that it will exit when the current time value becomes zero*

- *Creating simple animation*

- *Troubleshooting common problems associated with nested structures and custom variables*

Take a Look

CD-ROM

Before beginning the exercise, let's take a look at the exercise in its completed state so that you can clearly see what it is you are about to build.

1. Select File | Open and locate on the companion CD-ROM the directory named *Chapter13*. Within this directory, locate and double click on the file named *Exer13-3*.

2. The file *Exer13-3* should now appear in your copy of Authorware. Click on the Restart button to play the file from the top of the flowline. Note the following properties of this completed exercise.

- *After each button has been turned on, the countdown process starts with the countdown message and current time value displayed on screen.*

- *When the current time reaches zero, the rocket launches.*

Storyboard: On Screen

Figure 13-16 shows the completed presentation on screen.

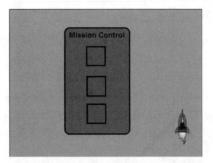

Fig. 13.16. Completed presentation on screen.

Storyboard: Behind the Scenes

Figure 13-17 shows the main flowline (with all icons, their placement, and their names) as it should look when you are finished with this exercise. The Map icon *Countdown* and the Calculation icon *Countdown -1* are shown in an open state in this illustration.

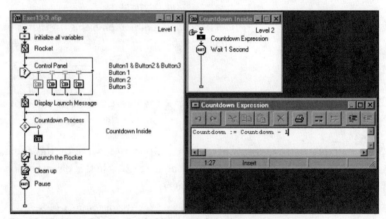

Fig. 13-17. Main flowline with Map and Calculation icons open.

Step-by-Step Instructions

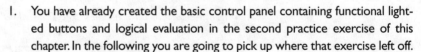

1. You have already created the basic control panel containing functional light-ed buttons and logical evaluation in the second practice exercise of this chapter. In the following you are going to pick up where that exercise left off.

    a) Open *Chap13-2.a6p* from the *SaveWork* directory on your computer's hard drive.

    Or

Go Solo

Open *Exer13-2.a6p* from the companion CD-ROM's *Chapter13* directory.

b) Select File | Save As and save this file as *Chap13-3.a6p* into the *SaveWork* directory on your computer's hard drive.

2. Take a look at what you are starting with. After the user has turned on all three buttons, the Conditional response evaluates this condition and exits the Interaction icon *Control Panel*.

3. You are ready to begin the countdown process. How do we represent a countdown?

a) Let's see if Authorware has a system variable for this purpose. There is a Time category. Click on the Variable Window button. Click on the Category field and select Time. Anything look good? Click on *ClickSeconds* and read the description. This does not serve the purpose. Click on Sec and read the description. This also does not serve the purpose. Try whatever else you want to look at. Close the window.

b) There is nothing obvious that jumps out. Therefore, let's create a variable for the purpose.

4. Create the variable. In the process you will be following good programming practice by using a Calculation icon to initialize all necessary variables. That is, you will set each of the variables to a known value before using it.

a) Drag a Calculation icon and place it at the very top of the flowline. Name it *Initialize All Variables*.

b) Double click on the Calculation icon. Make sure the cursor is inside the Calculation icon window. Click on the Variables Window button. In the Category field, select the option *Exer13-3.a6p* (current file name, at the very bottom of the list).

c) You should be able to see the three custom variables you created previously. Here you can use a shortcut. Single click on *Button1*. Click on the Paste button. Single click on *Button2*. Click on the Paste button. Single click on *Button3*. Click on the Paste button. Click on the Done button.

d) Click the cursor between *Button1* and *Button2*. Press the Enter key. Click the cursor between *Button2* and *Button3*. Press the Enter key.

e) After each variable, type in *:= False*. When you are finished, the expressions should look as follows:

Button1 := False
Button2 := False
Button3 := False

Remember that while creating a new variable the Initial Value field is where you provide Authorware with "starting information" as you first define the variable. In practice, if you always use a Calculation icon and initialize all variables you are about to use (that is, set them to known values), it does not matter too much what value you use in the Initial Value field as you first define a new variable.

f) Place the cursor at the end of the third line and press the Enter key, so that the cursor is now at the beginning of a fourth line.

g) Create the new variable, and assign a known value to it (to start the time value being displayed). Recall from the "Take a Look" section of this exercise that the countdown started with 10. Type in *Countdown := 10*.

h) Close the Calculation icon. Save the changes. The New Variables window opens, showing *Countdown* in the Name field. In the Initial Value field, type in *0* (zero). In the Description field, type in *This custom variable will hold the current value of the seconds left until launch*.

i) Click on the OK button to close the window. The window and the Calculation icon should have closed.

5. Display the countdown message, and show the time decreasing with each second. You will display this information using a Display icon.

a) Drag a Display icon and place it at the bottom of the flowline, below the Interaction icon. Name it *Display Launch Message*.

b) Double click on the Display icon. Select the Text tool. Set the text attributes to Arial, 14, and Bold.

c) This message is going to be a combination of regular text and the embedded variable you just created. Type in *Seconds to launch... *. Leave the text object open, with the cursor at the end of where you stopped typing. Click on the Variables Window button. The category *Exer13-3.a6p* should already be selected. Single click on the variable *Countdown*. Click on the Paste button. Click on the Done button. This should have pasted the custom variable into the text object on screen, surround by curly brackets. The text object should now look as follows:
Seconds to launch... {Countdown}

d) Select the Pointer tool to close the text object. The text object should now look as follows.:
Seconds to launch... 0

The zero value reflects the 0 you entered into the New Variable window, in the Initial Value field. You have not run the program yet, so Authorware has not yet encountered the Calculation icon *Initialize All Variables*, in which you set the value of *Countdown* to 10.

e) You are now displaying the current value of the variable *Countdown*. You want to display the changing values of this variable, and therefore need to tell Authorware to update this variable. Select Modify | Icon | Properties. The Properties/Display Icon dialog window has opened. On the Display tab, toward the top, you will see the option Update

Displayed Variables. Place a check mark in the box beside this option. Click on the OK button to close the dialog window.

    f)   Position the text toward the bottom of the screen. Close the Display icon.

6.   You can now display the launch message with the embedded *Countdown* variable. How are you going to represent the countdown? What expression can you use to do this? Think back to practice exercise 12-2, in which you built a simple calculator. You used a custom variable to hold the current calculated value and subtracted or added values to this current value. This concept will help you get started here. Let's give it a try.

    a)   Drag a Calculation icon and place it on the flowline below the Display icon *Display Launch Message*. Name the Calculation icon *Countdown Expression*.

    b)   Double click on the Calculation icon. Click on the Variable Window button. The category *Exer13-3.a6p* should already be selected. (If it is not, select it.) Single click on the variable *Countdown*. Click on the Paste button. Click on the Paste button a second time. Click on Done. Place the cursor between the two countdowns and press the space bar. Type in :=. Place the cursor to the right of the last variable. Press the space bar. Type in − 1. When you are finished, your expression should look as follows.

    Countdown := Countdown − 1

    In the Calculation icon *Initialize All Variables* at the top of the flowline, you set the value of the variable *Countdown* to 10. Therefore, *10 − 1* arrives at 9 (left side of equal sign). In other words, *New Value = Old Value − 1*.

7.   Let's test it.

    a)   Click on the Restart button. Click on all three buttons.

    b)   You should see the launch message. The value probably decreased to 9 before you had a chance to see the 10.

8.   You have an expression that can subtract 1 from the current value, and you have set the starting value at 10. How can you continue to subtract until you reach zero? You need to keep looping through the process to perform this task. Recall from practice exercise 6-2 that you created a repeating loop. The Decision icon associated with such a loop is the key.

    a)   Drag a Decision icon and place it on the flowline below the Calculation icon. Name the icon *Countdown Process*.

    b)   Drag the Calculation icon *Countdown Expression* and place it to the right of the Decision icon.

c) Double click on the Decision icon. The Properties/Decision Icon dialog window has opened.

d) Here is the magic! In the Repeat field, open the pull-down menu and select Until True.

e) After this selection, the previously inactive field becomes available.

f) You have just set Repeat to Until True. Until what becomes true?

g) You want to keep Authorware looping through this Decision icon, subtracting 1 until the current value of *Countdown* is 0, and then exit.

h) Click the cursor in the blank field below the Repeat field. Click on the Variable window. The category should already be set on *Exer13-3.a6p*. Single click on *Countdown*. Click on the Paste button. Click on the Done button to close the window. Type in *=0*. When finished, this dialog window should look like that shown in figure 13-18.

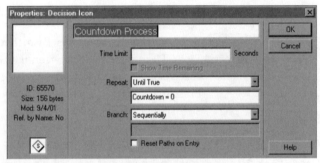

Fig. 13-18. Properties/Decision Icon dialog window.

9. Let's try another test.
   a) Click on the Restart button.
   b) Click on each of the three buttons to turn on each.
   c) You should see the launch message, and if your computer is slow enough, you might have seen the numbers very quickly descend to 0. If you have a faster computer, you just see a 0.

10. What's wrong? You have built a structure, using a variable expression that does what you want it to do. It starts with an initial value and subtracts 1 from it, displaying a new current value. The process repeats, subtracting another 1, and displays the next new current value, and so on. The computer is doing this as fast as it can, which is obviously too fast and not related to real time. How can you modify the structure so that the subtraction happens only once a second? In other words, a pause needs to follow the subtraction. You can accomplish it using a Wait icon.

    a) If you want to place a Wait icon beneath the Calculation icon *Countdown Expression*, you must first wrap a Map icon around the Calculation icon. Select the Calculation icon. Select Modify | Group. There should now be a Map icon wrapped around the Calculation icon. The Map icon made use of the Calculation icon's name. Let's change the name of the Map icon to *Countdown Inside*.

    b Double click on the Map icon to open it. Drag a Wait icon to the level 2 flowline and place it above the Calculation icon. Name the Wait icon *Wait 1 Second*.

    c) Double click on the Wait icon. Remove all check marks. Click the cursor in the Time Limit field. Type in *1*. Click on the OK button to close the dialog window.

11. Let's test once again.

    a) Click on the Restart button.

    b) Click on each of the three buttons to turn on each.

    c) You should see the launch message, and should see the seconds slowly decrease from 10 downward.

You could place the Display icon *Rocket* in a couple of places. However, it probably makes most sense to see it on screen from the very beginning, before the user starts working with the control panel. Hence, it needs to go at the top of the flowline.

12. You have completed the difficult part. After the countdown reaches 0, you need to launch a rocket using simple animation.

    a) Drag a Display icon and place it at the top of the flowline, immediately below the Calculation icon *Initialize All Variables*. Name the Display icon *Rocket*.

    b) Double click on the Display icon. Select File | Import. On the companion CD-ROM, in the *Chapter13* directory, locate and select the file *rocket.bmp*. Click on the Import button. Use the Mode inspector and set the graphic background to Transparent. Position the rocket at the lower right of the screen. Close the Display icon.

    c) When do you want the rocket to move? The answer is after the countdown reaches 0. Drag a Motion icon and place it at the bottom of the flowline, below the Decision structure. Name the icon *Launch the Rocket*.

    d) Drag a Wait icon and place it on the flowline, below the Motion icon. Name it *Pause*. Double click on the Wait icon. Remove all check marks. Place the cursor in the Time Limit field and type in *1*. Close the icon.

    e) Drag an Erase icon and place it at the very bottom of the flowline. Name it *Clean up*.

13. Set up the animation link.

    a) Click on the Restart button.

    b) Click on each of the three buttons to turn on each.

    c) You should see the launch message, and should see the countdown.

d) After the countdown reaches 0, you should see on screen the Properties/Motion Icon dialog window. In the Type field, Direct to Point is the default setting. Leave this setting. Click on the Layout tab.

e) Note the instructional message *Click object to be moved*. Click on the rocket. You should now see the rocket in the upper left-hand corner of the dialog window, indicating that this object is what the current Motion icon is linked to.

f) Note the second instructional message, *Drag object to destination*. Drag the rocket upward, leaving just a little bit of the tail section still on screen. Click on the OK button.

g) After a 1-second pause, you should have now encountered the Properties/Erase Icon dialog window. Click on every object you see on screen. Select a Transition effect if you wish to. Click on the OK button.

14. Let's run the program for the last time.
    a) Click on the Restart button.
    b) Click on each of the three buttons to turn on each.
    c) You should see the launch message, and should see the countdown.
    d) The rocket launches, moves, and then everything erases.

15. Select File | Save.

What if something goes wrong and you need to stop the launch? In the following exercise you will incorporate this possibility.

Practice Exercise 13-4: Controlling Perpetual Buttons with Custom Variables

Description

In this exercise you are going to pick up where the last exercise left off. You have successfully built a control panel with button lights. You also built a structure to count down (after all lights were on) and finally launch a rocket when the countdown reached 0. However, as in real life, what happens if you need to stop the countdown, or even stop additional buttons from being turned on before the countdown begins. In this exercise you will build a structure that is always available and that will stop all elements of the launch process. The following elements are covered in this exercise.

• *Creating an perpetual icon structure that is always available and contributes to the ability to stop the countdown process*

• *Creating a Decision icon structure that can evaluate whether to proceed with or stop the countdown*

• *Modifying the perpetual icon structure so that it can also resume the countdown*

- *Modifying Interaction responses so that conditions can make buttons active or inactive*

- *Troubleshooting common problems associated with nested structures and custom variables*

Take a Look

CD-ROM

Before beginning the exercise, let's take a look at the exercise in its completed state so that you can clearly see what it is you are about to build.

1. Select File | Open and locate on the companion CD-ROM the directory named *Chapter13*. Within this directory locate and double click on the file named *Exer13-4*.

2. The file *Exer13-4* should now appear in your copy of Authorware. Click on the Restart button to play the file from the top of the flowline. Note the following properties of this completed exercise.

- *After each button has been turned on, the countdown process starts with the countdown message and current time value displayed on screen.*

- *When the current time reaches zero, the rocket launches.*

- *If the Stop Launch button is selected prior to the countdown beginning, no button state (On or Off) can be changed until the Resume button has been pressed.*

- *If the Stop Launch button is selected after the countdown has begun, the countdown stops until the Resume Launch button is pressed.*

Storyboard: On Screen

Figure 13-19 shows the completed presentation on screen when the exercise has been completed.

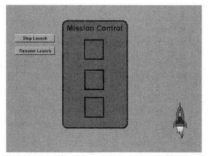

Fig. 13-19. Completed presentation on screen.

Storyboard: Behind the Scenes

Figure 13-20 shows the main flowline and representative level 2 flowlines (with all icons, their placement, and their names) as they should look when you are finished with this exercise.

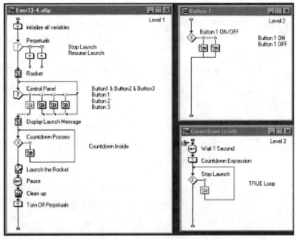

Fig. 13-20. Main flowline and representative level 2 flowlines.

Step-by-Step Instructions

Go Solo

1. You have already created the basic control panel with working lighted buttons, a countdown process, and a rocket launch. In the following you will pick up where the last exercise left off.

   a) Open *Chap13-3.a6p* from the *SaveWork* directory on your computer's hard drive.

   Or

   Open *Exer13-3.a6p* from the companion CD-ROM's *Chapter13* directory.

   b) Select File | Save As and save this file as *Chap13-4.a6p* into the *SaveWork* directory on your computer's hard drive.

2. You want a Stop Launch button to be available to a user from the very beginning. This tells you that the structure must be an Interaction icon (i.e., a user-controlled button). The requirement of the capability being constantly available tells you that this must be a perpetual response, placed at the top of the flowline. Let's create the perpetual structure.

   a) Drag an Interaction icon to the top of the flowline and place it below the Calculation icon, *Initialize All Variables*. Name the Interaction icon *Perpetuals*.

b) Drag a Calculation icon to the right of the Interaction icon. The Response Type dialog window opens. Leave the default, Button. Name this icon *Stop Launch*.

c) Drag a second Calculation icon to the right of the first Calculation icon. Name this icon *Resume Launch*.

d) Double click on the Response Type symbol for the first response, *Stop Launch*. The Button tab should be on top. On the bottom of this tab, click on the button for the Cursor library. Select the Hand cursor. Close the Cursor library. Click on the Response tab. Click on the small box next to the Scope/Perpetual field to place a check mark there. Click on the OK button to close the window.

e) Double click on the Response Type symbol for the second response, *Resume Launch*. The Response tab should be on top. Place a check mark in the Perpetual field. Click on the Button tab. Open the Cursor library. Select the Hand cursor. Close the Cursor library. Click on the OK button to close the window.

3. Create a logical variable that operates in such a way that with one value the countdown is allowed to continue but with another value, the countdown stops.

a) Double click on the Calculation icon *Stop Launch*. Type in *StopLaunch := True*. Note that there is no space in the variable name. Close the Calculation icon. Save the changes. The New Variable dialog window opens, with *StopLaunch* in the Name field. Click the cursor in the Initial Value field. Type in *false*. Click the cursor in the Description field. Type in *This variable will store either a TRUE value (which will stop the launch) or a FALSE value, which will allow the launch process to continue*. Click on the OK button to close the window.

b) Clicking on the Stop Launch button will assign a True value to the variable *StopLaunch*. This means that you need to start the exercise with this variable set to a False condition, so that you can go through the countdown unless the Stop Launch button is pressed.

c) Double click on the Calculation icon *Initialize All Variables*. Click the cursor at the very end of the last line and press the Enter key to create a new blank line. Click on the Variables Window button. In the Category field, select the category *Exer13-4.a6p* (current file name). You should see the new variable, *StopLaunch*. Single click on *StopLaunch*. Click on the Paste button. Click on the Done button. Type in *:= False*. When finished, the content of the Calculation icon should look like the expressions that follow. When you are finished, close the Calculation icon.

·T/P·

If you look at the flowline, it should be obvious that the Inter-action structure is currently not perpetual. Each Calculation icon has a Try Again branch, and the flowline is broken or discontin-uous. Simply changing the Try Again to Exit will "re-join" the flow-line but will still require that either of the buttons be pressed. Once the button is pressed, both buttons disappear from the screen.

Button1 := FALSE
Button2 := FALSE
Button3 := FALSE
Countdown := 10
StopLaunch := FALSE

d) *StopLaunch* starts in the False condition, allowing the countdown to proceed.

e) If stopped (condition is True), you need to be able to reset the variable to False so that the countdown can continue. Double click on the Calculation icon *Resume Launch*. Click on the Variable Window button. The category should already be set to *Exer13-4.a6p*. Single click on *StopLaunch*. Click on the Paste button. Click on the Done button. Type in *:= False*. When finished, the expression should look as follows.

StopLaunch := FALSE

Close the Calculation icon. Save the changes.

4. You now have the perpetual structure with variable conditions that will allow the user to stop and resume the countdown. However, how can you actually stop the countdown process? Where would this need to take place? It seems like a good bet that you need to build something in the same location the countdown icon structure is located. Look at the Decision icon *Countdown Process*; specifically, inside the attached Map icon *Countdown Inside*. This is where the "stop" has to happen. To build the "stop," you are going to use a Decision icon a little differently than you have previously. Let's build this icon first, and then come back and see how and why it works.

a) Double click on the Map icon *Countdown Inside*.

b) Drag a Decision icon to the level 2 flowline, below the Calculation icon you see there. Name the Decision icon *Stop Launch*.

c) Drag a Map icon to the right of the Decision icon. Name it *TRUE Loop*.

d) On the outside, so far this looks just like the countdown loop. However, this is where the similarity ends.

e) Double click on the Decision icon *Stop Launch*.

f) In the Branch field, select To Calculated Path. The field below, previously inactive, is now active.

g) Click the cursor in the blank field and then click on the Variables Window button. The category *Exer13-4.a6p* should still be selected. Single click on *StopLaunch*. Click on the Paste button. Click on the Done button. The Variables Window closes.

h) Go up to the Repeat field and select Until True. The field below, previously inactive, is now active.

i) Click the cursor in the blank field and then click on the Variables Window button. The category *Exer13-4.a6p* should still be selected. Single click on *StopLaunch*. Click on the Paste button. Click on the Done button. The Variables Window closes.

j) Type in = *False*. Notice that this time we did NOT include a colon before the equals sign. Here we are not assigning a value to the variable, but are evaluating the condition *StopLaunch = False*.

k) The Decision icon should now look like that shown in figure 13-21.

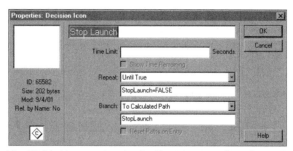

Fig. 13-21. New settings in the Decision icon Stop Launch.

l) Save the file.

5. Let's go back and see if we can figure out how this thing works. Either look at the Decision icon *Stop Launch* on your flowline or refer to figure 13-21 as you continue.

Let's examine the Branch settings first. In selecting To Calculated Path, Authorware will now refer to each icon attached to the Decision icon in terms of a numeric value. Authorware starts with a 0 (zero) for the Decision icon itself. Authorware then numbers the first attachment as 1, the second attachment as 2, and so on.

In the blank field below the Branch field, if you had "hard-coded" a numeric value (for example, by typing in a 1), Authorware would continually drop through path 1, the first response attached to the Decision icon. In this case, path 1 (TRUE Loop) is simply an empty Map icon. The result is that Authorware continually runs around in this loop.

Instead of entering a numeric value, however, you typed in a variable name. This is a logical variable. However, as you saw earlier, Authorware actually stores a 0 for a False value and a 1 for a True value. Hence, if the current value of *StopLauch* is 0, Authorware will drop straight through the Decision icon, and will continue to loop around the *Countdown Process* structure, subtracting 1 from the current value of *Countdown* as if the Decision icon *Stop Launch* were not there.

However, if the variable *StopLaunch* has a 1 value (i.e., is True, reset by pressing the Stop Launch button), Authorware will enter the Decision icon Stop Launch and drop into path 1 (an empty Map icon), circle around to the Decision icon again, drop into the empty Map icon again, and so on. With a True value for *StopLaunch*, Authorware will keep circling around this loop until the value of *StopLaunch* gets reset to False (this happens by pressing the Resume Launch button).

Go up to the Repeat field. The Until True setting really only deals with the situation in which *StopLaunch* has already been set to True. By entering the expression *StopLaunch = FALSE* in the field below, you now have a "way out" of the True loop. When the condition specified in the blank field becomes True, Authorware will stop repeating the loop and drop through the Decision icon. The Repeat setting really only affects the path 1 response (True loop), because a 0 value in the Calculated field will cause Authorware to immediately drop through the Decision icon. If you have not yet closed the Decision icon, do so now.

6. Try it.
   a) Click on the Restart button.
   b) Click on all three buttons, let the countdown start, and then click on the Stop Launch button. The countdown should stop after the next calculation is performed.
   c) Click on the Resume Launch button. The countdown should resume.

7. What if you want to stop the launch even earlier than the countdown, before all buttons have been turned on? In this case, you need to "deactivate" all buttons when the variable *StopLaunch* becomes True.
   a) Double click on the Response Type symbol for the Map icon *Button1*. Click on the Response tab. Click the cursor in the Active If field. Click on the Variable Window button. Single click on *StopLaunch*. Click on the Paste button. Click on the Done button. Type in = False. Again, note there is NO colon before the equals sign. Here we are not assigning a value to the variable, but are evaluating a condition. The completed expression in the Active If field should look as follows:

   StopLaunch = FALSE

   In other words, let the button be active if the variable has the condition that allows the process to continue (which is *StopLaunch = FALSE*). Use your cursor and highlight the entire expression. Select Edit | Copy. Close the dialog window.

b) Double click on the Response Type symbol for the Map icon *Button2*. In the Response tab, click the cursor in the Active If field. Select Edit | Paste. The completed expression should look as follows:

StopLaunch = FALSE

Close the dialog window.

c) Double click on the Response Type symbol for the Map icon *Button3*. In the Response tab, click the cursor in the Active If field. Select Edit | Paste. The completed expression should look as follows:

StopLaunch = FALSE

Close the dialog window.

d) Save the file.

8. Let's try stopping the buttons, prior to the countdown beginning.

a) Click on the Restart button.

b) Click on any two control panel buttons.

c) Click on the Stop Launch button.

d) Try clicking on any control panel button. All buttons should now be inactive.

e) Click on the Resume Launch button.

f) Click on the buttons so that all lights are on. The countdown should proceed. The rocket launches, and everything erases. Note, however, that the perpetual buttons are still there.

9. If the flowline were now to enter a different part of a program, where you did not want the perpetual buttons to show up at all, what could you do to get rid of the perpetual buttons where you no longer wanted them? Actually, there is a pretty simple solution. Let's create a custom variable that will have a True value when we are inside the current exercise and will have a False value when we leave the exercise.

a) Double click on the Calculation icon *Initialize All Variables*. Click the cursor at the end of the last line. Press the Enter key to create another blank line. Type in *InExercise := TRUE*. Note that we DO include the assignment operator (:=) here because we are assigning a value to the variable. Close the Calculation icon. Save the changes. The New Variables dialog window now opens, with *InExercise* in the Name field. In the Initial Value field, type in *FALSE*. In the Description field, type in *This variable will store a TRUE value when the current exercise is being performed and a FALSE value when Authorware exits the current exercise.* Close the dialog window.

b) Double click on the Response Type symbol for the Stop Launch perpetual button. Click on the Response tab. In the Active If field, type in

·T*i*P·

Remember to single click slowly. If you end up clicking several times quickly, because you are in the authoring mode you may end up pausing the program and entering the icon you double clicked on.

InExercise=TRUE (no colon). What this means is that the button will only be active if the custom variable *InExercise* has a current value of True. Now click on the Button tab. Click on the box next to the option, *Hide When Inactive*, to place a check mark there. When the button is inactive, it will be hidden, not just grayed out. You started at the top of the flowline (inside the Calculation icon *Initialize All Variables*), with a True value. Highlight this expression (*InExercise = TRUE*). Copy it to the clipboard. Close the Calculation icon. Save the changes.

c) Double click on the Response Type symbol for the Resume Launch perpetual button. On the bottom of the Button tab, click on the box next to the option, *Hide When Inactive*, to place a check mark there. Click on the Response tab. Click the cursor in the Active If field. Paste the expression from the clipboard. Close the dialog window. Save the changes.

d) Drag a Calculation icon to the very bottom of the flowline. Name the icon *Turn off perpetuals*. Double click on the Calculation icon. Paste the expression from the clipboard. Modify the expression so that is now reads *InExercise = False*. As Authorware exits the current exercise, this Calculation icon will deactivate the two perpetual buttons.

Excellent job! You are done here. Get your space suit; you are ready for NASA!

Summary

- *This chapter continued the use of custom variables within nested icon structures. Specifically, you explored linking logical conditions with visual indicators, evaluating logical conditions, building a second counter, and creating a perpetual icon structure capable of reassigning the value of variables from anywhere within the program.*

- *The first guided tour focused on creating a nested structure capable of capturing user data, leaving it on screen, and placing the information within Authorware's memory. Both system and custom variables were used.*

- *In the first practice exercise, a structure was built that allowed buttons to be visually turned on and off, each button independent of the other.*

- *In the second practice exercise, additional structures and variable expressions were created that were linked to visual conditions and made capable of evaluating multiple logical conditions.*

- *In the third practice exercise, a looping structure was created that would systematically subtract 1 from the current value and count down seconds in real time.*

- *In the last practice exercise, a perpetual structure, looping structure, and expressions were created that provided the ability to reassign variable values from anywhere within the program. Variables were used to deactivate and activate buttons.*

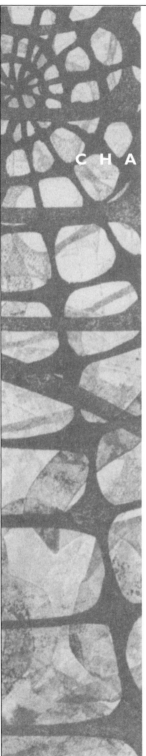

C H A P T E R

14

Application:

Creating

Interactive

Structures

Introduction

In this chapter you will create interactive structures that can be used as instructional learning strategies and quiz formats. The key to efficient Authorware development is creating interactive structures that require very little rework for reuse. Each of the exercises in this chapter emphasizes the benefits of carefully designing the learning activity interface before starting, and then making use of grid patterns developed during this design phase. As a side note, the question structures are intermediate-level structures, offering a generic capability without the complexity (or power) of the dynamic model you will explore in Chapter 27.

Application Exercise 14A:
Interactive Learning Strategy 1

Description

This learning activity illustrates an interactive strategy based on hot spots, which can be effectively used when there are multiple terms or concepts that must be learned or associated with additional information. Once the learning activity interface has been created, it can be reused with the same set of target words within seconds, or reworked with a different subject within moments. You will leave this exercise grouped within a Map icon that will be inserted into a topic structure (in Chapter 17).

Storyboard: On Screen

Figure 14-1 shows what the exercise will look like on screen when completed.

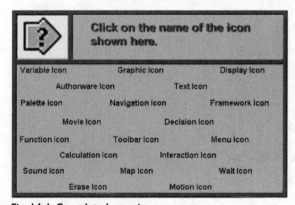

Fig. 14-1. Completed exercise on screen.

Storyboard: Behind the Scenes

Figure 14-2 shows the main and second-level flowlines (with all icons, their placement, and their names) as they should look when you are finished with this exercise.

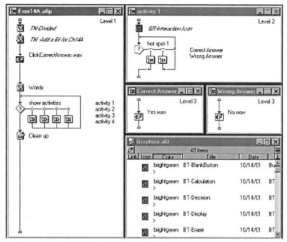

Fig. 14-2. Main and second-level flowlines.

Step-by-Step Instructions

Use the following generalized steps as guidance in completing this exercise on your own. Consult the completed exercise (*Exer14A.a6p*) on the companion CD-ROM for further guidance.

1. Open the file *Exer14A.a6p* located on the companion CD-ROM in the directory named *Chapter14*. Open the library file *Graphics.a6l* located in the same directory. Run the program and see how it works. Jump to the flowline and examine the various icons and structures.

2. Open the Calculation icons labeled READ ME and read their content.

3. Leave this file open in this copy of Authorware.

4. Open another copy of Authorware, starting a new file. Save the file as *App14A*. Open the library file *Graphics.a6l* located in the *SaveWork* directory of your hard drive.

5. When finished, make sure to save your exercise in the *SaveWork* directory on your computer's hard drive.

Application Exercise 14B:
Interactive Learning Strategy 2

Description

This learning activity illustrates using the Drag and Drop response to have learners correctly match descriptive labels to graphics. The key to rapid reuse is in effectively designing the interface, the objects, and a placement grid. You will leave this exercise grouped within a Map icon to be inserted within a topic structure (in Chapter 17).

Storyboard: On Screen

Figure 14-3 shows what the exercise will look like on screen when completed.

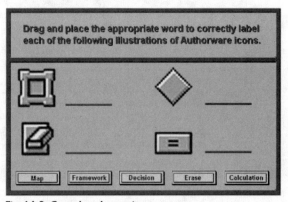

Fig. 14-3. Completed exercise on screen.

Storyboard: Behind the Scenes

Figure 14-4 shows the main and second-level flowlines (with all icons, their placement, and their names) as they should look when you are finished with this exercise.

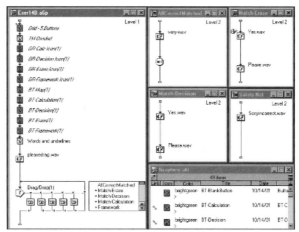

Fig. 14-4. Main and second-level flowlines.

Step-by-Step Instructions

Use the following generalized steps as guidance in completing this exercise on your own. Consult the completed exercise (*Exer14B.a6p*) on the companion CD-ROM for further guidance.

1. Open the file *Exer14B.a6p* located on the companion CD-ROM in the directory named *Chapter14*. Open the library file *Graphics.a6l* located in the same directory. Run the program and see how it works. Jump to the flowline and examine the various icons and structures.

2. Open the Calculation icons labeled READ ME and read their content.

3. Leave this file open in this copy of Authorware.

4. Open another copy of Authorware, starting a new file. Save the file as *App14B*. Open the library file *Graphics.a6l* located in the *SaveWork* directory of your hard drive.

5. When finished, make sure to save your exercise in the *SaveWork* directory on your computer's hard drive.

Application Exercise 14C:
Interactive Learning Strategy 3

Description

This learning activity uses the Drag and Drop response again, but this time to drag words to complete multiple sentences with missing phrases. The design and grid play an important part of efficient reuse. You will leave this exercise grouped within a Map icon to be inserted within a topic structure (in Chapter 17).

Storyboard: On Screen

Figure 14-5 shows what the exercise will look like on screen when completed.

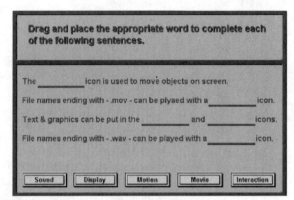

Fig. 14-5. Completed exercise on screen.

Storyboard: Behind the Scenes

Figure 14-6 shows the main and second-level flowlines (with all icons, their placement, and their names) as it should look when you are finished with this exercise.

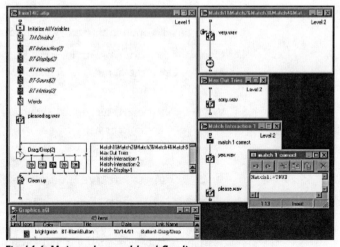

Fig. 14-6. Main and second-level flowlines.

Step-by-Step Instructions

Use the following generalized steps as guidance in completing this exercise on your own. Consult the completed exercise (*Exer14C.a6p*) on the companion CD-ROM for further guidance.

1. Open the file *Exer14C.a6p* located on the companion CD-ROM in the directory named *Chapter14*. Open the library file *Graphics.a6l* located in the same directory. Run the program and see how it works. Jump to the flowline and examine the various icons and structures.

2. Open the Calculation icons labeled READ ME and read their content.

3. Leave this file open in this copy of Authorware.

4. Open another copy of Authorware, starting a new file. Save the file as *App14C*. Open the library file *Graphics.a6l* located in the *SaveWork* directory of your hard drive.

5. When finished, make sure to save your exercise in the *SaveWork* directory on your computer's hard drive.

Application Exercise 14D: Interactive Learning Strategy 4

Description

In this learning activity, an interactive graphic is used to provide two layers of information to the learner. As the learner moves the cursor over a graphic of an icon, narration states what the icon is. If the user clicks on that same icon, a second layer of information is provided, including text and narration. The design and grid play an important part of efficient reuse. You will leave this exercise grouped within a Map icon to be inserted into a topic structure (in Chapter 17).

Storyboard: On Screen

Figure 14-7 shows what the exercise will look like on screen when completed.

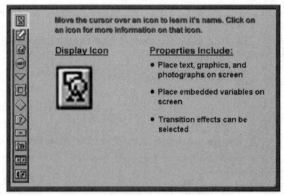

Fig. 14-7. Completed exercise on screen.

Storyboard: Behind the Scenes

Figure 14-8 shows the main and second-level flowlines (with all icons, their placement, and their names) as they should look when you are finished with this exercise.

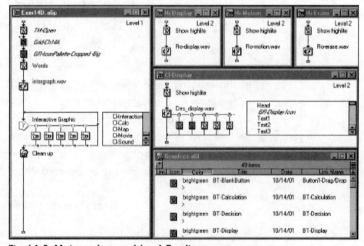

Fig. 14-8. Main and second-level flowlines.

Step-by-Step Instructions

Use the following generalized steps as guidance in completing this exercise on your own. Consult the completed exercise (*Exer14D.a6p*) on the companion CD-ROM for further guidance.

1. Open the file *Exer14D.a6p* located on the companion CD-ROM in the directory named *Chapter14*. Open the library file *Graphics.a6l* located in the same directory. Run the program and see how it works. Jump to the flowline and examine the various icons and structures.

2. Open the Calculation icons labeled READ ME and read their content.

3. Leave this file open in this copy of Authorware.

4. Open another copy of Authorware, starting a new file. Save the file as *App14D*. Open the library file *Graphics.a6l* located in the *SaveWork* directory of your hard drive.

5. When finished, make sure to save your exercise in the *SaveWork* directory on your computer's hard drive.

Application Exercise 14E:
Creating a Basic Generic Question

Description

In this exercise you will create a generic question structure that is both effective and efficient, requiring minimal effort to change content and scoring considerations. You will explore the details of the variables and structure used to facilitate this structure. The design and grid play an important part in efficient reuse. This exercise constructs an intermediate-level question structure, offering a generic capability without the complexity (or power) of the dynamic model you will explore in Chapter 27. You will leave this exercise grouped within a Map icon to be inserted into a topic structure (in Chapter 17).

Storyboard: On Screen

Figure 14-9 shows what the exercise will look like on screen when completed.

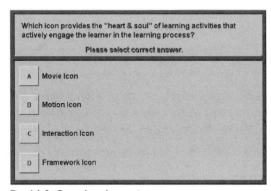

Fig. 14-9. Completed exercise on screen.

Storyboard: Behind the Scenes

Figure 14-10 shows the main and second-level flowlines (with all icons, their placement, and their names) as they should look when you are finished with this exercise.

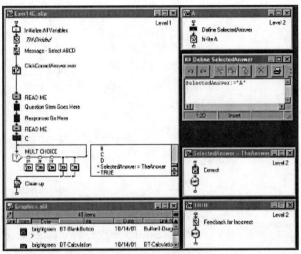

Fig. 14-10. Main and second-level flowlines.

Step-by-Step Instructions

Use the following generalized steps as guidance in completing this exercise on your own. Consult the completed exercise (*Exer14E.a6p*) on the companion CD-ROM for further guidance.

1. Open the file *Exer14E.a6p* located on the companion CD-ROM in the directory named *Chapter14*. Open the file. Open the library file *Graphics.a6l* located in the same directory. Run the program and see how it works. Jump to the flowline and examine the various icons and structures.

2. Open the Calculation icons labeled READ ME and read their content.

3. Leave this file open in this copy of Authorware.

4. Open another copy of Authorware, starting a new file. Save the file as *App14E*. Open the library file *Graphics.a6l* located in the *SaveWork* directory of your hard drive.

5. When finished, make sure to save your exercise in the *SaveWork* directory on your computer's hard drive.

Application Exercise 14F: Creating a Generic Question for Multiple Correct Answers

Description

In this exercise you will create a generic question structure in which there may be multiple correct answers. The learner may select and deselect answers until she is ready to have the answers evaluated by clicking on the Lock In Answers button. This structure is both effective and efficient, requiring minimal effort to change content and scoring considerations. This exercise is an intermediate-level question structure, offering a generic capability without the complexity (or power) of the dynamic model you will explore in Chapter 27. You will explore the details of the variables and the structure used to facilitate this interaction. You will leave this exercise grouped within a Map icon to be inserted into a topic structure (in Chapter 17).

Storyboard: On Screen

Figure 14-11 shows what the exercise will look like on screen when completed.

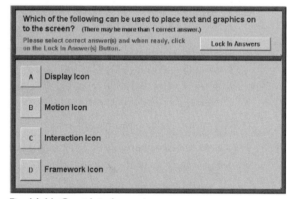

Fig. 14-11. Completed exercise on screen.

Storyboard: Behind the Scenes

Figure 14-12 shows the main and second-level flowlines (with all icons, their placement, and their names) as they should look when you are finished with this exercise.

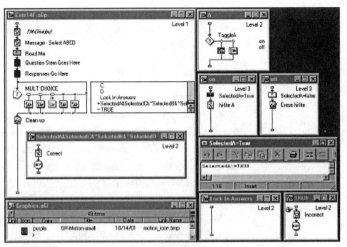

Fig. 14–12. Main and second-level flowlines.

Step-by-Step Instructions

Use the following generalized steps as guidance in completing this exercise on your own. Consult the completed exercise (*Exer14F.a6p*) on the companion CD-ROM for further guidance.

1. Open the file *Exer14F.a6p* located on the companion CD-ROM in the directory named *Chapter14*. Open the library file *Graphics.a6l* located in the same directory. Run the program and see how it works. Jump to the flowline and examine the various icons and structures.

2. Open the Calculation icons labeled READ ME and read their content.

3. Leave this file open in this copy of Authorware.

4. Open another copy of Authorware, starting a new file. Save the file as *App14F*. Open the library file *Graphics.a6l* located in the *SaveWork* directory of your hard drive.

5. When finished, make sure to save your exercise in the *SaveWork* directory on your computer's hard drive.

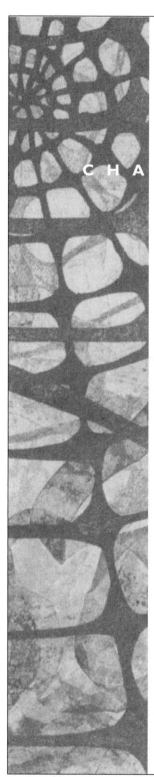

C H A P T E R

15

The Framework

Icon Structure

Introduction

To this point, the icon structures you have created have generally been small, single-event interactions or small, simple "page" sequences. You have worked extensively with the Interaction icon and the Decision icon, individually and in combination. What you have not encountered yet is an icon structure capable of easily presenting numerous "pages" with full learner control over navigational features such as moving forward, moving backward, accessing menus, and quitting.

The Framework icon will provide all of this and more. The Framework icon is the square donut-looking thing in the middle of the Icon palette. In one sense, it is like a super combination of the Interaction icon and the Decision icon. You will take a look at the Framework properties in the guided tour that follows.

This chapter focuses on using the Framework icon as the foundation of a generic paging structure, culminating in the creation of a fairly bulletproof topic-level structure. This topic-level structure includes the use of system and custom variables to activate/deactivate navigational buttons, provide status information to the user, and provide generic "replay the page" functionality. There are many approaches to creating topic-level structures. The approach taken in this chapter is use of the Framework icon as the foundation. Subsequently you will incorporate this topic-level structure into a larger-scale organizational structure based on the Interaction icon, which is covered in detail in the first half of Chapter 16.

In the second half of Chapter 16, you will be introduced to the Framework being used in a different context: as the foundation of a project's overall organizational and navigational structure. Both approaches are presented because you will need to use one or the other or both, depending on the nature of the project.

Closely related to the Framework icon is the Navigation icon (or Navigate icon), which looks like a small triangle and is located directly above the Framework icon on the Icon palette. The Navigate icon can only be used with a Framework icon and, as its name suggests, it provides directions as to where Authorware should branch to within a specified Framework structure. By the end of the Chapter you will be able to:

- *Create a simple paging structure using the Framework icon as the foundation*
- *Modify a Framework paging structure with the use of system variables to activate/deactivate navigational buttons and provide additional status information to the user*

- *Modify a Framework paging structure with the use of a system variable to provide page-level "replay" capability*

- *Modify a Framework paging structure by adding perpetual navigational controls, a self-contained glossary, and a self-contained reference section*

- *Modify a Framework paging structure by adding the capability to deactivate buttons while within a specified section, activating them again upon exit from a specified section*

- *List the general steps required to create a hypertext link*

- *List the general steps required to define an Authorware text style*

- *List the general steps required to apply an Authorware text style*

- *Modify a Framework paging structure by adding a second layer of information with the use of hyperlinks and multiple Framework icon structures*

Guided Tour 15A: Introduction to the Framework Icon and Navigate Icon

The Framework icon provides an easy means of setting up paging structures and providing navigation from one section to another within an Authorware file. The Framework icon comes with a full set of learner controls (buttons), which are built in and ready to go. Both the appearance of these buttons and their functionality can be modified. Let's just jump in and see how a Framework structure works.

1. Select File | New | File. Close the two Knowledge Object dialog windows.

2. Verify that you are now looking at a new flowline.

3. Set up the file properties.
    a) Select Modify | File | Properties.
    b) Select whatever background color you want.
    c) Make sure Size is set to 640 x 480.
    d) Remove the check marks beside the Tile Bar and Menu Bar options.
    e) Click on the OK button to close the window.

4. In the following you are going to quickly set up a very simple Framework structure and see what it is capable of right out of the box. You will then go back and "look underneath the hood" to see how it works.
    a) Drag a Framework icon to the flowline and name it *Boris* (after the character of Rocky and Bullwinkle fame).
    b) Drag a Display icon to the right of the Framework icon and drop it there. Note that unlike the Interaction icon there is no dialog window that opens. You can simply drop an icon in place.

c) Drag three (3) more Display icons to the right of the Framework icon. Name these Display icons *Page 1*, *Page 2*, *Page 3*, and *Page 4*.

d) Double click on *Page 1*. Select the Text tool and type in *This is page 1*. Select the text object and copy it to the clipboard. Close the icon.

e) Double click on *Page 2*. Paste the text object from the clipboard. Modify the text object so that it reads *This is page 2*. Move the text object to another location on screen. Close the icon.

f) Double click on *Page 3*. Paste the text object from the clipboard. Modify the text object so that it reads *This is page 3*. Move the text object to another location on screen. Close the icon.

g) Double click on *Page 4*. Paste the text object from the clipboard. Modify the text object so that it reads *This is page 4*. Move the text object to another location on screen. Close the icon.

5. Run the program to see what you have.

a) Click on the Restart button.

b) You should now see on screen, probably in the upper right-hand corner, a set of learner control buttons. See figure 15-1.

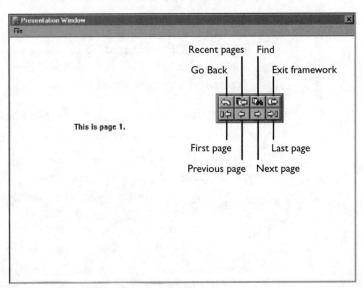

Fig. 15-1. Framework built-in learner controls.

c) Click on the Right Arrow (Forward) button 5 or 6 times. As you can see, Boris did not know that he ran out of pages, and after the last page (4), simply circled back and went to page 1 again.

For those of you who may not be familiar with the "super spy couple" Boris and Natasha (from the *Rocky and Bullwinkle Show*), Boris did *not* have the brains in the family. Out of the box, the Framework icon provides very easy-to-use learner controls, but they are not very "smart." Hence, our name for the Framework icon here, *Boris*. You will learn to "give smarts" to a Framework structure in Practice Exercise 15-1. Appropriate to the occasion, this Framework icon will be named *Natasha*.

d) Click on the Left Arrow (Backup) button 5 or 6 times. As you can see, Boris did not know that he ran out of pages, and after reaching page 1 simply circled back and went to page 4 again.

e) Now look at the control panel of buttons. Look at the button to the right of the Right Arrow. It looks like an arrow and a wall. Click on it. As you can see, this button takes the user to the last page in the current Framework.

f) Look at the button to the left of the Left Arrow button. Click on it. As you can see, this button takes the user to the first page in the current Framework.

g) Look at the top row of buttons in the control panel. What are these? What do they do?

h) Look at the button that looks like a pair of binoculars with a few sheets of paper. Click on it. The Find dialog window opens. From the icon of the binoculars, you might have guessed that this was a "find" button. Let's see how it works.

i) In the first field (Word/Phrase), type in *page*. Click on the Find button in the lower left-hand corner of the window. In the second field, you now have a list of the icons where this word is located. It is located in the four Display icons listed here. Single click on *Page 3* in the list. Click on the Go To Page button. As you can see, it takes you to the Display icon named *Page 3* and highlights the word you were looking for.

j) Let's try it again. In the first field (Word/Phase), type in 2. Click on the Find button. In the second field, you now have a list where this word is located. There is only one icon listed. Click on the Go To Page button. It takes you to the Display icon where this word is located and highlights the word.

k) Click on the Cancel button to close the Find dialog window.

l) So what do the other three buttons in the top row of the control panel do? For most people, it is not immediately obvious from looking at the icons on these buttons. You can look at the labels in figure 15-1 to see what these buttons do, but the user of an Authorware application will not have this labeled diagram. You will learn how you can modify the appearance of these buttons in Practice Exercise 15-1.

NOTE

If you are going to use "icons" (small graphic symbols that represent something), make sure the graphic symbol you use is immediately obvious to the typical user as to what the icon represents or what its function is.

m) Use figure 15-1 as a reference and click on each of the other three buttons in the top row of the control panel, just to see what each one does.

6. Let's take a very quick look at the Framework icon's properties.
   a) Jump to the flowline. Select the Framework icon.
   b) Select Modify | Icon | Properties. The Properties/Framework Icon dialog window is now open. See figure 15-2.

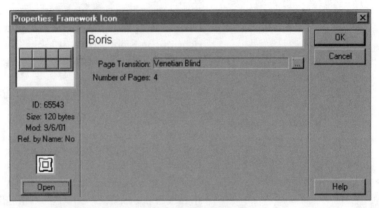

Fig. 15-2. Properties/Framework Icon dialog window.

c) There is only one option, the Page Transition field. Click on the button located to the right of the field name. The Page Transition window opens. This window is identical in function to the Transition window for both the Display icon (effects for displaying objects) and the Erase icon (transition effects as objects are erased). This field for the Framework sets the same transition for both the display and erase effects for each page attached to the Framework icon. Close the Transition window. Close the Properties window.

7. Now let's "lift the hood" and take a look at what the Framework "engine" looks like.

   Double click on the Framework icon. See figure 15-2. There are two basic parts to the Framework window: the Entry pane (above the line) and the Exit pane (below the line).

   Entry Pane: As Authorware moves down the flowline and encounters a Framework icon, it first enters the Entry pane flowline, regardless of the "page" it may be headed for. Anything located on the Entry pane flowline will be displayed or acted upon, before Authorware proceeds into any of the icons attached to the Framework icon.

Note that the Entry pane flowline has an Interaction icon on it (named *Navigation hyperlinks*), with several button responses attached to it. These buttons are in fact the buttons in the learner control panel you just looked at. You will take a closer look at these in material to follow. Note that every response attached to this Interaction icon is set to Perpetual. You can discern this because the flowline directly below the Interaction icon is directly connected to the Interaction icon.

As Authorware enters the Entry pane, all perpetual buttons appear on screen as Authorware continues down the Entry pane flowline. When Authorware reaches the bottom of the Entry pane flowline, unless specifically directed to do otherwise it will drop down into the first icon attached to the Framework icon. This is exactly what you saw when you ran the file: the buttons appeared, immediately followed by page 1 on screen. The navigational controls are active as long as Authorware remains within the current Framework or variables are used to modify this "active" condition.

You might use the Entry pane as the location to include a Display icon containing a screen background (or template) to be used for each page in the Framework. You will get some experience doing this in Practice Exercise 15-2.

Exit Pane: In the event of the user selecting the Exit Framework button (upper right-hand corner of the control panel), Authorware first jumps to the Exit pane flowline and will display or act on any icons located on the Exit pane flowline before dropping down to the main flowline. You might use the Exit pane to provide some feedback to the user before she totally exits the current frame. As an example, you could place a Display icon and a Wait icon here and display the message *You have just completed XYZ*, with a Continue button to proceed.

8. Let's now take a look at the Interaction icon *Navigation hyperlinks* and the Display icon *Gray Navigation Panel*, located on the Entry pane flowline.
   a) Double click on the Display icon *Gray Navigation Panel*. What you are looking at is a graphic background for the Framework's navigational buttons. Close the icon.
   b) Double click on the Interaction icon *Navigation hyperlinks*. What you are looking at are the actual buttons located on the control panel when the program is run. These buttons on screen are a function of the Button responses attached to this Interaction icon. Close the icon.
   c) Double click on the Response Type symbol for the first icon attached to the Interaction icon; in other words, the Response Type symbol

for *Go back*. The Properties/Response dialog window opens. You have seen this before. It is the same dialog window you first saw when looking at the Button response properties in Chapter 9. Look at the Button tab and the options here. Click on the Response tab and look at the options. Everything is the same and there is nothing to worry about. Close this dialog window.

9. Examine the Navigate icon and its various properties.

The Navigate (Navigation) icon can be used to set up a navigational link (branch) to any icon attached to a Framework icon. Navigate icons can be placed anywhere on the flowline, but they can only navigate to an icon directly attached to (or inside of an icon attached to) a Framework icon.

a) You should still be inside the Framework icon *Boris*, looking at the Entry pane. If not, reopen the Framework icon.

b) There are eight responses attached to the Interaction icon *Navigation hyperlinks*. Use the scroll bar located on the right to locate the response *Next page*. Double click on the Navigate icon itself. In other words, double click on the triangular icon in this response. The Properties/Navigate Icon dialog window has now opened. See figure 15-3.

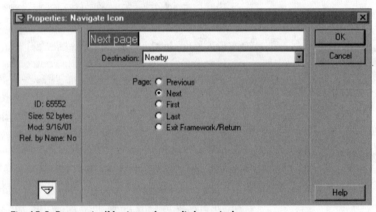

Fig. 15-3. Properties/Navigate Icon dialog window.

c) At the top of the dialog window there is a field named Destination. Click on the pull-down menu and look at the possibilities for where the Navigate icon can branch to. Whatever selection you choose in the Destination field will determine what options will be listed on the rest of the dialog window. The names of the destinations are fairly descriptive of what they do. Let's take a look at a 50,000-foot level.

d) Select the Nearby destination and look at the Page options below this field. These Page options illustrate settings for 5 out of the 8 buttons you just looked at on the Framework control panel. You are currently looking at the Next Page button. If you want Authorware to go to the next page (this next page is "nearby"), the Nearby destination makes sense. Close this dialog window.

e) Locate and double click on the Navigate icon for *Previous page*. The dialog window that opens looks identical to that you were just looking at. It has a Nearby destination but the Page option is set to Previous. This is a backup button for *Previous page*, and again the Nearby destination makes sense. It is next to the current page. Close this dialog window.

f) Locate and double click on the Navigate icon for *Last page*. Again, it is the same dialog window, with a destination of Nearby and the Page option set to Last.

g) If you would like to, open each of the *Next*, *First*, and *Exit Framework* Navigate icons and see that in each case the dialog window contains the Nearby destination, same Page options listed, and only differs in which page is selected (the Page selection corresponding to what the button does).

h) Locate and double click on the Navigate icon *Find*. Notice that the Destination field is set to Search. This makes sense. It is a destination that has to be "searched" for in order to "find" it. Look at the options listed here. See figure 15-4.

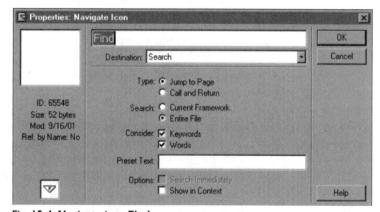

Fig. 15-4. Navigate icon Find.

i) In the Type field there are two options, as follows:

• **Jump to Page:** *Selecting this option calls for a "one-way" jump from the current Navigate icon to the destination icon. Authorware goes to the destination page and then continues to the next icon on the flowline.*

• **Call and Return:** *Selecting this option calls for "round-trip" navigation. Authorware will jump to the destination and return to the* *icon it came from when it encounters the* Exit Framework *icon in the destination framework.*

j)   In the Search field there are two options, as follows:

- **Current Framework:** *This option will limit Authorware to searching the current Framework only.*

- **Entire File:** *This option will allow Authorware to search all frameworks in the entire file. Depending on how many frameworks the file has, and how large each framework is, a search on this scope could take quite a while. You may want to be careful about setting the scope of the search this broadly.*

k)   In the Consider field there are two options, as follows:

- **Keyword:** *Searches for keywords attached to the pages.*

- **Word:** *Searches text contained in the text objects in the pages.*

l)   The Preset Text field is used to enter a word (or a variable containing a word) you want to appear automatically in the Find dialog box when the user clicks on the Find button. The user can change this word to look for other words, or can click on the Find button to start the search. If you enter a word (rather than a variable) in the Preset Text box, make sure to enclose it in quotation marks.

m)   The Options field contains two options that further define the search characteristics, as follows:

- **Search Immediately:** *Starts the search for the word entered in the Preset Text box when the user clicks on the Find button. If you enter a variable, such as* WordClicked *or* HotTextClicked, *Authorware immediately starts the search for the word or hot text when the user clicks on it, without displaying the Find dialog box.*

- **Show in Context:** *Displays the words Authorware finds together with the words that surround it. The found word appears highlighted. If you select this option, the Find dialog box is larger. The search also takes longer. This option applies to text only, not to keyword searches.*

n)   Close the Find dialog window.

o)   Locate and double click on the *Go back* Navigate icon. As you can see in the Destination field, this uses the Recent option. Under the Page field, there are two possibilities: Go Back (for the current icon, which is the seventh button on the control panel) and List Recent Pages (which is the eighth and final button on the control panel).

p)   Click on the Destination field and look again at the options listed. The only two you have not looked at yet are Calculate and Anywhere. Select the Calculate option. With the calculation destination, Authorware evaluates an expression that returns the ID number of a specific page. It then goes to that page. Look at the two options listed here.The Type field options are the same as you have seen before, as follows:

- ***Jump to Page:*** *Provides a "one-way" jump.*

- ***Call and Return:*** *Provides a "round-trip" jump.*

The Icon Expression field is where you type in the expression that will return an icon ID and provide the destination Authorware will jump to.

q) Click on the Destination field again, and select the Anywhere option. This Destination option is the one you will probably use most often when you create Framework icon structures. You will get hands-on experience working with this Navigate icon in exercises in this chapter and again in Chapter 16.

r) The Type field options are the same as those you have seen before, as follows:
- ***Jump to Page:*** *Provides a "one-way" jump.*

- ***Call and Return:*** *Provides a "round-trip" jump.*

s) The Framework field lists the names of all Framework icons located in the current file. As you can see, *Boris* is the only Framework icon in the current file.

t) The Page field lists all pages (by name) for the framework that has been selected in the Framework field.

u) The combination of the Framework field and the Page field provides you with the ability to "point and click" to the destination you want Authorware to go to from the current Navigate icon.

v) Click on the Cancel button.

10. One last note about the Entry and Exit panes. Note the black line between them. To the right of this line is a "handle" (black block). Click on the handle and drag the line down to increase the size of the Entry pane, or drag it up to make the Exit pane larger.

You are done with this tour. There is no need to save the file, unless you would like to.

Practice Exercise 15-1: Building a Framework with "Smarts," Custom Buttons, and User Features

Description

In the previous guided tour, you took your first step into the world of frames. On one hand, Authorware supplies ("out of the box") a very easy way to provide learner controls within a paging structure. On the other hand, you also saw that the framework "as is" cannot tell when it runs out of pages and needs some additional "nice to have" features.

Throughout this chapter, you will be working on a series of exercises that build upon one another. Beginning with the second exercise, you can either start with what you completed from the previous exercise or start with a completed "factory version" of the previous exercise, supplied on the companion CD-ROM. In this way you can skip an exercise if you want to.

The focus throughout this series of exercises is on how to build, modify, and control the Framework structure, rather than on content. Rather than taking a great deal of time creating numerous Display icons with text and graphics and importing sounds into Sound icons, the content will be supplied already built and placed within Map icons.

As a reflection of the "real-world" goal of increasing efficiency, you will also be introduced to Authorware's capability to import models. The models you will import contain the content needed for the exercises. The following are the exercises you will be working with in this chapter.

- *Practice Exercise 15-1:* Building a Framework with "Smarts," Custom Buttons, and User Features

- *Practice Exercise 15-2:* Adding a Glossary, Reference Section, and Replay Capability

- *Practice Exercise 15-3:* Adding a Second Layer of Content Using Hyperlinks

The generic topic structure you will create here will be used again in the first few exercises in Chapter 16, as you fit this structure into one approach to an organizational structure. There are many approaches to building Framework structures and many ways to create organizational structures within Authorware.

In the second half of Chapter 16 you will be introduced to a slightly different approach to a Framework structure, one that expands to a very different way of organizing navigational structures within Authorware. One approach is not necessarily better than the other; they both have certain advantages when used within particular situations. You will look at some of these situational details as you continue. The following elements are covered in this exercise:

- *Importing a model with prebuilt content*
- *Creating a basic paging structure based on the Framework icon*
- *Modifying the basic framework navigational buttons with the use of custom buttons*
- *Modifying the basic framework with the use of system variables to provide "smarts"*

Take a Look

CD-ROM

Before beginning the exercise, let's take a look at the exercise in its completed state so that you can clearly see what it is you are about to build.

1. Select File | Open and locate on the companion CD-ROM the directory named *Chapter15*. Within this directory locate and double click on the file named *Exer15-1*.

2. The file *Exer15-1* should now appear in your copy of Authorware. Click on the Restart button to play the file from the top of the flowline. Note the following properties of this completed exercise:

    - *There is a set of learner control buttons located in the bottom control panel.*

    - *Authorware recognizes that it is on the first page and "deactivates" the backup button on the first page.*

    - *Authorware recognizes when it reaches the last page and "deactivates" the Forward button on the last page.*

    - *In this exercise the Menu, Glossary, Reference, and Replay buttons do not work. You will add them in the next exercise.*

    - *Authorware displays the current page number out of how many pages there are in the framework.*

Storyboard: On Screen

Figure 15-5 shows you what the finished presentation will look like on screen.

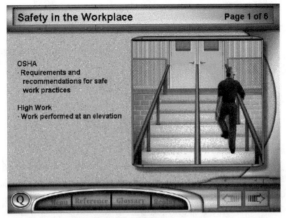

Fig. 15-5. Completed presentation on screen.

Storyboard: Behind the Scenes

Figure 15-6 shows the main flowline (with all icons, their placement, and their names) as it should look when you are finished with this exercise. Figure 15-6 also includes the Knowledge Object window, with the Model palette open showing the Authorware models you will use in this chapter. Figure 15-7 shows the Entry and Exit pane flowlines inside the Framework icon *Content*. Figure 15-8 shows the Properties/Response dialog window and Response tab for the Forward button. Figure 15-9 shows the Properties/Response dialog window and Response tab for the Backup button. Figure 15-10 shows the level 2 flowline inside the Map icon *Safety in the Workplace*, which is representative of the other content Map icons.

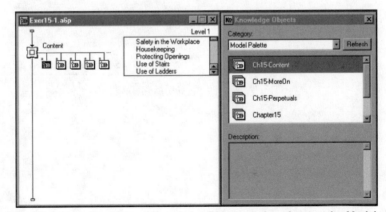

Fig. 15-6. Main flowline and Knowledge Object window showing the Model palette.

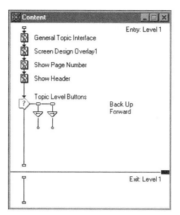

Fig. 15-7. Entry and Exit pane flowlines inside the Framework icon Content.

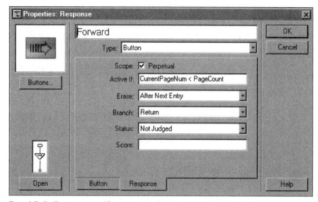

Fig. 15-8. Properties/Response dialog window and Response tab for the Forward button.

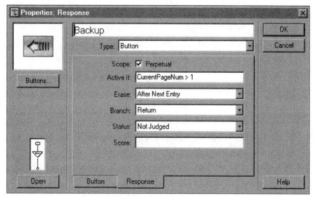

Fig. 15-9. Properties/Response dialog window and Response tab for the Backup button.

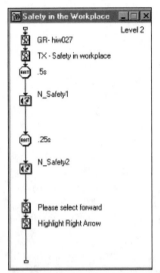

Fig. 15-10. Level 2 flowline inside the Map *icon* Safety *in the* Workplace.

Prework for Exercise

As you start creating structures on your own and you want to reuse them from project to project, you will probably want to start using Model Files. Creating a Model file is pretty easy. Simply select the structure you want to save, then select File | Save in Model.

Prior to starting the exercise, take a moment to copy three files from the companion CD-ROM to your hard drive. These files are Authorware models previously created to supply you with prebuilt content for the framework exercises. The models will help keep the focus on the framework and its controlling mechanisms rather than on assembling content.

You will need to copy these three files into the directory where Authorware is located on your computer's hard drive. If your copy of Authorware is located on a network server, you should consult your network administrator to receive assistance in accomplishing the file transfer.

If you did not accept the default directory settings that were suggested when Authorware was installed on your computer, you will have to modify the directory path shown in the following to accommodate the directory path on your computer.

1.   Make sure the companion CD-ROM has been appropriately placed within your computer's CD-ROM player.

2. Use your computer's My Computer button (or Windows Explorer) to locate the companion CD-ROM.

3. Locate and open the *Chapter15* directory.

4. Locate the following three files within this directory: *Ch15-Content.a6d*, *Ch15-MoreOn.a6d*, and *Ch15-Perpetuals.a6d*.

5. Copy these three files into the *Model Palette* directory using the following path (or modify the path based on how you installed Authorware on your computer).

   Root directory / Macromedia / Authorware 6 / Model Palette

6. After you open Authorware and the Knowledge Object window, you should see these three files within the *Model Palette* directory. (You may need to click on the Refresh button.)

You are ready to proceed to the first exercise.

Step-by-Step Instructions

Go Solo

1. Select File | New | File. Close the two Knowledge Object dialog windows.

2. Verify that you are now looking at a new flowline.

3. Set up the file properties.
   a) Select Modify | File | Properties.
   b) Select whatever background color you want.
   c) Make sure Size is set to 640 x 480.
   d) Remove the check marks beside the Tile Bar and Menu Bar options.
   e) Click on the OK button to close the window.
   f) Select File | Save and locate the *SaveWork* directory. Type in *Chap15-1* and click on the OK button.

4. Open the Knowledge Object window to access the models that contain the content for the framework you will build in this exercise.
   a) Select Window | Knowledge Objects. As you open a new Authorware file, two Knowledge Object windows open. You are routinely instructed in these directions to close these windows. The second of these two windows is in fact the window you have just opened.
   b) Use the pull-down menu in the Category field to locate and select the category Model Palette.
   c) Use the scroll bar in the field below Category and check to see if you can find the three model files you copied onto your computer in the "Prework" section. They are *Ch15-Content*, *Ch15-MoreOn*, and *Ch15-Perpetuals*.

CAUTION

To proceed with this exercise, you must first complete the "Prework" section. In the "Prework" section, you are instructed on how and where you need to copy the model files you are about to import into Authorware. If you have not yet copied these files into the *Model Palette* directory on your computer's hard drive, complete the "Prework" section now.

d) If you do not see these models, click on the Refresh button located in the upper right-hand corner of the Knowledge Object window.

e) Verify that you can now see the models in the window.

f) Double click on *Ch15-Content* and wait a couple of seconds. You should now see six (6) Map icons and three (3) Display icons located on the main flowline. Each icon's name is descriptive of the content located within it.

g) Double click on the Map icon *Safety in the Workplace*. As you can see, the Map icon simply contains a series of Display icons, Sound icons, and Wait icons.

h) Open and look at (or listen to) any of the icons located within this Map icon, any of the other Map icons, or other icons. Try not to move any of the objects on screen. If you do, do not worry about it; you will be able to readjust their positions later.

i) Leave the three Display icons on the very bottom of the flowline. These will be used in the last step of this exercise.

5. Put together the basic content for the Framework structure.

a) Drag a Framework icon and place it at the top of the flowline. Name it *Content*.

b) Drag each Map icon from its location on the flowline to the right of the Framework icon. Drag and place them in the following order, using figure 15-6 as reference.

- *Safety in the Workplace*
- *Housekeeping*
- *Protecting Openings*
- *Use of Stairs*
- *Use of Ladders*
- *Ladder Maintenance*

c) Drag a Display icon from the Icon palette to the top of the flowline. Name it *General Topic Interface*.

You might be asking why you placed the Display icon with the topic interface graphic on the main flowline above the Framework icon. You could leave it here, but actually will move it inside the Framework icon in material to follow. Placing it here simply allows you to get started.

d) Double click on the Display icon to open it. Select File | Import. Use the Look in field to locate the companion CD-ROM and the *Chapter15* directory on it. Inside the *Chapter15* directory, locate and select the file *Topic_Interface.gif*. Click on the Import button.

e) Verify that you are now looking at the basic interface template. There is room for subject and status information in the top (header) panel. There are complete navigational control "placeholders" located in the bottom panel. In the following you will add two custom buttons and place them directly over these placeholders. In the next exercise you will complete the learner control panel with the addition of other custom buttons.

The graphic you just imported contains the general screen background, the header panel on the top, and navigational control placeholders on the bottom. The central portion of the screen has been left open. In the following you will add another graphic, which overlays the basic screen design, to serve as a content layout design for the placement of text and graphics within this open area.

As you may remember from Chapter 2, the basic screen interface should remain consistent within a project, although the content area may include several to many different screen layout designs to accommodate varying graphic and text needs. By separating the basic screen background and interface from the content area screen design, you can change and replace the content area screen designs within the topic structure with very little effort and with no screen flash that generally accompanies replacing a full screen graphic with another.

f) Close the Display icon.

6. Let's see what you have at this point.
   a) Click on the Restart button.
   b) Authorware started at the top of the flowline; dropped into the Entry pane of the framework, where it encountered the Navigational hyperlinks (the perpetual buttons); and then dropped into the first Map icon (the *Safety in the Workplace* Map icon) attached to the framework. You should see text and a graphic on screen, as you listen to narration. Pause the program (Ctrl + P).
   c) Look in the upper right-hand corner to see the default navigational buttons. You will greatly modify these in material to follow. Note that the buttons at the bottom of the screen are still just placeholders.
   d) Note that the text and the graphic (in particular) look a bit naked and misplaced without any further screen layout design. You will also fix this in material to follow.
   e) Jump to the flowline.

7. Now you will greatly modify the default navigational buttons. Roll up your sleeves and get ready for mass destruction!
   a) Double click on the Framework icon. Look at the Entry pane flowline.

b) Drag the Display icon (*General Topic Interface*) from the main flowline and place it at the very top of the Entry pane flowline. (Again, you do not really have to do this; it just keeps things for the framework together.)

c) Select the Display icon *Gray Navigation Panel*. This icon contains the background for the buttons. Delete this icon.

d) Look at the Interaction icon *Navigation hyperlinks*. Attached to it are several Navigate icons.

e) Delete the following Navigate icons: *Go back*, *Recent pages*, *Find*, *Exit Framework*, *First page*, and *Last page*.

f) The only two Navigate icons that should be left are *Previous page* and *Next page*.

g) Select the Interaction icon and rename it *Topic Level Buttons*.

h) Select the Navigate icon *Previous page*. Rename it *Back Up*.

i) Select the Navigate icon *Next page*. Rename it *Forward*.

8. Save the file.

9. Now it is time to undertake a new venture: adding custom buttons to a Button response attached to an Interaction icon. It really is easy and can make a tremendous difference in how your interface looks. Before you begin this process, however, review the following background information on buttons and the Button editor.

As you will see in material to follow, you can use Authorware's Button Editor dialog box to create a custom button that is available whenever you want to use a button in any interaction within the current file. A button has four main states: Up, Down, Roll Over (or Mouse Over), and Disabled (or grayed out). You have the capability to make each button state appear differently and to include different sounds associated with the button state.

You can also show or hide a button's label in each state. Authorware's Button editor takes the different graphics and sounds associated with these different button states and creates the illusion that the button is 3D and that the button depresses when clicked on. Obviously the button is not 3D as it is displayed on a flat computer monitor. However, with the assumptions our eyes and brain make about light and shadow, combined with the Button editor's instant replacement of graphics, the illusion of depth and movement is created very well. You may want to review the beginning of Chapter 4, concerning creating visual depth, if you need a quick review of the principles of highlights and shadows. The button states are as follows.

- *Up: This is the normal position, as the button is ready to be selected. The button in the up position appears as if it rises above the surface.*

- **Down:** *This is what the button looks like when it is clicked on or depressed. It appears as if the down button is recessed below the surface. You will also add a sound to the "down" state, so that a "click" will be heard as the button is depressed.*

- **Over:** *This state provides the option to include a different visual appearance when the cursor is moved over the button but the user has not yet pressed the mouse button. You will be applying a "green glow" to represent this button state.*

- **Disabled:** *This is what the button will look like when the button has been deactivated. You are not going to use this state in the Button editor. As you have previously seen, the disabled or deactivated state of buttons is preestablished on the interface. Why this method was chosen is explained in material to follow.*

Creating a custom button is straightforward. For each of the button's states, you can import a graphic and sound and select a setting to show or hide the button's label. If you do not want a different graphic for each state, Authorware automatically uses the graphic you have already imported; or you can choose no graphic at all.

Before you use the Button editor with your own Authorware applications, you must create the graphics or select the clip art images you want to use for each of the button's states. You should also create or select a sound (perhaps a button "click") to be used with one or more button states.

10. You are now ready to create your first custom button. All graphics and a sound file for the buttons have been supplied on the companion CD-ROM, within the *Chapter 15* directory. The following naming convention is used for these button graphics: *NameOfButton-ButtonState.bmp*. The following are examples of this convention: *Left-Up.bmp*, *Left-Down.bmp*, *Left-Over.bmp*, *Menu-Up.bmp*, *Menu-Down.bmp*, and *Menu-Over.bmp*.

    a) The Framework icon *Entry Pane* should still be visible. If not, double click on the Framework icon to open it. Look at the Interaction icon *Topic Level Buttons,* which you previously renamed.

    b) Double click on the Response Type symbol above the Navigate icon *Back Up*. The Properties/Response dialog window has opened. If you look at the upper left-hand corner, you can see the graphic of the default Back Up (or Previous) button.

    c) Click on the Buttons button in the upper left-hand corner. This button will open the Button library.

d) The Button library should now be open. Use the scroll bar located on the right and scroll through the buttons included in the Button library by default. Your new buttons will appear there soon.

e) Notice that the graphic of the left arrow is currently highlighted in this list. Click on the Edit button located in the lower left-hand corner of the Button Library window. The Button editor now opens.

f) Note that the four button states are listed in four rows in the upper left-hand corner of this editor. There are also two columns: Normal (which you will use) and Checked (typically used only with radio buttons, and which you will not use).

g) Note that the visual indicator of a selected state of a button is fairly subtle, being a medium gray rectangle that surrounds the inside edge of the row/column selected. The rectangle currently resides in the Normal/Up state. Click on the Normal/Down state so that you can see the gray "highlight" change position. Again, this gray highlight is pretty subtle, so be certain you know what state is selected before you do anything.

h) Click on the Normal/Up state to return the gray highlight to this position. Look at the lower right-hand side and locate the Graphic field. By default, the option is set to Use Imported (as you can see, the other option is None). Leave the setting Use Imported. Click on the Import button located slightly to the right of this field. Use the Look in field to locate the companion CD-ROM and the *Chapter15* directory on it. Locate and single click on the file *Left-Up.bmp*. Make sure there is a check mark in the Show Preview field in the lower left-hand corner of the Import window. You should now be looking at a graphic of a custom left arrow in the right-hand side of the Import window. Click on the Import button. You should have seen a blue progress bar rapidly display on screen.

i) Click on the Normal/Down state. In the Graphic field, make sure Use Imported is selected. Click on the Import button located slightly to the right of this field. The Look in field should already be pointing to the *Chapter15* directory on the companion CD-ROM. Locate and single click on the file *Left-Down.bmp*. Click on the Import button. You should have seen the blue progress bar rapidly display on screen.

j) Link a "button click" sound with the down state of this button. (The Normal/Down state should still be selected, unless you accidentally changed it. Make sure it is still selected.) Locate the Sound field (slightly below the Graphic field). Click on the Import button located to the right of the Sound field. The Look in field should already be pointing to the *Chapter15* directory, with the *click.wav* file being the only file listed. Single click on this file. Click on the Import button. Click on the Play button to listen to what sound will now be heard as the button is clicked on (i.e., shows the activated state).

k) Click on the Normal/Over state. In the Graphic field, make sure Use Imported is selected. Click on the Import button, located to the right of this field. The Look in field should already be pointing to the *Chapter15* directory on the companion CD-ROM. Locate and single click on the file *Left-Over.bmp*. Click on the Import button. You should have seen the blue progress bar rapidly display on screen. There will be no sound with the Roll Over state.

l) Click on the OK button located at the lower right-hand corner of the Button editor to close the editor. You are now looking at your new button, located in the Button library. Note that there is some text that describes the button, and a small icon of a Display icon and a speaker. This indicates that there is a graphic being displayed and that there is a sound associated with the button. Click on the OK button in the lower right-hand corner to close the Button library.

m) You are back to the Properties dialog window. The Button tab should be on top (if not, select it). Click on the Cursor Library button at the bottom of this tab. Select the Hand cursor. Click on the OK button to close the Cursor library. In the Options field, place a check mark next to Hide When Inactive (instead of simply "graying it out").

n) Note that the X and Y coordinates for the Size field are grayed out. This is because you are using a custom button whose graphic cannot be resized (within Authorware, you can bring in whatever size of button you want, after you have created it using an external graphic package).

o) Note that the X and Y coordinates for the Location field currently show the button in the upper left-hand corner, close to where the default button resided before you modified it. Click the cursor in the *X coordinate* Location field. Type in *498*. Click the cursor in the *Y coordinate* field. Type in *431*.

For all of the steps in which you need to supply X and Y coordinates for new custom buttons, you are provided with numbers to type in. These numbers are based on a preestablished graphic interface and proper placement of buttons. Normally you would not have this information available and would have to experiment with the placement to find the proper location for each button. X and Y coordinates are provided to eliminate the guesswork and keep the focus on concepts.

p) Look at the Key(s) field, which is currently blank. To refresh your memory, this field can be used to input the name of any key you want to activate and to allow the user to press as a keyboard alternative to clicking the mouse on the button. This means that either a key press or a mouse click can trigger the button. Let's use it. Click the cursor in this field and type in *leftarrow*. (Consult your Authorware manual for the correct spelling of the names that can be entered here to represent other keys.)

q) Click on the OK button to close the Properties window.

11. Create a custom button for the Forward button.

a) Double click on the Response Type symbol above the Navigate icon *Forward*. The Properties/Response dialog window has opened. If you look at the upper left-hand corner of the screen, you can see the graphic of the default Forward (or Next) button.

b) Click on the Buttons button in the upper left-hand corner to open the Button library.

c) Note that the graphic of the right arrow is currently highlighted in this list. Click on the Edit button located in the lower left-hand corner of the Button Library window. The Button editor now opens.

d) Make sure the Normal/Up state is selected (click on it to make sure). Make sure that the Graphic field is set to Use Imported. Click on the Import button located slightly to the right of this field. The Look in field should already pointing to the *Chapter15* directory on the companion CD-ROM. Locate and single click on the file *Right-Up.bmp*. Click on the Import button. You should have seen the blue progress bar rapidly display on screen.

e) Click on the Normal/Down state. In the Graphic field, make sure Use Imported is selected. Click on the Import button, located to the right of this field. The Look in field should already pointing to the *Chapter15* directory on the companion CD-ROM. Locate and single click on the file *Right-Down.bmp*. Click on the Import button. You should have seen the blue progress bar rapidly display on screen.

f) Leave the Normal/Down state selected. Click on the Import button located to the right of the Sound field. The Look in field should already pointing to the *Chapter15* directory. Select *Click.wav*. Click on the Import button.

g) Click on the Normal/Over state. In the Graphic field, make sure Use Imported is selected. Click on the Import button, located to the right of this field. The Look in field should already pointing to the *Chapter15* directory on the companion CD-ROM. Locate and single click on the file *Right-Over.bmp*. Click on the Import button. You should have seen the blue progress bar rapidly display on screen. There will be no sound with the Roll Over state.

h) Click on the OK button located at the lower right-hand corner of the Button editor to close the editor. Click on the OK button at the lower right-hand corner to close the Button library.

i) You are back to the Properties dialog window. The Button tab should be on top (if not, select it). Click on the Cursor Library button at the bottom of this tab. Select the Hand cursor. Click on the OK button to close the Cursor library. In the Options field, place a check mark next to Hide When Inactive.

j) Click the cursor in the *X coordinate* Location field. Type in *558*. Click the cursor in the *Y coordinate* field. Type in *431*.

k) Click the cursor in the Key(s) field and type in *rightarrow*.

l) Click on the OK button to close the Properties window.

12. Let's take a look at what you have at this point.

a) Click on the Restart button.

b) You should be able to see the new custom buttons for Forward and Back Up. Click on the Forward and Back Up buttons. You should be able to see the Up, Down, and Roll Over states for these two buttons.

13. Save the file.

14. The framework is still "dumb," in that it does not recognize when it runs out of pages. In addition, the content area still needs a screen design to help it look better. Let's take care of both of these situations.

a) The Framework icon should still be open. Drag a Display icon and place it on the Entry pane flowline, below the Display icon (*General Topic Interface*) but above the Interaction icon. Name the Display icon *Screen Design Overlay1*.

b) Double click on the Display icon. Select File | Import. The Look in field should already be pointing to the *Chapter15* directory on the companion CD-ROM. Locate and single click on the file *ScreenDesignOverlay.gif*. Click on the Import button. Close the Display icon. You will reposition this graphic in a later step, if necessary.

c) Give this frame some "smarts." Double click on the Response Type symbol above the Back Up button. Click on the Response tab. Click the cursor in the Active If field. You want the Back Up button to be active on every page except the first page. You want to deactivate the Back Up button on page 1 because there is no page before page 1. (In the next exercise you will add a Menu button the user can use to go back to the menu from page 1.) How can you express this in terms Authorware understands? There are system variables that will do the trick. Click on the Variables Window button.

d) Use the pull-down menu in the Category field to locate and select the Framework category. In the *Framework variable* listing, locate and single click on *CurrentPageNum*. The label really says what this variable does. This variable stores the value of the current page number of an icon attached to the current Framework icon.

e) Click on the Paste button. Click on the Done button. Type in *> 1*. The expression should now be *CurrentPageNum > 1*.

Here, you are telling Authorware you want this button to be active if the current page number is greater than 1. On page 1, 1 is not greater than 1; therefore, on page 1 the Back Up button will be inactive. Recall that previously you set the Button tab's option to Hide if Inactive. Therefore, you take away the button completely if inactive. Also recall that the inactive state for each button is already on the interface graphic. One advantage of including the visual indication of the inactive buttons in the screen interface is that they can help you accurately line up the placement of the active buttons.

f) Click on the OK button to close the dialog window.

g) Double click on the Response Type symbol above the Forward button. Click on the Response tab. Click the cursor in the Active If field. In this case, you want the Forward button to be active if it is on any page except the last page. You want to deactivate the Forward button on the last page because there is no page after it. (In the next exercise you will add a Menu button the user can use to go to the menu from the last page.)

How can you express this in terms Authorware understands? Again, there are system variables that will do the trick. Click on the Variables Window button.

h) Category should already be set to Framework. Single click on *CurrentPageNum*. Click on the Paste button. Single click on the variable *PageCount*. Read the description, which reasonably describes what the variable does. The variable contains the value of how many pages (or icons) are attached to the current Framework icon. Click on the Paste button. Click on the Done button.

i) Click the cursor between the two variables you just pasted into the Active If field. Modify the expression so that it reads as follows.

CurrentPageNum < PageCount

In this case, you could have used the expression *CurrentPageNum < 6* instead of what you entered in step *i*. This alternative expression would work fine for this particular situation. However, the moment you add or subtract another page, *CurrentPageNum < 6* will no longer work, because there are no longer six pages. Using the system variable *PageCount* solves this problem and allows you to build a nice generic expression that will not need to be modified if you add or subtract pages.

    j)   Click on the OK button to close the window.

15. Save the file.

16. You have fixed several things, so let's see where you are.
    a)   Click on the Restart button.
    b)   On page 1, the Back Up button is inactive. Click on the Forward button several times to get to the last page. On the last page, the Forward button is now inactive. In addition, the content area of the screen now looks much better (if the screen design overlay has inadvertently been moved out of position, pause the program and realign it, using figure 15-5 as reference).

17. This is a good start, but there are several other features that would be greatly appreciated by future users of this program. First, it would be nice to know what page you are on, relative to how many pages there are in the topic (e.g., page 3 of 6). It would also be nice to have the current page or topic appear in the header bar at the top of the screen.

You could go into every page and use an ordinary text object to type in all of the page and subject information, but this would be labor intensive, especially if changes are made to the number of pages. As you have probably guessed, a far more efficient method would be to use variables. Let's give it a try.
    a)   If the Framework icon is no longer open, open it and look at what is currently in the Entry pane.
    b)   Drag a Display icon from the Icon palette to the Entry Pane flowline and place it just above the Interaction icon. Name it *Show Page Number*.
    c)   Double click on the Display icon. Select the text attributes Arial, 14, Bold, and Right alignment. Type in *Page* (press the space bar). Click on the Variables Window button. Select the Framework category. Single click on the variable *CurrentPageNum*. Click on the Paste button. Single click on the variable *PageCount*. Click on the Done button to close the Variables window. Modify the text object so that it reads *Page {CurrentPageNum} of {PageCount}*. Select the Pointer tool to close the text object.
    d)   Select Modify | Icon | Properties. Place a check mark next to the Update Displayed Variables option. Close the dialog window. Close the Display icon.

e) Click on the Restart button. As soon the page is displayed, pause the program (Ctrl + P). Click on the text object with page numbers and drag it to the upper right-hand side of the screen, so that it fits within the header area on the right.

f) You need to use a variable or variables to show the current page topic as a "headline" in the header area. Let's see what system variables might be available. Click on the Variable Window button. The Framework category should already be selected. Take a look at what is here. Read whatever descriptions you want. The Framework category was a good place to start, but unfortunately there is no variable that can help here.

g) In the Category field, select Icons. Single click on *ExecutingIconTitle*. Read the description. If you were to use the *ExecutingIconTitle* variable (set to update), you would see the name of every icon Authorware encounters, which is not what is needed. Click on *IconTitle* and read the description. Look at the name of each Map icon attached to the Framework icon (you may have to move some of the open windows around so that you can see the main flowline with the Framework icon and Map icons). The names of the Map icons are what you can use for the "topic" headline, which is why the Map icons were named as they are. But how can you use this variable? There is a little trick, which uses the system variable *IconTitle* and a custom variable you will create. Close the Variable window.

h) Let's perform the trick and then come back and see how it works.

i) Drag a Display icon from the Icon palette and place it on the Entry Pane flowline, below the Display icon *Show Page Number* but above the Interaction icon. Name this Display icon *Show Header*.

j) Double click on the Display icon. The text attributes are already set from the last time you used the Text tool. Simply change the alignment to Left. Type in {*PageTitle*}. Make sure to type in the curly brackets (these symbols are on the keys above the Enter key). Select the Pointer tool to close the text object. You should now see the New Variable window, with *PageTitle* as the name. Click the cursor in the Initial Value field. Type in "" (closed quotation marks with no space between them). Click the cursor in the Description field. Type in *This custom variable will be assigned the current value of the system variable* IconTitle *for each Map icon attached to the Framework.* Close the New Variable window.

k) Select the Map icon *Safety in the Workplace*. Select Modify | Icon | Calculation. As you can see, this has opened a Calculation icon, which will be attached directly to this Map icon. The cursor should already be inside the Calculation icon. Click on the Variables Window button. Select the category *Exer15-1.a6p* (name of current file). Single click on *PageTitle*. Click on the Paste button. Select the category Icons. Locate and single click on *IconTitle*. Click on the Paste button. Click on the Done button. Modify the expression so that it reads *PageTitle := IconTitle*. Do not close the icon yet.

l) Highlight the variable expression *PageTitle := IconTitle*. Click on the Copy button. Close the Calculation icon. Save the changes.

m) Select the Map icon *Housekeeping*. Select Modify | Icon | Calculation. The cursor should already be inside the Calculation icon. Click on the Paste button. The variable expression *PageTitle := IconTitle* should now appear here. Close the Calculation icon. Save the changes.

n) Select the Map icon *Protecting Openings*. Select Modify | Icon | Calculation. Click on the Paste button. The variable expression *PageTitle := IconTitle* should now appear here. Close the Calculation icon. Save the changes.

o) Select the Map icon *Use of Stairs*. Select Modify | Icon | Calculation. Click on the Paste button. The variable expression *PageTitle := IconTitle* should now appear here. Close the Calculation icon. Save the changes.

p) Select the Map icon *Use of Ladders*. Select Modify | Icon | Calculation. Click on the Paste button. The variable expression *PageTitle := IconTitle* should now appear here. Close the Calculation icon. Save the changes.

q) Select the Map icon *Ladder Maintenance*. Select Modify | Icon | Calculation. Click on the Paste button. The variable expression *PageTitle := IconTitle* should now appear here. Close the Calculation icon. Save the changes.

r) Click on the Restart button. As soon as the first page displays, pause the program (Ctrl + P). Click on and drag the "header" text object up to the upper left-hand corner of the screen, so that it fits within the header panel. Jump to the flowline.

s) Save the file.

18. In this last step, let's add another feature that is not a necessity but provides additional information to the user, and increases the "professional touch." You are going to add visual indicators signaling when the narration is finished and prompting the user to select the appropriate button.

a) At the bottom the flowline, there are three Display icons that were brought in when you imported the model in step 4. Two of these icons contain text objects that provide a prompt to the user to select the appropriate button. The third Display icon (*Highlight Right Arrow*) contains a graphic that will surround the Right Arrow key.

b) Select the first two Display icons, *Please select forward* and *Highlight Right Arrow*. Copy them to the clipboard.

c) Double click on the Map icon *Safety in the Workplace*. Click the Paste Hand cursor at the very bottom of the level 2 flowline inside this Map icon. Paste the two Display icons here. Close the Map icon.

d) Double click on the Map icon *Housekeeping*. Click the Paste Hand cursor at the very bottom of the level 2 flowline inside this Map icon. Paste the two Display icons here. Close the Map icon.

e) Double click on the Map icon *Protecting Openings*. Click the Paste Hand cursor at the very bottom of the level 2 flowline inside this Map icon. Paste the two Display icons here. Close the Map icon.

f) Double click on the Map icon *Use of Stairs*. Click the Paste Hand cursor at the very bottom of the level 2 flowline inside this Map icon. Paste the two Display icons here. Close the Map icon.

g) Double click on the Map icon *Use of Ladders*. Click the Paste Hand cursor at the very bottom of the level 2 flowline inside this Map icon. Paste the two Display icons here. Close the Map icon.

h) Select the third Display icon (*Please select Menu*) at the bottom of the main flowline. Copy it to the clipboard.

i) Double click on the Map icon *Ladder Maintenance*. Click the Paste Hand cursor at the very bottom of the level 2 flowline inside this Map icon. Paste the Display icon here. Close the Map icon.

j) Click on the Restart button. Allow the first page to play all the way through the narration. After the narration finishes, the prompt text and Right Arrow highlight should appear.

k) Click on the Right Arrow several times until you get to page 6. Let the narration play through. After the narration finishes, the prompt text appears for the Menu button. (The Menu button does not yet appear. You will activate it in the next exercise.)

l) Now that you have copied the three Display icons in place, you are finished with them and can get rid of the originals on the main flowline. Select the three Display icons on the bottom of the flowline. Delete them.

m) Save the file.

Practice Exercise 15-2: Adding a Glossary, Reference Section, and Replay Capability

Description

In this exercise you are going to pick up where the last exercise left off. Before talking "Authorware," let's back up a minute and consider instructional design. In most applications you will build, it is very likely the audience that will be viewing (or learning from) your application will have varied backgrounds. Some people will have greater experience and knowledge of the subject than others. To accommodate the varied needs of the audience, many CBT developers frequently include additional information about the subject. This additional information is only seen/heard if the user selects it.

One method of providing this additional information is by including Glossary and/or Reference buttons on the navigational control panel that allow the user to select them at any point within a topic structure. In this exercise, you will add a self-contained glossary and a shell (placeholder) for a reference section.

Another feature instructional designers/CBT developers frequently like to include is a replay capability. The user can click on a Replay button to "refresh" or replay the narration, text, or animation contained within the current page. This feature is included to provide greater help to the user. There may be many reasons for wanting to replay the current page. In this exercise, you will add a Replay button to the navigational controls. The following elements are covered in this exercise.

- *Importing a model containing prebuilt content*
- *Adding a glossary contained within the current Authorware file*
- *Adding a reference section placeholder that can be used to call an external program*
- *Adding a replay capability, so that the user can replay the content of the current page*
- *Creating custom Glossary, Reference, Menu, and Replay buttons*
- *Adding variables to further control the active/inactive state of all buttons*

Take a Look

Before beginning the exercise, let's take a look at the exercise in its completed state so that you can clearly see what it is you are about to build.

CD-ROM

1. Select File | Open and locate on the companion CD-ROM the directory named *Chapter15*. Within this directory, locate and double click on the file named *Exer15-2*.

2. The file *Exer15-2* should now appear in your copy of Authorware. Click on the Restart button to play the file from the top of the flowline. Note the following properties of this completed exercise.

    *   *The Quit, Menu, Glossary, Reference, Replay, Back Up, and Forward buttons are all functional.*

    *   *The Menu button will be fully activated in Practice Exercise 16-1.*

    *   *The Menu, Glossary, Reference, Replay, Back Up, and Forward buttons become inactive when the user is within either the glossary or reference section. The only buttons active in these sections are the Quit and Return buttons.*

    *   *The glossary provides additional information at the click of a button.*

    *   *The reference section provides a placeholder.*

Storyboard: On Screen

Figure 15-11 shows what the finished presentation will look like on screen.

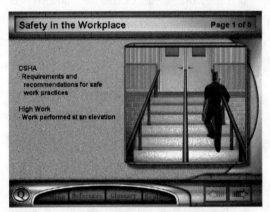

Fig. 15-11. Completed presentation on screen.

Storyboard: Behind the Scenes

Figure 15-12 shows the main flowline and a representative level 2 flowline (with all icons, their placement, and their names) as they should look when you are finished with this exercise. Figure 15-13 shows the Entry and Exit pane flowlines inside the Framework icon *Content*.

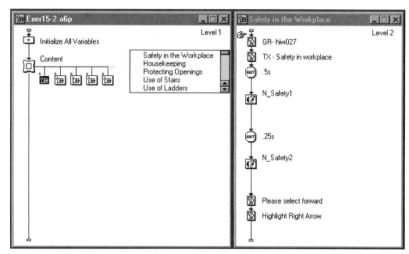

Fig. 15-12. Main flowline with a representative level 2 flowline from Content.

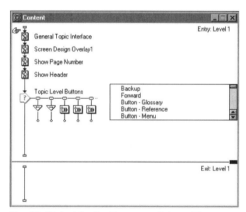

Fig. 15-13. Inside the Framework icon Content.

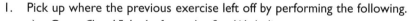

Step-by-Step Instructions

Go Solo

1. Pick up where the previous exercise left off by performing the following.
   a) Open *Chap15-1.a6p* from the *SaveWork* directory on your computer's hard drive.
      Or
      Open *Exer15-1.a6p* from the companion CD-ROM's *Chapter15* directory.
   b) Select File | Save As and save this file as *Chap15-2* into the *SaveWork* directory on your computer's hard drive.

2. Again, so that you can concentrate on the Authorware structures and variable expressions, the content for the glossary and reference section have been built for you. You will import them using a model you copied (in the "Prework" section) to your computer's hard drive.

  a) Let's clean up first. Close the Framework icon and any Map icons that may be open.

  b) Click the cursor on the bottom of the main flowline to place the Paste Hand cursor there.

  c) The Knowledge Objects window should already be open. If not, select Window | Knowledge Objects.

  d) Select the category Model Palette. Double click on *Ch15-Perpetuals* and wait a few seconds for it to load and paste into your flowline. You should now see three (3) Map icons at the bottom of the flowline: *Button – Glossary*, *Button – References*, and *Button – Menu*.

  e) Double click on the Framework icon.

  f) Select and drag the Map icon (*Button – Glossary*) to the far right of the Interaction icon (*Topic Level Buttons*) and to the right of *Forward*. Drop it here. Note that it has automatically taken the attributes (button response) of the icon to the left (*Forward*).

  g) Select and drag the Map icon *Button – Reference* to the right of *Button – Glossary* and drop it there.

  h) Select and drag the last Map icon (*Button – Menu*) to right of *Button – Reference* and drop it there.

3. Create custom buttons for these three new buttons and align them in their appropriate locations. Start with the Glossary button.

  a) Double click on the Response Type symbol above the Map icon *Glossary*. The Properties/Response dialog window has opened.

  b) Click on the Buttons button in the upper left-hand corner to open the Button library.

  c) Note that the graphic of the right arrow is currently highlighted in this list. Click on the Add button located in the lower left-hand corner of the Button Library window. The Button editor now opens.

  d) Make sure the Normal/Up state is selected (click on it to make sure). Click on the Import button located slightly to the right of the Graphic field. The Look in field should already be pointing to the *Chapter15* directory on the companion CD-ROM. Locate and single click on the file *Glossary-Up.bmp*. Click on the Import button. You should have seen the blue progress bar rapidly display on screen.

  e) Click on the Normal/Down state. Click on the Import button, located to the right of the Graphic field. The Look in field should already pointing to the *Chapter15* directory on the companion CD-ROM.

Locate and single click on the file *Glossary-Down.bmp*. Click on the Import button. You should have seen the blue progress bar rapidly display on screen.

f) Leave the Normal/Down state selected. Click on the Import button located to the right of the Sound field. The Look in field should already be pointing to the *Chapter15* directory. Select *Click.wav*. Click on the Import button.

g) Click on the Normal/Over state. Click on the Import button, located to the right of the Graphic field. The Look in field should already be pointing to the *Chapter15* directory on the companion CD-ROM. Locate and single click on the file *Glossary-Over.bmp*. Click on the Import button. You should have seen the blue progress bar rapidly display on screen. There will be no sound with the Roll Over state.

h) Click on the OK button located at the lower right-hand corner of the Button editor to close the editor. Click on the OK button at the lower right-hand corner to close the Button library.

i) You are back to the Properties dialog window. The Button tab should be on top (if not, select it). Note that the Hand cursor and Hide When Active options are already selected. These were the defaults (from the *Forward* response to the left) Authorware assumed you wanted when you dropped the Map icon here.

j) Click the cursor in the *X coordinate* location field. Type in *247*. Click the cursor in the *Y coordinate* field. Type in *427*.

Recall that these X and Y coordinates came from previously setting up the interface and buttons. You have been given the values to avoid "trail and error" placements.

k) Click on the OK button to close the Properties window.

4. Continue with the Reference button.
a) Double click on the Response Type symbol above the Map icon *Reference*. The Properties/Response dialog window has opened.

b) Click on the Buttons button in the upper left-hand corner to open the Button library.

c) Note that the graphic of the right arrow is currently highlighted in this list. Click on the Add button located in the lower left-hand corner of the Button Library window. The Button editor now opens.

d) Make sure the Normal/Up state is selected (click on it to make sure). Click on the Import button located to the right of the Graphic field. The Look in field should already be pointing to the *Chapter15* directory on the companion CD-ROM. Locate and single click on the file

Reference-Up.bmp. Click on the Import button. You should have seen the blue progress bar rapidly display on screen.

e) Click on the Normal/Down state. Click on the Import button located to the right of the Graphic field. The Look in field should already pointing to the *Chapter15* directory on the companion CD-ROM. Locate and single click on the file *Reference-Down.bmp*. Click on the Import button. You should have seen the blue progress bar rapidly display on screen.

f) Leave the Normal/Down state selected. Click on the Import button located to the right of the Sound field. The Look in field should already be pointing to the *Chapter15* directory. Select *Click.wav*. Click on the Import button.

g) Click on the Normal/Over state. Click on the Import button located to the right of the Graphic field. The Look in field should already pointing to the *Chapter15* directory on the companion CD-ROM. Locate and single click on the file *Reference-Over.bmp*. Click on the Import button. You should have seen the blue progress bar rapidly display on screen. There will be no sound with the Roll Over state.

h) Click on the OK button located at the lower right-hand corner of the Button editor to close the editor. Click on the OK button at the lower right-hand corner to close the Button library.

i) You are back to the Properties dialog window. The Button tab should be on top (if not, select it).

j) Click the cursor in the *X coordinate* Location field. Type in *154*. Click the cursor in the *Y coordinate* field. Type in *427*.

k) Click on the OK button to close the Properties window.

5. Create the Menu button.

a) Double click on the Response Type symbol above the Map icon *Menu*. The Properties/Response dialog window has opened.

b) Click on the Buttons button in the upper left-hand corner to open the Button library.

c) Note that the graphic of the right arrow is currently highlighted in this list. Click on the Add button located in the lower left-hand corner of the Button Library window. The Button editor now opens.

d) Make sure the Normal/Up state is selected (click on it to make sure). Click on the Import button located to the right of the Graphic field. The Look in field should already be pointing to the *Chapter15* directory on the companion CD-ROM. Locate and single click on the file *Menu-Up.bmp*. Click on the Import button. You should have seen the blue progress bar rapidly display on screen.

e) Click on the Normal/Down state. Click on the Import button located to the right of the Graphic field. The Look in field should already pointing to the *Chapter15* directory on the companion CD-ROM. Locate and single click on the file *Menu-Down.bmp*. Click on the Import button. You should have seen the blue progress bar rapidly display on screen.

f) Leave the Normal/Down state selected. Click on the Import button located to the right of the Sound field. The Look in field should already be pointing to the *Chapter15* directory. Select *Click.wav*. Click on the Import button.

g) Click on the Normal/Over state. Click on the Import button located to the right of the Graphic field. The Look in field should already be pointing to the *Chapter15* directory on the companion CD-ROM. Locate and single click on the file *Menu-Over.bmp*. Click on the Import button. You should have seen the blue progress bar rapidly display on screen. There will be no sound with the Roll Over state.

h) Click on the OK button located at the lower right-hand corner of the Button editor to close the editor. Click on the OK button at the lower right-hand corner to close the Button library.

i) You are back to the Properties dialog window. The Button tab should be on top (if not, select it).

j) Click the cursor in the *X coordinate* Location field. Type in *63*. Click the cursor in the *Y coordinate* field. Type in *427*.

k) Click on the OK button to close the Properties window.

6. Create the Replay button.

a) Drag a Navigate icon from the Icon palette to the far right of the Interaction icon (at the right of *Button – Menu*). Name the Navigate response *Replay*.

b) You will set the navigation link in material to follow. For now, let's simply add the custom button.

c) Double click on the Response Type symbol above the Navigate icon *Replay*. The Properties/Response dialog window has opened.

d) Click on the Buttons button in the upper left-hand corner to open the Button library.

e) Click on the Add button located at the lower left-hand corner of the Button Library window. The Button editor now opens.

f) Make sure the Normal/Up state is selected. Click on the Import button located to the right of the Graphic field. The Look in field should already be pointing to the *Chapter15* directory on the companion CD-ROM. Locate and single click on the file *Replay-Up.bmp*. Click on the Import button. You should have seen the blue progress bar rapidly display on screen.

g) Click on the Normal/Down state. Click on the Import button located to the right of the Graphic field. The Look in field should already be pointing to the *Chapter15* directory on the companion CD-ROM. Locate and single click on the file *Replay-Down.bmp*. Click on the Import button. You should have seen the blue progress bar rapidly display on screen.

h) Leave the Normal/Down state selected. Click on the Import button located to the right of the Sound field. The Look in field should already be pointing to the *Chapter15* directory. Select *Click.wav*. Click on the Import button.

i) Click on the Normal/Over state. Click on the Import button located to the right of the Graphic field. The Look in field should already be pointing to the *Chapter15* directory on the companion CD-ROM. Locate and single click on the file *Replay-Over.bmp*. Click on the Import button. You should have seen the blue progress bar rapidly display on screen. There will be no sound with the Roll Over state.

j) Click on the OK button located at the lower right-hand corner of the Button editor to close the editor. Click on the OK button at the lower right-hand corner to close the Button library.

k) You are back to the Properties dialog window. The Button tab should be on top (if not, select it).

l) Click the cursor in the *X coordinate* location field. Type in *340*. Click the cursor in the *Y coordinate* field. Type in *427*.

m) Click on the OK button to close the Properties window.

7. Let's take a quick look at the current state of the topic structure.

a) Click on the Restart button. The first page should be displayed with the narration running.

b) Move the mouse over the Menu, Reference, Glossary, and Replay buttons. The Roll Over states for these buttons should be working correctly.

c) Click on the Reference button. As you can observe, if the narration is playing as you click on the Reference button, the narration continues to play. You will change this so that it stops as you enter the reference section. Also note that all buttons are active.

You need to do something about this. If the user clicks on any of these buttons, the button will activate whatever task is assigned to it. Because the user is currently in a section unrelated to these buttons (Forward, Back Up, and so on), it is better from a design standpoint to deactivate these unrelated buttons.

8. Let's first look at how to interrupt narration if it is playing.

If you do not want the first sound interrupted when Authorware encounters a second Sound icon, you can tell Authorware to wait for the first sound to finish. Click on the Timing tab. At the bottom, place a check mark in the Wait for Previous Sound option to activate this functionality.

a) Click on the Restart button. As the narration starts to play for page 1, click on the Glossary button. Note that the narration is immediately stopped, the glossary is displayed, and the narration for the glossary begins. Let's see how this works.

b) Double click on the Framework icon (if it is not currently open). Double click on the Map icon (*Button – Menu*) attached to the Interaction icon. Look at the Sound icon, which is second from the top of the level 2 flowline. Double click on it. Click on the Play button in the upper left-hand corner of the dialog box. You hear nothing. This icon imported a very small blank *.wav* file. By default, Authorware will discontinue a currently playing Sound icon when it encounters a second Sound icon, and will begin to play the second sound. In this case, the second sound is a "blank" sound.

c) Close the Sound icon.

9. Let's look within the *Glossary* Map icon at some of the other icons. This may help you understand what is here, and how you will end up being able to deactivate the unrelated buttons.

a) Double click on the Display icon *Glossary*. As you can see, this icon contains the topic headline. Close the icon.

b) Double click on the Display icon *Scrolling*. This is where the glossary text exists. As you can see, it is a single text object, set to Scrolling (Text | Scrolling). The Scrolling text object makes it pretty easy to build a glossary of terms that can be stored within the current Authorware file. Close the icon.

c) The Sound icon *Audio* is the audio narration for the glossary.

d) The Interaction icon *Dummy* is empty. It has a Button response attached to it. This is the Return button. Double click on the Response Type symbol for Return. The Properties/Response dialog window opens. As you can see in the upper left-hand corner, the custom button for Return is already installed, just as you have already done for the other buttons. Click on the OK button to close the dialog window.

e) What about the Calculation icons? There is one at the top of the level 2 flowline and one at the bottom of the same flowline.

f) Double click on the Calculation icon *Turn OFF all buttons but Quit* at the top. The icon's label describes exactly what happens within the icon in regard to the use of custom variables. The following are the variable expressions you should see within this Calculation icon.

- *ButtonGlossary := FALSE*
- *ButtonReference := FALSE*

- *ButtonMenu := FALSE*
- *ButtonForward := FALSE*
- *ButtonBackup := FALSE*
- *ButtonReplay := FALSE*

g) You are looking at custom variables that were previously created by the authors and imported into the current Authorware file when you imported the model *Ch15-Perpetuals*. Let's verify this. Click on the Variable Window button. Select the Category option of the current file, *Exer15-2.a6p*. You should be able to see each of these variables, as well as the other custom variable you created, *PageTile*. Single click on *ButtonGlossary*. Read the description. Look at a few others if you wish. Close the Variable window.

h) This Calculation icon will assign a False value to these custom variables as soon as Authorware enters this flowline. But how can you use these variables to actually deactivate the buttons? Recall that you deactivated the Forward and Back Up buttons so that the Back Up button would not appear on the first page and the Forward button would not appear on the last page of the Framework structure. This was accomplished using the Response Type symbol for each button. Let's take a look. Close the Calculation icon.

i) Double click on the Response Type symbol for the Map icon *Button – Glossary*. Note that on the Button tab, at the bottom, there is already a check mark in the Hide When Inactive option. Click on the Response tab. Click the cursor in the Active If field. Click on the Variable Window button. Category should already be set to the name of the current file, *Exer15-2.a6p*. Single click on *ButtonGlossary*. Click on the Paste button. Click on the Done button. Finish the expression by typing in := *True*. The final expression should be *ButtonGlossary := True*. Close the dialog window.

j) Double click on the Response Type symbol for the Map icon *Button – Reference*. You should already be on the Response tab. Click the cursor in the Active If field. Click on the Variable Window button. Category should already be set to the name of the current file, *Exer15-2.a6p*. Single click on *ButtonReference*. Click on the Paste button. Click on the Done button. Finish the expression by typing in := *True*. The final expression should be *ButtonReference := True*. Click on the Button tab and verify that there is a check mark beside the Hide When Inactive option. Close the dialog window.

k) Double click on the Response Type symbol for the Map icon *Button – Menu*. You should already be on the Button tab. Verify that there is already a check mark beside the Hide When Inactive option. Click on the Response tab. Click the cursor in the Active If field. Click on the Variable Window button. Category should already be set to the name of the current file, *Exer15-2.a6p*. Single click on *ButtonMenu*. Click on the Paste button. Click on the Done button. Finish the expression by typing in := *True*. The final expression should be *ButtonMenu := True*. Close the dialog window.

l) Double click on the Response Type symbol for the Map icon *Button – Replay*. You should already be on the Response tab. Click the cursor in the Active If field. Click on the Variable Window button. Category should already be set to the name of the current file, *Exer15-2.a6p*. Single click on *ButtonReplay*. Click on the Paste button. Click on the Done button. Finish the expression by typing in := *True*. The final expression should be *ButtonReplay := True*. Click on the Button tab. Verify that there is already a check mark beside the Hide When Inactive option. Close the dialog window.

10. Provide deactivation of the Forward and Back Up buttons when in the glossary or reference section. This, with a slight twist, is similar to what you performed in step 9.

a) Double click on the Response Type symbol for the Navigate icon *Back Up*. Click on the Response tab if it is not on top. The Active If field already has one expression in it (*CurrentPageNum > 1*). This expression is what deactivates the button on the first page. You will now add a second expression, the conditions of which must also be met to activate the button. Click the cursor at the end of the current expression. Press the space bar. Type in &. Press the space bar. Click on the Variable Window button. Category should already set to the name of the current file, *Exer15-2.a6p*. Single click on *ButtonBackup*. Click on the Paste button. Click on the Done button. Finish the expression by typing in := *True*. The final expression should be *CurrentPageNum > 1 & ButtonBackup := True*. Close the dialog window. For this button to be active, two conditions must be simultaneously met. First, the current page must be greater than 1. Second, the variable *ButtonBackup* must be TRUE.

b) Double click on the Response Type symbol for the Navigate icon *Forward*. Click on the Response tab if it is not on top. The Active If field already has one expression in it *(CurrentPageNum < PageCount)*. This expression is what deactivates the button on the last page. You will now add a second expression, the conditions of which must also be met to activate the button. Click the cursor at the end of the current expression. Press the space bar. Type in &. Press the space bar.

Click on the Variable Window button. Category should already be set to the name of the current file, *Exer15-2.a6p*. Single click on *ButtonForward*. Click on the Paste button. Click on the Done button. Finish the expression by typing in := *True*. The final expression should be *CurrentPageNum < PageCount & ButtonForward := True*. Close the dialog window. For this button to be active, two conditions must be simultaneously met. First, the current page must be less than the number of pages attached to the framework. Second, the variable *ButtonForward* must be TRUE.

11. Let's take another look inside the Map icon *Button – Glossary*. Open it again, if you need to. Previously you saw how the Calculation icon at the top of this flowline assigns a False value to these custom variables. With these False values and the expressions in the Active If fields you just completed, the Glossary, Reference, Menu, Replay, Back Up, and Forward buttons should turn off. However, when Authorware returns to the topic, these buttons need to reactivate.

    a) Look at the Calculation icon *Turn on all buttons* at the bottom of the flowline. Double click on this Calculation icon. You should see the following expressions.

    - *ButtonGlossary := TRUE*
    - *ButtonReference := TRUE*
    - *ButtonMenu := TRUE*
    - *ButtonForward := TRUE*
    - *ButtonBackup := TRUE*
    - *ButtonReplay := TRUE*

    b) This is how you can turn the buttons back on. Close the Calculation icon.

12. Let's practice good programming and make sure that all variables will enter the Framework icon with the custom variables set to known values.

    a) Select the Calculation icon *Turn on all buttons*. Copy the icon to the clipboard.

    b) Move the other open windows around so that you can see level 1 of the main flowline. Click the Paste Hand cursor at the very top of the main flowline. Paste the Calculation icon there. Rename the Calculation icon *Initialize All Variables*.

    c) Double click on the Calculation icon *Initialize All Variables*. Earlier you created another custom variable that is not here. Click the cursor at the end of the last line. Press the Enter key to begin a new line. Click on the Variable Window button. The *Exer15-2.a6p* category should be selected. Click on *PageTitle*. Click on the Paste button.

Click on the Done button. Finish the expression by typing in := "". The final expression should be *PageTitle := ""*. Close the Calculation icon. Save the changes.

13. Let's try it.
    a) Click on the Restart button. As soon as the narration starts playing, click on the Glossary button. Note that all buttons (except the Return button) are inactive, as they should be.
    b) Click on the Return button. The glossary is still there, but should not be. Pause the program. Jump to the flowline. Double click on the Response Type symbol for *Button – Glossary*. Click on the Response tab. Look at the Erase field, which contains the problem. Select Before Next Entry. Close the dialog window.
    c) Double click on the Response Type symbol for *Button – Reference*. Click on the Response tab. In the Erase field, select Before Next Entry. Close the dialog window.

14. Link the Replay button. You want to create a button that allows the user to replay any narration or animation (and redisplay the text/graphics) that may exist within the current page.
    a) Double click on the Navigate icon *Replay* (open the Framework icon if you need to).
    b) In the Destination field, select Calculate.
    c) Leave the Type option set to Jump to Page.
    d) Click the cursor in the Icon Expression field. Click on the Variable Window button. In the Category field, select Framework. Single click on *CurrentPageID*. Read the description. This is the variable you want. Click on the Paste button. Click on the Done button.
    e) Click on the OK button to close the dialog window.

15. Save the file.

16. Let's try it.
    a) Click on the Restart button.
    b) Let the page 1 narration play through completely.
    c) Click on the Replay button.
    d) Click on the Forward button. Try out the Replay button on whatever other pages you want.

Guided Tour 15B: Creating Hyperlinked Pages

You have seen two methods of providing the user with additional information: a built-in glossary function and a reference section. The glossary function does not literally have to be used for a glossary but can be used with any type of additional information. The point of the access method is that it makes use of a Scrolling text object and allows the user to search for the word or subject she may be interested in. The reference section is included as a means of jumping to an external file (such as a Windows help file).

A third method of providing additional information is through a second layer of information that is context sensitive to what is on the current computer display (the first layer). With this method, everyone sees the first layer on screen, whereas the second layer is seen only by those users who click on a visual "hot spot" on screen that will link them to context-sensitive additional information about the subject they clicked on.

Before you actually create a hyperlinked second layer of information, let's take a 50,000-foot view of the process involved. Let's begin with the three steps involved, and then look more closely at the details of these steps. The following are the basic steps involved in creating hyperlinked pages.

1. Create the Framework icon containing the content for the general "layer 1" information, and a second Framework icon containing the content for the specific "layer 2" information.

2. Define the text style you will use for the hyperlink text.

3. Apply the hyperlink text style to all target words in the "layer 1" screens, linking them to the "layer 2" page associated with each.

There is really nothing additional to be said about the Framework icons. You have had some experience building a generic topic Framework structure. You will use this for the "layer 1" content. In the next exercise you will put together another framework to be used for the "layer 2" information. The following are the general steps for creating a text style within Authorware.

1. Select Text | Define Styles. The Define Styles dialog window opens.

2. Click on the Add button in the lower left to create a new style.

3. In the field above the Add button, type in a name that is descriptive of the style you are creating. Press the Enter key.

4. Select the text attributes you want to use for the style you are about to create, including font, size, color, and so on. (Hint: To change the color, you must first place a check mark next to Color, and then click on the color box next to it.)

5. On the right is an Interactivity section. Click on the Single Click and Cursor options.

6. In the lower right, click on the Done button.

It really is easy to create a new style. However, if as you are applying the style you created you discover you made a mistake in defining the style, it sometimes can be tricky to go back and redefine it. Go ahead and try to correct or change what you need to. On the other hand, note that sometimes it may be easier to just start over, assigning a new name to the style and proceeding more carefully as you recreate the style. The following are the general steps for applying a text style to be used as a hyperlink within Authorware.

1. Set the Start Flag above the "layer 1" framework that contains the general information.

2. Run the program from the Flag and advance through the framework using the Forward button until you are looking at the page where you want to add a hyperlink.

3. Pause the program (Ctrl + P).

4. Double click directly on the text you want to change. Select the Text tool and click the cursor within the text object that contains the word/phrase you want. Highlight the word/phrase you want.

5. Select Text | Apply Styles. A small Text Style window appears.

6. Place a check mark next to the style you want to use here.

7. The Properties/Navigation dialog window opens. The Destination field should already be set to Anywhere.

8. Locate and select the Call and Return option.

9. Use the Framework field to locate and select the Framework icon that you want to navigate to.

10. Use the Page field to locate the page within the selected framework that you want to navigate to.

11. Click on the OK button to close the dialog window.

12. Click on the Pointer tool to close the text object.

13. Press Ctrl + P to resume in the Play mode.

14. Use the Forward button to locate the next page where you want to apply the style.

Practice Exercise 15-3: Adding a Second Layer of Content Using Hyperlinks

Description

In this exercise you are going to pick up where the last exercise left off. In this exercise you will provide the user with the capability to access additional information that is context sensitive to information currently displayed on screen. Frequently designers refer to the general information on the current screen as the first layer of information, and as the user clicks on a hyperlink, the additional information that appears as a second layer of information.

You will be provided with the content for the second Framework icon, so that you can remain focused on the framework and the hyperlink functionality. The following elements are covered in this exercise.

- *Importing a model with prebuilt content*
- *Creating a framework to house the second-layer content*
- *Modifying the navigational controls for use as a second-layer overlay screen*
- *Defining a hyperlink text style*
- *Applying a hyperlink text style*

Take a Look

CD-ROM

Before beginning the exercise, let's take a look at the exercise in its completed state so that you can clearly see what it is you are about to build.

1.   Select File | Open and locate on the companion CD-ROM the directory named *Chapter15*. Within this directory, locate and double click on the file named *Exer15-3*.

2.   The file *Exer15-3* should now appear in your copy of Authorware. Click on the Restart button to play the file from the top of the flowline. Note the following properties of this completed exercise.

   - *Clicking on a word/phrase that is blue and underlined will jump to a context-sensitive screen containing additional information about whatever subject was selected.*

   - *The context-sensitive screen contains a Return button only.*

Storyboard: On Screen

Figure 15-14 shows what the finished presentation (with the hyperlink overlay) will look like on screen.

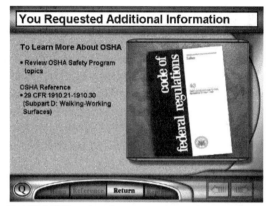

Fig. 15-14. Completed presentation with overlay screen.

Storyboard: Behind the Scenes

Figure 15-15 shows the main flowline and a representative level 2 flowline from the Framework icon *Second Layer* (with all icons, their placement, and their names) as they should look when you are finished with this exercise. Figure 15-16 shows the Entry and Exit panes within the Framework icon *Second Layer*.

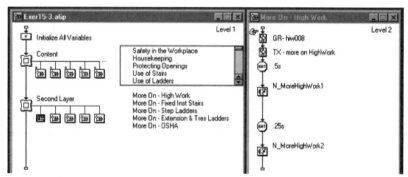

Fig. 15-15. Main flowline with a representative level 2 flowline from **Second Layer***.*

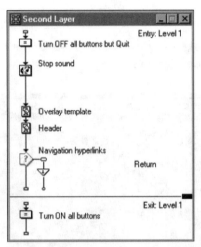

Fig. 15-16. Entry and Exit panes within the Framework Second Layer.

Step-by-Step Instructions

Go Solo

1. Pick up where the previous exercise left off.

   a) Open *Chap15-2.a6p* from the *SaveWork* directory on your computer's hard drive.

   Or

   Open *Exer15-2.a6p* from the companion CD-ROM's *Chapter15* directory.

   b) Select File | Save As and save this file as *Chap15-3* into the *SaveWork* directory on your computer's hard drive.

2. Again, so that you can concentrate on the Authorware structures and hyperlink functionality, the content for the second-layer framework has been built for you. You will import the content using the model you copied (in the "Prework" section) to your computer's hard drive.

   a) Let's clean up first. Close the Framework icon and any Map icons that may be open.

   b) Click the cursor on the bottom of the main flowline, so that the Paste Hand cursor appears there.

   c) The Knowledge Objects window should already be open. If not, select Window | Knowledge Objects.

   d) Select the category Model Palette. Double click on *Ch15-MoreOn* and wait a few seconds for it to load and paste into your flowline. You should now see five (5) Map icons and two (2) Display icons at the bottom of the flowline.

e) Drag a Framework icon to the main flowline and place it below the Framework icon *Content* and above the Map icon *More On – High Work*. Name this new Framework icon *Second Layer*.

f) Select and drag each of the Map icons you just imported to the right of the Framework icon. Place them in the following order, from left to right: *More On – High Work*, *More On – Fixed Inst Stairs*, *More On – Step Ladders*, *More On – Extension & Tres Ladders*, and *More On – OSHA*.

g) Leave the Display icons where they are.

3. You need to do some additional work to this new Framework icon before you can begin the hyperlink process. As you may recall from the "Take a Look" section, when the user clicks on a hyperlink, any sound that is playing is interrupted and all buttons except the Return button are deactivated. Actually, you did this same thing as a user enters the glossary or reference section. You need to do the same thing here.

a) Leave the Framework icon *Second Layer* open, but move it to the side.

b) Double click on the Framework icon *Content* (if it is not already open).

c) Locate and double click on the Map icon *Button – Glossary*. At the top of the level 2 flowline, there is a Calculation icon (*Turn OFF all buttons but Quit*) and a Sound icon (*Stop sound*). Select both of these icons and copy them to the clipboard. Leave this Map icon flowline open, but move it aside.

d) Move the flowline for the Framework icon *Second Layer* back to where you can work with it. Click the Paste Hand cursor at the very top of this level 2 flowline. Paste the two icons from the clipboard here. These two icons will now deactivate the buttons and will stop any sound currently playing.

e) Move back to the flowline for the open Map icon *Button – Glossary*. At the bottom of this flowline there is another Calculation icon that will reactivate all of the buttons. Select this Calculation icon (*Turn ON all buttons*) and copy it to the clipboard. Close the Map icon. Close the Framework icon *Content*.

f) Move the flowline for the Framework icon *Second Layer* back to where you can work with it. Click the Paste Hand cursor on the level 2 flowline in the Exit pane. Paste the Calculation icon from the clipboard here. As the user exits this second-layer Framework icon, all buttons will be reactivated.

4. Perform the following in regard to the Framework icon *Second Layer*.

a) Select the Display icon *Gray Navigation Panel*. Delete it.

b) Delete all icons attached to the Interaction icon except *Exit Framework*. See figure 15-16. Because you will use this Framework icon for context-sensitive direct links from the first framework, there is no need for any navigation within the framework. You do, however, need an Exit button. Create one and name it *Return*.

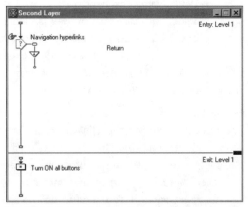

Fig. 15-17. Second Layer *Framework icon in progress.*

5.   Let's now create a custom button for the Return button.

a)   Double click on the Response Type symbol above the Navigate icon *Return*. The Properties: Response dialog window has opened. If you look on screen and in the upper left-hand corner, you can see the graphic of the default button.

b)   Click on the Buttons button in the upper left-hand corner to open the Button Library.

c)   Notice that the graphic of the default button is currently highlighted in this list. Click on the Add button located in the bottom of the Button Library window. The Button Editor now opens.

d)   Make sure the Normal / Up state is selected (click on it to make sure). Make sure that the Graphic field is set to Use Imported. Click on the Import button that is located slightly to the right of this field. The Look In field should already be pointing to the *Chapter15* directory on the CD-ROM. Locate and single click on the file *Return-Up.bmp*. Click on the Import button. You should have seen the blue progress bar rapidly display on screen.

e)   Now click on the Normal / Down state. In the Graphic field, make sure that Use Imported is selected. Click on the Import button, located to the right of this field. The Look In field should be already pointing to the *Chapter15* directory on the CD-ROM. Locate and single click on the file *Return-Down.bmp*. Click on the Import button. You should have seen the blue progress bar rapidly display on screen.

f)   Leave the Normal / Down state selected. Click on the Import button located to the right of the Sound field. The Look In field should already be pointing to the *Chapter15* directory. Select *Click.wav*. Click on the Import button. You should have seen the blue progress bar rapidly display on screen.

g) Now click on the Normal / Over state. In the Graphic field, make sure that Use Imported is selected. Click on the Import button, located to the right of this field. The Look In field should be already pointing to the Chapter15 directory on the CD-ROM. Locate and single click on the file *Return-Over.bmp*. Click on the Import button. You should have seen the blue progress bar rapidly display on screen. There will be no sound with the rollover state.

h) Click on the OK button located on the lower right-hand corner of the Button Editor, to close the editor. Click the OK button in the lower right-hand corner to close the Button Library.

i) You are back to the Properties dialog window. The Button tab should be on top (if not, select it). Click on the Cursor library button at the bottom of this tab. Select the Hand cursor. Click on the OK button to close the Cursor Library. In the Options field, place a checkmark next to Hide When Inactive.

j) Click the cursor in the Location field, X coordinate. Type in *246*. Click the cursor in the Y coordinate field. Type in *427*.

k) Click on the OK button to close the Properties window.

l) Save the file.

6. Now let's put into place a screen design that will overlay whatever was on screen before arriving at the Framework *Second Layer.*

a) Move the flowline for the Framework icon aside so that you can see the main flowline. When you imported the model at the beginning of this exercise, you brought in two Display icons (*Overlay template* and *Header*) that should still be located at the bottom of the main flowline.

b) Select both of these Display icons and copy them to the clipboard. Move the flowline for the Framework icon *Second Layer* back to where you can work with it.

c) Click the Paste Hand cursor above the Interaction icon *Navigational hyperlinks*. Paste the two Display icons here.

d) Using the mouse, click and hold down on the black handle to the right of the window. Drag down on the handle to make the Entry Pane flowline window a little larger.

e) Close the Framework icon.

f) Select the two Display icons (*Overlay template* and *Header*) that are on the very bottom of the flowline. Delete these icons.

7. You have just completed the first phase of creating hyperlinked material. In the previous exercise you completed the Framework icon (*Content*)

from which the hyperlink originates. You have just completed the Framework icon for the specific second-layer information that will be hyperlinked to. Continue with the following.

8. Define a hyperlink text style.
   a) Select Text | Define Styles. The Define Styles dialog window opens.
   b) Click on the Add button in the lower left to create a new style.
   c) In the field above the Add button, type in *Hyperlink*. Press the Enter key.
   d) Click next to the top field (Font) to place a check mark there. Use the pull-down menu to select Arial. Click next to the second field (Size) to place a check mark there. Select 12 in the pull-down menu next to it. Place a check mark next to the Bold option. Place a check mark next to the Underline option. Place a check mark next to the Color option. Click on the color box and click on a bright blue color. Click on the OK button in the Color window to close it.
   e) Locate the Interactivity section on the right. Click on the Single Click and Cursor options.
   f) In the lower right, click on the Done button. You should see a blue progress bar briefly appear on screen.

9. Apply the hyperlink text style.
   a) Because this exercise is the only thing in the current Authorware file, you can simply use the Restart button, instead of dragging the Start flag. Click on the Restart button.
   b) Run the program.
   c) As soon as the first page begins to play, pause the program (Ctrl + P).
   d) Double click directly on the text object. You should now see a toolbox on screen, with the icon label *TX – Safety in the Workplace*. Select the Text tool and click the cursor between the letters *S* and *H* in the word *OSHA*. Highlight the word *OSHA*.
   e) Select Text | Apply Styles. A small Text Style window appears.
   f) Place a check mark next to the Hyperlink style. The Properties/Navigation dialog window appears.
   g) In the Type field, select the Call and Return option.
   h) In the Framework field, use the pull-down menu to locate and select the Framework icon *Second Layer*.
   i) The Page field now lists the pages attached to the frame you selected in the Framework field. Locate the page More On – OSHA page and single click on it.
   j) Click on the OK button to close the dialog window.
   k) Click on the Pointer tool to close the text object.

l) You just finished the first hyperlink. Click on the Pointer tool to close the text object. You can now see what the hyperlinked text looks like (underlined blue text).

10. Let's take a quick look and see if it works.
    a) Click on the Restart button.
    b) Let the first page begin to play.
    c) Click on the hyperlinked word *OSHA*.
    d) You should now be looking at and listening to the More On – OSHA page from the *Second Layer* Framework icon.

11. In the following you will set up all links and then test them. Let's begin with the first page.
    a) Click on the Restart button to run the program.
    b) As soon as the first page begins to play, pause the program (Ctrl + P). You need to add another hyperlink to this page.
    c) Double click directly on the text object. You should now see a tool-box on screen, with the icon label *TX – Safety in the Workplace*. Select the Text tool and click the cursor between the words *High* and *Work*. Highlight the phrase *High Work*.
    d) The small Text Style window is probably already present (if not, select Text | Apply Styles).
    e) Place a check mark next to the Hyperlink style. The Properties/ Navigation dialog window appears.
    f) In the Type field, select the Call and Return option.
    g) In the Framework field, the Framework icon *Second Layer* is already selected.
    h) Locate the page *More On – High Work* and single click on it.
    i) Click on the OK button to close the dialog window.
    j) Click on the Pointer tool to close the text object.

12. Move to the next page.
    a) Resume Play mode (Ctrl + P). The first page is done. Click on the Forward button. Skip pages 2 and 3.
    b) When you reach page 4, pause the program (Ctrl + P).
    c) Double click directly on the text object. You should now see a tool-box on screen, with the icon label *TX – Use of Stairs*. Select the Text tool and click the cursor between the words *Fixed* and *Industrial*. Highlight the phrase *Fixed Industrial*.
    d) The small Text Style window is probably already present (if not, select Text | Apply Styles).
    e) Place a check mark next to the Hyperlink style. The Properties/ Navigation dialog window appears.

f) In the Type field, select the Call and Return option.

g) In the Framework field, the Framework icon *Second Layer* is already selected.

h) Locate the page *More On – Fixed Inst Stairs* and single click on it.

i) Click on the OK button to close the dialog window.

j) Click on the Pointer tool to close the text object.

13. Move to page 5.

a) Resume Play mode (Ctrl + P). Click on the Forward button.

b) When you reach page 5, pause the program (Ctrl + P).

c) Double click directly on the text object. You should now see a toolbox on screen, with the icon label *TX – Use of ladders*. Select the Text tool and click the cursor between the letters *p* and *l* in the word *Stepladders*. Highlight the word *Stepladders*.

d) The small Text Style window is probably already present (if not, select Text | Apply Styles).

e) Place a check mark next to the Hyperlink style. The Properties/Navigation dialog window appears.

f) In the Type field, select the Call and Return option.

g) In the Framework field, the Framework icon *Second Layer* is already selected.

h) Locate the page *More On – Step Ladders* and single click on it.

i) Click on the OK button to close the dialog window.

j) Click on the Pointer tool to close the text object.

14. Establish a second phrase for page 5.

a) Double click directly on the text object. You should now see a toolbox on screen, with the icon label *TX – Use of ladders*. Select the Text tool and click the cursor between the words *Trestle* and *ladders*. Highlight the phrase *Trestle ladders*.

b) The small Text Style window is probably already present (if not, select Text | Apply Styles).

c) Place a check mark next to the Hyperlink style. The Properties/Navigation dialog window appears.

d) In the Type field, select the Call and Return option.

e) In the Framework field, the Framework icon *Second Layer* is already selected.

f) Locate the page *More On – Extension & Tres Ladders* and single click on it.

g) Click on the OK button to close the dialog window.

h) Click on the Pointer tool to close the text object.

15. Let's try it.

a) Click on the Restart button.

b) Click on each hyperlinked word or phrase.

c) If you jump to a hyperlink and the basic interface erases, you probably forgot to place a check mark beside the Call and Return option.

d) If you find an error, repeat the steps for applying a text style for the word/phrase from which the incorrect hyperlink originates. Carefully go through the steps and make the appropriate selections.

16. Save the file.

You can see how easy it is with the use of Authorware's hyperlink capability to include a second layer of context-sensitive information for the user.

Summary

- *In the first practice exercise you used the Framework icon as the foundation of a generic paging structure, culminating in the creation of a fairly "bulletproof" topic-level structure. This topic-level structure included the use of system and custom variables to activate/deactivate navigational buttons, provide status information to the user, and provide generic "replay the page" functionality.*

- *In the second exercise, additional sections were added that provide the user with additional information. First, a glossary function provided an "in-the-same-file" access to a scrolling window containing additional information. The second section served as a placeholder into which a function can be placed to call an external file.*

- *The last exercise in this chapter added a hyperlink capability to provide context-sensitive information related to whatever word or phrase a user clicks on.*

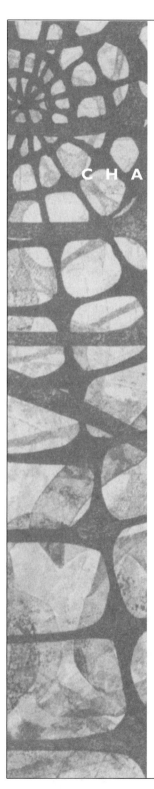

C H A P T E R

16

Organizational

and Navigational

Structures

Introduction

So far you have learned how to create media, interactions, and animation using Authorware. All of this interactivity is great, but at some point you need to know how to place all of these elements into a structure users can easily understand and easily navigate within, to see all of the content you have developed.

There are several organizational approaches that can be used in creating Authorware files based on the combination of the Interaction icon (serving as a menu) and the Framework icon (serving as a topic structure). You will take a few guided tours to examine some of these approaches.

In Chapter 15 you explored how to use the Framework icon as a tool for facilitating paging through content. This was Macromedia's original intention for the Framework icon; that is, an icon structure that would allow developers to quickly create paging structures. Like many Authorware features Macromedia has developed, the Authorware community has taken the Framework icon just a few steps further. What many Authorware developers realized when they first started using the Framework icon (back in the old Authorware 3.0 days) was that the powerful connection between the Framework icon and the Navigate icon made possible a new way of organizing content.

A Navigate icon can navigate to various parts of an Authorware file. More specifically, it can navigate to (or jump to) any page, attached to any Framework. If you move the destination page to another Framework, the link is maintained. If you delete the destination page, the Navigate icon renames itself as "Unlinked." These are powerful features, and the Framework icon has additional capabilities in its own right.

The Framework icon has an attribute that makes it perfect for navigational structures. Whatever is placed in the Entry pane of the Framework appears on every page of that Framework. In other words, anything you place inside the Entry pane of a Framework icon appears on every page attached to the Framework. This means, for example, that if you have a background graphic that needs to appear on every screen, you can place the graphic inside the Framework and it will appear on every subsequent page within that Framework icon. If you have a global functionality, such as a glossary or Quit button, that too can go inside the Framework icon, with the functionality always available, even if you run the program from the Start flag.

This type of navigational flexibility combined with the consistency of the Framework architecture makes for a perfect environment in which to create structural templates that can be used over and over. You can create a single Framework structure, commonly referred to as a Master Framework structure, which can accommodate your training applications, kiosks, or sales presentations. All of these types of programs can use the same flowline architecture. In this chapter, you will learn how to:

- *Create a single Authorware file that contains an organizational structure based on the Interaction icon and Framework icon*

- *Create an Authorware main menu "router" file branching to self-contained module files*

- *Create multiple Authorware menu "router" files branching to self-contained topic files*

- *Create a Master Framework structure*

- *Create global buttons and functionality*

- *Import custom buttons with rollover labels*

- *Incorporate existing paging models to expedite authoring*

- *Create a main menu structure that will allow users to navigate to different topics*

- *Create a "return to main menu" button*

- *Create a quit routine that will confirm whether or not the user wants to exit a program*

Methods of Organizing Information

Almost from the moment of birth, we all learn to distinguish, discern, label, and organize things as a means of learning how to live in a world in which we are bombarded with sensory information. To a certain extent, how well we organize our information determines how well we get along in life. Individuals organize information in any number of ways, heavily influenced by experience, personality, parental upbringing, religious conviction, political orientation, gender, nationality, and many other factors.

As a multimedia developer, it is part of your job to organize the information you want to present in a way that will help your viewers quickly access and better understand the information they are seeking. How you organize and present the content and provide a means of navigation within your program will need to accommodate the varying needs and backgrounds of your viewers, support the purpose behind the existence of your program, and facilitate the efficient development and maintenance of the program.

You may create a program that is linear, starting with the first page/screen and then move sequentially through the totality of what is to be presented. The typical PowerPoint presentation is a good example of this flat, linear organization. Here, there is basically "no choice"; just forward, back up, or quit.

Another possibility might offer the user categories to choose from, with each category consisting of numerous sublevels of choices. This organizational scheme is often referred to as a hierarchical structure, an example of which is shown in figure 16-1. As an example, you start out with a main menu that offers a choice of modules, with each module menu consisting of a choice of topics. Each topic will typically present the content in a sequential order, which may contain interactive learning strategies within the presentation of a "page" or make use of layered or hyperlinked additions.

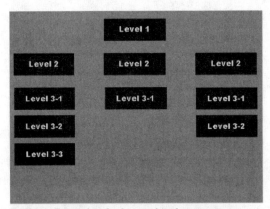

Fig. 16-1. Example of a hierarchical structure.

Generally, there is no wrong or right way to organize and structure your program. There will be many variables that will influence how you go about this. The primary motivating factor in how you organize and structure your program should be how to best communicate with your users.

Approaches to Creating Authorware File Structures

In addition to the need to organize and structure your program from the user's point of view, equally important is the need from a development standpoint to organize and structure the files and media elements being used to create the program. Although the organizational scheme and structure used "behind the scenes" (for the files and media elements) will probably reflect the organization and structure the user sees, it may not be an exact reflection.

Turning from the rather broad design/communication aspects of organizational structure, to focus on Authorware, there are several possibilities for how to create Authorware files to support the organizational decisions being made. As an authoring tool, Authorware is capable of importing or including almost all content (text, graphics, photographs, and sound) within its own self-contained file. The only general exception are movies, which are left as separate files Authorware can "call and run" within the program.

As an Authorware developer, however, you do have a choice as to whether you include all media elements within the Authorware file or elect to leave text, graphic, and sound elements in separate external files, using programming to call and play/display these elements within Authorware. Most developers tend to include most text, graphic, and sound elements within the Authorware application file, because it is generally easier to do so.

On one hand, including most elements within the application file means that it is much easier to keep track of things, avoiding the potential of forgetting to include what would otherwise be contained in many external files. On the other hand, including a lot of sound and graphic elements also means that the application file will tend to become quite large very quickly. If you are not careful, you may end up working with and delivering a single 200-megabyte file, which can be somewhat burdensome.

Guided Tour 16A: Organizational Structure Based on the Interaction and Framework Icons

The first three guided tours of this chapter take you through the process of three methods of structuring Authorware files. The same hierarchical design is used in each tour. Figure 16-2 shows the instructional hierarchy used here, which is typical of many CBT programs.

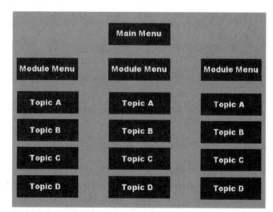

Fig. 16-2. Hierarchical structure.

In this first guided tour, you will see how the instructional structure and content are contained within only one Authorware file. You will first look at the program as the user sees it. You will then look at the file in Authoring mode, examining the nested structures it uses. The following examines the program as the user sees it.

1. Select File | Open and locate on the companion CD-ROM the directory named *Chapter16*. Within this directory, locate and double click on the file named *GuidedTour16A*.

2. The file *GuidedTour16A* should now appear in your copy of Authorware.

3. Click on the Restart button to play the file from the top of the flowline.

4. The first thing you encounter is the Main menu. Look at the text on screen and the navigational and module buttons.

5. Click on the Module 1 button. You should now be looking at the Module 1 menu. Look at the text on screen and the navigational and topic buttons.

6. Click on the Topic A button. You should now be looking at Module 1, Page 1, Topic A. Look at the text on screen and the navigational and topic buttons.

7. Make whatever other selections you want, such as going through the topic, returning to the Module 1 menu, or returning to the Main menu.

The following examines the program in Authoring mode.

1. Jump to the flowline.

2. Note that the Interaction icon named *Main Menu* is located directly on the main flowline.
    a) Double click on this Interaction icon to open it. You are now looking at where the content for the Main menu is located.
    b) Read the text objects as you now see them. Select the Text tool and click the I-bar cursor directly inside the text object labeled *Main Menu*. You have seen this system variable, *IconTitle*, in earlier exercises, and you will see it again in regard to the Module and Topic menus. Close the text object.
    c) The only navigational button on screen is the Quit button, located in the lower left. There are also three module buttons on screen. Close the Interaction icon.

3. Note that there are three Map icons attached to the Interaction icon.
    a) The name of each Map icon is also the name of one of the three module buttons you just saw on screen.
    b) Double click on the *Module 1* Map icon to open it. Note that there is another Interaction icon, with attached Map icons, located within this Map icon. The Interaction icon is named *Module 1 Menu*.
    c) On the level 2 flowline, double click on the Interaction icon named *Module 1 Menu*.

d) Note that the Module menu looks very similar to what you saw on the Main menu. Select the Text tool and click the I-bar cursor directly inside the text object *Module 1 Menu*. There is the system variable, *IconTitle*, again. Close the text object.

e) Note the names of the topic buttons on screen. These are also the names of the Map icons attached to this Interaction icon.

f) Also note that there is a new navigational button located in the lower left-hand corner. It is a button to return to the Main menu. You will look more closely at this button in material to follow.

g) Close the Interaction icon.

h) Note that there are four Map icons attached to the *Module 1 Menu* Interaction icon. These are the topic buttons you just saw on screen.

i) Double click on the *Topic A* Map icon. You are now looking at the same Framework structure you created at the end of Chapter 15.

j) Double click on the Framework icon to take a look at the Entry pane within. There is nothing new here; it is exactly the same as what you previously built. Close the Framework icon.

k) Close the *Topic A* Map icon.

4. Let's take a look at the properties of the Interaction icon *Main Menu* and the properties of the Map icons attached to it.

a) Double click on the Response Type symbol above the *Module 1* Map icon.

b) The Button tab is probably on top (if not, click on it). Note the presence of the Hand cursor and the check mark next to the Hide When Inactive field.

After a user has selected a module button and the program flow moves into the Map icon associated with the user selection, all buttons attached to the Interaction icon will become inactive while Authorware is inside the Map icon. However, unless you place a check mark in the Hide When Inactive field, the buttons will remain on screen (grayed out). Especially with a nested structure such as this, it is important to completely remove the appearance of the buttons when they are inactive. Placing the check mark in this field will do just that.

c) Click on the Response tab. Note that the Erase field is set to Erase Before Next Selection. This selection ensures that the Module menu (and all selections made from it) are erased as Authorware exits the Map icon and before it redisplays the Main menu in the Interaction icon located on the main flowline.

d) The properties of each Map icon attached to the Interaction icon contain the same properties as you have just seen. Close the Response dialog window.

e) Select the Interaction icon *Main Menu*. Select Modify | Icon | Properties. You are now looking at the properties for the Interaction icon. The Interaction tab should be on top (if not, click on it).

f) Note the setting After Next Entry in the Erase field. This is important, because the default setting of Upon Exit would leave the Main menu on screen, even after the user selected a module button and was looking at a Module menu. Close the dialog window.

5. Let's take a look at the Interaction icon *Perpetuals* at the top of the flowline. Note that the Quit and Main Menu buttons are located here. The first question you might have is why these two buttons were not also attached to the Interaction icon *Main Menu*. Why are they in a separate Interaction structure?

The answer is that all buttons attached to the Interaction icon will become inactive while Authorware is inside any of the Map icons attached to the interaction. If the Quit and Main Menu buttons were attached to the Interaction icon *Main Menu*, they would automatically become inactive while Authorware processed the flowline inside any of the Map icons attached.

Typically you want the Quit and Main Menu buttons to be available all of the time, from any screen, including the module menus and all screens within all topics. Placing these two buttons in a separate Interaction icon (set to Perpetual) at the top of the flowline accomplishes this task. Let's take a closer look.

a) Double click on the Interaction icon *Perpetuals*. Note that there is no content in the display area. Close the icon.

b) Double click on the Map icon *Main Menu*. Note that there is no content inside the Map icon. Using a perpetual Main Menu button with an empty Map icon placed at the top of the flowline is simply a technique to get Authorware back up to the top of the flowline so that it can then descend down the flowline and encounter the Interaction icon containing the Main Menu. Close the icon.

c) Double click on the Calculation icon *Quit*. *Quit* is a system variable. The option *(1)* means that when the user clicks on this button Authorware will close the current program and return to the Windows desktop. Close the icon.

d) Double click on the Response Type symbol for the Calculation icon. The Button tab should be on top (if not, click on it). Note that a custom button is displayed in the upper left-hand corner and the custom Hand cursor has been chosen. Click on the Response tab. The settings for the Erase field and the Branch fields really do not matter, because Authorware will quit and exit the program before it even reaches these settings. The Return branch is chosen here not out of necessity but to further distinguish this branch from the branch in the *Main Menu* response you will examine in the next step. Close the Response dialog window.

e) Note that the Main Menu branch looks different from the Quit branch. Double click on the Response Type symbol for the Main Menu response. The Response tab should be on top (if not, click on it).

f) Note that the Branch field is set to Exit Interaction. The branch returns to the main flowline. Why? Why not use the Return branch you have seen used in other perpetual buttons?

6. To answer the question of why use the Exit Interaction branch for the Main Menu response attached to the Interaction icon *Perpetuals*, let's run the program. As you run the program, examine figure 16- 3.

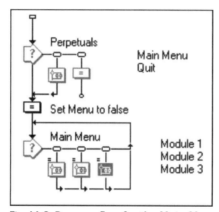

Fig. 16-3. Program flow for the Main Menu button.

a) Click on the Restart button. You are now on the Main menu. Click on the Module 1 button. You are now on the Module 1 menu. Note that there is a Main Menu button present on this screen. Click on the Topic A button. Note that there is a Main Menu button present on this screen. Click on the Forward button until you get to page 3. Note that there is a Main Menu button present on all topic-page screens.

b) Click on the Main Menu button. You should now be looking at the Main menu. Note that there is no Main Menu button present on this screen. It does not make sense to have a Main Menu button on the Main menu.

7. Let's consider the branching and program flow associated with the selections you have just made. Refer to figure 16-3. The Main Menu button was visible and active on every screen except the Main menu itself. From deep

inside the nested structure (page 3 in Topic A, Module 1), you clicked on the Main Menu button. Authorware's program flow jumped from page 3 up to the Perpetual button response *Main Menu*, where it then entered the empty Map icon *Main Menu*. With a branch of *Exit Interaction*, the program flow then exited to the main flowline, where it moved down the flowline and encountered the Interaction icon *Main Menu*. This is exactly what you wanted to do. If you had used a Return branch in the response for the Main Menu button, Authorware's program flow would have returned to page 3, which was not what you wanted.

8. But how do you remove the presence of the Main Menu button from the Main menu? Let's take a look.

a) Going up to the Interaction icon *Perpetuals*, double click on the Response Type symbol for the *Main Menu* response. Click on the Response tab. Note the entry in the Active If field. There is a variable expression, *InsideModule = TRUE*. This variable is what is used to turn off the Main Menu button. The expression states that the Main Menu button will be active if the variable *InsideModule* is true.

b) Click on the Button tab. Look at the bottom of the tab. Because there is a check mark in the Hide When Inactive field, the Main Menu button will be completely removed from the screen when the variable *InsideModule* is false. Close the Response dialog window.

c) Double click on the Calculation icon *Set Menu to False* at the very top of the flowline. Here is the custom variable *InsideModule := FALSE* again, which starts the file by setting the variable to a false condition. With a false condition, when Authorware first encounters the Main Menu perpetual button, it will be inactive and will not appear on screen. The Main menu remains inactive as Authorware encounters the Main menu for the first time. In other words, the Main Menu button will not appear on the Main menu screen. Close the Calculation icon.

d) After the user has selected a module (any module), the Main Menu button suddenly appears on screen from that point onward, as long as Authorware stays within the *Module* map icon. How was the button turned on?

e) Note each of the Map icons has a Calculation icon attached to it. Let's take a look inside one of these Calculation icons.

f) Select the Map icon *Module 1*. Select Modify | Icon | Calculation. You should now see the expression *InsideModule := TRUE*. Here is where you reassign the value of the custom variable and allow the Main Menu button to become active and appear on screen. The Main Menu button remains on screen as long as Authorware is within the Map icon *Module 1*. If the user clicks on the Main Menu button,

Authorware jumps up to the perpetual *Main Menu* response, and then exits to the main flowline and moves down to the Interaction icon *Main Menu*.

g) Note that the Interaction icon *Main Menu* also has a Calculation icon attached to it. Select the Interaction icon *Main Menu*. Select Modify | Icon | Calculation. You should now see the expression *InsideModule := FALSE*. This is where the Main Menu button is once again turned off as Authorware enters the Main menu again.

9. Take your time and look at any aspect of this structure or elements within the file.

Guided Tour 16B: Main Menu Router File Branching to Self-contained Module Files

In this second guided tour, what you will see on screen as a user will be no different than what you saw in the first guided tour. In fact, the third guided tour will also appear to the user as identical to the first guided tour. The difference is obviously not what is seen on screen but in how the content is structured "behind the scenes." The following examines the structure as the user sees it.

1. Select File | Open and locate on the companion CD-ROM the directory named *Chapter16*. Within this directory, locate and double click on the file named *Main-16B*.

2. The file should now appear in your copy of Authorware.

3. Click on the Restart button to play the file from the top of the flowline.

4. The first thing you encounter is the Main menu. Look at the text on screen and the navigational and module buttons.

5. Click on the Module 1 button.

6. Click on the Topic A button.

7. Make whatever other selections you want, such as going through the topic, returning to the Module 1 menu, or returning to the Main menu.

8. Everything on screen looks identical to what you saw in the first guided tour, except for one small difference. You might have noticed something right after you selected the Module 1 button. You may have seen the first file close as Authorware "jumped" to and opened a second file. However, you only see this close/open file process while in Authoring mode. Once the files have been packaged (you will learn more about this in Chapter 22), the user will not see this effect on screen as Authorware performs a *JumpFile* function. That is, the *JumpFile* function is totally transparent to the user.

9. Click on the Main Menu button.

The following examines the structure in Authoring mode.

1. Jump to the flowline. You should be in the file *Main-16B*.

2. Whoa. This does look different from what you saw in the first guided tour. The Interaction icon *Perpetuals* is missing, as are the Calculation icons on the main flowline. In addition, instead of Map icons attached to the Interaction icon there are Calculation icons.

3. Let's start with the Interaction icon.

   a) Double click on the Interaction icon *Main Menu*. This looks the same as what you saw in the first guided tour. Look around at whatever you want to here and then close the icon.

   b) Note that the Quit button is now directly attached to the Interaction icon *Main Menu*. It contains the same variable expression, *Quit (1)*, you saw in the first guided tour.

   c) Double click on the Calculation icon *Module 1*. The expression within this icon, which you have not seen before, is *JumpFile("Mod1-16B")*. This function will cause Authorware to "jump" from the current file to a file named *Mod1-16B*. Notice that the file name must be surrounded by double quotation marks, as do all alphanumeric strings.

   d) Click on the Functions Window button. Select the category Jump. Single click on the function *JumpFile*. Take a quick look at the Description field. There is a lot of information there. In a nutshell, the function *JumpFile* allows us to "jump" (branch) from one Authorware file to another. This is a one-way trip. Note that you can also pass the values of variables from one file to another as the jump is made. The function works with either unpackaged or packaged files.

   e) Single click on *JumpFileReturn*. This function also allows a jump from one Authorware file to another, but in this case it includes an automatic "round-trip." After Authorware has jumped from the first file to the second and the user is finished with the second file, selecting a Quit in the second file will automatically return Authorware (and the user) to the first file. In fact, Authorware returns to the very next location on the flowline from where the jump originated.

   f) Single click on *JumpOut*. This function allows a jump from an Authorware file to any other executable file (.exe) in the Windows environment. For example, this means you could jump from an Authorware file providing instruction on how to use Microsoft Word to the actual Microsoft Word program and automatically load a Word document as Word opens.

g) Single click on *JumpOutReturn*. This function provides an automatic round-trip, jumping from an Authorware file to any Windows-executable file. When the user quits the Windows-executable file, the user automatically returns to the original Authorware file. This function and the previous (*JumpOut*) can be especially useful functions in training applications.

h) Close the current Calculation icon.

i) Open the Calculation icon *Module 2*. You can see that this function will cause Authorware to jump to a file named *Mod2-16B*. Close the icon.

j) Open the Calculation icon *Module 3*. You can see that this function will cause Authorware to jump to a file named *Mod3-16B*. Close the icon.

4. You can clearly see at this point that the current file contains no content. It is simply the Main Menu screen and serves to route Authorware to whatever subsequent file is appropriate given the selection the user makes. Authorware developers refer to this type of file as a "router."

5. Click on the Restart button.

6. Click on the Module 1 button. You should now be looking at the Module 1 menu.

7. Jump to the flowline. You can see that you are now looking at a different file, *Mod1-16B*.

You can see that this file structure looks very similar to the one in the first guided tour. The main difference is that in the first guided tour the Authorware file contained a nested structure that was three levels deep: the Main menu, Module menu, and Topic Frameworks.

In this file the nested structure is two levels deep: Module menu and Topic Frameworks. The Main Menu is a separate file which is accessed with the use of a Main Menu button attached to the first Interaction icon *Perpetuals*. The Main Menu button consists of a Calculation icon that contains the *JumpFile* function.

Perhaps the largest advantage this file structure offers over the single-file structure is when several to many users might be accessing your Authorware course (project) at the same time. This structure removes all content from the first file, *Main Menu*. As you will learn about in much more detail in Chapter 22, you can package this first file with Authorware's "run" file, which creates the file in an executable file format (*.exe*). This executable file can then be distributed to each user's computer.

As each user accesses the program, he is using a copy of the executable Main menu. Given that the correct path names have been entered as part of the *JumpFile* function, each user can then access the module files located on a server. This technique can significantly increase "write-to-screen" performance of courseware being delivered over a network with multiple users.

A second very significant advantage of this second file structure is that you have distributed the content across multiple files (*Mod1-16B*, *Mod2-16B*, and *Mod3-16B*) instead of having everything in one file. In this case, it means you have reduced the maximum file size by about 66%, by distributing the content across the three Authorware files. The *Mod2-16B* and *Mod3-16B* files are identical in structure to the *Mod1-16B* file you are currently looking at.

In summary, the first guided tour showed a file structure in which everything is in one file. This second tour has shown you a file structure in which the content is distributed across three files, with *Main Menu* split out separately as a fourth file.

Guided Tour 16C: Multiple Authorware Menu Router Files Branching to Self-contained Topic Files

In this third guided tour, again what you will see on screen as a user is no different than what you saw in the first two guided tours. With this file structure, you have distributed all content to topic files, with both the Main menu and all module menus serving as routers. The following examines this structure as the user sees it.

1.   Select File | Open and locate on the companion CD-ROM the directory named *Chapter16*. Within this directory locate and double click on the file named *Main-16C*.

2.   The file *Main-16C* should now appear in your copy of Authorware.

3.   Click on the Restart button to play the file from the top of the flowline.

4.   The first thing you encounter is the Main menu. Look at the text on screen and the navigational and module buttons.

5.   Click on the Module 1 button.

6.   Click on the Topic A button.

7.   Make whatever other selections you want, such as going through the topic, returning to the Module 1 menu, or returning to the Main menu to select the Module 2 or Module 3 menu.

8.   Everything on screen looks identical to what you saw in the second guided tour.

9.   Click on the Main Menu button.

The following examines the structure in Authoring mode.

1. Jump to the flowline (Ctrl + P). You should be in the file *Main-16C*.

2. This Main menu router looks (and is) completely identical to the Main menu router in the second guided tour.

3. Click on the Restart button.

4. Select the Module 1 button. You should now be looking at the Module 1 menu.

5. Jump to the flowline (Ctrl + P). You should be in the file *Mod1Menu*.

6. This Module menu router looks (and is) completely identical to the Main menu router you just looked at. The only difference is that the *JumpFile* functions now jump to the topic files *Mod1TopA*, *Mod1TopB*, *Mod1TopC*, and *Mod1TopD*.

7. Click on the Restart button.

8. Select the Topic A button. You should now be looking at Page 1 in the Topic A of module 1.

9. Jump to the flowline (Ctrl + P). You should be in the file *Mod1TopA*.

10. You are now looking at the same Framework structure you built in Chapter 15. This structure was previously used for each of the topic structures in the first two guided tours, with some minor additions.

    a) Note that the Interaction icon *Perpetuals* now has both a Main Menu button and a Module Menu button. Both of these buttons contain Calculation icons in which the *JumpFile* function returns the user to the Main menu file or a particular Module menu file. Because you just came from Module 1, the *JumpFile* function will be for the *Module 1* file.

    b) Take a look at the expressions inside both of these Calculation icons.

This file structure repeats some of the advantages offered by the second file structure, and adds a couple more. The following are advantages of this distributed file structure:

- *Increased performance with network delivery with multiple and simultaneous users. This is achieved by providing each user with a copy of the Authorware executable file that is the main menu router file.*

- *Significantly reduces the size of any one Authorware file by distributing content over many topic files.*

- *Significantly increases the efficiency in reusing the entire topic with content or reusing the topic structure itself.*

The following is a disadvantage of this distributed file structure:

- *There are more files to keep track of. Unintentionally leaving out a file from your distributed product will be extremely noticeable and potentially disastrous.*

The *Mod2Menu* and *Mod3Menu* files, with their associated topic files, are identical in structure to what you have just looked at.

13. In summary, the first guided tour showed a file structure in which everything was in one file. The second tour has shown you a file structure in which the content is distributed across three content files, with the Main menu split out separately as a fourth file. The third file structure contains four menu routers (*Main-16C*, *Mod1Menu*, *Mod2Menu*, and *Mod3Menu*) and 12 content topic files (*Mod1TopA*, *Mod1TopB*, *Mod1TopC*, *Mod1TopD*, *Mod2TopA*, *Mod2TopB*, *Mod2TopC*, *Mod2TopD*, *Mod3TopA*, *Mod3TopB*, *Mod3TopC*, and *Mod3TopD*).

Practice Exercise 16-1: Building a Master Framework Structure

Description

Master Frameworks have evolved via use in the Authorware community into numerous applications. If you were to examine many developers' flowlines, however, you would see the same basic arrangement of icons over and over. This structure is typically a couple of introduction screens, some initialization Calculation icons, and then a single framework structure with Map icons attached as each page. Inside each Map icon there can be interactions, and media and other paging frameworks, but the result is the same: a single Framework holds everything together. Figure 16-4 shows an example of a Master Framework structure.

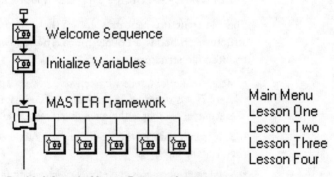

Fig. 16-4. Sample Master Framework structure.

In this exercise you will build a Master Framework structure that presents a common graphical user interface (GUI) to the end user with a Main menu that allows the user to view any one of four lessons. Each of the lessons will be a

Framework paging structure, but of course you could make each lesson anything you wanted it to be. The structure will also have some global features, such as buttons that launch a glossary, a quit, and a chance to have the end user exit the program. In this exercise you will:

- *Create a Master Framework structure*
- *Use Framework paging models for lesson structures*
- *Create placeholders for global features such as glossaries*
- *Import a custom button that graphically matches the GUI*
- *Build a Main menu that will launch each lesson*
- *Build a button that will return the user to the Main menu at any point in the training*

Take a Look

Before beginning the exercise, let's take a look at the Authorware file you are going to package.

CD-ROM

1. On the companion CD-ROM, locate the *Practice* folder. Open this folder and you will see a number of chapter folders.

2. Copy the *Chapter16* folder to your working directory and locate the file named *Exer16-1 – Master Framework.a6p*.

3. Double click on *Exer16-1 – Master Framework.a6p*. This file should now appear in your copy of Authorware.

4. Press the Restart button on the toolbar to play the file from the top of the flowline. Note the following properties of the completed exercise.

   - *The first screen you see is a Main menu with four lessons from which the user can choose.*
   - *Each item in the Main menu has a rollover that can describe the content of the lesson.*
   - *Lessons contain Next and Previous buttons that allow the user to page through the lesson.*
   - *There are page numbers at the lesson level.*
   - *There are three buttons that are always available on the left side of the GUI.*
   - *The global button for the Main menu returns the user to the Main menu from any lesson.*
   - *The global button for Quit presents a dialog box in which the user chooses whether or not to exit the program.*
   - *The Quiz button is a placeholder for a quiz you could create in another lesson.*

- *You can place a Start flag at any level of the flowline and always see all of the global buttons and GUI.*

Storyboard: On Screen

Figure 16-5 shows what the finished presentation will look like.

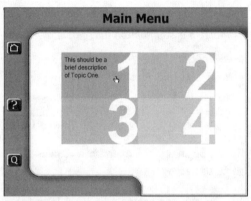

Fig. 16-5. Completed presentation on screen.

Storyboard: Behind the Scenes

Figure 16-6 shows the main flowline (with all icons, their placement, and their names) as it should look when you are finished with this exercise.

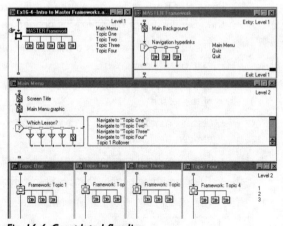

Fig. 16-6. Completed flowline.

Step-by-Step Instructions

Go Solo

1. Start a new Authorware file.
   a) Select File | New | File (Ctrl + N)
   b) Save the new file as *Exer16 – Master Framework.a6p*.

2. Set up the Master Framework.
   a) Drag a Framework icon to the flowline and label it *Master Framework*.
   b) Double click on the *Master Framework* icon.
   c) Select all of the icons inside the *Master Framework* icon and delete them.
   d) The Confirmation dialog box (see figure 16-7) appears, containing the message *Interaction, Decision, Framework, Digital Movie, and Sound icons cannot be deleted unless all of their attached icons are selected.* Click on the Select All Attached Icons button.
   e) Import the GUI interface. With the insertion finger pointing inside of the Entry pane of the Framework, import (Ctrl + Shirt + R) the *Main_Interface.gif* graphic from the *lesson 16* graphics folder.

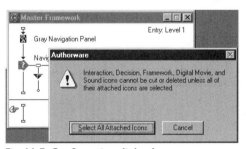

Fig. 16-7. Confirmation dialog box.

Once the display icon for the GUI is in place, you can prevent accidentally moving it while you are authoring by doing the following two things. First, right mouse click on the Display icon and enter the following expression: *Movable := FALSE.* This will prevent the object from moving while you are running the piece unpublished. Once a piece is published, all objects not purposely set to Movable will not be movable by the end user.

The second thing you can do is to set the X-Y positioning of a graphic so that even if you do accidentally move it while the program is paused the graphic will return to its original position the next time you run the file. Just open the Property dialog box for the Display icon and on the Layout tab select On Screen from the Positioning drop-down list. This sets the center of the X-Y screen position of the graphic. Note that no matter where you move the GUI when you run the program again, it displays in its initial position.

3. Set up the global navigation buttons.

   a) Drag an Interaction icon and place it beneath the *Main_Interface.gif* Display icon. Name it *Global Buttons*.

   b) Drag a Map icon to the right of the Interaction icon and select Button as the response type. Label it *Main Menu*.

   c) Open the Property Response dialog box for the button and change the cursor to the Hand. Click on OK.

   d) Drag two more Map icons to the right of the first one and label them *Quiz* and *Quit*.

   e) Run the piece and note that the buttons do not match the interface. In Practice Exercise 16-2 you will learn how to import custom buttons to Authorware.

The global buttons you have created are shown in figure 16-8.

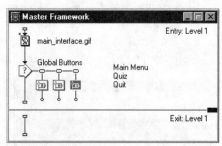

Fig. 16–8. Global buttons.

Practice Exercise 16-2: Importing Custom Buttons

In this exercise you will prepare the Master Framework buttons. These global buttons will be available to the learner at all times throughout the CBT. You will be building a custom button for returning to the Main menu, a link to a potential quiz, and a Quit button.

1. Double click on the Response Type symbol for the Main Menu button. The Property dialog box appears. See figure 16-9.

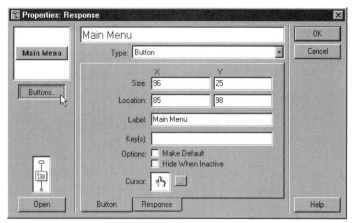

Fig. 16-9. Property dialog box for the Button response type.

2. Inside the Property dialog box, click on the Buttons button to open Authorware's Button library, shown in figure 16-10.

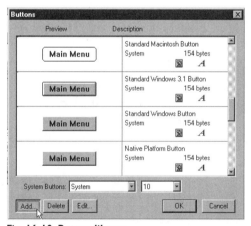

Fig. 16-10. Button library.

3. Click on the Add button to display the Button editor, shown in figure 16-11.

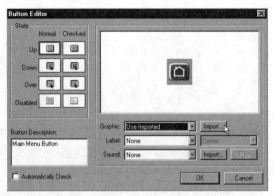

Fig. 16-11. Button editor.

4. Import the states for the Main Menu button.

    a) In the upper left-hand part of the Button editor, select the *UP* state by single clicking on it.

    b) In the Button editor, click on the Import button next to the Graphic setting.

    c) Select the graphic file *Main_Menu_up* from the *CBT Class Files/Graphics/Buttons* folder from the Import dialog box.

    d) Click on Import.

    e) Repeat the import process for all four states of the button.

5. Add a *Roll Over* label to the button. This will ensure that when the user's mouse is on top of the button a pop-up will show the button's label (see figure 16-12). This way, the user does not have to memorize what all of the iconic buttons represent.

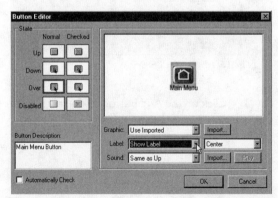

Fig. 16-12. The Over state of the button shows its label.

    a) On the *Over* state, select Show Label to show the button's label. When the user's mouse is over the button, the text label will appear.

b) Select Center as the alignment setting for the label.

c) In the Preview window in the Button editor, single click on the label to select it. With the label selected, you can change the font, size, and color of the label's text.

d) Select Text | Font and select Arial Narrow in the menu.

e) Select Text | Size and select 10 as the point size in the menu.

f) Select Text | Menu and select Anti-Aliased in the menu.

g) Select Windows | Inspectors | Colors (Ctrl + K) and select White as the text color in the menu. (White text looks good on the colored background of the GUI.) You will no longer be able to see the white label inside the Button editor because it is on a white background. However, as displayed on the interface this is very effective.

h) Click on OK to close the Button editor, and then click on OK again to close the Buttons dialog box.

6. Repeat the process for the other two buttons, Quiz and Quit.

7. Run the program and position your buttons on the left-hand side of the CBT interface.

·T/P·

You can use the Alignment tool (shown in figure 16-13) via Modify | Align (Ctrl + Alt + K) to line the buttons up in a straight line. Hold down the Shift key while selecting all three buttons. Then use the Alignment tool to align the buttons vertically.

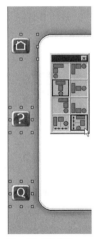

Fig. 16-13. Alignment tool.

Creating the Main Menu Page

In this section you will create the Main menu page, incorporating hot spots for navigating to the lessons, and rollover hot spots that display details of what is in each lesson.

Step-by-Step Instructions

1. Populate the Master Framework with topic Map icons. There is a prepared model for the lessons so that you do not have to recreate the paging model for each lesson.

   a) Access the folder *My Models* in the *Chapter 16* folder on the companion CD-ROM. In the *My Models* folder, access the Authorware model file *Paging Model.a6d* and place it on your hard drive inside the *Authorware 6\Knowledge Objects* directory. (To learn more about using and creating models, see Chapter 20.)

   b) In Authorware, open the Window | Knowledge Objects (Ctrl + Shift + K) window and click on the Refresh button.

   c) In the Category drop-down list you should see the category My Models (the name of the folder you added to the *Knowledge Objects* folder). Drag the *Paging* model to the right of your Master Framework.

   d) Change the title of each Map icon to reflect its topic. You can use generic titles such as *Topic One*, or you can be more descriptive. Whatever title you enter will be the title that appears on the screen.

2. Bring in the graphics for the Main menu. The populated Master Framework is shown in figure 16-14.

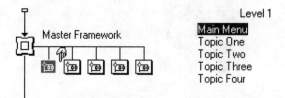

Fig. 16-14. Populated Master Framework.

   a) Attach a Map icon to the right of the Master Framework and label it *Main Menu*.

   b) Open the Map icon and drag a Display icon to its flowline.

   c) Title the Display icon *Menu Background*.

   d) Open the Display icon, and select File | Import (Ctrl + Shift + R).

   e) In the graphics folder, click on the plus sign (+) in the lower right-hand corner of the Import menu and then add the following graphics: *main_menu_button1 – 4.gifs*. Click on Import. By using the plus sign on the import dialog you are able to import more than one graphic at a time. See figure 16-15.

CD-ROM

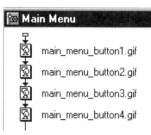

Fig. 16-15. Imported Main menu graphics.

    f)   Arrange the graphics on screen using the Alignment tool (Ctrl + Alt + K or Modify | Align) so that they are positioned in the middle of the screen.

    g)   Using the Text tool, type the title *Main Menu* across the top of the screen.

3.   Build the Interaction loop for the Main menu.

    a)   Jump to the flowline. Drag an Interaction icon and place it beneath the Main Background display. Name this Interaction icon *Which Topic?* Continue with the following steps to build the rollovers for the Main menu. These rollovers will give a brief description of the lesson to the user when the mouse is passed over a lesson number.

    b)   Drag a Display icon to the right of the Interaction icon. Select Hot Spot as the response type and label the icon *Topic 1 Rollover*.

    c)   Double click on the Response Type symbol.

    d)   On the Hot Spot tab, change the cursor to Hand and change the Match option to Cursor in Area.

    e)   On the Response tab, set Erase to Before Next Entry and then set Branching to Try Again.

    f)   Close the dialog box by clicking on OK.

    g)   Run the piece and then pause the program once the Main menu is visible.

    h)   Reposition the hot spot on top of the large numeral 1. Play the piece and fill in text that describes lesson 1 when the toolbox for that display icon appears.

    i)   Repeat steps *a* through *h* to add rollovers for topics 2, 3, and 4. See figure 16-16.

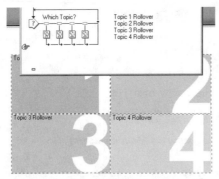

Fig. 16-16. *Hot spot rollovers positioned on top of graphics for the Main menu.*

4. Set up the hot spots that trigger the navigation to each topic.
   a) Drag a Navigate icon to the first position of the *Which Topic?* inter-action.
   b) Select Hot Spot as the response type.
   c) Open the Navigate icon and set it to navigate to *Topic One*. Note that the Navigate icon names itself *Navigate to "Topic One."* This is a great feature of the Navigate icon.
   d) Run the piece and then pause at the Main menu to reposition the hot spot on top of the graphic for Topic 1.
   e) Repeat the same steps for Topics 2, 3, and 4.

5. Fill in the rollover text and confirm that you are navigating to the correct topic.
   a) Run the program to check your work.
   b) When you place your cursor on top of any of the menu numbers, Authorware should pause the program and present you with a tool-box because of the blank display icon it encounters for the rollover. Using the Text tool, fill in some sample text for each possible rollover, as shown in figure 16-17.

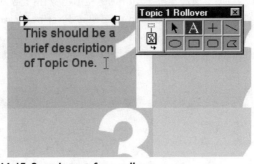

Fig. 16-17. *Sample text for a rollover.*

c) Continue playing the program until all of the text is filled in. Also confirm that when you click on a topic number you are in fact navigated to that topic.

6. Set up the Return to Main Menu button (see figure 16-18). Once a user has navigated to a topic, there is currently no way to return to the Main menu. In this step you will activate the global Main Menu button so that the user can return to the Main menu at any time.

   a) Open the *Master Framework* icon.
   b) Open the global button Map icon labeled *Main Menu*.
   c) Drag a Navigate icon and place it inside the Map icon. Open the Navigate icon.
   d) Set the Navigate icon to jump to the Framework *Master Framework* page *Main Menu*.

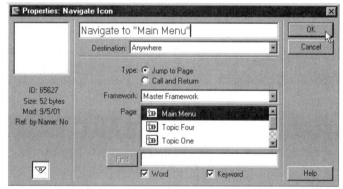

Fig. 16-18. Navigate icon Property dialog box containing the Return to Main Menu button.

You can see from the flowline that every time the user activates the global button Main Menu the Navigate icon will return the user to the first page of the Master Framework.

Creating a Quit Feature

The global buttons displayed on the GUI background are intended as examples of the functionality you can incorporate in your own piece. The Quit feature is one of those components typical of all programs. In this section you will create a simple dialog box that appears when the user clicks on the Quit button. This dialog box will ask the user for confirmation of exiting the Authorware file. You will use the Quit function to supply the functionality that when the Quit button is clicked on the program is exited.

1. Open the Master Framework and then open the *Quit* Map icon.

2. Build the dialog box.
   a) Drag an Interaction icon and place it inside the *Quit Map* icon. Name this icon *Are you sure?* See figure 16-19.

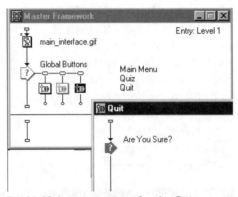

Fig. 16-19. Interaction icon for the Quit sequence.

   b) Double click on the Interaction icon and import the background graphic for the dialog box from the *Graphics* folder on the companion CD-ROM.
   c) Once the background is imported, use the Text tool to label the box *Quit* and to supply the user prompt *Are you sure you want to exit the program at this time?* See figure 16-20.

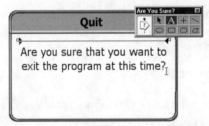

Fig. 16-20. On-screen text for the Quit interaction.

   d) Position the text on the Presentation window and then jump to the flowline.

3. Set up the buttons for the Quit sequence.
   a) Drag a Map icon to the right of the Interaction icon and set the response type to Button.
   b) Drag a second Map icon to the right of the first.
   c) Label the two Map icons *Yes* and *No*, respectively.

4. Create the *Quit* action when the user presses the Yes button. When the user clicks on the Yes button, you want Authorware to shut down. To do this you will use the system function *Quit*.

a) Open the *Yes* Map icon. Drag a Calculation icon and place it inside this Map icon. Label the Calculation icon *Quit*.

b) Open the Calculation icon and either paste from the Functions window or type the following command: *Quit(0)*.

```
Quit(0)
```

c) Save. Restart the program and test the Quit button. Note that when you click on the Yes button that Authorware does not close down, but rather the Presentation window closes. This is a feature of unpackaged Authorware files. Instead of exiting Authorware, the Presentation window is closed when in the unpublished state so that you are aware that the functionality is working. Once you have published your piece, the Authorware file will terminate.

5. Make the No button work properly. While you are testing the *Quit* routine, note that nothing happens when you select the No button. What you want is for the dialog box to disappear and the user returned to her place in the program before she clicks on the Quit button. You will not have to add any icons to the flowline to achieve this.

a) Double click on the Response Type symbol for the No button.

b) On the Response tab, change the Branch setting to Exit Interaction.

c) Close the dialog box by clicking on OK.

d) Test the piece again. Note now that when you click on the No button the Quit dialog box closes, in which case the user continues running the program from the same point as before she clicked on the Quit button. This is pure flowline logic. See figure 16-21.

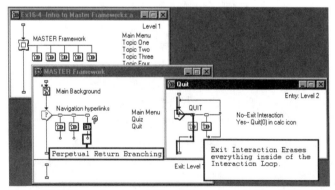

***Fig. 16-21.** Taking advantage of branching options to make the Quit dialog box erase automatically.*

If you look at the flowline you will see that by changing the No button's branching to Exit Interaction you are exiting the interaction loop. When you exit the loop, all of the graphics contained in that loop are automatically erased. Then the magic happens. Authorware flows out the bottom of the *Quit* map icon and then encounters the Branch option Perpetual Return. This is indicated by the small loop you see below the Quit map. This branch option literally makes a round-trip, returning to where Authorware's focus was before it jumped to the *Quit* routine. This type of branching is used primarily within Framework icons. The following are debugging tips.

- **Check icon settings.** *Check the settings used for the icons involved in a section of the piece that may not be working properly. An icon may be set differently from how you intended, and changing one setting can sometimes resolve a problem.*

- **Use the Start and Stop flags.** *When you can locate the section where the problem is occurring, use the Start and Stop flags to identify that section. Keep moving the flags until you isolate the section.*

- **Recreate the section.** *In a new file, recreate the sequence of icons contained in a section that has problems. If your new version does not work properly, the logic could be incorrect. If the new version works, compare it to the original to see how they differ. You may want to copy the section into the original piece and see if that fixes the problem.*

- **Make one change at a time.** *When you make changes to fix a problem, make one change and see if it solves the problem. Then change it back and try a different approach. Otherwise, it will be difficult to identify which change solved the problem.*

Summary

In this chapter you learned how to:

- *Create a single-file organizational structure using the Interaction icon as its foundation*

- *Create a two-level file organizational structure using the Interaction icon as its foundation*

- *Create a three-level file organizational structure using the Interaction icon as its foundation*

- *Create a Master Framework structure*

- *Create global buttons and functionality*

- *Import custom buttons with rollover labels*

- *Incorporate existing paging models to expedite authoring*

- *Create a Main menu structure that will allow users to navigate to different topics*

- *Create a Return to Main Menu button*

- *Create a Quit routine that will confirm whether or not the user wants to exit a program*

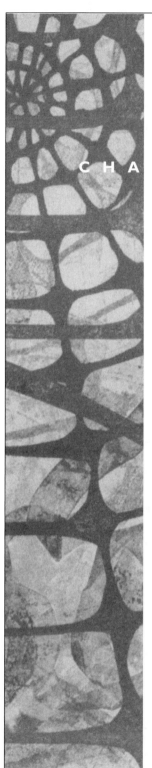

CHAPTER

17

Application:
Basic-level
Menu/Topic
Structures

Introduction

In this chapter you will create the organizational and navigational structures for the overall application project. You will first create the graphical user interface (GUI) and Main menu structure. This will include visual bookmarks on the Main menu to indicate which topics have been selected. You will then create topic-level structures and will go back to the earlier application chapters to gather the content you created in those. Everything you build within this chapter results in a course and topic-level structure that meet the needs of most CBT applications. This represents a basic-level interface and navigational controls. In Chapter 27 you will replace some of this structure with a more sophisticated, dynamic structure that offers easier maintenance and updating.

Application Exercise 17A: Interface and Main Menu Framework

Description

In this exercise you will create a GUI, Main menu framework, and global navigational controls with "smarts." The Main menu will include visual status markers to indicate which topics have been selected. You will also add a Flash movie at the beginning of the file.

Storyboard: On Screen

Figure 17-1 shows what the exercise will look like on screen when completed.

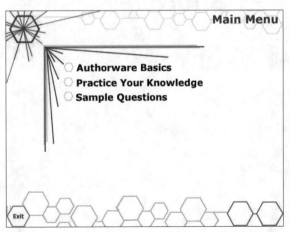

Fig. 17-1. Completed exercise on screen.

Storyboard: Behind the Scenes

Figure 17-2 shows the main and second-level flowlines (with all icons, their placement, and their names) as they should look when you are finished with this exercise.

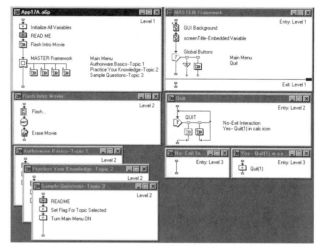

Fig. 17-2. Main and second-level flowlines.

Step-by-Step Instructions

Use the following generalized steps to complete this exercise on your own. Consult the completed exercise (*Exer17A.a6p*) on the companion CD-ROM for further guidance.

1. Open the file *Exer17A.a6p* located on the companion CD-ROM in the directory named *Chapter17*. Open the library file *Graphics.a6l* located in the same directory. Run the program and see how it works. Jump to the flowline and examine the various icons and structures.

2. Open the Calculation icons labeled READ ME and read their content.

3. Leave this file open in this copy of Authorware.

4. Open another copy of Authorware, opening the file (*App17A.a6p*) you completed in the previous exercise, located in the SaveWork directory of your computer's hard drive. Or you can first copy *Exer17A.a6p* (located on the companion CD-ROM, in the *Chapter17* directory) into the *SaveWork* directory on your computer and then open this file. Save the file as *App17A*. Open the library file *Graphics.a6l* located in the *SaveWork* directory of your hard drive.

5. When finished, make sure to save your exercise in the *SaveWork* directory on your computer's hard drive.

Application Exercise 17B:
Topic Structures with "Smart" Navigation

Description

In this exercise you will create three topic structures for the content you created in chapters 8 and 14: Authorware 6 features, interactive learning strategies, and interactions. Each topic structure will include topic-level navigational controls with "smarts." You will also add a Replay button so that the content (text, narration, and animation) of each "page" can be replayed.

Storyboard: On Screen

Figure 17-3 shows what the exercise will look like on screen when completed.

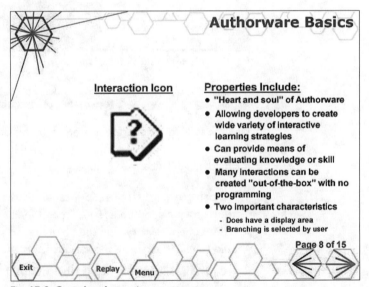

Fig. 17-3. Completed exercise on screen.

Storyboard: Behind the Scenes

Figure 17-4 shows the main and second-level flowlines (with all icons, their placement, and their names) as they should look when you are finished with this exercise.

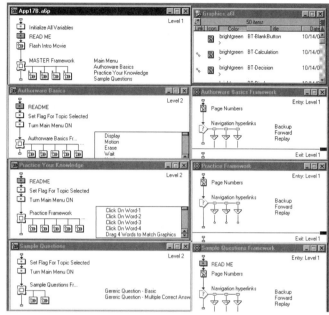

Fig. 17-4. Main and second-level flowlines.

Step-by-Step Instructions

Use the following generalized steps to complete this exercise on your own. Consult the completed exercise (*Exer17B.a6p*) on the companion CD-ROM for further guidance.

1. Open the file *Exer17B.a6p* located on the companion CD-ROM in the directory named *Chapter17*. Open the library file *Graphics.a6l* located in the same directory. Run the program and see how it works. Jump to the flowline and examine the various icons and structures.

2. Open the Calculation icons labeled READ ME and read their content.

3. Leave this file open in this copy of Authorware.

4. Open another copy of Authorware, opening the file (*App17A.a6p*) you completed in the previous exercise, located in the *SaveWork* directory of your computer's hard drive. Or you can first copy *Exer17A.a6p* (located on the companion CD-ROM, in the Chapter17 directory) into the *SaveWork* directory on your computer and then open this file. Save the file as *App17B*. Open the library file *Graphics.a6l* located in the *SaveWork* directory of your hard drive.

5. When finished, make sure to save your exercise in the *SaveWork* directory on your computer's hard drive.

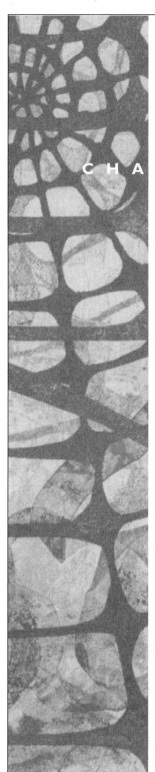

CHAPTER 18

Creating a Basic User Sign-on Application

Introduction

Most interactive training projects have three components: content presentation, testing, and tracking of student progress. In this chapter you will explore methods of tracking a student's progress through a course. Log-ins can be very simple or very complex. They can be very inexpensive to implement or they can be corporate-level integrations that cost millions of dollars, but the philosophy of a log-in is always the same: ask users to identify themselves, store that information, and be able to recall it on the user's subsequent visits.

The first thing you need to do is capture the student's ID information. You will accomplish this by creating a log-in that will store the user's name, job title, and a password. Once you have this basic information about who is taking the training, you can then track all sorts of information about the student, such as time in course, quiz scores, and completed lessons. The possibilities are limitless.

From an Authorware perspective, log-ins can be programmed with a few interactions or with very complex scripting solutions. Regardless of the level of complexity, the fundamental authoring practices are always the same: you need the user to enter information about themselves, you need to store that information, and you need to be able to recall that information. You will accomplish this by first using the Interaction icon to prompt the user's entry. Then you will store the entry to a variable so that it is not overwritten. Finally, you will store the variable to a text file so that it is stored for later recall. This is what you will concentrate on in this chapter: the fundamental principles associated with almost any log-in flowline. By the end of this chapter, you will be able to:

- *Set up a Text Entry interaction that can accept any user input*
- *Store the user's text entry as a variable*
- *Display the content of a variable so that the user can view the data*
- *Create string variables that can be added to an external text file*
- *Create external text files*
- *Read information into Authorware from an external text file*
- *Parse information read in from a text file*
- *Use a Decision icon to judge if a user has already logged in or not*
- *Create a masked password*
- *Verify that a user is entering the correct password*

Practice Exercise 18-1: Creating a Structure for Capturing User Information

Description

In this exercise you are going to build a text entry interaction that will prompt the user to enter her name. Once entered, the text the user has entered will be saved in the system variable *UserName*. Then you will use the Authorware system function *Capitalize()* to make sure the first letter of each name is uppercase. Once you have reformatted the text, a Display icon will display the user's name on screen and the user will then be prompted to enter her job title. The same procedures will be used to get the job title, but instead of using a system variable to store the data you will create a custom variable. In this exercise, you will:

- *Create a text entry interaction that allows the user to enter his name*
- *Store the user's entry to a system variable*
- *Format the name so that the first letter of each word is capitalized*
- *Display the resulting variable on screen for the user to see*
- *Perform the same steps for the user's job title*

Take a Look

CD-ROM

Before beginning the exercise, let's take a look at the exercise in its completed state so that you can clearly see what it is you are about to build.

1. Select File | Open and locate the *Practice* folder on the companion CD-ROM. Open this folder and you will see a number of chapter folders. Open the *Chapter18* folder and locate and double click on the file named *Exer18-1*.

2. The *Exer18-1* file should now appear in your copy of Authorware. Select Control | Restart or press the Restart button (Ctrl + R) on the toolbar to play the file from the top of the flowline. Note the following properties of this completed exercise.

    - *When the user is prompted to enter his name, the label for the Name field is highlighted in darker letters. Once the name is entered, the label reverts to gray and the next field becomes highlighted.*

    - *If a name is entered in lowercase, once entered, the first letter of each word becomes capitalized.*

    - *When all information is entered, there is a welcome message that displays the user's name and job title in the text.*

    - *Once the Continue button is pressed, all elements on screen are erased.*

Storyboard: On Screen

Figure 18-1 shows what the finished question will look like on screen.

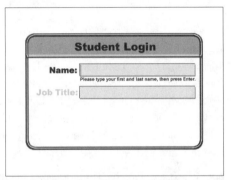

Fig. 18-1. Completed log-in interface.

Storyboard: Behind the Scenes

Figure 18-2 shows the flowline (with all icons, their placement, and their names) as it should look when you are finished with this exercise.

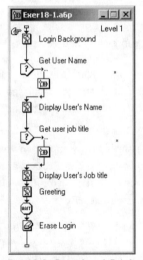

Fig. 18-2. Completed flowline.

Step-by-Step Instructions

Go Solo

1. Open a new file for this exercise.
   a) Select File | New | File.
   b) Close the two Knowledge Object dialog windows that open by clicking on the X in the upper right-hand corner.
   c) Verify that you are now looking at a blank flowline.

2. Save the file on your hard drive.
   a) Select File | Save and use the Scroll window to locate the *SaveWork* directory.
   b) Type in the name *Chap18-Ex1* and click on OK.

3. Display the background graphic for the log-in.
   a) Drag a Display icon to the top of the flowline.
   b) Name this icon *Login Background*.
   c) Open the Display icon.
   d) Select File | Import.
   e) Browse on the companion CD-ROM to the *Chapter18* folder and import the graphic called *LoginBkg.gif*.

4. Position the background graphic on the Presentation window and add text to the blank graphic.
   a) Align the background graphic in the center of the screen.
   b) Using the Text tool, type *Student Login* and position the text at the top of the log-in box.
   c) Create text to highlight the Name and Job Title fields, as shown in figure 18-3.

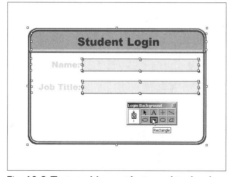

Fig. 18-3. Text and boxes that need to be drawn on the log-in background.

   d) Make sure the text is a light gray color and there is adequate room on the bottom of the box for error messages to be displayed.

5. Create the Text Entry interaction for capturing the user's name.
   a) Drag an Interaction icon to the flowline.
   b) Name this icon *Get User Name*.
   c) Press Shift and double click on the *Get User Name* Interaction icon to open it.
   d) In the Presentation window, enter the following text: *Please type your first and last name, then press Enter.*
   e) Type *Name:* in a dark color and place it on top of the light gray version of the label.

NOTE

This makes the Name field appear active to the user. Once the user presses the Enter key, the interaction is exited and the dark color of the text *Name:* will automatically be erased. The text *Job Title:* will then be displayed in a darker color. See figure 18-4.

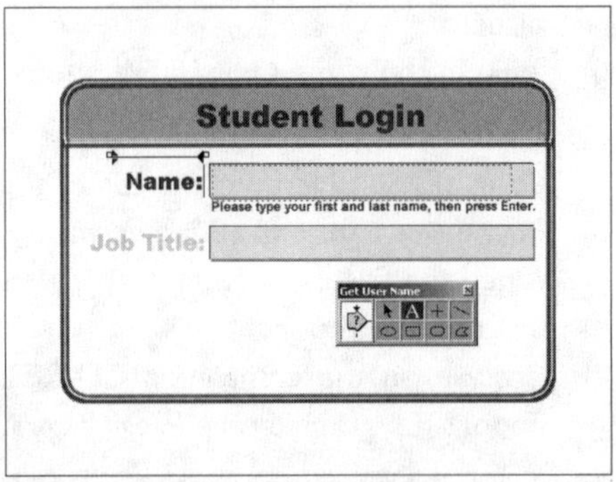

Fig. 18-4. Text created inside the Interaction icon Get User Name.

6. Set up the Text Entry response.
   a) Drag a Map icon to the right of the Interaction icon.
   b) Select Text Entry as the response type.
   c) Name the icon *.

NOTE

In a Text Entry interaction, the asterisk is a wildcard indicating that any text a user enters will be accepted. For this interaction, you do not want a particular response from the user. You simply want the user's name, and can therefore store it and then display it in a different part of the screen. See figure 18-5.

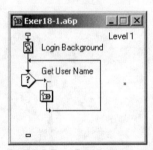

Fig. 18-5. Text Entry interaction set to match a wildcard pattern.

7. Set the response properties for the Text Entry response.
   a) Double click on the Response Type symbol to open the Response Properties dialog box.

NOTE

The purpose of this interaction is to capture the user's name. After that, you want Authorware to exit the interaction and move down the flowline to the next interaction you will build: getting the user's job title.

b)   On the Response tab, select Exit Interaction from the Branch menu.
c)   Click on OK to close the Property Response dialog box.

8.   You Assign the user's entry to a variable so that you can use it later. You will use the variable *UserName* to track the entry.
a)   Open the Map icon *.
b)   Drag a Calculation icon inside this Map icon.
c)   Name this Calculation icon *Store User's Name*.
d)   Open the Calculation icon.
e)   Open the Variables dialog box and from the Interaction category select the system variable *UserName*.
f)   Click on Paste.

UserName now appears in the Calculation dialog box. This system variable is designed to store the user's name, which can be assigned a value. Any acceptable text entered here will be assigned to *UserName*. Take a moment to read the description of the variable *UserName*. See figure 18-6.

NOTE

Note that this variable is based on another system variable called *EntryText*. The description of entry text says that *EntryText* "contains the text of the user's last response in the last interaction." This means that every time the user types information prompted by an Interaction icon the value of the system variable *EntryText* changes to reflect the new entry. You are storing the results of the user's entry to the variable *UserName* so that it is not overwritten by the next text entry.

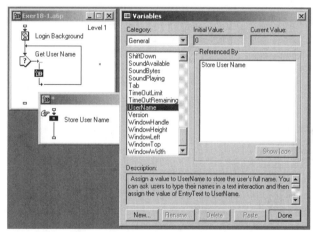

*Fig. 18-6. Variable window with **UserName** system variable displayed.*

g)   Return to the Calculation window.
h)   After the pasted variable *UserName*, type the assignment operator :=.
i)   Return to the Variables window and in the Interaction category locate the variable *EntryText*.
j)   Paste the variable *EntryText* after the assignment operator.
k)   The expression should now read *UserName := EntryText*.

This statement takes the text the user just entered and assigns or stores the text to the system variable *UserName*.

There is another way to accomplish this. Note in the description for the *EntryText* variable that it states, "Use *EntryText@"IconTitle"* to get the text of the user's response at a specific interaction." You could merely reference the user's name using *EntryText@"Get User Name"*.

Any variable with a @ symbol is referred to as an Icon variable. An Icon variable holds the value of a variable at a specific location on the flowline. At any point in the piece you can simply reference *EntryText@"interaction icon name"* and see the value that was entered at that interaction. You will not track the information with this method because you want to facilitate readability of the code. Instead, you will use some of the built-in features of the variable *UserName*; namely, the ability to automatically reference the user's first name only.

l)   Close the Variables dialog box.

9.   Format the user's entry so that each name (first and last) begins with a capital letter.

a)   Open the Functions dialog box.

b)   Locate the function *Capitalize()* and click on Paste.

c)   Read the description for the function *Capitalize()*.

d)   Replace the content within parentheses with the *EntryText* variable so that the expression reads:

```
UserName := Capitalize(EntryText)
```

e)   Close the Calculation window.

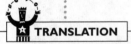

TRANSLATION

UserName:=Capitalize(EntryText)

This expression sets what the user just typed in *(EntryText)* as the name *(UserName)* by which you will track the user. The function *Capitalize* makes sure the first letter of every word in the name is capitalized. Use caution: The Capitalize function will not lowercase things before capitalizing the first letter. For example, if you were to enter a code string like:

resultString := Capitalize("some text tHat hAs fuNky caPS")

The variable *resultString* would end up looking like this: Some Text That Has FuNky CaPS. If you want to be sure that only the first letter is capitalized, first use the LowerCase function to set the entire string to lowercase letters and then apply the Capitalize function. For example:

resultString := Capitalize(Lowercase(EntryText))

But this can cause problems in last names like MacPherson with two capital letters. So use with caution.

See the descriptions for these Authorware variables and functions for more information.

10. Display the resulting user entry on screen. In this task, you will start to create the text in the Response icon that appears after users type their

names and press Enter. When you have completed the next three tasks, this text will include embedded variables. When users run the piece, they will not see the variable name. Instead, they will see the current value of that variable, which will be whatever text they typed in the Text Entry field in the interaction.

a) Add a Display icon under the *Get User Name* interaction.

b) Name this icon *Display User's Name*. See figure 18-7.

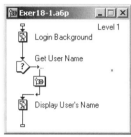

Fig. 18-7. Flowline showing interaction for Get User Name *and the new display icon* Display User's Name *at the bottom.*

c) Press Shift and double click on the *Display User's Name* Display icon to open it.

When you hold down the Shift key in opening the Display icon, you should see the text you created in the previous task, the Text Entry field, and the tool-box title reminding you that you are in the *Display User's Name* Display icon. If you do not, simply restart the piece and enter a user name. Authorware will pause automatically when it encounters the blank Display icon.

11. Embed the *UserName* variable in the icon, which will display the most recent text the user entered.

a) Open the Variables window.

b) Locate *UserName* in the Interaction category.

c) Click on Paste to paste *UserName* into the display. See figure 18-8.

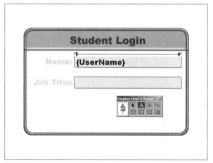

Fig. 18-8. Presentation window with the variable UserName *being pasted to the screen.*

Authorware pastes the variable name where the text cursor is placed. Note that *UserName* appears between curly brackets. Authorware provides curly brackets whenever you paste a variable into a display. When you enter a variable into a Display icon by typing it, remember to type the curly brackets.

    d)   Click on Done to close the Variables window.

    e)   Click on the Pointer tool in the toolbox.

The name of the variable and the curly brackets disappear. What you now see is the current value of the variable. In this case, there is no value because no text has been entered in the Text Entry field. To embed a variable in a Display icon, use the Text tool. The value of the variable is what you want users to see.

12. Test the interaction.

    a)   Run the piece and type in your name in lowercase characters.

    b)   Press Enter and note that your name displays in the capitalized format.

    c)   Pause the program and align the *Embedded Variable* text inside the text entry box as shown in figure 18-9.

    d)   You can change the font, style, and color of the entry text by clicking on the Text Field button in the Interaction Icon Properties dialog box and then clicking on the Text tab.

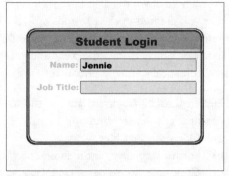

Fig. 18-9. Paused program with the user's name aligned in the Name area of the Login dialog box.

13. Perform a final test.

    a)   Save, and then restart the piece to be sure the alignment is correctly set up.

Now that you have the user's name, you will repeat the same process to get the user's job title. A good challenge for your own learning would be to try to create the Job Title interaction on your own. Consult the following steps if you need assistance.

You could also attempt to copy and paste the *Get User Name* interaction, but be very cautious when doing this. Make sure you change all references to the user's name and change the variable from *UserName* to the custom variable *Job_Title*. You will also have to reposition the Text Entry field and the embedded variable in the Display icon. With very careful attention to detail, copying and pasting can speed your authoring, but until you know all details to change, this strategy can sometimes slow you down.

14. Create the Text Entry interaction for capturing the user's job title.
    a) Drag an Interaction icon to the flowline.
    b) Name this icon *Get User Job Title*.
    c) Press Shift and double click on the *Get User Job Title* Interaction icon to open it.
    d) In the Presentation window, enter *Please type your job title, then press Enter.*
    e) Type *Job Title:* in a dark color and place it on top of the light gray version of the label.

This makes the Job Title field appear active to the user. Once the user presses the Enter key, the interaction is exited and the dark color of *Name:* will automatically be erased. The text *Job Title:* will then be displayed in a darker color. See figure 18-10.

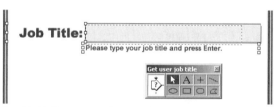

Fig. 18-10. Text created inside the Interaction icon **Get User Job Title.**

15. Set up the Text Entry response.
    a) Drag a Map icon to the right of the Interaction icon.
    b) Select Text Entry as the response type.
    c) Name the icon *.

In a Text Entry interaction, the asterisk is a wildcard indicating that any text a user enters will be accepted. For this interaction, you do not want a particular response from the user. You simply want the user's job title, and can therefore store it and then display it in a different part of the screen. See figure 18-11.

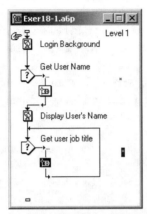

Fig. 18-11. Text Entry interaction set to match a wildcard pattern.

16. Set the response properties for the Text Entry response.

   a) Double click on the Response Type symbol to open the Response Properties dialog box.

   b) On the Response tab, select Exit Interaction from the Branch menu.

The purpose of this interaction is to capture the user's job title. After that, you want Authorware to exit the interaction and move down the flowline to the next interaction you will build: getting the user's job title.

   c) Click on OK to close the Response Properties dialog box.

17. Assign the user's entry to a variable so that you can use it later. There is no system variable for tracking a user's job title, so you must create a custom one.

   a) Open the Map icon .

   b) Drag a Calculation icon inside this Map icon.

   c) Name this icon *Store User's Job Title*.

   d) Open the Calculation icon.

   e) Type in the custom variable *jobTitle*.

   f) After the custom variable, type the assignment operator :=.

   g) Return to the Variables window and in the Interaction category locate the variable *EntryText*.

   h) Paste the variable *EntryText* after the assignment operator.

   i) The expression should now read:

```
jobTitle := EntryText
```

You have undoubtedly noticed that when you create a custom variable in Authorware it does not appear in the All category of the variable window. Instead, it is listed in a custom category that contains the name of your

·T/P·

To avoid opening the Response Properties dialog box to change the Branch option, merely hold down the Ctrl key and click on the branching arrow on the flowline. Notice when you do this that the arrow cycles through the three branching settings.

Authorware file. Sometimes when you are looking at code you may find it confusing to distinguish between custom variables and system variables. The frustrating experience of scrolling through the All category looking in vain for a variable (deciding that you are going crazy because you cannot find it, only to then remember that there is a separate category for custom variables) only happens a few times before you develop a method for distinguishing the custom and system variables. One way to avoid this confusion is to simply memorize the hundreds of system variables or, more feasibly, to establish a naming convention for all of your custom variables so that they are visually different from the system variable.

Note that all system variables have an uppercase first word and each subsequent word begins with an uppercase character, but there are no spaces within the variable name.

There are dozens of strategies for distinguishing custom variables. You could place your initials at the start of each variable. This is effective when working in a large development team in which many different developers may be creating variables. You can rename the variables once multideveloper code is brought together. Variable names can begin with a few letters to show functionality. For example, all variables having to do only with the functionality of the quiz could begin with the letters "qz," or navigation variables could use "nav." This practice will sort the variables together in the category list. The method you will use in this book is to make the first letter of the variable lowercase. This will provide for an instant visual cue that the variable is custom and will not compete with other variable naming standards.

18. Define the new custom variable.
    a) Save your Authorware file with the Calculation icon still open. This will trigger the New Variable window to open.
    b) Enter an initial value of empty quotes (" ") to distinguish this variable as a string variable that holds text.
    c) Enter a detailed description for your new custom variable *jobTitle*. Suggested description:
        This variable tracks what the user enters as a job title in the Login section of the program. This variable is based on the content of the system variable EntryText.
    d) Close the New Variable dialog box by clicking on OK.

19. Format the user's entry so that the job title is properly capitalized.
    a) Open the Functions dialog box.
    b) Locate the function *Capitalize()* and click on Paste.

c) Replace the content inside the parentheses with the *EntryText* variable so that the expression reads:

```
jobTitle := Capitalize(EntryText)
```

d) Close the Calculation window.

20. Display the resulting user entry on screen.
    a) Add a Display icon under the *Get User Job Title* interaction.
    b) Name this icon *Display User's Job Title*. See figure 18-12.

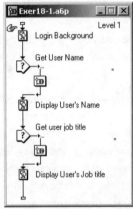

Fig. 18-12. Flowline showing interaction for Get User Job Title and the new display icon Display User's Job Title at the bottom.

c) Press Shift and double click on the *Display User's Job Title* Display icon to open it so that you can add content.

21. In the icon, you will embed the *jobTitle* variable, which will display the formatted job title the user just entered.
    a) Open the Variables window.
    b) Locate *jobTitle* in the category listed with the name of our Authorware file.
    c) Click on Paste to paste *jobTitle* into the display. See figure 18-13.

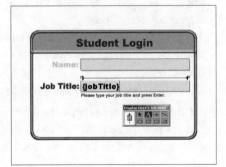

Fig. 18-13. Presentation window with the variable jobTitle being pasted to the screen.

    d)   Click on Done to close the Variables window.

    e)   Click on the Pointer tool in the toolbox.

22. Test the interaction.

    a)   Run the piece and type in your name in lowercase characters.

    b)   Press Enter and note that your name displays in the capitalized format.

    c)   Enter your job title.

    d)   Pause the program and align the *Embedded Variable* text inside the Text Entry box as shown in figure 18-14.

    e)   Change the font, style, and color of the entry text by clicking on the Text Field button in the Interaction Icon Properties dialog box and then clicking on the Text tab.

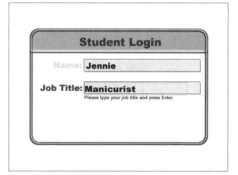

Fig. 18-14. Paused program with the user's job title aligned in the Job Title area of the Login dialog box.

23. Check the alignment.

    a)   Save. Then restart the piece to be sure the alignment is correctly set up. If there are any problems, pause the program and fix them.

24. Add a welcome statement after the user has successfully completed the log-in. Build the flowline for the welcome message.

    a)   At the very bottom of the flowline, drag a Display icon under the *Display User's Job Title* icon.

    b)   Name this icon *Greeting*.

    c)   Drag a Wait icon to the flowline.

    d)   Drag an Erase icon to the flowline and name it *Erase Login*. See figure 18-15.

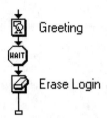

Greeting

Erase Login

Fig. 18-15. The Display, Wait, and Erase icons that constitute the welcome sequence.

25. Run the piece to populate the screen and variables.
    a) Restart the program from the top.
    b) Enter your name and press Enter.
    c) Enter your job title and press Enter.

26. Authorware automatically pauses the program when it encounters the blank display icon *Greeting*. Complete the settings for the welcome message.

Inside this display icon you want to welcome the user to the course by name. To use the system variable *UserName*, you would get the entire name (first and last name) on screen. This is very formal. You want to simply use the user's first name. This is where the advantage of using the system variable *UserName* comes in.

Read the description for the *UserName* variable. Note the first sentence of the second paragraph of the description: *When you assign a string to UserName, Authorware assigns either the first word or, if the string contains a comma, the first word after the comma to FirstName.* This is a wonderful feature. If the user entered the name *Jamil Zainasheff*, the system variable *UserName* would contain the value *Jamil Zainasheff*, and the system variable *FirstName* would contain *Jamil*. If the user had entered *Zainasheff, Jamil*, the *FirstName* variable would be "smart" enough to store the value *Jamil*.

   a) Using the Text tool, create the following text and embedded variables. See figure 18-16.

   ```
   Greetings, {FirstName}! Click on the Continue button
   and be on your way to becoming a better {jobTitle}.
   ```

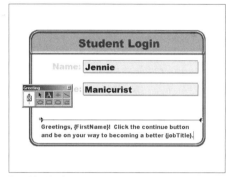

Fig. 18-16. **Greeting** *Display icon with text and embedded variables.*

    b) Play the program.

    c) When the Wait button appears on screen, you can pause the program and reposition it if necessary.

    d) Play the program again.

    e) When the Property dialog box for the Erase icon appears, click on all elements of the log-in to erase them.

    f) Click on OK to close the dialog box. See figure 18-17.

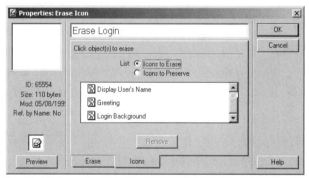

Fig. 18-17. **Property** *dialog box with all log-in elements selected.*

27. Save the exercise by selecting File | Save.

Practice Exercise 18-2: Storing User Information by Writing Data to Text Files

Description

External files can be very useful in tracking data within a piece. In the following exercises you will learn how to write to an external text file. In the following you will build an external text file that contains the course title, learner's name and job title (from the log-in), and the date and time the learner logs into the course. In this exercise you will:

- *Learn the arguments and uses of the WriteExtFile system function*
- *Create an external text file with data gathered from the learner*
- *Learn to create strings of data with variable and literal information combined*

Take a Look

CD-ROM

Before beginning the exercise, let's take a look at the exercise in its completed state so that you can clearly see what it is you are about to build.

1. Select File | Open and locate the *Practice* folder on the companion CD-ROM. Open this folder and you will see a number of chapter folders. Open the *Chapter18* folder and locate and double click on the file named *Exer18-2*.

2. The *Exer18-2* file should now appear in your copy of Authorware.

3. Save this file to your working directory so it can save the external files to your hard drive. If you don't do this you will get an error that the file cannot write data to the read-only CD-ROM. Select Control | Restart or press the Restart button on the toolbar to play the file from the top of the flowline. Note the following properties of this completed exercise:

- *Once the user has entered her information, a text file named Student Data is created as a subfolder of the location the piece is saved.*

- *The text file will contain the user's name and job title as entered by the user.*

Storyboard: On Screen

Figure 18-18 shows what the external text file will look like on screen.

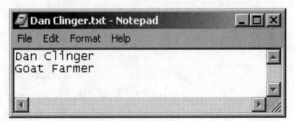

Fig. 18-18. Completed text file.

Storyboard: Behind the Scenes

Figure 18-19 shows the Calculation icon that will create the text file when you are finished with this exercise.

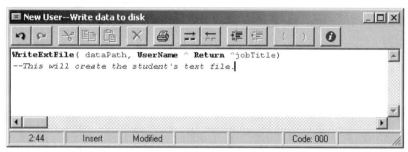

```
New User--Write data to disk
WriteExtFile( dataPath, UserName ^ Return ^jobTitle)
--This will create the student's text file.
```

| 2:44 | Insert | Modified | | | Code: 000 | |

Fig. 18-19. Completed Calculation icon.

Step-by-Step Instructions

Go Solo

1. Create your working file for this exercise. You will need to start with the flowline that was completed in the previous exercise, 18-1. If you have completed that exercise, keep working in that file. If you want to start working now, you will need to open the completed 18-1 exercise that is on your CD-ROM.

    a) If opening an existing file, select File | Open and locate the *Practice* folder on the companion CD-ROM.

    b) Open this folder and you will see a number of chapter folders. Open the *Chapter18* folder and locate the file named *Exer18-1*.

    c) Double click on *Exer18-1*.

2. Save the file on your hard drive.

    a) Select File | Save As and use the Scroll window and locate the *SaveWork* directory.

    b) Type in the name *Exer18-2* and click on OK.

3. Create the file path for student records to be stored on the user's hard drive.

    a) Insert a Calculation icon under the *Display User's Job Title* Display icon.

    b) Name this icon *Storage Location for Student Records*.

    c) Open the Calculation icon.

    d) In the Calculation window, type *dataPath :=*.

The custom variable *dataPath* will store the path location on the learner's hard drive to which all of the records will be sent. The location of where the records are being sent will be referenced every time you want to record data about the learner's progress. If you were to make an absolute path (i.e., *C:\StudentData*) and then decided you wanted to change that location, you would have to change it every time you sent data to the file. For convenience sake, you are creating a custom variable to store the file path so that if you need to change the location of student records it is much easier to do so once here than in hundreds of places all over the flowline. If you are interested in sending the student data to a database, reference chapter 19 to see how to accomplish this.

e) Open the Variables dialog box.

f) From the File category, select the variable *FileLocation*, and then click on Paste.

g) The expression in the Calculation icon should read *dataPath :=* *FileLocation*.

The *FileLocation* system variable holds the values of where the Authorware piece is saved on the learner's hard drive. By default, in Windows, the file will be stored in the same folder as *your* Authorware piece. *You* can specify a path name if *you* want the file to be stored in a different location.

h) At the end of *FileLocation* in the Calculation window, type ^.

The caret (^) is the concatenation symbol. You use it to join strings that are otherwise unrelated. Without it, Authorware will interpret the content of the string as incorrect syntax and return an error message.

i) Click on *UserName* in the General category of the Variables dialog box, and then click on Paste. The expression in the calculation should read:

```
dataPath := FileLocation ^ UserName.
```

j) At the end of *UserName* in the Calculation window, type ^.

k) After the caret, type "*.txt*". The Calculation window should read:

```
dataPath := FileLocation ^ UserName ^ ".txt"
```

Be sure you include the period before *txt*. The period separates the file name from its extension. The quotation marks are important, too. They tell Authorware that what is in quotes is a literal text string, not a variable, function, or number. The text file with the student records will be kept where the final Authorware piece is installed on the learner's hard drive. The file name will be the user's name with the extension .TXT. For example, if the user's name were Jane Doe, the file name would be "*Jane Doe.txt*". See figure 18-20.

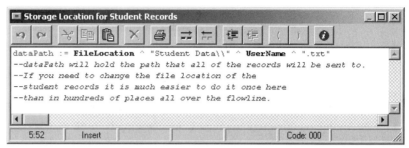

Fig. 18-20. Completed Calculation icon **Storage Location for Student Records.**

4. Now that you have created the path location for all data to be sent, you can concentrate on actually creating the text file and sending data to it.

   a) Drag a new Calculation icon to the flowline just below the Display icon *Storage Location for Student Records* and name it *New User – Write data to disk.*

   b) Open the Functions dialog box, and from the File category click on *WriteExtFile*, and then click on Paste. The expression in the Calculation icon should read:

   ```
   WriteExtFile("filename","string")
   ```

WriteExtFile writes an external text file containing whatever text string you instruct Authorware to place there.

   c) In the Calculation window, select the entire first argument, *"filename"*, and replace it with the custom variable *dataPath*. The expression in the Calculation icon should read:

   ```
   WriteExtFile( dataPath, "string")
   ```

   d) Select the argument *"string"*.

   e) In the Variables dialog box, select the File category and click on *FileName*. Click on Paste. Now *"string"* has been replaced with *FileName*.

   f) In the Calculation dialog box after *FileName*, type ^ *Return* ^.

Return causes Authorware to input a carriage return in the text file. In this case, a carriage return will be placed after *FileName*, so that the name of the course is placed on the first line of the text file.

·T/P·

The *WriteExtFile* function writes normal text files, but you can use whatever extension you want. Instead of ".txt" you could write a ".dan" file and, assuming there was nothing associated with that extension, you would have added one level of security to your file.

g) Continue typing in variables until you have the following expression on one line of your Calculation icon.

    WriteExtFile(dataPath , FileName ^ Return ^ UserName ^ Return ^ jobTitle ^ Return)

h) Close the Calculation icon.

i) Save and restart your piece. After you log in, a text file should appear at the same path location where you saved your working file, as shown in figure 18-21.

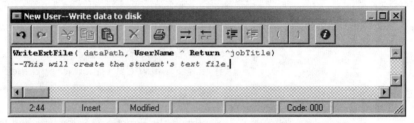

Fig. 18-21. Completed Calculation icon New User – Write data to disk.

Practice Exercise 18-3:
Checking for Previous Log-in Records

Description

If the user has logged in previously, it is important to retrieve the student's records and append new information to that record. You would not want to create a new record each time the user logged in, nor would you want to overwrite their previous record. You will set up a decision structure to test whether the user has logged in before. In this exercise you will:

- *Read in data from a text file created by the user's last entry (if one exists) to the course*

- *Save the data that has been read in and compare it to the data the user just entered*

- *Welcome (if the data matches) the user back to the course and append his records file with his reentry date*

- *Establish (if the data does not match) the user as a first-time student and generate her records*

Take a Look

Before beginning the exercise, let's take a look at the exercise in its completed state so that you can clearly see what it is you are about to build.

CD-ROM ✴

1. Select File | Open and locate the *Practice* folder on the companion CD-ROM. Open this folder and you will see a number of chapter folders. Open the *Chapter 18* folder and locate and double click on the file named *Exer18-3*.

2. The *Exer18-3* file should now appear in your copy of Authorware. Select Control | Restart or press the Restart button on the toolbar to play the file from the top of the flowline. Note the following properties of this completed exercise:

   - *Once the user has entered their information, a text file is created at the same location where the file is saved (FileLocation).*

   - *This text file contains the name of the Authorware file, the user's name and their job title.*

   - *There is a Calculation icon that will read the contents of this text file into the custom variable* readUserData.

   - *The* readUserData *variable is then parsed into separate data elements using the* GetLine *function. This determines if the user has logged into the course before or not.*

   - *If the user has been to the course before, they are welcomed back and their text file is opened with the return to course date.*

   - *If the user is new to the course, their text file is created.*

Storyboard: On Screen

Figure 18-22 shows what the external text file will look like on screen.

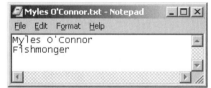

Fig. 18-22. Completed text file.

Storyboard: Behind the Scenes

Figure 18-23 shows the completed flowline for this exercise.

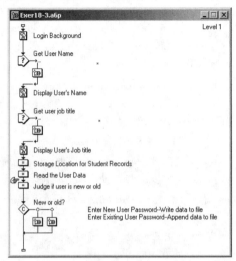

Fig. 18-23. Completed Calculation icon.

Step-by-Step Instructions

1. Open an existing file or continue with the file you used in the previous exercise.

    a) If opening an existing file, select File | Open and locate the *Practice* folder on the companion CD-ROM.

    b) Open this folder and you will see a number of chapter folders. Open the *Chapter18* folder and locate the file named *Exer18-2*.

    c) Double click on *Exer18-2*.

2. Save the file on your hard drive.

    a) Select File | Save As and use the Scroll window to locate the *SaveWork* directory on your computer.

    b) Type in the name *Exer18-3* and click on OK.

3. Build the decision loop that will control which greeting message the user sees, the message for a first-time user or a returning user.

    a) Drag a Decision icon to the very bottom of the flowline.

    b) Type *New or Exiting User?* as the title of the Decision icon.

    c) Drag the *New User – Write data to disk* Calculation icon to the right of the Decision icon.

    d) Group the Calculation icon to form a Map icon. See figure 18-24.

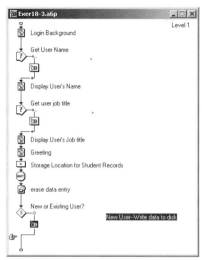

Fig. 18-24. Modified flowline.

4. Assemble the greeting screen for the first-time user. You will move the greeting icons inside the Map icon to form the basis of the new user greeting screen.
   a) Open the new Map icon.
   b) From the level I flowline, drag the Display icon *Greeting*, the Wait icon, and the Erase icon *Erase Login* into the Map icon. See figure 18-25.

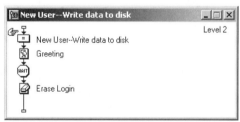

Fig. 18-25. Modified flowline.

5. Create the path for the existing user.
   a) Copy the *New User* Map icon.
   b) Paste this icon in the second position of the *New or Exiting User?* Decision icon.
   c) Retitle the pasted Map icon *Existing User – Append Data*.
   d) Open the new Map icon.
   e) Inside the Map icon for the existing user change the name of the Display icon *Greeting* to *Welcome Back*. See figure 18-26.

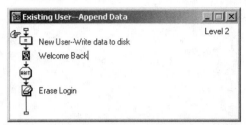

Fig. 18-26. Modified flowline with Welcome Back icon.

   f)   Open the Display icon *Welcome Back.*

   g)   Using the Text tool, change the text to read as follows. See figure 18-27.

> `" Welcome back {FirstName}! Click the continue button`
> `to return to your training."`

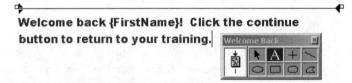

Fig. 18-27. Completed Calculation icon.

   h)   Close the Presentation window.

6.   Change the Calculation icon to add the student's return information to the text file.

   a)   Change the name of the Calculation icon to *Append data to text file.*

   b)   Open the Calculation icon.

   c)   Change the *Write* statement to an *Append* statement, as follows:

> `AppendExtFile( dataPath, Return ^ "Return to Course:`
> `" ^ Date ^ Tab ^ Time ^ Return)`

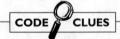

CODE   CLUES

AppendExtFile("filename","string")

AppendExtFile has two arguments. The first, *"filename,"* is the path location where the external file is expected to be located on the user's hard drive. The second argument, *"string,"* contains the information that will be added to that text file.

This function differs from the *WriteExtFile* function in that it does not overwrite a text file if it encounters one with the same path name. Rather, it will add the content of the string argument to the end of the existing text file. This function has the added benefit of creating a text file if one does not already exist at the *filename* argument location. As a default, if no path is declared for *filename,* Authorware uses the system variable *FileLocation* as the path. See figure 18-28.

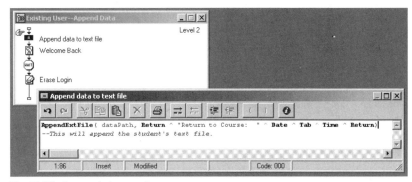

Fig. 18-28. **Append** *data code.*

> d) Close the Calculation icon and save the piece.
> e) Run the piece.

Now you will improve the log-in screen. Whenever the log-in screen is encountered, you will want to check whether it is the user's first time logging in and if there is already a password set. By reading the content of the text file, Authorware can determine which decision path to go down.

In the following steps, you will read from the text file using the *ReadExtFile* function, and you will place that information into user-defined variables. Finally, you will use the *GetLine* function to parse the user name from the text file into new user variables.

Here, you will place the *ReadExtFile* expression into a Calculation icon. The icon will follow the "Sign In" portion of the flowline. You will use the name the user types in to locate the file, if it exists.

> 7. Create a Calculation icon that will read the content of the external text file.
>   a) Drag a new Calculation icon below the *Storage Location for Student Records* Calculation icon.
>   b) Name this icon *Read the User Data.*
> 8. Evaluate the content of the text file.
>   a) Open the Calculation icon, and then open the Functions dialog box by selecting Windows | Functions or by pressing Ctrl + Shift + F .
>   b) In the File category, click on *ReadExtFile.* Click on Paste, and then click on Done.

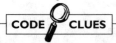

CODE CLUES

string := ReadExtFile("filename")

ReadExtFile is a function that reads the content of an external file. As the statement implies, you must assign the content of the file to a variable. *ReadExtFile* can read the content of a web-based file but the Authorware piece must be running in "trusted" mode for this to work. When specifying a URL for the path to *filename,* it must be an absolute URL that begins with either *http://servername* or *file:///*. CAUTION: *Authorware can only read in 32K of data at a time. Make sure you account for this when storing information in text files.*

⚠ CAUTION

Be sure to delete the quotation marks in the *"filename"* argument. It is important to remove the quotation marks or Authorware will try to evaluate the information as a literal string. You will be placing the custom variable *dataPath* in place of *"filename"*.

c) You should now see the following expression in the Calculation window: *ReadExtFile("filename")*. In the Calculation window, delete *"filename"*. See figure 18-29.

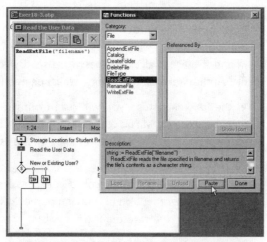

Fig. 18-29. Paste in the ReadExtFile *command.*

d) Open the Variables dialog box, and from the Custom category click on *dataPath*.

e) Click on Paste, and then click on Done to close the Variables dialog box.

f) The expression in the Calculation window should read:

```
ReadExtFile(dataPath)
```

NOTE

When you run the program and enter a user name, Authorware will read the content of the text file, if it exists. If the text file does not exist, the string read back will be blank, or a null string.

9. Assign the content of the text file to a variable for storage. You just used a function to read the text of an external file. However, you need to assign what the *ReadExtFile* function reads to a variable; otherwise, you will be unable to access the content of the file.

a) Before the *ReadExtFile* expression, type *readUserData:=* in the Calculation window.

b) The expression should read:

`readUserData :=ReadExtFile(dataPath)`

Now the content of the entire file is assigned to the *readUserData* variable, and you can use the string data from the text file in other expressions. See figure 18-30.

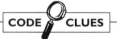
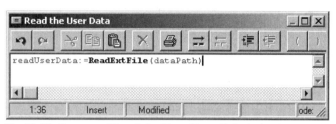

Fig. 18-30. Content of Read the User Data *Calculation icon.*

10. Parse the lines of the text file. You need to place the first line of the text file into a variable. Remember that the first line contains the user's name. You also need to place the second line of the text file into a variable. Recall that the second line contains the user's job title. By doing this, you can compare the user name from the text file to the name the user has just typed. In this step, you will create several custom or user-defined variables and assign values to them.

a) Type *existingName:=* on the next line of the Calculation window.

b) Open the Functions dialog box, and from the Character category click on *GetLine*. Click on Paste. The line should now read:

`existingName := GetLine("string", n , m, delim)`

CODE CLUES

resultString := GetLine("string", n [, m, delim])

GetLine is a function that returns the content of a specified line from a text string. There are two required arguments for this function. The first is the name of the string you want to get data from. The second is shown in the previous example as the letter *n*. This is the line number you want to retrieve. *GetLine* retrieves line *n* from *string*.

If you needed to get multiple lines from the string, you could use the third, optional, argument *m*. This would allow you to specify a series of lines. For example, lines 1 through 4 would be *n* = 1 *m* = 4, and the expression would read *GetLine(myString, 1 , 4)*.

By default, each line in *string* is separated (delimited) by a Return character. If a different separator were required, you could list it in the fourth argument (e.g., the Tab character could be listed as *Tab*). As an example of all four arguments in use, imagine a string of student test scores separated by tabs. The function would read *GetLine(studentScores, 1 , 4 , Tab)*. Remember that to use the fourth argument you must also use the third argument, even if the range of lines is only one line. For example: **GetLine(studentScores, 3 , 3 , Tab)**

c) Click on Done to close the Functions dialog box.

d) Replace *"string"* with *readUserData*.

e) Delete the *m* and *delim* arguments.

f) Replace *n* with *1*.

g) The line should now read:

```
ExistingName := GetLine( readUserData, 1)
```

Authorware will assign the content of the first line of *readUserData* and place it in the variable *existingName*.

h) Close the Calculation icon. See figure 18-31.

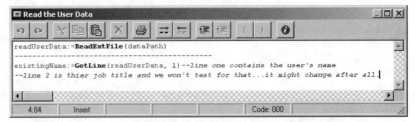

Fig. 18-31. *Content of the finished* **Read the User Data** *Calculation icon.*

11. Define new variables. Because you have not defined the new variables, the New Variable dialog box is displayed.

a) For the new variable *existingName*, place the initial value in double quotes to denote a *string* variable.

b) The description for a *string* variable should be: *Contains the user's name as read in from the external text file.*

c) Click on OK.

d) The initial value for *readUserData* should be empty quotes.

e) The description should be: *Contains the content of the text file that stores the user's name and password.*

You have just created, defined, and assigned values to three custom or user-defined variables. You assigned values to these variables based on the text from line 1 of the text file.

12. You need to use the Decision icon to determine if this is a new user or an existing user. Based on that decision, the user will be presented with different text (i.e., *Greetings* or *Welcome Back*). If this is a new user, a text file will be created. If a returning user, the date of the return will be appended to the text file.

a) Drag a new Calculation icon to the flowline under the *Read the User Data* Calculation icon.

b) Name this icon *Judge if user is new or old*.
c) Open the Calculation icon.
d) Inside the Calculation icon, type the following code. See figure 18-32.

```
if existingName = UserName then
   path := 2
else
   path := 1
end if
```

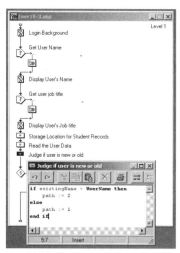

Fig. 18-32. Content of the Judge if user is new or old *Calculation icon*.

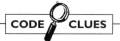 **CODE CLUES**

if condition then Statement

An *if/then* statement allows Authorware to perform different tasks based on the logical (true or false) result of a condition. For example, you can use an *if/then* statement to give different feedback to a student based on a quiz score. The statement would look as follows.

```
if PercentCorrect >= 80 then
      message := "You pass the quiz."
else
      message := "You failed the quiz."
end if
```

As you can see, the structure of an *if/then* statement has three parts: the condition Authorware is checking, what Authorware is to do if the condition is true, and what Authorware is to do if the condition is false. The syntax of the statement is important to follow. If there are both true and false conditions, the *if/then* statement must be executed on different lines, and the closing command, *end if*, must accompany the statement.

Here, if *UserName* and *existingName* are the same, what you place in the true expression will occur; otherwise, what you place in the false expression will occur. In relation to the *if/then/else* statement, the expression is such that *if* the user's name from the text file and what the user just typed in match, then *path* = 1, else *path* = 2.

If *UserName* = *existingName* is true (i.e., if the name the user enters matches the one in the text file), the decision will branch to the first path. If the condition is false, meaning that the names are different, the decision will branch to the second path.

 e) Close the Calculation window. The New Variable window appears for the custom variable path.

 f) The initial value should be 0, because this variable tracks a number.

 g) Enter the following description:

> **Temporary variable that holds which path of a calculated decision icon the user is being directed down.**

Temporary variables are used frequently by programmers to store a value for just a few seconds or for a current action. This value will not be stored permanently, and therefore it is important to let other developers know this in the description of the variable.

By naming this variable *path*, you will only use it for the path settings of Decision icons. This is a subtle point in Authorware: icons attached to Decision icons are referred to as paths; the icons of Interaction icons are referred to as Responses; and the icons attached to Framework icons are referred to as pages. You will notice this subtle naming convention in the names of Authorware system variables.

13. Set up the calculated Decision icon.

 a) Open the *New or Existing User?* decision icon.

 b) From the Branch menu, select To Calculated Path.

c) Type the custom variable path in the calculation space.

d) Click on OK to close the Decision Icon dialog box. See figure 18-33.

·T/P·

Based on the value of the variable *path*, Authorware will direct the user to view the *New User* Map icon or the *Existing User* Map icon. Remember that the paths of a Decision icon are numbered from left to right by Authorware. Thus, the first Map icon is path 1, the second Map icon is 2, and so on.

Question: What would be considered the "0" path? That's right! The flowline is the zero path of a Decision icon structure. You can use this if you want to create a structure in which Authorware will not branch to any of the paths of a Decision icon. Simply set the calculated path to 0.

This is often used in testing. Placing icons that you do not want to execute on a Decision icon set to branch path 0 skips them so you can see what happens without them.

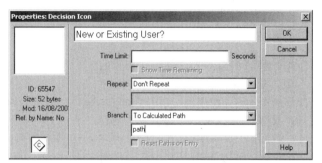

Fig. 18-33. **New or Existing User?** *Decision icon properties.*

14. You have set up the decision structure with a path for new users and one for existing users. Now you can try it out and see how it works.

a) Restart the program and type a new name and job title.

b) Verify that you see the *Welcome/New User* greeting message. In the background, Authorware writes the data to disk.

c) Restart the program again and enter the same name and password.

The program now reads from the text file and retrieves the user's name. The decision structure determines that *UserName* and *existingName* are the same. Therefore, it selects path 2.

Practice Exercise 18-4: Adding a Password

Description

So far you have created a log-in structure that tracks a user logging in and that will time stamp a text file with the date and time when a user logs on in subsequent visits. In the following you will add the extra measure of a simple, user-defined password. If a new user logs on, you will prompt him to enter a password and then confirm that password before he is welcomed to the course and a text file created. If the user's name is already present in the roster (text files), you will ask the user to provide a password. If the password the user entered the first time he entered the course matches the password he enters this time, the user will be welcomed back to the course. If, however, the passwords do not match after three tries, the user will be returned to the top of the log-in to reenter his name. In this exercise you will:

• *Create an interaction that will appear to the first-time user, asking her if she wants to create a password, retype her name, or quit the log-in.*

- *Create a keypress interaction that masks the user's password as she enters it.*
- *Write the user's password to her data file to store it for future use.*

Take a Look

Before beginning the exercise, let's take a look at the exercise in its completed state so that you can clearly see what it is you are about to build.

1. Select File | Open and locate the *Practice* folder on the companion CD-ROM. Open this folder and you will see a number of chapter folders. Open the *Chapter18* folder and locate and double click on the file named *Exer18-4*.

2. The *Exer18-4* file should now appear in your copy of Authorware. Select Control | Restart or press the Restart button on the toolbar to play the file from the top of the flowline. Note the following properties of this completed exercise.

    - *After a user logs on for the first time, he is prompted to create a password, retype his name, or quit the log-in.*
    - *The password entered is masked or unreadable to the user.*
    - *The user is prompted to confirm his password by reentering it.*
    - *If the passwords do not match, the user is told to try again.*
    - *If the user has logged on in the past, he is prompted to enter a password.*
    - *If the user enters his password incorrectly, he is told to try again.*
    - *If the user incorrectly enters his password three times, he is sent to the beginning of the log-in to reenter his name.*
    - *If the password does match, he is shown a "Welcome Back" message.*

Storyboard: On Screen

Figure 18-34 shows what the final log-in will look like with the Password field active.

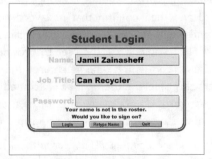

Fig. 18-34. Completed log-in screen.

Storyboard: Behind the Scenes

Figure 18-35 shows the interactions that will be required to build the password interactivity.

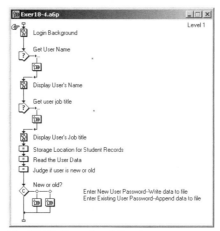

Fig. 18-35. Completed flowline.

Step-by-Step Instructions

Go Solo

1. You need to open an existing file for this exercise or continue with the file you used in the previous exercise.
   a) If opening an existing file, select File | Open and locate the *Practice* folder on the companion CD-ROM.
   b) Open this folder and you will see a number of chapter folders. Open the *Chapter18* folder and locate the file named *Exer18-3*.
   c) Double click on *Exer18-3*.

2. Save the file to your hard drive.
   a) Select File | Save As and use the Scroll window to locate the *SaveWork* directory.
   b) Type in the name *Exer18-4* and click on OK.

3. Create the sign-on interaction loop for the new user.
   a) Open the Map icon *Enter New User Password – Write data to file* next to the Decision icon *New or old?*.
   b) At the top of the level 2 Map icon, drag a new Interaction icon to the flowline.
   c) Name the Interaction icon *Login?*.
   d) Drag a Map icon to the right of the Interaction icon.

e) Select Button as the response type.

f) Name the new Map icon *Login*.

g) Double click on the Response Type symbol to open the button's Property dialog box.

h) On the Button tab, check the Make Default check box.

i) Change the cursor to a hand.

j) On the Response tab, change the Branch pull-down list to Exit Interaction. See figure 18-36.

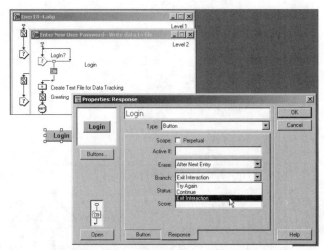

Fig. 18-36. Log-in button properties.

k) Drag two Calculation icons to the right of the Map icon.

l) Name these icons *Retype Name* and *Quit*.

4. Create the on-screen instructions and align the buttons for the user.

a) Double click on the Interaction icon *Login?*.

b) Using the Text tool, type the following instructions:

    Your name is not in the roster.
    Would you like to sign on?

c) Using the Pointer tool, align the buttons under the text.

d) Save your work. See figure 18-37.

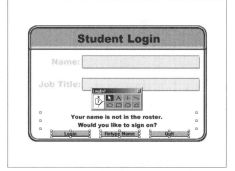

Fig. 18-37. Text and button layout.

5. Complete the quit functionality.
   a) Open the Calculation icon *Quit*.
   b) Enter the following function expression:

   `Quit(1)`

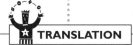

TRANSLATION

Quit(option)

The system function *Quit* immediately closes the Authorware file. The *only* argument sends an instruction to Windows about what to do after the Authorware piece closes. Each option is described in further detail in the description of the *Quit* function. The option you are using, 1, quits Authorware and displays the Desktop (Windows 95, 98, NT 4.0, and Windows 2000), or Finder (Macintosh). Notice that Quit option 3 will automatically shut down Windows. There can be hours of fun using that option and not telling your co-workers about it.

   c) Close the Calculation icon and save changes.

6. Create the *Retype Name* Calculation icon. In this icon, you will send the user back to the top of the log-in so that she can start the log-in process over. Before you send the user back to the top, however, you want to make sure that all of the variables for the log-in are set back to their initial values. You will accomplish all of this by using one function, *Restart()*.
   a) Open the *Retype Name* Calculation icon.
   b) Open the Functions window.
   c) In the category General, locate and paste the function *Restart()*.

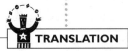

TRANSLATION

Restart()

Restart causes Authorware to branch to the beginning of the file and initialize all variables, even if the file is set to resume in the File Properties dialog box. Use *Restart* only in Calculation icons.

e) Close the Calculation icon and save changes. See figure 18-38.

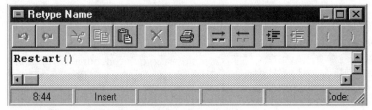

Fig. 18-38. Retype the **Name** *Calculation icon.*

7. Build the keypress interaction loop for entering the password.
   a) Drag an Interaction icon under the *Password Box* Display icon.
   b) Name this icon *Enter Password*.
   c) Drag a Calculation icon to the right of the Interaction icon.
   d) Set the response type to Keypress.
   e) Drag two more Calculation icons to the right of the first one.
   f) Open the Response Properties dialog box for the first one.
   g) On the Keypress tab, set the key to Enter.
   h) On the Response tab, change the branching to Exit Interaction.
   i) Close the dialog box.
   j) Name the next Calculation icon *Backspace|Delete*.
   k) Name the final Calculation icon *?*. See figure 18-39.

·T/P·

Note that when you enter the action key(s) that will activate this keypress response, the title of this icon changes its name from "untitled" to Enter. Keypress is one of those unique instances in which Authorware looks directly at the title to get its information. You can use this as a shortcut on the flowline by merely changing the title of the icon to reflect the name of the active key to be pressed.

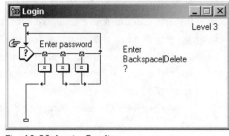

Fig. 18-39. Login flowline.

·T/P·

When tracking individual keypresses, the question mark symbol (?) allows any key to be entered as a wildcard entry.

8. Build the background for the password log-in.
   a) Open the Interaction icon *Enter password*.
   b) Inside this Display icon, build the password entry ground graphic.
   c) Using the Text tool, type *Password:*.
   d) Draw a box next to the text for the entry for the password. See figure 18-40.

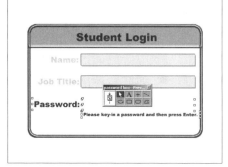

Fig. 18-40. Password text design.

9. Track the user's password entry.

   a) Open the Calculation icon *?*.
   b) On the first line, type the following expression:

   ```
   passwordEntry := passwordEntry ^ Key
   ```

This expression is activated every time the user presses a key on the keyboard because the response type is set to *keypress* and the key being tracked is the wildcard *?*. Once the user presses a key, you want to capture it. You will store the variable the user types in the custom variable *passwordEntry*. Every time the user presses a key (this is an Authorware system variable), you will append (using the concatenation operator [^]) that key to the password. This will effectively build the password as the user types it.

   c) Save your file.
   d) Save the new variable *passwordEntry* as *Initial value: 0*.
   e) *Description:* tracks the user's password as the user enters it one keypress at a time.

10. Create a masked password that will be displayed on screen as the user enters her password.
    a) On the next line of the *?* Calculation icon, type the following expression:

    ```
    passwordDisplayed := passwordDisplayed ^ "*"
    ```

CAUTION ⚠

If the user were to use one of the extra keys on the keyboard (i.e. Ctrl or Alt), that keypress would be added to the *passwordEntry* string. A way around this is to put a check like this:

If CharCount(Key) = 1 then
    passwordEntry := PasswordEntry ^ Key
end if

Another caution is that the typical Authorware keyboard shortcuts no longer work while the piece is running. For example, Ctrl+J will not jump you back to the icons anymore because the keypress interaction is trapping it.

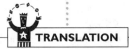

TRANSLATION

passwordDisplayed := passwordDisplayed ^ "*"

As the user types his password, you want him to see an asterisk appear for each key pressed. Behind the scenes you can see what you are doing. You are not formally encrypting the password; rather, you are just showing the user an asterisk symbol for every key pressed. The custom variable *passwordDisplayed* will be embedded on screen. Thanks to the concatenation symbol, you are able to join the * with the existing string for *passwordDisplayed*. See figure 18-41.

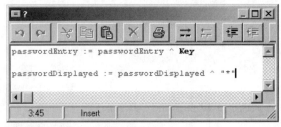

Fig. 18-41. Calculation icon ?.

   b) Save your file.
   c) Save the new variable *passwordDisplayed* as *Initial value: ""*.
   d) The *Description* variable is embedded on the password entry background and displays an asterisk (*) symbol every time the user presses a key on the keyboard. This will appear as a masked password.

11. Store the password once the user presses the Enter key.
    a) Open the Calculation icon *Enter*.
    b) On the first line, type the following expression:

    passwordEntry := UpperCase(passwordEntry)

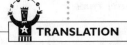

TRANSLATION

passwordEntry := UpperCase(passwordEntry)

In this expression you are using the function *UpperCase* to force all of the characters in the user's entry to be uppercase. This way you will not have to check for case-sensitive options. If the user is required to enter his password using exactly the same case each time, then this step can be eliminated.

    c) On the next line of the calculation type the following expression:

    passwordFirst := passwordEntry

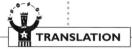

TRANSLATION

passwordFirst := passwordEntry

In this expression you are assigning the password the user just entered to the new custom variable *passwordFirst*. You are doing this because you are going to have the user reenter his password and you will need to know what he typed in the first time so that you can compare the two entries. If what the user typed both times matches, the user will proceed to the course. If the passwords do not match, you will have the user try again.

d) Save your file.

e) Save the new variable *passwordFirst* as *Initial value:""*.

f) The *Description* variable stores the password the user enters. Once entered, the user is asked to confirm her password. If this variable matches the user's second entry, the user is allowed to process the program.

h) On the last line of this Calculation icon, enter the following expression. See figure 18-42.

```
Initialize( passwordEntry , passwordDisplayed)
```

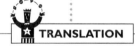

TRANSLATION

Initialize(passwordEntry , passwordDisplayed)

In this expression, you are resetting the password entry variables for the next interaction. If users are required to enter their passwords using exactly the same case each time, then this step can be eliminated.

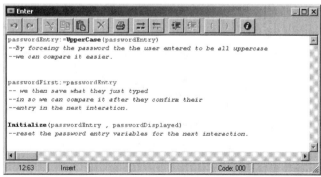

Fig. 18-42. Enter *Calculation icon.*

12. Create the backspace and delete functionality for the key press entry. If the user were typing in a password and made a mistake, his fingers would invariably go to the Backspace or Delete key on the keyboard. Because you are using the *?* key to capture every key the user touches, you must first check for a Delete key press in this interaction. You will need to subtract the last character the user typed. You will do this using the *Substring* and *Character Count* functions.

a) Open the Calculation icon *Backspace | Delete*.

b) On the first line, type the following expression:

    passwordEntry :=

c) Paste the function *SubStr()* from the Character category. The expression should now read:

    passwordEntry := SubStr("string", first, last)

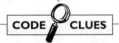

CODE CLUES

resultString := SubStr("string", first, last)

SubStr will return just a part of any string. Identify the string you want to get a portion of in the *"string"* argument. Then place the first character position number you want to get down to the last. In this example, you will look at the *passwordEntry* variable and subtract the last character.

d) Replace the *"string"* argument with the custom variable *passwordEntry*. The expression should now read:

    passwordEntry := SubStr(passwordEntry, first, last)

e) Replace the argument *first* with the number *1*. The expression should now read:

    passwordEntry := SubStr(passwordEntry, 1, last)

f) Find the total number of characters in the variable *passwordEntry*. Replace the argument *last* with the system function *CharCount*. The expression should now read:

    passwordEntry := SubStr(passwordEntry, 1, CharCount("string"))

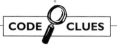

CODE CLUES

number := CharCount("string")

The system function *CharCount* (short for Character Count) returns the number of all characters, including spaces or special characters, found in the specified string. You will be using this function to get the total number of characters in the variable *passwordEntry*.

g) Replace the argument for the *CharCount* function with the custom variable *passwordEntry last*. The expression should now read:

```
passwordEntry := SubStr( passwordEntry, 1, CharCount
( passwordEntry))
```

h) Subtract I from the total *CharCount* by placing a – *I* between the two sets of closing parentheses.

```
passwordEntry := SubStr( passwordEntry, 1, CharCount
( passwordEntry) — 1 )
```

This statement will subtract one character from the total number of characters in the variable *passwordEntry*. Then Authorware will strip out that last character and save the rest to the custom variable *passwordEntry*.

13. Set up the same procedure for the string of asterisks the user sees on screen. The previous step subtracted one character from the actual password every time the user pressed the Backspace or Delete key. Now you must make sure the password displayed on screen follows the same behavior.

a) With the *Backspace|Delete* calculation icon still open, copy the first line of code.

b) Replace the custom variable *passwordEntry* with the *passwordDisplayed* variable. The content of the Calculation icon should read:

```
passwordDisplayed := SubStr( passwordDisplayed , 1 ,
CharCount( passwordDisplayed) — 1 )
```

c) Save your file. See figure 18-43.

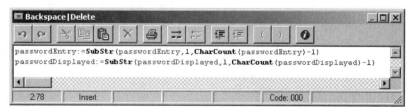

*Fig. 18-43. Finished **Backspace|Delete** Calculation icon.*

14. Now you will set up the visual elements of this password entry. First you will embed a variable to display the user's password as a series of asterisks. Then you will add prompt text and highlight the label of the Entry field.

a) Right-click on the Interaction icon to open the Properties dialog box.

c) On the Display tab, check the Update Displayed Variables box. See figure 18-44.

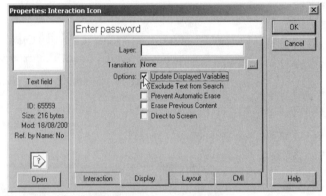

Fig. 18-44. Update Displayed Variables box.

d) Close the dialog box.

f) Open the Interaction icon's Presentation window so that you can see the entire log-in background. (Hold down the Shift key when you double click.)

g) Using the Text tool, embed the variable *passwordDisplayed* where the user is entering his password.

h) Type the following statement under the password entry box: *Please key in a password and then press Enter.*

i) On top of the grayed-out label that says *Password:*, type the same word, but in a darker color. See figure 18-45.

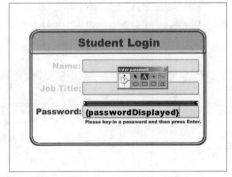

Fig. 18-45. Password screen design.

15. Create the confirmation prompt for the user's password entry.
    a) Select the entire interaction loop you just created and copy the loop.
    b) Place the paste hand under the interaction loop you just copied and paste it to the flowline.
    c) Change the name of the second Interaction icon to *Confirm password*.
    d) Open the Interaction icon and change the prompt text to read *Please confirm your password by pressing Enter.*

16. Change the password variables the user's entries are stored as.
    a) Open the first Calculation icon attached to the *Confirm Password* interaction icon.
    b) Change the first line to read *password := UpperCase(passwordEntry).*
    c) Delete the line *passwordFirst := passwordEntry.*To the initialization function, add the variable *password* inside the parentheses. See figure 18-46.

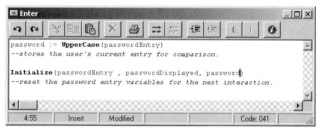

Fig. 18-46. Enter *Calculation* icon.

17. Finally, you need to judge the two passwords the user just entered and decide if they match or not. If they do match, the user's data file will be created. If the passwords do not match, the user will be sent to reenter his password.
    a) Drag a Map icon to the top of the *Login* Map icon.

b) Name this icon *Jump for wrong password – Do Not Delete.*

c) Drag a Calculation icon to the bottom of this Map icon and title it *Do the Passwords Match? Write Data File or Reenter the Password.* See figure 18-47.

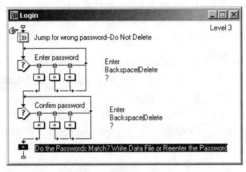

Fig. 18-47. Modified flowline.

As we mentioned earlier, when you begin to make strings of information inside a Calculation window using the concatenation symbol (^), the line can sometimes get quite long and scroll off the other side of the calculation. This makes reading the string very difficult. To get around this you can have text wrap to the next line of the calculation with the soft break symbol immediately following a concatenation symbol. The soft break symbol is achieved by holding the Alt and Enter keys at the same time. The soft break symbol looks like this: ¬. The soft break can only be used right after a concatenation symbol with no spaces. If we wanted the string for *WriteExtFile* to appear on separate lines we would type:

```
WriteExtFile( dataPath , UserName ^ Return ^¬

jobTitle ^ Return ^¬

password ^ Return)
```

d) Open the Calculation icon and enter the following code:

```
if password = passwordFirst then

    WriteExtFile( dataPath , ¬

                    UserName ^ Return ^¬

                    jobTitle ^ Return ^¬

                    password ^ Return)

else

    Initialize( passwordEntry , passwordDisplayed,
password)
```

> **NOTE**
>
> Sometimes there are icons on the flowline that are referenced by other icons or code expressions. If these icons are deleted from the flowline, the program will stop working properly, but no error message will appear when you delete the icon. As a bit of safety code, you are including the comment to not delete this Map icon.

```
    GoTo( IconID@"Jump for wrong password--Do Not
Delete")

    end if
```

This *if/then* statement judges if the first password the user entered is confirmed by the second entry. The structure of an *if/then/else* is fairly simple to read. The first line is the condition you are judging. In this case, you are checking to see if the values of the two custom variables match. If they do, you create an external text file that contains the user's name and password. If they do not match, using the *GoTo()* function you will send the user back to the top of the password log-in. See figure 18-48.

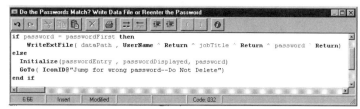

Fig. 18-48. **Do the Passwords Match?** *Calculation icon.*

18. Create the log-in for an existing user. To do this you will read the user's text file and have the user enter a password. If the password matches the text file, the user will continue through the program. If the passwords do not match, the user will be prompted to try again.

a) Inside the *Login* Map icon you have been working on, select the second interaction loop, named *Confirm Password*.

b) Copy the *Confirm Password* interaction loop.

c) Close the *Login* Map icon.

d) On the level 1 flowline, open the Map icon *Enter Existing User Password – Append data to disk*.

e) Place the Paste Hand cursor at the top of the level 2 flowline and paste the interaction loop. Group the first Calculation icon of the pasted interaction loop into a Map icon. See figure 18-49.

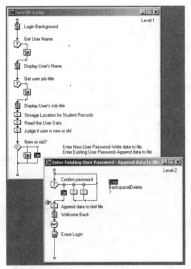

Fig. 18-49. Modified flowline.

g) Open the new Map icon *Enter*.

h) Inside the Map icon, rename the Calculation icon *Compare Passwords*, and open the Calculation icon.

i) Keep the first line of code, but delete the rest of the content of this Calculation icon.

j) On the next few lines of the Calculation icon, enter the following *if/then/else* statement:

```
if existingPassword = password then
   BranchPath := 1
else
   BranchPath := 2
end if
```

In this *if/then/else* statement, you are checking to see if the password the user just entered (*password*) matches the password the user entered in his previous visit (*existingPassword*). If these two values are equal, the user will exit the interaction and continue down the flowline. Otherwise, the branch of the response will prompt the user to try again.

BranchPath is a system variable that stores the branch path of the last interaction response the user matched. The settings for *BranchPath* correspond to the branch settings of an interactive response as follows: *0=Continue*, *1=Exit Interaction*, *2=Try Again*, and *3=Return*.

In this example you are checking to see if the old and new passwords match. If they do, the branching exits. Otherwise, the branching is set to try again. If you assign a number to *BranchPath*, the branching for that response changes. This change in the branch arrow's direction is not visible on the flowline. See figure 18-50.

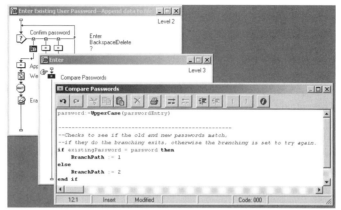

Fig. 18-50. *Inside the* **Compare Passwords** *Calculation icon.*

19. Determine if the password the user entered the first time through the log-in matches the second password entry.

   a) Inside the *Enter* Map icon, drag a Decision icon under the *Compare Passwords* Calculation icon you worked with in step 18.

   b) Name this Decision icon *Wrong?*.

   c) Open the Decision icon.

   d) Change the branching to Calculated Path.

   e) In the text field under the Branch option, enter the following expression. See figure 18-51.

   ```
   Test( existingPassword = password , 0 , 1 )
   ```

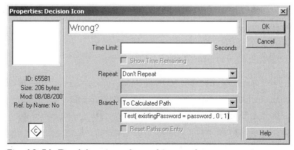

Fig. 18-51. Decision *icon branching code.*

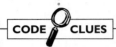

CODE CLUES

Test(condition , true expression [, false expression])

The system function *Test* evaluates the condition you specify exactly like an *if/then* statement. If the condition is true, *Test* executes the true expression; if the condition is false, *Test* executes the false expression. The false expression is optional. You use this function instead of an *if/then* statement because it is evaluated on a single line. In Authorware, text fields in property dialog boxes cannot contain the multiple lines of code *if/then* statements require.

In this example, the condition is if the password read in from the text file *(existingPassword)* has the same value as the password the user just entered. If these two values match, the true expression is 0. Zero will be the path number Authorware branches to from this Decision icon because you are trying to find the **calculated** path number. Zero represents the flowline and will bypass display of an error message to the user. If the passwords do not match, the *false* expression is executed and the user is branched to the first path of this decision loop. You will place an error message in the first path. Another way to write this decision branching code would be:

existingPassword <> password

If the statement is true (that the two values are not equal), they get the true (1) branch path. If it is false they get the zero path. Same end result.

20. Count how many times the user attempts to enter the correct password. After three mistakes, you will return the user to the beginning of the log-in and prompt the user to reenter her name and job title.
    a) Drag a Map icon to the right of the Decision icon and name it *Display Error Message*.
    b) Open the Map icon and drag a Calculation icon inside it.
    c) Name this Calculation icon *Incorrect Password Counter*.
    d) Inside the Calculation icon, enter the following code:

    ```
    Initialize( passwordEntry , passwordDisplayed)
    ```

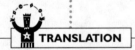

TRANSLATION

Initialize([variable1, variable2, ..., variable 10])

The *Initialize* function resets the variables specified to their initial values. You can specify up to 10 variables, and commas must separate all. If you do not include any parameters (i.e., just type *Initialize()*), Authorware will reset all custom variables and any system variables that have been assigned a value. This will clear the *password* variable so that the user can try again without the wrong password being stored in the system's memory.

    e) On the next line of the Calculation icon, enter:

    ```
    passwordWrong := passwordWrong + 1
    ```

After the user has entered the wrong password three times, you want to return the user to the beginning of the log-in to reenter her name. You will do this by counting how many times the user has viewed the error message.

In this expression you are incrementing the custom variable *passwordWrong* by 1 and then storing that new value to the same variable. Thus, the first time the user goes through this interaction the value of *passwordWrong* is 0. You add 1 to that and then store the result, 1, to the variable *passwordWrong*.

    f)   In the Calculation icon, enter the following. See figure 18-52.

```
if passwordWrong > 3 then
  Beep()
  Restart()
end if
```

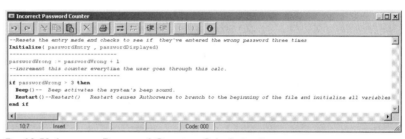

Fig. 18-52. Incorrect **Password Counter** *Calculation icon.*

This *if/then* statement only activates if the user has entered her password incorrectly more than three times. Once the counter variable (*passwordWrong*) is greater than 3, the computer's system "beep" plays and the log-in restarts at the top of the flowline. *Beep()* plays the system's alert sound. *Restart()* causes Authorware to branch to the beginning of the file and initialize all variables, even if the file is set to Resume in the File Properties dialog box.

    g)   Close the Calculation icon and save.

21. Create the error message the user will see if he enters the wrong password.
    a)   Drag a Display icon to the flowline under the *Incorrect Password Counter* Calculation icon.
    b)   Open the Display icon and, using the Text tool, type the following text in the password entry box: *That is not the password we have on file for you. Try again.* See figure 18-53.

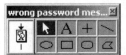

That is not the password we have on file for you. Try again.

Fig. 18-53. Incorrect password text.

c) Close the Presentation window.

d) Double click on the Path Properties symbol above the icon *Display Error Message*.

e) Change the Erase Contents setting to Don't Erase, and then click on OK to close the dialog box. See figure 18-54.

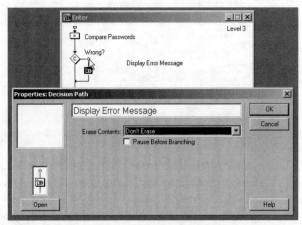

Fig. 18-54. Changing the Erase Contents dialog box.

22. Verify that you are reading in the user's password from the text file.

a) At the top of the *Enter Existing User Password – Append data to file* Map icon, drag a Calculation icon and name it *Gather Data and Initialize Variables*.

b) Inside the Calculation icon, enter the following code:

```
Initialize( passwordWrong)
```

This is considered safety code. It is unlikely the user will get to this part of the program if the *passwordWrong* variable has a value, but to make sure it is cleared out you can initialize it at this point.

c) On the next line of the Calculation icon, enter the following. See figure 18-55.

```
existingPassword := GetLine( readUserData , 3 )
```

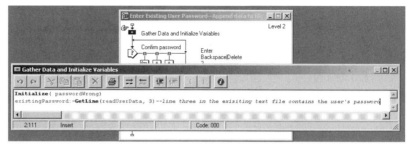

Fig. 18-55. **Gather Data and Initialize Variables** *Calculation icon.*

This will store the previous value of the user's password as it was found in the external text file. Recall that the text file data was gathered earlier, on the flowline in the Calculation icon *Read the User Data*.

Guided Tour 18A: The Resume File Setting and Jumping Between Authorware Files

Description

Typically you will build a single interactive course using Authorware. At the beginning of the course, there is a log-in. At the end of the course, you gather quiz scores and send them to a data file, but over time you may add more and more courses to your curriculum. Making the user log in for every course would be tedious, and making the user start from the top of the training course every time would be frustrating. Therefore, developers create a single log-in that can branch to one of numerous courses. Every time the user logs into a course he has entered previously, his progress in that course is saved like a bookmark.

This strategy of "chunking" courses into individual Authorware files is great for two reasons. First, this will separate the information for the end user into groups of information easily processed within a certain time frame (e.g., 1/2 hour of chair time). Second, the individual Authorware files are smaller, and thus load quicker.

Just like building a log-in, there are many strategies and methods to link Authorware files. You are going to explore some of the methods built into the Authorware program, including solutions that would work well for a user with an intermediate level of Authorware knowledge. There are some files that have been created and exist on the companion CD-ROM. You will use these files in exploring strategies for linking files. In this guided tour you will learn:

- *How to use the* JumpFile *function to link multiple Authorware files*
- *How to pass variable values between Authorware files*
- *Authorware's Resume setting*
- *How to use Authorware's native record keeping locations*

Take a Look

CD-ROM

1. Save two files to your working directory on your hard drive. Both files are located in the *Practice* folder on the companion CD-ROM. Open the *Chapter18* folder and locate the files named *Exer18-5 – Login File.a6p* and *Exer18-5 – Main Program.a6p*. Save these files to your working directory. These files must be saved to your hard drive because they create data-tracking files that must be written to your hard drive. If you leave them on the CD-ROM, they will not be able to create the data files on the read-only format of the CD.

2. Open *Exer18-5 – Login File.a6p*. The file should appear in your copy of Authorware. You need to save this file to your working directory on your hard drive.

3. Select Control | Restart or press the Restart button on the toolbar to play the file from the top of the flowline. Note that when you complete the log-in you are then prompted to "jump" to another file, named *Exer18-5 – Main Program.a6p*.

4. Once inside *Exer18-5 – Main Program.a6p*, you will see that this is a simple navigational framework structure, such as that created in Chapter 16. There is one major addition, however: when the user has "completed" a lesson (by viewing all three pages), a check mark of completion appears next to the lesson number on the Main menu.

5. As you run through the program, gathering check marks, quit the program, select File | Open, and then select the *Exer18-5 – Login File.a6p* file.

6. Log in as the same user a second time and note that when you jump to the main program file your check marks are recalled.

JumpFile()

Open *Exer18-5 – Login File.a6p* and look inside the *Jump to Course* Calculation icon at the bottom of the flowline. Inside this Calculation icon you will note that you are using the system function *JumpFile*. Jumping to another

Authorware file is very easy with the *JumpFile()* function in Authorware. In this example, you are jumping from the log-in file to the main program. Sometimes if your curriculum is large enough you may want to break up your files into separate Authorware files to save file space and allow other developers to work on separate files to speed development and avoid version control problems.

The *JumpFile()* function has three arguments. If you look at the example of the format of *JumpFile()* you will see the following:

```
JumpFile("filename"[, "variable1, variable2, ...",
["folder"]])
```

The three arguments that make up *JumpFile* are very simple to understand. Jumping between two Authorware files is very similar to taking a vacation. You need three things when you go on a holiday: (1) you need to know where you are going, (2) you have to pack your suitcase, and (3) you need to know where to send postcards to your friends back home.

The first argument, *"filename"*, is your destination. This is the file you want Authorware to launch. In this example, you are jumping to the *Exer18-5* main program file. You do not need to include the extension of the file to which you plan to jump because Authorware automatically searches for files with an *.A6P* extension when it executes a jump. Similarly, *RunA6W* automatically searches for files with an *.EXE* or *.A6R* extension.

The second argument, *"variable list"*, is optional. This would represent the clothes you pack in your suitcase. What do you need to take with you on your trip? This second argument allows you to specify which variable values will be transported to the file you are jumping to. In this example, you are taking the value of the variables *UserName*, *FirstName*, and *jobTitle*. With this information, you can then display the user's name on screen while they are taking the training. By defining the argument variable in *JumpFile*, you can pass the value in that variable to the file to which you are jumping. When passing custom variables, make certain they have been created in both files. If you list several variables, be sure to separate them with commas and enclose the entire list in quotation marks. As a shortcut, you can use an asterisk (*) to list variable names with a common prefix or to list all variables.

The final argument, *"folder"*, is optional. Just like the address of a friend back home, this argument will specify where data is returned from the next file. By defining the argument *"folder"*, you can change the value of the *RecordsLocation* system variable from the default location (the *A6W_DATA* folder in the Windows directory). This is the only method of changing the *RecordsLocation* variable. In this example you are passing the information to the default Authorware *RecordsLocation*, but then you are creating a custom folder for each user. This will allow students who take the course on this computer to have their own set of files.

Resume File Settings

•T/P•

To see another example of the Resume and *JumpFile* functionality look at the Macromedia Show Me files in your installed Authorware directory called *Logon.a6p* and *Content.a6p*.

There are many methods for having a user return to an Authorware file he has visited previously and retrieve his status in the course. Among the options are retrieving data from a database (see Chapter 19) or sending variable data to a local text file and then reading that information back into Authorware, as you did in Exercise 18-3. There is another option native to Authorware: *On Return/Resume*. The Resume setting restarts the piece where the user quit. Authorware keeps track of the user's location in the piece and of the values of all variables, and stores this information in a user records file. Authorware creates a user records file for every Authorware piece and assigns to it the piece's file name with an REC file extension. Authorware stores the user records file either in the *A6w_data* folder (in the Windows folder) or in the folder you specify.

Take a Look

1. Open *Exer18-5 – Main Program.a6p* from your working directory.

2. Select File | Modify | Properties (Ctrl + Shift + D) to open the Properties dialog box for the program.

3. Click on the Interaction tab to display the Interaction options.

4. Note that the On Return setting is set to Resume. See figure 18-56.

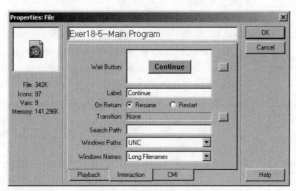

Fig. 18-56. On Return option set to Resume.

The default setting is Restart. You are by now very familiar with how Authorware behaves every time a packaged file is run. Every time you launch your Authorware application, the file starts from the first screen. The Resume setting records the value of all system and custom variables every time the user runs the course. The Resume setting creates a records file on the user's hard drive. All values of the variables are saved to that file, and every time the Authorware piece is restarted the variable values return to their previous values.

The record file created is placed by default on the user's hard drive at *C:\WIN-DOWS\A6W_DATA*. This value is also stored in the system variable *RecordsLocation*. The file created at the record location is the name of the Authorware file with a *.rec* extension. This file is scrambled and can only be read by Authorware. If you were to attempt to open the "Rec" file, Windows would not have a program associated with that file type to open it. You can look at the content of the Rec file using the Notepad text editor, but what you will see is mostly garbled text.

You can change the location of the record directory with the third argument of the *JumpFile* and *JumpFileReturn* functions. You can also specify the location of the record directory in the *A6W.INI* file. This file should be placed in either the Authorware application directory or in the *Windows* directory. For pieces packaged with the Authorware runtime, the *A6W.INI* file may be placed in the directory that contains the executable (*.EXE*) file. If Authorware does not locate the *A6W.INI* file, it creates a new file in the *Windows* directory.

Summary

In this chapter you learned how to create a basic user log-in with password and data-tracking capabilities. Log-ins can be more complex or even more simple based on your requirements, but all log-ins have the following features in common.

- *Text entry interaction that can accept any user input*
- *Storage of the user's text entry*
- *Capability to create a method for storing user data*
- *Recall of information the user entered into the course the last time they logged on*
- *Checking of information the user has entered to make sure it is correct*

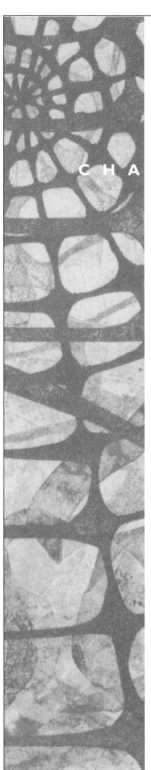

CHAPTER

19

Connecting

to Databases

Introduction

In Chapter 18 you wrote data out to text files that stored user data such as names, but you now need something more powerful, something to handle a lot more data, robustly and possibly across a network. You have looked into the options and have discovered that finally you have to learn how to connect Authorware to a database.

 This is a step forward in thinking, but it really is the least painful and most rewarding step you can take in your Authorware career. Once you understand how to use databases, you will never look back. In this chapter you will learn how to use Authorware to read and manipulate databases on a local machine, across a corporate LAN, and via the Web through an intranet or on the Internet. To perform the exercises in this chapter you will need a computer with Microsoft Access installed. By the end of this chapter you will:

* *Understand the fundamentals of connecting Authorware and databases*

* *Know the basics of SQL*

* *Connect to a database on our own machine*

* *Connect to a database over the Web*

Guided Tour 19A: Databases and Standards: ODBC Versus ASP Solutions

Understanding the basics is really the key to becoming comfortable with databases and Authorware, and all Authorware database solutions are structured in the same manner, as depicted in figure 19-1.

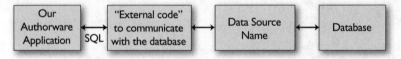

Fig. 19-1. An overview of Authorware communicating with a database.

Let's go through the diagram shown in figure 19-1. Each database solution you build will consist of these four boxes, the only difference in the solutions being what these boxes contain. The Authorware applications here communicate with the "external code" (e.g. ASP or ColdFusion) using SQL (Structured Query Language). Again, do not worry; this is not something you have to master. You simply need to know four commands, explained in the material that follows. There are many different types of "external code" you can use to communicate with the database. Many times you will be forced into one or the other by the environment in which you are working.

The data source name contains the location of the database and must be set up on the machine or server where the "external code" to communicate to the database resides. The only way the "external code" can communicate with the database is if it has this location information residing in the same place where it is. The final box can be any ODBC-compliant database type, such as Microsoft Access, Sybase, Oracle, dBase, FoxPro, and so on. It does not matter here, as all of the databases will understand the SQL you use.

Setting up this Authorware database system requires four subsystems to be set up correctly. The remainder of this chapter examines this piece by piece for both a direct database connection system and a Web-enabled system. The diagram of figure 19-1 shows how these pieces fit together.

The biggest issue to deal with first is to decide which "external code" to communicate with your database. All of the dozens of these third-party solutions fall into two categories. These categories are via direct database connection or via a Web connection. You are going to explore the standard ODBC solution and the ASP solution for the direct and Web connection methods, as these are two of the most common, and both are free.

To know which of these two systems to use is very simple. This has to do with how the computers running the Authorware piece are connected to the computer or server containing the database. If your Authorware piece is going to use a database on a user's computer or on a LAN, it is easier, simpler, and faster to use a direct connection, such as the ODBC solution. If, however, you have an Authorware piece that is only able to connect over the Internet or an intranet, you must use a Web connection, such as the ASP solution.

For example, you might have an Authorware piece running on client machines linked to the Internet but not to one another. In this case, you would have to use a Web solution to link all these machines to a database on a remote server. If, on the other hand, you had a piece running in one company and all machines linked via LAN, including the server or computer with the database, you could use the direct ODBC method.

Imagine you are going to create a CBT for a global company with offices in America, Singapore, and Holland. The CBT will be distributed by CD-ROM to the remote offices in Singapore and Holland but will run over the intranet in America. The American users all sit in the head office, and all are connected via LAN and via intranet to their database server. The Singapore workers use laptops and have only Internet access, whereas in Holland the computers are also LAN connected to the servers in America, but the Dutch office is forbidden to use the Internet or intranet.

The American version of a CBT could use either direct ODBC connection or a Web-based ASP solution. The Singapore users would have to use a Web-based solution, as their only connection to the database server is via the Web. The Dutch office would have to use a direct ODBC solution, as its only connection to the database server is via a LAN. Let's take a look at these two systems. First, let's take a closer look at the ODBC solution, an example of which is shown in figure 19-2.

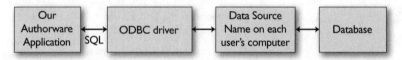

Fig. 19-2. Overview of Authorware communicating with a database using ODBC.

Note that the ODBC driver and DSN must be set up on each end user's computer. Figure 19-3 shows an example of the ASP solution.

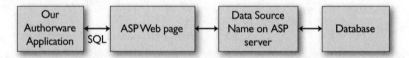

Fig. 19-3. Overview of Authorware communicating with a database using ASP.

Note that the data source name must be set up on the Web server that hosts the ASP page. Understand that it is the method of communication available between your Authorware piece and the database that determines the choice of using ODBC or a Web-based solution, not whether you are running a Web-packaged or runtime-packaged Authorware piece.

Guided Tour 19B: Using SQL, the Language of the Database

Description

In this guided tour you will learn how to use SQL, the language of databases. This is the standard language used to read and manipulate databases. You will learn by using a finished Authorware piece and a database, manipulating the database using four basic SQL commands. No matter what type of database, connection or Authorware application you build, a basic knowledge of this language goes a long way. In this exercise, you will:

- *Open and view a basic Access database*
- *Practice the four main SQL commands*

Take a Look

Let's take a look at the Authorware application that is communicating with a database.

CD-ROM

1. Select File | Open and locate the *Practice* folder on the companion CD-ROM. Open this folder and you will see a number of chapter folders. Open the *Chapter19* folder and locate and double click on the file named *Db19-1.mdb*.

2. Save this database to your working directory so you do not get a "read-only" error using this file from the CD-ROM.

3. The *Db19-1* file should now appear in our copy of Access, and the main Database dialog box should be displayed containing the table *Address_Data*. See figure 19-4.

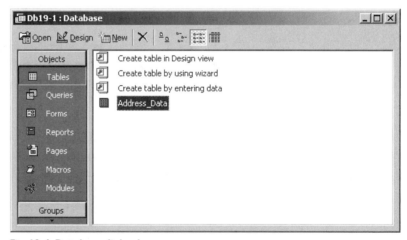

Fig. 19-4. Database dialog box.

4. Double click on the *Address_Data* table field to open the *Address_Data* table view. See figure 19-5.

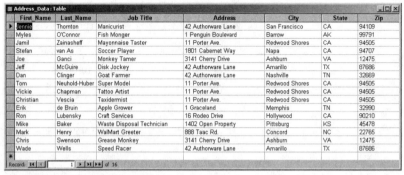

Fig. 19-5. Address_Data *table view.*

5. Note how the database table is built. It has been given seven columns and all required fields. Each row is another entry, one row per user. This table has been built to hold user names, addresses, and job titles. It is useful to know at this stage that a single database can contain many tables that can be linked by rules, or relationships. This database is of the simplest format, having just one table.

6. Now that you have seen the database in its raw format, close the database and Access down by clicking on the X in the upper right-hand corner of the main Access window.

7. Let's look at a completed Authorware application that can communicate with this database. Select File | Open and locate the *Practice* folder on the companion CD-ROM. Open this folder and you will see a number of chapter folders. Open the *Chapter19* folder and locate and double click on the file named *Exer19-1*.

8. The *Exer19-1* file should now appear in your copy of Authorware. Select Control | Restart or press the Restart button on the toolbar to play the file from the top of the flowline.

9. The database *Db19-1.mdb* is read into Authorware and displayed in a table. See figure 19-6.

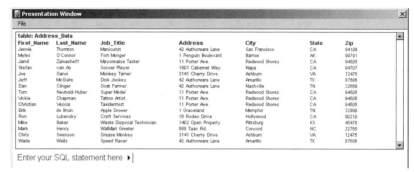

Fig. 19-6. Presentation Window of the database.

10. The first SQL command you will learn will be *SELECT. SELECT* allows you to view the database, or parts of it. With any SQL command you must also give it parameters to use so that it knows what to do. *SELECT* requires that you send parameters that specify what to return and from what table. In SQL, an asterisk is the wildcard. You see here that the entire table has been brought into the top window of the Presentation window. Beneath this window is the space for typing in SQL commands. The results appear in the bottom window.

a) Type in *SELECT * FROM Address_Data;*. Remember to include all of the SQL in uppercase and always end a command with a semicolon.

b) Press Enter and you will see the entire table *Address_Data* displayed in the bottom box.

c) Type *SELECT Last_Name FROM Address_Data;*. You will see that all last names have been selected from the table. See figure 19-7.

SQLString Executed
SELECT Last_Name FROM Address_Data;

Result:
Thornton
O'Connor
Zainasheff
van As
Ganci
McGuire
Clinger
Neuhold-Huber
Chapman
Vescia
de Bruin
Lubensky
Baker
Henry
Swenson
Wells

Fig. 19-7. Last names.

d) Type *SELECT First_Name,Last_Name FROM Address_Data ORDER BY Last_Name;*. You will examine how first and last names have been selected and the results ordered alphabetically. See figure 19-8.

SQL String Executed
SELECT First_Name,Last_Name FROM Address_Data ORDER BY Last_Name;

Result:

Mike	Baker
Vickie	Chapman
Dan	Clinger
Erik	de Bruin
Joe	Ganci
Mark	Henry
Ron	Lubensky
Jeff	McGuire
Tom	Neuhold-Huber
Myles	O'Connor
Chris	Swenson
Jennie	Thornton
Stefan	van As
Christian	Vescia
Wade	Wells
Jamil	Zainasheff

Fig. 19-8. Alphabetical list of names.

e) Try some more *SELECT* commands yourself. Note that SQL does not return an error message if you make a typo; it simply says "Completed!"

11. Now that you can read a database, how do you insert values into it? The answer is with the *INSERT* command.

a) Type *INSERT INTO Address_Data values ('Super','Man','Hero','1 North Pole Road','San Francisco','CA',22222);*. You will see that a new line is entered at the bottom of the database. Also note that any character columns must be entered using single quotes.

Numerical values can be entered without quotes. Always be consistent with the database. In many database applications, you can set a column up to be either characters, dates, numerical values, or binary numbers. Always use single quotes for character columns and date columns, even if entering a number. The number sign (#) is preferred for the Date format when using Access. In Access, if you open the database, open the table, and then select the View/Design View, you will see the different data types of the columns. See figure 19-9.

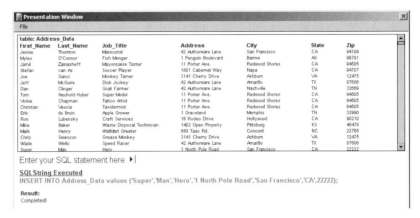

Fig. 19-9. Inserting a new row of information.

b) Type *INSERT INTO Address_Data (First_Name,Last_Name) VALUES ('Fred','Bassett');*. You will see that this is another way of using the *INSERT* command to insert values into a table. See figure 19-10.

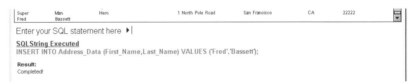

Fig. 19-10. Inserting the name Fred Bassett.

12. Assume a student represented in the database, Myles, did not pass his quiz and has been fired from the company. How do you delete him from the records? Easy; use the *DELETE* command.

a) Try typing *DELETE FROM Address_Data WHERE First_Name = 'Myles';*. You will see that now Myles needs a job and is no longer in the records. Be aware that this command will delete everyone with the first name of Myles.

b) Let's try a more specific delete so that you make sure you only delete one person. Let's sack Jennie, too. Type *DELETE FROM Address_Data WHERE First_Name = 'Jennie' AND Last_Name = 'Thornton';*. This will remove the name Jennie Thornton from the database. If you wanted to be even more specific, you could add the *Delete* command to this job title and city, and so on. See figure 19-11.

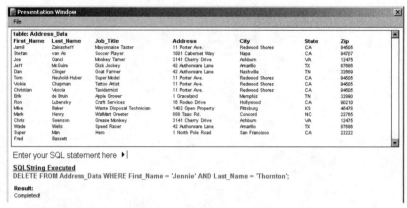

Fig. 19-11. Deleting the name Jennie Thornton.

13. Now that you can select, insert, and delete, all that is left to do is to learn how to update records. For this you use the command *UPDATE*. Let's give Jamil a well-deserved promotion.

   a) Type *UPDATE Address_Data SET Job_Title = 'Authorware Guru' WHERE First_Name = 'Jamil';*. Note how quickly Jamil is promoted. Notice that anyone in the database with the first name of Jamil would also be promoted to guru status. In this type of situation a single unique piece of data like a social security number, or employee ID number is very handy. See figure 19-12.

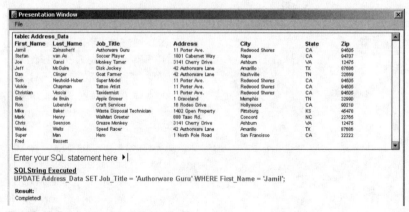

Fig. 19-12. Promoting Jamil Zainasheff.

This is a useful
trick if you are
using dates. By using
Date < 01/01/2000,
you can update all data
before the specified
date, which in this
case is 2000.
See figure 19-13.

14. Let's say you wanted to update all people whose zip codes are greater than 94000, as the postal service has allocated a new zip code to all of these areas.

a) Type *UPDATE Address_Data SET Zip = 12345 WHERE Zip > 94000;*. You will see all changes made to the zip codes.

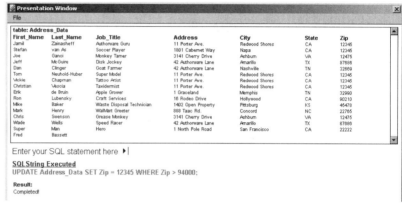

Fig. 19-13. Updating zip codes.

Practice Exercise 19-1: Creating a Database and Setting Up a Data Source Name

Description

Now that you are familiar with SQL and the difference between setting up a direct ODBC system and setting up a Web system, you can start looking at building these systems. You are going to start with a simple ODBC system. Figure 19-14 shows the missing parts of the system.

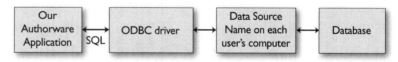

Fig. 19-14. Overview of Authorware communicating with a database using ODBC.

The missing parts are a database, the data source name, the ODBC driver, and the Authorware file. In this section you are going to build a database and set the data source name. In the section on building an ODBC log-in example you will write the Authorware code and use the ODBC commands.

Building a Database

The type of database you choose will depend on many things. More user-friendly database systems such as Microsoft Access are great for prototyping but are not often used in large organizations due to other systems being more reliable and having greater scalability options. Among many systems you may come across are Sybase, Oracle, or SQL Server. Most of the time, if an organization uses a database system you do not know, this is good news, not bad. It probably means the organization has database administrators (DBAs) who can help you build the database.

Whichever database system you use, the first tasks are to specify what fields, tables, and relationships are necessary to the database and then build the database. For this system, you are going to use one table with no relationships. In this exercise you will:

- *Open and view a basic Access database*
- *Practice the four main SQL commands*

Step-by-Step Instructions

1. On your computer, create a folder named *C:\Authorware Exercises*.

2. Open your copy of Microsoft Access.

3. Select Create Blank Database. See figure 19-15.

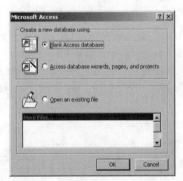

Fig. 19-15. Select Blank Access Database.

4. Save the database as *Db19-2* in the *C:\Authorware Exercises* folder. See figure 19-16.

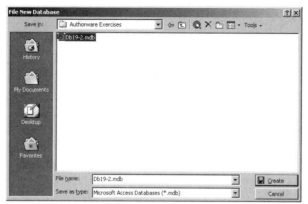

Fig. 19-16. Save the database.

5.   Select the option Create Table in Design View. See figure 19-17.

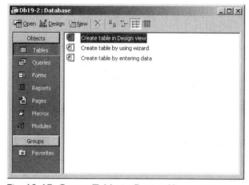

Fig. 19-17. Create Table in Design View option.

6.   Type in the following field names and corresponding data types.

First_Name	*Text*
Last_Name	*Text*
Job_Title	*Text*
Password	*Text*
Date	*Date/Time*

Note how each field must have a data type set, as shown in figure 19-18. It is very important to know what the data type is of each field, as your SQL must be written with this in mind. Remember the use of single quotes.

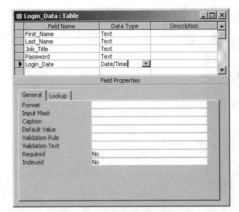

Fig. 19-18. Field names and types.

7.   Select View | Datasheet View. See figure 19-19.

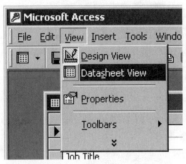

Fig. 19-19. Select Datasheet View.

8.   Fill out the *Address_Data* table as follows. Note in this example that the American MM/DD/YYYY format is used. (If you were outside America, you would probably use DD/MM/YYYY.) Also make sure you do not use column headings that are SQL commands. For example, never use *Date* as a column heading, as SQL will not understand the difference between a column heading and a command. See figure 19-20.

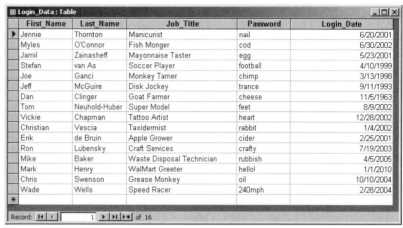

Fig. 19-20. **Address_Data** *table information.*

9.   Close the table and when asked to save the table type *Login_Data.* See fig-
     ure 19-21.

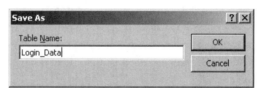

Fig. 19-21. Save the table.

10. If Access asks for a primary key, select No, as you are not going to have
     multiple tables with relationships. See figure 19-22.

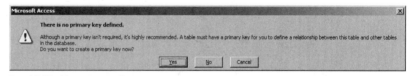

Fig. 19-22. No primary key.

11. Close and save the database.
     You have created your first database to use with Authorware.

Creating the Data Source Name

The data source name is a way for the machine to keep track of where the
database is stored so your application doesn't need to. If you had twenty calls
to the database, and each time you had to specify where the database was, that

would be twenty references. But if you have to change the location of that database, instead of twenty places to change the reference in your code, you simply can change one place on the system, and your calls will still work. As long as the name of the data source does not change, it will find the database connected to it. Now that you have built the database, the next thing to put in place will be the data source name. The data source name resides on the machine either in the location of the ODBC drivers for the direct LAN connections (typically the machine the student is using to run your Authorware file) or on the same Web server as the ASP Web page for the Web connections. For ODBC solutions, the most usual place to set up the DSN is on each computer running the Authorware file. For Web solutions, you must find out who the server administrator is and ask them to set one up for you. You must tell the server administrator the name and location of your database, information the DBA (database administrator) should have told you.

As the Web server DSN will be set up by someone else, here you will only run through setting up a DSN for individual computers. While you do this, remember that all the Web server administrator is doing is something very similar to this but on the server rather than on a desktop computer. If you are working by yourself and do not have the benefit of working with a Web server administrator, you may have to set up a Web server yourself. This solution is covered later in this chapter under "Guided Tour 19C: Web Solutions and Setting Up a Personal Web Server."

1. If you did not create the previous database manually, create a folder named *Authorware Exercises*.

2. Locate the *Practice* folder on the companion CD-ROM. Open this folder and you will see a number of chapter folders. Open the *Chapter19* folder and locate the file named *Db19-2*. Copy this file to *C:\Authorware Exercises*.

3. Open the *Data Sources* (ODBC) icon from the control panel or from the Administrative Tools palette on the control panel. See figure 19-23.

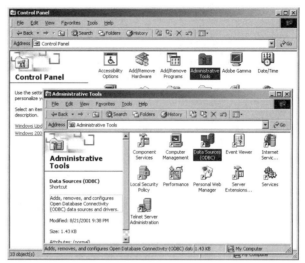

Fig. 19-23. Data Sources (ODBC) icon.

4.   Select the System DSN tab in the Data Source Administrator dialog box
so you can create a DSN that will be accessible by all users of this
machine. Click on Add. See figure 19-24.

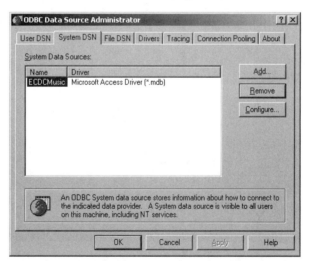

Fig. 19-24. ODBC Data Source Administrator dialog box.

5.   Select the database type. For this example, you are using an Access database. Therefore, click on Driver do Microsoft Access (*.mdb*) option and
then click on the Finish button. See figure 19-25.

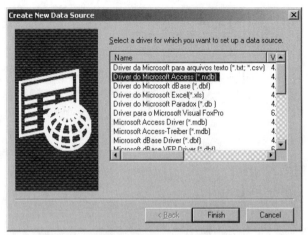

Fig. 19-25. Create New Data Source dialog box.

6. Create a descriptive name for the DSN. For this example, type *Login Database DSN* and type in a description of what this DSN is connecting. Click on Select. See figure 19-26.

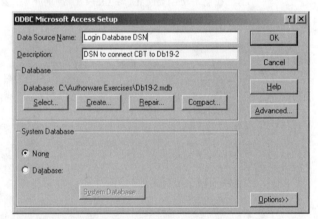

Fig. 19-26. Naming the data source parameters.

7. Locate the *Db19-2.mdb* file in *C:\Authorware Exercises* and click on OK. See figure 19-27.

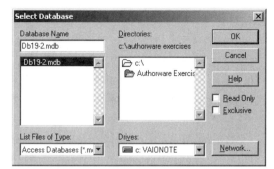

Fig. 19-27. Select the database you just created.

8. You will now see that the DSN has been created. Now the ODBC drivers will know where the database is when Authorware calls the database. See figure 19-28.

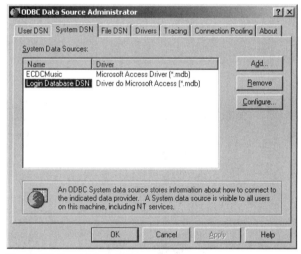

Fig. 19-28. Completed DSN.

You now know how to manually create a DSN on a PC. There are also third-party tools that allow you to do this within Authorware. Therefore, if you do not have access to the client's machines, you can generate this automatically. This is also useful if you have a large number of client machines and you do not wish to work on each one individually. You will use one of these automated methods in the next section.

Practice Exercise 19-2: Building an ODBC Log-in

Description

In this exercise you are going to adapt the log-in sequence from Chapter 18 to utilize the database knowledge you have so far, and substitute the text data for a database. In this exercise you will:

- *Make a fully functional log-in routine connected to a database*
- *Learn the ODBC functions*
- *Discover a faster way of setting up a DSN*

Take a Look

CD-ROM

Before beginning the exercise, let's take a look at the exercise in its completed state so that you can clearly see what it is you are about to build.

1. Select File | Open and locate the *Practice* folder on the companion CD-ROM. Open this folder and you will see a number of chapter folders. Open the *Chapter19* folder and locate and double click on the file named *Exer19-3*.

2. The *Exer19-3* file should now appear in your copy of Authorware. Select Control | Restart or press the Restart button on the toolbar to play the file from the top of the flowline. Note the following properties of this completed exercise.

   - *The program works identically to the log-in you created in Chapter 18.*
   - *Make sure you open the Access database in* C:\Authorware Exercises\Db-19-2.mdb *to see what the program is doing.*
   - *You can log in as anyone from the database in* C:\Authorware Exercises\Db-19-2.mdb.
   - *The job title can be changed in each entry and is updated in the database.*
   - *The Login_Date field is updated every time you log in.*
   - *If you log in as a new user, a new line is added to the database.*

Storyboard: On Screen

Figure 19-29 shows what the finished exercise will look like on screen.

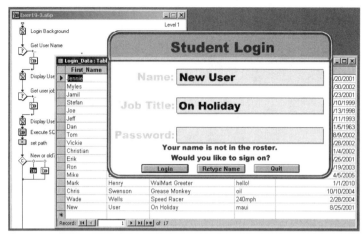

Fig. 19-29. Entering a new user.

Storyboard: Behind the Scenes

Figure 19-30 shows the flowline (with all icons, their placement, and their names) as it should look when you are finished with this exercise.

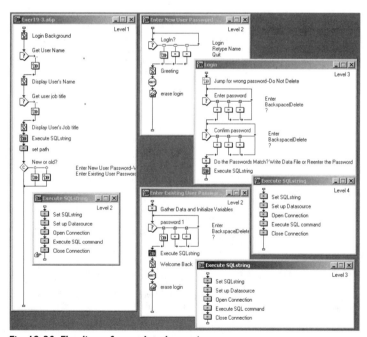

Fig. 19-30. Flowline of completed exercise.

Step-by-Step Instructions

Go Solo

1. Open *Exer19-2* and resave it as *Exer19-3.a6p* to create a new file for this exercise, continuing from the log-in example in Chapter 18.

    a) Select File | Open and locate the *Practice* folder on the companion CD-ROM. Open this folder and you will see a number of chapter folders. Open the *Chapter19* folder and locate and double click on the file named *Exer19-2*.

    b) Select Save As from the File/Open option and select the file name *Exer19-3.a6p*.

    c) This exercise assumes you have built the database and copied it to *C:\Authorware Exercises\Db-19-2.mdb* on your computer, and have created the DSN, all as described in the previous section. If you copy the database *DB19-2* from the CD-ROM, make sure you set the read-only attribute to *off* by right-clicking on the file, selecting Properties, and unchecking the Read Only checkbox.

2. Remove the old code that reads the text files from the main flowline and replace it with code for reading the database.

    a) Delete the three Calculation icons named *Storage Locations for Student Records*, *Read the User Data*, and *Judge if the user is new or old*.

    b) Drag a Map icon under the icon *Display User's Job Title* and name it *Execute SQLstring*. See figure 19-31.

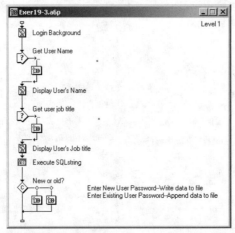

Fig. 19-31. Deleted text file code and new Map icon.

    c) Double click on the empty Map icon you just created.

3. Create the database communication code.

    a) To talk to the database, perform the following steps:

- *Set the SQL command*
- *Know the name of the data source that points to the database*
- *Open the ODBC connection*
- *Execute the ODBC connection*
- *Close the ODBC connection*

b) Drag five (5) Calculation icons (one under another) into the Map icon and name them as follows. See figure 19-32.

- *Set SQLstring*
- *Set up Datasource*
- *Open Connection*
- *Execute SQL command*
- *Close Connection*

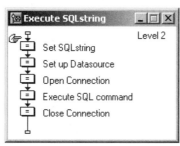

Fig. 19-32. Five Calculation icons for communicating with the database.

c) Double click on the first icon, *Set SQLstring*.

d) Type in the following:

```
lastName:=SubStr(UserName,CharCount(FirstName)+2,
CharCount(UserName))
```

This is needed, as Authorware has only a *FirstName* variable, not a *lastName*.

e) Type in the following.

```
lastName:=Replace("'","''",lastName)
```

Remember that SQL will understand any single quotes as the beginning and end of a value (e.g., *SET last_Name = 'O'Connor'* would be read as *SET Last_Name = 'O' to SQL*). For this reason, you must always use a double single quote (e.g., *SET Last_Name = 'O"Connor'*).

f) Type in the following.

```
if lastName = "" then
```

635

```
        lastName := "None"

    end if
```

You need this in case a user types in a first name only.

g) The last line should read as follows:

```
sqlString:="SELECT * FROM Login_Data WHERE First_Name
= '"^FirstName^"' AND Last_Name = '"^lastName^"';"
```

h) This is the SQL statement that will pull out the data for the user who has just logged in. Study this line and note the use of single and double quotes. For example, if Myles O'Connor had just logged in, you would want *SQLstring* to be something like *SELECT * FROM Login_Data WHERE First_Name = 'Myles' AND Last_Name = 'O"Connor'*. See figure 19-33.

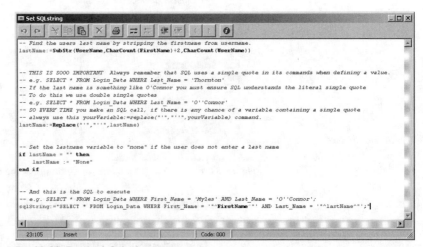

Fig. 19-33. Finished Calculation icon.

i) Close and save the icon, and make sure you add a description for the *last_Name* and *SQLstring* variables.

4. The next Calculation icon, *Set up Datasource*, is just used to store the correct DSN you have already set up on your PC.

a) Double click on the Calculation icon to open it, and type in the following.

```
database := "Login Database DSN"

dbUser := ""

dbPassword := ""
```

b) This sets the variable database to your DSN, and sets a database user and password. Every database can have permissions set so that users of the database can have access to different portions. In this case, you have no users or passwords set in the database and therefore user and password are set to "". Understand that this is a user and password for access to the database, not the user and passwords of the actual data. Setting these allows you to keep the database on a shared network location, but without knowing the password, the users can't see the data inside. The course will know the information it needs. See figure 19-34.

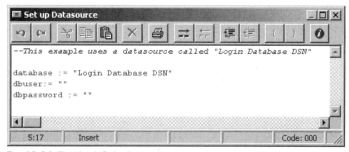

Fig. 19-34. Finished Calculation icon.

c) Close and save the icon and be sure to write a description for each new variable.

5. The next Calculation icon, *Open Connection*, is the first time you talk to the database.

a) This line uses the command *ODBCOpen*:

```
ODBCHandle := ODBCOpen(WindowHandle, "ErrorVar",
database, dbUser, dbPassword)
```

There are only three ODBC commands used here: *Open*, *Execute*, and *Close*. The *ODBCOpen* command opens an ODBC connection between your Authorware piece and the database. Imagine your Authorware piece as a fire truck that pulls up near a fire hydrant. The *ODBCOpen* command is the hoseman sent to find the hydrant. The database variable contains the name of the hydrant, and the DSN you set up earlier is the map the hoseman uses to find the connection for the hose. This entire connection is then stored in the variable *ODBCHandle*.

b) The parameters of the ODBC command are as follows. See figure 19-35.

• WindowHandle *is the identifier of your Authorware piece.*

- "Error Var" *is the name of the variable that holds errors returned during the communication. This name must be in quotes. It is the name of the variable, not its current value.*

- database *is the name of the DSN.*

- dbUser *and* dbPassword *are set to* "" *, unless you are using a username and password.*

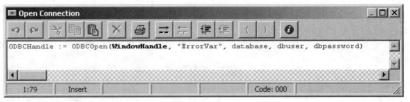

Fig. 19-35. Finished Calculation icon.

c) Close the Calculation icon. Again, make sure to add a description for each variable.

d) When you close the Calculation icon, you will get a dialog box Where is function ODBCOpen()?. This is because the ODBC drivers are external to Authorware.

e) Select the file *ODBC.U32* in your Authorware directory, and click on Open. See figure 19-36.

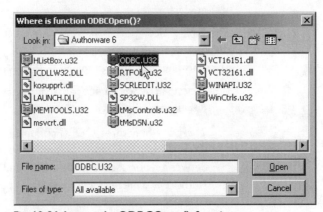

Fig. 19-36. Import the **ODBCOpen()** *function.*

f) Save the Calculation icon.

6. Open the next Calculation icon *Execute SQL command*.

a) Type:

```
ODBCData := ODBCExecute(ODBCHandle, sqlString)
```

This executes the previously entered SQL string.

b) The output of the SQL is placed in the variable *ODBCData*. See figure 19-37.

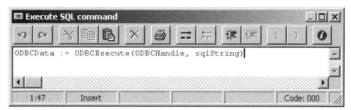

Fig. 19-37. ODBCExecute *function.*

c) Close and save the icon.

d) Again, when the pop-up window reads *Where is function ODBCExecute(),* double click on the *ODBC.U32* file to import it. It might seem silly to keep closing and opening the connection, and if you perform a series of SQL statements this may be an inefficient way to operate. However, you must ensure that each open connection is closed as soon as you have finished using it. This ensures the proper operation of this function.

7. In the last Calculation icon, ensure the connection is closed.

On closing connections: Windows 98 could support 100 open connections at a time. Once you have 100, the functions stop functioning. It is possible to open the connection to the database at the beginning of your file, communicate during your course, then when the user clicks the Quit button, you close the connection. If the user finishes correctly, this would be fine. But if the user quits by clicking on the X instead of your Quit button, that close is never called. More likely what will happen is that in your testing, you will run the file from the top, opening the connection, use the Ctrl+J to get back to the icons, then run again the next time you want to test something else. Each time you do this a new connection is made, and its identifier is put into the *ODBCHandle* variable. The old one is not destroyed, but you no longer have any way to close it. This is why you want to close the connection as soon as you are finished with it.

a) Type *ODBCClose(ODBCHandle).*

b) Close the icon and import the function *ODBCClose* from *ODBC.U32.* See figure 19-38.

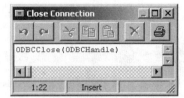

Fig. 19-38. **ODBCClose** *function.*

8. Close the Map icon *Execute SQLstring*. You have now replaced the code so that it will read the database instead of reading the text files. Provide the decision functionality for determining if this is a new or old user.

   a) Drag a Calculation icon under the Map icon *Execute SQLstring*. Name the Calculation icon *set path*.

   b) Type the following lines:

```
if ODBCData = "" then
 path := 1
else
 path := 2
end if
```

   c) Close and save the icon. See figure 19-39.

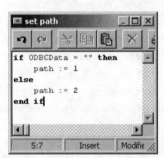

Fig. 19-39. Calculation icon **set path.**

9. Change the code in the *New User Password* Map icon attached to the *New* or *Old* Decision icon.

   a) Double click on the Map icon *Enter New User Password – Write data to file*.

   b) Double click on the Map icon *Login*. See figure 19-40.

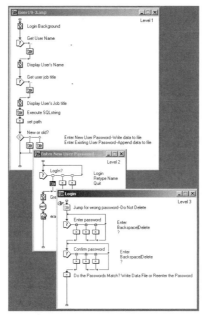

Fig. 19-40. Login *Map icon*.

    c)   Double click on the Calculation icon *Do the Passwords Match? Write Data File or Reenter the Password.*

    d) Comment out the *WriteExtFile* line. See figure 19-41.

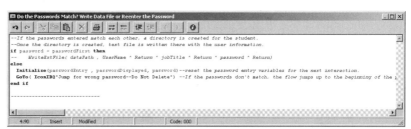

Fig. 19-41. *Modified Calculation icon code.*

10. Now that you have removed the text code, add some code to write to the database.

    a)   On the level 1 flowline, select and then copy the *Execute SQLstring* Map icon.

    b)   Paste this icon under the *Do the Passwords Match? Write Data File or Reenter the Password* icon in the level 3 flowline. See figure 19-42.

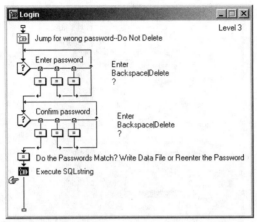

Fig. 19-42. Pasted Execute SQLstring Map icon.

c) Double click on the pasted *Execute SQLstring* icon in the level 3 flow-line.

d) Double click on the first Calculation icon, *Set SQLstring*.

e) Edit the last line to read:

```
sqlString:="INSERT INTO Login_Data VALUES
('"^FirstName^"','"^lastName^"','"^jobTitle^"',
'"^LowerCase(password)^"','"^Year^"-"^Month^"-
"^Day^"');".
```

f) This code is for adding a new user. Therefore, you use the SQL command *INSERT*. The first name, last name, job title, and password are simple enough, but you must be careful with the date. Although in Access the date is set to MM/DD/YYYY for American PCs and DD/MM/YYYY for most others, SQL defaults to YYYY-MM-DD, so this is the format you must use. You can also add time, as in YYYY-MM-DD HH:MM:SS (24-hour clock). As long as it is a valid format, you should be able to enter it using the Authorware *var* Date. You can reformat it later if you need to, but it will adjust based on the system Date format. See figure 19-43.

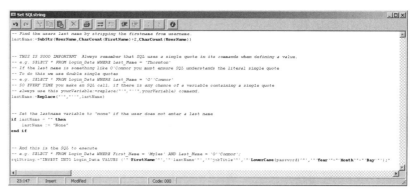

Fig. 19-43. Modified Calculation icon.

    g)   Close and save the Calculation icon.

    h)   Close all windows to the level 1 flowline.

11. Let's now change the existing user code.

    a)   Double click on the Map icon *Enter Existing User Password – Append data to file*.

    b)   Double click on the first Calculation icon, *Gather Data and Initialize Variables*.

    c)   Edit the last line to read:

```
existingPassword:=UpperCase(GetLine(ODBCData,
4,4,"\t"))
```

    Line four in the existing text file contains the user's password.

This grabs the existing password from the variable *ODBCData*, which contains the line of information from the database about the existing user. You do this using the *GetLine* function. We will separate the pieces of data with a Tab symbol. This is called a Tab Delimited string. The password is the fourth tab-delimited piece of information. An example of such a line is *Chris\tSwenson\tGrease Monkey\toil\t10/10/2004*. See figure 19-44.

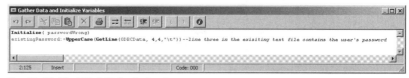

Fig. 19-44. Modified Calculation icon.

    d)   Save and close the Calculation icon.

    e)   Delete the Calculation icon *Existing User – Append data to disk*.

    f)   As before, copy the Map icon *Execute SQLstring from the level 1 flowline*.

g) Paste the Map icon where the deleted Calculation icon was in the level 2 flowline, just above the *Welcome Back* Display icon. See figure 19-45.

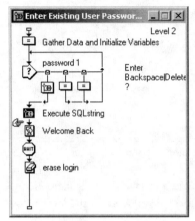

Fig. 19-45. Modified flowline.

h) Double click on the *Execute SQLstring* icon in the level 2 flowline.
i) Double click on the *Set SQLstring* Calculation icon.
j) Change the last line to:

```
sqlString:="UPDATE Login_Data SET Job_Title =
'"^jobTitle^"', Login_Date = '"^Year^"-"^Month^"-
"^Day^"' WHERE First_Name = '"^FirstName^"' AND
Last_Name = '"^lastName^"';"
```

k) Note that because you are dealing with an existing user, you use the SQL command *UPDATE* to update a row in the database. This command will update the job title and log-in date for the line where the first and last names match the current user.

l) Update the job title and log-in date for the line where the first and last names match the current user. See figure 19-46.

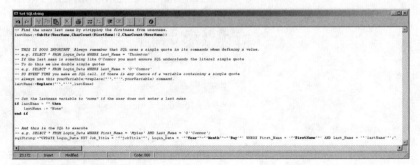

Fig. 19-46. Modified Calculation icon.

m) Close and save the Calculation icon.

12. Run the file and open the database in Access. You can see how the rows are added and updated as you use the application.

If you package this file you must include the *ODBC.U32* file with the finished piece. See Chapter 22 on publishing for more information.

The U32 Solution

In this exercise you used a manually set up DSN named *Login Database DSN*. Sometimes in the trenches it is inconvenient to go to every computer where the ODBC drivers will run and manually set this up. Luckily, there is an easy solution to this, available for free download by the Authorware development firm, The Media Shoppe (*www.mediashoppe.com*). It is a U32 named *tmsDSN.U32,* which contains a function that can automatically set up a DSN on a PC.

1. Let's try this out. Go back into the control panel and find the *ODBC Data Source* icon. Double click and in the System DSN select *Login Database DSN*. Click on Remove, and then on Yes. See figure 19-47.

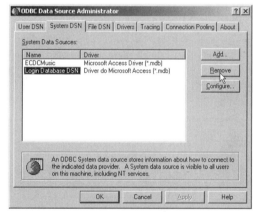

Fig. 19-47. Remove the current DSN.

2. Close the ODBC administrator and run *Exer19-3.a6p*. You will note that because the DSN is not present the file cannot read or write to the database, and every user will be treated like a new user.

3. Insert the *tmsDSN.U32* code.

    a) Insert a Calculation icon at the very beginning of the flowline and name it *Data Source (tmsDSN.U32)*.

    b) Type the following lines. See figure 19-48.

    ```
    db ReqType:=4
    ```

```
db Type:="Microsoft Access Driver (*.mdb)"

db List:="DSN=Login Database DSN;"

db List:=db List^"Description=DSN to connect CBT to
DB19-2;"

db List:=db List^"Access;"

db List:=db List^"DBQ=C:\\Authorware Exercises\\
Db19-2.mdb;"

ODBC DriverInstalled:=tMsDBRegister(db ReqType, db
Type, db List)
```

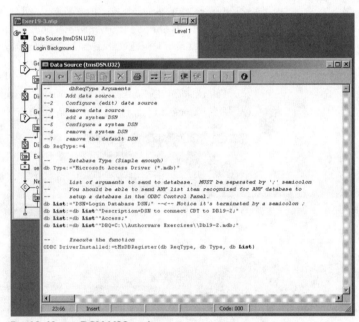

Fig. 19-48. tmsDSN.U32 code.

4.   Close and save the Calculation icon and import the function *tmsRegister()* from the *tmsDSN.U32* in the Authorware program folder.

5.   When you run the file, you will note that it connects straight to the database.

The DSN must be in the same location as the external code, which in this case is the *ODBC.U32* file. This means that you can use the *tmsDSN.U32*. In a Web solution in which the database is connected via the Internet, the DSN must be on the Web server where the database is. The *tmsDSN.U32* cannot set up a DSN on a remote Web server; it can only set one up on a local or network

PC. In the Web solution you must therefore get the Web server administrator to set up the DSN.

Guided Tour 19C: Web Solutions and Setting Up a Personal Web Server

Description

You now know how to set up an ODBC system. What happens if you have a Web-packaged Authorware file running globally and all users access a central database? You need a Web solution. In this and the next section you are going to build a Web solution that simply reads in the database you have been using in the previous ODBC example, using an ASP page. In a Web solution, you need some external code to connect the Authorware application to the database. You will be performing a task very similar to the "ODBC drivers" work that used *ODBC.U32*.

There are many ways to accomplish this (such as using CGI, ColdFusion, PHP, and so on), and all operate in a very similar manner. ASP was chosen for this example because most PCs can be configured relatively simply for experimenting with this. In the following you will simulate a real-world example on your PC. In a real-world application you would probably have a database server, a Web server, and a client PC running a Web browser with your Authorware piece running in it.

In this example, you will configure your PC as the database server, Web server, and client machine all in one. Because of this, as you go through the next two sections remember that normally these servers are different machines, connected via the Internet or an intranet. Figure 19-3 shows you the parts you need, including a database server. You also need to set up the Web server, set the DSN up on the Web server, and write the Authorware application. In this section you will:

- *Enable your computer to act as a database server and a Web server*
- *Set up the database "server" on your PC*
- *Set up the "Web server" on your PC*

Setting Up the Database

For this exercise, assume that the database server is the database you copied to *C:\Authorware Exercises\Db19-2.mdb* from the companion CD-ROM in the ODBC example. If you did not complete the ODBC example, copy this database from the companion CD-ROM to *C:\Authorware Exercises\Db19-2.mdb* and set the database so that it is *not* "read only" by right-clicking on the database, selecting Properties, and then enabling the Read Only checkbox.

For this exercise, setting up the database is as simple as this. In a corporate environment or for databases like SQLServer that are not file-based, this process would be more complex and would require the help of a database administrator.

Setting Up the Web Server

To use your PC as a Web server, you need to install Personal Web Server (PWS). The process is outlined in the following for a Windows 98 computer and a Windows 2000 computer.

Windows 98

There are two places you can get PWS, both of which are free. The Windows 98 CD includes it, and you can download it from the Microsoft Web site.

1. To download PWS from *Microsoft.com*, perform the following.
    a) Go to *http://www.microsoft.com/msdownload/ntoptionpack/ askwiz.ASP*.
    b) Select Option 1.
    c) Run the downloaded file.

2. If you are installing from the Windows 98 CD, perform the following. The Windows 98 CD includes PWS, but you need to run a separate setup program to fully install and configure it. To start the installation, perform the following.
    a) Insert your Windows 98 CD in its drive.
    b) Click on Start and then click on Run.
    c) In the Run dialog box, type *x:\add-ons\pws\setup.exe*.
    d) Substitute the letter of your CD drive for x, and click on OK.

Whichever method you use, run the program. The screen shown in figure 19-49 will appear.

·T/P·

If you do not have the Windows 98 CD, you can download the NT4 Option Pack, which contains PWS for Windows 95 and 98. Be aware that the download is 34 Mb, which will take nearly 3 hours to download with a 28.8 modem.

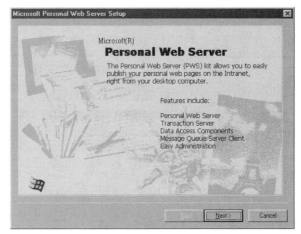

Fig. 19-49. PWS installation introductory screen.

3.   Run through the installation screens.
     a)   Click on Next. See figure 19-50.

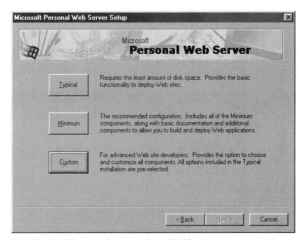

Fig. 19-50. Options for installing PWS.

     b)   Because you are installing PWS specifically for running ASP applica-
          tions, you need to override Microsoft's standard install options by
          clicking on the Custom button.
     c)   The typical installation does not include the excellent ASP docu-
          mentation. Therefore, in the Web Server Setup dialog box you will
          specify this to be installed.
     d)   Click on Custom in the Web Server Setup dialog box. See figure 19-51.

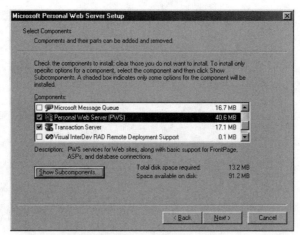

Fig. 19-51. Web Server Setup dialog box.

e) The custom installation has all options of the Typical field selected. Therefore, all you need to do is find the checkbox for the ASP documentation, and enable it. It is three levels down.

f) Highlight Personal Web Server (PWS), being careful not to deselect the box. Select Show Subcomponents.

g) Highlight Documentation, again without deselecting the checkbox. Select Show Subcomponents. See figure 19-52.

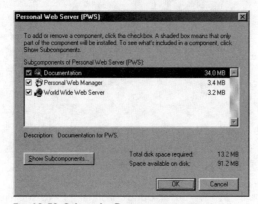

Fig. 19-52. Select the Documentation option.

h) Enable the Active Server Pages checkbox. (See figure 19-53.) Click on OK.

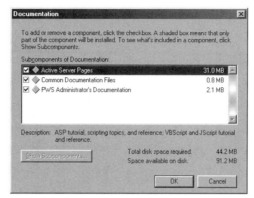

Fig. 19-53. Select the Active Server Pages option.

i) Click on OK once more, and then click on Next to continue with the next step of the installation. See figure 19-54.

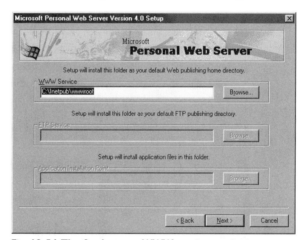

Fig. 19-54. The final screen: WWW service settings.

j) Accept the default path and click on Next.

4. After the installation is complete, you will be asked to restart your computer. After restarting your system, you will see something new in your system tray on the task bar at the bottom right-hand corner of your display which shows that your PWS is now up and running. See figure 19-55.

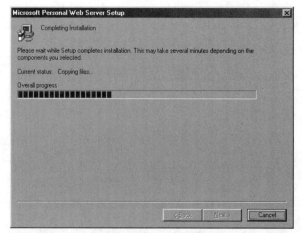

Fig. 19-55. Dialog box showing the PWS installation progress.

5. A quick way to test whether PWS is functional is to go to the URL *http://localhost/iishelp*. (Write this URL down, bookmark it in your browser, and review the documentation.) If the site is displaying successfully, you are assured that you have set up PWS correctly. This site brings up the excellent Help that covers PWS, including an ASP reference. See figure 19-56.

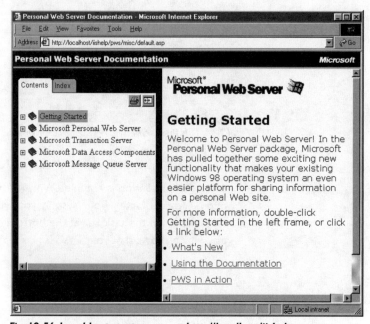

Fig. 19-56. Local host start screen at http://localhost/iishelp.

Windows 2000

To load PWS under Windows 2000, perform the following steps:

1. Open the control panel.
2. Double click on Add/Remove Programs. See figure 19-57.

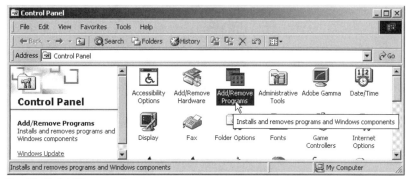

Fig. 19-57. Add/Remove Programs option.

3. Click on the Add/Remove Windows Components option in the left-hand column of the dialog box. See figure 19-58.

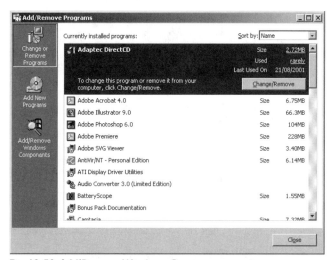

Fig. 19-58. Add/Remove Windows Components option.

4. Select the Internet Information Services (IIS) option. See figure 19-59.

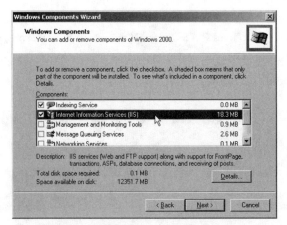

Fig. 19-59. Internet Information Services option.

5. Click on Next.

6. Wait for the Windows Components wizard to copy all of the files. See figure 19-60.

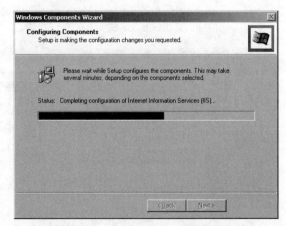

Fig. 19-60. Windows Components wizard.

7. Click on Next when the wizard is finished.

8. Click on Finished. See figure 19-61.

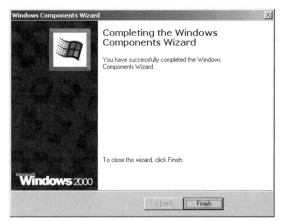

Fig. 19-61. Finished wizard.

9. To test the installation, open a browser window and type in *http://local-host*. See figure 19-62.

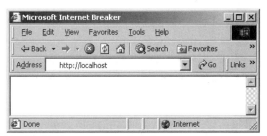

Fig. 19-62. Browser set to localhost.

10. You will see the help screens once the IIS ASP engine fires up. See figure 19-63.

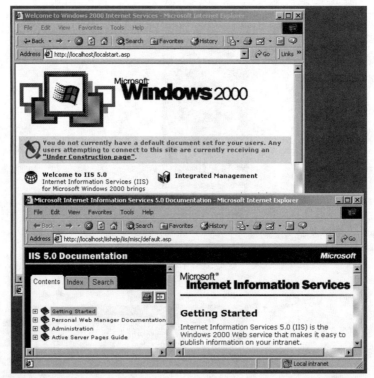

Fig. 19-63. IIS Welcome pages.

Now that you have set up your computer as the database server and Web server, you are ready to build the application, create the ASP page, and set up the DSN.

Practice Exercise 19-3: A Basic ASP Solution

Description

In this exercise you are going to set up the DSN, build an ASP page, and build a very simple Authorware file for reading a database to demonstrate that the system works. The Authorware file will call an ASP page with a command line *SQL* statement. The ASP page will look up the DSN and connect to the database. The ASP page will then return the result to the Authorware application. In this exercise you will:

- *Set up the Web server DSN*
- *Make an ASP page*
- *Make a very simple Authorware application for reading the database*

Step-by-Step Instructions

Setting Up the Web Server DSN

Go Solo

Note that you must set the DSN up on the Web server. Normally, this would be done by asking the Web server administrator to do this for you. In this example, however, you are the Web server administrator because you have set your computer up as the Web server. To set up a DSN on a PWS is exactly the same as setting up a DSN on a normal PC. Therefore, if you have completed the ODBC example, there is no need to set another one up, as you are going to use the same "Login Database DSN" you configured previously.

If you did not perform the "Creating the Data Source Name" section of Practice Exercise 19-3, or have removed the old DSN, perform that section of exercise 19-3. Make sure also that you have the database *Db19-2.mdb* copied into *C:\Authorware Exercises\Db19-2.mdb*.

Creating an ASP Page

ASP is a language in itself, specifically designed to display dynamic Web pages by pulling data from databases. Rather than learn the entire language, however, you are going to take a shortcut. You are going to use an ASP page specifically written to accept an SQL command and return the results in a Web page.

1. Copy the finished ASP page to the correct location and then have a look at it.
   a) Select File | Open and locate the *Practice* folder on the companion CD-ROM. Open the folder and you will see a number of chapter folders. Open the *Chapter19* folder and locate the file named *dbaction.ASP*. Create a folder named *C:\Inetpub\wwwroot\ASP* and copy this file to *C:\Inetpub\wwwroot\ASP\ dbaction.ASP*.
   b) Open Notepad and browse to *C:\Inetpub\wwwroot\ASP\dbaction.ASP*.

The file should look as shown in figure 19-64.

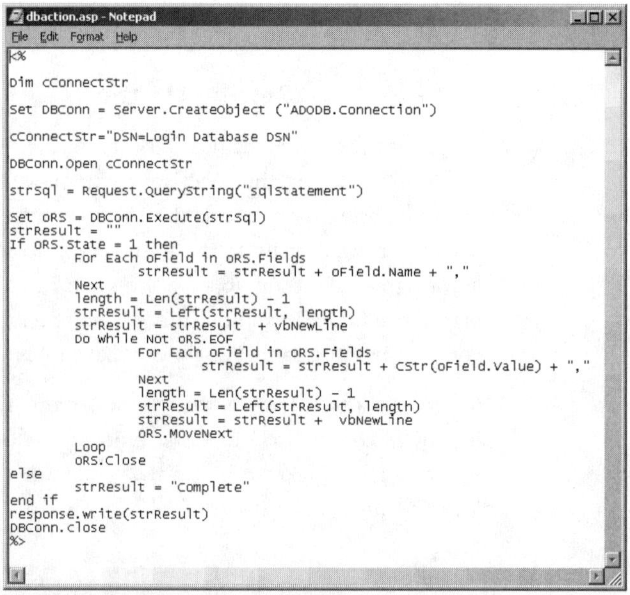

```
dbaction.asp - Notepad
File  Edit  Format  Help

<%

Dim cConnectStr

Set DBConn = Server.CreateObject ("ADODB.Connection")

cConnectStr="DSN=Login Database DSN"

DBConn.Open cConnectStr

strSql = Request.QueryString("sqlStatement")

Set oRS = DBConn.Execute(strSql)
strResult = ""
If oRS.State = 1 then
        For Each oField in oRS.Fields
                strResult = strResult + oField.Name + ","
        Next
        length = Len(strResult) - 1
        strResult = Left(strResult, length)
        strResult = strResult + vbNewLine
        Do while Not oRS.EOF
                For Each oField in oRS.Fields
                        strResult = strResult + CStr(oField.Value) + ","
                Next
                length = Len(strResult) - 1
                strResult = Left(strResult, length)
                strResult = strResult + vbNewLine
                oRS.MoveNext
        Loop
        oRS.Close
else
        strResult = "Complete"
end if
response.write(strResult)
DBConn.close
%>
```

Fig. 19-64. ASP page dbaction.ASP.

If you wish to learn ASP, there are many resources on the Web, such as *www.learnASP.com*, which incorporate hundreds of tutorials. To use this ASP page again and again, the only line you need to know is line 7, *cConnectStr="DSN=Login Database DSN"*. This line tells the ASP page which DSN to use, and hence from the DSN the page will communicate with the correct database. To reuse this code for your own work, you can just simply change *Login Database DSN* to whatever DSN you set up.

c)   Close Notepad.

2.   As the ASP page and DSN are in place, there is no reason you cannot test the ASP page.

a)   Open a browser window.

b)   Type in the location (with no spaces): *http://localhost/ASP/dbaction.ASP?sqlStatement=select%20*%20 from%20Login_Data.*

c)   Note the use of *%20* for spaces, all in lowercase and no semicolon at the end. This is because you are entering the line into a browser, the rules for which are slightly different from standard SQL.

d)   Press Enter. See figure 19-65.

·T/P·

Do not use an editor such as Word or Front Page, as these will add all sorts of rubbish in the ASP code and the ASP will not work.

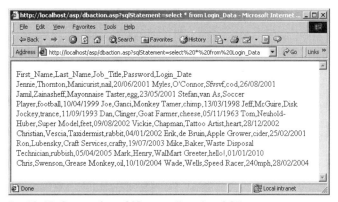

Fig. 19-65. Output from ASP page dbaction.ASP.

Note that you have just pulled the entire database into a Web page. Now all you have to do is create an Authorware file that can send out SQL statements in this URL format, and bring back the results. Authorware has a limit of 30,000 characters. Because of this it is often a better practice to bring in a single line of data at a time. A relatively small database can easily have over 30,000 characters.

Creating a Simple Authorware Application

1. Create the Authorware file.
   a) Open a copy of Authorware and select File | New.
   b) Select File | Save and name the file *Exer19-4.a6p*.
   c) Drag a Calculation icon to the flowline and name it *Set up variables*.
   d) Double click on this Calculation icon to open it.
   e) Type the following lines. See figure 19-66.

   ```
   sqlStatement:="select * from login_data;"
   sqlStatement:=Replace(" ","%20",sqlStatement)
   sqlStatement:="?sqlstatement="^sqlStatement
   ASPLocation:=http://localhost/ASP/dbaction.ASP
   ```

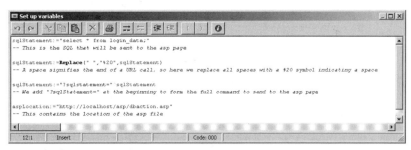

Fig. 19-66. Set up variables *Calculation* icon.

f) The first line is where your SQL statement goes. Remember to use lowercase for the Web version. You do not need a semicolon at the end. Normally, this is the only line you have to change.

g) The second line replaces the spaces with *%20* so that the URL is continuous. A space is considered the end of the command in a URL.

h) The third line adds a *"?sqlStatement"* string so that the URL will be in the correct format for the ASP page.

i) The last line is the location of the ASP page. In a large program, you could set this up at the beginning of a program in an easily modifiable form.

Most developers have two databases: a test and a production database. The idea is that if in the course of developing you make a mistake, you do not obliterate all of your good data. To do this you can simply have two ASP pages with different DSNs: one to the production database and one to the test. By setting *aspLocation* to *http://localhost/asp/dbactiontest.asp*, you will point to your test database and can easily switch between test and production.

j) Close and save the Calculation icon.

3. Set up the calculation to execute the ASP page.

a) Drag another Calculation beneath the first and name it *Execute ASP page*.

b) Double click on this Calculation icon to open it.

c) Type the following. See figure 19-67.

```
aspResult:=ReadURL(aspLocation^sqlStatement)
```

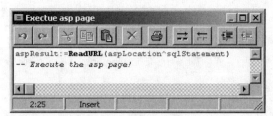

Fig. 19-67. Execute ASP Calculation icon.

d) This uses the command *ReadURL* to read in the result of the SQL statement. In this case, the line would read:

```
aspResult:=ReadURL("http://localhost/ASP/dbaction.ASP?
sqlStatement=select%20*%20from%20Login_Data")
```

This code uses the function *ReadURL*. *ReadURL* typically is calling things using the URL to send data. There is a character limit of 255 in any URL. As long as you don't post more that 255 characters at a time *ReadURL* is fine, but if you need to post more data, use the *PostURL* function.

PostURL is often a better solution if you are calling CGI pages. *PostURL* may be a better bet if you need to send more data to your ASP file, but in my experience, *ReadURL* seems to works in the vast majority of cases. The only way to find out is to experiment.

e) Close and save the Calculation icon.

4. Display the results of the ASP call.

a) Drag a Display icon beneath and name it *Display the results*. See figure 19-68.

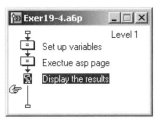

Fig. 19-68. Completed flowline.

b) Double click on the Display icon and embed the variable *ASPResult* in curly brackets. See figure 19-69.

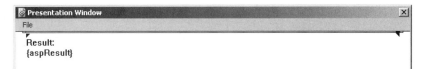

Fig. 19-69. Display icon.

c) Close the Display icon.
d) Save your application. Whenever working with ASP and external code, always save your application before you run it.
e) Run the program.
f) The entire database should be pulled into the display window. See figure 19-70.

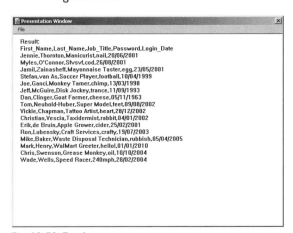

Fig. 19-70. Final screen.

Now that you have an understanding of SQL, you can adapt this program to do anything you wish to the database. You can substitute any SQL line for the *sqlStatement* variable (including one from a text entry) to perform updates, deletions, and insertions in the database.

Remember that the Internet does not always work. You should always incorporate error-checking code into your Authorware piece. If the Web page returns nothing, wait for half a second and try again. After five or six tries without success, verify that your application can still operate, but place it in a "database off" mode until the database starts working again. You might even try having your program send you an e-mail with the current user's name and the data your application cannot upload, so that you are alerted as soon as there is a problem. By default ASP files will time out after 90 seconds. This involves planning from the beginning of your project.

Summary

- *In the first guided tour, you learned the differences between ODBC and ASP solutions.*

- *In the second guided tour, you learned some of the most common commands of SQL and the syntax of the language.*

- *In the first practice exercise, you created a database and set up a data source name.*

- *In the second practice exercise, you added two-way database communication to the log-in routine from Chapter 18.*

- *In the third guided tour, you learned how to set up a personal Web server.*

- *In the final practice exercise, you learned how to implement a basic ASP solution.*

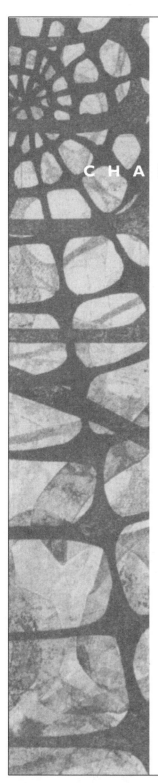

CHAPTER

20

Power Tools

Chapter Topics:

- *Introduction*

- *Guided Tour 20A:
  Working with Models*

- *Guided Tour 20B:
  The RTF Objects Editor
  and Knowledge Objects*

- *Guided Tour 20C:
  External Media*

- *Guided Tour 20D:
  ActiveX Controls*

- *The Commands menu*

- *Guided Tour 20E: Using
  XML with Authorware*

Introduction

An advanced Authorware user is not necessarily someone who can program a Calculation icon to play "Space Invaders" or program Xtras, but more often one who knows where to find and how to use the Authorware tools needed to create powerful multimedia efficiently. These Authorware gurus all have one thing in common: they know where to look for a simple solution to a difficult problem. You can be one who spends three months programming, icon by icon, a simulation of Internet Explorer, or you can spend the time to learn enough to be able to do the same with one icon. By the end of this chapter you will be able to:

- *Use the RTF editor and Knowledge objects*
- *Link external media for changing graphics in a packaged piece*
- *Use ActiveX controls in your application*
- *Easily make you way around the Commands menu*
- *Use XML in Authorware*

Guided Tour 20A: Working with Models

If you ever find yourself needing to copy and paste an Authorware structure many times or reuse the same segment in numerous Authorware pieces, consider making it a model. A model is like saving a template you want to reuse at will. Models represent a great means of sharing standard components among the members of a development team. For example, if you want to use the same set of buttons and text styles in more than one file, create an interaction that contains all buttons and styles and then turn the interaction into a model. Drag the model into any piece in which you want to use the features, save the piece, and then delete the interaction. All buttons will remain available in the Button library, and all text styles will be in your Apply Styles menu.

A model typically consists of various icons. Every time you want to use the functionality of a model, you simply drag a version of it from your Model palette and that saved combination of icons will appear on the flowline, ready for you to edit.

Models should not to be confused with Library icons. Simply, libraries store media only (e.g., sound and display icons); a model is an Authorware structure (e.g., an interaction loop). For example, you can store a single Interaction icon in a library, but to save an entire interaction structure, you need to turn it into a model.

Unlike Library icons, models do not link to anything. Each time you add a model to the flowline, you are pasting the content of the model in its entirety. Thus, you do not save any disk space by using a model. On the other hand, you can change the structure of the model to tailor it to the particular context. Changing the structure of a model after you have pasted it into a piece has no effect on the model itself, nor will such changes affect other places you have pasted the model.

Once a model is in a piece, it is a totally independent piece of code. If you go to the original model and make changes to it, the changes will *not* be reflected in the flowline of your Authorware files. In addition, a model placed on the flowline has no link to the original file. When using models, keep the following points in mind.

- *Models let you create a permanent copy of a chunk of functionality.*
- *The copy of the model you add to the flowline is not linked to the model; it is a duplicate.*
- *Changing the icons contained in the model after you add them to the flowline has no effect on the model. Models can contain Library icons or linked external content provided the libraries or external files are available to the file you paste the model into.*
- *A development team can use the same set of models to standardize its work.*

Creating Models

Models are easy to create and use. To create a model, select the segment of the flowline you want to copy and save it in a model. Place the model file in the *Knowledge Objects* folder on your hard drive (in the same folder as Authorware). Models in the *Knowledge Objects* folder appear in the Knowledge Objects window and in the model palettes. To use the model, drag it from the Knowledge Objects window to the flowline.

There are two methods of adding an icon structure to your model collection. The first method is to use the File menu. The second method uses the Model palette. The sections that follow take you through the steps involved in each method.

Save In Model Method

1. Use the mouse to select the segment of icons you want to use as a model. See figure 20-1.

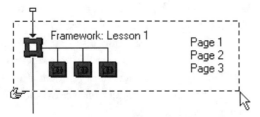

Fig. 20-1. Selecting icons for a model.

2. Select File | Save in Model.

3. Select a folder, and then name the file in the *File name* field. Notice that when you save a model, the Save Model As dialog box prompts you to save the model inside of the Authorware Knowledge Objects file structure. See figure 20-2. In order for Authorware to access your collection of models, you must save all your models into this location on your hard drive. Unless you customize your installation of Authorware, this path will be: *C:\Program Files\Macromedia\Authorware 6\Knowledge Objects*.

T/P

Creating new model categories: If you want to create your own categories in which to organize your models, all you have to do is create a new folder inside the *Knowledge Objects* folder. Whatever you name that folder will appear as a new category of models within Authorware. Notice in figure 20-2 that the folder the model is being saved to is called *My Models*. This is a custom folder.

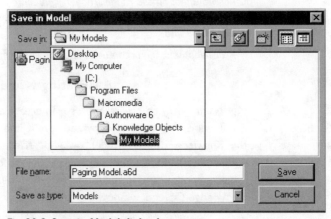

Fig. 20-2. Save in Model dialog box.

4. Click on Save. The model is saved as a separate file, with the *A6D* extension.

5. Click on the Refresh button in the Window/Knowledge Objects dialog box to see the model there. See figure 20-3.

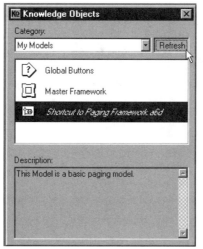

Fig. 20-3. Knowledge Objects window with new model selected.

Model Palette Method

You can also add models to your collection by using the Models Palette option. To create a model using this method, perform the following steps.

1. Select Windows | Panels | Model Palette (Ctrl + 3). Note that a small gray box appears under your primary Icon palette on the left side of your screen. See figure 20-4.

Fig. 20-4. Empty Model palette.

2. Right-mouse click on the gray part of that panel to see the list of all folders that reside within your *Knowledge Objects* folder on your hard drive. Select one of the categories.

3. If you want to create your own category, right-mouse click a second time on the gray area and select New Category. See figure 20-5.

·T*i*P·

Did you notice that all of the Knowledge objects that ship with Authorware have descriptions on them? These descriptions can be used to give information to your users about how your models should be used, or even step-by-step instructions of how to use your models in their Authorware files. If you want to add a description for your model to appear in the description field of the Knowledge Objects window, perform the following steps:

1. Before saving the model, right-click on the first icon of the structure.

2. Select Description from the drop-down list and enter a description in the field.

3. Select File | Save in Model.

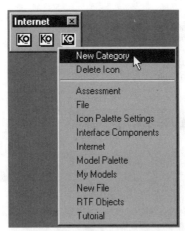

Fig. 20-5. New Category option in the Model palette.

4. The New Category dialog box appears so that you can name the category. Name this category *My Models*. Click on OK. See figure 20-6.

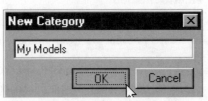

Fig. 20-6. New Category dialog box.

5. Once you have a category established, drag and drop icons onto the Model palette. Using your mouse, select the segment of icons you want to use as a model. See figure 20-7.

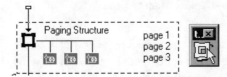

Fig. 20-7. Selecting icons to drag to the new Model palette.

6. Drag the selected icons to the top of your new Model palette.

T/P

Network your models: Models are great when working with a team of developers sharing a network drive.

To share models from a network drive:

1) Save the models in a shared folder on the network.

2) Create a Windows shortcut to the model.

3) Place the shortcut inside each developer's \Authorware\ Knowledge Objects\ models folder.

Each time a model is replaced/updated on the network drive, all deveopers will have instant access to it without having to reinstall the model on their hard drive.

Inserting Models

Knowledge Objects Window Method

If the model file is not in the *Knowledge Objects* folder (in the same folder as Authorware), move it there or to a subfolder within the *Knowledge Objects* folder. Alternatively, place a shortcut to the model in the *Knowledge Objects* folder. To place a model on the flowline, perform the following steps.

1. In the Knowledge Objects window, select the category where the model is located. (To display the Knowledge Objects window, select Window | Knowledge Objects.) If you have just added the model to the *Knowledge Objects* folder, click on the Refresh button in the Knowledge Objects window. Each category name is the name of a subfolder within the *Knowledge Objects* folder. See figure 20-8.

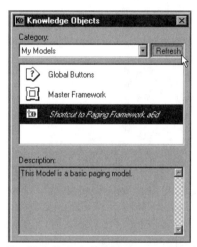

Fig. 20-8. Knowledge Objects window displaying new model.

2. Drag the model to the flowline.

Model Palette Method

You can see in your Knowledge Objects window all of your custom models as well as the Knowledge Object wizards that ship with Authorware. The Knowledge Objects window, however, can be unmanageably large on a small monitor display. There is another way of viewing your models and getting them onto the flowline: via use of Model palettes.

1. Select Windows | Panels | Model Palette (Ctrl + 3). Note that a small gray box appears under your primary Icon palette on the left side of your screen. See figure 20-9.

Fig. 20-9. New model palette.

2. Right mouse click on the gray part of that panel to see the list of all folders that reside within the *Knowledge Objects* folder on your hard drive. See figure 20-10.

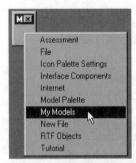

Fig. 20-10. Selecting a new model category.

3. Select a category and note that the box expands to fit the number of Knowledge Objects or models in that category. You can resize the box by dragging the edge of the box. You can also open more than one model palette. See figure 20-11.

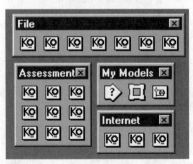

Fig. 20-11. Multiple model palettes opened within Authorware.

Guided Tour 20B: The RTF Objects Editor and Knowledge Objects

Using the RTF Objects editor and Knowledge objects allows for seamless integration of external RTF files in your Authorware piece. This provides non Authorware developers a means of updating the course material. The RTF Objects editor can produce all normal formatting, as well as other polygon shapes. The editor can also link external RTF and external text files within RTF files, use all Authorware variables and functions within RTF files, and print from the RTF objects editor. In this tour you will:

• *Explore the use of external RTF files within Authorware, the RTF Objects editor, and Knowledge objects used to display RTF objects*

• *Examine a file that includes an example of each feature of the RTF objects*

Using and displaying external RTF files in Authorware requires that you design RTF files using the RTF Objects editor and then use RTF Knowledge objects to display these files. In the following you will take a brief look at the editor and the Knowledge objects and then explore an example file that uses all features of the external RTF available to you.

1. Examine the RTF Objects editor.

   a) Open Authorware with a new, empty file. Select Commands | RTF Objects Editor. See figure 20-12.

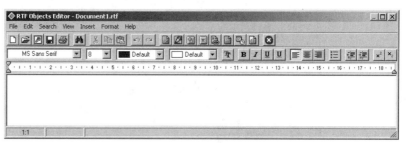

Fig. 20-12. RTF Objects editor.

   b) Type some example text, close the editor, and save the RTF file as *C:\Authorware Exercises\example text.rtf*. Close the RTF Objects editor. See figure 20-13.

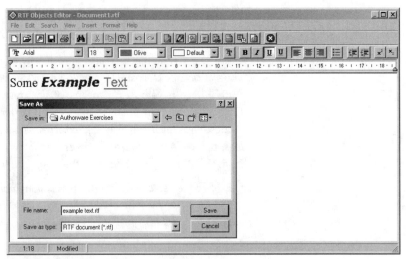

Fig. 20-13. Save file.

2. Examine the Knowledge objects.

   a) Open the Knowledge Object dialog box if it is not already open, by pressing Shift + Ctrl + K. Scroll down to the RTF category. Select Create RTF Object and drag it to the flowline. The wizard will launch for the Knowledge Object and you will be prompted to save your file, if you have not done so already. Save your Authorware file in the same directory as the RTF file *C:\Authorware Exercises*. See figure 20-14.

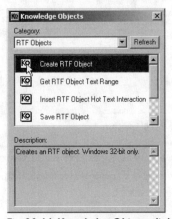

Fig. 20-14. Knowledge Objects dialog box.

   b) In the Create RTF Object wizard, click on Next to leave the Introduction screen. On the following screen, titled Source, click on the ellipses and locate the RTF file. Click on Open. Click on Done to close the Create RTF Object source. See figure 20-15.

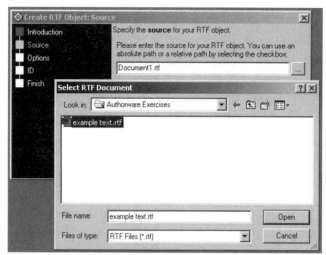

Fig. 20-15. Locating the RTF file.

c) Run the file. You will see the RTF file displayed within the Presentation window. With the piece paused, you can resize the displayed RTF file if necessary. See figure 20-16.

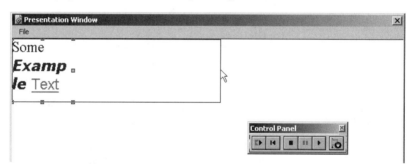

Fig. 20-16. Resizing the RTF file.

d) The other main Knowledge object you will use is the Insert RTF Object Hot Text interaction. When this is dragged onto the flowline, the Hot Text interactions are automatically set up. In the following you will examine this interaction and many other features of an example file. First, however, close this copy of Authorware.

3. Examine the example file.

a) Select File | Open and locate the *Practice* folder on the companion CD-ROM. Open this folder and you will see a number of chapter folders. Open the *Chapter20* folder. Open the *RTF* folder and locate and double click on the file named *Exer20-1.a6p*.

b) The *Exer20-1* file should now appear in your copy of Authorware. See figure 20-17. Select Control | Restart or click on the Restart button on the toolbar to play the file from the top of the flowline.

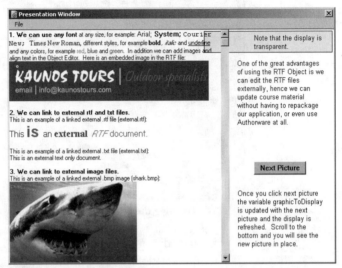

Fig. 20-17. Presentation window.

c) As you scroll down, you will see the following features.

- *You can use any available font in the RTF file; that is, any font size, color, style, and alignment. You can also embed images.*

- *From the external RTF file, you can link to other RTF and text files.*

- *You can link to external graphics files.*

- *You can embed Authorware variables and expressions.*

- *You can embed a variable to call different external graphics. Try clicking on Next Picture and scrolling back down the display.*

- *You can embed hot text. In this example, you can create a "beep" or a "quit." Try them!*

d) Examine the RTF file in the editor to see how all of this is achieved.

e) Select Commands | RTF Objects Editor. Locate the file *rtffiletodisplay.rtf* in the *RTF* folder on the companion CD-ROM. Select and open this file. Note the following.

- *Producing the RTF text is similar to the process under most word processing applications.*

- *To link to an external rtf or text file, select Insert | File and select the file you wish to link to. In the dialog that pops up, you can select to link or to import.*

- *To link to an external image is the same, except that you select Insert | Image.*

- *To use variables and expressions, select Insert | Authorware Expression.*

- *To embed a variable to display a graphic, embed the variable as described previously and in Authorware set the variable to "{myGraphic.jpg}" using a string and using curly brackets.*

- *Hot text can be added by selecting Insert | Hot Text. Once this is done, you must go back to your Authorware piece and use the Insert RTF Object Hot Text interaction Knowledge object to enable the hot text to work. When you use this Knowledge object, the interaction is created, as in the example file.*

f) The last, and very powerful, feature (not shown in the example) is the use of the RTF features with a database. In the RTF Objects editor, you will notice an Access database icon in the toolbar. This allows you to view values in the memo fields of an Access database. The RTF Objects editor can be used to store RTF information in a database. Therefore, instead of having to use multiple RTF files you can now use a single database.

Guided Tour 20C: External Media

When is a good time to use external content? Several situations come to mind. The first is an example of a recent project. The project was a CD-ROM-based marketing tool for a computer company. The products featured for the international sales force changed about twice a year. Every six months a new CD-ROM was sent out with the new product listing, but the design of the content always remained the same. The client was having to go through the Authorware piece twice a year and replace all the graphics and text and then repackage the Authorware file. They were using libraries, but still had to change the Authorware source every time a new product was featured. By linking the text and graphics externally, the Authorware piece itself never had to be touched again. The new content was sent to the marketing people in the field, and they would change the folder that was being called on by their laptop hard drive. Using external content allowed the program to be easily updated outside Authorware without having to run through the Authorware file and change the imported information.

Authorware files that are Web-enabled are another good application of external content. Because external files can reside on a Web server, this is a good application for using external content. In this tour you will:

• *See how to link external graphics to display icons*

• *Experiment with using variables to control the display*

In the following you will work through two Authorware applications to explore how external media works in practice.

CD-ROM

1. Select File | Open and locate the *Practice* folder on the companion CD-ROM. Open this folder and you will see a number of chapter folders. Open the *Chapter20* folder and locate the file named *Exer20-2b.a6p* and the subfolder *graphics*. Select both the file and the subfolder and press Ctrl + C to copy them. Locate (or create) the folder *C:\Authorware Exercises* on your PC. When you are here, press Ctrl + V to copy the files onto your PC. See figure 20-18.

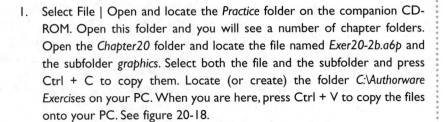

Fig. 20-18. Copying the files to your PC.

2. Open your copy of Authorware and select File | Save. Navigate to the *C:\Authorware Exercises* folder, type the file name *Exer20-a.a6p*, and press Enter. See figure 20-19.

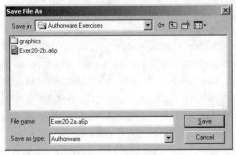

Fig.. 20-19. Saving the new file.

3. Create a file with an external link.
   a) Select File | Import. Navigate to *C:\Authorware Exercises\graphics* and select the file *picture2.jpg*. Check the box Link To File. This ensures the media will be kept external. Click on Import. See figure 20-20.

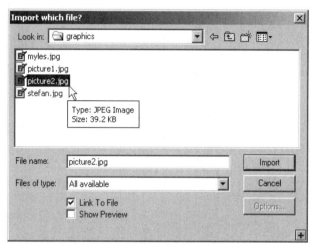

Fig. 20-20. Importing the external file.

   b) Restart the file. See figure 20-21.

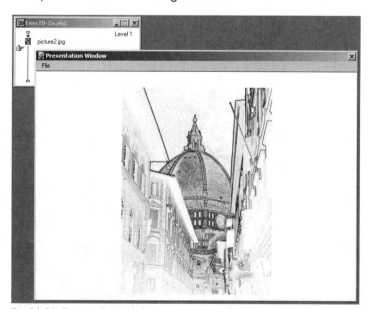

Fig. 20-21. Externally-linked graphic displayed in the Presentation window.

c) Assume you have a large packaged file and need to change a graphic. Rather than edit the file, because you have used external graphics you can now simply replace the graphic. Let's replace *picture2.jpg*. Open Windows Explorer and navigate to the *C:\Authorware Exercises\graphics* folder. Right-click on the file *picture2.jpg* and select Rename. Change the file name to *picture3.jpg*. Right-click on *picture1.jpg* and select Rename. Change the file name to *picture2.jpg*. See figure 20-22.

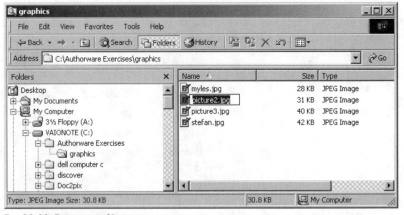

Fig. 20-22. Renaming files.

d) Return to your Authorware file, and without changing anything restart the file. Note that the image has been replaced! See figure 20-23.

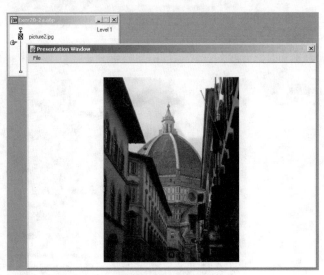

Fig. 20-23. Updated externally-linked image.

4. Use a variable expression to select an external file.
    a) When using external files, you can also change which picture is being displayed by using expressions within Authorware. Pause the presentation and double click on the image to open the *picture2.jpg* Display icon. Double click on the image again to bring up the Properties dialog box. See figure 20-24.

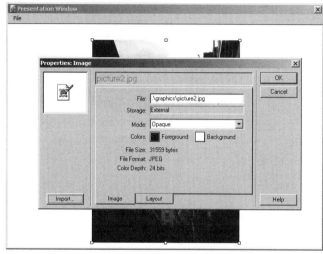

Fig. 20-24. Display element's Properties dialog box.

    b) Note that the File field reads *.\graphics\picture2.jpg*. This is the file location of this display element. You can edit this field in different ways:
        - *To manually change the graphic type in* .\graphics\picture3.jpg *to display a different file, the ".\" is the indicator to Authorware that you are assuming path relative to where your piece is saved.*
        - *To display a graphic that resides on the Internet you need to place the URL in the File field and, if you are connected to the Internet, it will be displayed. You need to include the entire URL including the* http:// *prefix.*
        - *To display the graphic using a code expression, use the equal sign before the rest of the expression. After the equal sign you can use variables, functions or strings to dynamically update the graphic. For example, you could type:*

```
=FileLocation ^ "graphics\" ^IconTitle
```

        With this variable expression the image that has the same name as this display icon will appear on the screen. See Figure 20-25. Application Chapter 21 has an excellent example of this strategy.

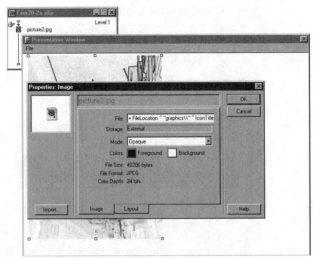

Fig. 20-25. Variable expression in the File field.

    c)   Click on OK and then restart the file. You will see the original picture in place.

5.   Examine a more powerful example.

    a)   Open the *C:\Authorware Exercises* folder. Open the *Chapter20* folder and locate and double click on the file named *Exer20-2b.a6p*.

    b)   The *Exer20-2b* file should now appear in your copy of Authorware. Select Control | Restart or click on the Restart button on the toolbar to play the file from the top of the flowline.

    c)   Click on one of the pictures. See figure 20-26.

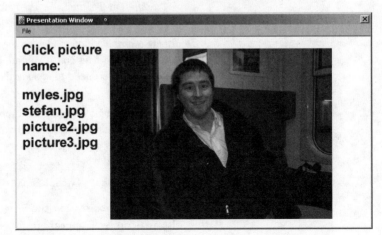

Fig. 20-26. Presentation window.

d) As you click on the other names, the other images appear.

e) So how can you get this much functionality from just two icons? If you open the Interaction icon, you see that there is a *Catalog* function bringing in the names of all files in the *graphics* folder. Using this file, you could have as many graphics as you wanted in this directory and all could be displayed using this application. Try adding your own graphics in the folder to see how they display.

f) If you open the display element by double clicking on the graphic element, you see that the following expression brings in the external files.

```
= FileLocation ^ "graphics\\" ^ GetLine( Catalog(
FileLocation ^ "graphics"), LineClicked)
```

This expression calls the *LineClicked* of the *Catalog* function and opens this file.

Guided Tour 20D: ActiveX Controls

Authorware 6 now ships with a very good ActiveX control. It is very easy to insert almost any ActiveX control directly onto the flowline and fully control it using Calculation and Interaction icons. There are tens of thousands of pre-built ActiveX controls, from custom browsers to music programs. See *http://browserwatch.internet.com/activex.html* for a list. You can use your own ActiveX components by developing them yourself or getting a developer to do this for you. In this tour you will:

- *Learn how to install an ActiveX control on your user's machine*

- *Control a Web browser ActiveX control*

- *Get and send events to an ActiveX control*

Placing an ActiveX control in your Authorware piece is as easy as adding any icon. Controlling the ActiveX requires a little more thought. Each ActiveX control has properties, methods, and events. If you imagine creating an Authorware application to display a Web page, and compare this to a Web browser ActiveX, you see that the Authorware file uses variables. In the ActiveX, these are called properties. They can be read and assigned new values, just as Authorware variables can. Your Authorware piece could incorporate functions (e.g., you might have programmed a "go back" function).

In an ActiveX control, these are called methods. Therefore, if you use the *GoBack* method in a Web browser, ActiveX will go back a page. In your Authorware piece, you might also have included sending an event if a particular action occurs. For example, you might send a little message out when a page has completed its download. In the ActiveX control, this is called an event. If you are using an ActiveX control in your Authorware piece, you can read and set its variables (properties), use its functions (methods), and "listen" for it triggering an event (events).

Installing ActiveX Controls

There are two negatives to using ActiveX controls: the control must be installed on the target machine, and ActiveX only works on Windows machines. If you are planning to run your piece on a Macintosh, you cannot use ActiveX commands. To overcome the first problem, there is an easy way install the controls in Authorware.

1) Place a Calculation icon on the flowline before you plan to use the ActiveX control (usually at the top of your flowline is best). Title the control Install ActiveX Control.

2) Inside of the calculation enter the following script:

```
if ActiveXControlQuery("A26A2C5F-6B79-11D1-BF3C-
000000000000") = 0 then

ActiveXControlRegister(FileLocation^"GTprogss.ocx")

end if
```

This code will check to see if the control with the classID listed is already installed on the machine; if not, the file named .ocx will be installed from where your piece is running.

Working with the ActiveX Control

Let's take a look at the Authorware application to explore how ActiveX works in practice. For this tour, it is useful although not essential to have an Internet connection running on your PC.

1. Select File | Open and locate the *Practice* folder on the companion CD-ROM. Open this folder and you will see a number of chapter folders. Open the *Chapter20* folder and locate and double click on the file named *Exer20-3.a6p*.

2. The *Exer20-3 file* should now appear in your copy of Authorware. Select Control | Restart or click on the Restart button on the toolbar to play the file from the top of the flowline. See figure 20-27.

·T/P·

ActiveX functions: There is a category of functions called "Xtra ActiveX." Inside this category are all the functions that allow you to manipulate different ActiveX controls.

CD-ROM

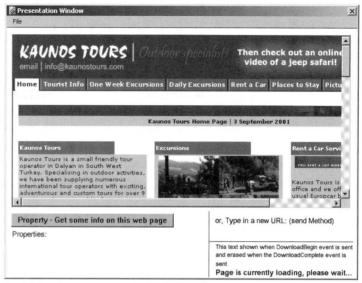

Fig. 20-27. Opening screen of the Authorware program.

3. Note the three ideas (i.e., properties, methods, and events) depicted in the Presentation window. The ActiveX object is displaying the Web page. You are controlling this ActiveX using a method, using events to turn on and off the text in the bottom right-hand portion of the Presentation window, and getting the Web page URL and name via properties. Try entering a new URL (or a local *txt* or *htm* file if you are off line) and then using the Property button to see how the application functions.

4. Once you have used the application, stop the application and look at the flowline. See figure 20-28.

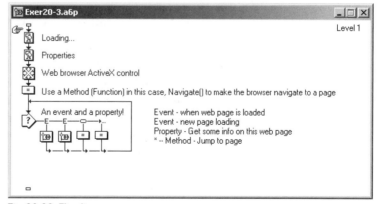

Fig. 20-28. Flowline.

5. Examine the application in more detail.

   a) The first icon, *Loading*, displays the text in the bottom right-hand corner, informing you that a Web page is in the process of loading. You will use events to turn this on and off. The second display icon is *Properties*, which contains the custom variable *WebPageProperties* and is set to "update displayed variables."

   b) The third icon is the ActiveX itself. To insert a new ActiveX icon, you select Insert | Control | ActiveX. As this is already in place, let's have a look at it now. Double click on this icon and then click on the Options button on the right-hand side. See figure 20-29.

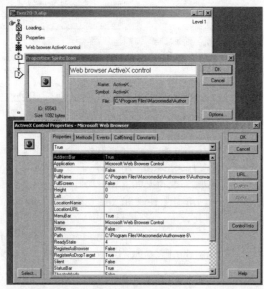

Fig. 20-29. ActiveX control properties.

Controlling ActiveX Properties

In the ActiveX Control Properties dialog box you can see all properties, methods, and events available to you in Authorware. Look through these, remembering that the properties are variables you can read and some you can set, the methods are functions you can use to ask the ActiveX to do something, and the events are things the ActiveX sends back to Authorware. The sections that follow explore using these methods, events, and properties in your Authorware piece.

Methods

The Calculation icon below the ActiveX is a method used to make the Web browser ActiveX display a Web page. Double click on the Calculation icon to see how this is done. See figure 20-30.

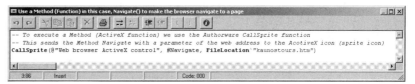

Fig. 20-30. Calling an ActiveX method.

All methods are called in the following manner. You use the Authorware function *CallSprite* to tell Authorware you want to send a call to the ActiveX icon. The three parameters of the CallSprite function are: 1) the icon containing the ActiveX control you are changing, 2) the name of the method, and 3) the parameter to be sent for that method. In the previous example you can see that you are 1) calling to the ActiveX icon titled *Web browser ActiveX control*, 2) using the method *Navigate*, and 3) will be navigating the user to the Web page *kaunostours.htm* stored in your *pieces* working directory. To see all methods for comparing them with the ActiveX, double click on the ActiveX icon and click on Options. In the Methods tab, you see the *Navigate* method.

Events

Every time an ActiveX command does something, it can send an event. All events available for use are listed in the Events tab of the ActiveX icon, and in this application you are going to use *DownloadComplete* and *DownloadBegin* to determine if the *Loading* Display icon should be displayed.

1. Double click on the Response Symbol for *Event – when Web page is loaded* (it looks like a capital "E") See figure 20-31.

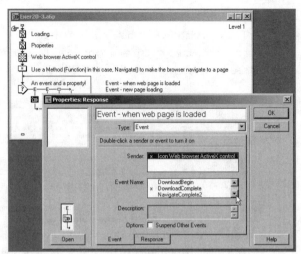

Fig. 20-31. Event Property Response dialog box

2. In the Properties Response dialog box, you see that the Type option is set to Event. For an event, you have two lists to select from. The first is a list of all ActiveX icons in your application (in this case, only one). Click on this "sender" once to see the events you can manipulate. Scroll down to *DownloadComplete* and you see an X beside this event. For each "sender" (or ActiveX icon in your file) you can manipulate multiple events by double clicking on the "x" next to the event name to turn the setting on or off.

3. Try experimenting with these dialog boxes so that you get used to them. Now whenever the Web browser ActiveX triggers a *DownloadComplete* event your flowline matches and your icons below this Event interaction are run.

Below the events all you have is an Erase icon for when the page has downloaded completely and a display for the loading message when a new download begins.

Properties

In the interaction there is a button labeled *Property – Get some info on this Web page*. When you click on this button, you get the values of the URL of the current Web site (LocationURL) and the Web site name (LocationName) from the ActiveX.

1. Double click on the Calculation icon to see how this is done. See figure 20-32.

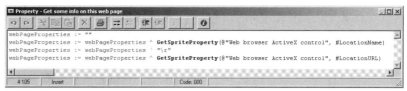

Fig. 20-32. A property.

2. Note that to find the value of a property you use the Authorware function *GetSpriteProperty*. The function *SetSpriteProperty* is used to set these properties, but not all properties can be set, as in Authorware. For example, the Authorware variable *FileLocation* can be read, but not set.

3. Note that in this example you read the properties *#LocationName* and *#LocationURL* from the ActiveX icon.

The last icon in the interaction is another method, which allows the user to enter a URL and send this method to the ActiveX.

The Commands Menu

In Authorware 6, you can create and add your own custom commands to the new, extensible Commands menu. You can add any kind of executable (*.EXE*) file to the Commands menu. You do not have to create it using Authorware. However, only Authorware *.EXE*, *A6R*, or *A6P* files, or files built with an SDK like the Delphi SDK (included on the Authorware CD-ROM), will be able to communicate with Authorware directly. The Commands menu allows you to access powerful commands with just one click. You can use the predefined commands or edit and add your own commands. The Commands menu displays any applications in the *Commands* subfolder of Authorware and executes them with one click. Any *.EXE* or *.A6R* file can be placed in this directory. The main two applications of the Commands menu are as a shortcut to your favorite programs and as a shortcut to your own Knowledge objects. In this discussion you will:

*   *Learn how to add your own commands*

*   *Understand how you can place your own Knowledge objects in the Commands menu*

Adding Commands

Adding your own commands in the Commands menu is straightforward enough. Say, for example, you use Dreamweaver in your work very often and are forever opening and closing it. Let's add this to our menu! You do this by making a shortcut to Dreamweaver and placing it in the *Commands* subfolder of Authorware. Try this by dragging and dropping (while holding down the Shift and Control keys) the *dreamweaver.exe* file from the *dreamweaver* folder to the *commands* folder, as shown in figure 20-33. Then close Authorware and reopen it. You will see Dreamweaver in your Commands menu. See figure 20-34.

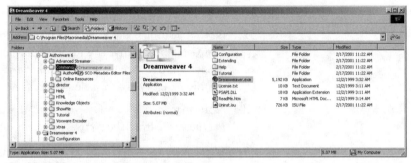

Fig. 20-33. Creating a Dreamweaver shortcut.

Try the following: Locate the *commands* folder under the *Program Files/ Authorware* folder and select it by clicking once on it. Select File | New | New Shortcut. When the wizard pops up, type the following:

C:\Documents and Settings\All Users\Start Menu\Programs Win2000

C:\WINDOWS\Start Menu\Programs Win98

Close and then restart Authorware. You will see that every program on your PC is now in your Commands menu!

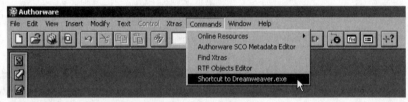

Fig. 20-34. New Commands menu.

If you edit the file name of the shortcut to *Dreamweaver* in Windows Explorer, the changes will be reflected in the Commands menu the next time you open Authorware. As well as placing files in the *commands* directory, you can create new directories and place files within these, making a "tree" of commands, as in the *commands/online resources/macromedia* tree and directory structure. The Commands menu copied the directory structure you have in place.

Using Knowledge Objects in the Commands Menu

Launching external programs may be useful as a shortcut. More importantly, it is possible to place your own programs in the Commands menu that interact with the application you used to launch the command. For example, it is possible to incorporate a command that will go through your entire Authorware piece and check for any icons named *Untitled*. You could in fact create a command for changing the flowline, editing icon properties, editing Calculation icons automatically, and creating an AutoSave program. The list of possibilities here is limited only by imagination. Once you build the application, you copy the packaged *.EXE* or *.A6R* file to the *commands* directory and restart Authorware.

Guided Tour 20E: Using XML with Authorware

XML is a format for holding data. Although similar in appearance to HTML, it is more appropriate to think of XML as a database than to confuse it with HTML, which is used for Web page layout. XML is a very useful data format both for its readability and ease of transmission across the Internet. No ODBC connections or DSN need be set up. Data can be easily communicated from any system to any system as virtually all have a text-based mode of transmission. Now Authorware has the ability to import and parse XML data into usable chunks. It does not contain the ability to modify or export XML. In this tour you will:

- *Learn how the XML parser handles XML*

- *See an example of how the parser works in Authorware*

Authorware has always been able to read XML files because XML is a text format. The problem has always been how to use the XML information once you have it stored in a variable. The XML parser now allows you to use many functions on the XML to pull out the data you need without very lengthy character manipulation.

The first thing you must still do is import the XML file into a variable using the *ReadExtFile* or *ReadURL* function. You must then create a new instance of the XML parser object. For example, if you needed to read in XML code from a locally stored file you would enter the following code inside a Calculation icon:

```
myXMLText := ReadExtFile(FileLocation ^ "magicXML.xml")
```

Creating a new instance of an object is something you will do all the time. Every time you drag a new Display icon to the flowline you are "making a new instance of the display object." The Display icon will always display a graphic, but each instance of the graphic object can have its own property values (e.g., where on screen it should appear). Think of it this way: Display Icons are just that – Icons. To see their properties, you can right click on the icon, then choose Properties. XML objects are not created as icons on the flowline, but by code in Calculation icons. In a Calculation icon for creating a new instance of an object, you use the *NewObject* function. Therefore, to create a new XML parser object, you use the following:

```
myXMLObj := NewObject( "XMLParser")
```

You end up with a value in the *myXMLObj* variable, even though there is no visible icon on the flowline. This is similar to the icon ID of an icon. Each icon has a unique *iconid*, and you can therefore use functions such as *IconTitle(IconID)* to find out the title of the icon. The same is true when you create a new object using the *NewObject* function. You now have a unique identifier, and can therefore use functions (methods) on the object.

Once you have an instance of the XML Parser object, you must ask the object to "parse" the XML document. At the moment, the XML parser does not know what information you are trying to get from the file. To do this, you use the *ParseString* function of the XML object. To call this, you use the following.

```
CallObject( myXMLObj, "ParseString", myXMLText )
```

CallObject is simply asking the *myXMLObj* you have already set up to use the function *ParseString* on the Authorware variable *myXMLText*. Errors can be asked for by using the following.

```
myErrorStr := CallObject( myXMLObj, "GetError" )
```

Again, this is asking *myXMLObject* to use the function *GetError* and return the value to the Authorware variable *myErrorStr*.

Once you have achieved this you are ready to read the data from the XML. The XML parser creates "nodes" from the XML file so that you can access the information. A node, representing each level and element, is called using a comma-delimited string. Examine the following code.

```
<Level1>

<Level2PartA>

MyTitle

</Level2PartA>

<Level2PartB>

MyText

</Level2PartB>

</Level1>
```

The XML parser will break up the XML so that node 1 is *<Level1>*; node 1,1 is *<Level2PartA>*; node 1,1,1 is *MyTitle*; and node 1,2,2 is *MyText*. As you can see, each new level of the structure is another comma and number in the node structure. Once you understand nodes, you can use the XML parser with the *Call* object, and use all methods. The following are examples.

- *XmlNode := "1,2,2"*
- *contentStr := CallObject(myXMLObj, "getText", xmlNode)*
- *contentType := CallObject(myXMLObj, "getType", xmlNode)*
- *childxmlNode := CallObject(myXMLObj, "GetChild", 1, xmlNode)*

- *childCount := CallObject(myXMLObj, "getCount", #Child, xmlNode)*

Attributes can also be extracted, such as the following.

```
<contact>
 <name email="myles@kaunostours.com" phone="90 252 284
2816">Myles O'Connor</name>
 <notes>Leave deliveries at rear door</notes>
</contact>
xmlNode := "1,1"
emailAddr := CallObject( myXMLObj, "getAttributeValueByName",
"email", xmlNode )
```

Let's now look at an example that uses all of these techniques.

1. Select File | Menu and locate the *Practice* folder on the companion CD-ROM. Open this folder and you will see a number of chapter folders. Open the *Chapter20* folder and locate and double click on the file named *Exer20-4.a6p*.

2. The *Exer20-4* file should now appear in your copy of Authorware. Select Control | Restart or click on the Restart button on the toolbar to play the file from the top of the flowline. See figure 20-35.

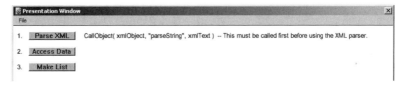

Fig. 20-35. Results of the CallObjects function.

3. The XML file has already been read in using the *ReadExtFile* function, as in the following:

```
myxmlText := ReadExtFile( FileLocation ^ "example.xml")
```

a) Inform the XML parser to use the *xmlText* variable to parse. Click on the Parse XML button. This calls the following code.

```
CallObject( xmlObject, "parseString", xmlText )
```

b) Click on the Parse XML Text button. See figure 20-36.

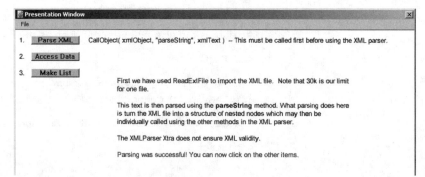

Fig. 20-36. Results of the Parse XML code.

4.   The XML file is now parsed and you are now in position to access the data. Click on the Access Data button. Press Enter. See figure 20-37.

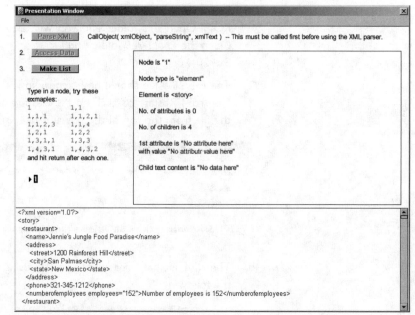

Fig. 20-37. Results of accessing the XML data.

a)   The node you entered is 1, which is the very first element in any XML file (in this case, *<story>*). This is displayed in the box on the right-hand side of the screen. Beneath this is the node type, element, description, number of attributes and children (e.g., *<restaurant>*, *<review>*, *<body>*, and *<menu>*), details of the attributes, and content of any text.

b) Go through all node examples and choose some of your own until you are completely happy with the idea of nodes and the information you can extract. See figure 20-38.

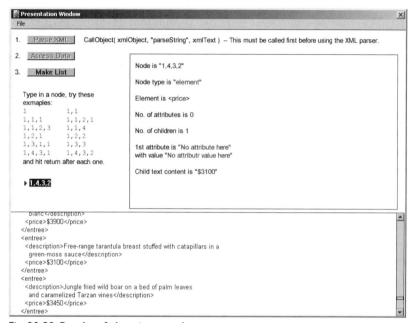

Fig. 20-38. Results of changing a node.

5. The XML parser can also create a list of the entire XML file. Most of the time you will know the format of the XML files your Authorware file is receiving, as well as which tags must be present, in which order, and how they should be nested. If you do not know these details, it may well be useful to convert the entire XML file to a list and use Authorware functions to search through the list. Click on the Make List button to see what this looks like. See figure 20-39.

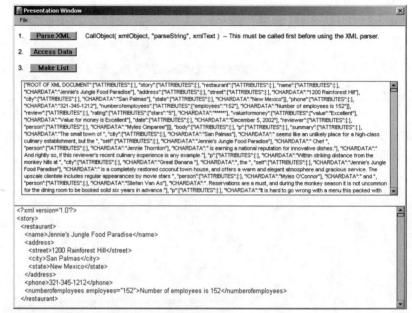

Fig. 20-39. Results of listing all the XML data.

6. Open the flowline and compare the Calculation icons incorporating XML functions (described previously) with what is displayed in the Presentation window.

Summary

In this chapter you learned how to:

- *Use the RTF editor and Knowledge objects*
- *Link external media so that you can change graphics in a packaged piece*
- *Use ActiveX controls in your application*
- *Add your own shortcuts to the Commands menu*
- *Use XML in Authorware*

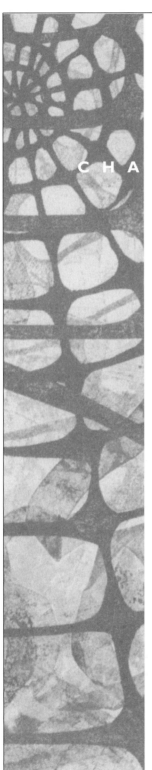

C H A P T E R

21

Application:

Creating a Sign-on

and Using Extra

Features

Introduction

In this chapter you will add to the navigational structures of the overall application project. Building on the navigation structure created in Chapter 17, you will now add more content and user tracking. First, you will create a log-in structure to track the user's entry into the Authorware file. Then you will see how to use the RTF Editor command to make Rich Text files that can be brought into Authorware or linked externally to make updating content easier than ever. Once you have your RTF text in place, you will learn to incorporate externally linked graphics for each page of text and use variables to make these graphics update automatically based on the page of text being viewed. You will use the Expression feature to dynamically pull in graphics based on the icon title of a display. Then you will use an ActiveX control to display Web pages within Authorware.

Application Exercise 21A: Creating a Sign-on Application and Connecting to a Database

Description

In this exercise you will create a log-in structure to track the user's entry into the Authorware file and then save that information to a custom variable. Every time the user returns to the file, she will be prompted for name and password to confirm user status. This exercise demonstrates the implementation of the log-in file created in Chapter 18. Once the user has confirmed her identity, the information entered will be used to create a text file on the user's hard drive. You will also see how to send the information to a database, using the structure outlined in Chapter 19.

Storyboard: On Screen

Figure 21-1 shows what the exercise will look like on screen when completed.

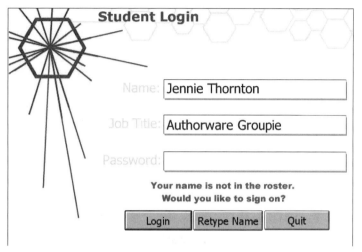

Fig. 21-1. Completed exercise on screen.

Storyboard: Behind the Scenes

Figure 21-2 shows the Main, second- and third-level flowlines (with all icons, their placement, and their names) as they should look when you are finished with this exercise.

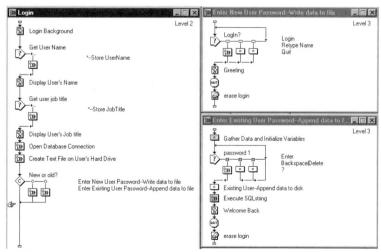

Fig. 21-2. Main, second- and third-level flowlines.

Step-by-Step Instructions

Use the following generalized steps to complete this exercise on your own. Consult the completed exercise (*Exer21A.a6p*) on the companion CD-ROM for further guidance.

1. Open the file *Exer21A.a6p* located on the companion CD-ROM in the directory named *Chapter14*. Open the library file *Graphics.a6l* located in the same directory. Run the program and see how it works. Jump to the flowline and examine the various icons and structures.

2. Open the blue Calculation icons labeled READ ME and read their content.

3. Leave this file open in this copy of Authorware.

4. Open another copy of Authorware, starting a new file. Save the file as *App21A*. Open the library file *Graphics.a6l* located in the *SaveWork* directory of your hard drive.

5. When finished, make sure to save your exercise in the *SaveWork* directory on your computer's hard drive.

Application Exercise 21B: Using the RTF Editor and Creating RTF Knowledge Objects

Description

In Chapter 20, you learned how to use the new RTF Editor command to make Rich Text files that can be brought into Authorware or linked externally to make updating content easier than ever. In this exercise you will use the Create RTF Knowledge object to import a multipage RTF document that will introduce you to some of the more recognizable names in the Authorware community. This RTF file will be displayed via a Framework paging structure. Using the system variable *CurrentPageID*, you will be able to display one page of the RTF document at a time.

Storyboard: On Screen

Figure 21-3 shows what the exercise will look like on screen when completed.

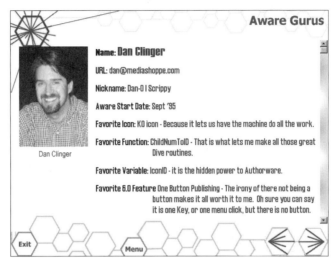

Fig. 21-3. Completed exercise on screen.

Storyboard: Behind the Scenes

Figure 21-4 shows the completed flowline and the Create RTF Object Knowledge Object dialog box as they should look when you finish this exercise.

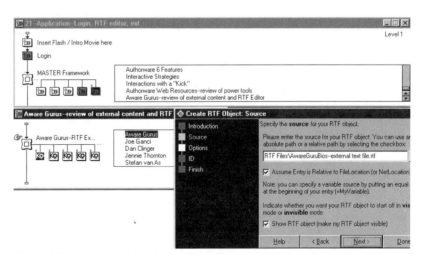

Fig. 21-4. The completed flowline and the Create RTF Object Knowledge Object dialog box.

Step-by-Step Instructions

Use the following generalized steps to complete this exercise on your own. Consult the completed exercise (*Exer21B.a6p*) on the companion CD-ROM for further guidance.

1. Open the file *Exer21B.a6p* located on the companion CD-ROM in the directory named *Chapter21*. Run the program and see how it works. Jump to the flowline and examine the various icons and structures.

2. Open the blue Calculation icons labeled READ ME and read their content.

3. Leave this file open in this copy of Authorware.

4. Open another copy of Authorware, starting a new file. Save the file as *App21B*. Open the library file *Graphics.a6l* located in the *SaveWork* directory of your hard drive.

5. You will also have to copy the files for the text file from the companion CD-ROM. Copy the folder named *RTF File* to your working directory.

6. When finished, make sure to save your exercise in the *SaveWork* directory on your computer's hard drive.

Application Exercise 21C: Linking to External Graphics

Description

In Chapter 20, you learned how to use the external media features in Authorware to speed your development and update files remotely. In this exercise, you will use the expression feature to dynamically pull in graphics based on the icon title of a display.

Storyboard: On Screen

Figure 21-5 shows what the exercise will look like on screen when completed.

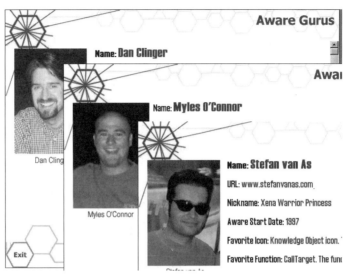

Fig. 21-5. Completed exercise on screen.

Storyboard: Behind the Scenes

Figure 21-6 shows the second-level flowline, the entry pane of the Topic Framework, and the Property dialog box for the externally-linked image.

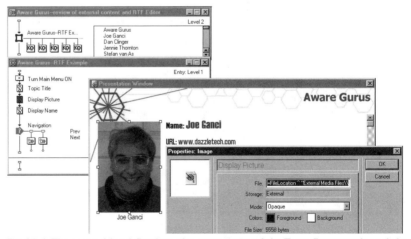

Fig. 21-6. The second-level flowline, the entry pane of the Topic Framework, and the Property dialog box for the externally-linked image.

Step-by-Step Instructions

Use the following generalized steps to complete this exercise on your own. Consult the completed exercise (*Exer21C.a6p*) on the companion CD-ROM for further guidance.

1. Open the file *Exer21C.a6p* located on the companion CD-ROM in the directory named *Chapter21*. Run the program and see how it works. Jump to the flowline and examine the various icons and structures.

2. Open the blue Calculation icons labeled READ ME and read their content.

3. Leave this file open in this copy of Authorware.

4. Open another copy of Authorware, starting a new file. Save the file as *App21C*.

5. You will also have to copy the files for the external graphics files from the companion CD-ROM. Copy the folder named *External Media Files* to your working directory.

6. When finished, make sure to save your exercise in the *SaveWork* directory on your computer's hard drive.

Application Exercise 21D: Using ActiveX Controls and Event Responses

Description

In Chapter 20, you learned how to use ActiveX controls for displaying Web pages within Authorware. In this exercise, you will create an interaction in which users can view various Web pages about the Authorware community and the properties about each page.

Storyboard: On Screen

Figure 21-7 shows what the exercise will look like on screen when completed.

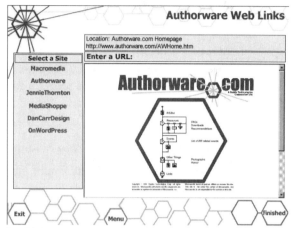

Fig. 21-7. Completed exercise on screen.

Storyboard: Behind the Scenes

Figure 21-8 shows the second- and third-level flowlines (with all icons, their placement, and their names) as they should look when you are finished with this exercise.

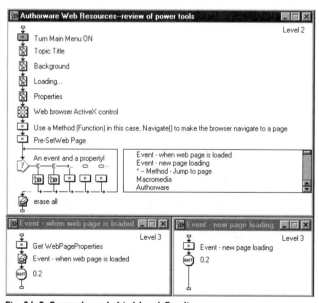

Fig. 21-8. Second- and third-level flowlines.

Step-by-Step Instructions

Use the following generalized steps to complete this exercise on your own. Consult the completed exercise (*Exer21D.a6p*) on the companion CD-ROM for further guidance.

1. Open the file *Exer21D.a6p* located on the companion CD-ROM in the directory named *Chapter21*. Open the library file *Graphics.a6l* located in the same directory. Run the program and see how it works. Jump to the flowline and examine the various icons and structures.

2. Open the blue Calculation icons labeled READ ME and read their content.

3. Leave this file open in this copy of Authorware.

4. Open another copy of Authorware, starting a new file. Save the file as *App21D*. Open the library file *Graphics.a6l* located in the *SaveWork* directory of your hard drive.

5. When finished, make sure to save your exercise in the *SaveWork* directory on your computer's hard drive.

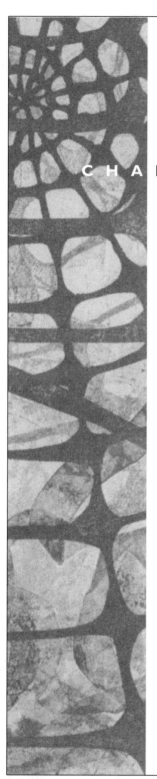

C H A P T E R

22

Publishing and

Distributing Your

Application

Introduction

A published Authorware piece is the format you will distribute to end users. The end user of the program you have created does not necessarily need to have Authorware installed on his machine to play your piece, but the file must be prepared for distribution, and certain accompanying files are required for Authorware to run on other computers. These issues are explored in this chapter. By the end of the chapter you will be able to:

- *Determine what sort of delivery environment your piece will run on*
- *Use the One-Button Publishing feature to speed your publishing*
- *Publish an Authorware file as an executable file for local delivery*
- *Publish an existing Authorware file for delivery over the Internet*
- *Identify the required supporting files for distribution*
- *Batch process many files with one click*

Determining Your Delivery Environment

At the beginning of your project you should know what your delivery environment is. Is your piece going to be deployed on a CD-ROM or sent over the World Wide Web? Will your program be displayed on multiple computers in a training lab with a database tracking system, or will all of your video run from CD-ROM, with users having the executable installed to their hard drives?

Delivering on CD-ROM or Disk

When delivering to a CD-ROM or some other type of disk, realize that you are publishing your Authorware file as an executable (.exe) file. The following are points to keep in mind regarding various media in this category of delivery.

- **Hard drive:** *If you are lucky enough to deliver your Authorware piece directly to the user's hard drive, you will get the optimal performance. You will have to be able to ensure that the user's hard drive contains enough space to store your piece.*
- **CD-ROM:** *A single CD-ROM can store up to 740 Mb of data. The popularity of CD-ROM drives and CD mastering devices makes this a good choice for multimedia programs. The cost of duplication can be very inexpensive.*
- **Removable disks:** *Many other types of removable disks are available – from floppy disks to cartridges that can hold a gigabyte of information. Make sure your users have the appropriate disk drive to read the delivery medium you choose. Also perform speed tests early in the design process, to ensure that large media files will load smoothly.*

Delivering on Networks

Network delivery is accessible to users across vast distances. You can easily revise files, and users can run the piece at their convenience. You can also track the progress and results of everyone who runs the piece.

This delivery medium also allows you to distribute a piece over a local area network (LAN) when your users' computers are all connected to the same network. The piece can be stored on a hard disk attached to the server, or on the server itself. Users save disk space on their local computers because many of the external files, such as libraries, remain on the server.

The server does not have to be the same platform as on users' computers, as long as the local computers can mount it. For example, a Windows computer can obtain files from a UNIX server as long as it can mount the server.

Delivery over the Internet or via a company intranet has the advantage of being timely, with changes implemented to all of your users instantaneously. In addition, you do not need to produce CDs for each update.

The main limitation of Internet or intranet delivery is the connection speed of users' computers and the network that carries your piece. Design your piece with the benefits of the Internet in mind – interactivity, discussion, and access to other resources – and try to keep large images and movies at a minimum. A key strategy for Internet delivery can be to use Authorware for interactive lessons and simulations and traditional Web pages for text presentation.

Authorware Publishing Overview

Publishing is a very simple process, quite often possible with a single click of the mouse (referred to as "one-button publishing," or OBP). In the following you will examine the various settings and talk about the differences in publishing for local (i.e., hard drive, CD-ROM, or intranet) delivery versus delivering over the Internet through a browser. When using Authorware's OBP functionality, published files are organized as either local or Web-based.

Local Publishing

If you need to convey your Authorware file via CD-ROM or hard drive, you need to include the published Authorware file, all linked libraries, supporting drivers for any video, Xtras that enable various media elements to display, and the Authorware Runtime engine. The Runtime is a play-only version of Authorware that takes the place of the regular Authorware application in running the piece. The Runtime engine, *Runa6w32.exe*, adds approximately 1.4 Mb to your final piece.

There are two options for Authorware local delivery. You can package your Authorware file as an executable Authorware file (i.e., an .exe file), with the Runtime program included within the executable. Alternatively, you can publish without the Runtime player and include the player as a separate file when you distribute your piece, which will give your published file an *.a6r* extension.

Web Publishing

Deploying your Authorware piece over the Web is a very different process. For end users to view your piece via a browser, they must have the Authorware Web Player (a free plug-in) installed on their system. Once this plug-in is installed, an Authorware piece can be viewed through a browser. The Authorware Web packaging process breaks your Authorware file into small data chunks called segments, and then streams these chucks as required by the plug-in. The result for the end user is a consistent stream of interactions and content.

Practice Exercise 22-1: One-button Publishing

Description

One of the most empowering new features of Authorware 6.0 is One-Button Publishing. Via the Publish setting of the File menu, you can create a folder containing all of the components you need to distribute your piece for local or Internet delivery. In this exercise you will publish a basic Authorware file. In subsequent exercises and tours, you will explore the settings that allow you to fine-tune and control how your piece is packaged. In this exercise you will:

- *Open an existing file and check it for accuracy*
- *Save the file with a different name to ensure you have a final version*
- *Publish the file*
- *Examine the output of the publishing process*

Take a Look

Before beginning the exercise, let's take a look at the Authorware file you are going to package.

CD-ROM

1. On the companion CD-ROM, locate the *Practice* folder. Open this folder and you will see a number of chapter folders.

2. Copy the *Chapter22* folder to your working directory and locate the file named *Exer22-1 – Publishing Sample.a6p*.

3. Double click on *Exer22-1 – Publishing Sample.a6p*. This file should now appear in your copy of Authorware.

4. Click on the Restart button on the toolbar to play the file from the top of the flowline. Note the following properties of this sample file.

    - *There is a library containing various media files (audio and video for Windows) that are all linked to the Authorware file.*

    - *There is a "Video for Windows" file (.avi) on page 2 of lesson 4.*

    - *The background graphics are imported .gif images.*

    - *The text on screen is antialiased.*

All of these elements will require supporting files called Xtras in order to appear in a published file. Once you publish this piece, you will see a series of directories that produces both the local and Web-enabled versions of the program.

Step-by-Step Instructions

Go Solo

1. Open the sample Authorware file.
    a) If you have not already done so, copy the *Chapter22* folder from the companion CD-ROM *Practice* folder to your working directory and locate the file named *Exer22-1 – Sample File.a6p*.
    b) Double click on *Exer22-1 – Sample File.a6p*. This file should now appear in your copy of Authorware, as shown in figure 22-1.

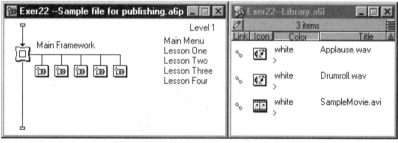

Fig. 22-1. Sample Authorware file and accompanying library.

Before publishing, it is a good idea to perform the following tasks to make sure your Authorware file is ready to go.

- *Save the file with a different name. Do this for archival purposes only. Try changing the name to something that indicates that this is a final product (e.g., Final CBT.a6p or CBT – TestingVersion-1.a6p).*

- *Search the Authorware file for any unlinked Navigate icons. Do this by selecting Edit | Find and then searching for the icon title* Unlinked. *As you know, if a*

Navigate icon has been named by Authorware and becomes unlinked, its title will reflect that broken link. If you find any unlinked icons, fix them.

• *Select Xtras | Library Links. Once open, click on the radio button Broken Links. If there are any Library icons in your piece that have no library source, they will become unlinked and will not display in your presentation. Fix any broken links at this time.*

2. Publish the Authorware file using the One-Button Publishing settings. See figure 22-2.

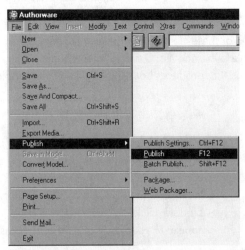

Fig. 22-2. File menu with Publish option selected.

    a) Select File | Publish (F12). Note that a publishing progress indicator appears, showing the process taking place. See figure 22-3.

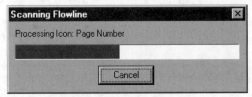

Fig. 22-3. Publishing progress indicator.

3. Launch the packaged piece. The packaged Authorware files will be located on your hard drive in the same directory your .A6P file is saved.
    a) Locate and open the file *Published Files*.
    b) Open the file *Local*.
    c) Double click the file with the *.A6R* extension to view what your piece looks like packaged. See figure 22-4.

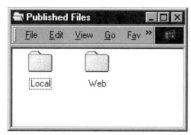

Fig. 22-4. Organization of published files.

Note that when you run the final published piece all elements of the Authorware software program are gone and the file plays in a standalone window.

Guided Tour 22A: Overview of Published Files

Description

A published piece takes the form of an Authorware file, as well as any Xtras, DLLs, libraries, and external files the Authorware file may use. To run properly, a piece requires that these supporting files are on the computer running the packaged piece. With few exceptions, these files need to be in the same directory as the final Authorware piece. If they are not already installed, you must ensure that they accompany your final piece. To distribute an Authorware piece, you need the following files:

- *The published Authorware file*
- *The Runtime engine*
- Xtras *folder containing the Xtras required*
- *Library files used in the piece, if not packaged internally*
- *External media files used in the piece*
- *Drivers for any media that require them, such as QuickTime movies*
- *Fonts used in the piece that might not be available on the user's computer*
- *UCDs, DLLs, and U32s used by the piece*

Before the advent of Authorware 6, all external files had to be located and identified by the developer manually. With the advent of the One-Button Publishing feature, the files a published piece requires are determined by the types of media the piece uses, as well as by other functions you are taking advantage of. In this tour you will examine all of the various types of supporting files. In this guided tour you will learn:

- *When to package with Runtime*
- *What Runtime is*
- *Files you need for distributing various media types, including sounds, images, and movies*
- *How to publish libraries*
- *How to distribute an Authorware piece that uses a database*
- *Listing of Xtras and when to use them*
- *Listing of UCDs, U32s, and DLLs and when to use them*
- *Listing of video drivers and what types they support*

Take a Look

1. If you have not already done so, open the *Exer22 – Publishing Sample.a6p* file and publish it as outlined in Practice Exercise 22-1.

2. Examine the supporting files for local delivery. Once the files are published, Authorware will create a *Packaged Files* directory in your working folder. See figure 22-5.

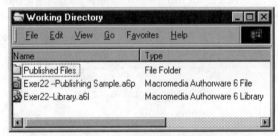

Fig. 22-5. Organization of published files on developer's hard drive.

a) Open the *Packaged Files* directory. See figure 22-6.

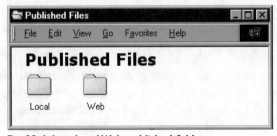

Fig. 22-6. Local and Web–published folders.

b) Open the *Local* folder. See figure 22-7.

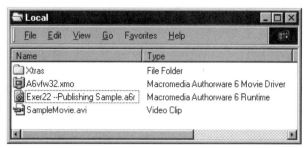

Fig. 22-7. Content of the Local folder.

Within the *Local* folder you will see three files and one folder. Let's examine why each is needed to play your piece properly.

- ***Exer22 – Publishing Sample.A6R:*** *This is your Authorware file published without the Runtime engine. This piece runs correctly without the Runtime engine in this directory because you have Authorware installed elsewhere on your machine. When an .A6R file is launched, the Runtime engine is searched for. If the engine is not found in the same directory as the .A6R file, the path where Authorware is typically installed is searched (i.e.,* C:\Program Files\Macromedia\Authorware 6\). *If you were to distribute this piece without the Runtime engine accompanying this file, other users would not be able to view it.*

- ***SampleMovie.avi:*** *This is the .avi (Video for Windows) file stored externally to the Authorware piece to save file size (see Chapter 5 for more information). Because video files are always external to Authorware, the video file must accompany the final published piece wherever it is distributed.*

- ***A6vfw32.xmo:*** *This is the Authorware 6 Video for Windows 32-bit video driver. This driver communicates with the user's machine and with Authorware, telling the computer how to play the video. Without this driver in the same directory as the published file, the video will not run. There are 10 different .XMOs for different types of video, including MPEG and QuickTime. All .XMOs are stored where Authorware was installed on your system (e.g.,* C:\Program Files\Macromedia\Authorware 6\). *(See Appendix B for a complete listing of all supporting files included with Authorware.)*

- ***Xtras folder:*** *Xtras are plug-ins that let you add functional elements to the Presentation window. For example, Authorware cannot natively produce .GIF files, but with the GIFIMP.x32 Xtra distributed with your published piece, GIFs can be displayed in the Presentation window. (See Appendix B for a complete listing of all supporting files included with Authorware.) See figure 22-8.*

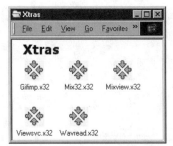

Fig. 22-8. Content of the Xtras folder.

When you use a transition, media, or scripting Xtra in a piece, you need to distribute the Xtras files along with the Authorware files. Remember the following rules when working with Xtras. For a complete listing of Xtras and their functions, see Appendix B.

• Xtras cannot be packaged within an Authorware piece. You need to distribute them as separate files.

• Xtra files must be placed in an *Xtras* folder within the folder that contains your Authorware piece.

• There are 16-bit and 32-bit versions of Xtras for Windows computers. 16-bit Xtras run on all Windows systems, but 32-bit Xtras are much faster and more efficient on Windows 95, Windows 98, Windows NT, and Windows 2000 systems. Do not use 32-bit Xtras on Windows 3.1 systems.

Let's take a look at the Web-packaged version.

1. If you have not already done so, open the *Exer22 – Publishing Sample.a6p* file and publish it as outlined in Practice Exercise 22-1.

2. Examine the supporting files for Web delivery. Once these files are published, Authorware will create a *Packaged Files* directory in your working folder. See figure 22-9.

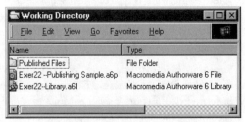

Fig. 22-9. Organization of published files on developer's hard drive.

a) Open the *Packaged Files* directory. See figure 22-10.

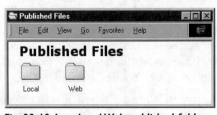

Fig. 22-10. Local and Web-published folders.

b) Open the *Web* folder. See figure 22-11.

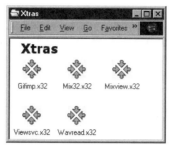

Fig. 22-11. Content of the Web folder.

Within the *Web* folder you will see 11 files and one folder. All of these files would need to be uploaded to your sever for the piece to play through a browser. Note that there is no *.A6R* or *.exe* file. When you are publishing over the Web, you will not need either of these two files. Instead, you will embed your Authorware media in an HTML page and then upload all supporting files to your server. Let's examine what each file is and why it is needed to play your piece properly through a Web browser.

- ***exer0000.aas – exer0006.aas:*** *These are called "segment" files. Each of these segments is a small chunk of your Authorware file. The segments are "streamed" to your users as needed. Because of this technology, your Authorware file that might be 10 Mb is chunked into smaller segments that are easily downloaded one at a time. Segment files can be between 1 K and 2.4 Mb.*

- ***exer22 – publishingsample.aam:*** *This is the Authorware map file. The map file is the file embedded in your HTML page. This file communicates to the browser which segments need to be downloaded, and in which order. The map file also contains information on the size your Authorware piece will run in the browser, what Xtras are required, and any external media required. You can edit and view the content using the Authorware Web Packager program installed with your copy of Authorware.*

- ***exer22 – publishingsample.htm:*** *This is a basic HTML page that contains the commands the browser needs to read your map file and display the Authorware window at the correct size.*

- ***SampleMovie.avi:*** *This is the .avi (Video for Windows) file stored externally to the Authorware piece to save file size (see Chapter 5 for more information). Because this video file is stored externally, it must accompany the Authorware file wherever it is distributed.*

- ***A6vfw32.xmo:*** *This is the Authorware 6 Video for Windows 32-bit video driver. This driver communicates with the user's machine and with Authorware, telling the computer how to play the video. Without this driver in the same server directory as the map file, the video will not run. (See Appendix B for a complete listing of all supporting files included with Authorware.)*

- **Xtras folder:** *Xtras are plug-ins that let you add functional elements to the Presentation window. For example, Authorware cannot natively produce .GIF files, but with the GIFIMP.x32 Xtra distributed with your published piece, GIFs can be displayed in the Presentation window. (See Appendix B for a complete listing of all supporting files included with Authorware.)*

NOTE

Why are Xtras External? Many developers wonder why the *Xtras* folder is kept external to the final Authorware packaged piece. One of the main reasons is that if you have a program made up of four Authorware files, and each one must have the .gif viewer internal to it, that would be an extra 53k each. As it works now, you only need that 53k once. If you are delivering over a network and you have hundreds of titles, this can be a major savings.

Practice Exercise 22-2: Customizing Publishing Settings

Description

One of the most empowering new features of Authorware 6 is One-Button Publishing (OBP). Using the Publish setting from the File menu, you can create a folder with all the components you need to distribute your piece for local or Internet delivery. As you have seen, the results of the OPB process may not be in the exact format you need for your project. In this exercise you will customize the publishing settings to create a single executable file with no Web version. In this exercise you will:

- *Customize the publishing settings to make an executable file*
- *Publish the file*
- *Examine the output of the publishing process*

Take a Look

Before beginning the exercise, let's take a look at the Authorware file you are going to package.

CD-ROM

1. If you have not done this in previous exercises, locate the *Practice* folder on the companion CD-ROM. Open this folder and you will see a number of chapter folders.

2. Copy the *Chapter22* folder to your working directory and locate the file named *Exer22-1 – Publishing Sample.a6p*.

3. Double click on *Exer22-1 – Publishing Sample.a6p*. This file should now appear in your copy of Authorware.

4. Click on the Restart button on the toolbar to play the file from the top of the flowline. Note the following properties of this sample file.

   - *There is a library with various media files (audio and video for Windows) that are all linked to the Authorware file.*
   - *There is a Video for Windows (.avi) file on page 2 of lesson 4.*
   - *The background graphics are imported .gif images.*
   - *The text on screen is antialiased.*

All of these elements require supporting files called Xtras in order to appear in a published file. Once you publish this piece, you will see a series of directories that produces both the local and Web-enabled versions of the program.

Step-by-Step Instructions

Go Solo

1. Open the sample Authorware file.
   a) If you have not already done so, copy the *Chapter22* folder from the companion CD-ROM *Practice* folder to your working directory and locate the file named *Exer22-1 – Sample File.a6p*.
   b) Double click on *Exer22-1 – Sample File.a6p*. This file should now appear in your copy of Authorware. See figure 22-12.

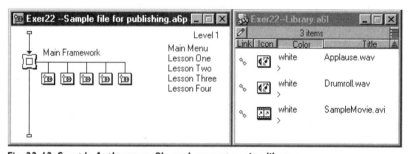

Fig. 22-12. Sample Authorware file and accompanying library.

2. Open the Publish Settings dialog box.
   a) Select File | Publish Settings (Ctrl + F12). See figure 22-13.

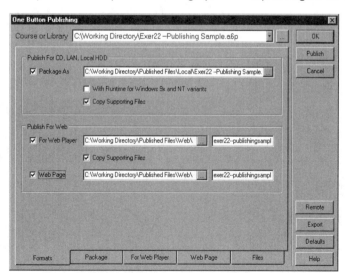

Fig. 22-13. Opening the Publish Settings dialog box.

3. Customize the settings to produce an executable and no Web version.

   a) On the Formats tab, select the checkbox *With Runtime for Windows 9x and NT variants*.

   b) Deselect the checkboxes titled For Web Player and Web Page. Note that when you deselect the Web options the last two tabs disappear.

   c) Change the name of the file to be published from *Exer22 – Publish Sample.exe* to *FINAL.exe*. See figure 22-14.

> **·T/P·**
>
> If you package a piece with the Runtime application, the piece becomes an executable (.exe) application. However, sometimes you want to keep the Runtime application separate. For example, if you have a lot of packaged files that are part of one project, all of them can use the same Runtime application if it is not packaged. In Windows, there are two versions of the Runtime application: *Runa6w16.exe* (for Windows 3.1) and *Runa6w32.exe* (for Windows 95, Windows 98, Windows NT, and Windows 2000). You can find the Runtime application files in the Authorware program folder.

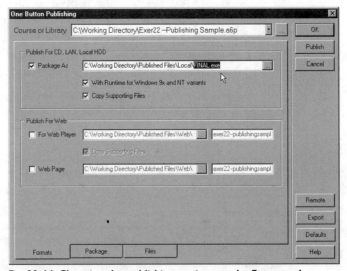

Fig. 22-14. Changing the publishing settings on the Format tab.

4. Publish the file and examine the resulting files.

   a) Click on the Publish button in the OBP dialog box.

   b) Once you get the One-Button Publishing Completed dialog box, click on the Details button.

   c) Click on the Files List button. See figure 22-15.

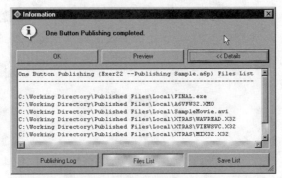

Fig. 22-15. OBP Completion dialog box with supporting files displayed.

·T*i*P·

F12: the Power Key. The most dazzling thing about OBP is that once you make the settings for how you want your piece published – to the web, uploaded automatically to your remote server, or whatever combination of files you have – all you need to do is press the F12 key on your keyboard, and viola! One keypress and all the work is done for you.

Note that all of the files that will be required to distribute the piece are being copied to the working directory. You can also review each of the settings and customize them as needed. Once you save your customized publishing settings, you do not have to reenter them if you need to package and publish your files again.

Guided Tour 22B: One-button Publishing Settings

Description

There are two advantages to using the OBP system. The first is that you as developer can rely on Authorware to identify the supporting files you need to distribute your piece, and can publish pieces without changing the default settings. The second advantage is that you can fine-tune the settings to produce any combination of published files. Then you can save your customized publishing settings so that you do not have to reenter them if you need to package and publish your files again.

Take a Look

1. Open the sample Authorware file.
    a) If you have not already done so, copy the *Chapter22* folder from the companion CD-ROM *Practice* folder to your working directory and locate the file named *Exer22-1 – Sample File.a6p*.
    b) Double click on *Exer22-1 – Sample File.a6p*. This file should now appear in your copy of Authorware.
2. Select File | Publish | Publish Settings (Ctrl + F12) to open the One Button Publishing dialog box and view the Formats tab. See figure 22-16.

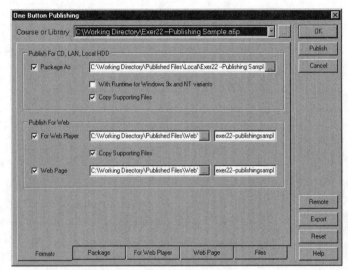

Fig. 22-16. One Button Publishing Formats tab.

3. You should be looking at the One Button Publishing window with the Formats tab selected. At the top of the window is a drop-down list labeled "Course and Library." The default value of this list is the path and file name of the current piece. Opening this will show the libraries connected to this file. To the right of the drop-down list is an Ellipses button. Clicking this button will let you select a file other than the current one to package.

Note the following about the area for publishing to CD, LAN, and HHD.

- **Package As:** *A check mark to the left of the label indicates that the file will be packaged for local delivery. The text field with ellipses indicates the location the file will be published to.*

- **With Runtime for Windows 9x and NT variants:** *With Runtime packages a piece with the Runtime application Runa6w32.exe (for Windows 95, Windows 98, Windows ME, Windows NT, and Windows 2000), and creates the piece as a completely self-contained application. This selection publishes an .exe file.*

- **Without Runtime:** *Publishes a piece without the Runtime application. Users will need Runa6w32.exe, available in the Authorware program file directory, to run this piece. Click on the Ellipses (...) button next to the Without Runtime option to change the default file name or directory for the package. This selection publishes an .A6R file.*

- **Copy Supporting Files:** *Locates and copies any supporting files you need for the packaged piece to the Package As location. This box is selected by default.*

Note the following about the area for publishing to the Web. All of these settings apply only to an Authorware file that will be viewed via a Web browser.

- **For Web Player:** *A check mark to the left of the label indicates that the file will be packaged for Web delivery. Click on the Ellipses (...) button next to the For Web Player option to change the default file name and directory for the package. This option creates an AAM file that is launched with the Authorware Web Player. Users' hard drives will need the Authorware Web Player, available at www.macromedia.com/support/authorware. This can also be set up to automatically download if the user does not have it. This is seen in the Web Page tab.*

- **Copy Supporting Files:** *Copies all supporting files to the map file.*

- **Web Page:** *Creates an HTML file with the necessary embedded tags for the Authorware map file so that the piece will display within a browser.*

4. Click on the Package tab. Use the Package tab to review the packaging options for libraries and externally linked media. See figure 22-17.

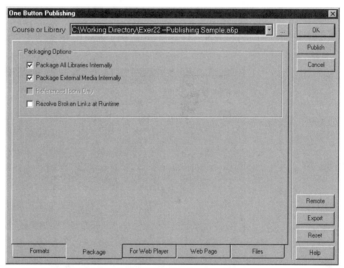

Fig. 22-17. One Button Publishing Package tab.

Note the following about the packaging options:

- **Package All Libraries Internally:** *Includes libraries in the packaged piece. If you do not package the library internally to the published piece, you will have to set up one-button publishing settings for the library (as well as the piece) by selecting the library in the Course or Library drop-down list at the top of the dialog box. Libraries that are not published internal to the piece have an .a6e extension.*

- **Package External Media Internally:** *Includes external media referenced by the library in the packaged piece. This does not include movie files. Digital movie files (AVI, MPEG, etc.) are always stored externally to your packaged piece.*

- **Referenced Icons Only:** *Packages only the icons that are referenced by the library. Referenced icons have a small link symbol next to them in the library. This setting is only active when the library you want to package is selected from the Course or Library drop-down list at the top of the dialog box. You might ask, "Why would you have things in your library that you didn't want to package? And why is leaving them there a bad thing?" Well, you might have graphics that were not used in this piece but are used in other courses that use the same library. By not packaging the files that are unlinked, you will save significant file space.*

- **Resolve Broken Links at Runtime:** *Checks for broken links when the piece is run, and allows the user to locate the files.*

5. Click on the For Web Player tab. Use this tab to review the Map File and Advanced Streamer settings. The For Web Player tab is available only if you have selected the For Web Player publishing option on the Formats tab.

Note the following about the settings within the Map File option of the For Web Player tab. See figure 22-18.

If you are using one-button publishing, you have the option of packaging your libraries internally, in which case they do not have to be distributed with the piece. However, if you do not package your libraries internally, you will need to set up publishing settings for each library, as well as the piece.

When you package libraries separately, store packaged library files in the same folder as the piece. Placing packaged libraries in this location ensures that the Runtime application can find them. If the Runtime application cannot find a library file when opening the piece, a standard dialog box appears that asks the user to locate the library file.

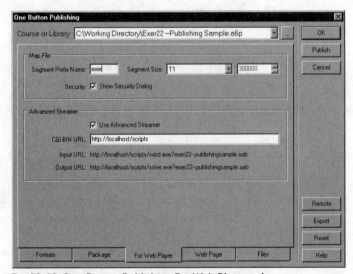

Fig. 22-18. One Button Publishing For Web Player tab.

- **Segment Prefix Name:** *This is the prefix for the segments (called by the map file) the Authorware Web Packager will produce. This prefix is for the Web player's use only, and therefore you do not have to worry about creating meaningful names for your own or others' use. The default name consists of the first four characters of the source file's name and the second four characters in the name are the segment numbers that the Web publisher assigns. Thus the segment's name is only eight characters in length — the DOS default.*

- **Segment Size:** *Using this drop-down list, you can select the connection speed at which your users will be viewing your piece. Once you have selected your connection speed, Authorware generates an average size for each of the segments.*

- **Show Security Dialog:** *This is selected by default. Select this if users need the opportunity to run the piece in trusting mode. (For more information on security settings see the "Planning for Web Delivery" section in this chapter.)*

Authorware Advanced Streamer improves downloading performance for a Web-packaged piece. Authorware Advanced Streamer records the general file access patterns users make when running a piece. It uses that information to download file segments in the background when subsequent users run the piece.

Authorware Advanced Streamer uses probability calculations to determine how future users will navigate through the piece, based on past users. As a user spends time reading information or interacting with the current segment of a piece, Authorware Advanced Streamer downloads the next segments it predicts will be requested by the user. By productively using this idle time, Authorware Advanced Streamer reduces the amount of time users spend waiting for material to download. Note the following about Advanced Streamer.

- **Use Advanced Streamer:** *Select this to use Authorware's Advanced Streamer.*

- **CGI-BIN URL:** *Indicates the location of the directory on the server that hosts the Advanced Streamer.*

- **Input URL:** *Indicates the location of the probabilities file Authorware Web Player uses to download segments of the piece. For the URL, enter an absolute URL to the sstrd.exe application as follows:*
  http://www.myserver.com/scripts/sstrd.exe?mypiece.aab. *Here,* mypiece *is the name of the Authorware piece you have selected to publish.*

- **Output URL:** *Indicates the location you want to save the probability file you are creating for the piece. For the URL, enter an absolute URL to the sstwr.exe application as follows:*
  http://www.myserver.com/scripts/sstwr.ext?mypiece.aab. *Here,* mypiece *is the name of the Authorware piece you have selected to publish.*

6. Click on the Web Page tab. Use this tab to set up how the HTML file that is generated by OBP behaves. The Web Page tab is available only if you have selected the Web Page publishing option on the Formats tab. See figure 22-19.

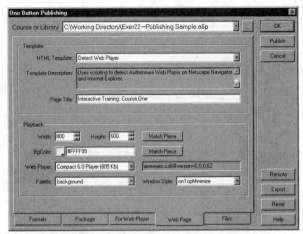

Fig. 22-19. One Button Publishing Web Page tab.

Note the following about the Template section.

- *HTML Template is used to select from the following pre-formatted HTML templates to use when publishing your piece to a Web page.*

    Default: *Uses both an OBJECT tag for Internet Explorer and an EMBED tag for Netscape Navigator to display Authorware.*

    Data Tracking: *Uses an EMBED tag with the HTTP AICC CMI protocol (HACP).*

    Detect Web Player: *Uses scripting to detect the Authorware Web Player on Netscape Navigator and Internet Explorer.*

    Internet Explorer Only: *Uses an Internet Explorer OBJECT tag to display Authorware.*

    Netscape Navigator Only: *Uses a Netscape Navigator EMBED tag to display Authorware.*

- **Template Description:** *Describes the selected template.*

- **Page Title:** *Used to change the name of your published Web page. The default name is* Untitled Document. *This is the title that shows in the browser's title bar.*

In the Playback section, you can change the following options for playing the piece.

- **Width and Height:** *These settings determine the width and height of the window in which the piece runs. The default is to play the piece at a width of 640 and a height of 480. You can use the arrows to change these options, or click on the Match Piece button to match the size of your Presentation window.*

- **BgColor:** *Determines what background color is used. The default is to use #FFFFFF for the background color. You can type in another background color, or click on the Match Piece button to match the background color of your Presentation window.*

·TiP·

You can easily modify and customize these HTML templates to fit your needs. They are located in the Authorware 6 HTML folder. Just modify the templates with your own settings and graphics and then overwrite the originals. Or better yet, add your own templates to the HTML folder and they will appear in the OBP Template list.

- **Web Player:** *Determines what version of the Authorware Web Player is used. The default is to use the Full Player option. You can also select Minimal Player. The Full Player player is approximately a 5Mb-sized file. It includes all the Xtras and UCDS that ship with Authorware. Using the full player ensures that your users will always have access to all of Authorware's features. The Minimal Player is about 2Mb in size and contains only the most frequently used supporting file. Use the Minimal Player option when download size is an issue.*

- **Palette:** *Allows you to set the color palette — the one you used in Authorware or the one the browser uses. You have two options, as follows.*

    Foreground: *Loads the color palette of the Authorware piece. This can cause a noticeable color shift in other images displayed in the browser. (The color shift is corrected when the browser reloads its own color palette once the Authorware piece finishes.) If the palette setting is not specified, the default is* PALETTE=Foreground.

    Background: *Uses the browser's color palette. Using the Background setting avoids the color shift that happens when you use the Foreground setting, but this has the disadvantage of changing the appearance of the Authorware piece. (The colors you used when you created the Authorware piece are replaced with the colors in the browser's palette.) The default is Background.*

- **Window Style:** *Allows you to determine how the window that plays the Authorware piece is displayed in relation to the browser window. The default is to leave it in place, within the browser window. Other options are to leave it on top, in its own separate window, with the browser running in the background. The third, and most unique, choice is to minimize the browser window to the toolbar and display the Authorware file to a separate window. This will make the application seem to be running on its own, not in a browser. It allows you the entire screen real estate.*

7. Click on the Files tab. Use this tab to set up where the individual files included in the publishing process are handled. For instance, you can change the directory from which different files are published. See figure 22-20.

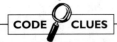

CODE CLUES

Working with Tokens

Tokens are very similar to the system variable *FileLocation* in that they track a predetermined path on your user's system. Tokens are only used in the One Button Publishing Settings dialog box and are powerful because they allow you to specify the destination folder of one or more files from within OBP. If several files need to be grouped in the same directory, and that directory can change, then instead of changing the absolute path in multiple places, you just update the path of the token and the change is reflected in all associated files. Basically, you can modify the destination directory for multiple files at a single location without having to manually change each destination path in OBP.

Here's how you can set tokens: Right click in any Destination field on either the Formats tab or the Files tab and then select Edit Token from the drop-down menu. The token will get inserted into the "destination" field at the caret position. You can also customize existing tokens to save files to a unique file path.

For example, if your piece contains multiple files that require installation into *C:\Windows\System*, you can define a custom token (such as: *$TOKEN1*); now all the files that use this token will be installed in *C:\Windows\System*. If you want to change the destination folder of the files using the *$TOKEN1* token, you only have to make one change in the Edit Tokens dialog box rather than change every file in OBP's Files tab to the new destination.

The built-in tokens such as *$FONTS* are very handy, too. Suppose you need to publish a *.TTF* along with your piece. The preset Token will load all the custom fonts directly to your user's system folder where the fonts are stored.

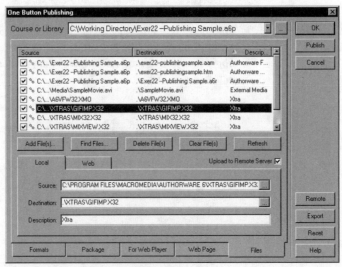

Fig. 22-20. One Button Publishing Files tab.

Note the following about the Files tab options:

- **Source:** *Indicates the name and path of all files selected for publishing. Note the following about this option.*

  Files that will be published are indicated with a check mark.

  To add a listed file to the package, make sure the file is selected with a check mark.

  Working links are indicated with a blue Link icon, and broken links are indicated with a red Link icon. Content location that is based on variables may show as a broken link if the file has not been run to set the current values of those variables. But that doesn't mean there is a problem. When the piece runs, the file name or location will resolve correctly.

  Sort the files by clicking on any of the headings in the list of displayed files.

- **Destination:** *Indicates the name and path where files will be published.*

- **Description:** *Indicates the name and path of files selected for publishing.*

- **Add File(s):** *Used to add additional, unlisted, files to the package, such as a reference from Flash, QuickTime, or ActiveX. Click on this button, and then select the file(s).*

- **Find Files:** *Used to find additional, unlisted, files and add them to the package. Click on this button. The Find Supporting Files dialog box displays. Select U32s/DLLs, Standard Xtras, or External Media, and indicate where to copy them. Authorware one-button publishing scans your piece, locates the files, and places them in the list of files.*

- **Delete Files:** *Used to remove a file you have manually added. Select the file, and then click on this button.*

- **Clear Files:** *Used to clear (remove) all supporting files. Click on this button and all supporting files will be removed.*

- **Refresh:** *Used to relocate moved files and restore broken links. For example, if you have changed the file path to a piece of external media, click on this button to refresh the link to that file.*

- **Upload to remote server:** *This checkbox is used to indicate whether the selected file should be uploaded to the remote server. This is useful when you are republishing a piece and only want to load specific files on the server. This setting requires that you set up the settings inside the Remote button on the lower right-hand side of the One Button Publishing window*

- **Local tab:** *Displays Source, Destination, and Description fields for the selected file. You can change any of these fields for supporting files, but you cannot change them for files that will be published.*

- **Web tab:** *Displayed next to the Local tab if you manually select an Xtra, U32, or a movie for adding the list of files to be published. Use this tab to indicate whether the selected file is added to the map (AAM) file for the Authorware*

Web Player, and to select options for handling the way an external file is downloaded.

- **Include with aam:** *This checkbox determines whether or not the selected file is to be added to the AAM map file for the Authorware Web Player.*

- **PUT:** *Indicates where the file is placed locally (relative to the Web Player folder).*

- **Platform:** *For selecting the publishing platform for the file.*

- **Preempt:** *If a given external file is available on a user's hard disk or CD-ROM, selecting this checkbox tells Authorware to disregard that file and instead download the file from the network.*

- **OnDemand:** *Select this checkbox to download the external file only when the piece calls for it.*

- **Recycle:** *Select this checkbox so that the file is not deleted when the Authorware piece ends. When the piece starts again, it uses the same file again, instead of downloading it a second time.*

- **MacBinary:** *Select this checkbox to create an AAB file, combining the resource fork and the data fork of the file into a single MacBinary file. This preserves the Macintosh "create" and "type" information and is needed to ensure that movies, Xtras, and XCMDs download properly (because HTTP transfers over the Internet would not otherwise preserve this information).*

8. Note the following buttons on the right side of the OBP dialog box. Click on the Files tab. Use this tab to set up where the individual files included in the publishing process are handled. For instance, you can change the directory from which different files are published.

    - **Reset:** *Select this button to restore your one-button publishing settings and selected files to the default settings for one-button publishing.*

    - **Export:** *Select this button to save your one-button publishing settings in a registration (REG) file. The registration file is connected to your Authorware piece, so that whenever you publish the piece the settings will already be in place.*

    - **Remote:** *Select this button to set one-button publishing to publish to a remote FTP site. This allows you to automatically upload your files to the Web server that is hosting it.*

    - **FTP Host:** *Enter the host name of the server to which you intend to upload the Authorware files. The specific information required to make an FTP connection is unique to each server. If you are not sure about some of this information, ask your ISP or your system administrator.*

    - *Your FTP host name is the full Internet name of a computer system, such as ftp.pathware.com. Enter the full host name without any additional text (such as the protocol name* http://) *in front of the host name; for example, as follows:*

Correct: *ftp.interaction.com*

Correct: *134.245.555.550*

Incorrect: *ftp://ftp.interaction.com*

Incorrect: *interaction.com*

- **Host Directory:** *Enter the name of the folder on the remote site where you want to store the documents to make them visible to the public. This folder or directory on the server corresponds to the local root folder on your local disk. In some cases, a server may be configured to automatically route you to the correct directory by default. In that case, you may leave the Host Directory text box blank. If your server is not set up like that, however, you need to enter a host directory.*

- **Login and Password:** *Enter the log-in name and password you use to connect to the FTP server. Optionally, if the status line at the bottom of the Remote Settings dialog box indicates that the FTP host is disconnected, you can click on Test to determine if the settings are correct. If they are correct, you will be connected to the FTP site.*

- **Publish:** *This button publishes the piece using the settings you selected. If publishing is successful, an Information dialog box is displayed. In the Information dialog box, you can select the following buttons.*

  OK: *Closes the One Button Publishing dialog box and saves your current publishing settings.*

  Preview: *Displays a preview of the published piece.*

  Details: *Displays a publishing log. You can click on Save Log to save the log in a log file. You can also click on Files List to display a list of files that were published and where they were published. If you click on Files List, you can then click on Save List to save the list of files in a text file.*

Guided Tour 22C: Batch Publishing

Description

In addition to using one-button publishing to publish several versions of a single Authorware piece, you can publish several Authorware pieces at the same time, using the batch publishing settings. You might want to do this if you are working on a series of curricula that are all being updated at the same time. You could set up the setting for publishing your files and then with a click of the mouse publish all of your courseware at once, with the same supporting files to the same directory structure. In this guided tour you will learn:

- *When to use the Batch Publishing feature*
- *The basic operation of the Batch Publishing dialog box*

Take a Look

1. Batch publish several pieces at once.
   a) Select File | Publish | Batch (Shift + F12). The Batch Publish dialog box opens, displaying a new batch. See figure 22-21.

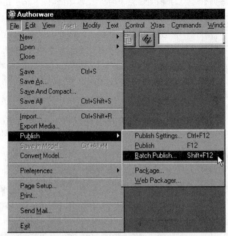

Fig. 22-21. Batch Publish dialog box.

   b) To open an existing batch, select Batch | Open and select the batch file.
   c) To add files to the batch, click on Add.
   d) Verify that the Select File dialog box has displayed.
   e) Locate the file and select it, and then click on Open.
   f) Verify that the Batch Publish dialog box is displayed, with the selected file included in the list of files to be published.
   g) Continue adding pieces until you have selected all pieces you want to publish. See figure 22-22.

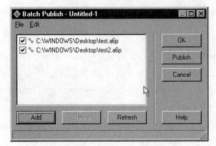

Fig. 22-22. Multiple files added to the Batch Publish dialog box.

h) To save the batch, select Batch | Save, and enter a file name.

i) To publish the batch, click on Publish. The selected files are published. An Information window is displayed, informing you that batch publishing was completed. Note the following buttons in the Batch Publishing dialog box.

- **Refresh:** *Clears all files from the screen and starts over.*
- **Delete:** *Deletes an individual file.*

Web Publishing Overview

An Authorware piece downloaded over the Web must be designed differently from a piece that runs from the user's hard disk. The two environments have different strengths and constraints. The major strength of streaming technology is its flexibility; its major constraint is network speed.

Managing Content in Web-packaged Pieces

Content can be embedded in, or external to, a Web-packaged piece, just as it can in any Authorware piece. A consideration to keep in mind when designing a piece is to avoid delays when content is downloading.

If you are using Authorware Advanced Streamer, avoid using external content whenever possible. This is less efficient than using embedded content.

Embedded Content

Authorware one-button publishing includes embedded content in one of the segments it creates when you package the piece for the Web. Note the following.

- *If you are using Authorware Advanced Streamer, avoid using the* NetPreload *function. NetPreload does manually what Authorware Advanced Streamer attempts to do automatically: download segments when the transfer is least noticeable.*

- *If you are not using Authorware Advanced Streamer, use the* OnDemand *option and* NetPreload *to control when Authorware Web Player downloads the segments that contain content.*

External Content

Authorware handles external content in accordance with how you have set up the content. Note the following.

- *If the path to an external media file points to your local hard disk or your local server, one-button publishing adds a path that points to the folder on the user's computer where the player will download the file.*

- Use the OnDemand *option to download the file only when actually needed. The player first checks for the file in the folder on the user's computer. If it finds a copy there, it uses it rather than downloading the file again.*

- *If the path to an external media file is a URL, one-button publishing leaves the path as it is.*

- *Use Preload to load an external sound or graphics file directly from a URL into memory.*

- *If you use* NetDownload *to download an external media file, Authorware Web Packager leaves the path to the file as it is.*

- *Use the OnDemand option in the map file to control precisely when the player downloads the file.*

- *Custom fonts are difficult to handle because they need to be installed after they are downloaded.*

Planning for Web Delivery

Internet users are an increasingly impatient bunch. In situations such as training, if learners are expected to sit and wait for a download, they may become frustrated and unmotivated. If there is a long download time on a Web site, many users simply cancel the page and go somewhere else. You need to avoid these pauses during downloading. Design a project so that long downloads and data transfers are not necessary. Create the flow of your project to keep new information in front of the user at all times. In this regard, keep the following guidelines in mind:

- *Always test and remember your target network speed. Your file may look great at your T3 development station, but could be painfully slow on a 56-K modem for someone in the field.*

- *Use more interactions and avoid large graphics and long sound files. The interactivity in Authorware is very small in file size; it works well at standard modem speeds.*

- *Nonstandard presentation windows can look great on Web pages, and smaller sizes run faster. Set a smaller Presentation window size by selecting Modify | File | Properties. You can set the File | Properties selection to Variable and then at the top of the flowline insert a Calculation icon with the variables ScreenHeight and ScreenWidth for setting the size of screen you want.*

- *Experiment with really small color depths. See how creative you can be with 4-bit images, which are half as big as 8-bit images. Try using 1-bit images. These are black-and-white, but you can add two colors (one foreground and one background) using the Colors palette in Authorware.*

- *Save graphics in PNG, JPEG, and GIF formats, which are smaller than their BMP counterparts. Macromedia Fireworks is an excellent tool both for determining which format produces a more compact file and for saving the file in the most appropriate format.*

- *Save voice audio files in Voxware (VOX) format. (The Voxware encoder ships with Authorware and is installed in your Authorware directory.) Save other audio files in Shockwave Audio (SWA, available via Xtras | Other | Convert .wav to .swa) or MP3 format.*

- *Use NetDownload, NetPreload, and Preload functions before large files are needed to begin the download process while the user is reading a page or in an interaction.*

- *When you use one-button publishing to package a piece for Authorware Web Player, experiment with different sizes of segments.*

Connection Speed

The speed at which you can play a piece across a network or download it, or download linked external content, always depends on the same things: the speed of data transmission across the network and the amount of information being transferred. On all types of networks – LANs, intranets, and the Internet – network speed varies depending on the specific network configuration and the amount of activity on the network. Intranets that use T1 or T3 servers can be quite fast, but if users are dialing into the intranet from a modem, the connection will be only as fast as their modem.

The Internet is typically slower than an intranet, primarily because unless users have DSL or other high-speed connections users dial in at relatively slow speeds. If traffic is heavy at the Internet access point or on the Internet host, or if there is network congestion, the rate drops even lower – to as low as a few hundred bytes per second.

Authorware Web Player

When you publish your piece as an executable you can end up with a 20-Mb file. To expect users to download that file size across the Internet is ludicrous. Authorware's Web publishing feature takes your 20-Mb file, chops it into many smaller chunks (called segments), and plays each chunk in the correct order via the browser. The browser knows what order in which to display the segments because the Authorware map (.*aam*) file gives it that information. Streaming involves the use of four file types, described in the sections that follow.

Map File (.aam)

The map file, created by the OBP feature, communicates between the browser and the Authorware Web Player. The map file tells Web Player what to download, when to download it, and where to place the downloaded segments. If you were to open a map file and look at its settings, you would see a list of segment files, numbers, and external media. The best thing about Web Player is that you really do not need to understand what is going on; you simply need to be able to upload it to a directory on your server.

Segment File (.aas)

One of the big advantages of Web packaging a piece is that the piece is divided into segments. The segments can be as small or as large as you establish. In addition, the player downloads segments only as they are needed. This makes it possible to produce large applications – 20 or 30 Mb and larger – that run efficiently and continuously. If you have installed Authorware Advanced Streamer on a Web server, Authorware Web Player will even attempt to download in advance the segments users are most likely to want next. But, if you have a large audio file, it will not be broken up into smaller segments. The segment containing that piece will end up at least the size of that file.

HTML File (.htm)

For your Web-published file to display via a browser it must be called from an HTML page that contains the commands the browser needs to read your map file and display the Authorware window at the correct size. The HTML page can also contain Java Script that checks to see if your user has the Authorware Web Player installed. If the user does not have the plug-in, the user will be directed to a site from which to download it. If you are running in an "Internet Explorer only" environment, you can automatically download the Web Player ActiveX command to the user's system. For more information on this process, consult the Authorware help files article "Using the Authorware Web Player Control for ActiveX."

Authorware Web Player Plug-in

Users need the correct version of Authorware Web Player installed on their machine to run a Web-packaged piece created in Authorware 6. There are two methods for displaying Web-packaged Authorware pieces: Authorware Web Player and Authorware Web Player Control for ActiveX. Although both Internet Explorer and Netscape Navigator support Authorware Web Player, only Internet Explorer in Windows supports ActiveX controls.

The benefit of ActiveX controls is that if the user is missing the Authorware plug-in the ActiveX controls can be downloaded to the user's machine without her permission. The controls can be downloaded and installed without user intervention, which reduces the chance of user error.

If you are not working in an environment in which you can distribute the player to users directly, have them download it (at no cost) from the Macromedia Web site. For information on setting up a link to the Macromedia Web site, visit the Authorware Support Center. (Select Help | Developer's Center, or visit *www.macromedia.com/support/authorware.*)

Avoiding Trouble

The following are tips for avoiding problems when working with Web-packaged pieces.

- **DLLs, drivers, and Xtras:** *Make sure you have not marked any DLLs, drivers, and Xtras onDemand. DLLs, drivers, and Xtras need to download before the piece starts. OnDemand is best used with long AVI files or other large content.*

- **Disk cache:** *Clear your browser's disk cache after posting new versions of a Web-packaged piece.*

- **Libraries:** *It is often easier to manage Web-packaged content if you package libraries internally. Package libraries externally only if they need to be shared among multiple pieces or files.*

- **Prefs.ini file:** *You can provide your users with a default setup by having them use a non Web-packaged installation program to install the Prefs.ini file in the Np32asw folder in the Netscape plug-ins folder. One of the benefits of such a default setup is that you can configure it to automatically trust your site. Use the Authorware Web Player Security Knowledge Object to install the Prefs.ini file.*

- **NetDownload and ReadExtFile:** *"File not Found" or "Invalid version in map file" errors may be caused by NetDownload or ReadExtFile failures that are not explicitly mentioned in the AAM file.*

- *Authorware run-time location: Do not change the location of the Authorware Runtime application relative to Authorware Web Player. For example, in Windows 95, the player file, Np32asw.dll, is located in the Netscape plug-ins folder. Inside the Netscape plug-ins folder is a folder named Np32asw, which contains the Authorware 3.5 Runtime application. Inside the Np32asw folder are three more folders: Aw40, which contains the Authorware 4 version of the Runtime application; Aw50, which contains the Authorware 5 version of the Runtime application; and Aw60, which contains the Authorware 6 version of the Runtime application.*

Authorware's Advanced Streamer

Authorware Advanced Streamer is a separate installation on your Web server that keeps track of the order in which users view your files. As more users view your content, the Advanced Streamer begins to anticipate which segment files might be called upon next and starts pre-loading them in the background. This improves downloading performance for a Web-packaged piece.

Authorware Advanced Streamer uses probability calculations to determine how future users will navigate through the piece based on past users. As a user spends time reading information or interacting with the current segment of a piece, Authorware Advanced Streamer downloads the next segments it predicts will be requested by the user. By productively using this idle time, Authorware Advanced Streamer reduces the amount of time users spend waiting for material to download.

Installing Authorware Advanced Streamer

The following specify server requirements for using Authorware's Advanced Streamer.

- *Authorware Advanced Streamer supports Microsoft Internet Information Server (IIS) version 4 running on Windows NT.*

- *Authorware Advanced Streamer consists of two CGI applications that must be installed in the* scripts *folder of your server.*

- *With IIS, the* scripts *folder is generally c:\inetpub\scripts. You must have system administration rights to the server to install the scripts.*

- *In addition, the scripts must be able to write data to the SST folder that contains the probabilities data the Authorware Advanced Streamer uses.*

- *This can be done by granting the generic Web user write access to the \scripts\sst folder and all of its subfolders.*

Server Installation

To install Authorware's Advanced Streamer, perform the following steps.

1. Open the Authorware Advanced Streamer folder inside the Authorware 6 application folder.

2. Copy the content of the Authorware Advanced Streamer folder to the *scripts* directory of your Web server. Do not copy the Authorware Advanced Streamer folder itself, just its content. This includes *sstrd.exe*, *sstwr.exe*, and the folder *SST*.

File Preparation

To use a piece with Authorware Advanced Streamer, you edit the piece's map file using the One Button Publishing For Web Player tab's Advanced Streamer options. See figure 22-23.

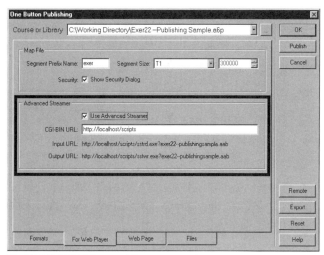

Fig. 22-23. OBP Advanced Streamer settings.

Maintaining Authorware Advanced Streamer Files

Authorware Advanced Streamer has an *INI* file that controls various options and error messages users may encounter when running a piece. You can edit the file using Notepad or any text editor. The file is located in *\sst\prog\sst.ini*. To delimit comment lines in the *INI* file, use the pound sign (#) at the beginning of the line. You can set options as follows.

- *Serial Number: The valid serial number for this copy of Authorware Advanced Streamer. Without a valid serial number, only five users can simultaneously run the piece. You can obtain a valid serial number from the Authorware Support Center at* www.macromedia.com/support/authorware.

- *ShowLicenseErrors: Determines if users see an error message if more than the licensed number of users are running the piece.*

- *LicenseErrorMessage: Specifies the error message users encounter if the* ShowLicenseErrors *option is set to Yes. Include the error string within quotation marks and do not place a carriage return in the quoted string.*

- *NumberOfUsers: Controls the number of simultaneous users that can run the piece when a valid serial number has been entered. The number of users can be set as high as 60,000.*

- *ShowGenericErrors: Determines if users see an error message when an unexpected error occurs (e.g., if the disk on the server were to become full, thereby prohibiting Authorware Advanced Streamer from writing probability information at the end of a session).*

- **GenericErrorMessage:** *Specifies the error message users encounter if a generic error occurs. Place the error message within quotation marks with no carriage returns. A good strategy is to enter a help desk phone number or e-mail address for people to contact.*

- **LogErrors:** *Determines if an error log is maintained for license and generic errors. The error log file is located in \sst\prog\errorlog.txt.*

Authorware Advanced Streamer writes a small (typically less than 100 K) probability file to the *\sst\data* folder each time the piece is run. The name of this file is formed by concatenating the unique ID in the piece's map file with the name you provided for the *AAB* file as part of the *InputPredictiveURL* and *OutputPredictiveURL*. For example, if you specify *mypiece.aab* and the Unique ID for the piece is 12345, the data file generated is named *mypiece000001 2345.aab*.

If you are not using one-button publishing, each time you package a piece for the Web, you may want to manually delete the old data files from the *\sst\data* folder on the Web server that correspond to the IDs of old pieces. For external libraries, the data file name consists of the unique ID of the main piece's map file, followed by an underscore, and then the unique ID from the library map file itself.

Authorware Web Player Security Features

Authorware Web Player has built-in security features that protect the integrity of a user's system from unwanted downloads or potential hacking. Before the player runs a Web-packaged piece, it displays a dialog box that asks whether the user wants to trust the site the Web-packaged piece is coming from.

The appearance of the Security dialog box interrupts the flow of a piece, so take it into consideration when you are designing how you want a piece to work. Security features are handled in the One Button Publishing For Web Player tab.

Trusting Mode

A user can choose to trust a site either temporarily (by clicking on OK in the Security dialog box) or permanently, by adding the site's URL to the Security Options dialog box. If a user chooses to trust a site, the Web-packaged piece can take full advantage of Authorware features, including Xtras, UCDs, and DLLs. If you are developing a course for a corporate or educational intranet, you can set up a *Prefs.ini* file that trusts any piece that is part of the course, without the user needing to choose.

Nontrusting Mode

Nontrusting mode protects users from running Web-packaged pieces that might cause damage to their system, infect their system with a virus, or read confidential files from their hard disk and transmit them back to the server. You can bypass the Security dialog box and allow users to run a piece in non-trusting mode.

If you allow users to run a piece in nontrusting mode, the player will not download external content files, Xtras, UCDs, and DLLs. Certain variables and functions (such as *DeleteFile, SaveRecords, WriteExtFile*, and *FileLocation*) are also disabled restrictions in nontrusting mode. There are two security restrictions in nontrusting mode, as follows:

- *All writing to the user's hard disk, including renaming or deleting files, is prevented.*

- *The player does not look for Xtras in the following locations on the user's hard drive.*

Disabled variables in nontrusting mode:

DiskBytes	**OrigWorkingDirectory**
FileLocation	**RecordsLocation**
FileType	**SearchPath**

Disabled functions in nontrusting mode:

AppendExtFile	**PrintScreen**
Catalog	**Quit(2)**
CreateFolder	**Quit(3)**
DeleteFile	**QuitRestart(2)**
JumpFileReturn	**QuitRestart(3)**
JumpOut	**RenameFile**
JumpOutReturn	**SaveRecords**
JumpPrintReturn	**WriteExtFile**
NetDownload	

If an Authorware file is operating in nontrusting mode, Authorware Web Player makes the *FileLocation* variable return an empty (zero-length) string. If the course is operating in trusted mode, the *FileLocation* variable returns the location of the player directory on the file system. To determine the security mode, place the following code in a Calculation icon at the beginning of the file.

```
-- Test for security in trusting/non-trusting mode.

if FileLocation = "" then

-- Security is enabled. Operating in non-trusting mode.

 netSecurity := 1
```

```
else

-- Security is disabled. Operating in trusting mode.

netSecurity := 0

end if
```

The Authorware file can then use the custom variable *netSecurity* to trigger warnings to the user or otherwise modify the operation of the course. If a Web-packaged piece uses features prohibited in nontrusting mode, the player still runs the piece. However, it will not work as you intended it to.

Guided Tour 22D: Bypassing the Authorware Web Player Security Dialog

Description

Normally, before Authorware Web Player downloads a Web-packaged piece, it displays the Security dialog box. The Security dialog box can sometimes be both unnecessary and undesirable; for example, when students are taking a training course over a corporate intranet. You can create a preferences file (*.ini*) that tells Authorware Web Player which URLs it can trust and thereby prevent the Security dialog box from appearing on subsequent visits.

Take a Look

1. Use the Authorware One Button Publishing For Web Player tab to turn off the Show Security Dialog option. See figure 22-24.

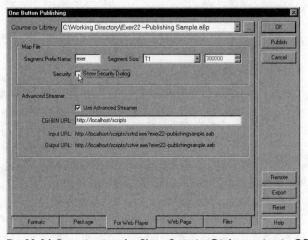

Fig. 22-24. Deactivating the Show Security Dialog option in OBP.

2. Once you deactivate the Show Security Dialog option in OBP you can view the map file and see that *BypassSecurityDialog=TRUE*. This will keep the box from appearing to sites that are trusted. See figure 22-25.

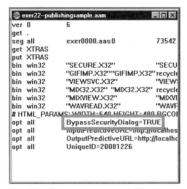

Fig. 22-25. Resulting map file (.aam).

You can include the Knowledge Object icon in the first web-packaged piece in the curriculum or web-package it as a separate piece that uses the *JumpFile()* function to launch the main file.

3. To add to the list of trusted sites, place the Authorware Web Player Security Knowledge object on your flowline. See figure 22-26.

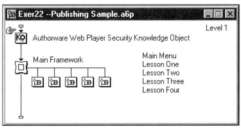

Fig. 22-26. Adding the Authorware Web Player Security Knowledge object to the flowline.

4. On the Trusted URLs page of the Knowledge object, enter the entire sub-domain (such as *http://www.jenniethornton.com*) you want the Web Player to trust. You must include the *http://* for the URL to be trusted.

5. To trust all sites at one domain, enter an asterisk after the *http://*. That is, *http://*.jenniethornton.com*. (The asterisk must come immediately after *http://*.) See figure 22-27.

You need to set up the Authorware Web Player Security Knowledge object only once. It does not need to change with each revision of Authorware or with each new corporate training piece you develop, as long as you post the piece in a trusted domain. You can make it possible for the security dialog box to never show to a user, but you must place the *Awshkwv.ini* file on each student's hard drive. Because this file is not an executable, but just a text file, most corporate IT departments will assist you in copying it to end-user hard drives before the training is launched.

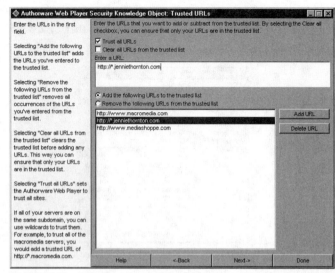

Fig. 22-27. Trusted URLs page of the Web Player Security Knowledge object.

6. On the Security Dialogs page of the Knowledge object, check the appropriate box to determine if and when the security box displays on subsequent visits to the Authorware file. See figure 22-28.

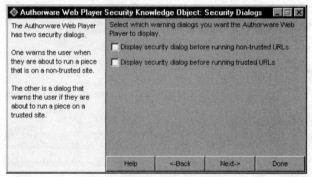

Fig. 22-28. Security Dialogs page of the Web Player Security Knowledge object.

7. When you upload the file to your server, the first time the file runs you will get the Security dialog box. After the Knowledge object and the preferences *.ini* file (called *Awshkwv.ini* and placed in the user's system directory) run, every subsequent visit there will be no dialog box. See figure 22-29.

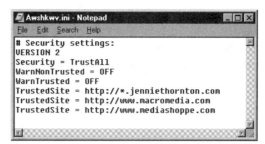

Fig. 22-29. Content of the **Awshkwv.ini** *file.*

Guided Tour 22E: Configuring Your Server

You need to set up the Web server where you place the HTML page and the Web-packaged Authorware piece so that it recognizes the Multipurpose Internet Mail Extensions (MIME) type that identifies a Web-packaged Authorware file. This is a matter of adding a few lines to the server's configuration settings.

The following instructions provide an idea of how to configure a basic server to recognize and handle the MIME types for Macromedia products. However, because there are so many different types of Web servers, you may need to consult the documentation for your Web server to configure it properly.

Naming Web Files

For proper downloading of segments, the file names in the map file must match the file names on the HTTP server. Authorware Web Packager creates the file names in all lowercase characters. Unfortunately, however, certain types of FTP client software can alter the case of file names during the upload process.

If you have a UNIX server, make sure you are using FTP client software that does not alter the capitalization of file names (because UNIX servers are case sensitive in handling file names). If you find that the file names between the map file and the server have different capitalization – and you cannot change your FTP client software – you will need to either rename the files on the server or change the file names in the map file to match what is on the server.

Authorware MIME Type Mappings

The following are the MIME types for Authorware:

AddType application/x-authorware-map aam

AddType application/x-authorware-seg aas

AddType application/x-authorware-bin aab

> ### CAUTION ⚠️
>
> This section assumes that you are already familiar with maintaining or administering a web server. If this is not the case, do not attempt to follow these directions. Have your system administrator configure the server for you.

The format of the MIME type directive will change from server to server. For example, on an NCSA server, the server administrator updates the *srm.conf* file to include the appropriate MIME type lines. On some servers, you may need to specify the extension with a period; for example, as follows.

```
AddType application/x-authorware-map .aam
```

On Netscape servers, the entries are in the file *mime.types* and are formatted as follows. Once the file is updated, you should restart the server.

```
type=application/x-authorware-map   exts=aam

type=application/x-authorware-seg   exts=aas

type=application/x-authorware-bin   exts=aab
```

Configuring MIME Types

Some Web servers allow you to configure a single directory as an alternative to changing the configuration for the entire server. For example, if your Internet service provider (ISP) does not add the Authorware MIME types to its server, as a user you could create a file to add the MIME types in your personal Web directory. On an NCSA server, this file is called *.htaccess*, and the format is the same as for *srm.conf* in the previous MIME-type mappings directives.

Practice Exercise 22-3: Web Delivery

Description

After you have completed a piece you can package it for delivery over the World Wide Web. To package a piece for the Web, use one-button publishing, which segments and compresses the file to make downloading faster. You can also use one-button publishing to set up how external files (libraries, Xtras, digital movies, and so on) are downloaded. Authorware one-button publishing for the Web Player does two things.

- *Divides the piece into segments the Authorware Web Player can download. (You can set the size of the segments to get the best performance.)*

- *Creates a map file, which tells the player what to download, when to download it, and where to place the downloaded segments.*

You must embed the Web-packaged piece in an HTML page. You must also configure a Web server and place the Web-packaged piece and all of its external files there. This is all done with one-button publishing. Users of a Web-packaged piece must have the Authorware Web Player to run it. You can supply the player with the piece, or users can download it from the Macromedia Web site. In this exercise you will:

- *Open an existing file and check it for accuracy*
- *Change the OBP settings to produce a Web version only*
- *Publish the Web files to a remote server*
- *Examine the output of the publishing process*

Take a Look

Before beginning the exercise, let's take a look at the Authorware file you are going to package.

CD-ROM

1. On the companion CD-ROM, locate the *Practice* folder. Open this folder and you will see a number of chapter folders.

2. Copy the *Chapter22* folder to your working directory and locate the file named *Exer22-2 – Web Sample.a6p*.

3. Double click on *Exer22-2 – Web Sample.a6p*. This file should now appear in your copy of Authorware.

4. Click on the Restart button on the toolbar to play the file from the top of the flowline. Note the following properties of this sample file.

   - *An Authorware Web Player Security Knowledge object is used.*
   - *The graphic is an imported .bmp image.*
   - *The text on screen is antialiased.*
   - *There is a concurrent animation sequence.*
   - *There is a perpetual Quit button.*

All of these elements will require supporting files called Xtras in order to appear in a published file. Once you publish this piece, you will see a series of directories that produces the Web-enabled version of the program.

Step-by-Step Instructions

Go Solo

1. Open the sample Authorware file. See figure 22-30.

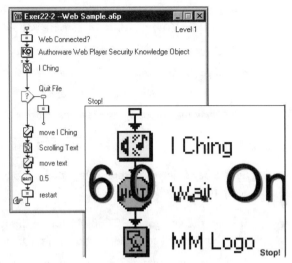

Fig. 22-30. Sample Authorware file.

a) If you have not already done so, copy the *Chapter22* folder from the companion CD-ROM *Practice* folder to your working directory and locate the file *Exer22-2 – Web Sample.a6p*.

b) Double click on *Exer22-2 – Web Sample.a6p*. This file should now appear in your copy of Authorware.

2. Change the OBP settings to publish a Web version only. See figure 22-31.

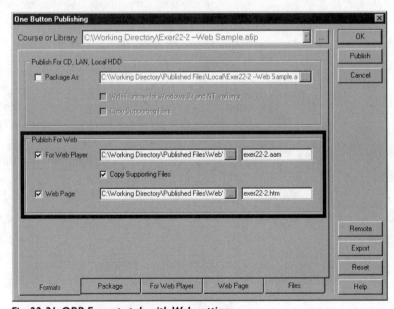

Fig. 22-31. OBP Formats tab with Web settings.

a) Select File | Publish Settings (Ctrl + F12). The One Button Publishing dialog box is displayed, with the Formats tab showing.

b) Select the course (*A6P*) file to be published.

c) Deselect the Package As checkbox, as you will not be producing a version for local delivery.

d) Select For Web Player to publish for the Authorware Web Player.

e) Change the name of the map file and HTML file to *exer22-2*.

f) Select Copy Supporting Files (i.e., Xtras) if you want all supporting files to be copied to the map file.

3. Set up the Web Player settings. By default, the piece's file name is preceded by the first four characters of the source file's name, Segment Size is set to 56 kbps modem at 16000 baud, and Show Security Dialog is selected. See figure 22-32.

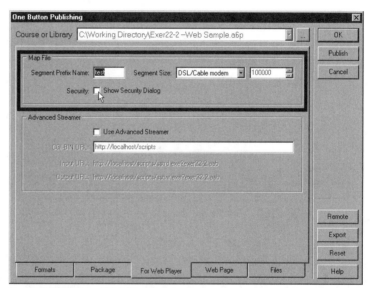

Fig. 22-32. OBP For Web Player tab.

a) Click on the For Web Player tab and review the Map File settings. The For Web Player tab is available only if you have selected the For Web Player publishing option on the Formats tab.

b) Change the prefix name to *test*. This is the prefix for the segments the Authorware Web Packager will produce.

c) Change the Segment Size to DSL/Cable Modem, or select Custom and enter your own speed. The speed changes based on the segment size selected.

d) Deselect the Show Security Dialog checkbox. Select this box if users need the opportunity to run the piece in trusting mode.

4. Set up the Web Page settings. Web browsers understand HTML, so the way to get a browser to download a Web-packaged piece for the player is to make the piece part of an HTML page. You can use the one-button publishing Web page option to add the Web-packaged piece to a Web page. The Authorware Web Player cannot connect with the Web on its own. It works in conjunction with a Web browser such as Netscape Navigator or Internet Explorer. See figure 22-33.

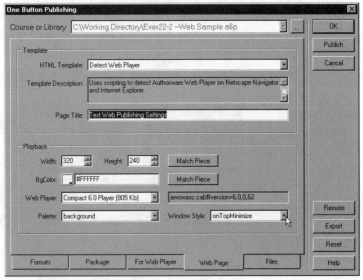

Fig. 22-33. OBP Web Page tab.

·T/P·

You can easily modify and customize these HTML templates to fit your needs. They are located in the Authorware 6 *HTML* folder. Just modify the templates with your own settings and graphics and then overwrite the originals. Or better yet, add your own templates to the *HTML* folder and they will appear in the OBP Template list.

a) If you are publishing to a Web page, click on the Web Page tab and review the settings. The Web Page tab is available only if you have selected the Web Page publishing option on the Formats tab.

b) In the Template section, you can select from several pre-formatted HTML templates to use when publishing your piece to a Web page. Select the Detect Web Player template. This template will use scripting to detect the Authorware Web Player on Netscape Navigator and Internet Explorer.

c) Change the Page Title option to Test Web Publishing Settings. This will change the name of your published Web page. The default name is *Untitled Document.*

d) In the Playback section, you can change the Web Player options for playing the piece. The default is Full 6.0 Player. Select Minimal 6.0 Player.

e) Window Style allows you to determine how the window that plays the Authorware piece is placed on the user's desktop. The default is to leave the Authorware piece inside the browser window. The other options are to leave it on top of the browser or to minimize the browser and display the Authorware file on top. Try selecting *OnTopMinimize*.

You can also set one-button publishing to publish to a remote FTP site. If you have a user name and password access to an FTP site, you can have your Authorware file and all supporting files directly uploaded to the appropriate directory when you click on the Publish button. See figure 22-34.

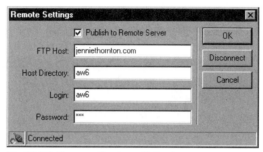

Fig. 22-34. Remote Settings dialog box.

5. Enter the host name of the server to which you intend to upload the Authorware files. The specific information required to make an FTP connection is unique to each server. If you are not sure about some of this information, ask your ISP or your system administrator. Your FTP host name is the full Internet name of a computer system, such as *ftp.authorware.com*. Enter the full host name without any additional text (such as the protocol name *http://*) in front of the host name. The following are examples of correct and incorrect format:

Correct: *ftp.authorware.com*

Correct: *411.42.18.70*

Incorrect: *ftp://ftp.authorware.com*

Incorrect: *authorware.com*

6. Enter the name of the folder on the remote site where you want to store the documents to make them visible to the public. This folder or directory on the server corresponds to the local root folder on your local disk. In some cases, a server may be configured to automatically route you to the correct directory by default. In that case, you may leave the Host

Directory text box blank. If your server is not set up like this, however, you need to enter a host directory.

7. Enter the log-in name and password you use to connect to the FTP server.

8. Click on Test to determine if the settings are correct. If they are correct, you will be connected to the FTP site.

9. Select the Publish to Remote Server checkbox. This will automatically connect and upload your files to the FTP site when you click on the Publish button.

Once you have finished publishing your Web-enabled Authorware piece, you can check to see if the files are all in the proper order by viewing the Information dialog that appears at the successful completion of the publishing process. See figure 22-35.

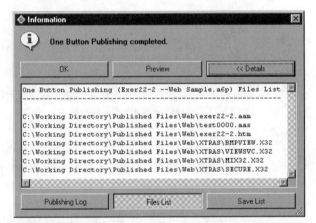

Fig. 22-35. OBP Completion dialog with supporting files listed.

You can also click on the Preview button and view your Authorware file in the Web browser. See figure 22-36.

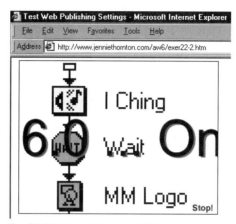

Fig. 22-36. Piece playing in Web browser.

Summary

- *At the beginning of the design process you must identify your delivery environment. Will you be developing to the Web or to CD-ROM? Wherever your piece will reside, you must begin testing sample files immediately.*

- *Authorware publishes files into two formats: local delivery and Web-browser streamed.*

- *Authorware requires a series of supporting files for the piece to run smoothly in different environments. To display different types of media and effects, Xtras are used. For added functionality, DLLs and UCDs are used.*

- *One Button Publishing is a new feature of Authorware 6.0 that provides a more efficient way of publishing files expediently and with more control of output.*

- *Using Authorware's batch publishing settings you can publish many Authorware files with one click of the mouse.*

- *To publish to the Web you must take into account connection speeds, media types, storage locations, and streaming technologies.*

- *Utilizing Authorware's Advanced Streamer software can make your pieces download segments in anticipation of learners' most typical paths through your piece.*

- *Authorware is capable of running over the Internet and placing files on the user's hard drive, and therefore there is a security dialog box that appears asking the user if she wants to trust the piece or not. If the user does not trust the piece, various functions and variables will not work.*

- *To bypass the security dialog box, the Authorware Web player .INI file must include the URL of your Web sever. You can add to the .INI file using the Authorware Web Player Security Knowledge object.*

- *To house Authorware files on your server, MIME types need to be added by your system administrator.*

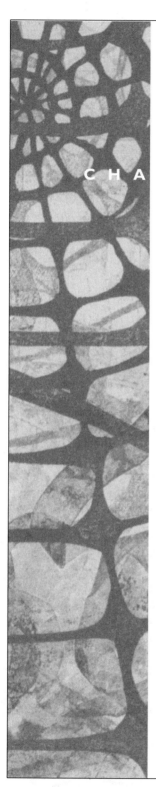

CHAPTER

23

Subroutines

Introduction

Among the skills you will find yourself needing as you advance in Authorware programming is the use of what are known as subroutines. A subroutine is a group of coded icons that perform a task needed multiple times within a project, and even from project to project. A subroutine appears only once on the flowline but may be called and executed many times from various parts of the program. This practice makes the flowline more efficient and easier to update.

This chapter introduces the concept of the subroutine by building two separate subroutine structures: a multiple-choice question and a slider used for gathering end-user evaluation data. By the end of this chapter you will be able to:

- *Describe the concept of subroutines*
- *Create custom variables that hold content*
- *Build a quiz randomizer subroutine using the Decision icon*
- *Build an evaluation subroutine using a slider*
- *Set up navigation links*

The Philosophy of Subroutines

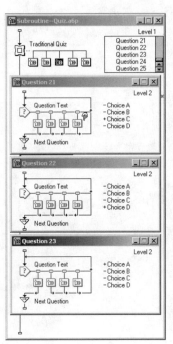

After you have built an Authorware structure that does what you want it to do, you will probably want to reuse that structure again and again. Why reinvent the wheel? As an example, in an earlier chapter you built a generic multiple-choice question structure, with sections for the question stem, responses, buttons, and feedback. At this point, the structure does what you want a question structure to do. To create a 25-item quiz, you could place this structure inside a Map icon and copy/paste this Map icon 24 additional times to the right of a Framework icon. See figure 23-1.

Fig. 23-1. Traditional quiz structure.

After you have copied and pasted the question structure, you would then need to go into each question to change the question stem and responses, and to indicate which answers are correct or incorrect. There is nothing wrong with creating a quiz this way, but there are some disadvantages.

- *First, it will be time consuming to manually go into each of the 25 structures to make the initial set of content changes, make any corrections or changes to the interactive structure in the future, and make content changes in the future.*

- *Second, going into 25 separate structures to make programming fixes or changes will increase the likelihood of human error. This is especially true if you plan to make multiple changes to each structure, in which case it will be very easy to forget to make a change here or there.*

- *Third, pasting the structure into the flowline 24 additional times will increase file size unnecessarily. A small file size is important for loading your Authorware program quickly, especially over the Web. If you have duplicated a code structure many times (especially if it contains large graphic or sound elements), it will increase the size of your Authorware program and could cause it to load more slowly. Reusing code by cutting and pasting is generally not a good practice if you are concerned about file size.*

The subroutine to the rescue! This is where a subroutine can save you valuable authoring time, reduce the possibility of error, and reduce file size.

Let's consider another way to build our quiz, but this time using a subroutine. See figure 23-2. Imagine being able to have a 25-question multiple-choice quiz with only one interaction structure for the entire quiz. This way, if you need to change the way the question behaves, you simply make the change in a single location and this change is reflected in all 25 questions automatically.

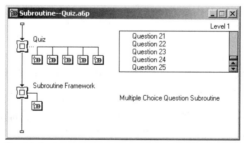

Fig. 23-2. Quiz using a subroutine.

But how does this work? The answer is pretty simple: by separating the question structure from the content. With the use of custom variables, the Framework icon, and the Navigate icon, you can easily build one structure that will systematically store and sequence content (see figure 23-3), and another structure that will display the content (see figure 23-4) within a single framework/interaction structure. You will see the details of how this works in the practice exercise that follows.

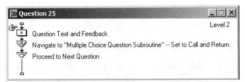

Fig. 23-3. Question content within a Calculation icon.

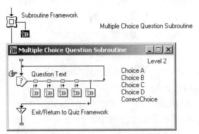

Fig. 23-4. Single interaction within a Framework icon.

To the end user there is no visible difference between our first quiz (25 separate interactions) and the subroutine quiz you will create in Practice Exercise 23-1. The real difference lies behind the scenes. Let's take a closer look.

Practice Exercise 23-1: Multiple-choice Question Subroutine

Description

In this exercise you are going to build a subroutine for creating a simple multiple-choice quiz. There will be a single question structure that will display on screen, a question stem, four responses (labeled A, B, C, and D), and feedback concerning the choice selected. Only one answer is correct. The user will have two tries to get the question correct, with feedback if this limit is exceeded.

The interaction loop is located in just one place on the flowline. As each new content chunk (question and responses) is encountered, it is sent to the interaction loop for display. After the user has responded either correctly or has exceeded the "tries" limit, Authorware returns to the content area to select the next content chunk. Behind the scenes you can update the structure for the question in one place and have the entire quiz appear to change for all questions. In this exercise you will:

- *Create a Decision icon structure to randomly select question content*
- *Create the custom variables for the quiz*
- *Set up the subroutine framework structure*

- *Build the question structure using an Interaction icon, Display icons, and embedded variables*
- *Complete the navigation links*
- *Add additional quiz questions*

Take a Look

Before beginning the exercise, let's take a look at the exercise in its completed state so that you can clearly see what it is you are about to build.

CD-ROM

1. Select File | Open and locate the *Practice* folder on the companion CD-ROM. Open this folder and you will see a number of chapter folders. Open the *Chapter23* folder and locate and double click on the file named *Exer23-1*.

2. The *Exer23-1* file should now appear in your copy of Authorware. Select Control | Restart or click on the Restart button on the toolbar to play the file from the top of the flowline. Note the following properties of this completed exercise.

   - *When the cursor passes through a response, the normal "arrow" cursor will change to a "hand." As soon as the cursor leaves the response area, it changes back to the normal cursor symbol.*

   - *If the user selects a wrong answer, feedback is provided and is then returned to the interaction to try again.*

   - *Once the correct choice is selected and feedback is given, a Continue button appears. Once the Continue button is selected, the feedback window and Continue button erase and the user exits the current interaction.*

   - *If the user selects the correct answer, Authorware moves to the next question.*

   - *If the user fails to answer the question correctly after two tries, feedback is provided and then the user exits the interaction by clicking on the Continue button.*

   - *All questions follow the exact same format. The fonts used, the screen position of the text, and the color of the feedback are identical in all quiz questions.*

   - *There are no Erase icons used in this icon structure. All erasing is accomplished using automatic erase functions of the Interaction icon and response paths.*

   - *The three questions attached to the Question Randomizer Decision icon contain no interactions, just Calculation icons that contain the content. Each Calculation icon contains a series of custom variables that are assigned "strings" containing each question stem, responses, and feedback.*

   - *The only Interaction icon in the file is located within the MC Question Subroutine Map icon attached to the subroutines framework.*

- *All of the questions use a Navigate icon, set to Call and Return, to navigate to the subroutine and then return to the Question Randomizer icon to get the content for the next question.*

Storyboard: On Screen

Figure 23-5 shows what the finished question will look like on screen.

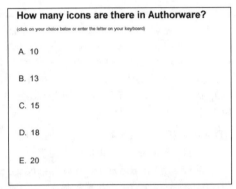

Fig. 23-5. Multiple-choice Question 1 on screen.

Storyboard: Behind the Scenes

Figure 23-6 shows the level 1 and level 2 flowlines (with all icons, their placement, and their names) as they should look when you are finished with this exercise.

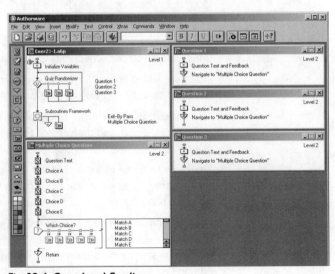

Fig. 23-6. Completed flowlines.

Step-by-Step Instructions

1. Open a new file for this exercise. Select File | New | File. Close the two Knowledge Object dialog windows that open by clicking on the X in the upper right-hand corner.

2. Verify that you are now looking at a blank flowline.

3. Save the file on your hard drive by selecting File | Save. Use the Scroll window to locate the *SaveWork* directory on your computer, which you created previously. Type in the name *Exer23-1* and click on OK.

4. Drag a Calculation icon to the flowline and name it *Initialize Variables*.

5. Open the Calculation icon and enter the following expressions.

```
correct_Choice := 0
question_Text := " "
choice_A := " "
choice_B := " "
choice_C := " "
choice_D := " "
choice_E := " "
feedback_Correct := " "
feedback_Incorrect := " "
feedback_Tries_Limit := " "
```

·T/P·

You will be creating 10 custom variables as you type the information into the Calculation icon. By placing all of your custom variables at the top of the flowline, you will always be able to reference them quickly, and other developers who look at your code will be able to quickly see what you have done.

6. Save your file. When you do this, Authorware prompts you to define the new variable you have created. Use the information in the following steps to define each new variable.

   a) *correct_Choice* should have an initial value of 0. You can give it the following description: *This variable tracks the correct answer for each question. Must be set by the programmer for each question.*

   b) *question_Text* should have an initial value of " ". You can give it the following description: *This variable contains the text for the question stem that is embedded and displayed within the multiple-choice question subroutine.*

   c) *choice_A* should have an initial value of " ". You can give it the following description: *This variable contains the text for answer A that is embedded and displayed within the multiple-choice question subroutine.*

   d) *choice_B* should have an initial value of " ". You can give it the following description: *This variable contains the text for answer B that is embedded and displayed within the multiple-choice question subroutine.*

   e) *choice_C* should have an initial value of " ". You can give it the following description: *This variable contains the text for answer C that is embedded and displayed within the multiple-choice question subroutine.*

f) *choice_D* should have an initial value of " ". You can give it the following description: *This variable contains the text for answer D that is embedded and displayed within the multiple-choice question subroutine.*

g) *choice_E* should have an initial value of " ". You can give it the following description: *This variable contains the text for answer E that is embedded and displayed within the multiple-choice question subroutine.*

h) *feedback_Correct* should have an initial value of " ". You can give it the following description: *This variable contains the text for the correct answer feedback that is embedded and displayed within the multiple-choice question subroutine.*

i) *feedback_Incorrect* should have an initial value of " ". You can give it the following description: *This variable contains the text for the wrong answer feedback that is embedded and displayed within the multiple-choice question subroutine.*

j) *feedback_Tries_Limit* should have an initial value of " ". You can give it the following description: *This variable contains the text for the feedback if the maximum number of tries has been exceeded. This variable is embedded and displayed within the multiple-choice question subroutine.*

As you complete and close the last New Variable window, Authorware will complete the saving process. At this point you can further comment the code within this Calculation icon for documentation purposes and clarity. Using the descriptions you entered for each variable would make great comments. See figure 23-7.

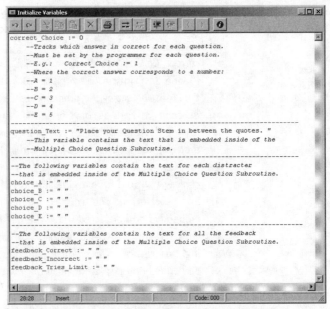

Fig. 23-7. Completed content within the Calculation icon.

NOTE

Remember that a double hyphen (--) tells Authorware to ignore whatever follows on that line. The dashed lines that separate the question stem, the choices, and the feedback do not show up on screen (they follow the --). They are used here to visually make it easier to quickly distinguish the various parts of the question content.

7. Create the content structure. This structure will select the question content in a random order. Once all questions have been viewed, Authorware will exit the loop.

    a) Drag a Decision icon to the flowline. Name this icon *Quiz Randomizer*.

Use a Decision icon because you want to "randomly" select the question. The Decision icon provides this random selection capability "out of the box," with no programming necessary.

    b) Drag a Map icon and place it to the right of the Decision icon. Name this Map icon *Question 1*. See figure 23-8.

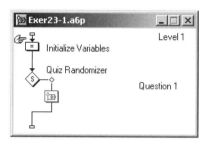

Fig. 23-8. Decision icon with Map icon attached.

8. Let's set the Decision icon to randomly select questions.
    a) Double click on the Decision icon to open it.
    b) Change the setting for the Repeat field to Until All Paths Used.
    c) Change the setting for the Branch field to Randomly To Unused Path.
    d) Click on OK to close the Dialog window.

9. Set up variables that will contain each question's text and feedback.
    a) Double click on the *Question 1* Map icon to open it.
    b) Drag a Calculation icon inside the Map icon and name it *Question Text and Feedback*.

TIP

To save time you can copy and paste the *Initialize Variables* Calculation icon you created in steps 3 and 4 and rename it *Question Text and Feedback*. Then you will have all variables you need already set in the icon.

    c) Double click on the *Question Text and Feedback* Calculation icon and type in the following information exactly as shown.

```
correct_Choice := 1

-------------------------

question_Text := "Place your Question Stem between
the quotes. "

-------------------------

choice_A := "Enter Text for distracter A here."

choice_B := "Enter Text for distracter B here. "
```

```
choice_C := "Enter Text for distracter C here."

choice_D := "Enter Text for distracter D here."

choice_E := "Enter Text for distracter E here."

------------------------

feedback_Correct := "That is Correct."

feedback_Incorrect := "That is incorrect, try again."

feedback_Tries_Limit := "That is not correct. The
correct answer is A."
```

10. Close the Calculation icon and save changes.

11. Now that all of the variable information has been entered in the Calculation icon, you can begin creating the subroutine. First, create a framework structure with no internal navigation, as it will just serve as a jump point for all of the question/content subroutine calls.

   a) Drag a Framework icon to the level 1 flowline, placing it below the Decision icon. Name this icon *Subroutines Framework*.

   b) Double click on the *Subroutines Framework* icon and delete the Display icon named *Gray Navigation Panel and Interaction Icon with all of the Navigation Hyperlinks*. The Framework entry pane should be totally empty when you finish. Close the Framework icon.

   c) Drag a Map icon to the right of the Framework icon and name it *Multiple-choice Question*. Your flowline should look like that shown in figure 23-9.

The beauty of using a Framework icon here is that you will be able to use Navigate icons in the *Quiz Randomizer* icon to jump to this location, which contains the interaction structure, and then return to where the jump originated. Remember that the Navigate icon can only jump to a location attached to a Framework icon.

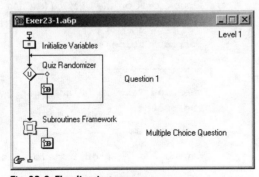

Fig. 23-9. Flowline in progress.

12. Begin building the question interaction structure.

You are going to place separate Display icons (each containing an embedded variable) above the Interaction icon. As an alternative, you could embed these variables inside the display area associated with the Interaction icon. However, if you do this, you would encounter other considerations. As stated, there are often many ways to correctly build an Authorware structure. Using the method chosen here will provide easy access for realigning each element, and will allow you to use the Display icons as Hot Objects so that you do not have to worry about the size and location of each "hot spot."

a) Double click on the *Multiple-choice Question* Map icon.

b) Drag a Display icon to the flowline inside the Map icon and name it *Question Text*.

c) Double click on *Question Text* to open this Display icon.

d) Select the Text tool from the toolbox and click the cursor near the upper left-hand corner of the Presentation window.

e) Select the Variables window in the menu bar. In the dialog window that opens, in the Category field, scroll to *Exer23-1* (this is the Custom Variable category at the bottom of the list). Locate and paste the *question_Text* variable into the open text object in the Display icon. Close the Variables window.

f) Using the Pointer tool, widen the margins of the text object so that it occupies almost the full width of the screen. Close *question_Text*.

13. Set up each response to the question as a Hot Object by placing each response (A, B, C, and D) in its own Display icon.

a) Drag five (5) Display icons to the flowline and inside the Map icon, placing them beneath *question_Text*.

b) Name each new Display icon as follows: *Choice A*, *Choice B*, *Choice C*, *Choice D*, and *Choice E*.

c) Hold the Shift key down and double click on *Choice A*.

d) Select the Text tool and click the cursor to open a text object below where you placed the embedded variable *question_Text*.

e) Select the Variables window in the menu bar. In the dialog window that opens, in the Category field, scroll to the *Exer23-1* Custom Variable category. Locate and paste the *choice_A* variable into the open text object in the Display icon. Close the Variables window.

f) Using the Pointer tool, widen the margins of the text object so that it occupies almost the full width of the screen. Close *Choice A*.

g) Repeat steps 10c through f for Display icons *Choice B*, *Choice C*, *Choice D*, and *Choice E*. When you are finished, each of these five Display icons will contain its own corresponding embedded custom variable

NOTE

Holding the Shift key down as you open a Display icon will bring back on screen the last image that was there. This is so that you can use it as a point of reference for the current Display icon. What you see on screen is not in the current Display icon, but is an image of the last one.

for displaying the current value of the variable. Because each response is in its own Display icon, you will be able to set up these icons as Hot Objects. See figure 23-10.

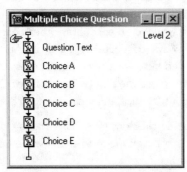

Fig. 23-10. Display icons containing embedded custom variables

14. Create the interaction structure. Start with the Interaction icon.

    a) Drag an Interaction icon to the flowline and inside the Map icon and name it *Which Choice?*.

    b) With the Interaction icon highlighted, select Modify | Icon | Properties (you can also either hold down the Ctrl key and double click on the icon or right click and select Properties). The Interaction Icon Properties dialog window opens.

    c) Select the Interaction tab and activate the options (place a check mark next to) *Pause before Exiting* and Show Button.

15. Add responses to the Interaction icon.

    a) Drag a Map icon to the right of the Interaction icon. In the dialog window that opens, select Hot Object as the response type. Click on OK. Name the Map icon *Match A*.

    b) Double click on the Response Type symbol for *Match A*. A dialog window opens.

    c) Select the Response tab, and change the Branching option to Continue.

    d) Select the Hot Object tab, and change the Cursor option to Hand. Click on OK to close the window.

    e) Drag four (4) more Map icons to the right of *Match A* and name them *Match B*, *Match C*, *Match D*, and *Match E*. See figure 23-11.

·T/P·

You are going to want a Pause and a Continue button for each response to this interaction. Earlier in the book you created and used the *Pickup Truck* interaction model, which placed Wait icons inside each Map icon. This was done to help you troubleshoot interactive structures. In this example, by selecting the options Pause and Show Button in the Interaction icon, you can save time and effort.

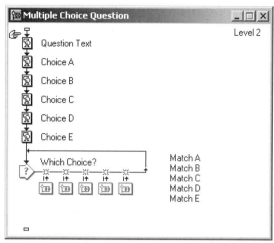

Fig. 23-11. Interaction icon in progress.

16. Create a response that will check to see whether the Hot Object (response) the user clicked on was the correct answer. You cannot use Authorware's automatic response tracking of "Correct Answer/Wrong Answer/Not Judged" because you do not want to change this option every time you display a new question. What you will do instead is capture and store this necessary information within a custom variable named *correct_Choice*. The value of this variable is defined for each question, back in the content section. Therefore, within the interaction structure you can set up a Conditional response type to evaluate whether or not the object the user clicked on matches the current value of the *correct_Choice* variable.

a) Drag a Map icon to the right of the *Match E* Map icon.

b) Double click on the Response Type symbol for this new Map icon. Using the pull-down menu in the Type field, change the type from Hot Object to Conditional.

c) Select the Response tab and change the Branch field to Exit Interaction.

d) Select the Conditional tab and change the Automatic field to On False to True.

e) In the Condition field, type in *ChoiceNumber = correct_Choice*. Note that this expression now also becomes the name of this Map icon.

ChoiceNumber is a system variable that contains the number of the response selected by the user in the last Interaction icon. Authorware numbers the responses attached to an Interaction icon (in this case, the Map icons) from left to right as 1, 2, 3, 4, and so on. This system variable allows you to easily "grab" the value associated with the user's response and evaluate whether this value equals the value for the custom variable *correct_Choice*.

Note that there is also a system variable *CorrectChoice* (no underscore between the words). The reason you have created your own custom variable (instead of using this system variable) is that you want to redefine the value of the variable for every question. You cannot set or redefine values such as these using system variables.

f)   Click on OK. See figure 23-12.

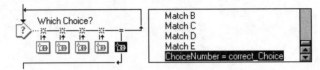

Fig. 23-12. Conditional response type.

17. Add the feedback for when the user selects the correct response.
    a)   Double click on the *ChoiceNumber* Map icon and drag a Display icon to the flowline and place it inside this Map icon. Name the Display icon *Correct Feedback*.
    b)   Double click on *Correct Feedback* and select the Text tool. Click the cursor on the bottom of the screen to open a text object. Open the Variables window. Select the *Exer23-1* category. Locate and paste *feedback_Correct* into the open text object. Close *Correct Feedback*. See figure 23-13.

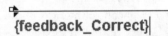

Fig. 23-13. Embedded variable for correct feedback.

18. Create the functionality for evaluating if the user clicked on the wrong object (response).
    a)   Drag another Map icon to the right of the Conditional Map icon you have been working on.
    b)   Name the new Map icon *ChoiceNumber <> correct_Choice*.
    c)   Hold down the Ctrl key and click on the branching arrow to change the branching to Try Again. See figure 23-14.

Try Again is the only property you need to change. There is no need to open the Response Type symbol Properties dialog window because this new response can use all other properties as the *Conditional* response to the left (the one you just created).

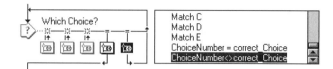

Fig. 23-14. Response for incorrect answers.

19. Add feedback for the incorrect answer.
    a) Double click on the "incorrect" Map icon you just created and then drag a Display icon to the flowline and place it inside this Map icon. Name the Display icon *Incorrect Feedback*.
    b) Double click on *Incorrect Feedback* and select the Text tool. Click the cursor on the bottom of the screen to open a text object. Open the Variables window. Locate and paste in the custom variable *feedback_Incorrect*.
    c) Change the color of the text to red by selecting Windows | Inspectors | Color (or hold down Ctrl + K, or double click on the circle tool on the tool palette). See figure 23-15.

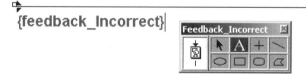

Fig. 23-15. Embedded variable for incorrect feedback.

20. Limit the user to a maximum number of tries. If a user guesses wrong twice, they will receive feedback, exit this interaction, and then be presented with the next question.
    a) Drag a Display icon to the right of the Interaction icon and place it between the two Conditional response type Map icons. Name this icon *2 tries*. This will be the "tries limit" response.
    b) Double click on the Response Type symbol for the *2 tries* Display icon. In the Type field, change this option to Tries Limit.
    c) Select the Tries Limit tab and in the Maximum Tries field type in *2*.
    d) Click on OK to close the Property window.
    e) Double click on the *2 tries* Display icon. Select the Text tool. Click the cursor on the bottom of the screen. Open the Variables window.

Locate and paste the custom variable *feedback_Tries_Limit* into the open text object. Close the Display icon.

21. Set up the navigation links between the *Subroutines Framework* icon and the *Quiz Randomizer* icon.
    a) The *Multiple-choice Question* Map icon attached to the Framework icon should still be open. If it is not, open it.
    b) Drag a Navigate icon to the bottom of the flowline and place it inside the *Multiple-choice Question* Map icon. Name this Navigate icon *Return*. See figure 23-16.

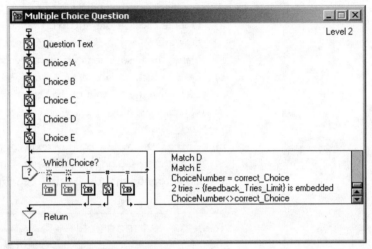

Fig. 23-16. Return Navigate icon.

    c) Double click on the Navigate icon and set the options as follows. See figures 23-16 and 23-17. When finished setting these options, close the icon.

Destination: Nearby

Page: Exit Framework/Return

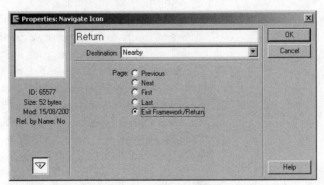

Fig. 23-17. Property dialog box for the Navigate icon.

You set this Navigate icon to Exit/Return because you want to return to the content section *Quiz Randomizer*. In material to follow you will use several other Navigate icons within the content section to jump within the interaction structure (subroutine framework). These other Navigate icons will be set to Call and Return, and therefore all you need to do here with this Navigate icon in the subroutine framework is to set it to Exit/Return. Authorware will know where to return.

22. Close the *Multiple-choice Question* Map icon.

23. Add the navigation in the content section.
    a) Return to the main flowline and double click on the *Question 1* Map icon attached to the *Quiz Randomizer* Decision icon.
    b) Drag a Navigate icon to the bottom of the flowline and place it inside this Map icon.
    c) Double click on the Navigate icon. Set the options as follows. When finished setting these options, close the Navigate icon.
       Destination field: Anywhere
       Type field: Call and Return
    d) Using the pull-down menu in the Page field, locate and select Subroutines Framework. Select the *Multiple-choice Question* Map icon.
    e) The setting for this Navigate icon should look like that shown in figure 23-18.

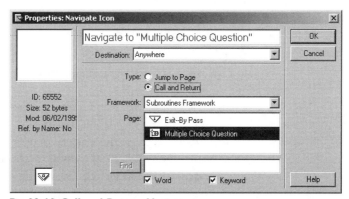

Fig. 23-18. Call and Return *Navigate* icon.

The Calculation icon on the flowline, above the Navigate icon you just added, will gather the current values (text) of the question and responses. With the Navigate icon, Authorware will jump to the multiple-choice subroutine where the embedded variables will display (as text) the current values of the embedded variables. Because of the Call and Return setting set here in the Navigate icon, once the user finishes the question and exits the interaction Authorware will execute the *Return* Navigate icon (in the subroutine framework) and return to the Navigate icon. This looping process will continue until all of questions have been seen.

24. Add a few more quiz questions to the *Quiz Randomizer* icon.
   a) Copy the *Question 1* Map icon to the clipboard.
   b) Click the Paste Hand cursor to the right of *Question 1* and paste. Rename the Map icon *Question 2*.
   c) Double click on the Calculation icon *Question Text and Feedback* and using figure 23-19 as reference change the string information for each variable within the Calculation icon.

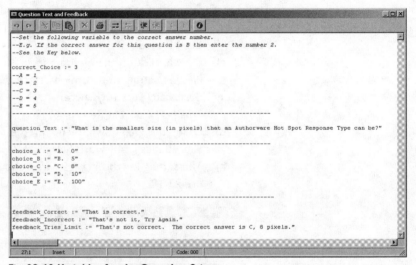

*Fig. 23-19. Variables for the **Question 2** icon.*

   d) Click the Paste Hand cursor to the right of *Question 2* and paste. Rename the Map icon *Question 3*.
   e) Double click on the Calculation icon *Question Text and Feedback* and using figure 23-20 as reference change the string information for each variable inside the Calculation icon.

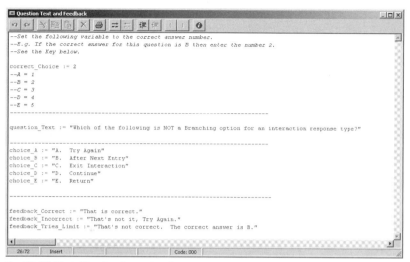

Fig. 23-20. Variables for Question 3.

    f)   Your Flowline should now look like that shown in figure 23-21.

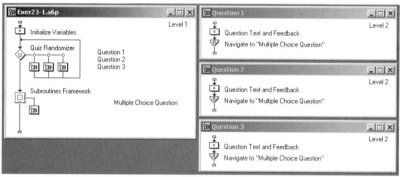

Fig. 23-21. Flowline in progress.

25. Let's go back and finish the subroutine framework. You need to add something here so that when the user is finished with the quiz Authorware will not get hung up in the Framework icon. How would this happen? As you have the structure now, as Authorware leaves the *Quiz Randomizer* icon and drops down the flowline it will encounter the *Subroutine Framework* icon and automatically drop into the *Multiple-choice Question* Map icon and get caught in an endless loop.

The solution is simple. You need to add an exit in the first page position for this framework. In this way, when Authorware drops down the flowline and encounters the *Subroutine Framework* icon it will automatically drop into a new first page, where it will exit the framework.

a) Look at the *Subroutine Framework* icon.
b) Drag a Navigate icon to the first page position (first position to the right of the framework). Name it *Exit – ByPass*. See figure 23-22.

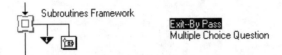

Fig. 23-22. **Exit – ByPass** *Navigate icon.*

c) Double click on the Navigate icon and set the options as follows. When finished setting these options, close the icon. See figure 23-23.
Destination field: Nearby
Page field: Exit Framework/Return

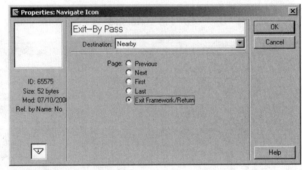

Fig. 23-23. Bypass settings.

26. Save your work.

27. Run the program and try it.

Practice Exercise 23-2:
Subroutine for Student Evaluation

Description

In this exercise you are going to try a completely different use of a subroutine. The benefits are similar to those associated with the previous subroutine. You can create a useful structure once and reuse it over and over. In this exercise you are going to look at another "real-world" issue many multimedia developers face.

Too frequently developers become consumed in the process of trying to get a CBT project delivered on time and within budget. Budgets shrink and time sometimes seems to disappear. Unfortunately, part of the development process is often overlooked: the evaluation phase. Does the newly created CBT accomplish what it was supposed to accomplish? Does it meet the business need, the primary training goal, the learning objectives, and the learner's needs? Too often, the best-laid plans for insightful evaluation of the CBT drop by the wayside.

One way to help improve the odds of getting learner feedback about the CBT is to make the evaluation questionnaire part of the CBT program. The learner, as part of finishing up the course, can quickly fill out a questionnaire. The questionnaire itself might be as simple as a few questions, or further up the scale it might involve an on-line data-tracking database. The learner evaluation you are going to construct in this exercise can grow as you need it to, but most importantly it can easily be placed in your CBT now, without delay.

You will create a unique way of collecting student data using a moving slider that allows the student to rate questions on a scale of 1 to 10. This data will be sent to an easy-to-read text file. In this exercise you will:

- *Create a slider mechanism*
- *Use embedded custom variables*
- *Create a subroutine structure*
- *Create an evaluation feedback question interface*
- *Capture the path position of the slider and round that number to a whole number*

Take a Look

Before beginning the exercise, let's take a look at the exercise in its completed state so that you can clearly see what it is you are about to build.

CD-ROM

1. Select File | Open and locate and open the *Practice* folder on the companion CD-ROM. Open the *Chapter23* folder and locate and double click on the file named *Exer23-2*.

2. The file *Exer23-2* should now appear in your copy of Authorware. Select Control | Restart or press the Restart button on the toolbar to play the file from the top of the flowline. Note the following properties of this completed exercise.

   - *The on-screen slider can be moved from left to right on the scale, but not off the scale.*
   - *Once the Continue button is selected, another question is displayed.*

- *Each question is in the same position within the Presentation window.*

- *Once three questions have been viewed, the screen goes blank and the interaction is exited.*

- *The three questions attached to the Evaluation Question Framework icon do not contain an interactive structure. The Interaction icon and structure is contained in the Slider Subroutine Map icon attached to the Subroutine Framework icon.*

- *All of the content for each question is located inside a Calculation icon (Set Slider Text), where a series of custom string variables are assigned the values for that particular question.*

- *All of the questions use a Navigate icon set to Call and Return to navigate to the subroutine, return to the Evaluation Framework icon, and then proceed to the next question.*

Storyboard: On Screen

Figure 23-24 shows what the finished question will look like on screen.

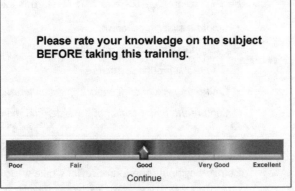

Please rate your knowledge on the subject BEFORE taking this training.

Poor   Fair   Good   Very Good   Excellent
Continue

Fig. 23-24. Evaluation slider Question 1.

Storyboard: Behind the Scenes

Figure 23-25 shows the level 1 and level 2 flowlines (with all icons, their placement, and their names) as they should look when you are finished with this exercise.

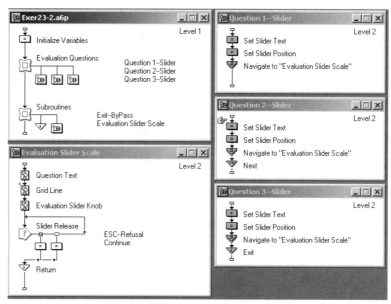

Fig. 23-25. Completed level 1 and level 2 flowlines.

Step-by-Step Instructions

1. Open a new file for this exercise. Select File | New | File. Close the two Knowledge Object dialog windows that open by clicking on the X in the upper right-hand corner.

2. Verify that you are looking at a new flowline.

3. Save the file on your hard drive by selecting File | Save and using the Scroll window to locate the *SaveWork* directory on your computer. Type in the name *Chap23-2* and click on OK.

4. The rating scale for each question will be created using a subroutine. The first step is to create the necessary custom variables and settings for each question.

   a) Drag a Calculation icon to the top of the flowline and name it *Initialize Variables*. Open the Calculation icon.

   b) Inside the Calculation icon, type the following code.

   ```
   screen_Text := " "

   --------------------

   slider_Text_1 := " "

   slider_Text_2 := " "
   ```

```
slider_Text_3 := " "

slider_Text_4 := " "

slider_Text_5 := " "

--------------------

slider_Base := 0

slider_End := 0

slider_Initial := 0

--------------------

data_Path := " "

choice_ := " "
```

c) Close the Calculation icon and save the changes you have made by clicking on Yes in the Save dialog box.

d) In the New Variable windows that open, use the following information to define each new custom variable. Close each New Variable window as you finish each custom variable.

- screen_Text should have an initial value of " ". *You can give it the following description:* Contains the text for the question that the user will see on the screen. This variable is used so that the questions always appear in the same position on screen in an embedded variable within the subroutine.

- slider_Text_1 should have an initial value of " ". *You can give it the following description:* This variable is used to store the current value of point 1 on the slider.

- slider_Text_2 should have an initial value of " ". *You can give it the following description:* This variable is used to store the current value of point 2 on the slider.

- slider_Text_3 should have an initial value of " ". *You can give it the following description:* This variable is used to store the current value of point 3 on the slider.

- slider_Text_4 should have an initial value of " ". *You can give it the following description:* This variable is used to store the current value of point 4 on the slider.

- slider_Text_5 should have an initial value of " ". *You can give it the following description:* This variable is used to store the current value of point 5 on the slider.

- slider_Base should have an initial value = 0. *You can give it the following description:* Contains the current numeric value for the base position for the scale used by the slider.

- slider_Initial should have an initial value = 0. *You can give it the following description:* Contains the current numeric value for the starting position.

- slider_End should have an initial value = 0. *You can give it the following description:* Contains the current numeric value for the ending position.

- data_Path should have an initial value = " ". *You can give it the following description:* A custom variable that contains the File Location of the Text File that is being used to record the evaluation results.

- choice_ should have an initial value of = " ". *You can give it the following description:* This variable contains the user's answer for each question as it is asked and is sent to the text file. It is overwritten by the next question the user is asked.

5. The entire evaluation questionnaire will be built using a Framework icon so that each question can be a separate page and can be navigated to easily. Start with the basic framework structure.

a) Drag a Framework icon to the flowline and name this icon *Evaluation Questions*. See figure 23-26.

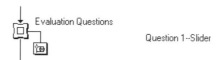

Evaluation Questions

Question 1--Slider

Fig. 23-26. Evaluation Questions *Framework icon.*

b) Double click on the Framework icon to open it, and delete all icons in the Entry pane inside. Close the Framework icon.

c) Drag a Map icon to the right of the *Evaluation Questions Framework* icon and name it *Question 1 – Slider*.

d) Double click on the *Question 1 – Slider* Map icon to open it.

e) Drag a Calculation icon to the level 2 flowline, place it inside the Map icon, and name it *Set Slider Text*.

6. Create some custom variables that will store and display the question and the various points (labels) on the scale (Poor, Fair, Good, and Excellent).

a) Double click on the Calculation icon to open it and type in *screen_Title:="Place your question text here"*.

You could have used ordinary text objects as labels for the slider scale, in which case they would not appear here in the Calculation icon but be placed in the same Display icon that holds the background for the slider. However, you are going to use custom variables now so that in the future if you want to reuse this slider subroutine in another application you can easily change the labels to whatever is appropriate for the new use.

Another good reason to use this method is in case some of your questions have different labels. Some might have "Poor /Fair / Good" labels, and some might have "Sometimes / Always / Never" labels. If they were all the same, hard coding would be better, but this method allows flexibility.

b) Press Enter to drop to the next line, and type in the following information.

```
slider_Text_1:="Poor"
slider_Text_2:="Fair"
slider_Text_3:="Good"
slider_Text_4:="Very Good"
slider_Text_5:="Excellent"
```

c) Close the Calculation window. Click on Yes to save.

7. Create custom variables for the slider so that the scale values can be changed, if needed, for different question types you may have in the future.

a) Drag a Calculation icon to the level 2 flowline and place it below *Set Slider Text*.

b) Name this Calculation icon *Set Slider Position*. See figure 23-27.

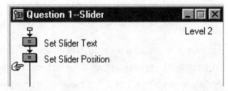

Fig. 23-27. Inside the **Question 1 – Slider** *Map icon.*

c) Double click on the *Set Slider Position* Calculation icon and type in the following information.

```
slider_Base := 1
slider_End := 10
slider_Initial := 5.5
```

d) Close the Calculation window. Click on Yes to save.

8. Let's move on to build the *Slider Subroutine* Framework icon.

a) Drag a Framework icon to the main flowline (below the *Evaluation Framework* icon) and name it *Subroutines*.

b) Double click on *Subroutines* and delete all icons inside the Entry pane of this Framework icon. Close the Framework icon.

c) Drag a Navigate icon to the first page position in the *Subroutines Framework* icon and name this Navigate icon *Exit – ByPass*.

d) Double click on the Navigate icon and set the options as follows. When finished setting these options, close the icon. See figure 23-28.
Destination: Nearby
Page: Exit Interaction/Return

> **NOTE**
>
> This bypass structure will allow Authorware to bypass the *Subroutines* Framework icon if the program enters this framework from the flowline and not through a Call and Return icon from the *Evaluation Questions* Framework icon.

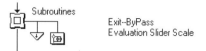

Fig. 23-28. Subroutines Framework *icon with* **Exit – ByPass** *Navigate icon.*

9. Set up the background elements for the slider.
   a) Drag a Map icon to the right of the *Subroutines* Framework icon and name this Map icon *Evaluation Slider Scale.*
   b) Double click on the *Evaluation Items Scale* Map icon to open it.
   c) Drag three (3) Display icons to the level 2 flowline and place them inside this new Map icon.
   d) Name the three Display icons *Question Text*, *Grid Line*, and *Evaluation Slider Knob.* See figure 23-29.

At first glance, these three Display icons may not look like they provide any interactivity. In reality, the third icon will have properties set that will allow the user to position it on a defined path.

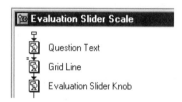

Fig. 23-29. *Display icons inside the* **Evaluation Slide Scale** *Map icon.*

   e) Double click on the *Question Text Display* icon. Select the Text tool and click on the background (in the top-center portion of the screen). Open the Variable window. Locate and paste the *screen_Text* custom variable into the open text object. Close the Display icon. See figure 23-30.

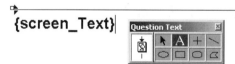

Fig. 23-30. *Embedded* **screen_Text** *variable.*

   f) Double click on the *Grid Line Display* icon. Select File | Import. Use the browse function to locate the *Chapter23* folder inside the *Practice* folder on the companion CD-ROM. Locate and import the graphic *rainbow_gridline.gif.*

g) Place the graphic of the grid line toward the bottom-center of the Presentation window.

h) Select the Text tool and open five (5) text objects, pasting each of the following custom variables in its own text object. Place the following "labels" in the appropriate location next the graphic of the slider. When finished, close the Display icon. See figure 23-31.

```
{slider_Text_1}
{slider_Text_2}
{slider_Text_3}
{slider_Text_4}
{slider_Text_5}
```

i) Select Modify | Icon | Calculation and type in *Movable=False*.

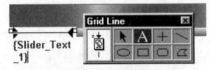

Fig. 23-31. Embedded slider labels.

10. Set up the slider knob. This icon will contain the knob the user moves along the track of the slider.

a) While holding down the Shift key, double click on the *Evaluation Slider Knob* Display Icon. Select File | Import. Use the browse function to locate the *Chapter23* folder inside the *Practice* folder on the companion CD-ROM. Locate and import the graphic *slider_knob.gif*.

b) Position the knob on the left side of the grid-line graphic. See figure 23-32.

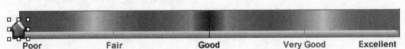

Fig. 23-32. Knob located on slider.

11. With the *Evaluation Slider Knob* Display icon still open, select Modify | Icon | Properties.

a) Select the Layout tab. Set the options as follows.
Positioning field: On Path (will place the knob on the path when it is first displayed)
Movable: On Path (will allow the user to move the knob on the path only)

NOTE

Movable is a system variable that can be defined as either True (allowing objects contained within this icon to be moved around on screen) or False (locking any object inside so that it cannot be moved). In this case you want to "lock it down" so that you do not accidentally pull the slider apart when developing. Once packaged, all icons are locked down, unless you tell them not to be.

CD-ROM

·T/P·

Holding down the Shift key will allow you to see the grid line (from the last Display icon) on screen as you try to position the slider knob in the proper place on the slider.

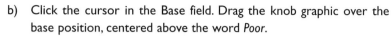

When you are inside
an icon's Property
dialog window,
instructions appear
under the Title field,
telling you what
Authorware needs to
complete the task.

b) Click the cursor in the Base field. Drag the knob graphic over the
base position, centered above the word *Poor*.

c) Click the cursor in the End field. Drag the knob graphic over the end
position, centered above the word *Excellent*. Carefully reposition the
path marker (small triangle) so that the line between the base and
end positions is straight and not jagged. See figure 23-33.

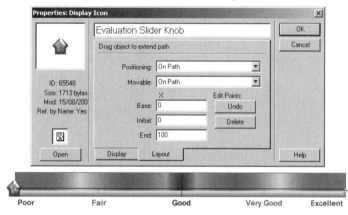

Fig. 23-33. Straight line between base and end positions.

Pasting these custom
variables into the Base,
End, and Initial fields
will allow you (in the
future) to change the
values of the scale from
within the *Set Slider
Position* Calculation
icon without coming
back to this location
to change hard-coded
values.

d) Click the cursor in the Base field. Open the Variable window. Locate
and paste the custom variable *slider_Base* into this field. See figure 23-34.

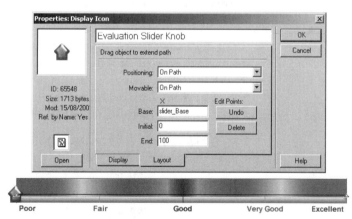

Fig. 23-34. Custom variables.

e) Click the cursor in the End field. Open the Variable window. Locate
and paste the custom variable *slider_End* into this field.

f) Click the cursor in the Initial field. Open the Variable window. Locate
and paste the custom variable *slider_Initial* into this field.

g) Close the Properties dialog window.

12. You need to be able to tell where the user will place the knob along the scale. This mechanism must capture the user's answer when he positions the slider at different points along the scale. You can do this using Authorware's system variable that can track the position of the slider along the defined path. Once the user has made his choice, he will click on a Continue button that will include a function for sending the value a text file.

a) Drag an Interaction icon to the level 2 flowline and place it inside the *Evaluation Slider Scale* Map icon. Name this icon *Slider Release*.

b) Drag a Calculation icon to the right of the Interaction icon and select Key Press as its response type.

c) Name this Calculation icon *ESC*. Double click on the Response Type symbol and set the branching to Exit Interaction.

Setting up this Esc key is optional, but it is recommended that you use it. This key will allow the user to *not* answer the question. This type of option is especially important when gathering evaluation data. A user should never feel forced to respond to an optional or personal question. It is also recommended that you explain this option to the user in an introductory screen.

This Esc key is also important if you are tabulating user responses. If the user decides to not answer a question and just presses the Continue button, a score of 5 will be recorded for the response. This "non" score may affect the statistics you are gathering.

Using the Esc key on the keyboard instead of showing a button on screen will tend to protect your data-gathering efforts from a user who might otherwise just click a "refuse" button on screen to quickly bypass the questions without answering them. Once the Esc key is pressed you might want to send a record of this choice to your data file to record the nonresponse.

d) Double click on the Calculation icon and type in the following information (or just type in a double hyphen as a placeholder).
This allows the user to NOT answer the question.
Once the Esc key is pressed, you might want to record this non-response.
You might use AppendExtFile(data_Path, "No Answer"^Return).

e) Close the Calculation icon. In the New Variable window that opens, define the new custom variable using the following information. See figure 23-35.
data_Path should have an initial value = " ". You can give it the following description: *A custom variable that contains the file location of the text file being used to record the evaluation results.*

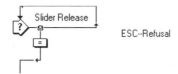

Fig. 23-35. ESC Keypress response.

13. Set up the Continue button that will record the results and send the user to the next question.

    a)   Drag a Calculation icon to the right of the *ESC* icon. Double click on the Response Type symbol and select Button as its response type.

    b)   Name the Calculation icon *Continue*. See figure 23-36.

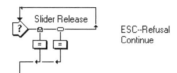

Fig. 23-36. Slider release interaction in progress.

    c)   Double click on the *Continue* Calculation icon to open it.

    d)   Capture the user's response by using the system variable *PathPosition* and placing this value into the custom variable *choice_* by typing the following expression inside the Calculation window. See figure 23-37.

```
choice_:=PathPosition@"Evaluation Slider Knob"

- - First, capture the number the user finally
decided on
```

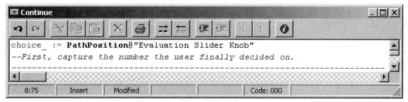

Fig. 23-37. Capturing the slider's position on the path.

PathPosition is an Authorware system variable that contains the position of the slider in relation to the defined path. At the time the user clicks on the Continue button, you will record the last position of the slider and place this value into the custom variable *choice_*. The only possible downside to using this variable is that it tracks the position of the slider to about nine decimal points. This can be corrected by using the *Round* function, which you will do in step 16.

14. To get rid of the decimal points *PathPosition* will automatically report, you need to do some "rounding off." Authorware's system function *Round* will remove the decimal points associated with the value in *PathPosition* and will round the value to the nearest whole number. While still in the same Calculation icon, press the Enter key to drop to the next line and type in the following code. See figure 23-38.

> `choice_ := Round(choice_)`

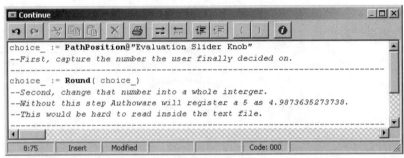

```
choice_ := PathPosition@"Evaluation Slider Knob"
--First, capture the number the user finally decided on.
-----------------------------------------------------------------
choice_ := Round( choice_)
--Second, change that number into a whole interger.
--Without this step Authoware will register a 5 as 4.9873635273738.
--This would be hard to read inside the text file.
-----------------------------------------------------------------
```

Fig. 23-38. Rounding the value of PathPosition.

·T/P·

The two lines you entered in this Calculation icon could be combined onto one line, as follows: *choice_ := Round(PathPosition@ "Evaluation Slider Knob").*

15. Capture the information the user just entered regarding the student's text file; in this case, located on your hard drive in the *SaveWork* folder. In this example you will send the question text (*screen_Text*) and the learner's response (*choice_*) to a text file. This string information will be formatted using the concatenation symbol (^).

   a) Open the Functions window and paste in the function *AppendExtFile* from the File category.

   b) Replace the first argument within the parentheses ("*Filename*") with the custom variable *data_Path*.

   c) After the first comma, replace the argument for "*string*" with the following expression.

   > `screen_Text^":"^choice_^Return`

·T/P·

When inside the Calculation icon you can use the hot key combination Ctrl + H to launch a completion window of all system variables and functions. This is a great tool when you already know the variable or function you need to use because it will paste in the code without any typos. In the case of pasting in a function, the Ctrl + H hot key combination includes all arguments for that function.

d) The complete statement should read:

```
AppendExtFile( data_Path , screen_Text ^ ": " ^
choice_ ^ Return)
```

e) Close the Calculation icon and save the changes you have made.

16. Once you are out of the interaction loop, you want to return to the content to update the custom variables with information for a new question. Therefore, you have to give the command to Authorware to return to the point in the content where it was first gathered. To do this you will use the Navigate icon again.

a) Place a Navigate icon the flowline below the interaction loop to return to the content. See figures 23-39 and 23-40.

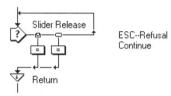

Fig. 23-39. Return navigation.

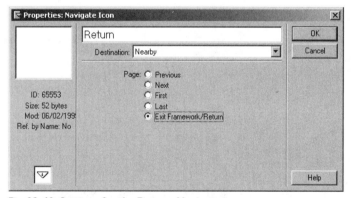

Fig. 23-40. Settings for the Return Navigate icon.

b) Drag a Navigate icon to the level 2 flowline and place it below the Interaction icon. Name this Navigate icon *Return*.

c) Double click on the icon and set the options as follows.
Destination field: Nearby
Page radio button: Exit Interaction/Return

d) Close the icon when finished.

e) Close the *Evaluation Slider Scale* Map icon.

17. Set up the navigation link between the content for the question and the subroutine code. The setting Call and Return is the magic behind framework subroutines. The Call and Return navigation setting allows Authorware to jump to one part of the program and then once a Navigate icon (set to Return) is encountered to return to where it was on the flowline before the jump. This is why you are able to separate the content from the code and make reusable structures.

a) Drag a Navigate icon to the level 2 flowline and place it inside the *Question 1 – Slider* Map icon below the *Set Slider Position* icon.

b) Double click on the Navigate icon and set the options as follows. See figure 23-41.
    Destination field: Anywhere
    Type field: Call and Return
    Framework field: Subroutine Framework
    Page field: Subroutines and Evaluation Slider Scale

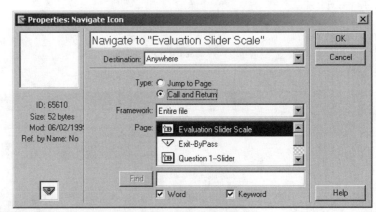

Fig. 23-41. Navigation link to the subroutine.

c) Click on OK to close the dialog window.

18. Run and test. Change the positioning of any text on screen. Note what happens when you click on the Continue button: the screen goes blank. What you want here is to have another question displayed using the same slider.

19. To do this, you must copy and paste the first *Question* Map icon and change the screen text to display the new question. You must also add navigation to move from one question to the next.

a) At the level 1 flowline, copy the Map icon *Question 1*.

b) Click to the right of the *Question 1* Map icon to set the Paste Hand cursor.

c) Paste the *Question 1* Map icon twice.

d) Name these two new Map icons *Question 2* and *Question 3*.

20. Place new content into each of the new questions.
    a) Open the *Question 2* Map icon.
    b) Open the *Set Slider Text* Calculation icon.
    c) Change the assigned value of the variable *screen_Text* to anything you want. (Simply change the text within the quotation marks.)
    d) If you want to change any of the slider text labels, you may do so at this time.
    e) Repeat the same steps for the *Question 3* Map icon.

21. Run and test. What do you notice? You may expect to see all three questions, but you do not. What are you seeing? Currently, you may only get the first question and then the screen goes blank. You can trace this problem by looking at the flowline or running a trace in the Control Panel window. This is happening because Authorware is jumping form the *Question 1* Map icon to the subroutine but not proceeding to the next question. Authorware is not going to the next question because it did not issue the command to go to the next page.

    Once Authorware returns from the subroutine, it goes back to the next icon after the Navigate icon set to Call and Return. At this point of the flowline, you must tell Authorware to go to the next question. There are a few ways to do this. One solution would be to incorporate a navigation set to destination *Anywhere* and then assign that icon to navigate to the *Question 2* Map icon. This is called absolute navigation. The downside to absolute navigation is that if the Map icon were to be deleted and a new Map icon placed in the same location Authorware would not go to that new Map icon. The navigation for taking you there would become unlinked. A better solution would be to incorporate a relative navigation link, as follows.
    a) Open the *Question 1* Map icon.
    b) Drag a Navigate icon to the bottom of the Map icon.
    c) Open the Navigate icon.
    d) Change the Destination drop-down list selection to Nearby.
    e) Change the Page radio button setting to Next.
    f) Close the Navigation dialog box.
    g) Repeat steps *a* through *f* for the *Question 2* Map icon.

22. For the *Question 3* Map icon, you have to set up the navigation differently because it is the last question in the series. If you placed a *Next* Navigate icon as soon as the user got to the last question, the *Next* icon would loop the user back to the first page of the framework. Instead, you will have the user exit the current framework.
    a) Open the *Question 3* Map icon.
    b) Drag a Navigate icon to the bottom of the *Question 3* Map icon.

   c)   Open the Navigate icon.

   d)   Change the Destination drop-down list selection to Nearby.

   e)   Change the Page radio button option to Exit Framework.

   f)   Close the Navigation dialog box.

23. Run and test. Success! You should now see all three questions only once. After the third question, the screen goes blank.

24. Save the file.

Summary

In this chapter you learned how to work with subroutines. Subroutines can be used easily in Authorware because of the functionality of the Call and Return settings of a Navigate icon. Subroutines have the following advantages.

- *Code logic appears only once on the flowline.*

- *Making a single update to the logic will fix problems in numerous content areas.*

- *The overall file size of your Authorware piece is kept smaller.*

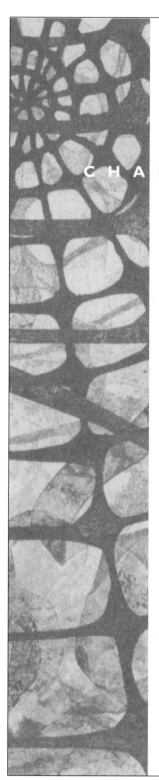

CHAPTER

24

Introduction

to Scripting

Introduction

This chapter covers the fundamentals of scripting and provides you with a solid foundation in the language of Authorware. So far you have used variables and functions in controlling how Authorware works. Here you will begin to understand that the scripting in Authorware is a language in itself, capable of helping you make Authorware do what you want it to do. By the end of this chapter you will:

- *Understand operators*
- *Use* If/Then/Else *statements*
- *Use repeat and nested repeat loops*
- *Have an understanding of the* IconID *functions*

Guided Tour 24A: Overview of Operators

Description

In this guided tour you will learn all of the operators available in Authorware for assigning values to variables, concatenating strings, and using the logical, relational, and arithmetic operators. You will also examine the order in which the operators work and how to control the order with brackets. In this exercise you will:

- *Learn the assignment operator, concatenation, and the logical, relational, and arithmetic operators*
- *Examine the order of operators and brackets*

Take a Look

Let's take a look at the Authorware application to explore how the operators function.

CD-ROM

1. Select File | Open and locate the *Practice* folder on the companion CD-ROM. Open this folder and you will see a number of chapter folders. Open the *Chapter24* folder and locate and double click on the file named *Exer24-1.a6p.*

2. The *Exer24-1* file should now appear in your copy of Authorware. Select Control | Restart or press the Restart button on the toolbar to play the file from the top of the flowline. See figure 24-1.

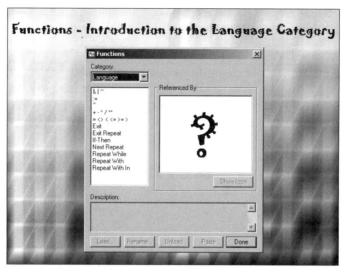

Fig. 24-1. Opening screen of Authorware program.

3. Examine the assignment operator.

a) The first and most commonly used operator is the assignment operator (:=). This operator assigns the value on the right to the variable you specify on the left.

b) Note in the application *Exer24-1.a6p* that the first calculation to appear is *carrots := 45*. See figure 24-2.

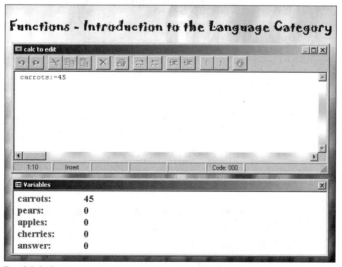

Fig. 24-2. Assignment operator Carrots := 45.

The assignment operator (:=) is functionally different from the equal sign (=). The assignment operator is setting a value to a variable, whereas the equal sign (=) compares two values and returns the result as True or False.

    c)   Note in the application that the calculation appears in the top window and the output of the variables in the bottom window.

    d)   Edit the Calculation icon to experiment with the expression.

    e)   In the flowline, open the *Calculation to edit* icon by double clicking on it. See figure 24-3.

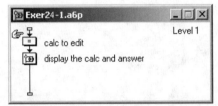

Fig. 24-3. Flowline showing Calculation to edit icon.

    f)   Edit the Calculation icon to read:

       carrots := "Rabbit Food"

    g)   Close and save the icon and restart the application. See figure 24-4.

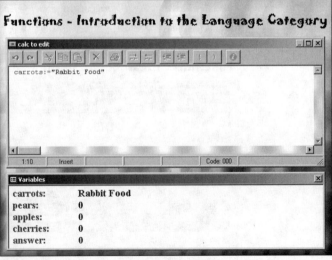

Fig. 24-4. Results of the assignment operator.

4.   Examine the concatenation operator.

    a)   If you have two strings and wish to join them, use the concatenation operator (^).

b) Open the Calculation icon *Calculation to edit* and modify the code to read:

carrots := "Rabbit Food"^"Galore".

c) Close and save the Calculation icon and restart the program. See figure 24-5.

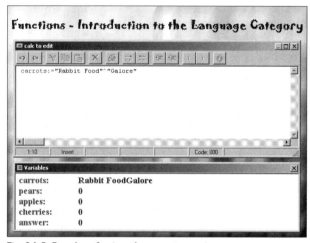

Fig. 24-5. Results of using the concatenation operator.

d) Note that the strings are joined, without a space between them.
e) You can concatenate as many times as necessary, and variables can also be concatenated. Type the following:

carrots := "Rabbit Food"^" "^"Galore"

pears := "Little Duckling Food"

answer := carrots^" "^pears

f) Close and save the Calculation icon and restart the program. See figure 24-6.

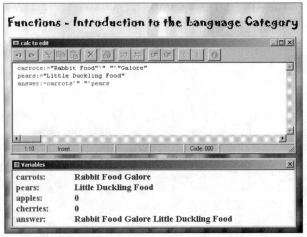

Fig. 24-6. Results of using multiple concatenation operators.

5. Examine the logical operators.

   a) The logical operators are *not* (~), *and* (&), and *or* (|). Among other uses, these are typically used with binary numbers. The binary equivalents for 0 are FALSE and OFF. The binary equivalents for 1 are TRUE and ON.

The generic names of the operator symbols are tilde (~), ampersand (&) and pipe (|).

   b) Enter the following code inside the Calc To Edit icon.

   ```
   carrots := ~0

   pears := ~TRUE

   apples := OFF & ON

   cherries := 1 & ON

   answer := ~1 | ~0
   ```

   c) Close and save the Calculation icon and restart the program. See figure 24-7.

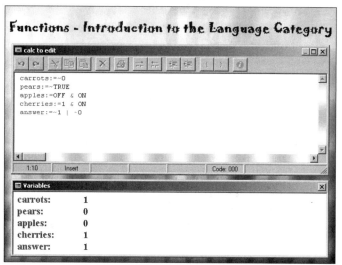

Fig. 24-7. Output window.

Note the following about the logical results of the code you just entered.

- *The results default to 1s and 0s.*

- *The not (~) operator reverses a 1 or 0 to its opposite. In the case of the TRUE, it reverses it to a 0.*

- *The and (&) operator will only give a 1 if all entries are a 1. For example: 1 & 1 & 1 & 1 is 1; 1 & 1 & 0 & 1 is 0.*

- *The or (|) operator will return a 1 if any of the entries is a 1. For example: 0 | 0 | 1 | 0 is 1; 0 | 0 | 0 | 0 is 0.*

  d) Enter the following code inside the Calc To Edit icon. Before you run the program to view the results, take a moment and try to guess what you will see as a result. See figure 24-8.

  ```
  carrots := ~TRUE

  pears := 0

  apples := carrots | pears | 0

  cherries := TRUE & apples & 1

  answer := ~cherries & 1
  ```

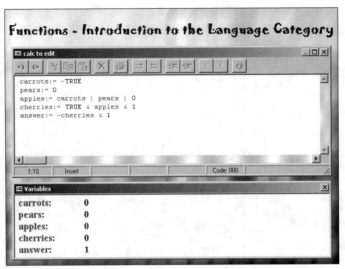

Fig. 24–8. Results of the logical operator code.

The relational operators are used to compare values and then return a binary result. There are six relational operators, as follows:

• equal *(=)*

• not equal *(<>)*

• less than *(<)*

• less than or equal to *(<=)*

• greater than or equal to *(>=)*

• greater than *(>)*

    e)   Again, see if you can work out what the variable answer will be before you run the code. Then close and save the Calculation icon and restart the application. Try the following code in the Calculation icon. See figure 24-9.

```
carrots := 45 = 90

pears := 45 = 45

apples := 45 <> 90

cherries := 45 <> 45

answer := pears = apples
```

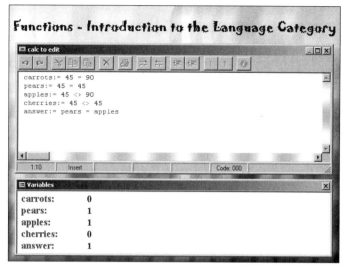

Fig. 24-9. Results of the relational operator code.

To explain the code, the variable *pears* will become equal to 1 (as 45 does equal 45). The variable *apples* will become 1 (as 45 does not equal 90). The answer is 1 because both the *pears* and *apples* variables are equal to 1.

f) Again, see if you can work out what the variable answer will be before you run the code. Then close and save the Calculation icon and restart the application. Now try the following code. See figure 24-10.

```
carrots := 45 < 90

pears := 45 <= 45

apples := 45 > 90

cherries := 45 >= 90

answer := pears = apples
```

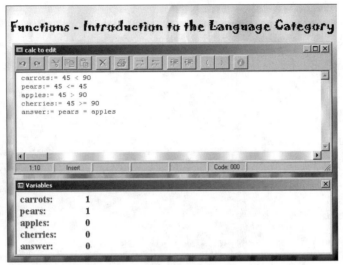

Fig. 24-10. Results of the relational operators code.

To see what is going on here, let's look through each line in turn.

- carrots *will become 1 as 45 is less than 90. Notice how with all these operators you can speak through the line of code.*

- *In the next line, is 45 less than or equal to 45? The answer is yes, so* pears *is assigned the value 1.*

- *For* apples, *is 45 greater than 90? No, so* apples *is assigned a 0.*

- *For* cherries, *is 45 greater than or equal to 90? No, so again* cherries *is assigned a 0.*

- *For the last line, is* pears *(1) equal to* apples *(0)? Answer is no, so* answer *is assigned a 0.*

6. Examine the arithmetic operators. There are five arithmetic operators, as follows:

   - add *(+)*
   - subtract *()*
   - multiply *(*)*
   - divide *(/)*
   - exponentiate *(**)*

   a) Try the following code.

   ```
   carrots := 4

   pears := -carrots
   ```

```
apples := carrots + 6

apples := apples + 10

cherries := carrots * 4

answer := cherries / 10
```

b) Note that *pears* is the negation of 4; that is, it is –4. Close and save the Calculation icon and restart the program. See figure 24-11.

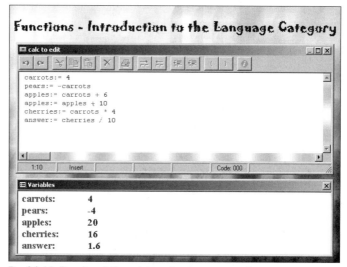

Fig. 24-11. Results of the arithmetic operators code.

c) Try the following lines in the Calculation icon.

```
carrots := 4

carrots := carrots ** 2

pears := carrots ** 3

apples := carrots ** 4

cherries := carrots ** 5

answer := cherries / 1000000
```

d) Close and save the Calculation icon and restart the program. See figure 24-12.

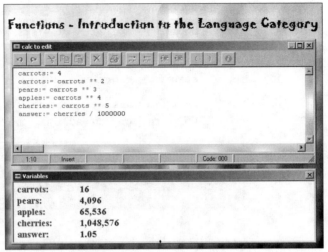

Fig. 24-12. Output window.

Note what the exponential operator is doing. It takes the initial value, in this case 4, and multiplies it the number of times stated after the operator. For example, in the 45th line, cherries is assigned the value of 4 * 4 * 4 * 4 * 4, which is 1048576.

7.   Let's examine the order of operators. When you read a page in a book, you read from left to right. This is not always so in operator land.

   a)   Type the following in the Calculation icon, and close, save, and restart the application. See figure 24-13.

```
carrots := 4 + 3 * 2
```

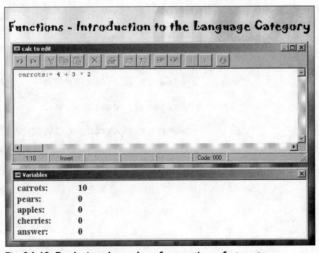

Fig. 24-13. Exploring the order of execution of operators.

So what's going on? 4 plus 3 is 7, times 2 should be 14, but we have 10. The answer is that operators work in an order of precedence, and all multiplications are done before additions. The order of operators is: (), ~, unary, **, *, /, +, -, ^, =, <>, <, >, <=, >=, &, |, and :=.

b) Try the following in the Calculation icon.

```
carrots := 4 + 3 * 2

pears := (4 + 3) * 2

apples := 4 + (3 * 2)

cherries := 7 = 7 / 2

answer := (7 = 7) / (2 + 2)
```

c) Close and save the Calculation icon and restart the application. See figure 24-14.

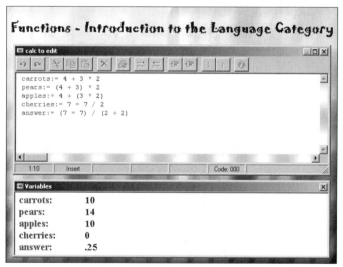

Fig. 24-14. Results of the code example in step 7b.

The second line gives you the answer of 14! This is because you have used brackets to alter the order of operation. This is all that brackets do: change the order of the operators. As *4 + 3* is inside brackets, this gets evaluated first. Then the result, 7, is multiplied by the 2.

The fourth line, *cherries*, is interesting. As the divide operator has higher precedence than the equal relational operator, the 7 divided by 2 is calculated first. This result, 3.5, does not equal 7, and thus the binary result of 0. In the last line, 7 does equal 7, giving a 1. 2 plus 2 is 4. The result, 1/4, is 0.25.

Brackets can be nested. Always work from the middle brackets out in evaluating an expression.

    d)   Can you work out what the answer will be without running the application? Try the following lines in the Calculation icon.

```
carrots := 4 * (3 - (2 + 1))

pears := ((4 * 3) - 2) + 1

apples := 1 * -2 + 3 / 6

cherries := 1 * ((-2 + 3) / 6)

answer := ((pears - 1) * -(apples - 0.5)) - 30 * cherries
```

    e)   Restart the application to see how you did. See figure 24-15.

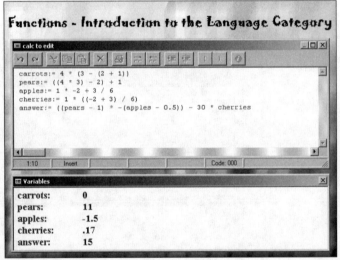

Fig. 24-15. Results of the code in step 7d.

You have now covered the operators in the Language category of the Functions dialog box. There are many more functions in the Math section, which are often overlooked and are very powerful. See figure 24-16.

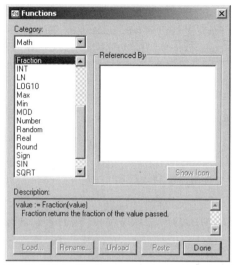

Fig. 24-16. The Math category in the functions box.

Guided Tour 24B: If/Then Statements

Description

If/Then statements are one of the cornerstones of any language, and this is just as true in Authorware scripting. As in real life, if you have more pears, you might make a fruit salad; if you have more carrots, you might make a carrot salad. In Authorware, you come across Ifs like this quite often. If/Then statements can make the Authorware application perform different tasks based on the logical (True or False, 1 or 0) result of a condition. In this exercise you will:

- *Learn how to use If/Then statements*
- *Learn the* else *parameter*
- *Have a peek at the* Test() *function*

Take a Look

Let's take a look at the Authorware application to explore how If/Then statements work.

CD-ROM

1. Select File | Open and locate the *Practice* folder on the companion CD-ROM. Open this folder and you will see a number of chapter folders. Open the *Chapter24* folder and locate and double click on the file named *Exer24-1.a6p*.

2. The *Exer24-1* file should now appear in your copy of Authorware.

3. Format the If/Then statement. The simplest form is "If this condition is true, then do the following statement." Type the following into the first Calculation icon in the flowline in the file *Exer24-1.a6p*.

```
if TRUE then

    answer := 1

end if
```

a) Close the Calculation icon, save, and restart the application. See figure 24-17.

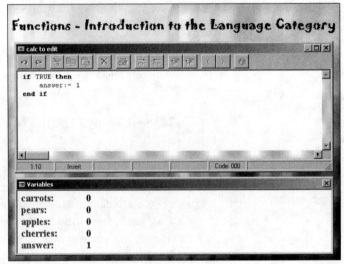

Fig. 24-17. Results of the If/Then statement.

Note that as TRUE is true, the command *answer := 1* is carried out.

b) Let's try something more complex. Type the following into the Calculation icon.

```
carrots := 7

pears := 9

if pears > carrots then

    answer := "Make a Fruit Salad"

end if
```

c) Close and save the Calculation icon and restart the program. See figure 24-18.

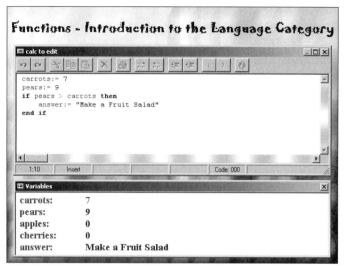

Fig. 24-18. Results of a variable condition in an If/Then statement.

Note the format of the If/Then statement. After the If/Then, you must have an *end if* so that Authorware knows where the If/Then statement finishes.

d) You can also program an alternative condition using the Else statement. Say you have 9 carrots and only 7 pears. Type in the following:

```
carrots := 9

pears := 7

if pears > carrots then

   answer := "Make a Fruit Salad"

else

   answer := "Make a Normal Salad"

end if
```

e) Close and save the Calculation icon and then restart the application. See figure 24-19.

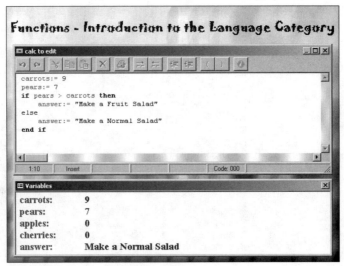

Fig. 24-19. Using the else statement.

Now the *else* statement is executed, as *pears* is not greater than *carrots* and *answer* is to *make a normal salad*.

f) Assume you need to check for more than one condition. Let's say the number of pears you have will dictate what size of a fruit salad you make. If you have up to 4 pears you can make a small fruit salad. If you have between 4 and 7 you can make a medium salad, and if you have 7 or more pears, then you can make a huge fruit salad. Type the following code into the Calculation icon.

```
pears := 5

if pears < 3 then

    answer := "Make a Small Fruit Salad"

else if pears < 7 then

    answer := "Make a Medium Fruit Salad"

else

    answer := "Make a Huge Fruit Salad"

end if
```

g) Close and save the Calculation icon and restart the application. See figure 24-20.

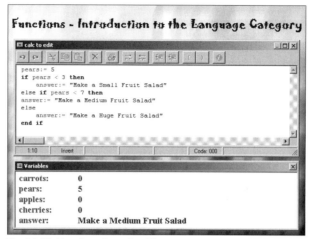

Fig. 24-20. Results of an **else if** statement.

4. There is an alternative to the simple If/Then statement that is often over-looked. This is the *Test()* function. It operates in a very similar manner to the If/Then statement. The format is *Test(condition, statement if condition true, statement if condition is false)*. This function is often used in places like the Calculated Path field of a Decision icon where you cannot enter multiple lines of code. It is very uncommon to see it used instead of an If/Then/Else structure in Calculation icons.

a) Type the following into the Calculation icon.

```
cherries := 3

Test(cherries > 2, answer := "Jennie's Cherry Salad",
answer := "No Salad")
```

b) Close and save the Calculation icon and restart the application. See figure 24-21.

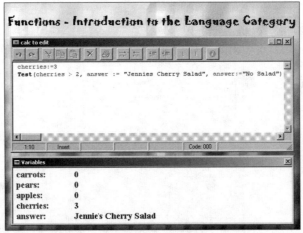

Fig. 24-21. Results of using the Test function.

Because you have more than *3* cherries, the *Test* function executes only the first parameter, and therefore sets the variable answer to *"Jennie's Cherry Salad"*. The *Test* function does not need the third parameter if you do not wish to have an *else* as part of it. For example, *Test(cherries > 2, answer := "Jennie's Cherry Salad")* will work, but if *cherries* has a smaller or equal value to 2, *answer* will not be assigned a value.

Guided Tour 24C: Repeat Loops

Description

In this lesson you will use a repeat loop to find a value from a list and then exit the loop once the value is found. Repeat loops allow you to repeat an instruction or a series of instructions in a script for a defined number of times or until a condition is met. Repeat loops execute instructions more quickly than Decision icon branching, allowing data to be gathered and managed efficiently. Each repeat type is briefly discussed before you try your hand at creating a repeat loop. There are three types of repeat loops, as follows:

- *Repeat With loops are used to execute an instruction or set of instructions repeatedly for a given number of times.*

- *Repeat With In loops are used to execute an instruction or set of instructions for each position in a list variable.*

- *Repeat While loops are used to execute an instruction or set of instructions while a given condition remains true.*

In this exercise you will:

- *Learn situations for which repeat loops can be used*
- *Script a repeat loop*
- *Learn how to skip loops and exit from loops*
- *Look at nested repeat loops*

Take a Look

Let's take a look at the Authorware application to explore how a repeat loop works.

CD-ROM

1. Select File | Open and locate the *Practice* folder on the companion CD-ROM. Open this folder and you will see a number of chapter folders. Open the *Chapter24* folder and locate and double click on the file named *Exer24-1.a6p*.

2. The *Exer24-1* file should now appear in your copy of Authorware.

3. The Repeat With loop is the most common loop by far, and is used to repeat a statement a certain number of times.

    a) Type the following code into the first Calculation icon in the flowline.

```
carrots := ""

repeat with counter := 1 to 10

   carrots := carrots ^ counter ^ " "

end repeat
```

    b) Close and save the Calculation icon and then restart the application. See figure 24-22.

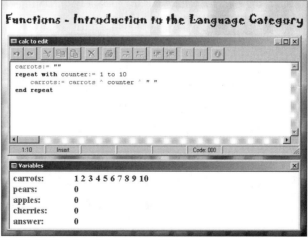

Fig. 24-22. Results of the Repeat With script.

Note that the repeat loop works 10 times, and each time the loop goes around the variable counter is incremented by 1. It is also possible to loop backward from a high number to a low number.

c) Type the following code into the Calculation icon.

```
cherries := ""

repeat with counter := 10 down to 5

    cherries := cherries ^ counter ^ " "

end repeat
```

d) Close and save the Calculation icon and then restart the application. Note how the loop goes down from 10 to 5. See figure 24-23.

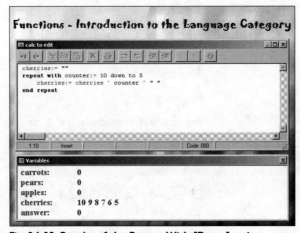

Fig. 24-23. Results of the Repeat With [Down] script.

e) You can also use variables in the repeat statement. Type the following:

```
cherries := ""

pears := 19

apples := 24

repeat with counter := pears to apples

    cherries := cherries ^ counter ^ " "

end repeat
```

f) Close and save the Calculation icon and restart the application. See figure 24-24.

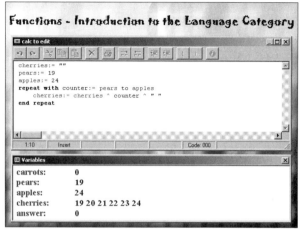

Fig. 24-24. Results of the Repeat With using variables.

4.   The Repeat With In loop is used with lists and will loop the number of times there are elements in a list (lists are covered in detail in Chapter 25). For example, a list of [10,20,30] will loop three times, and with each loop the counter is assigned the appropriate value from the list (i.e., 10 then 20 then 30).

a)   Try the following code in the Calculation icon.

```
carrots := [10, 20, 30]

answer := 0

repeat with counter in carrots

    answer := answer + counter

end repeat
```

b)   Close and save the Calculation icon and then restart the application. See figure 24-25.

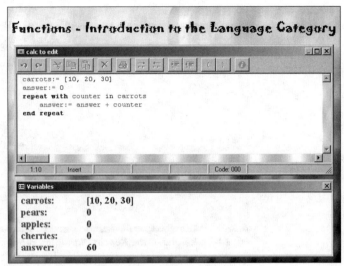

Fig. 24-25. Results of the Repeat With In script.

Using a Repeat With In loop, you can alter the list as the loop is progressing.

c) Try the following:

```
carrots := [10, 20, 30]

answer := 0

repeat with counter in carrots

   if counter = 20 then

      AddLinear(carrots, 40 , 4)

   end if

   answer := answer + counter

end repeat
```

d) Close and save the Calculation icon and restart the application. See figure 24-26.

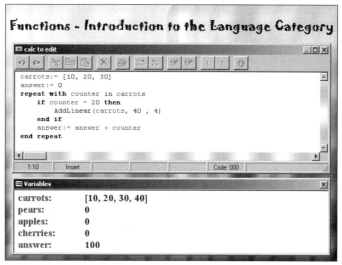

Fig. 24-26. Using an If/Then statement inside a Repeat With In script.

As the counter increments to the second list item, 20, the *AddLinear* command adds another entry into the list, and the loop repeats 4 times, not 3, as would normally be expected.

5. Repeat While loops are used when you want to continue looping as long as a condition is true. Once that condition listed becomes false, the loop quits.

    a) Type the following to test this loop.

        ```
        carrots := 40

        answer := " "

        repeat while carrots > 20

           answer := answer ^ carrots ^ " "

           carrots := carrots - 3

        end repeat
        ```

b) Close and save the Calculation icon and then restart the application. See figure 24-27.

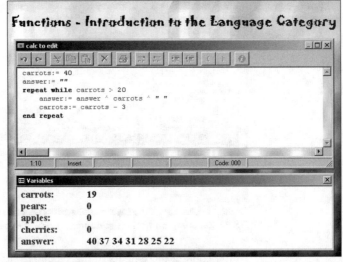

Fig. 24-27. Results of the Repeat While script.

Each time the loop repeats, *carrots* is reduced by 3 until *carrots* are not greater than 20 and the loop exits. Note the following about skipping loops and exiting from loops.

- *There are two extra repeat commands you can use to control the behavior of all loops:* Next Repeat *and* Exit Repeat. *These can be used anywhere within the repeat loop.*

- Next Repeat *skips over any remaining steps in the loop and immediately starts to execute the next loop from the top.*

- Exit Repeat *exits the loop and starts executing the next line in the Calculation icon after the repeat loop.*

c) Type the following code into the Calculation icon.

```
carrots := 7

answer := ""

repeat with counter = 1 to carrots

    if counter = 5 then

      Next Repeat

    end if

    answer := answer ^ counter ^ " "

end repeat
```

d)   Close and save the Calculation icon and then restart the application. See figure 24-28.

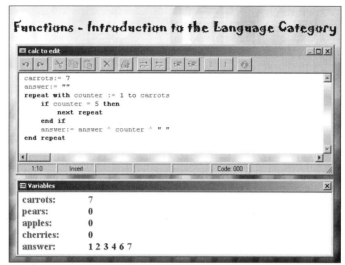

Fig. 24-28. Results of the Repeat Next script.

Note how the repeat loop skips the *answer := answer ^ counter ^ " "* line when *carrots* is equal to 5.

e)   Let's try the *Exit Repeat* on the same loop. Type the following into the Calculation icon.

```
carrots := 7

answer := ""

repeat with counter = 1 to carrots

  if counter = 5 then

    Exit Repeat

  end if

  answer := answer ^ counter ^ " "

end repeat
```

f)   Close and save the Calculation icon and restart the application. See figure 24-29.

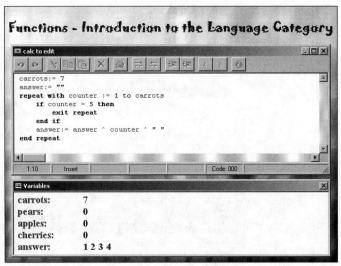

Fig. 24-29. Results of using the Exit Repeat command inside a repeat loop.

Note how the loop simply exits when *counter* is equal to 5.

6. Repeat loops become very powerful when they are nested, and all sorts of functionality can be gained form using them in this manner.

   a) Type the following in a Calculation icon to see what is happening.

   ```
   carrots := 4

   cherries := 3

   answer := ""

   repeat with counter1 = 1 to carrots

      repeat with counter2 = 1 to cherries

         answer := answer ^ counter2 ^ " "

      end repeat

   end repeat
   ```

   b) Close and save the Calculation icon and then restart the application. See figure 24-30.

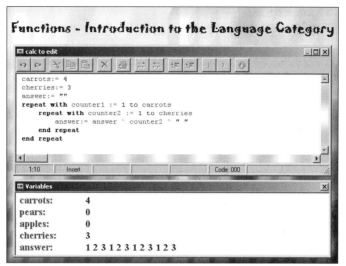

Fig. 24-30. Results of a nested repeat loop structure.

Here, the middle loop, with *counter2*, repeats itself 4 times by the outer loop, *counter1*, so that you end up with 4 lots of 1 2 3. Let's say you have a list of numbers (for example, 1 , 2 , 10 , 20) and you wish to add not the numbers but all individual digits (1 + 2 + 1 + 0 + 2 + 0). One way to accomplish this would be to use a nested loop, or a "loop within a loop."

c) Try the following in the Calculation icon.

```
carrots := [24,45,56,78,90]

cherries := 0

answer := ""

repeat with counter1 in carrots

  cherries := cherries + counter1

repeat with counter2 = 1 to CharCount(counter1)

answer := answer + SubStr(counter1,counter2,counter2)

  end repeat

end repeat
```

d) Close and save the Calculation icon and restart the application. See figure 24-31.

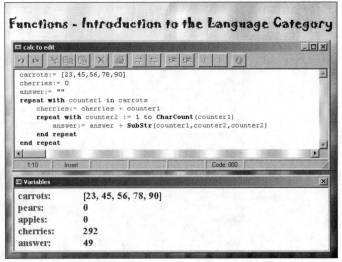

Fig. 24-31. Results of a nested repeat loop calculation.

Here the loop *counter2* adds the values of the individual number, whereas the *counter1* loop repeats for each list item.

Guided Tour 24D: Introduction to IconID Functions

Description

Understanding IconIDs can facilitate authoring, as it allows for a better understanding of how Authorware works, and allows you to start using Authorware to start examining the flowline. Once you understand *IconIDs*, a lot more functions become easier to understand because so many reference this idea. In this exercise you will:

- *Learn what an* IconID *is*
- *Use* IconIDs *to analyze a program*
- *Use the* IconID *variable to reprogram Authorware*

Take a Look

Let's take a look at the Authorware application to explore how *IconIDs* work.

CD-ROM

1. Select File | Open and locate the *Practice* folder on the companion CD-ROM. Open this folder and you will see a number of chapter folders. Open the *Chapter24* folder and locate and double click on the file named *Exer24-2.a6p*.

2.   The *Exer24-2* file should now appear in your copy of Authorware. Select
     File | Save As and save it to your PC as *Exer24-3.a6p*. See figure 24-32.

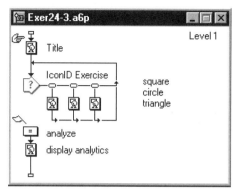

Fig. 24-32. Flowline of **Exer24-3.a6p.**

3.   Locate the "*analyze*" Calculation icon on the flowline and right click on it.
     Select Properties. See figure 24-33.

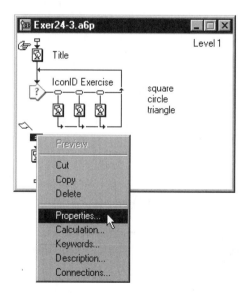

Fig. 24-33. Properties selection.

A dialog box will pop up containing the information about this icon. See
figure 24-34.

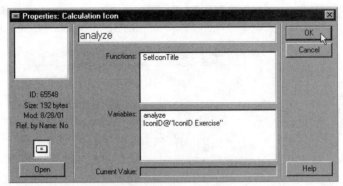

Fig. 24-34. Icon Properties dialog box.

On the left-hand side of this box will be several lines of text, the first one being *ID: 65548*. The actual number 65548 may well be different in your version of this file. The *IconID* number is unique to each icon. However, the value of an individual icon may well change when you edit, save, or package a piece as all the *IconIDs* get shuffled around.

   a) Write down what your *IconID* was for this icon. Open the Calculation icon *analyze* by double clicking on it. Inside you will see the following code.

```
analyze := IconID
```

   b) Close the Calculation icon and click on Restart from Flag in the Control menu. See figure 24-35.

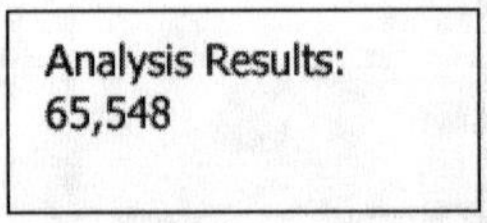

Analysis Results:
65,548

Fig. 24-35. Presentation window.

You will see the same number in the Presentation window. This is because the variable *IconID* holds the value of the *IconID* of the icon in which it is placed.

   c) Open the Calculation icon *analyze* again and edit it to read as follows:

```
analyze := IconID@"IconID Tutorial"
```

   d) Close and save the icon and restart from the flag. See figure 24-36.

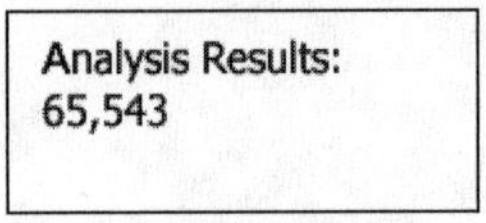

Analysis Results:
65,543

Fig. 24-36. Presentation window.

You may well have a different number displayed here, but if you open the properties of the icon *IconID Tutorial* you see that the *IconID* has been extracted from this icon. The "at" (@) symbol makes the variable use the local value from the icon specified in the quotes. Now that you know how to find out the *IconID* of an icon, let's look at two examples of how you could use this information.

e) Type the following into the Calculation icon *analyze*.

```
analyze := IconNumChildren(IconID@"IconID Tutorial")
```

f) Close and save the Calculation icon and restart from the flag. See figure 24-37.

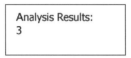

Analysis Results:
3

Fig. 24-37. Presentation window.

Here, by extracting the *IconID* of the icon *IconID Tutorial* you can use another function to find out how many children this icon has. In this case, three children: *square*, *circle*, and *triangle*.

g) Type the following into the Calculation icon *analyze*.

```
analyze := SetIconTitle(IconID@"IconID Tutorial", "My
Super Lesson")
```

h) Close and save the Calculation icon and restart from the flag. Close the Presentation window to look at the flowline. See figure 24-38.

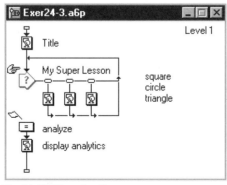

Fig. 24-38. New flowline.

You can see here that the title on the Interaction icon has changed from *IconID Tutorial* to *My Super Lesson*. You have just written a computer program that has programmed itself. This capability is dealt with further in Chapter 25.

Summary

In this chapter you examined the syntax of Authorware scripting. You should now:

- *Understand the differences among the Authorware operators*
- *Understand the assignment operator, concatenation, and the logical, relational, and arithmetic operators*
- *Be aware of the order in which operators and brackets are executed*
- *How to use If/Then/Else statements*
- *Understand the Else/If parameter*
- *Have an understanding of how the Test() function can be used*
- *Use repeat loops with counters to evaluate statements*
- *How to nest repeat loops to check for multiple instances*
- *Understand that every icon has a unique IconID that is assigned by Authorware*

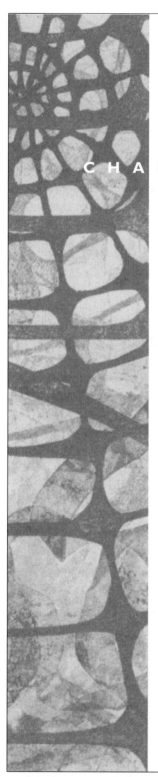

25

Lists and Arrays

Introduction

As you author more and more, you will find that you use more and more custom variables. Once there are hundreds of custom variables in your applications, they become very difficult to understand and also very cumbersome to program. For example, if you have 150 pages in a tutorial and wish to store each page's name in a variable, you could make 100 variables, from *pageName001* to *pageName150*.

However, imagine what the code for this would look like, especially if you also wanted to store page lengths, and page information such as which user has visited which page. You are already up to 600 or so variables! Wouldn't it be good if you could have one variable to store all page names, one variable to store all page lengths, and only one variable to store all user progress data? You can. This is where lists come into play. By the end of this chapter you will be able to:

- *Describe the concept of lists*
- *Create and use custom linear, property, and multidimensional lists*
- *Build a list capable of holding student progress information*

Guided Tour 25A: Linear Lists

Description

A linear list is the simplest list Authorware can work with. A linear list consists of items of data stored in a sequence. For example, if you have four sections and wish to store the names of each section, you simply list them separated by commas; for example, as follows: *Repeat Loops, Nested Repeat Loops, Linear Lists, Multi-Dimensional Lists – Arrays*. This is a list of data. In Authorware, you use the following format:

```
MyList := ["Repeat Loops","Nested Repeat Loops","Linear
Lists","Multi-Dimensional Lists — Arrays"]
```

Note the square brackets used to enclose the list. In this exercise you will:

- *Learn how to create a linear list*
- *Add values to a linear list*
- *Get values from a linear list*
- *Copy linear lists*
- *Sort linear lists*

Step-by-Step Instructions

Let's take a look at the exercise in its completed state and then experiment with the application to learn about linear lists.

CD-ROM

1. Select File | Open and locate the *Practice* folder on the companion CD-ROM. Open this folder and you will see a number of chapter folders. Open the *Chapter25* folder and locate and double click on the file named *Exer25-1*.

2. The *Exer25-1* file should now appear in your copy of Authorware. See figure 25-1.

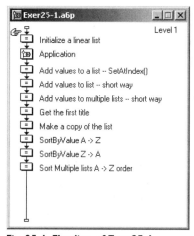

Fig. 25-1. Flowline of **Exer25-1.**

3. Each Calculation icon is another command you will learn for controlling the list. The application Map icon simply shows the output of the Calculation icon and then stops at this position so that the Calculation icons underneath do not operate. Go through each Calculation icon to discover what it does.

4. Initialize the linear list.
    a) Double click on the first icon, *Initialize a linear list.* You will see the following code. See figure 25-2.

    ```
    unitTitlesList := []
    ```

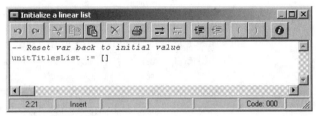

Fig. 25-2. Calculation icon.

b) This is how you initialize a linear list, by basically assigning a variable to be a new list. Just as we saw the initial value of a string variable was "", and a numeric variable was a zero, the initial value of a list is [].

c) Close this icon and restart the application. See figure 25-3.

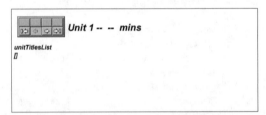

Fig. 25-3. Initial value of list displayed in the Presentation window.

d) Page through the four units that constitute the application. As you have not assigned any values to the list, only the unit numbers are displayed as you page through the tutorial.

5. Add values and data to a list.

a) Return to the flowline and drag and drop the *Application* Map icon below the *Add values to a list – SetAtIndex()* Calculation icon. See figure 25-4.

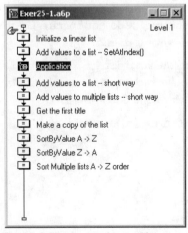

Fig. 25-4. Flowline with new Map icon.

b) Double click on the *Add values to a list – SetAtIndex()* Calculation icon. You will see the following code:

```
SetAtIndex( unitTitlesList, "Linear Lists", 1)

SetAtIndex( unitTitlesList, "Repeat Loops", 2)

SetAtIndex( unitTitlesList, "Multi-Dimensional List", 3)

SetAtIndex( unitTitlesList, "Nested Repeat Loops", 4)
```

c) This is the "long" way of assigning data to a linear list. The command *SetAtIndex* has three parameters. The first is the list to assign the data to, the second is the data itself, and the third is the position to assign the data to.

d) Close this icon and restart the application. See figure 25-5.

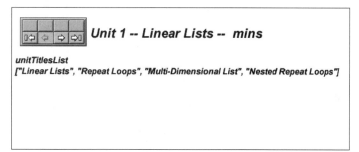

Fig. 25-5. Populated list displayed in the Presentation window.

e) Page through the sections and note how the *unitTitlesList* variable is used to see which unit you are looking at. Also make sure you fully see the format of the list, enclosed in square brackets.

6. Add values and data to the list.

a) Return to the flowline and drag and drop the *Application* Map icon below the *Add values to a list – short way* Calculation icon. See figure 25-6.

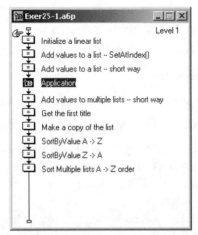

Fig. 25-6. Application Map icon's new position on the flowline.

b) Double click on the *Add values to a list – short way* Calculation icon. You will see the following code:

```
unitTitlesList[1] := "Linear Lists"

unitTitlesList[2] := "Repeat Loops"

unitTitlesList[3] := "Multi-Dimensional List"

unitTitlesList[4] := "Nested Repeat Loops"
```

c) This is the "short" way of assigning data to a linear list and the most common method used by Authorware developers. The list and position is specified on the left and the value to assign is on the right.

d) Close this icon and restart the application. See figure 25-7.

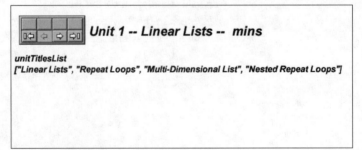

Fig. 25-7. Results of assigning data to a linear list.

e) Page through the sections and note that this method has assigned the same values as the "long" method.

7. Add values/data to multiple lists.

a) Return to the flowline and drag and drop the *Application* Map icon below the *Add values to multiple lists – short way* Calculation icon. See figure 25-8.

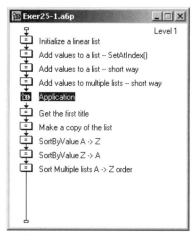

Fig. 25-8. Application Map icon's new position on the flowline.

b) Double click on the *Add values to multiple lists – short way* Calculation icon. You will see the following code:

```
unitTitlesList[1] := "Linear Lists"

unitTitlesList[2] := "Repeat Loops"

unitTitlesList[3] := "Multi-Dimensional List"

unitTitlesList[4] := "Nested Repeat Loops"


unitTimesList[1] := 20

unitTimesList[2] := 30

unitTimesList[3] := 60

unitTimesList[4] := 25
```

c) Here all you have done is assign values to two different lists. Note how *linear lists* in the first list corresponds to 20 in the second list, *Repeat Loops* corresponds to 30, and so on. This is an important relationship to maintain.

d) Close this icon and restart the application. See figure 25-9.

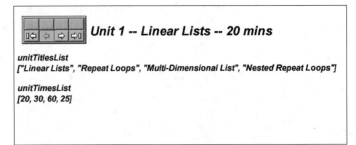

Unit 1 -- Linear Lists -- 20 mins

unitTitlesList
["Linear Lists", "Repeat Loops", "Multi-Dimensional List", "Nested Repeat Loops"]

unitTimesList
[20, 30, 60, 25]

Fig. 25-9. Results of the populated list on the Presentation window.

    e)   Page through the sections and notice that now you have lengths of each course displayed in minutes.

8.   Get data from lists.

    a)   Return to the flowline and drag and drop the *Application* Map icon below the *Get the first title* Calculation icon. See figure 25-10.

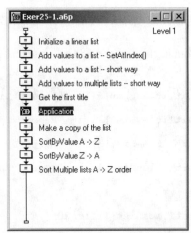

Fig. 25-10. New position of the Application Map icon below the **Get the first title** *Calculation icon.*

    b)   Double click on the *Get the first title* Calculation icon. You will see the following code:

```
tempVar:=ValueAtIndex(unitTitlesList, 1)

-- or

tempVar := unitTitlesList[1]
```

    c)   As there are two ways to assign a value, there are also two ways to get the values. Again, the most common way is the short, latter method, using *tempVar := unitTitlesList[1]*. In this method, *tempVar* is the variable in which to store the value, *unitTitlesList* is the list, and [1] signifies which position in the list you are interested in. In this case, it is the first title.

d) Close this icon and restart the application. See figure 25-11.

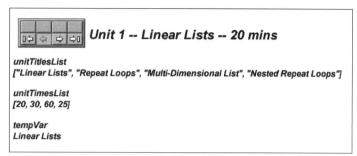

Fig. 25-11. Lists sorted by title.

e) Note how the variable *tempVar* now equals *Linear Lists*, the first value in the *unitTitleList* list.

9. Copy lists.

a) Return to the flowline and drag and drop the *Application* Map icon below the *Make a copy of the list* Calculation icon. See figure 25-12.

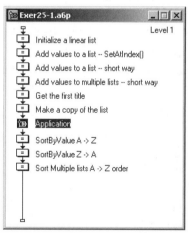

Fig. 25-12. New position of the Application Map icon below the **Make a copy of the list** *Calculation icon.*

b) Double click on the *Make a copy of the list* Calculation icon. You will see the following code:

```
tempVar := []

tempVar := CopyList( unitTitlesList)
```

c) This first creates a new empty list and assigns it to *tempVar*. Then you use the *CopyList* function to make a carbon copy of the list and assign it to *tempVar*.

Why do you not just use the format *tempVar := unitTitleList*? You can, but this works in a different way from the *CopyList* function. If you use the *CopyList* function, you now have two independent lists. This is normally what you want when you copy a list. If you assign *unitTitleList* to *tempVar* by the line *tempVar := unitTitleList*, you have not copied the list but have assigned *tempVar* to the list. If after this line you change *unitTitleList*, *tempVar* is also going to reflect these changes. That is, you still only have one list, but now with two variables pointing at it.

d) Close this icon and restart the application. See figure 25-13.

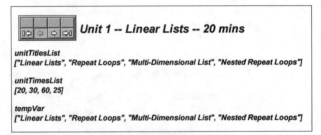

Unit 1 -- Linear Lists -- 20 mins

unitTitlesList
["Linear Lists", "Repeat Loops", "Multi-Dimensional List", "Nested Repeat Loops"]

unitTimesList
[20, 30, 60, 25]

tempVar
["Linear Lists", "Repeat Loops", "Multi-Dimensional List", "Nested Repeat Loops"]

Fig. 25-13. Results of the CopyList function.

e) Note how the variable *tempVar* is now a copy of the list *unitTitlesList*.

10. Sort lists in alphanumeric order.
   a) Return to the flowline and drag and drop the *Application* Map icon below the *SortByValue A -> Z* Calculation icon. See figure 25-14.

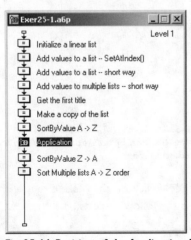

Fig. 25-14. Position of the Application Map icon below the SortByValue A-> Z Calculation icon.

b) Double click on the *SortByValue A -> Z* Calculation icon. You will see the following code:

```
SortByValue( unitTitlesList, TRUE)
```

c) The *SortByValue* function sorts the list *unitTitlesList* in alphanumeric order.

d) Close this icon and restart the application. See figure 25-15.

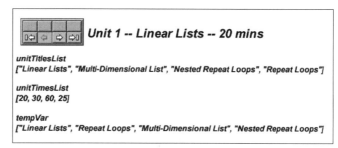

Fig. 25-15. Results of the SortByValue A -> Z function.

e) Note how the list *unitTitlesList* is now sorted.

11. Sort lists in reverse alphanumeric order.

a) Return to the flowline and drag and drop the *Application* Map icon below the *SortByValue Z -> A* Calculation icon. See figure 25-16.

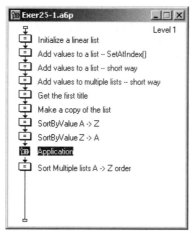

Fig. 25-16. Position of the Application Map icon below the SortByValue Z-> A Calculation icon.

b) Double click on the *SortByValue Z -> A* Calculation icon. You will see the following code:

```
SortByValue( unitTimesList, FALSE)
```

c) The *SortByValue* function sorts the list *unitTimesList* in reverse alphanumeric order because you have set the second parameter to FALSE.

d) Close this icon and restart the application. See figure 25-17.

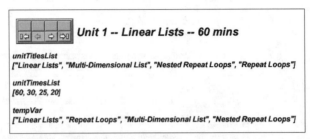

unitTitlesList
["Linear Lists", "Multi-Dimensional List", "Nested Repeat Loops", "Repeat Loops"]

unitTimesList
[60, 30, 25, 20]

tempVar
["Linear Lists", "Repeat Loops", "Multi-Dimensional List", "Nested Repeat Loops"]

Fig. 25-17. Results of the SortByValue Z -> A *function.*

e) Note how the list *unitTitlesList* is sorted in alphanumeric order and the list *unitTimesList* in reverse alphanumeric order. Because TRUE is the default choice, it is optional.

```
SortByValue(unitTitlesList, unitTimesList)
```

12. Sort multiple lists together.

a) The problem with the last two sorts is that one list is sorted without the other. Therefore, now the titles and times do not match. If you do any sort on one list and not the other, you will lose the relevance of the two lists. Let's look at how you can sort one list and keep the other list's values matched to the first list. Say, for example, you wish to put the *unitTitlesList* in alphanumeric order and sort the *unitTimesList* so that the times still match the intended units.

b) Return to the flowline and drag and drop the *Application* Map icon below the *Sort Multiple Lists A -> Z* Calculation icon. See figure 25-18.

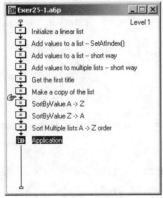

Fig. 25-18. Position of the Application Map icon below the Sort Multiple Lists A -> Z *order Calculation icon.*

c) Double click on the *Sort Multiple Lists A -> Z* Calculation icon. You will see the following code:

```
SortByValue(unitTitlesList, unitTimesList, TRUE)
```

d) The *SortByValue* function sorts the list *unitTitlesList* in alphanumeric order as the last parameter is set to TRUE, and shuffles around the *unitTimesList* to keep in step with the *unitTitlesList* list.

e) To stop the other sorts from confusing the results, drag and drop both *SortByValue* icons below the *Application* Map icon. See figure 25-19.

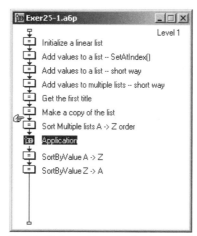

Fig. 25-19. Reposition the *Application Map* icon below the Sort Multiple Lists A -> Z order *Calculation* icon.

f) Restart the application. See figure 25-20.

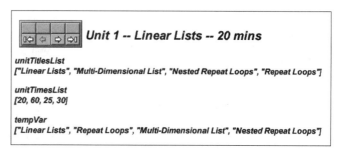

Fig. 25-20. Results of the Sort Multiple Lists A -> Z order *function*.

g) Note how the list *unitTitlesList* is sorted in alphanumeric order and the list *unitTimesList* has been rearranged so that the correct times refer to the correct units (e.g., *Linear Lists* is still 20 and *Repeat Loops* is still 30).

Guided Tour 25B: Property Lists

Description

Imagine you wish to store someone's log-in details. If you use a linear list you could store their first name in position 1, second name in position 2, job title in position 3, and password in position 4. Without looking at the last sentence, if all this were stored in a linear list *userInformationList*, what would be the value of *userInformationList[3]*? If this piece of code were halfway through the program, you might well forget if in position 3 you were storing the password or the job title.

This problem gets much worse when you have many lists with many values. The solution to this is to use a property list. With a property list, if you wish to store or retrieve a user's password, all you do is use *userInformationPropList[#password]*. All individual values can be assigned a property; for example, as *#firstName*, *#lastName*, and *#jobTitle*. If you are using many strings, using property lists makes the code much more readable. In this exercise you will:

- *Learn how to create a property list*
- *Add values to a property list*
- *Get values from a property list*
- *Sort property lists*

Step-by-Step Instructions

Let's take a look at the exercise in its completed state and then experiment with the application to learn about property lists.

 CD-ROM

1. Select File | Open and locate the *Practice* folder on the companion CD-ROM. Open this folder and you will see a number of chapter folders. Open the *Chapter25* folder and locate and double click on the file named *Exer25-2*.

2. The *Exer25-2* file should now appear in your copy of Authorware. See figure 25-21.

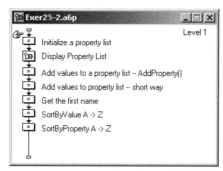

Fig. 25-21. Flowline of Exer25-2.

3.   Each Calculation icon is another command you will learn for controlling the list. The *Display Property List* Map icon simply shows the output of the Calculation icons and then stops at this position so that the Calculation icons underneath do not operate. Go through each Calculation icon to discover what it does.

4.   Initialize a property list.

    a)   Double click on the first icon, *Initialize a property list.* You will see the following code:

```
userInformationPropList := [:]
```

    b)   This is how you initialize a property list; basically, by assigning a variable to a new property list. Note the insertion of a colon to denote a property list rather than a normal linear list.

    c)   Close this icon and restart the application. See figure 25-22.

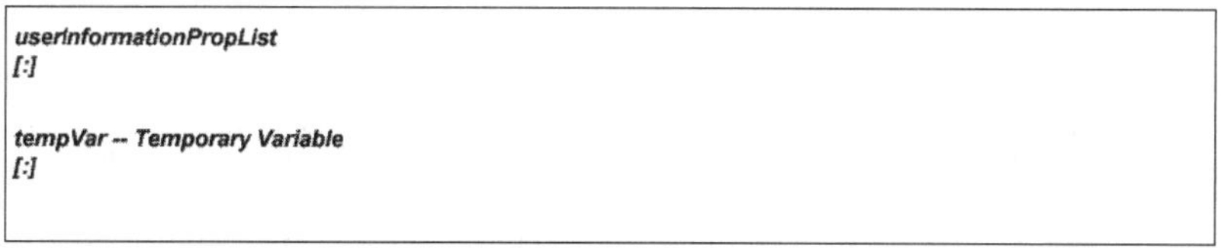

> *userInformationPropList*
> *[:]*
>
> *tempVar -- Temporary Variable*
> *[:]*

Fig. 25-22. Results of the initialized property list.

    d)   Note that both the *userInformationPropList* and *tempVar* are new lists. *tempVar* is set to a new property list in the Initial Values setting in the Variables dialog box.

5.   Add values/data to a property.

    a)   Return to the flowline and drag and drop the *Display Property List* Map icon below the *Add values to a property list – AddProperty()* Calculation icon. See figure 25-23.

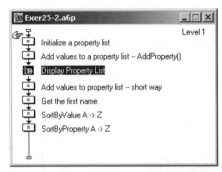

Fig. 25-23. Flowline position of the Display Property List Map icon.

b) Double click on the *Add values to a property list – AddProperty()* Calculation icon. You will see the following code:

```
AddProperty( userInformationPropList, #firstName,
"James")

AddProperty( userInformationPropList, #lastName,
"Brown")

AddProperty( userInformationPropList, #jobTitle,
"Godfather of Soul")

AddProperty( userInformationPropList, #password,
"reality")
```

c) This is the "long" way of assigning data to a property list. The function *AddProperty()* has three parameters. The first is the list to assign the data to, the second is the property, and the third the data itself.

d) Close this icon and restart the application. See figure 25-24.

---

userInformationPropList
[#firstName:"James", #lastName:"Brown", #jobTitle:"Godfather of Soul", #password:"reality"]

tempVar -- Temporary Variable
[:]

Fig. 25-24. Results of the AddProperty function.

e) You can now see the format of the property list *userInformationPropList*.

6. Add values/data to a property.

a) Return to the flowline and drag and drop the *Display Property List* Map icon below the *Add values to a property list – short way* Calculation icon. See figure 25-25.

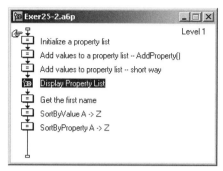

Fig. 25-25. Flowline position of the Display Property List Map icon under the Short Way Calculation icon.

b) Double click on the *Add values to a property list – short way* Calculation icon. You will see the following code:

```
userInformationPropList[#firstName] := "James"

userInformationPropList[#lastName] := "Brown"

userInformationPropList[#jobTitle] := "Godfather of
Soul"

userInformationPropList[#password] := "reality"
```

c) This is the "short" way of assigning data to a property list. The list and property are specified on the left, and the value to be assigned on the right. This is the most commonly used method.

d) Close this icon and restart the application. See figure 25-26.

---

userInformationPropList
[#firstName:"James", #lastName:"Brown", #jobTitle:"Godfather of Soul", #password:"reality"]

tempVar -- Temporary Variable
[:]

Fig. 25-26. Results of the populated Property List.

e) You can see that the format of the property list *userInformationPropList* is the same as before.

7. Get values from a property list.
   a) Return to the flowline and drag and drop the *Display Property List* Map icon below the *Get the first name* Calculation icon. See figure 25-27.

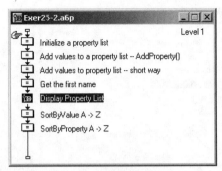

Fig. 25-27. *Flowline position of the* **Display Property List** *Map icon under the* **Get the first name** *Calculation icon.*

b) Double click on the *Get the first name* Calculation icon. You will see the following code:

```
tempVar:=PropertyAtIndex(userInformationPropList,
#firstName)

-- or

tempVar := userInformationPropList[#firstName]
```

c) As there are two ways to assign a value, so there are two ways to retrieve these values. In most cases you will want to use the latter, shorter method, in which *tempVar* is assigned the property *#firstName* from the list *userInformationPropList*.

d) Close this icon and restart the application. See figure 25-28.

```
userInformationPropList
[#firstName:"James", #lastName:"Brown", #jobTitle:"Godfather of Soul", #password:"reality"]


tempVar -- Temporary Variable
James
```

Fig. 25-28. *Results of the* **Get the first name** *function*

e) Here you can see that the variable *tempVar* is assigned the *#firstName*, which is *James*.

8. Sort by value.
    a) As property lists have both properties and values, there are two ways to sort these lists, either by the values or by the properties. Here you will first sort by the values.
    b) Return to the flowline and drag and drop the *Display Property List* Map icon below the *SortByValue A -> Z* Calculation icon. See figure 25-29.

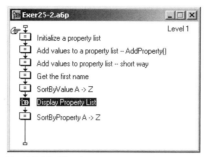

Fig. 25-29. *Flowline position of the* **Display Property List** *Map icon under the* **SortByValue A -> Z** *Calculation icon.*

    c)   Double click on the *SortByValue A -> Z* Calculation icon. You will see the following code:

```
SortByValue( userInformationPropList, TRUE)
```

    d)   Note the two parameters. The first is the list to sort and the latter is the order, in this case alphanumerically.

    e)   Close this icon and restart the application. See figure 25-30.

---

userInformationPropList
[#lastName:"Brown", #jobTitle:"Godfather of Soul", #firstName:"James", #password:"reality"]

tempVar -- Temporary Variable
James

Fig. 25-30. *Results of the* **SortByValue** *function.*

    f)   Here you can see that the property list is sorted by the values in alphanumerical order: *Brown, Godfather of Soul, James,* and *reality*.

9.   Sort by property.

    a)   Return to the flowline and drag and drop the *Display Property List* Map icon below the *SortByProperty A -> Z* Calculation icon. See figure 25-31.

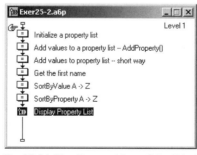

Fig. 25-31. *Flowline position of the* **Display Property List** *Map icon under the* **SortByProperty A -> Z** *Calculation icon.*

b) Double click on the *SortByProperty A -> Z* Calculation icon. You will see the following code:

```
SortByProperty( userInformationPropList, TRUE)
```

c) Note the two parameters. The first is the list to sort and the latter is the order, in this case alphanumerically.

d) Close this icon and restart the application. See figure 25-32.

---

userInformationPropList
[#firstName:"James", #jobTitle:"Godfather of Soul", #lastName:"Brown", #password:"reality"]

tempVar -- Temporary Variable
James

Fig. 25-32. Results of the SortByProperty function.

e) Here you can see that the property list is sorted by the properties in alphanumerical order: *#firstName*, *#jobTitle*, *#lastName*, and *#password*.

Guided Tour 25C: Multidimensional Lists and Arrays

Description

You should now be comfortable with lists and property lists. Now let's say you have 16 users and each takes five tests. You could use 16 lists and a user name list. Well why not use a list of lists? This is all a multidimensional list is, commonly referred to as an array. This way you can store a very large amount of information in a single variable.

You can picture an array easily by imagining a table. Think of the columns being the first names and test results and the rows being the users. (See figure 25-33.) In this exercise you will:

• *Learn how to create an array*

• *Add values to an array*

• *Get values from an array*

·TiP·

Just as in linear lists, if you were to have multiple property lists and wished to sort two without losing the order of one relative to the other, you could use the extra parameter in the *SortByValue* or *SortByProperty* functions (e.g., *SortByValue(userInformationPropList, userInformationCheckList , and TRUE)*).

User	Results1	Results2	Results3	Results4	Results5
Jennie	36	66	63	12	35
Myles	20	4	80	87	78
Jamil	4	55	63	76	38
Stefan	61	78	75	61	53
Joe	47	43	94	57	84
Jeff	17	35	89	52	14
Dan	57	35	41	74	68
Tom	4	68	10	88	51
Vickie	81	54	28	30	89
Christian	51	10	76	55	14
Erik	16	16	4	87	38
Ron	78	55	16	75	71
Mike	0	92	5	71	14
Mark	55	7	1	76	23
Chris	69	22	91	46	25
Wade	24	53	35	79	29

Fig. 25-33. Array of results data.

Step-by-Step Instructions

Let's take a look at the exercise in its completed state and then experiment with the application to learn about property lists.

CD-ROM

1. Select File | Open and locate the *Practice* folder on the companion CD-ROM. Open this folder and you will see a number of chapter folders. Open the *Chapter25* folder and locate and double click on the file named *Exer25-3*.

2. The *Exer25-3* file should now appear in your copy of Authorware. See figure 25-34.

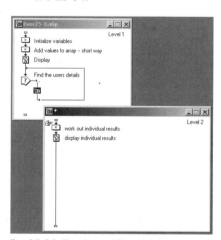

Fig. 25-34. Flowline of Exer25-3.

3. This application sets up a list with 16 user names and an array of five quiz results for each of the users, as in the table in figure 25-33. Then you can enter a number and the details of this individual user will be extracted from the array.

4. Run through the flowline.
   a) On the flowline, double click on the Calculation icon *Initialize variables*.
   b) The code now reads as follows:

   ```
   passMark := 50

   userNameList := []

   userInformationArray := [[]]
   ```

   c) The first line sets a variable for a pass mark, the second is a linear list, and the third line is the initialization of a multidimensional list (in this case a 2D array).
   d) Close this Calculation icon and open the *Add values to array – short way* Calculation icon. The code will read as follows:

   ```
   userNameList := [ "Jennie","Myles","Jamil",
   "Stefan","Joe","Jeff","Dan","Tom","Vickie",
   "Christian","Erik","Ron","Mike","Mark","Chris","Wade" ]

   userInformationArray[1] := [ 36,66,63,12,35 ]

   userInformationArray[2] := [ 20,4,80,87,78 ]

   userInformationArray[3] := [ 4,55,63,76,38 ]

   userInformationArray[4] := [ 61,78,75,61,53 ]

   userInformationArray[5] := [ 47,43,94,57,84 ]

   userInformationArray[6] := [ 17,35,89,52,14 ]

   userInformationArray[7] := [ 57,35,41,74,68 ]

   userInformationArray[8] := [ 4,68,10,88,51 ]

   userInformationArray[9] := [ 81,54,28,30,89 ]

   userInformationArray[10] := [ 51,10,76,55,14 ]

   userInformationArray[11] := [ 16,16,4,87,38 ]

   userInformationArray[12] := [ 78,55,16,75,71 ]

   userInformationArray[13] := [ 0,92,5,71,14 ]

   userInformationArray[14] := [ 55,7,1,76,23 ]

   userInformationArray[15] := [ 69,22,91,46,25 ]

   userInformationArray[16] := [ 25,53,35,79,29 ]
   ```

e) The *userNameList* is a linear list with all 16 user names. The *userInformationArray* is what you have to concentrate on here. Compare this to the table in figure 25-33 to see how alike this is to a table of data. Each line is a linear list. The variable *userInformationArray* is a list of these lists. The *userInformation* variable will look as follows:

```
[[ 36,66,63,12,35 ] , [ 20,4,80,87,78 ] ,
[ 4,55,63,76,38 ] ….. [ 25,53,35,79,29 ]]
```

f) Note that the lists are enclosed in another pair of square brackets to denote that they are themselves in a list. To set or get the values, use a format similar to a linear list, with one more parameter. The following are examples:

```
userInformationArray[1,1] := 36

userInformationArray[1,2] := 66

userInformationArray[1,3] := 63

userInformationArray[2,1] := 20

userInformationArray[2,4] := 87
```

g) You can see that the first number is the row and the second is the column.

h) Close the Calculation icon and open the Map icon * attached to the Interaction icon *Find the users details*. See figure 25-35.

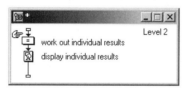

*Fig. 25-35. Flowline of *.*

i) This code gets executed when you enter a number from 1 to 16 as the application is running. Double click on the Calculation icon *Work out individual results*. The code will read as follows:

```
if EntryText > 0 & EntryText < 17 then
  name := userNameList[EntryText]
  result1 := userInformationArray[EntryText,1]
  result2 := userInformationArray[EntryText,2]
  result3 := userInformationArray[EntryText,3]
  result4 := userInformationArray[EntryText,4]
  result5 := userInformationArray[EntryText,5]
end if
```

j) The *if* statement ensures that you have entered a valid number. The variable name is assigned the value of the user's name. For example, say you entered 2 into the *entrytext*. The name should be *Myles*.

k) Examine the following line:

```
result4 := userInformationArray[EntryText, 4]
```

If *entrytext* is 2, the line will read as follows:

```
result4 := userInformationArray[2, 4]
```

l) If you refer to the table, you see that the result of row 2, column 4, is 87.

5. Run the application.

a) Restart the application. See figure 25-36.

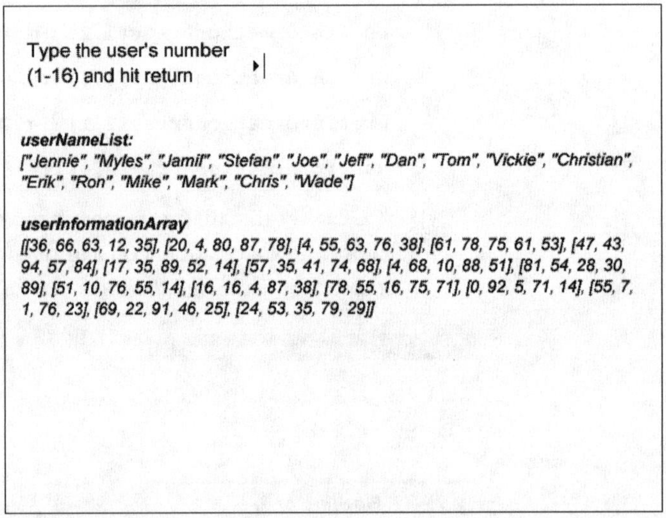

Type the user's number ▸|
(1-16) and hit return

userNameList:
["Jennie", "Myles", "Jamil", "Stefan", "Joe", "Jeff", "Dan", "Tom", "Vickie", "Christian", "Erik", "Ron", "Mike", "Mark", "Chris", "Wade"]

userInformationArray
[[36, 66, 63, 12, 35], [20, 4, 80, 87, 78], [4, 55, 63, 76, 38], [61, 78, 75, 61, 53], [47, 43, 94, 57, 84], [17, 35, 89, 52, 14], [57, 35, 41, 74, 68], [4, 68, 10, 88, 51], [81, 54, 28, 30, 89], [51, 10, 76, 55, 14], [16, 16, 4, 87, 38], [78, 55, 16, 75, 71], [0, 92, 5, 71, 14], [55, 7, 1, 76, 23], [69, 22, 91, 46, 25], [24, 53, 35, 79, 29]]

Fig. 25-36. Results of the **userInformationArray.**

b) The two variables you see straight away are the *userNameList* of all user names and the array *userInformationArray* containing all results.

c) Type in 2 and press Enter. See figure 25-37.

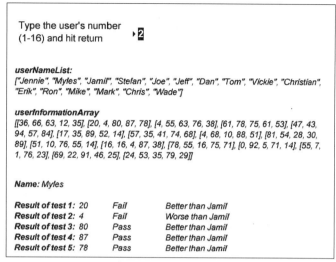

Fig. 25-37. Results of the **userInformationArray** *sorted by user.*

d) If you look near the bottom, at *Result of test 4*, you see that the answer is 87!

e) In this application, the fail and pass scores are below or above the *passMark* variable. There is also a comparison. Open the Variables dialog box in Authorware and find the variable *betterThan*. See figure 25-38.

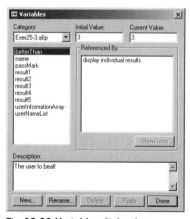

Fig. 25-38. Variables dialog box.

f) Change the initial value to 1. Click on Done. Restart the application.

g) Type in 4 and press Enter. See figure 25-39.

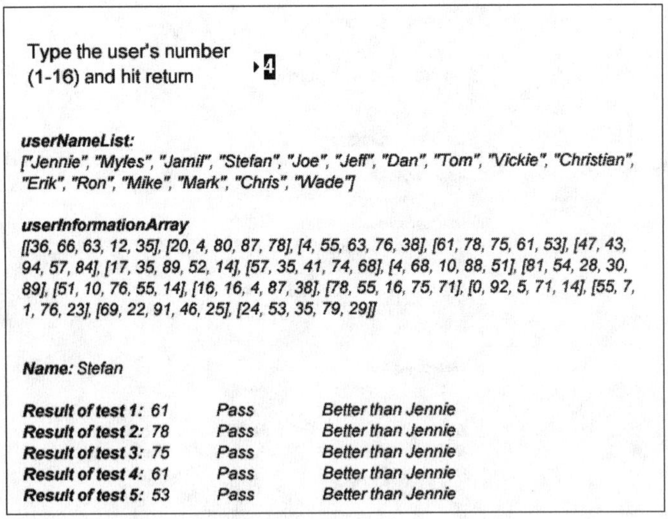

Type the user's number
(1-16) and hit return ▸4

userNameList:
["Jennie", "Myles", "Jamil", "Stefan", "Joe", "Jeff", "Dan", "Tom", "Vickie", "Christian", "Erik", "Ron", "Mike", "Mark", "Chris", "Wade"]

userInformationArray
[[36, 66, 63, 12, 35], [20, 4, 80, 87, 78], [4, 55, 63, 76, 38], [61, 78, 75, 61, 53], [47, 43, 94, 57, 84], [17, 35, 89, 52, 14], [57, 35, 41, 74, 68], [4, 68, 10, 88, 51], [81, 54, 28, 30, 89], [51, 10, 76, 55, 14], [16, 16, 4, 87, 38], [78, 55, 16, 75, 71], [0, 92, 5, 71, 14], [55, 7, 1, 76, 23], [69, 22, 91, 46, 25], [24, 53, 35, 79, 29]]

Name: Stefan

Result of test 1: 61	Pass	Better than Jennie
Result of test 2: 78	Pass	Better than Jennie
Result of test 3: 75	Pass	Better than Jennie
Result of test 4: 61	Pass	Better than Jennie
Result of test 5: 53	Pass	Better than Jennie

Fig. 25-39. Stefan is on top of Jennie in every situation.

h) You can see that Stefan is better than Jennie in every test. You can see how using multidimensional lists is so powerful. By changing one variable you can alter the functionality of the application.

You have used a two-dimensional array. It is very easy now to make a list of two-dimensional arrays. From this you would get a three-dimensional array. Authorware allows you to have up to 10 dimensions. The following is an example of a three-dimensional array:

my3dArray := [[[1,2],[3,4]],[[5,6],[7,8]]]

If you now say *tempVar := my3dArray[2,1,2]*, you would work it out as follows:

• *The first number is a 2, so you are looking at the second element in the topmost array: [[5,6],[7,8]].*

• *The second number is a 1, so you are looking at the first element: [5,6].*

• *The third number is a 2, so you are looking at the second element: 6.*

Practice Exercise 25-1:
Creating a Student Progress List

Description

This is a universal example of an array. The array almost every tutorial will have is of course the "how much of the course is completed" array. A simple course may consist of units, each unit incorporating pages. Say, for example, you have five pages. You can keep a record of whether or not a user has completed the pages using an array of Boolean numbers (e.g., [1,1,1,0,0]). In this instance, the user has completed three of the pages and has not completed the last two. If there are four units, you will have a 2D array, as follows:

[[1,1,1,0,0], [0,0,0,0,0], [0,0,0,0,0], [0,0,0,0,0]]

From this array you can see that the user has completed the first three pages of unit 1 only. All other units have not been attempted. In this exercise you will:

- *Build an example course*
- *Use the array idea to keep track of a user in a course*

Take a look

Before beginning the exercise, let's take a look at the exercise in its completed state so that you can clearly see what it is you are about to build.

1. Select File | Open and locate the *Practice* folder on the companion CD-ROM. Open this folder and you will see a number of chapter folders. Open the *Chapter25* folder and locate and double click on the file named *Exer25-4*.

2. The *Exer25-4* file should now appear in your copy of Authorware. Select Control | Restart or click on the Restart button on the toolbar to play the file from the top of the flowline. Note the following properties of this completed exercise:

   - *Clicking through the units and pages, be sure to concentrate on the pagesCompleted variable and see which element in the array is being updated.*

Storyboard: On Screen

Figure 25-40 shows what the finished question will look like on screen.

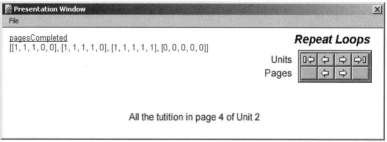

Fig. 25-40. Completed exercise.

Storyboard: Behind the Scenes

Figure 25-41 shows the level 1 and level 2 flowlines (with all icons, their placement, and their names) as they should look when you are finished with this exercise.

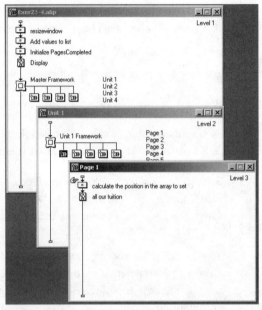

Fig. 25-41. Completed level 1 and level 2 flowlines.

Step-by-Step Instructions

Go Solo

1. Open a new file for this exercise. Select File | New | File. Close the two Knowledge Object dialog windows that open by clicking on the X in the upper right-hand corner. You should now be looking at a blank flowline.

2. Save the file on your hard drive by selecting File | Save. Use the Scroll window to locate the *SaveWork* directory on your computer. Type in the name *Exer25-4* and click on OK.

3. Initialize and set up the variables.
    a) Drag a Calculation icon onto the flowline and name it *resizewindow*. See figure 25-42.

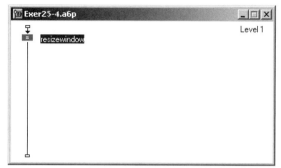

Fig. 25-42. *Resizing the Presentation window.*

b) Double click on the Calculation icon and type in the following code. See figure 25-43.

```
ResizeWindow(640,180)
```

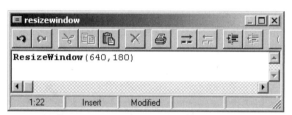

Fig. 25-43. *Resizing the presentation window Calculation icon.*

c) Close and save the *resizewindow* Calculation icon. Drag another Calculation icon below the previous Calculation icon and name it *Add values to list*. See figure 25-44.

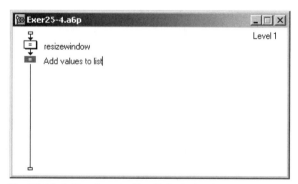

Fig. 25-44. Add values to list *Calculation icon.*

d) Type the following code into the icon. See figure 25-45.

```
-- Populate the title list
unitTitlesList[1] := "Linear Lists"
unitTitlesList[2] := "Repeat Loops"
unitTitlesList[3] := "Multi-Dimensional List"
unitTitlesList[4] := "Nested Repeat Loops"
```

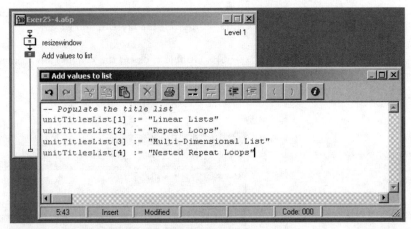

Fig. 25-45. Add values to list *Calculation icon.*

e) Close and save the Calculation icon.
f) When the New Variable dialog box pops up, type in *initial value as []* and type in a description. See figure 25-46.

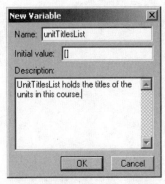

Fig. 25-46. New Variable dialog box.

g) Click on OK. Drag another Calculation icon onto the flowline and name it *Initialize PageCompleted.* Double click on the Calculation icon and type in the following code. See figure 25-47.

```
pagesCompleted := Array( 0, 4, 5)
```

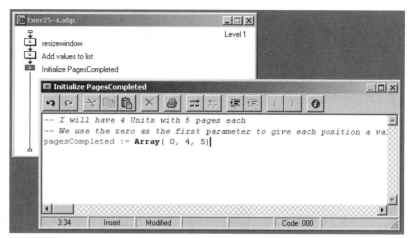

Fig. 25-47. **Initialize PageCompleted** *Calculation icon.*

h) Close and save the Calculation icon. In the New Variable dialog box, type in *[[]]* for the initial value and type in a description. See figure 25-48.

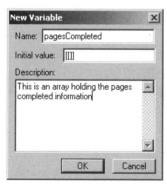

Fig. 25-48. Revised New Variable dialog box.

i) Click on OK. Drag a Framework icon to the flowline and name it *Master Framework*.

j) Drag a Display icon above the Framework icon and name it *Display*. Type the following in the top right-hand corner.

```
{unitTitlesList[ CurrentPageNum@"Master Framework"]}
```

k) Type the following in the top left-hand corner.

```
{pagesCompleted}
```

l)   Type in the labels *Units* and *Pages*. The final screen should look like that shown in figure 25-49.

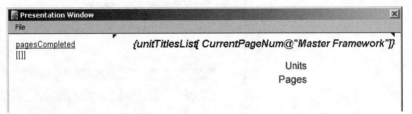

Fig. 25-49. Presentation window at authoring time.

m)   Close the Display icon and then double click on the *Master Framework* icon. See figure 25-50.

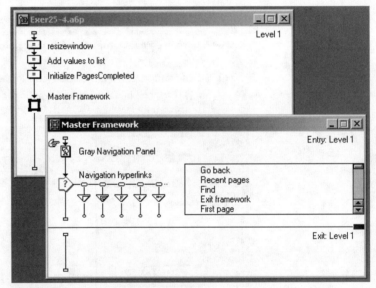

Fig. 25-50. Master Framework icon.

4.   Set up the navigation.

a)   In the *Master Framework* icon, delete the *Go Back* Navigate icon, the *Recent Pages* Navigate icon, the *Find* icon, and the *Exit Framework* Navigate icon.

b)   Double click on the Previous Page button to open the button properties. Click on the Response tab.

c)   In the Active If field, type the following code, so that the user cannot click to access a page before the first page. See figure 25-51.

```
CurrentPageNum@"Master Framework" > 1
```

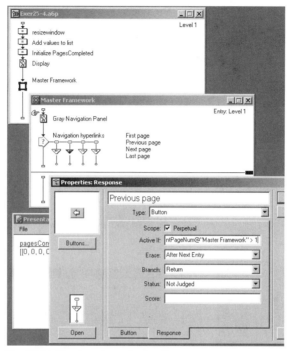

Fig. 25-51. Previous page properties.

d) Click on OK. Double click on the Next Page button to access the properties. Click on the Response tab and type the following:

```
CurrentPageNum@"Master Framework" < PageCount@"Master
Framework"
```

e) Click on OK. Close the *Master Framework* icon.

f) Drag a new Framework icon under the *Master Framework* icon. It will automatically group itself as a Map icon. See figure 25-52.

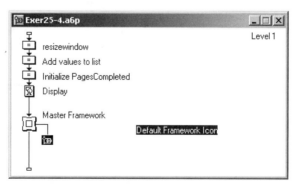

Fig. 25-52. New subframework.

g) Make the pages. Rename the default Framework icon *Unit 1*. Double click on the *Unit 1* icon and rename the Framework icon from *Untitled* to *Unit 1 Framework*. Double click on this Framework icon. Delete all Navigate icons attached to the Interaction icon except the *Previous Page* and *Next Page* icons. See figure 25-53.

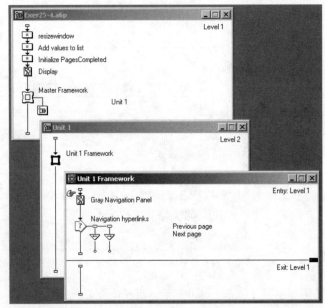

Fig. 25-53. Unit 1 *Framework icon.*

h) Delete the *Gray Navigation Panel* Display icon. Double click on the Previous Page button response symbol to open the button properties. Click on the Response tab and type the following in the Active If field.

```
CurrentPageNum@"Unit 1 Framework" > 1
```

i) Click on OK. Double click on the Next Page button to open the button properties. Click on the Response tab and type the following in the Active If field.

```
CurrentPageNum@"Unit 1 Framework" < PageCount@"Unit 1
Framework"
```

j) These will ensure that you cannot overrun the units by disabling the Previous and Next buttons at the first and last chapters, respectively.

k) Close the *Unit 1* Framework icon. Drag a new Map icon beneath the *Unit 1* Framework icon and name it *Page 1*. Open this new Map icon by double clicking on it and then drag a new Calculation icon into it.

Rename this *Calculate the position in the array to set.* Double click on this Map icon to open it and type in the following code. See figure 25-54.

```
pagesCompleted[ CurrentPageNum@"Master Framework",
CurrentPageNum@"Unit 1 Framework"] := 1
```

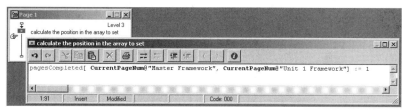

Fig. 25-54. Calculating the position.

l) This code assigns a 1 to the 2D array *pagesCompleted* at *unit number, page number.* Take a minute now to study this line so that you know how it is functioning. Refer to the section on multidimensional arrays if necessary.

m) Close and save the Calculation icon. Drag a new Display icon under the Calculation icon and name it *All our tuition.* In a "real" course this is where you could place course material. See figure 25-55.

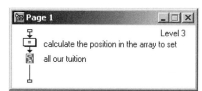

Fig. 25-55. Course material.

n) Double click on the new Display icon *All our tuition* and type in the following code. See figure 25-56.

```
All the tuition in page {CurrentPageNum@"Unit 1
Framework"} of Unit {CurrentPageNum@"Master
Framework"}
```

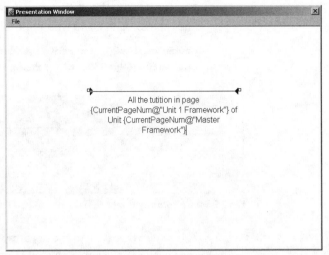

Fig. 25-56. Embedded variables used to display the current page number.

o) Close the Display icon. The only thing left to do with the navigation is to realign the unit selection buttons. To do this, return to the level I flowline. Double click on the *Master Framework* icon. Double click on the *Gray Navigation Panel* icon. Close the Display icon. Press Shift and double click on the Interaction icon *Navigation hyperlinks*. See figure 25-57.

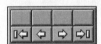

Fig. 25-57. Gray Navigation Panel icon.

p) Click the leftmost mouse button once. Using the Up Arrow key, move the button up exactly 22 pixels. See figure 25-58.

Fig. 25-58. Gray Navigation Panel icon edited.

q) Repeat step *p* for all buttons. See figure 25-59.

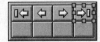

Fig. 25-59. Gray Navigation Panel icon edited.

r) Close the Navigation Hyperlinks interaction display. Return to the level 1 flowline.

5. Create the pages.

a) Double click on the *Unit 1* Map icon. Select the *Page 1* icon attached to the *Unit 1* Framework icon. Copy this icon by pressing Ctrl + C. Set the Paste Hand cursor to the right of this icon and press Ctrl + V. Repeat this another three times. Rename the icons so that they read *Page 1*, *Page 2*, *Page 3*, *Page 4*, and *Page 5*. See figure 25-60.

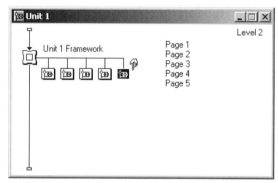

Fig. 25-60. Pages created.

b) Close the *Unit 1* Map icon so that you are back at the level 1 flowline. Select the *Unit 1* Map icon and copy it by pressing Ctrl + C. Set the Paste Hand cursor to the right of this icon and press Ctrl + V. Repeat this another two times. Rename the icons so that they read *Unit 1*, *Unit 2*, *Unit 3*, and *Unit 4*. See figure 25-61.

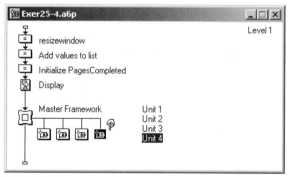

Fig. 25-61. Units created.

c) Double click on the *Unit 2* Map icon. Authorware has renamed the Framework icons so that they all have unique titles. This is necessary because the Framework icons are references (with "@" symbols) so the titles must be unique. By default, Authorware has merely added a number to the end of each title. Rename *Unit 1 Framework2* to *Unit 2 Framework*. Close the *Unit 2* icon. See figure 25-62.

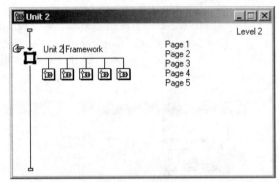

Fig. 25-62. Renaming the unit Framework icons.

d) Repeat the renaming for the Framework icons in units 3 and 4.

6. Restart the application.

Summary

• *List variables are specifically designed to store multiple instances of data, incorporating easy methods for populating and retrieving data.*

• *Lists allow you to group similar data into a single variable.*

• *A linear list stores the values in a variable from left to right by position number.*

• *Property lists store data as a property identifier and a value. Property lists differ from other lists in that you can assign a distinct number, character, or name as the property identifier for storing a value within the property list.*

• *A multidimensional list is a list of lists, commonly referred to as an array. This way you can store a very large amount of information in a single variable.*

• *In this chapter you learned about linear lists for storing and sorting values; created and used custom linear, property, and multidimensional lists; and built a list capable of holding student progress information.*

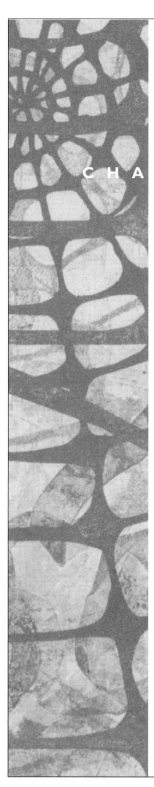

C H A P T E R

26

Dynamic

Structures

Introduction

When you develop your first few Authorware pieces, you are usually more concerned with just getting everything to work than with making models (Chapter 20) you can reuse on the next project or with expediting the process with subroutines (Chapter 23). As you create more projects, however, you start realizing that there are many things that can be re-purposed between projects. As you have more success with Authorware, the demand on you to produce more projects increases. To streamline your process, you might start using models and Knowledge Objects. Working with external content to update files easily is a great trick as well. Ultimately, you will need a template you can supply to other people (such as subject matter experts in your team). This allows others to simply start plugging content into the template without having to worry about setting up navigation and GUI structures.

The ideal is that you can give a template to a beginning Authorware developer (conformable with the skills outlined in chapters 1 through 10) and she can start adding content to the program. The program's navigation, GUI, titling, and tracking would already be in place, and could be reused for as many new programs as you need. This type of template integration is the aim of the Application Knowledge Object (see Appendix D), but most of the time you can create your own template without the need for an elaborate wizard/Knowledge Object interface.

The aim of this chapter is to show you the strategies for creating a dynamically updating navigational structure. This template can be saved and reused anytime you start a new project. Starting with the "master framework" concept (Chapter 16), you can use calculated navigation to build a navigation structure that works no matter how many pages or topics are added to a course. In this chapter you will explore:

- *The parent and child relationship of icons*
- *How icon functions work*
- *How to use icon functions to produce on-screen titles*
- *What a dynamic structure is*
- *What types of icons constitute a dynamic flowline structure*
- *How to create a dynamically generated menu*
- *Dynamic page navigation*

Exploring the Parent/Child Relationship of Icons

There is an entire category of functions and variables, called "icons," that depend on and return information about the parent/child relationship. The use of "parent" and "children" functions is perhaps the least understood topic in Authorware, and potentially the most powerful concept you can learn on your way to becoming an Authorware guru. Practical use of the functions is not intuitive without good examples. Before using calculated navigation icons, you must have a working knowledge of the parent/child relationship between icons in Authorware.

Simple Parent/Child Relationships

A Map icon that has any icons in it is a parent to those icons. Any icon in the Map icon is a child of that Map icon. The first icon in the Map icon is the first child, the second icon is the second child, and so on. Children are ordered from top to bottom in Map icons. The top icon in a Map icon is the first child of the Map icon, and the last icon of the Map icon is the last child. Figure 26-1 shows a simple animation introduction sequence. Note that the Map icon is named *Parent* and that the subsequent children are also labeled.

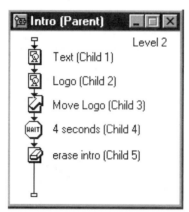

Fig. 26-1. Map icon as a parent.

There are no "grandparents" or "grandchildren" in Authorware. The term *grandparent* is simply not used in Authorware. If a parent icon has a Map icon inside it, that Map icon is a child, but the icons inside that Map icon are children only of the Map icon; they are not grandchildren of the first level. Figure 26-2 shows a Display icon as a child of the Map icon labeled *Parent*.

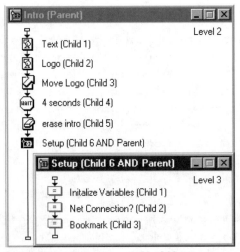

Fig. 26-2. Display icon as child of Map icon.

Branching Icons

Map icons are not the only parent icons. Branching icons such as interactions, decisions, sounds, and digital movie icons are also parents to any icons attached to them. The difference between Map icon parents and Branching icon parents is the ordering. Children to Branching icon parents are ordered left to right instead of top to bottom. See figure 26-3.

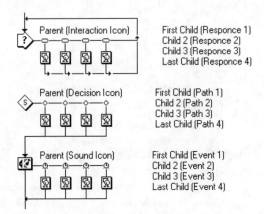

Fig. 26-3. Various Branching icons with attached children.

Framework Icons

Framework icons follow the same relationship. The Framework icon is the parent and the attached pages are children of that framework. You might ask, what about icons inside the Entry and Exit panes of the framework? Great question. These are obviously children of the Framework icon as well, but if you were talking about the first child of a framework would you be talking about the first page or the first icon inside the Entry pane? The answer is simple: in Authorware there is a *Flag* argument used when dealing with frameworks. In figure 26-4 you see that the pages of a Framework icon are *Flag = 0*, any icons in the Entry pane are *Flag = 1*, and the Exit pane is *Flag = 2*.

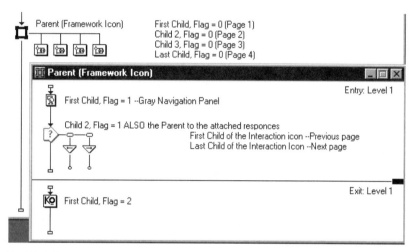

Fig. 26-4. Framework icon showing page and Entry and Exit pane flag number assignments.

Guided Tour 26A: Parent/Child Functions

There is a category of Authorware system functions called the Icon category. These functions take advantage of the inherent parent/child relationship between Authorware icons. Take a minute and open the Functions window and read some of the descriptions for the functions. As you read these descriptions you will see countless references to the *IconID* of various icons. Nearly all of these functions return the value of an *IconID*. See figure 26-5.

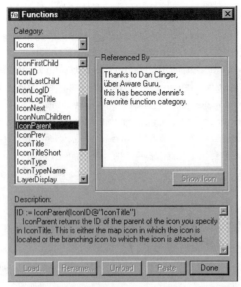

Fig. 26-5. Functions window showing the Icon category.

Take a Look

1. Examine the syntax of the function *IconParent*.
   a) Open a new Authorware file.
   b) Open the Functions window and look at the description for the *IconParent* function.
   c) Note that the first line of the description demonstrates the most common syntax for the function.

   ```
   ID := IconParent(IconID@"IconTitle")
   ```

Most commonly *IconParent* will return an *IconID* number (in Chapter 23 there is an overview of the *IconID* concept). Inside the parentheses you need to provide the function with an ID number of a specific icon. If you know the name of the icon, you can simply place the title inside the quotes and the function will determine the parent of that icon and return its ID number. See figure 26-6.

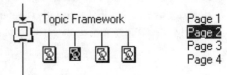

Fig. 26-6. Sample flowline.

·T/P·

The format that is usually used in *Icon* functions is: IconID@"IconTitle" The shortcut is to drop the IconID, as long as you keep the @ symbol. IconParent(@"IconTitle") will work just as well.

For example, examine the flowline in figure 26-6. Let's say the user was currently viewing page 2. If you wanted to get the *IconID* of the *Topic* Framework icon, you could enter the following code.

```
topicID := IconParent(IconID@"Page 2")
```

If you wanted to make this more dynamic, instead of typing *"Page 2"* in quotes you could use a variable (such as *CurrentPageID*) that returns the ID number of the page currently being viewed. This expression would read as follows:

```
topicID := IconParent(CurrentPageID)
```

The custom *topicID* variable would then contain the ID number of the *Topic* Framework icon, which is **65544**. (This number may be different in your copy of Authorware.) See figure 26-7.

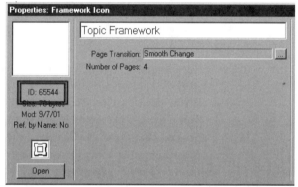

Fig. 26-7. Property dialog box for the Topic *Framework* icon, with ID number highlighted.

Guided Tour 26B:
Using Icon Functions for On-screen Titles

Take a Look

Let's look at a simple example of how the icon functions can streamline a simple master framework structure (Chapter 16).

CD-ROM

1. On the companion CD-ROM, locate the *Practice* folder for Chapter 26. Open this folder and open and double click on the file named *Exer26-1 – Icon Functions.a6p.* This file should now appear in your copy of Authorware.

2. Run the file. Note that this is the same master framework structure you were working on in chapters 16 and 18. It behaves the same way, but try

pausing the program and double clicking on the screen title at the top of the GUI.

    a)   Once you see the toolbox, select the Text tool and select the screen title. Note that the title is in fact an embedded variable. This Display icon's properties have been changed to Update Displayed Variables. See figure 26-8.

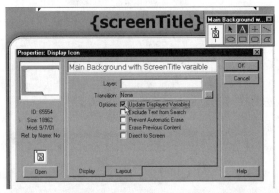

Fig. 26-8. Embedded screenTitle *variable on the main GUI background graphic.*

    b)   If you open the first Map icon (named *Main Menu*) attached to the *Master Framework* icon, you will see a Calculation icon named *Update Screen Title*. Within this Calculation icon you will see the string *"Main Menu"* assigned to the *screenTitle* variable that is embedded in the main background. See figure 26-9.

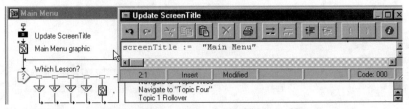

Fig. 26-9. The screenTitle *variable used in the* **Main Menu** *Map icon.*

With this method of updating the screen variable, you never have to worry about pixel shifts of your title again. In addition, if you want to change the color or font size of all titles in your piece, you simply employ this method once and these items are updated automatically. Anytime you need the screen to say something else, you would just drag a Calculation icon to the flowline and change what is inside the quotes. The downside is that you still have to go through the piece icon by icon and change what is inside the quotes. Let's look at the *Topic One* Map icon to see a slightly more stream-lined way of getting a screen title.

3. Open the Map icon *Topic One*.

    a) Note that the first icon inside this Map icon does not say *"Update Screen Title."* Instead, it reads as follows:

        ```
        screenTitle := "Topic One" --Icon Title method.
        ```

    b) Open the Calculation icon and you will see the following expression. See figure 26-10.

        ```
        EvalAssign(IconTitle)
        ```

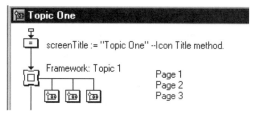

Fig. 26-10. **EvalAssign** *method of updating the* **screenTitle** *variable.*

This expression looks at the icon title and then evaluates the statement to see if it is a valid Authorware code expression. Because the syntax of the Calculation icon's title is accurate, the screen title updates on the GUI. With this method of updating the screen variable, all you have to do is change the text in the quotes of this icon. No more double clicking to open the Calculation icon. The downside is that you still have to go through the piece icon by icon and change what is inside the quotes. In addition, if there is a syntax error in the title, Authorware will not generate an error message. Instead, the title simply will not update. This seeming "shortcut" is ripe with peril.

4. Open the *Topic Two* Map icon.

    a) Note that the title of the first Calculation icon is as follows. See figure 26-11.

        ```
        Topic Two --Change the text before the "--"
        ```

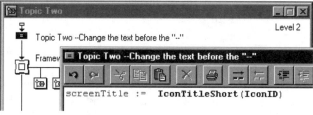

Fig. 26-11. **IconTitleShort( )** *method.*

    b) Inside the Calculation icon you will see the following expression.

```
screenTitle := IconTitleShort(IconID)
```

With this method of updating the screen variable, all you have to do is change the title of this icon. The function *IconTitleShort* has the added benefit that if it encounters the *rem* symbol ("--") it will ignore anything past that point. The downside is that you still have to go through the piece icon by icon and change the title. Note that the title *Topic Two* is already on the flowline (i.e., it is the name of the Map icon you are inside of). Let's look at the *Topic Three* Map icon to see if we can capitalize on this coincidence.

5. Open the *Topic Three* Map icon.
    a) Note that the Calculation icon is back to its most descriptive name, *Update Screen Title*. See figure 26-12.

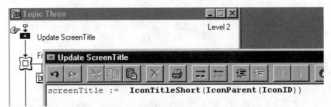

Fig. 26-12. **IconParent( )** *method; the most dynamic so far.*

    b) Inside the Calculation icon you will see the following multifunction statement.

```
screenTitle := IconTitleShort(IconParent(IconID))
```

This statement may look confusing at first, but just read it one element at a time and you will see its simplicity. First, start reading the innermost variable, *IconID*. This statement starts with the *IconID* number of the Calculation icon you are inside. Examine this icon's parent. Once Authorware's focus is on the *Parent* Map icon, you get the icon title of the Map icon, ignoring anything after the two dashes. That title is then saved to the custom variable *screenTitle*.

This statement is an example of what is meant by dynamic flowlines. This has great potential. Imagine that a developer simply drags a model for topic paging to the flowline, titles it, and the title appears on screen. The only downside here is that if someone were to delete this icon or place it inside a Map icon (adding another level of "parenting") this would not work.

6. Open the *Topic Four* Map icon to see one final improvement.
    a) Note that the Calculation icon is now gone altogether. How does the screen title get updated? Note the attached Calculation symbol on the Framework *Topic 4* icon. See figure 26-13.

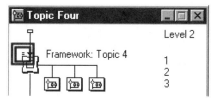

Fig. 26-13. Attached Calculation method.

> b) Open the attached Calculation icon (right-click on the Framework icon and select Calculation). Inside note the same expression you had in the previous, *Topic Three*, example, as follows:

```
screenTitle := IconTitleShort(IconParent(IconID))
```

The advantage of placing this expression as an attached Calculation icon is that it is more likely no other developer will accidentally erase it or place it inside a Map icon. The previous five examples show a nice progression of the logic behind the dynamic flowlines you will begin to examine in the following material.

Overview of Dynamic Structures

With the announcement of Authorware 4.0, the community was introduced to a new way of designing navigational structures. In Authorware 4.0 there were a series of templates that if used together could create a fully functional CBT. These templates were the precursors of the Application Knowledge Object released as part of Authorware 5.0. The templates relied on the following three things.

- *The Master Framework structure (Chapter 16)*

- *A repeat loop (Chapter 23) that would gather the icon ID numbers of all icons and save them to an array (Chapter 24)*

- *Calculated navigation based on the IconID array generated at the start of the program (this chapter)*

These templates allowed users to add and subtract topics and pages of content from the master framework, with the paging, bookmarking, and title functionality always working the same. This represented groundbreaking code in the Authorware community. The only problem with it was that it was so script/code intensive that it was indecipherable to most intermediate-level Authorware developers. These templates and the style of "diving" the flowline inspired a new philosophy for developing with Authorware. Just like the Framework icon had changed things in version 3.0, the "dive" and the concept of dynamic structures altered the way advanced Authorware users were building their structures.

To see a truly inspired example of diving the flowline, examine any of the "Show Me" files in your *Authorware 6* directory. In the flowline for every Show Me there is a red icon named *Run to View Documentation*. Attached to this Map icon is a Calculation icon. Open the Calculation icon and you will see a repeat loop structure that stores the ID number of various types of icons on the flowline, saves their titles to a list, and then sets the icons to *Movable := FALSE*.

Guided Tour 26C:
Examining a Dynamic Flowline Structure

Description

What makes this type of Authorware development so exciting is the flexibility you will begin to enjoy in your own development career. Creating these types of structures will finally employ all of the skills you have learned to this point. You will be setting up framework structures for organizing content, combining repeat loops and lists to compile a list of *IconID* numbers for navigation, and creating a list of topic titles that will constitute a main menu.

The code that makes this possible looks intimidating at first, but keep in mind that if you have been following this book in a linear order every concept covered in the following is old news to you. As you look at each icon and each line of code you will see the logic and ease of use of this system. You do not necessarily need a programming background to master these concepts. You will be employing the same logic you have since learning what an icon is and how to create simple interactions.

Undoubtedly, the best reason to embark on developing these dynamic structures is the time it will save you in the long run. If you can get all of your navigation and tracking to work regardless of how many topics you add to future projects, you can concentrate on other things, such as making the learner experience more interactive.

For the rest of this chapter you will be looking at one Authorware file found on the companion CD-ROM. This file is named *EX26-2 – Dynamic Structure.a6p*. This file represents one way of setting up a dynamically updatable Authorware file. This file may not cover all possible configurations and situations, but it does cover all of the concepts you will need to create your own dynamic templates.

Take a Look

Before beginning the exercise, let's take a look at the Authorware file you are going to learn about.

CD-ROM

1. On the companion CD-ROM, locate the *Practice* folder. Open this folder and you will see a number of chapter folders.

2. Copy the *Chapter26* folder to your working directory and locate the file named *Exer26-2 – Dynamic Structure.a6p*.

3. Double click on *Exer26-2 – Dynamic Structure.a6p*. This file should now appear in your copy of Authorware.

4. Select Save As to save this file to the working directory of your hard drive.

5. Click on the Restart button on the toolbar to play the file from the top of the flowline. Note the following properties of this sample file.

   - *The first screen you see is a main menu with three lessons from which the user can choose.*

   - *There is a title at the top of every screen.*

   - *There are page numbers that update on every topic screen.*

   - *Within each lesson are Next and Previous buttons that allow the user to page through the lesson.*

   - *There are page numbers at the Topic level.*

   - *There are two buttons that are always available on the left-hand side of the GUI.*

   - *The Global button for the Main Menu returns the user to the main menu from any lesson.*

   - *The Global button for quitting presents a dialog box for verifying that the user wants to exit the program.*

Storyboard: On Screen

Figures 26-14 and 26-15 show what the finished presentation will look like.

Main Menu

Topic One
Topic Two
Topic Three

Fig. 26-14. Completed main menu presentation on screen.

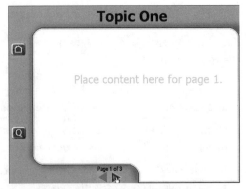

Fig. 26-15. Completed topic paging structure.

Storyboard: Behind the Scenes

Figure 26-16 shows the main flowline (with all icons, their placement, and their names) as it should look when you are finished with this exercise.

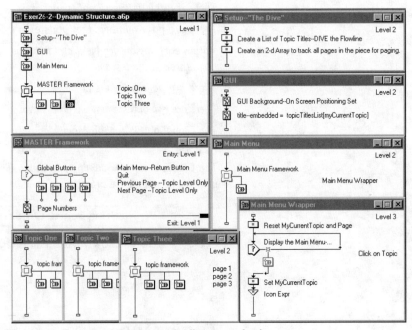

Fig. 26-16. Completed flowline with all icons and titles.

Step-by-Step Instructions

1. Examine the level 1 flowline. See figure 26-17.

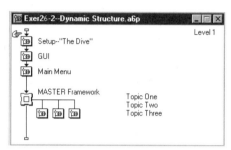

Fig. 26-17. Level 1 flowline.

Note that there are three Map icons above the master framework. This is different from previous examples. So far, all navigation, menuing, and GUI elements have been within the structure of the master framework. Now, because you will be looking at the *IconIDs* of the topics attached to the master framework, it is much easier to simply have the content portion of the flowline attached to the Framework icon and all of the setup in icons above the Framework icon. In a development situation, the three icons at the top of the flowline would be manipulated by a senior developer. The topic Map icons would be where the content integration took place.

2. Look inside the first Map icon named *Setup – "The Dive."* See figure 26-18.

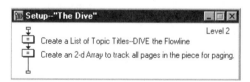

Fig. 26-18. Calculation icons that will dive the flowline for information.

This Map icon contains two Calculation icons. Each icon uses repeat loops and lists to build a list of topic titles for the main menu and a count of all pages of content in each topic for navigation purposes. These two dives will be the focus of the next two guided tours of this chapter.

3. The Map icon named *GUI* contains two Display icons. See figure 26-19.

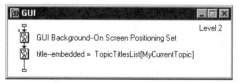

Fig. 26-19. GUI setup.

The first icon is the main background graphic. The screen positioning has been set to On Screen, and a Calculation icon has been attached to keep the background from being accidentally moved while developing the piece.

In the second icon, *title – embedded = topicTitlesList[myCurrentTopic]*, the variable expression that will display the title as embedded. Previously in this chapter, you used a custom variable (*screenTitle*) to display the titles of the topic Map icons on screen. You will see that in this lesson you are taking the titling to the next step. Inside this Display icon you will see the following embedded code.

```
Test(myCurrentTopic = 0 ,"Main Menu," topicTitlesList[myCurrentTopic])
```

This expression first checks with the *test* statement to see if the user is on a topic at all. If the *myCurrentTopic* variable is equal to zero, you know that the user is not inside a topic Map icon, and that therefore you can safely assume that the user is still in the main menu (with that phrase displayed on screen). If *myCurrentTopic* is *not* equal to zero, then the title from the list is displayed. You will see how this list is populated in the next guided tour.

4. The last of the three setup Map icons is the Map icon named *Main Menu*. When you open this Map icon, you see an empty Framework icon with another Map icon named *Main Menu* attached to it. See figure 26-20.

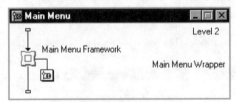

Fig. 26-20. Menu framework wrapper.

This second Map icon is attached to a Framework icon to provide it with a jump point for a Navigate icon. When a Framework icon is used in this manner, it is referred to as a "wrapper." Open the *Main Menu* wrapper Map icon. See figure 26-21.

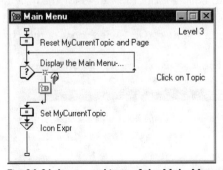

Fig. 26-21. Inner workings of the Main Menu wrapper icon.

This *Main Menu* icon is one part slight-of-hand and one part intimate knowledge of Authorware variables and functions, the result being an eloquent structure that works regardless of the number of topics added to the master framework. You will explore this menu in more detail in the next guided tour.

5.   Open one of the topic Map icons attached to the *Master Framework* icon. Note that inside each Map icon there is a Framework icon with Map icons that are merely placeholders for the content that would be added later by a content integration developer. What is most interesting about these topic Map icons is the fact that there are no icons whatsoever inside each Framework icon. See figure 26-22.

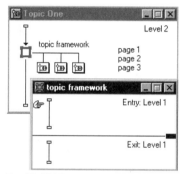

Fig. 26-22. Topic-level framework.

This is totally different from the methods you have been taught in this book so far. The magic of this structure is that all of the navigational elements are inside the master framework. This includes global buttons such as Main Menu and Quit, as well as buttons you see only at the topic level, such as the Previous and Next buttons. This means that the master framework can be totally off limits to other developers on your team. There will be no elements that can stop working at the topic level. Just add a blank framework to the flowline and you are a puppeteer of new topics!

6.   Open the *Master Framework* icon. This icon now contains global elements such as buttons and page numbers. See figure 26-23.

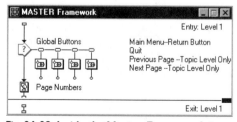

Fig. 26-23. Inside the **Master Framework** *icon.*

The most intriguing elements of this Entry pane are the Previous and Next buttons and the page numbers. These are elements you have placed inside the paging framework. However, with the dive done at the top of the flowline, you have a list of all page ID numbers and can use calculated navigation icons to move between pages. This is explored in the last guided tour of this chapter.

Guided Tour 26D: Dynamically Generating a Menu

Description

You have learned about lists, arrays, repeat loops, frameworks, variables, and functions. You now have the opportunity to use them all together. The menu you will be looking at is created by listing the titles of all topic Map icons attached to the *Master Framework* icon. This list is then displayed on screen and the user is prompted to click on the topic he wants to view first. When the user clicks on the topic item, the click is captured and the user is sent to that topic. There are three main elements of this menu: dive, click, and jump.

The dive involves searching down the flowline, finding the *Master Framework* icon, and determining how many Map icons are attached to it and what their titles are. Then these titles are saved to a list that can be displayed on the page level for the main menu and as titles on screen.

The click is the process in which you will capture the user's choice (or click) when the user clicks on one of the topics on the main menu. You will capture this click using the Hot Object response type. Once the user clicks, using the Authorware system variable *ParagraphClicked*, you will determine which list item she clicked on. The jump happens once you know which topic the user has chosen. You will then use a Navigate icon set to Destination/Calculated to jump to the appropriate topic page of the master framework.

Take a Look

1. If you have not already done so, locate the *Practice* folder on the companion CD-ROM. Copy the file named *Exer26-2 – Dynamic Structure.a6p* to the working directory on your hard drive.

2. Double click on *Exer26-2 – Dynamic Structure.a6p*. This file should now appear in your copy of Authorware. Select Save As to save this file to the working directory of your hard drive.

3. Examine the dive. Open the *Setup – The Dive* Map icon. Inside this Map icon you will see the first Calculation icon, *Create a List of Topic Titles – DIVE the Flowline*. Open this Calculation icon. Note that this Calculation

icon is divided by dashes into four tasks. You can right click in the Calculation icon, and choose Insert | Divider Line. You will examine each task in turn. The tasks are as follows:

- *Find the ID number of the* Master Framework *icon without using the literal string* "Master Framework."
- *Get the total number of topic Map icons attached to the master framework.*
- *Populate a list with the total number of topic titles.*
- *Populate the variable* mainMenu *with the titles of the topics.*

4. Find the ID number of the *Master Framework* icon without using the literal string *"Master Framework."*

You might ask why you cannot simply type in *IconID@"Master Framework"* as a literal string expression when you need to reference the ID number. Why go to all the trouble of diving down the flowline checking for Framework icons? The answer is all about safety code.

Have you every created a model that uses referenced Navigate icons? What happens to references when the model is pasted into an Authorware piece? The navigation is unlinked. The same thing happens if the reference is deleted from your Authorware piece. This problem can be avoided by using calculated navigation icons to jump to an *IconID* number that is dynamically generated. This way, even if a junior-level developer deletes the *Master Framework* icon and starts over, the menuing will still work.

This dive is designed to find the first Framework icon on the level 1 flowline and save its ID. This dive really only works if the *Master Framework* icon is the first Framework icon on level 1 of the flowline. You would have to make sure the Framework icon is not placed into a Map icon (that would throw it to level 2).

a) Examine the first line of code, which follows:

```
repeat with Index := 1 to IconNumChildren(RootIcon)
```

RootIcon is a very interesting (and until recently unpublished) Authorware system variable. *RootIcon* contains the *IconID* of the "theoretical" Map icon that encapsulates the level 1 flowline. If you look at the title bar of any Authorware file, you will see a Map icon symbol next to the file name. By using the *IconNumChildren* function to count how many children are on the first level of the flowline, you can set a repeat loop to keep checking icons for as many icons as are on the level 1 flowline.

b) The block of code is what is referred to as safety code. The first line determines whether or not the icon currently being examined in the repeat loop is a Framework icon (*IconType* = *12*), as follows:

```
if IconType(ChildNumToID(RootIcon, Index)) = 12 then
```

The *IconType* function requires an *IconID* inside its parentheses. It then looks at that icon and returns its type (see the description for *IconType* in the Functions window for a list of the icon type numbers). With the help of the *ChildNumtoID* function, you can get the child number of each icon on the level 1 flowline (*RootIcon*) as it cycles through the loop (index).

c) When *12* = *12*, you will execute the next line of code, as follows:

```
masterFrameID := ChildNumToID(RootIcon, Index)

end if

end repeat
```

This line stores the *IconID* of the *Master Framework* icon. With this information, you will be able to count the number of Map icons attached to it and then know how many topics are being covered.

5. Get the total number of topic Map icons attached to the master framework. Thanks to the previous step, this task is easy, written as follows:

```
topicCount := IconNumChildren(masterFrameID)
```

Because you have no idea how many topics (or children) you may have, you must populate a variable that can change with the number of children attached to the master framework.

6. Populate a list with the total number of topic titles.
   a) Create the list and initialize it for Authorware, as follows:

   ```
   topicTitlesList := []
   ```

This list will store all titles of all topics. The titles will be the same as the titles of the topic Map icons attached to the *Master Framework* icon.

b) Populate the list the same number of times as there are topics. Establish the repeat loop as follows:

```
repeat with Index:= 1 to topicCount
```

c) Each time you go through the loop you will store the ID number of the topic Map icon (child of the *Master Framework* icon) as follows:

```
topicChildID := ChildNumToID( masterFrameID, Index)
```

d) Populate the list each time through the loop. You will populate the list by assigning the icon title of each topic ID number as follow.

```
topicTitlesList[Index]:=
IconTitleShort(topicChildID)

    end repeat
```

e) As a check to see if the list is populating correctly, you can use the *Trace* function to show the content of the list in the Control Panel window, as follows:

```
Trace( "TopicTitlesList= ")

Trace( topicTitlesList)
```

·T*i*P·

When tracing lists, try placing the description string on a separate line so that the description does not appear at each position of the list.

If you have to trace on one line, or write out to a file, or other places where concatenation is needed, use the String() function around the list.

7. Populate the variable *mainMenu* with the titles of the topics. You will create a return-delimited list that is displayed on screen. The reason you are placing returns between each of the topic titles is because in the main menu the topic the user clicks on will be determined using the system variable *ParagraphClicked* which is based on the return character.

a) Verify that the variables are initialized, as follows:

```
tempString := ""

mainMenu := ""
```

The *tempString* variable will hold each title of the list for the loop. The *mainMenu* variable will contain the completed return-delimited list that will be embedded and clicked on by users.

b) Count how many positions are in the list, as follows:

```
repeat with tempString in topicTitlesList
```

The *Repeat/With/In* loop type is used only for looping through a list.

c) As Authorware repeats through the list, each list item will be appended to the *mainMenu* variable with a return after each title, as follows:

```
mainMenu := mainMenu ^ tempString ^ Return

    end repeat
```

8. Close the *Dive* Calculation icon. Examine how the menu, with all of this information gathered in the dive, captures a user's click.

9. To capture the user's click, open the *Main Menu* Map icon and the main menu wrapper to reveal the inner workings of the main menu. See figure 26-24.

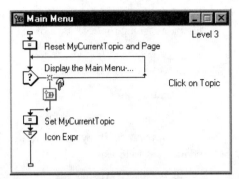

Fig. 26-24. Main menu flowline.

a) The first icon, *Reset MyCurrentTopic and Page*, merely resets the variables used to their initial values, as follows:

```
myCurrentTopic := 0

myCurrentPage := 1
```

b) The next icon, the Interaction icon *Display the Main Menu*, contains the embedded variable {*mainMenu*}.

c) Note that the *Click on Topic* Map icon attached to the Interaction icon is grayed out (meaning that there is nothing inside it) and is set to the Hot Object response type. If you open the Response Properties dialog box for this hot object, you will see that it is associated with the Interaction icon as its object. See figure 26-25.

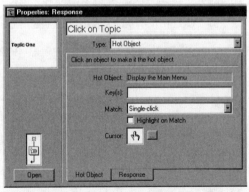

Fig. 26-25. Response Properties dialog box for the main menu hot object.

d) If you follow the flowline, after the user's click is registered there is a Calculation icon named *Set MyCurrentTopic*, with the following code inside it.

```
myCurrentTopic := ParagraphClicked
```

Obviously you are saving what the user clicked on into the custom variable *myCurrentTopic*, but why did you use the variable *ParagraphClicked* instead of *LineClicked*? The answer is that if one of the topic titles were to text wrap to the next line, the variable *LineClicked* would count each line. Therefore, if for example topic 3 wrapped to the next line, if you clicked on it you would be navigated to topic 4, which would be incorrect. The variable *ParagraphClicked* will only separate a line at a hard return character.

10. The final piece of the main menu is the calculated Navigate icon that actually performs the jump to the user-chosen topic.

    a) Open the calculated Navigate icon. See figure 26-26.

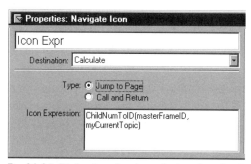

Fig. 26-26. Dialog box for the calculated navigation.

To use a calculated Navigate icon you only need one thing: an *IconID* number of where you want Authorware to jump to. For this example you already know which child of the *Master Framework* icon you want to jump to, so all you have to do is convert the child number into an ID number. To do this you will use the *ChildNumToID* function. This function has two main arguments. The first thing this function needs is the ID number of the parent of the icon ID you want. The second argument is the number of the icon you need. You will get the topic the user chose (*myCurrentTopic*), which is attached to the Master Framework icon (*masterFrameID*).

Guided Tour 26E: Dynamic Page Navigation

Description

One of the primary advantages of creating a dynamic structure is that all of your delicate navigation and GUI elements you do not want other developers (or content integrators) to accidentally alter can live in one place on the flowline. It is much easier to protect one place than many scattered all over your flowline.

In this tour you are going to look at the topic-level paging structure. Even though there are three topics and there could be many more, there is only one set of Next and Previous buttons in the entire file. If you need to change the positioning or functionality of the buttons, you can do so in one place. This paging takes place in two places on the flowline: the dive for all Topic Page ID numbers, and the buttons inside the *Master Framework* icon.

Take a Look

1. If you have not already done so, locate the *Practice* folder on the companion CD-ROM. Copy the file named *Exer26-2 – Dynamic Structure.a6p* to your working directory on your hard drive.

2. Double click on *Exer26-2 – Dynamic Structure.a6p*. This file should now appear in your copy of Authorware. Select Save As to save this file to the working directory of your hard drive.

3. Examine the dive. Open the *Setup – The Dive* Map icon. Inside this Map icon you will see the last Calculation icon, *Create a 2-d Array*, for tracking all pages in the piece for paging. Open this Calculation icon. This Calculation icon is a dive. To be specific, this is a four-level dive (i.e., the repeat loops are nested four deep). Examine figure 26-27 to see where the four levels come from.

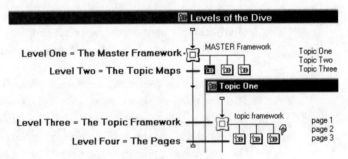

Fig. 26-27. Four levels required for the dive.

To get the *IconID* numbers for every page attached to each topic Framework icon, you must first get the *Master Framework* icon, and then the topic Map icon IDs. Once you have these, you can get the icon IDs of the Framework icons inside the topic Map icons and finally the pages attached to the topic Framework icons. This is a four-level dive down the flowline.

4. When you look at the nested repeat loops for this dive one line at a time, it is very clear what is happening. (Note: many elements of this code are repeated in the first Calculation icon viewed in the last tour in this chap-

ter.) You could combine these in your project, but for purposes here you are repeating some of the steps.

a) Examine the level I flowline for the *Master Framework* icon, as follows:

```
repeat with Index := 1 to IconNumChildren(RootIcon)

    if IconType(ChildNumToID(RootIcon, Index)) = 12 then
```

The first Framework icon encountered on the flowline will have its *IconID* saved, as follows:

```
masterFrameID := ChildNumToID(RootIcon, Index)
```

Then you will create the array that has all *IconID* numbers of all individual pages for every topic. There are currently three lessons attached to the main menu so that this array will start as 3 by 1 (one list for each topic and one placeholder for each potential page). With arrays, only the second dimension can grow.

b) In the next repeat loop you will dive for the ID numbers of the topic Map icons, as follows. The topic Map icons are the number of children of the master framework.

```
repeat with Index2 := 1 to
    IconNumChildren(masterFrameID)

    topicMapID := ChildNumToID(masterFrameID, Index2)
```

c) In the next level of the dive you are once again looking for a Framework icon, and will therefore include that safe code in the dive, as follows:

```
repeat with Index3 := 1 to IconNumChildren(topicMapID)

    tempIconID := ChildNumToID(topicMapID , Index3)

if IconType(tempIconID) = 12 then--safety code

topicFrameID := tempIconID
```

d) In the last level of the dive, you can begin recording the page ID numbers in the array. Loop for all children attached to the topic Framework icon, as follows:

```
repeat with Index4:= 1 to
    IconNumChildren(topicFrameID)
```

Each time through the loop you will convert the page number into an *IconID* number and store that to a temporary variable, as follows:

```
topicPageID := ChildNumToID(topicFrameID, Index4)
```

Once you have the page ID stored, you can populate it into the appropriate position of the array, as follows:

```
pageIDArray[Index2 , Index4] := topicPageID
```

e) The most gratifying part of any multilevel dive is as follows:

```
        end repeat --close level 4

                    end if

                 end repeat --close level 3

              end repeat-- close level 2

           end if

        end repeat -- close level 1
```

5. The other vital component of making the navigation work is creating the buttons the user can interact with. This setup is fairly simple, based on all icon IDs gathered in the dive.

a) Open the *Master Framework* icon. See figure 26-28.

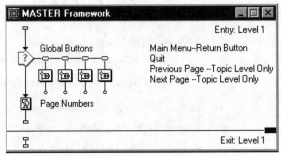

Fig. 26-28. Inside the Master Framework icon.

b) Examine the properties of the buttons. You will note when you run this piece that the Previous and Next buttons do not wrap around the pages. That is, when the user is viewing page 3, for example, the Next button is disabled and the user cannot move forward to page 1. In Chapter 15 you learned to place the expression *CurrentPageNum < PageCount* in the Active If field of the Next button. You are doing the same type of control on these buttons, but instead of using the system variables you looking at the array to see what page number the user is viewing. Open the Properties/Response dialog box for the Previous button. See figure 26-29.

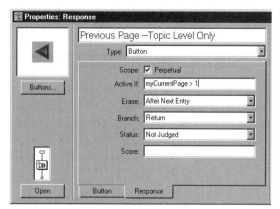

Fig. 26-29. Properties/Response dialog box for the Previous button.

Note in the Active If field that you are using the following custom variable.

`myCurrentPage > 1`

Thus, the back arrow is only enabled if the page the user is viewing is greater than one. Close this dialog box and open the Next Page response dialog box. See figure 26-30.

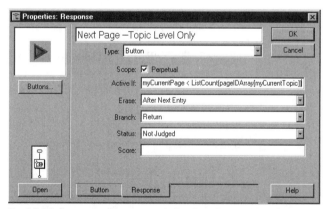

Fig. 26-30. Properties/Response dialog box for the Next button with Active If field displayed.

Note the following Active If statement in this box. What is it saying?

`myCurrentPage < ListCount(pageIDArray[myCurrentTopic])`

It is saying that the Next button is only active if the page the user is currently viewing (*myCurrentPage*) is less than the total number of pages for this particular topic. Using the function *ListCount*, you can look at the number of positions in the topic dimension of *pageIDArray*.

c) Examine what happens when the user clicks on the Previous button. See figure 26-31.

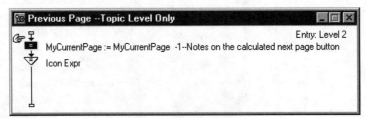

Fig. 26-31. Inside the Previous button Map icon.

The first thing that happens every time the user clicks on the black arrow is that 1 is subtracted from the *myCurrentPage* variable. This will keep the button's active state behaving as anticipated. The second thing that happens is the calculated navigation. This navigation is based on the following expression.

```
pageIDArray[myCurrentTopic , myCurrentPage ]
```

In this array position you are getting the exact page to go to.

d) If you understood the previous, the Next button should be perfectly clear. Everything is the same except for the subtraction of 1. Inside the Next button you add 1 every time the user clicks on the button. See figure 26-32.

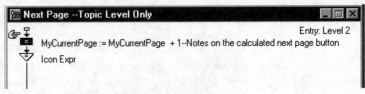

Fig. 26-32. Inside the Next button Map icon.

Summary

In this chapter you learned:

- *The parent/child relationship of icons*
- *How the icon functions work*
- *How to use the icon functions to produce on-screen titles*
- *What a dynamic structure is*
- *What types of icons constitute a dynamic flowline structure*
- *How to create a dynamically generated menu*
- *How to create dynamic page navigation*

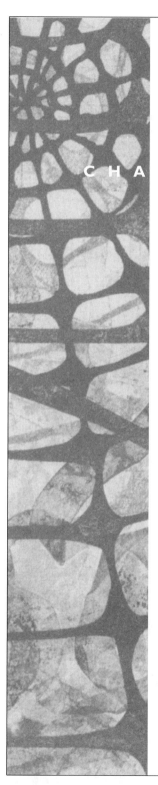

CHAPTER **27**

Application:

Creating Dynamic

Navigation

Structures

Introduction

In this chapter you will see how all of the advanced scripting techniques you have learned in chapters 23 through 26 can be used together to create an application structure that can be updated very easily. First, you will see a subroutine-based quiz that calls all of its questions from an external text file. Next, you will see an improved navigational structure for the overall application project. In Chapter 17, you created a basic menu/topic structure that works fine, but as you learned in Chapter 26 you can create a more "advanced" structure that is much easier to maintain and update. In these exercises you will enhance the menu and topic structures to provide an end result in which content can be added or subtracted, without affecting the dynamic structure.

Application Exercise 27A: Creating a Subroutine Quiz

Description

In Chapter 23 you learned how to separate the content from the code, with the result of a flowline that is easier to update and to troubleshoot. In chapters 24 and 25 you learned how to populate lists with the repeat loop function. In this exercise, you will bring it all together to create a subroutine quiz with all of its data being called from an external file. The data will be stored in a list and will populate the quiz as needed. This exercise provides a good example of the power and ease of use accomplished by separating content from structure.

Storyboard: On Screen

Figure 27-1 shows what the exercise will look like on screen when finished.

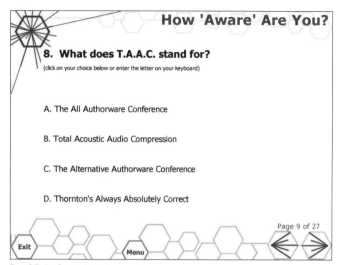

Fig. 27-1. Completed exercise on screen.

Storyboard: Behind the Scenes

Figure 27-2 shows the level 2, 3, and 4 flowlines (with all icons, their placement, and their names) as they should look when you are finished with this exercise.

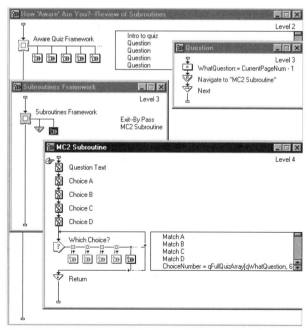

Fig. 27-2. Level 2, 3, and 4 flowlines of the completed exercise.

Step-by-Step Instructions

Complete this exercise on your own, guided by following the general steps. See the completed exercise on the CD-ROM copy of Authorware for further guidance.

1. The completed version of the exercise is *Exer27A.a6p*, located on the companion CD-ROM in the directory named *Chapter14*. Open this file.

2. Open the *Quiz.txt* file located in the same directory. Run the program and see how it works. Jump to the flowline and examine the various icons and structures.

3. Make sure to open the blue Calculation icons labeled READ ME and read what is inside.

4. Leave this file open in this copy of Authorware.

5. Open another copy of Authorware, starting a new file. Save the file as *App27A*.

6. Copy all of the supporting files from this folder to the working folder on your hard drive.

7. When finished, make sure to save your exercise in the *SaveWork* directory on your computer's hard drive.

Application Exercise 27B: Creating a Dynamic Menu and Navigation

Description

In Chapter 17 you created a basic menu/topic structure that works fine, but as you learned in Chapter 26 you can create a more "advanced" structure that is much easier to maintain and update. In this exercise, using variables, you will enhance the menu and topic structures and the parent/child relationships to provide an end result in which content can be added or subtracted, without affecting the dynamic structure.

Storyboard: On Screen

Figure 27-3 shows what the exercise will look like on screen when finished.

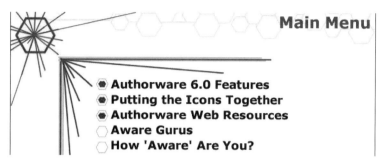

Fig. 27-3. Completed main menu on screen.

Storyboard: Behind the Scenes

Figure 27-4 shows the main and levels 2 and 3 flowlines (with all icons, their placement, and their names) as they should look when you are finished with this exercise.

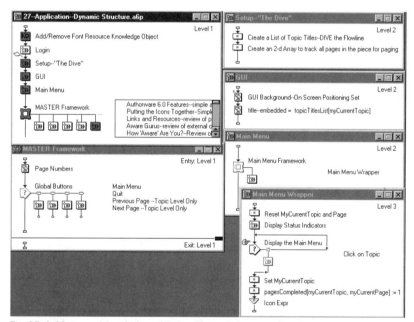

Fig. 27-4. Main and levels 2 and 3 flowlines of the completed exercise.

Step-by-Step Instructions

Complete this exercise on your own, guided by following the general steps. See the completed exercise on the CD-ROM copy of Authorware for further guidance.

1. The completed version of the exercise is *Exer27B.a6p,* located on the companion CD-ROM in the directory named *Chapter27.* Open this file. Run the program and see how it works. Jump to the flowline and look at the various icons and structures.

2. Make sure to open the blue Calculation icons labeled READ ME and read what is inside.

3. Leave this file open in this copy of Authorware.

4. Open another copy of Authorware, starting a new file. Save the file as *App27B.*

5. When finished, make sure to save your exercise in the *SaveWork* directory on your computer's hard drive.

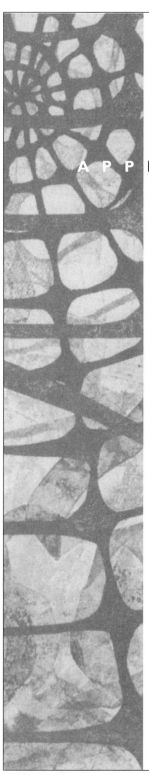

Frequently Used Functions and Variables

There are hundreds of Authorware system variables and functions. Learning what every one of them can help you build is the true secret to becoming a guru-level author. This abbreviated list contains some of the most common variables and some of the most interesting functions. To better learn what the possibilities are, try reading some of the descriptions of the functions and variables each day. The first time you are exposed to the idea you may not see a use for it, but there will come a day when you are presented with an Authorware problem and in the back of your mind a voice will call out, "There is a function for that!" and you will be using Authorware like a guru.

Functions

AppendExtFile

Syntax
```
number := AppendExtFile("filename", "string")
```

Description
AppendExtFile simply adds the text you specify in *"string"* to the end of the file you specify in *"filename."* Remember, this function will only work with files you have on local or network disks; it cannot work over the Internet. For this you must use the FTP functions.

Example
The following statement adds the content of *NewUser* to the end of DATA.TXT.

```
AppendExtFile(RecordsLocation^"DATA.TXT", NewUser)
```

Beep

Syntax
```
Beep()
```

Description
Beep triggers the sound you have set up as the system beep. This can be set in Control Panel | Sounds.

Example
Beep is useful when you want to attract the user's attention. For example, you could have a beep sound when the user selects an incorrect response.

CallTarget

Syntax
```
result := CallTarget("SystemFunctionName" [, arguments, ...])
```

Description
CallTarget sends the function and parameters you specify to the target piece that launched it. *CallTarget* is the powerhouse behind making your own Knowledge Objects. It allows you as a Knowledge Object developer to build an Authorware file remotely, just like using your TV remote control. You point the remote at the TV and change the channel. With *CallTarget* you identify a Target piece (which is just another Authorware file) and then send a function command to that target file. The command is then executed in the target file.

There are great articles in the Authorware Help pages about using *CallTarget* to build Knowledge Objects.

Example

The following statement retrieves the content of the *FileName* variable in a target piece.

```
TargetFileName := CallTarget("GetVariable", "FileName")
```

ChildNumToID

Syntax

```
ID := ChildNumToID(IconID@"Parent", n [, flag])
```

Description

You might well find the entire Icon category essential to any project in Authorware. The Icon category is the link from icons to script and makes complex navigation possible as well as writing Knowledge Objects and BOTs. The magic of *ChildNumToID* is discussed in detail in Chapter 26. What makes this function so powerful is its simplicity: If you know the name of a parent icon, and you know which number the child is, this function will return to you the ID# of that icon. Once you have an icon's ID#, you can bookmark it, navigate to it, copy it, and so on. This function is the power behind most dynamic structures that advanced users are creating. The *ChildNumToID* function returns the *IconID* of the child specified in the *n* attribute.

The flags are used for finding the children of Framework icons. Framework icons have three sets of children: those attached to them as pages, those in the Entry pane, and those in the Exit pane. Use flag as 0, 1, and 2, respectively, for these icons.

Example

```
ChildNumToID(@"Module 2",2)
```

Eval, EvalAssign

Syntax

```
result := Eval("expression" [, decimal, separator])
result := EvalAssign("expression" [, decimal, separator])
```

Description

Eval and *EvalAssign* work out the string expression and return the result. This enables you to build an expression with strings (e.g., *"45" ^ "+ 32"*). *EvalAssign* allows you to use expressions with an assignment operator to assign a value to a variable, as in *EvalAssign("myVar := 34 + 23")*. Therefore, you can make expressions and variable names with strings and evaluate them. The variables must have been created previously in Authorware or the *EvalAssign* will not work.

Example
The following example shows how to read in an initialization file and assign its values to variables. The external text file *demo.ini* contains the following lines:

```
LastSection := 3
UserName := "John"
```

Within a Calculation icon, the following lines read in the text file and pass the content of the file to *EvalAssign* line by line. Even though the previous lines are kept in an external file, Authorware executes them as if they were entered in a Calculation icon.

```
FileContents := ReadExtFile(FileLocation^"demo.ini")
repeat with X:=1 to LineCount(FileContents)
        Line := GetLine(FileContents, X)
        EvalAssign(Line)
end repeat
```

GetIconProperty, SetIconProperty

Syntax
```
result := GetIconProperty(IconID@"IconTitle", #property)
SetIconProperty(IconID@"IconTitle", #property, value)
```

Description
This gets the value for the property of the specified icon or sets the property for the specified icon. Use this function in concert with many of the functions in the Icon category and the function *CallTarget* and you can make Authorware build its own files.

Example
The following statement gets the value of the *#awMotionObject* property of the Motion icon named *Move Planet*.

```
CurrentPlanet := GetIconProperty(IconID@"Move Planet",
#awMotionObject)
```

In this case, the value of *CurrentPlanet* is an *IconID*.

GoToNetPage

Syntax
```
GoToNetPage("URL" [, "windowType"])
```

Description

A *Net* function that will only work when your piece is running in a Web browser. The *GoToNetPage* function opens the Web page you specify in *"URL"*. Window type is a must to know. If you do not specify a window type or type in *"_self,"* your Authorware piece will terminate and the Web page will open. If you wish to launch another browser with the Authorware piece running, you must use *"_blank"* as the second parameter.

Example

The following displays the Macromedia home page in the current browser window and then closes the current piece.

```
GoToNetPage("http://www.macromedia.com/index.html")
```

The following displays the Macromedia home page in a blank window while keeping the window displaying the current piece open.

```
GoToNetPage("http://www.macromedia.com/index.html", "_blank")
```

IconTitle and IconTitleShort

Syntax
```
string := IconTitle(IconID)
string := IconTitleShort(IconID)
```

Description

IconTitle returns the icon title of the icon you specify in *IconID*. *IconTitleShort* returns the icon title with any comments stripped.

Example

If you were using icon titles to display text on screen (i.e., *ScreenText := IconTitleShort(IconID)*), the title of the icon might read *Click the mouse to continue*. As the primary developer, if you saw this unlikely icon title on the flowline, you would know that this text would appear on screen, but another developer might miss that and rename the icon. The advantage of *IconTitle Short* is that if you place a *rem* symbol in the title (the comment out "--"), anything after is dropped. Therefore, you could name your icon *Click the mouse to continue. -- don't change this text it appears on the screen*. Only the information before the double hyphen would be displayed on screen.

IconType

Syntax
```
number := IconType(IconID@"IconTitle")
```

Description

Returns the icon type as a number.

0	Invalid icon ID
1	Display icon
2	Animation icon
3	Erase icon
4	Interaction icon
5	Decision icon
6	Map icon
7	Wait icon
8	Calculation icon
9	Digital movie icon
10	Sound icon
11	Video icon
12	Framework icon
13	Navigate icon
14	Sprite Xtra icon
15	Knowledge Object icon

Example

The following might return the number 7 for a Wait icon. *IconType* is especially helpful when diving down the flowline. We use this function in Chapter 26 to look for the Master Framework into which all the dynamic navigation is incorporated.

```
IconType(@"Wait 2")
```

Initialize

Syntax
```
Initialize([variable1, variable2, , variable10])
```

Description

Sets all custom variables to their initial state. If used with the parameters it can be used to set only the specified variables to their initial state.

Example

This function allows you to reset variables when a user exits a sequence, so that the user can return and run through the same sequence again. Initializing specific variables allows you to clear or reset certain variables while continuing to change others.

```
Initialize(Score,TimeOutLimit,UserName)
```

JumpFile, JumpFileReturn

Syntax
```
JumpFile("filename", ["variable1, variable2, ","folder"])
JumpFileReturn("filename", ["variable1, variable2,
","folder"])
```

Description
JumpFile launches the Authorware file you specify in *filename* and then quits. Any lines after the function are ignored, so use it at the end of a Calculation icon.

JumpFileReturn launches the other Authorware file and quits. Upon the new Authorware file quitting, the original file reopens at the point where it left off.

The parameters allow variables to be sent to the next file. To specify all variables, use an asterisk. The final parameter specifies a new location for the records. See *RecordsLocation*.

To jump to a non-Authorware file, use *JumpOut*.

Example
The following statement jumps to the history file and passes the value of subjects.

```
JumpFile("history", "subjects")
```

The following statement jumps to the history file, passes no variables, and changes the record location.

```
JumpFileReturn("history", "", FileLocation ^"User Records")
```

NetDownload, NetDownloadBackground

Syntax
```
string := NetDownload("URL")
netId := NetDownloadBackground("URL" [,"filename"])
```

Description
NetDownload and *NetDownloadBackground* only work in the Web player. *NetDownload* downloads the specified file and returns a string of where the file has been downloaded to.

Example
The following statement downloads the *README.TXT* file and returns the *pathname* to a variable named *string*.

```
string := NetDownload("http://www.company.com/readme.txt")
```

NOTE

When jumping between files that have the same Presentation window size, Authorware places the file you are jumping to in the same screen location as the file you are jumping from. This provides a better transition between files. To disable this automatic positioning, make the Presentation window for one of the files one pixel larger than the other.

NetPreload, Preload

Syntax
```
NetPreload(IconID@"IconTitle <mailto:IconID@"IconTitle>")
number := Preload(IconID@"IconTitle" [, option])
```

Description
NetPreload uploads the icon to the user's PC so that it is ready when you need it. This is different from *Preload*, which you use in non-Web-packaged pieces to load a file into memory.

Example
```
NetPreload(IconID@"MyVeryBigGraphic")
```

PackageFile

Syntax
```
Result := PackageFile("OutputFile", Runtime,
ResolveLinksAtRuntime, PackLibsInternal, PackMediaInternal,
UseDefaultNames, [LibraryLocations])
```

Description
Packages the current file when used via the *CallTarget* function from an unpackaged file. This function, new in Authorware 6, allows you to create an Authorware file that can package another Authorware file.

Example
```
PackageSuccessful := PackageFile( "c:\myFile.exe", 2, 1, 1, 1, 1)
```

PasteModel, SetPasteHand

Syntax
```
PasteModel("ModelFileName")
SetPasteHand(IconID@"IconTitle", #position [, flag ])
```

Description
PasteModel inserts the specified model file into a piece at the Paste Hand cursor. The file name may be absolute or relative. When you use *PasteModel*, Authorware updates two system variables (*IOStatus* and *IOMessage*) and returns the value of *IOStatus*. If no error occurs, *IOStatus* contains 0 and *IOMessage* is empty.

SetPasteHand moves the Paste Hand cursor to the icon you specify. *#position* can be either *#before*, *#after*, *#beforeFirstChild*, or *#afterLastChild*. *Flag* is used in Framework icons to be a page of the framework, in the Entry pane, or in the Exit pane (as 0, 1, or 2, respectively).

Example

To set the position of the Paste Hand cursor, use the *CallTarget* function, as follows:

```
VariableForID := CallTarget("IconID","IconTitle")
CallTarget("SetPasteHand",VariableForID,#position)
```

PressKey

Syntax
```
PressKey("keyname")
```

Description

Activates the key you specify as if the key were pressed on the keyboard.

Example

Use *PressKey* to generate a user response. For example, in a text response, use *PresetEntry* to preload the text entry area, and then use *PressKey* to automatically select the answer: *PressKey("Return")*.

Quit(3)

Syntax
```
Quit([option])
```

Description

The *Quit* function leaves Authorware. Mostly it is used with option 0 to just quit Authorware and return to an Authorware file if it was opened with *JumpFileReturn*. Option 1 leaves Authorware even if a *JumpFileReturn* has been used. Option 2 leaves Authorware and restarts Windows. This is a very useful trick for kiosk applications. Option 3 shuts down Windows completely. Use Quit(3) if you are installing new drivers on a Windows machine or if you need to wake up your learner audience.

Example
```
Quit(3)
```

ResizeWindow

Syntax
```
ResizeWindow(width, height)
```

Description

Resizes the Presentation window to the width and height you specify. If the user menu bar and title bar are present, be sure you get the required results.

Example

In the following, Authorware resizes the Presentation window to fill the top half of the screen.

```
MoveWindow(0, 0)
ResizeWindow(WindowWidth, WindowHeight/2)
```

RGB

Syntax

```
RGB(red, green, blue)
```

Description

Use to set the RGB color for use with Authorware's draw functions. RGB is a method of describing colors. The letters stand for Red, Green, and Blue. You can describe all the colors you see on your screen as varying intensities of red, green and blue.

The range for each value is 0 to 255. Use the *RGB*, *SetFrame*, and *SetFill* functions to determine what color Authorware uses for the drawing functions. For example, RGB(0,0,0) is black while RGB(255,255,255) is white.

Example

```
SetFill(1 , RGB(242, 242, 242))
Box(0, 11,53,184,166)
```

SyncPoint, SyncWait

Syntax

```
SyncPoint(option)
SyncWait(seconds)
```

Description

These are really useful to sync displays and animations or video. If you use Wait icons, you can become very out of step.

Use *SyncPoint(1)* to set the timer after the icon it is attached to is displayed. Then use *SyncWait* functions further down the flowline. The way to do this is to attach *SyncWait* functions in icons with the number of seconds specified. The flowline will not go beyond this point until the number of seconds past the *SyncPoint* function has elapsed.

Example

```
SyncPoint(0)
SyncWait(30)
```

Test

Syntax
```
Test(condition, true expression [, false expression])
```

Description
Test evaluates the condition and executes the *true* expression if it is true and the *false* expression if the condition is false.

Example
The following shows how to use the *Test* function to determine how Authorware proceeds based on the value of a user's score. One of these paths displays remedial materials; the other displays a challenge quiz.

The following expression, entered in a Decision icon's To Calculated Path field, checks whether the value of the variable *Score* is less than 50.

```
Test(Score<50, path:=1, path:=2)
```

If the value is less than 50, Authorware takes path 1 through the decision structure. If the score is 50 or more, Authorware takes path 2.

Trace

Syntax
```
Trace("string")
```

Description
This is a powerful debugging tool. When this command is *string*, it is placed into Authorware's trace list. Use this in conjunction with the Authorware Control Panel window to see the results.

Example
Put *Trace* in a Calculation icon at the point where you want to make sure something has happened. The following statement displays *"Checkpoint 1"* in the trace window when Authorware encounters it.

```
Trace("Checkpoint 1")
```

You can also preview the value of variables while you are authoring. To do this, place the variable inside the Trace function:

```
Trace(IconTitle)
```

To better label the results of the trace in the control panel window place a string label inside the argument:

```
Trace("Icon Title = " ^ IconTitle)
```

Variables

CharCount

Type
Numeric

Description
Contains the number of characters the user typed into a text response. Not to be confused with the Authorware function *CharCount()*, which returns the number of characters in a string.

Example
```
Test( Charcount > 9, returnString := "Too long Jennie! Try a
shorter one.")
```

In this example the Test function asks the question, If the Character Count is greater than 9 then return the text, "Too Long!"

ChoiceNumber

Type
Numeric

Description
This contains the number of responses attached to an Interaction icon.

Example
Use *ChoiceNumber* to select a decision path based on which option the user selected in an interaction. Place an Interaction icon at the beginning of your application that asks the user to make a choice, and then use that *ChoiceNumber* throughout the rest of the file to determine which information to present. We used *ChoiceNumber* in Chapter 23, "Subroutines" to judge the user's response to the quiz question.

ControlDown, AltDown, ShiftDown, MouseDown, RightMouseDown

Type
Logical

Description
The variable is true if the key is currently being pressed. This is vital information if you are trying to simulate software.

Example
```
Test(ControlDown = True, stepForward := 5)
```

CorrectChoicesMatched

Type
```
Numeric
```

Description
Contains the number of choices the user has matched that have their status set to correct.

Example
These variables can be used to summarize users' performances in an interaction. If users are matching the same wrong responses, you may need to give them more direction or redesign the interaction.

CursorX, CursorY

Type
```
Numeric
```

Description
Very useful and update very quickly. These variables contain the pixels from the left and top of the screen, respectively.

Example
If the user does not respond within a certain length of time or responds incorrectly, use the values of *CursorX* and *CursorY* to determine where the user is placing the cursor on the screen and give feedback accordingly.

Date

Type
```
Numeric
```

Description
Contains the current date in numeric format (e.g., MM/DD/YY). The exact order will depend on the user's settings on his PC.

Example
Date is useful for labeling information you are writing to an external file, such as test results. When you write a user's results to a file, include the user's name and the current date.

e

Type
`Numeric`

Description
e is the transcendental constant used as the base for natural logarithms (2.718281828459).

Example
Use this variable in an exponential calculation, such as the following.

```
Result := 75**3.2
```

EntryText, PresetEntry, UserName, FirstName

Type
`Character`

Description
EntryText contains the text the user entered in a text interaction. *PresetEntry* can be used to set a string to be set into a text entry as it is displayed. *UserName* and *FirstName* are very useful, as Authorware will automatically get the first name from the *UserName* variable.

Example
Use this variable, such as follows, whenever you need to use the user's text response. *EntryText* is commonly used to capture data such as the user's name. Once the user has entered some text, you can assign it to another variable.

```
UserName := EntryText
```

EvalMessage, EvalStatus, IOMessage, IOStatus

Type
`Character`

Description
Essential for error trapping. *EvalMessage* contains an error message about the last syntax error generated from using *Eval* or *EvalAssign*. *EvalStatus* contains a number referring to the error.

IOMessage and *IOStatus* are the same but are used for errors returned from using the functions *WriteExtFile*, *ReadExtFile*, *AppendExtFile*, *CreateFolder*, *DeleteFile*, *RenameFile*, and *SaveFile*.

Example

Use these variables at run time to verify the success of a file operation and to alert a user if it was unsuccessful. Insert a decision structure after the file operation, and put *IOStatus* in the To Calculated Path field of the Decision Icon Properties dialog box. If *IOStatus* does not equal 0, an error occurred and the first path is taken. You can then display the *IOMessage* for the user and provide options for quitting or recovering. Use these error-catching variables with a *Trace* function to see the results of various function calls in the control panel window. For example:

```
Trace("Error Code: " ^ IOStatus ^ "Error: " ^ IOMessage)
```

FileLocation, RecordsLocation

Type
```
Character
```

Description

Contains the location of the file. In a Web-packaged piece, it will contain the location of the Authorware downloaded files.

Example

The following shows how to use the system variable *FileLocation* to specify the location of a text file.

```
template := ReadExtFile(FileLocation^"datatemp.txt")
```

When the Authorware Web Player is running a piece in nontrusting mode, it disables this variable.

IconTitle, IconID

Type
```
Character
```

Description

These contain the icon title or ID in which they appear. *IconID* is the base information that Authorware requires for all dynamic navigation, bookmarking, and tracking. It is used extensively in Chapter 26.

Example
```
myTitle := IconTitle
```

Key

Type
`Character`

Description
Contains the last key the user pressed.

Example
Use in a text entry and use with preset entry to show a different character than the one the user pressed. *Key* is used in Chapter 18 to make a masked password.

MediaPlaying

Type
`Logical`

Description
This is true if any medium (such as movies, video, or sound) specified with *"MediaPlaying@IconTitle <mailto:MediaPlaying@IconTitle>"* is playing.

Example
Use *MediaPlaying* to synchronize events by activating or deactivating icons, depending on whether *MediaPlaying* is true. Use *MediaPlaying* in the Begin field in the Sound Icon Properties dialog box to start a sound when a movie is playing.

Movable

Type
`Logical`

Description
This is true if the icon is movable. This variable can be set, so no displays can be accidentally moved while in authoring mode.

Example
Movable@"IconTitle" is true if the user can move the object displayed by the specified icon. You can assign a value of TRUE or FALSE to this variable to make any display movable or immovable.

By default, the user cannot move objects in a packaged application, unless you make them movable through the icon's Properties dialog box or if they are part of a target area interaction. You can move all displayed objects while authoring, but you can accidentally move background elements. To avoid moving an object unintentionally during authoring, attach a Calculation icon to the icon you want to make immovable and enter the following expression:

```
Movable := FALSE
```

NetConnected

Type
Logical

Description
Important when any piece may be delivered both on local drives and Web-packaged formats. *NetConnected* is true if the piece is currently in the Web-packaged mode.

Example
Use *NetConnected* within your piece to display different icons or external media, depending on whether the piece is running under the Authorware Web Player. The following statement determines which external graphic Authorware displays:

```
if NetConnected then
        graphic := NetLocation^"SmallPhoto.jpg"
else
        graphic := FileLocation^"LargePhoto.bmp"
end if
```

PageCount, CurrentPageNum

Type
Character

Description
PageCount contains the number of pages attached to a Framework icon. *CurrentPageNum* is the number of the page the user is currently in. These variables are used extensively in Chapters 15 and 16.

Example
Use *CurrentPageNum* to prevent wraparound paging in a framework. When a framework reaches the last page, it wraps back to the first page of the framework.

To make the Next page button unavailable when displaying the last page of a framework, place the following statement in the *Active If* field of the button:

```
CurrentPageNum<PageCount
```

To prevent wraparound paging from the first page to the last, place the following statement in the Previous page button:

```
CurrentPageNum>1
```

ParagraphClicked

Type
Numeric

Description
Contains the number of the paragraph the user clicked in a text object. This function is used in Chapter 26 to track which main menu item the user selected from the list.

Example
Display several paragraphs of text in an interaction and use *ParagraphClicked* and *LastParagraphClicked* to retrieve the paragraph the user clicked, as in the following:

```
TextSelected := GetLine(TextObject, ParagraphClicked)
```

RootIcon

Type
Numeric

Description
Contains the *IconID* of the highest level of logic in an Authorware flowline. The *RootIcon* is the icon that houses all other icons in your piece. You may have noticed that at the top of your level one flowline, there is a picture of a Map icon in the title bar. That map is the implied *RootIcon* in which your piece resides. This variable is used in Chapter 26 to "dive" the main flowline looking for the *IconID* of the Master Framework.

Example
The following returns the *IconID* of the first icon on the flowline.

```
firstIcon := IconFirstChild(RootIcon)
```

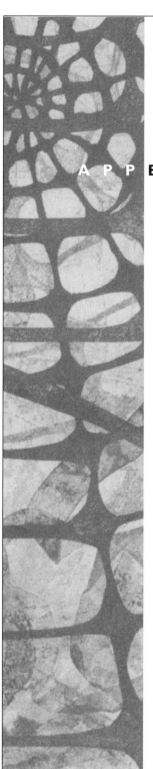

Authorware 6

Xtras

Introduction

Authorware has core functionality. The rest is gained from Xtras. Because of this, you need to include the Xtras with your packaged piece in a subfolder named *Xtras* when you distribute it. The following is a comprehensive guide to all of the Xtras you are likely to come across.

Images

If you import any media (including: graphics, sounds, or digital movies) into an Authorware file, you will require these two Xtras.

Windows 95 and up (All 32-bit versions of Windows)	Windows 3.1 (16-bit version of Windows)
Viewsvc.x32	Viewsvc.x16
Mix32.x32	Mix16.x16

In addition, if you have used any of the image formats listed in the first column in the following table, make sure you distribute the format's corresponding Xtra.

Image Formats	Windows 95 and up (All 32-bit versions)	Windows 3.1 (16-bit version)
BMP, DIB, RLE	Bmpview.x32	Bmpview.x16
GIF	Gifimp.x32, Mixview.x32	Gifimp.x16, Mixview.x16
JPEG	Jpegimp.x32, Mixview.x32	Jpegimp.x16, Mixview.x16
LRG (xRes format)	Lrgimp.x32, Mixview.x32	Lrgimp.x16, Mixview.x16
Photoshop 3.0	Ps3imp.x32, Mixview.x32	Ps3imp.x16, Mixview.x16
PICT	Pictview.x32, QuickTime 2.0 or later for Windows*	Pictview.x16, QuickTime 2.0 or a later for Windows*
PNG (Portable Network Graphic)	Pngimp.x32, Mixview.x32	Pngimp.x16, Mixview.x16
TGA (Targa)	Targaimp.x32, Mixview.x32	Targaimp.x16, Mixview.x16
TIF (TIFF)	Tiffimp.x32, Mixview.x32	Tiffimp.x16, Mixview.x16
WMF (Windows MetaFile)	Wmfview.x32	Wmfview.x16
EMF (Extended MetaFile)	Emfview.x32	n/a

Sounds

All sound formats require the Xtras outlined in the following table.

Windows 95 and up (All 32-bit versions of Windows)	Windows 3.1 (16-bit version of Windows)
Viewsvc.x32	Viewsvc.x16
Mix32.x32	Mix16.x16
Mixview.x32	Mixview.x16

In addition, if you have used any of the sound formats listed in the first column in the following table, make sure you distribute the format's corresponding Xtra.

Sound Formats	Windows 95 and up (All 32-bit versions of Windows)	Windows 3.1 (16-bit version of Windows)
Authorware 3.x sound	A3sread.x32	A3sread.x16
AIF (AIFF)	Aiffread.x32	Aiffread.x16
AIFF with IMA compression	Aiffread.x32, Ima4dcmp.x32	Aiffread.x16, Ima4dcmp.x16
AIFF with MACE compression	Aiffread.x32, Macedcmp.x32	Aiffread.x16, Macedcmp.x16
MP3	awmp3.x32	—
SWA (Shockwave Audio)	Swaread.x32, Swadcmpr.x32	Swaread.x16, Swadcmpr.x16
PCM	Pcmread.x32	Pcmread.x16
VOX (Voxware)	Voxread.x32, Voxdcmp.x32	Voxread.x16, Voxdcmp.x16
WAV (WAVE)	Wavread.x32	Wavread.x16

When you distribute an Authorware piece, create an *Xtras* folder in the folder that contains either the Runtime application *(Runa6w32.exe* or *Runa6w16.exe)* or in the Authorware piece you are distributing (if you packaged it with the Runtime application). Put the Xtras in the *Xtras* folder. The files listed in the following table need to be distributed and placed in the same folder as Authorware or the Authorware Runtime application *(Runa6w32.exe* or *Runa6w16.exe).*

Sound Formats	Windows 95 and up (All 32-bit versions of Windows)	Windows 3.1 (16-bit version of Windows)
VOX (Voxware)	Mvoice.vwp, Vct32161.dll	Mvoice.x32, Mvoice16.vxr, Vct16151.dll

Movies

If you want to include a QuickTime movie, also consider using the QuickTime Asset Xtra, which allows you to play up to QuickTime 4. ActiveMovie 1.0 enables Windows 95 and Windows NT 4 computers to play MPEG movies without an MPEG card. Movie formats are outlined in the following table.

Movie Formats	Windows 95 and up (All 32-bit versions of Windows)	Windows 3.1 (16-bit version of Windows)
QuickTime 2.0*	A5qt32.xmo, QuickTime 2.0 for Windows (32-bit)	A5qt.xmo, QuickTime 2.0 for Windows (16-bit)
Video for Windows (AVI)	A5vfw32.xmo, Video for Windows	A5vfw.xmo, Video for Windows
MPEG	A5mpeg32.xmo, ActiveMovie 1.0** or MPEG playback board and software drivers	A5mpeg.xmo, MPEG playback board and software drivers

Director Movies

For the most recent information concerning files you need to distribute with Director movies, go to Macromedia's Authorware Support Center. The files your users need to play a Director 6 or 6.5 movie in Authorware 6 – and the folder where each file needs to be located – are listed there. [Project Folder] or [Proj_dir] in the sections that follow stands for the folder or directory that contains either the Runtime application (Runa6w or RunA6M) or the Authorware piece you are distributing (if you packaged it with the Runtime).

- Xtras in Director 4, Director 5, and Director 6
- Files for Windows 95, Windows 98, Windows NT 3.5.1 or 4.0, Windows 2000
- Files for Windows 3.1

Xtras in Director 4, Director 5, and Director 6

The sections that follow describe how Xtras work in relation to movies created in Director 4, Director 5, and Director 6.

Xtras and Director 4 Movies

Movies created in Director 4 do not require any Xtras. If you have used only Director 4 movies in an Authorware piece, you do not need to distribute any of the Xtras stored in the following folders.

- Windows 95, Windows 98, Windows NT, and Windows 2000: *[Project Folder] \Director \Xtras*

- Windows 3.1: *[Proj_dir]\Director\Xtras*

Xtras and Director 5 Movies

Movies created in Director 5 require only the Xtras that were used during authoring (for example, the *Sharkbyte* transitions Xtras from *g/matter*). If you have used only Director 5 movies in an Authorware piece, distribute only the Xtras you used during authoring in the following folders.

- Windows 95, Windows 98, Windows NT, and Windows 2000: *[Project Folder]\Director\Xtras*

- Windows 3.1: *[Proj_dir]\Director\Xtras*

Xtras and Director 6 Movies

The Xtras used by the Director 6 movie drivers are located in the following folders. The Director 6 Xtras are not interchangeable with the Authorware 6Xtras located in the Authorware *Xtras* folder. Do not mix them.

- Windows 95, Windows 98, Windows NT, and Windows 2000: *[Project Folder]\Director\Xtras*

- Windows 3.1: *[Proj_dir]\Director\Xtras*

Files for Director 6 Movies

If the Director 6 movie contains external links to any of the following types of external content, you will also need to distribute the file listed in the following table.

Sound	[Project Folder]\Director\Xtras\MIXSND.X16
GIF images	[Project Folder]\Director\Xtras\MIXGIF.X32
JPEG images	[Project Folder]\Director\Xtras\MIXJPEG.X32
Any linked medium	mix32.x32

Files for Shockwave

If the Director 6 movie is a Shockwave movie (DCR), you will also need to distribute *[Project Folder]\Director\Xtras\SWADCMPR.X32*.

- *[Project Folder]:Director:Xtras:SWA Decompression 68K Xtra*

Files for Windows 95, Windows 98, Windows NT 3.5.1 or 4.0, Windows 2000

To play a Director 6 movie in Windows 95, Windows 98, Windows NT, or Windows 2000, you need to distribute the following:

- *[Project Folder]\A5DIR32.XMO*
- *[Project Folder]\Director\M5DRVR32.EXE*
- *[Project Folder]\Director\M5DRVR32.RSR*
- *[Project Folder]\Director\ M5IF32.DLL*
- *[Project Folder]\Director\XOBGLU32.DLL*
- *[Project Folder]\Director\D60XTRA.MCH*
- *[Project Folder]\Director\ASIPORT.RSR*
- *[Project Folder]\Director\ASIFONT.MAP*
- *[Project Folder]\Director\FONTMAP.TXT*
- *[Project Folder]\Director\MACROMIX.DLL*
- *[Project Folder]\Director\DIRDIB.DRV*
- *[Project Folder]\Director\LINGO.INI*
- *[Project Folder]\Director\FILEIO.DLL*

Files for Windows 3.1

To play a Director 6 movie in Windows 3.1, you need to distribute the following:

- *[Proj_dir]\A5DIR.XMO*
- *[Proj_dir]\Director\M5DRVR16.EXE*
- *[Proj_dir]\Director\M5DRVR16.RSR*
- *[Proj_dir]\Director\ M5IF16.DLL*
- *[Proj_dir]\Director\XOBGLU16.DLL*
- *[Proj_dir]\Director\D60XTRA.MCH*
- *[Proj_dir]\Director\ASIPORT.RSR*
- *[Proj_dir]\Director\ASIFONT.MAP*
- *[Proj_dir]\Director\FONTMAP.TXT*
- *[Proj_dir]\Director\MACROMIX.DLL*

- *[Proj_dir]\Director\DIRDIB.DRV*
- *[Proj_dir]\Director\LINGO.INI*
- *[Proj_dir]\Director\FILEIO.DLL*
- *[Proj_dir]\Director\Xtras\MIX16.X16*

Flash Movies

Xtras required for Flash movies are outlined as follows:

Flash movie – internal	Flash Asset.x32
Flash movie – linked to a local file	Flash Asset.x32 MoaFile2.x32
Flash movie – linked via URL	Flash Asset.x32 Netfile.x32 Ineturl.x32

Flash Asset Xtras required for Flash movies are outlined as follows:

Flash Asset Options.x32	This file provides support for Flash movies while authoring movies in Authorware. Do not distribute this file with Authorware pieces. This file is not licensed for redistribution.
Flash Asset.x32	Distribute this file with any Authorware pieces you create using the Flash Asset Xtra.

Animated GIFs

In addition to the Xtra *(animgif.x32)*, Authorware requires that *Awiml32.dll* and *msvcrt.dll* are included in order to play animated GIFs. Both *Awiml32.dll* and *msvcrt.dll* need to be included in the same folder as the Runtime application, *runa6w32.exe*. They are located in the Authorware folder on the hard drive. When developing for the Web and using the minimal version of the player, add a *put* statement to place these in the *aw60* folder next to the runtime, as follows:

```
put aw60
```

Then add bin lines to actually download the files, as follows:

```
bin     win32     awiml32.aab     awiml32.dll

bin     win32     msvcrt.aab      msvcrt.dll
```

Make sure the files are named with the file extension *.aab* on the server. Then put them in the same directory on the server as the *.aam* file. Alternatively, the Get function can also be used to put them in a subdirectory on the server. All binary files on the server must have the file extension *.aab* to prevent servers such as IIS from misinterpreting the file data type.

ActiveX

Two components of the Macromedia Control Xtra for ActiveX come with Authorware, as follows. There is no 16-bit version of the Macromedia Control Xtra for ActiveX.

- ActXPriv.X32 *contains components of the Macromedia Control Xtra for ActiveX that you need only for authoring. Do not include it with the project files you distribute. It is not licensed for redistribution.*

- ActiveX.X32 *contains everything users need to use an ActiveX control you have embedded in a piece. Include ActiveX.X32 with the project files you distribute.*

Database

In addition to the external files you must otherwise include with a piece, there are several items you must include when distributing a piece that connects to a database, as follows. The data sources you set up when you author must also be set up on the computer that runs the piece. For the user's convenience, it is a good idea to provide an installer that automatically installs the drivers and sets up data sources in addition to installing the rest of the piece.

- *The ODBC UCD, which contains the ODBC functions, ODBC.U32, and ODBC.UCD*

- *The data source for any databases the piece uses and a license to distribute the drivers you are using*

- *The database file*

Other Xtras

The following are other Xtras you might want to consider.

- **a6dir.u32:** *Used for Director files.*
- **budapi.u32:** *Needed if any functions from* budapi *are used.*
- **budunzip.u32:** *Needed if any functions from the* budunzip *utility are used.*
- **fileio.x32:** *Needed for all* fileio *functions.*
- **ftp.u32:** *Used for all FTP functions in Authorware.*

- **INETURL.X32:** *Required if you are using a URL to point to a linked file.*
- **MEMTOOLS.U32:** *Used for all the memory tool functions.*
- **PWInt.x32:** *Any application using Pathware CMI functions.*
- **RTFObj.u32:** *Used with the new RTF Objects editor.*
- **SCRLEDIT.U32:** *Used for scrolling edit boxes.*
- **secure.x32:** *Used for the Authorware security dialog.*
- **tMsControls.u32:** *Windows-based controls.*
- **tMsDSN.u32:** *For setting up a data source name.*
- **winapi.u32:** *Used for direct communication with the windows API.*
- **WinCtrls.u32:** *For using all of the new Windows controls.*
- **XmlParser.x32:** *Used with the XML parser.*

Video Overlay Devices

The following are needed if you are using a video overlay device, depending on the manufacturer.

- *a6bravo.vdr*
- *a6mci.vdr*
- *a6mci32.vdr*
- *a6mmotn.vdr*
- *a6vblast.vdr*
- *a6vlogic.vdr*
- *a6vsvw.vdr*

Laser Disc Devices

The following are needed if you are using a laser disc player, by manufacturer.

- *a6pioclv.vdr*
- *a6pioclv32.vdr*
- *a6pion32.vdr*
- *a6pioner.vdr*
- *a6sony.vdr*
- *a6sony32.vdr*

Transitions

The following are transitions with which you will want to be familiar.

- **COVERIN.X32:** *Zeus Productions transitions*
- **COVEROUT.X32:** *Zeus Productions transitions*
- **CROSSIN.X32:** *Zeus Productions transitions*
- **DIRTRANS.X32:** *Cover, Dissolve, Other, Push, Reveal, Strips, and Wipe*
- **THEBYTE.X32:** *Shark Byte transitions*

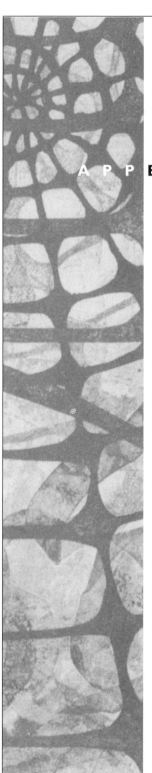

Authorware

Resources

Local

Authorware Help Pages - F1

Believe it or not, the built-in help pages can usually answer all of your questions. Look here first.

CD-ROM

The CD-ROM that your version of Authorware shipped on is full of extra tools. Make sure you browse the *goodies* folder!

Macromedia

Support Center

The Authorware Support Center site is a rich and continuously growing source of information about Authorware.

http://www.macromedia.com/support/authorware/

TechNotes

The TechNotes site contains the most up-to-date information on Authorware. You can find answers to your questions by browsing or searching more than 300 technical documents on known Authorware issues.

http://www.macromedia.com/support/authorware/technotes.html

Authorware Publications

http://www.macromedia.com/support/authorware/ts/documents/tn3002-awpubs.html

Authorware Mailing Lists

http://www.macromedia.com/support/authorware/ts/documents/tn3001-awmaillists.html

Tip of the Day

http://www.macromedia.com/support/tipoftheday/?product=authorware

Macromedia Press

http://www.macromedia.com/support/mmpress/

Support by E-mail

http://www.macromedia.com/support/email/complimentary/

Submit Feature Request

http://www.macromedia.com/support/general/ts/documents/tn3536-feedback.html

Macromedia Support Programs

http://www.macromedia.com/support/one_to_one/

Third Party

The AWARE listserve

This is the hangout of the Authorware community. Make sure you read all of the literature before you start to post.

http://www.e-media.nl/aware/

Stefan van As Multimedia Software

A collection of tools, plug-ins, and utilities for Authorware.

http://www.stefanvanas.com

Information on Macromedia Authorware

Reviews of books about Authorware, links to news groups, Web sites, download sites, magazines, and newsletters.

http://www.betsybruce.com/books/

Media Shoppe

Downloads, FAQs, and links to other sites. The number one Authorware training house.

http://www.mediashoppe.com/

Dazzle Technologies Corporation

Joe Ganci's Web page, with information on his books, Authorware Intelligence Reports, and user group information.

http://www.dazzletech.com/

Authorware.com

A Dazzle Technologies Corporation site.

http://www.authorware.com

The Life and Times of Jennie Thornton

Information about Authorware, instructional design, and Jennie's life philosophies.

http://www.jenniethornton.com

DirectXtras

DirectXtras creates Xtras for Authorware and Director.

http://www.directxtras.com

Authorware Resource Center

A full resource for Authorware and developer information, including over 50 downloadable examples in Authorware 4 and 5 formats.

http://www.stingray-interactive.com/awunder/

Nowhereroad

Great resource for building games, simulation, and computer-based training (CBT).

http://www.nowhereroad.com

Apurva Lawale

This site provides advanced code and concepts for Authorware developers.

http://home3.pacific.net.sg/%7Eapudeepa/

Authorware Web Ring 1

http://www.ix-software.nl/authorware/

Authorware Web Ring 2

http://phoebe.bomis.com/ring_home.fcgi?ring=authorware

Add-ons, Xtras, and ActiveX Sources

The following are add-ons, Xtras, and ActiveX sources you might find helpful.

Gary Smith's UCD Download Page

Many good UCDs for Authorware, including the essential *buddyapi*.

http://www.mods.com.au/frameset.htm

Comprehensive list of Xtras

http://www.neommug.org/AWxtras.htm

Complete list of ActiveX controls

http://browserwatch.internet.com/activex.html

Graphics and Sounds

The following are sources dedicated to computer graphics and sounds.

Picture libraries

http://www.photodisc.com/

Many more picture libraries

http://www.gettyimages.com/

Thousands of sound effects

http://www.wavcentral.com/

Sound effects generator

http://www.windowsgames.co.uk/effects.html

Bell Laboratories text to speech

http://www.bell-labs.com/project/tts/voices.html

Conferences

The following are leading conferences in this area.

TAAC (The Alternative Authorware Conference)

Held annually in the USA, a must for every Authorware developer.

http://www.rlinteractive.com/html/taac/

EuroTAAC

European Alternative Authorware Conference, for Authorware developers on the other side of the pond.

http://www.eurotaac.com

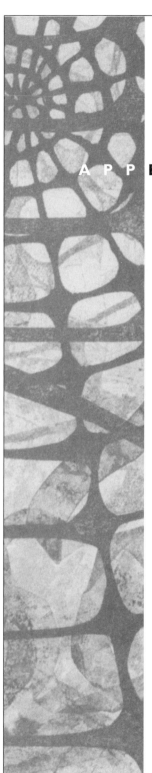

APPENDIX D

Standard
Authorware
Knowledge
Objects

Most users get so in the habit of closing down the Knowledge Object window that they forget how many amazing time-saving Knowledge objects there are. Read through these so that you see how much free code you get with Authorware. If you can, use them.

Assessment

The following are Assessment Knowledge objects associated with Authorware.

Drag-Drop Question

Creates a drag-drop question. Works in conjunction with the Assessment Login and Scoring Knowledge objects.

Hot Object Question

Creates a hot object question. Works in conjunction with the Assessment Login and Scoring Knowledge objects. Compatible with IMS QTI version 1.1 XML specification.

Hot Spot Question

Creates a hot spot question. Works in conjunction with the Assessment Login and Scoring Knowledge objects. Compatible with IMS QTI version 1.1 XML specification.

Login

Implements the log-in sequence and selects storage type to facilitate score recording for assessment questions in assessment scoring.

Multiple Choice Question

Creates a multiple-choice question. Works in conjunction with the Assessment Login and Scoring Knowledge objects. Compatible with IMS QTI version 1.1 XML specification.

Scoring

Implements score accumulation, display, and recording for assessment questions.

Short Answer Question

Creates a short answer question. Works in conjunction with the Assessment Login and Scoring Knowledge objects.

Single Choice Question

Creates a single-choice question. Works in conjunction with the Assessment Login and Scoring Knowledge objects. Compatible with IMS QTI version 1.1 XML specification.

True-False Question

Creates a true-false question. Works in conjunction with the Assessment Login and Scoring Knowledge objects. Compatible with IMS QTI version 1.1 XML specification.

File

The following are File Knowledge objects associated with Authorware.

Add-Remove Font Resource

Adds or removes TrueType font resources. Adding a font resource makes the font available to applications that draw text using the font.

Copy File

Copies one or more files to a directory.

Find CD Drive

Locates the first CD-ROM drive on the computer running your piece.

Jump to Authorware File

Jumps to a specified Authorware file.

Read INI File

Reads a value from a Windows INI file.

Set File Attribute

Sets the following file attributes for one or more files: No Attributes, Read Only, Hidden, System, and Archive.

Write INI Value

Writes a value to a Windows INI file.

Icon Palette Settings

The following is the Knowledge object for customizing Icon palettes.

Customizable Icon Palette

These contain the icons you have customized for use in the Icon palette.

Interface Components

The following are Knowledge objects associated with Interface components.

Browse Folder Dialog

Displays a dialog box for selecting a directory. Stores the absolute path to the selected directory in a variable. Windows 32-bit only.

Checkboxes

Creates a checkbox interaction.

Message Box

Creates a Windows-style message box.

Move Cursor

Moves the cursor to a set location on the screen. The cursor's movement can be instant or animated over time.

Movie Controller

Creates a control panel for digital movies.

Open File Dialog

Displays a dialog box for selecting a file to open. Stores the absolute path to the selected file in a variable. Windows 32-bit only.

Radio Buttons

Creates a radio button interaction.

Save File Dialog

Displays a dialog box for specifying a file name and location. Stores the absolute path to the specified file in a variable. Windows 32-bit only.

Set Window Caption

Changes the caption in the title bar of the Authorware Presentation window.

Slider

Creates a slider.

Windows Control

Displays a common Windows Control. Windows 32-bit only.

Windows Control: Get Property

Retrieves a Windows Control property value. Windows 32-bit only.

Windows Control: Set Property

Modifies a Windows Control property value. Windows 32-bit only.

Internet

The following are Knowledge objects associated with Internet use.

Authorware Web Player Security

Sets the list of trusted URLs for Authorware Web Player. Includes options for displaying the security dialogs.

Launch Default Browser

Launches the specified URL with the system's default Web browser.

Send Email

Sends an e-mail message via SMTP (Simple Mail Transfer Protocol). Windows 32-bit only.

Model Palette

The following Knowledge object is associated with the Model palette.

Customizable Model Palette

This contains the icons you have customized for use in the Model palette.

New File

The following Knowledge objects are associated with creating new files.

Application

Creates an Authorware application suitable for creating training pieces. Includes numerous options.

Quiz

Creates a quiz application. Includes the following question types.

- *Drag-and-drop*
- *Hot object*
- *Hot spot*
- *Multiple choice*
- *Short text*
- *Single choice*
- *True/false*

RTF Objects

The following Knowledge objects are associated with RTF use.

Create RTF Object

Creates an RTF object. Windows 32-bit only.

Get RTF Object Text Range

Returns the text in an RTF object range. Windows 32-bit only.

Insert RTF Object Hot Text Interaction

Inserts an Interaction icon with hot spot responses for your RTF object. Windows 32-bit only.

Save RTF Object

Exports an RTF object. Windows 32-bit only.

Search RTF Object

Searches an RTF object for specific terms or phrases. Windows 32-bit only.

Show or Hide RTF Object

Makes an RTF object visible or invisible. Windows 32-bit only.

Tutorial

The following Knowledge objects are associated with Authorware tutorials.

Camera Parts

Used in Authorware tutorial.

Take Pictures

Used in Authorware tutorial.

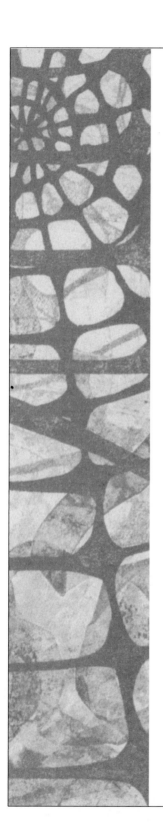

Index